The Earth and Its Peoples

A Global History

BRIEF EDITION   SIXTH EDITION

Volume I: To 1550

The Earth and Its Peoples

A Global History

Richard W. Bulliet
Columbia University

Pamela Kyle Crossley
Dartmouth College

Daniel R. Headrick
Roosevelt University

Steven W. Hirsch
Tufts University

Lyman L. Johnson
University of North Carolina–Charlotte

David Northrup
Boston College

CENGAGE
Learning·

Australia • Brazil • Mexico • Singapore • United Kingdom • United States

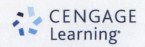

The Earth and Its Peoples: A Global History,
Brief Edition Sixth Edition
Volume I: To 1550
Richard W. Bulliet, Pamela Kyle Crossley,
Daniel R. Headrick, Steven W. Hirsch,
Lyman L. Johnson, David Northrup

Product Director: Suzanne Jeans

Product Manager: Brooke Barbier

Senior Content Developer: Tonya Lobato

Content Coordinator: Cara Swan

Product Assistant: Katie Coaster

Media Developer: Kate MacLean

Marketing Brand Manager: Kyle Zimmerman

Senior Content Project Manager: Carol Newman

Senior Art Director: Cate Barr

Manufacturing Planner: Sandee Milewski

Senior Rights Acquisition Specialist: Jennifer
Meyer Dare

Production Service/Compositor: Lachina
Publishing Services

Text and Cover Designer: Dick Hannus, Hannus
Design Associates

Cover Image: Net Fishing in the Reeds,
ca. 2323–2150 B.C. Alfredo Dagli Orti/The Art
Archive/Corbis

For product information and technology assistance, contact us at
Cengage Learning Customer & Sales Support, 1-800-354-9706

For permission to use material from this text or product,
submit all requests online at **www.cengage.com/permissions**.
Further permissions questions can be emailed to
permissionrequest@cengage.com.

Library of Congress Control Number: 2013946152

ISBN-13: 978-1-285-44552-6
ISBN-10: 1-285-44552-X

Cengage Learning
200 First Stamford Place, 4th Floor
Stamford, CT 06902
USA

Cengage Learning is a leading provider of customized learning solutions with office locations around the globe, including Singapore,
the United Kingdom, Australia, Mexico, Brazil and Japan. Locate your
local office at **international.cengage.com/region**.

Cengage Learning products are represented in Canada by Nelson
Education, Ltd.

For your course and learning solutions, visit **www.cengage.com**.

Purchase any of our products at your local college store or at our
preferred online store **www.cengagebrain.com**.

Instructors: Please visit **login.cengage.com** and log in to access
instructor-specific resources.

Printed in Canada
1 2 3 4 5 6 7 17 16 15 14 13

BRIEF CONTENTS

CONTENTS

PART TWO

The Formation of New Cultural Communities, from 1500 B.C.E.   80

4

Greece and Iran, 1000–30 B.C.E.   82

PART THREE

Growth and Interaction of Cultural Communities, 300 B.C.E.–1200 C.E.   184

The Sasanid Empire and the Rise of Islam, 200–1200   206

Christian Societies Emerge in Europe , 600–1200   228

Southern Empires, Southern Seas, 1200–1500   328

MAPS

FEATURES

ENVIRONMENT & TECHNOLOGY

ISSUES IN WORLD HISTORY

DIVERSITY & DOMINANCE

MATERIAL CULTURE

PREFACE

In preparing the sixth edition of this book, we examined the flow of topics from chapter to chapter and decided that certain rearrangements within chapters and in the order of chapters would accommodate the needs of instructors and students better than the template they had followed since the first edition. The first change was reversing the order of the third and fourth chapters to have early Mediterranean and Middle Eastern history directly follow the discussion of the origins of civilization in the Nile Valley and Mesopotamia.

The second change addressed the problem of when and how to discuss the history of pre-Columbian America. The time span to be covered, ranging from roughly 1500 B.C.E. to 1500 C.E., was too long to fit easily into the book's division into eight parts. The new structure we have adopted relocates the long pre-Aztec and pre-Inka narrative from Part Three, Growth and Interaction of Cultural Communities, to the end of Part Two, The Formation of New Cultural Communities. This change puts the status of the earliest civilizations in the Western Hemisphere on the same footing as the early civilizations of Greece, China, and South and Southeast Asia. It has the added benefit of making the history of East Asia in the Tang and Song periods directly precede the history of the Mongol empire, which allows instructors to have an uninterrupted focus on East Asia. The histories of the Aztecs and Inkas have been shifted to the chapter on tropical history located in Part Four, Interregional Patterns of Culture and Contact. This allows for a discussion of the overall influence of tropical environments and places them in close proximity to our treatment of the coming of Europeans to the New World.

A third structural change has shortened the length of the book by one chapter. To lessen the impression that Europe's domination of the world should always be the primary focus of student attention between the eighteenth and mid-twentieth centuries we have combined the two separate chapters on European imperialism, Chapters 22 and 24 in previous editions, into one. We feel that this change provides a better balance between the saga of European imperialism, accounts of resistance to imperialism, and the rise of independence movements in different parts of the world.

In a related change, we have relocated the chapter dealing with the histories of India, Latin America, and Africa in the first half of the twentieth century from after World War II, the former Chapter 27, to a position between the world wars. The aim of this largely new chapter, titled "Revolutions in Living," is to portray that period not only as a time of political change in parts of the world subjected to European imperialism, but also as one of transformation of daily lives of people in both the industrialized and nonindustrialized worlds. The added focus of the chapter fills a gap between discussion of the Industrial Revolution in the eighteenth and nineteenth centuries and the advent of major technological changes in the post-World War II era.

Finally in this new edition, contributor and East Asian specialist Michael Wert of Marquette University brought a fresh perspective to many of our chapters dealing with East Asia, helping ensure that our coverage is at the forefront of emerging scholarship.

The authors believe that these changes, along with myriad smaller changes detailed below, significantly enhance the overall goal of *The Earth and Its Peoples*, namely, to be a textbook that speaks not only for the past but also to today's student and teacher. Students and instructors alike should take away from this text a broad, and due to the changes, more flowing impression of human societies beginning as sparse and disconnected communities reacting creatively to local circumstances; experiencing ever more intensive stages of contact, interpenetration, and cultural expansion and amalgamation; and arriving at a twenty-first-century world in which people increasingly visualize a single global community.

Process, not progress, is the keynote of this book: a steady process of change over time, at first differently experienced in various regions, but eventually connecting peoples and traditions from all parts of the globe. Students should come away from this book with a sense that the problems and promises of their world are rooted in a past in which people of every sort, in every part of the world, confronted problems of a similar character and coped with them as best they could. We believe that our efforts will help students see where their world has come from and learn thereby something useful for their own lives.

Central Themes and Goals of the Text

We have subtitled *The Earth and Its Peoples* "A Global History" because the book explores the common challenges and experiences that unite the human past. Although the dispersal of early humans around the world resulted in many different economic, social, political, and cultural systems, all societies displayed analogous patterns in meeting their needs and exploiting their environments. Our challenge was to select the particular data and episodes that would best illuminate these global patterns of human experience.

To meet this challenge, we adopted two themes to serve as the spinal cord of our history: "technology and environment" and "diversity and dominance." The first theme represents the commonplace material bases of all human societies at all times. It grants no special favor to any cultural group even as it embraces subjects of the broadest topical, chronological, and geographical range. The second theme expresses the reality that every human society has constructed or inherited structures of domination. We examine practices and institutions of many sorts: military, economic, social, political, religious, and cultural, as well as those based on kinship, gender, and literacy. Simultaneously we recognize that alternative ways of life and visions of societal organization continually manifest themselves both within and in dialogue with every structure of domination.

With respect to the first theme, it is vital for students to understand that technology, in the broad sense of experience-based knowledge of the physical world, underlies all human activity. Writing is a technology, but so is oral transmission from generation to generation of lore about medicinal or poisonous plants. The magnetic compass is a navigational technology, but so is a Polynesian mariner's hard-won knowledge of winds, currents, and tides that made possible the settlement of the Pacific islands.

All technological development has come about in interaction with environments, both physical and human, and has, in turn, affected those environments. The story of how humanity has changed the face of the globe is an integral part of this central theme. Yet technology and the environment do not explain or underlie all important episodes of human experience. The theme of "Diversity and Dominance" informs all our discussions of politics, culture, and society. Thus, when narrating the histories of empires, we describe a range of human experiences within and beyond the imperial frontiers without assuming that the imperial institutions are a more suitable topic for discussion than the economic and social organization of pastoral nomads or the lives of peasant women. When religion and culture occupy our narrative, we focus not only on the dominant tradition but also on the diversity of alternative beliefs and practices.

Organization

The brief edition of *The Earth and Its Peoples*, sixth edition, retains the eight broad chronological divisions of previous editions to define its conceptual scheme of global historical development.

In **Part One: The Emergence of Human Communities, to 1500 B.C.E.**, we examine important patterns of human communal organization primarily in the Eastern Hemisphere. Small, dispersed human communities living by foraging spread to most parts of the world over tens of thousands of years. They responded to enormously diverse environmental conditions, at different times and in different ways discovering how to cultivate plants and utilize the products of domestic animals. On the basis of these new modes of sustenance, populations grew, permanent towns appeared, and political and religious authority, based on collection and control of agricultural surpluses, spread over extensive areas.

Part Two: The Formation of New Cultural Communities, from 1500 B.C.E. introduces the concept of a "cultural community," in the sense of a coherent pattern of activities and symbols pertaining to a specific human community. While all human communities develop distinctive cultures, including those discussed in Part One, historical development in this stage of global history prolonged and magnified the impact of some cultures more than others. In the geographically contiguous African-Eurasian landmass, as well as the Western Hemisphere, the cultures that proved to have the most enduring influence traced their roots to the second and first millennia B.C.E.

Part Three: Growth and Interaction of Cultural Communities, 300 B.C.E.–1200 C.E. deals with early episodes of technological, social, and cultural exchange and interaction on a continental scale both within and beyond the framework of imperial expansion. These are so different from earlier interactions arising from more limited conquests or extensions of political boundaries that they constitute a distinct era in world history, an era that set the world on the path of increasing global interaction and interdependence that it has been following ever since.

In **Part Four: Interregional Patterns of Culture and Contact, 1200–1550**, we take a look at the world during three centuries that saw both intensified cultural and commercial contact and increasingly confident self-definition of cultural communities in Europe, Asia, Africa, and the Americas. The Mongol conquest of a vast empire extending from the Pacific Ocean to eastern Europe greatly stimulated trade and interaction. In the West, strengthened European kingdoms began maritime expansion in the Atlantic, forging direct ties with sub-Saharan Africa and entering into conflict with the civilizations of the Western Hemisphere.

Part Five: The Globe Encompassed, 1500–1750 treats a period dominated by the global effects of European expansion and continued economic growth. European ships took over, expanded, and extended the maritime trade of the Indian Ocean, coastal Africa, and the Asian rim of the Pacific Ocean. This maritime commercial enterprise had its counterpart in European colonial empires in the Americas and a new Atlantic trading system. The contrasting capacities and fortunes of traditional land empires and new maritime empires, along with the exchange of domestic plants and animals between the hemispheres, underline the technological and environmental dimensions of this first era of complete global interaction.

In **Part Six: Revolutions Reshape the World, 1750–1870**, the word *revolution* is used in several senses: in the political sense of governmental overthrow, as in France and the Americas; in the metaphorical sense of radical transformative change, as in the Industrial Revolution; and in the broadest sense of a perception of a profound change in circumstances and worldview. Technology and environment lie at the core of these developments. With the rapid ascendancy of the Western belief that science and technology could overcome all challenges, technology became not only an instrument of transformation but also an instrument of domination, to the point of threatening the integrity and autonomy of cultural traditions in nonindustrial lands and provoking strong movements of resistance.

Part Seven: Global Diversity and Dominance, 1850–1945, examines the development of a world arena in which people conceived of events on a global scale. Imperialism, international economic connections, and world-encompassing ideological tendencies, such as nationalism and socialism, present the picture of a globe becoming increasingly involved with European political and ideological concerns. Two world wars arising from European rivalries provide a climax to these developments, and European exhaustion affords other parts of the world new opportunities for independence and self-expression.

Part Eight: Perils and Promises of a Global Community, 1945 to the Present, divides at the turn of the millennium not because 2000 is a round number but because the terrorist attacks of 9/11 triggered, and now symbolize, so many changes in the world's political, economic, social, and ideological attitudes. Where the challenges of the Cold War and postcolonial nation building dominated the second half of the twentieth century, the promises and perils of globalization have been the hallmark of the twenty-first. Technology is a key topic in Part Eight because the threat of nuclear weapons and the urgency of supplying the growing world demand for oil overshadowed the late twentieth century, and the transformation of information technology has shaped the twenty-first, with worries about the impact of new technologies on the environment forming a constant and growing concern throughout the period.

The brief edition is produced in two formats: A complete edition covers the entire chronology from prehistory to the present, and a two-volume edition can be used for the two-semester survey. Volume I covers the period from prehistory to 1550, and Volume II covers 1500 to the present. There is a brief introduction to

Volume II that orients students to the general political and social climate of the world before and up to 1500.

Changes in the Brief Sixth Edition

Several changes have been made to the organization of the text to make the narrative more logical and accessible. In Part One, Chapters 2 and 3 have been swapped for better continuity with Part Two. Chapter 3 now contains a substantial new section on pastoral nomadism in the Eurasian steppe. Additionally, descriptions of early civilizations in the Western Hemisphere have been shifted to Chapter 7 in order to facilitate a more unified discussion of Pre-Columbian America. The placement of Chapter 8 has been corrected in this edition, moving from Part Two to Part Three where it fits logically with the part focus on the growth and interaction of cultural communities.

Part Four features a new organization and contains heavily revised chapter material. Chapter 13 (formerly Chapter 14) has expanded coverage of eastern Europe and the Ottoman empire. A largely new Chapter 14 bears a new title, "Southern Empires, Southern Seas," and includes treatment of the Aztec and Inka empires that were previously covered much earlier in the book. Chapter 15 reflects new research on South Asian and Polynesian maritime cultures.

In Part Five, Chapter 18 has expanded to include the history of Russia, hence a new opening featuring a Russian popular hero and the change of title to "Territorial Empires Between Europe and China." Chapter 19 has a new discussion of Korean history and the Imjin War.

The organization of Part Six has been modified as well. Chapters 20 and 21 have been reversed in sequence to provide better continuity to discussions of revolutions in Europe and parallel changes in the Americas. Chapter 20 includes a new discussion of proto-industrialization as well as augmented discussions of the spread of industrialization to continental Europe and North America and the early career of Karl Marx. The section "Protest and Reform" has been broadly revised to include machine breaking in the textile sector and rural resistance to mechanization in the Captain Swing riots.

Part Seven has been the focus of our revision efforts and features a new organization highlighting global issues, much streamlined content, and one brand new chapter on culture and technology. The opening chapter of Part Seven now combines accounts of European imperialism that were previously contained in Chapters 22 and 24. Chapter 24 features a revised discussion of early Japanese industrialization as well as an expanded treatment of Marx and Marxism and a new discussion of Mikhail Bakunin and anarchism. Chapter 26 combines in a new chapter a discussion of technology and lifestyle changes that occurred between 1900 and 1945 with accounts of political movements in India, Latin America, and Africa that were previously located in Chapter 27.

The final Part Eight includes an updated discussion about the Cold War confrontation between West and East plus a revised discussion of apartheid and South Africa's struggle for independence. The final chapter updates world affairs through the first half of 2013.

Features and Pedagogical Aids

As with previous editions, the sixth edition offers a number of valuable features and pedagogical aids designed to pique student interest in specific world history topics and help them process and retain key information.

Our **Material Culture** feature calls particular attention to the many ways in which objects and processes of everyday life can help us understand human history on a broad scale. Thus essays like "Wine and Beer in the Ancient World" and "Cotton Clothing" are not only interesting in and of themselves but also suggestive of how today's world historians find meaning in the ordinary dimensions of human life.

The **Environment and Technology** feature, which has been a valuable resource in all prior editions of *The Earth and Its Peoples*, serves to illuminate the major theme of the text by demonstrating the shared material bases of all human societies across time.

Historical essays for each of the eight parts called ***Issues in World History*** were specifically designed to alert students to broad and recurring conceptual issues that are of great interest to contemporary historians; this feature has proved to be an instructor and student favorite.

Finally, **Diversity and Dominance**, also core to the theme of the text, is the primary source feature that brings a myriad of real historical voices to life in a common struggle for power and autonomy.

Pedagogical aids include the following:

Chapter Opening Focus Questions These questions are keyed to every major subdivision of the chapter through a system of color-coding and serve to help students focus on the core chapter concepts. The unique color-coded system helps students keep track of where they are in the text and easily identify which focus question corresponds to each section of the chapter. The color-coding carries through to the end of each chapter, where the focus questions for each section are answered and summarized.

Section Reviews Short bullet-point reviews appear at the end of each major section in every chapter and remind students of key information.

Chapter Conclusions Every chapter ends with a comparative conclusion that will help students synthesize chapter material and understand how it fits into the larger picture.

Key Terms with Definitions Students can handily find definitions for bolded key terms right on the page of the text where the term first appears.

Chapter Reviews Keyed to the chapter opening focus questions through a system of color-coding, the chapter reviews summarize the most important concepts addressed in the chapter, making studying more efficient and effective.

Pronunciation Guide Phonetic spellings for unfamiliar names and terms have been integrated into the text.

Supplements

A wide array of supplements accompany this text to assist students with different learning needs and to help instructors master today's various classroom challenges.

Instructor Resources

MindTap™ [ISBN: 9781285843056] The Personal Learning Experience. MindTap for *The Earth and Its Peoples* is a personalized, online digital learning platform providing students with *The Earth and Its Peoples* content and related interactive assignments and app services—while giving you a choice in the configuration of coursework and curriculum enhancement. Through a carefully designed chapter-based learning path, students can access the ebook (MindTap Reader, see description below); Aplia™ assignments developed for the most important concepts in each chapter (see Aplia description below); brief quizzes; and a set of web applications known as MindApps to help you create the most engaging course for your students. The MindApps range from ReadSpeaker (which reads the text out-loud to students) to Kaltura (allowing you to insert inline video and audio into your curriculum) to ConnectYard (allowing you to create digital "yards" through social media—all without "friending" your students). MindTap for *The Earth and Its Peoples* goes well beyond an eBook, a homework solution/ digital supplement, a resource center web-site, or a Learning Management System. It is truly a Personal Learning Experience that allows you to synchronize the text reading and engaging assignments and quizzes. To learn more, ask your Cengage Learning sales representative to demo it for you—or go to www.cengage.com/MindTap.

Aplia™ [ISBN: 9781285780382] is an online interactive learning solution that improves comprehension and outcomes by increasing student effort and engagement. Founded by a professor to enhance his own courses, Aplia provides automatically graded assignments with detailed, immediate explanations on every question. The interactive assignments have been developed to address the major concepts covered in *The Earth and Its Peoples* and are designed to promote critical thinking and engage students more fully in learning. Question types include questions built around animated maps, primary sources such as newspaper extracts, or imagined scenarios, like engaging in a conversation with a an historical figure or finding a diary and being asked to fill in some blanks; more in-depth primary source question sets address a major topic with a number of related primary sources and questions that promote deeper analysis of historical evidence. Many of the questions incorporate images, video clips, or audio clips. Students get immediate feedback on their work (not only what they got right or wrong, but why), and they can choose to see another set of related questions if they want more practice. A searchable eBook is available inside the course as well so that students can easily reference it as they work. Map-reading and writing tutorials are also available to get students off to a good start.

Aplia's simple-to-use course management interface allows instructors to post announcements, upload course materials, host student discussions, e-mail students, and manage the gradebook; a knowledgeable and friendly support team offers assistance and personalized support in customizing assignments to the instructor's course schedule. To learn more and view a demo for this book, visit www.aplia.com.

MindTap Reader for *The Earth and Its Peoples* is an eBook specifically designed to address the ways students assimilate content and media assets. MindTap Reader combines thoughtful navigation ergonomics, advanced student annotation, note-taking, and search tools, and embedded media assets such as video and MP3 chapter summaries, primary source documents with critical thinking questions, and interactive (zoomable) maps. Students can use the eBook as their primary text or as a multimedia companion to their printed book. The MindTap Reader eBook is available within the MindTap and Aplia online offerings found at www.cengagebrain.com.

Online PowerLecture with Cognero® [ISBN: 9781285455075] This PowerLecture is an all-in-one online multimedia resource for class preparation, presentation, and testing. Accessible through cengage.com/login with your faculty account, you will find available for download: book-specific Microsoft® PowerPoint® presentations; a Test Bank in both Microsoft® Word® and Cognero® formats; an Instructor Manual; Microsoft® PowerPoint® Image Slides; and a JPEG Image Library. The Test Bank, offered in Microsoft® Word® and Cognero® formats, contains multiple-choice and essay questions for each chapter. Cognero® is a flexible, online system that allows you to author, edit, and manage test bank content for *The Earth and Its People*, sixth edition. Create multiple test versions instantly and deliver through your LMS from your classroom, or wherever you may be, with no special installs or downloads required.

The **Instructor's Manual** contains for each chapter: an outline and summary; critical thinking questions; in-class activities; lecture launching suggestions; a list of key terms with definitions; and suggested readings and Web resources. The Microsoft® PowerPoint® presentations are ready-to-use, visual outlines of each chapter. These presentations are easily customized for your lectures and offered along with chapter-specific Microsoft® PowerPoint® Image Slides and JPEG Image Libraries. Access your Online PowerLecture at www.cengage.com/login.

CourseReader CourseReader is an online collection of primary and secondary sources that lets you create a customized electronic reader in minutes. With an easy-to-use interface and assessment tool, you can choose exactly what your students will be assigned—simply search or browse Cengage Learning's extensive document database to preview and select your customized collection of readings. In addition to print sources of all types (letters, diary entries, speeches, newspaper accounts, etc.), their collection includes a growing number of images and video and audio clips.

Each primary source document includes a descriptive headnote that puts the reading into context and is further supported by both critical thinking and multiple-choice questions designed to reinforce key points. For more information visit www.cengage.com/coursereader.

Cengagebrain.com Save your students time and money. Direct them to www.cengagebrain.com for choice in formats and savings and a better chance to succeed in your class. Cengagebrain.com, Cengage Learning's online store, is a single destination for more than 10,000 new textbooks, eTextbooks, eChapters, study tools, and audio supplements. Students have the freedom to purchase a-la-carte exactly what they need when they need it. Students can save 50% on the electronic textbook, and can pay as little as $1.99 for an individual eChapter.

Reader Program Cengage Learning publishes a number of readers, some containing exclusively primary sources, others a combination of primary and secondary sources, and some designed to guide students through the process of historical inquiry. Visit Cengage.com/history for a complete list of readers.

Custom Options Nobody knows your students like you, so why not give them a text that is tailor-fit to their needs? Cengage Learning offers custom solutions for your course—whether it's making a small modification to *The Earth and Its Peoples* to match your syllabus or combining multiple sources to create something truly unique. You can pick and choose chapters, include your own material, and add additional map exercises along with the Rand McNally Atlas to create a text that fits the way you teach. Ensure that your students get the most out of their textbook dollar by giving them exactly what they need. Contact your Cengage Learning representative to explore custom solutions for your course.

Student Resources

Writing for College History, **First Edition [ISBN: 9780618306039]** Prepared by Robert M. Frakes, Clarion University. This brief handbook for survey courses in American history, Western Civilization/European history, and world civilization guides students through the various types of writing assignments they encounter in a history class. Providing examples of student writing and candid assessments of student work, this text focuses on the rules and conventions of writing for the college history course.

The History Handbook, **Second Edition [ISBN: 9780495906766]** Prepared by Carol Berkin of Baruch College, City University of New York and Betty Anderson of Boston University. This book teaches students both basic and history-specific study skills such as how to read primary sources, research historical topics, and correctly cite sources. Substantially less expensive than comparable skill-building texts, The History Handbook also offers tips for Internet research and evaluating online sources.

Doing History: Research and Writing in the Digital Age, **Second Edition [ISBN: 9781133587880]** Prepared by Michael J. Galgano, J. Chris Arndt, and Raymond M. Hyser of James Madison University. Whether you're starting down the path as a history major, or simply looking for a straightforward and systematic guide to writing a successful paper, you'll find this text to be an indispensable handbook to historical research. This text's "soup to nuts" approach to researching and writing about history addresses every step of the process, from locating your sources and gathering information, to writing clearly and making proper use of various citation styles to avoid plagiarism. You'll also learn how to make the most of every tool available to you—especially the technology that helps you conduct the process efficiently and effectively.

The Modern Researcher, **Sixth Edition [ISBN: 9780495318705]** Prepared by Jacques Barzun and Henry F. Graff of Columbia University. This classic introduction to the techniques of research and the art of expression is used widely in history courses, but is also appropriate for writing and research methods courses in other departments. Barzun and Graff thoroughly cover every aspect of research, from the selection of a topic through the gathering, analysis, writing, revision, and publication of findings, presenting the process not as a set of rules but through actual cases that put the subtleties of research in a useful context. Part One covers the principles and methods of research; Part Two covers writing, speaking, and getting one's work published.

***Rand McNally Historical Atlas of the World*, Second Edition** [ISBN: 9780618841912] This valuable resource features over 70 maps that portray the rich panoply of the world's history from preliterate times to the present. They show how cultures and civilization were linked and how they interacted. The maps make it clear that history is not static. Rather, it is about change and movement across time. The maps show change by presenting the dynamics of expansion, cooperation, and conflict. This atlas includes maps that display the world from the beginning of civilization; the political development of all major areas of the world; expanded coverage of Africa, Latin America, and the Middle East; the current Islamic World; and the world population change in 1900 and 2000.

Acknowledgments

In preparing the sixth edition, we benefited from the critical readings of many colleagues. Our sincere thanks go in particular to contributor Michael Wert of Marquette University who lent his fresh perspective to our coverage of East Asia. We thank Beatrice Manz of the History Department at Tufts University who provided guidance on the new Pastoral Nomads section in Part One. We are also indebted to the following instructors who lent their insight over various editions: Hedrick Alixopuilos, Santa Rosa Junior College; Hayden Bellenoit, U.S. Naval Academy; Dusty Bender, Central Baptist College; Cory Crawford, Ohio University; Adrian De Gifis, Loyola University New Orleans; Peter de Rosa, Bridgewater State University; Aaron Gulyas, Mott Community College; Darlene Hall, Lake Erie College; Vic Jagos, Scottsdale Community College; Adrien Ivan, Vernon College; Andrew Muldoon, Metropolitan State College of Denver; Percy Murray, Shaw University; Dave Price, Santa Fe College; Anthony Steinhoff, University of Tennessee-Chattanooga; Anara Tabyshalieva, Marshal University; Susan Autry, Central Piedmont Community College; Anna Collins, Arkansas Tech University; William Connell, Christopher Newport University; Gregory Crider, Winthrop University; Shawn Dry, Oakland Community College; Nancy Fitch, California State University, Fullerton; Christine Haynes, University of North Carolina at Charlotte; Mark Herman, Edison College; Ellen J. Jenkins, Arkansas Tech University; Frank Karpiel, The Citadel; Ken Koons, Virginia Military Institute; David Longfellow, Baylor University; Heather Lucas, Georgia Perimeter College; Jeff Pardue, Gainesville State College; Craig Patton, Alabama A & M University; Linda Scherr, Mercer County Community College; Robert Sherwood, Georgia Military College; Brett Shufelt, Copiah-Lincoln Community College; Kristen Walton, Salisbury University; Christopher Ward, Clayton State University; William Wood, Point Loma Nazarene University.

When textbook authors set out on a project, they are inclined to believe that 90 percent of the effort will be theirs and 10 percent that of various editors and production specialists employed by their publisher. How very naïve. This book would never have seen the light of day had it not been for the unstinting labors of the great team of professionals who turned the authors' words into beautifully presented print. Our debt to the staff of Cengage Learning remains undiminished in the sixth edition. Brooke Barbier, product manager, has offered us firm but sympathetic guidance throughout the revision process. Tonya Lobato, senior product developer, offered astute and sympathetic assistance as the authors worked to incorporate many new ideas and subjects into the text. Carol Newman, senior content project manager, moved the work through the production stages to meet a challenging schedule. Abbey Stebing did an outstanding job of photo research.

We thank also the many students whose questions and concerns, expressed directly or through their instructors, shaped much of this revision. We continue to welcome all readers' suggestions, queries, and criticisms. Please contact us at our respective institutions.

ABOUT THE AUTHORS

RICHARD W. BULLIET Professor of Middle Eastern History at Columbia University, Richard W. Bulliet received his Ph.D. from Harvard University. He has written scholarly works on a number of topics: the social and economic history of medieval Iran (The Patricians of Nishapur and Cotton, Climate, and Camels in Early Islamic Iran), the history of human-animal relations (The Camel and the Wheel and Hunters, Herders, and Hamburgers), the process of conversion to Islam (Conversion to Islam in the Medieval Period), and the overall course of Islamic social history (Islam: The View from the Edge and The Case for Islamo-Christian Civilization). He is the editor of the Columbia History of the Twentieth Century. He has published four novels, coedited The Encyclopedia of the Modern Middle East, and hosted an educational television series on the Middle East. He was awarded a fellowship by the John Simon Guggenheim Memorial Foundation and was named a Carnegie Corporation Scholar.

PAMELA KYLE CROSSLEY Pamela Kyle Crossley received her Ph.D. in Modern Chinese History from Yale University. She is currently the Robert and Barbara Black Professor of History at Dartmouth College. Her books include The Wobbling Pivot: An Interpretive History of China Since 1800; What Is Global History?; A Translucent Mirror: History and Identity in Qing Imperial Ideology; The Manchus; Orphan Warriors: Three Manchu Generations and the End of the Qing World; and (with Lynn Hollen Lees and John W. Servos) Global Society: The World Since 1900.

DANIEL R. HEADRICK Daniel R. Headrick received his Ph.D. in History from Princeton University. Professor of History and Social Science, Emeritus, at Roosevelt University in Chicago, he is the author of several books on the history of technology, imperialism, and international relations, including The Tools of Empire: Technology and European Imperialism in the Nineteenth Century; The Tentacles of Progress: Technology Transfer in the Age of Imperialism; The Invisible Weapon: Telecommunications and International Politics; Technology: A World History; Power Over Peoples: Technology, Environments and Western Imperialism, 1400 to the Present;

and When Information Came of Age: Technologies of Knowledge in the Age of Reason and Revolution, 1700–1850. His articles have appeared in the Journal of World History and the Journal of Modern History, and he has been awarded fellowships by the National Endowment for the Humanities, the John Simon Guggenheim Memorial Foundation, and the Alfred P. Sloan Foundation.

STEVEN W. HIRSCH   Steven W. Hirsch holds a Ph.D. in Classics from Stanford University and is currently Associate Professor of Classics and History at Tufts University. He has received grants from the National Endowment for the Humanities and the Massachusetts Foundation for Humanities and Public Policy. His research and publications include The Friendship of the Barbarians: Xenophon and the Persian Empire, as well as articles and reviews in the Classical Journal, the American Journal of Philology, and the Journal of Interdisciplinary History. He is currently completing a comparative study of ancient Greco-Roman and Chinese civilizations.

LYMAN L. JOHNSON   Professor Emeritus of History at the University of North Carolina at Charlotte, Lyman L. Johnson earned his Ph.D. in Latin American History from the University of Connecticut. A two-time Senior Fulbright-Hays Lecturer, he also has received fellowships from the Tinker Foundation, the Social Science Research Council, the National Endowment for the Humanities, and the American Philosophical Society. His recent books include Workshop of Revolution: Plebeian Buenos Aires and the Atlantic World, 1776-1810; Death, Dismemberment, and Memory; The Faces of Honor (with Sonya Lipsett-Rivera); Aftershocks: Earthquakes and Popular Politics in Latin America (with Jürgen Buchenau); Essays on the Price History of Eighteenth-Century Latin America (with Enrique Tandeter); and Colonial Latin America (with Mark A. Burkholder). He also has published in journals, including the Hispanic American Historical Review, the Journal of Latin American Studies, the International Review of Social History, Social History, and Desarrollo Económico. He has served as president of the Conference on Latin American History.

DAVID NORTHRUP   David Northrup earned his Ph.D. in African and European History from the University of California, Los Angeles. He has published scholarly works on African, Atlantic, and world history. His most recent books are How English Became the Global Language, the third edition of Africa's Discovery of Europe, 1450–1850, and the Diary of Antera Duke, an Eighteenth-Century African Slave Trader. He taught at a rural secondary school on Nigeria, Tuskegee Institute in Alabama, Boston College, and Venice International University and is a past president of the World History Association.

NOTE ON SPELLING AND USAGE

Where necessary for clarity, dates are followed by the letters C.E. or B.C.E. The abbreviation C.E. stands for "Common Era" and is equivalent to A.D. (anno Domini, Latin for "in the year of the Lord"). The abbreviation B.C.E. stands for "before the Common

Era" and means the same as B.C. ("before Christ"). In keeping with our goal of approaching world history without special concentration on one culture or another, we chose these neutral abbreviations as appropriate to our enterprise. Because many readers will be more familiar with English than with metric measurements, however, units of measure are generally given in the English system, with metric equivalents following in parentheses.

In general, Chinese has been Romanized according to the pinyin method. Exceptions include proper names well established in English (e.g., Canton, Chiang Kaishek) and a few English words borrowed from Chinese (e.g., kowtow). Spellings of Arabic, Ottoman Turkish, Persian, Mongolian, Manchu, Japanese, and Korean names and terms avoid special diacritical marks for letters that are pronounced only slightly differently in English. An apostrophe is used to indicate when two Chinese syllables are pronounced separately (e.g., Chang'an).

For words transliterated from languages that use the Arabic script—Arabic, Ottoman Turkish, Persian, Urdu—the apostrophe indicating separately pronounced syllables may represent either of two special consonants, the hamza or the ain. Because most English-speakers do not hear the distinction between these two, they have not been distinguished in transliteration and are not indicated when they occur at the beginning or end of a word. As with Chinese, some words and commonly used place-names from these languages are given familiar English spellings (e.g., Quran instead of Qur'an, Cairo instead of al-Qahira). Arabic romanization has normally been used for terms relating to Islam, even where the context justifies slightly different Turkish or Persian forms, again for ease of comprehension.

Before 1492 the inhabitants of the Western Hemisphere had no single name for themselves. They had neither a racial consciousness nor a racial identity. Identity was derived from kin groups, language, cultural practices, and political structures. There was no sense that physical similarities created a shared identity. America's original inhabitants had racial consciousness and racial identity imposed on them by conquest and the occupation of their lands by Europeans after 1492. All of the collective terms for these first American peoples are tainted by this history. Indians, Native Americans, Amerindians, First Peoples, and Indigenous Peoples are among the terms in common usage. In this book the names of individual cultures and states are used wherever possible. Amerindian and other terms that suggest transcultural identity and experience are used most commonly for the period after 1492.

There is an ongoing debate about how best to render Amerindian words in English. It has been common for authors writing in English to follow Mexican usage for Nahuatl and Yucatec Maya words and place-names. In this style, for example, the capital of the Aztec state is spelled Tenochtitlán, and the important late Maya city-state is spelled Chichén Itzá. Although these forms are still common even in the specialist literature, we have chosen to follow the scholarship that sees these accents as unnecessary. The exceptions are modern place-names, such as Mérida and Yucatán, which are accented. A similar problem exists for the spelling of Quechua and Aymara words from the Andean region of South America. Although there is significant disagreement among scholars, we follow the emerging consensus and use the spellings khipu (not quipu), Tiwanaku (not Tiahuanaco), and Wari (not Huari). In this edition we have introduced the now common spelling Inka (not Inca) but keep Cuzco for the capital city (not Cusco), since this spelling facilitates locating this still-important city on maps.

The Earth and Its Peoples

A Global History

Part One

The Emergence of Human Communities, to 1500 B.C.E.

© Cengage Learning

	8000 B.C.E.	7000 B.C.E.	6000 B.C.E.	5000 B.C.E.
AMERICAS		• **7000** Incipient plant domestication in Peru		• **5000** Maize, beans, and squash domestication in Mesoamerica
EUROPE	Spread of Indo-European languages		• **6000** Farming in southern Europe	
AFRICA	• **8000** Farming in eastern Sahara		• **5500** Farming in Egypt	
MIDDLE EAST	• **8000** Domestication of plants and animals in Fertile Crescent			• **5000** Irrigation in Mesopotamia
ASIA AND OCEANIA		• **6500** Rice cultivation in China		• **5000** Farming in India

Human beings evolved over several million years from primates in Africa. Able to walk upright and possessing large brains, hands with opposable thumbs, and the capacity for speech, early humans used teamwork and created tools to survive in diverse environments. They spread relatively quickly to almost every habitable area of the world, hunting and gathering wild plant products. Around 10,000 years ago some groups began to cultivate plants, domesticate animals, and make pottery vessels for storage. This led to permanent settlements—at first small villages but eventually larger towns as well.

The earliest complex societies arose in the great river valleys of Iraq, Egypt, Pakistan, and northern China. In these arid regions agriculture depended on river water, and centers of political power arose to organize the labor required to dig and maintain irrigation channels. Kings and priests dominated these early societies from the urban centers, helped by administrators, scribes, soldiers, merchants, craftsmen, and others with specialized skills. Surplus food grown in the countryside by a dependent peasantry sustained the activities of these groups.

Certain centers came to dominate broader expanses of territory, seeking access to raw materials, especially metals. This development also stimulated long-distance trade and diplomatic relations between major powers. Artisans made weapons, tools, and ritual objects from bronze. Culture and technology spread to neighboring regions, such as southern China, Nubia, Syria-Palestine, Anatolia, and the Aegean.

4000 B.C.E.	3000 B.C.E.	2000 B.C.E.	1000 B.C.E.
• **4000** Quinoa and potato domestication in Peru	• **3000** Farming in central Mexico	• **2000** Farming in Peru	• **1200** Rise of Olmec civilization in Mesoamerica • **900** Rise of Chavín civilization in Peru
• **4000** Megaliths	**3000–1100** Aegean civilization		• **1000** Iron metallurgy
	• **3100** Unification of Egypt **2575–2134** Old Kingdom Egypt	**2040–1640** Middle Kingdom Egypt • **2000** Rise of Kush in Nubia **1532–1070** New Kingdom Egypt	• **800** Rise of Nubian Kingdom at Napata
	• **3100** Mesopotamian civilization Advent of horses in western Asia **2000** • • **2350** Akkadian kingdom	• **1750** Hammurabi's law code **1700–1200** Hittites dominant in Anatolia	• **911** Rise of Neo-Assyrian Empire
	Bronze metallurgy in China **2000** • **2600–1900** Indus Valley civilization	**1600–1027** Shang kingdom in China **1027–221** Zhou kingdom in China	

Nature, Humanity, and the First River-Valley Societies

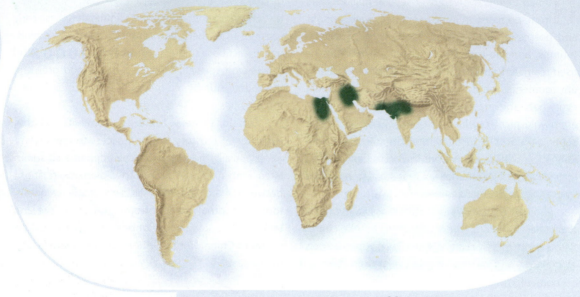

© Cengage Learning

CHAPTER PREVIEW

EARLY HUMANS

- *In light of scientific advances in our understanding of human origins, what have we learned about our relationship to the earth and other living species?*

THE AGRICULTURAL REVOLUTIONS

- *How did plant and animal domestication set the scene for the emergence of complex societies?*

MESOPOTAMIA

- *How did Mesopotamian civilization emerge, and what technologies promoted its advancement?*

EGYPT

- *What role did the environment and religion play in the evolution of Egyptian civilization?*

Conclusion

MATERIAL CULTURE: Lamps and Candles

Were the people who lived tens of thousands of years ago different from people today? Did their eyes see beauty, their ears hear music, and their minds wonder at the meaning of the world around them and the celestial bodies above them? Biologically, members of *Homo sapiens* have not changed much over time, but very little evidence exists to tell us what our ancestors were like inside—in their thoughts, imaginations, and emotions.

We might find clues in the splendid creative abilities of early humans that first came to light in 1940 near Lascaux in southwestern France, where youths stumbled upon a vast underground cavern whose walls were covered with paintings of animals, including many that had been extinct for thousands of years. Such art immediately suggested that those who made it were as sophisticated as the people who live today. Even though the original significance of these paintings is a mystery, we have a sense of these cave artists' common humanity with ourselves.

Paintings and engravings on stone created tens of thousands of years ago by early humans have been found on every continent. The oldest recognizable human art, a carefully crosshatched bone from Blombos Cave east of Cape Town, South Africa, dates from over 70,000 years ago. The oldest cave paintings discovered in southwestern France date from 32,000 years ago. To even the most skeptical person, these artistic troves reveal rich imaginations and sophisticated skills, qualities also apparent in the stone tools and in the evidence of complex social relations uncovered from prehistoric sites. Just as the skeletal remains of *Homo sapiens* of tens of thousands of years ago show they had modern bodies, the art they made suggests they had modern minds.

The production of such artworks and tools over wide areas and long periods of time demonstrates that skills and ideas were not simply individual expressions but were deliberately passed along within societies. These learned patterns of action and expression constitute **culture**. Culture includes material objects, such as dwellings, clothing, tools, and crafts, along with nonmaterial values, beliefs, and languages. Although it is true that some animals also learn new ways, their activities are determined primarily by inherited instincts. Only human communities trace profound cultural developments over time. The development, transmission, and transformation of cultural practices and events are the subject of **history**.

EARLY HUMANS

■ *In light of scientific advances in our understanding of human origins, what have we learned about our relationship to the earth and other living species?*

Since Charles Darwin argued in *The Descent of Man* (1871) that human beings had come into existence through the process of natural selection called **evolution**, it has been popular (and controversial) to say that we are descended from apes. In fact, apes and humans share a common ancestor. Over 99 percent of human DNA, the basic genetic blueprint, is identical to that of the great apes. But three traits distinguish humans from apes and other primates. The first of these traits to appear was walking upright on two legs. This frees the forelimbs from any role in locomotion and enhances the development of a thumb that can manipulate objects skillfully. Modern humans' second distinctive trait was a very large brain. Besides enabling humans to think abstractly, experience profound emotions, and construct complex social relationships, this larger brain controls the fine motor movements of the hand and of the tongue, increasing humans' tool-using capacity and facilitating the development of speech. The physical possibility of language, however, depends on a third distinctive human trait: the location of the larynx (voice box). In humans it lies much lower in the neck

culture Socially transmitted patterns of action and expression. *Material culture* refers to physical objects such as dwellings, clothing, tools, and crafts. Culture also includes arts, beliefs, knowledge, and technology.

history The study of past events and changes in the development, transmission, and transformation of cultural practices.

evolution The biological theory that, over time, changes occurring in plants and animals, mainly as a result of natural selection and genetic mutation, result in new species.

than in any other primate, making it possible to create a wide range of sounds.

About 65 million years ago, primates—members of a class of four-limbed, social animals known as mammals—came to prominence. Biologists classify humans as members of a family of primates known as **hominids** (HOM-uh-nids). The first hominids are now dated to about 7 million years ago. Beginning approximately 4.5 million years ago, several species of hominids known as **australopithecines** (aw-strah-loh-PITH-uh-seens) evolved in southern and eastern Africa.

In northern Ethiopia in 1974, Donald Johanson unearthed a well-preserved skeleton of a twenty-five-year-old female whom he nicknamed "Lucy," supporting the 1924 finding by Raymond Dart that a transitional "human" he named *Australopithecus africanus* (aw-strah-loh-PITH-uh-kuhs ah-frih-KAH-nuhs) (African southern ape) walked upright like a human but had a brain the size of an ape's. A wealth of fossil evidence had been mounting that the tropical habitat of the African apes was the cradle of humanity. The discovery of fossilized footprints in Tanzania in 1977 provided spectacular visual evidence that australopithecines walked on two legs.

Bipedalism evolved because it provided australopithecines an advantage for survival. Some studies suggest that walking and running on two legs is very energy efficient. Another theory is that bipeds survived better because they could carry armfuls of food back to their mates and children.

Climate Change, Food, and Stone Tools

Climate changes between 2 and 3 million years ago led to the evolution of a new species. Falling temperatures culminated in the **Great Ice Age**, or Pleistocene (PLY-stuh-seen) epoch, extending from about 2 million to 11,000 years ago, when it was followed by our era, the Holocene (HOH-loh-seen). These temperature changes and altered rainfall and vegetation imposed great strains on plant and animal species. What most distinguished **Homo habilis** (HOH-moh HAB-uh-luhs) (handy human) from the australopithecines was a brain nearly 50 percent larger. Greater intelligence may have enabled Homo habilis to locate things to eat throughout the seasons of the year. Seeds and other fossilized remains

John Reader/Science Source

Fossilized Footprints Archaeologist Mary Leakey (shown at top) found these remarkable footprints of a hominid adult and child at Laetoli, Tanzania. The pair had walked through fresh volcanic ash that solidified after being buried by a new volcanic eruption. Dated to 3.5 million years ago, the footprints are the oldest evidence of bipedalism yet found.

hominid The biological family that includes humans and humanlike primates.

australopithecines The several extinct species of humanlike primates that existed from about 4.5 million years ago to 1.4 million years ago (genus *Australopithecus*).

bipedalism The ability to walk upright on two legs, characteristic of hominids.

Great Ice Age Geological era that occurred between ca. 2 million and 11,000 years ago.

Homo habilis The first human species (now extinct). It evolved in Africa about 2.3 million years ago.

Chronology

	Geological Epochs	Species and Migrations	Technological Advances
7,000,000 B.C.E.		7,000,000 B.C.E. Earliest hominids	
4,000,000 B.C.E.		4,500,000 B.C.E. Australopithecines	
		2,300,000 B.C.E. Early *Homo habilis*	2,600,000 B.C.E. Earliest stone tools; hunting and gathering (foraging) societies
2,000,000 B.C.E.	2,000,000–9000 B.C.E. Pleistocene (Great Ice Age)	1,800,000–350,000 B.C.E. *Homo erectus*	2,000,000–8000 B.C.E. Paleolithic (Old Stone Age)
1,000,000 B.C.E.		400,000–100,000 B.C.E. Archaic *Homo sapiens*	500,000 B.C.E. Use of fire
100,000 B.C.E.		100,000 B.C.E. Anatomically modern *Homo sapiens* in Africa	
		50,000 B.C.E. Behaviorally modern *Homo sapiens* possessing language	
		Migrations to Eurasia	
		46,000 B.C.E. Modern humans in Australia	30,000 B.C.E. First cave paintings
		18,000 B.C.E. Modern humans in Americas	
10,000 B.C.E.	9000 B.C.E.–present Holocene		8000–2000 B.C.E. Neolithic (New Stone Age); earliest agriculture

found in ancient Homo habilis camps indicate that the new species ate a greater variety of more nutritious foods than did australopithecines.

Moreover, unlike australopithecines, *Homo habilis* made tools. Abundant evidence of stone tools first appeared at ancient human sites around 2.6 million years ago, causing this period to be called the **Stone Age**. The **Paleolithic** (or Old Stone Age) period lasted until 10,000 years ago. Specimens of crude early tools found in the Great Rift Valley of eastern Africa reveal that *Homo habilis* made tools by chipping flakes off the edges of volcanic stones. Lacking the skill to hunt and kill large animals, *Homo habilis* probably obtained animal protein by scavenging meat. The razor-sharp edges of the volcanic flakes would have been highly effective for skinning and butchering wild animals. These two changes—increased meat eating and toolmaking—appear to be closely linked.

By 1 million years ago *Homo habilis* and all the australopithecines had become extinct. In their habitat lived a new hominid, **Homo erectus** (HOH-moh ee-REK-tuhs) (upright human), which first appeared in eastern Africa about 1.8 million years ago. (It is uncertain whether *Homo erectus* evolved from *Homo*

Stone Age The historical period characterized by the production of tools from stone and other nonmetallic substances.

Paleolithic The period of the Stone Age associated with the evolution of humans.

Homo erectus An extinct human species. It evolved in Africa about 1.8 million years ago.

habilis or both species descended from *Australopithe-cus.*) A nearly complete skeleton of a twelve-year-old male of the species discovered in 1984 in Kenya shows that *Homo erectus* closely resembled modern people from the neck down. These creatures possessed brains a third larger than those of *Homo habilis*. Members of *Homo erectus* were also scavengers, but they were more clever. They created the multipurpose hand ax, for example, that could be used for scraping skins, digging up edible roots, or hurling at animals. *Homo erectus* even hunted elephants by driving them into swamps, where they became trapped and died. These early humans may have also used fire; evidence suggests that fires were deliberately set as early as 1.4 million years ago, and hearths were being kept as early as 500,000 years ago. Very successful in dealing with different environments, *Homo erectus* underwent hardly any biological changes for over a million years.

DNA and fossil evidence indicates that **Homo sapiens** (HOH-moh SAY-pee-enz) (wise human) first evolved in Africa sometime between 400,000 and 100,000 years ago. The brains of *Homo sapiens* were a third larger than those of *Homo erectus*, whom they gradually superseded. Members of *Homo sapiens* were far more skillful hunters. Using their superior intelligence, they could track animals and make a spear. Despite these abilities, anthropologists believe early humans would have reserved meat for feasts.

Archaeological and genetic evidence suggest that a further development, probably connected to the emergence of language, produced the first behaviorally modern humans, with the intellectual and social capabilities that we have. There is no scholarly consensus on when, why, or how humans developed the capacity to speak. Assuming that the shape of the throat and low position of the larynx are essential, it ought to be relevant that these features were still evolving in *Homo habilis* and *Homo erectus*. Some scholars link the development of language in the fullest sense to the period around 50,000 years ago when *Homo sapiens* began to migrate out of Africa.

Early humans first expanded their range in eastern and southern Africa. Then they ventured out of Africa, perhaps following migrating herds of animals or searching for more abundant food supplies in a time of drought. Early migrations from Africa into southern Eurasia were followed by treks across land bridges during ice ages, when giant ice sheets lowered ocean levels. About 46,000 years ago, modern humans also traveled by boat to New Guinea and Australia. The reasons for these migrations are uncertain, but the end results are vividly clear: an ancestral group from which all humans are descended (which may have comprised as few as 5,000 individuals) successfully colonized every habitable environment across the globe, including deserts and arctic lands.

Life in Paleolithic Communities

Archaeological evidence from Ice Age campsites suggests that early humans lived in highly mobile bands of **foragers** (hunting and food-gathering peoples)—big enough to defend their members from predators and divide responsibilities and small enough not to deplete the food supply in the vicinity. The band would move regularly to follow migrating animals and take advantage of seasonally ripening plants. Where the climate was severe or where natural shelters like caves did not exist, people erected huts of branches, stones, bones, skins, and leaves.

Although the oldest evidence of fibers woven into cloth dates from about 26,000 years ago, the appearance of the body louse around 70,000 years ago has been linked to people beginning to wear close-fitting garments. Early peoples would have likely worn animal skins. An "Iceman" from 5,300 years ago, whose frozen remains were found in the European Alps in 1991, was wearing many different garments made of animal skins sewn with cord fashioned from vegetable fibers and rawhide.

Ice Age women would have done most of the gathering and cooking, which they could do while caring for small children. Researchers studying present-day foragers infer that day-to-day nourishment would have come mostly from wild plant foods that women collected in skins or baskets woven from leaves. They would have dug edible roots out of the ground. Men,

Homo sapiens The current human species. It evolved in Africa sometime between 400,000 and 100,000 years ago.

foragers People who support themselves by hunting wild animals and gathering wild edible plants and insects.

© Smetek/STERN/Picture Press

The Iceman This is an artist's rendition of what the Iceman might have looked like. Notice his tools, remarkable evidence of the technology of his day.

with stronger arms and shoulders, would have been better suited for hunting animals, particularly large animals, and some early cave art suggests male hunting activities. Since male hunters only occasionally succeeded in bringing down their prey, women gatherers provided the bulk of the band's daily diet, and it is likely that women held a respected position for this reason. Women past childbearing age would have

been the most knowledgeable and productive food gatherers.

Even before *Homo sapiens*, the two-parent family would have been common. While other large mammals are mature at two or three years of age, humans are not able to care for themselves until much later, making the nurturing of children a biological imperative. The human reproductive cycle was also unique. In many other species sexual contact only occurs during a special mating season or when the female is fertile. In contrast, an enduring bond between human parents made it much easier for vulnerable offspring to receive the care they needed during the long period of their childhood.

Early music and dance have left no traces, but there is abundant evidence of painting and drawing. Because many cave paintings feature wild animals that were hunted for food, some believe they were meant to record hunting scenes or formed part of magical and religious rites to ensure successful hunting. However, a newly discovered cave in southern France features rhinoceroses, panthers, bears, and other animals that probably were not hunted. Other drawings include people dressed in animal skins and smeared with paint. In many caves there are stencils of human hands. Are these the signatures of the artists or the world's oldest graffiti? Some scholars suspect that other marks in cave paintings and on bones from this period may represent efforts at counting or writing. Other theories suggest that cave and rock art represent concerns with fertility, efforts to educate the young, or elaborate mechanisms for time reckoning.

Without written texts it is difficult to know about the religious beliefs of early humans. Sites of deliberate human burials from about 100,000 years ago give some hints. The fact that an adult was often buried with stone implements, food, clothing, and red-ochre powder suggests that early people revered their leaders, relatives, and companions enough to honor them after death and implies a belief in an afterlife.

Today we recognize that the Old Stone Age, whose existence was scarcely dreamed of two centuries ago, was a formative period. Although accidents, erratic weather, and disease might take a heavy toll on a foraging band, day-to-day existence was probably not particularly hard or unpleasant. Studies suggest that,

SECTION REVIEW

- In Charles Darwin's theory of evolution, natural selection of traits that promote survival and reproduction accounts for the gradual development of modern humans from primate ancestors.

- Bipedalism, a large brain, and a lower location of the larynx that enables speech are advantages that humans have over other primates.

- About 50,000 years ago early humans began to migrate out of Africa to the other continents, using land bridges during glacial periods with low sea levels, and even boats.

- Early humans made tools, foraged for food, and hunted. They found natural shelters or built temporary shelters, and they provided themselves with clothing.

- In early hunter-gatherer societies, women gathered the plant foods that provided most of the band's diet, while men did the hunting. The two-parent family offered children protection and a long period to mature.

- This lifestyle left them leisure to develop art and religion. Although the remains of their art and religion are difficult to interpret, it is clear that early modern humans had the mental capabilities that we have.

in plant- and game-rich areas, obtaining necessary food, clothing, and shelter would have occupied only from three to five hours a day. This would have left a great deal of time for artistic endeavors, toolmaking, and social life. Important in its own right, this period also laid the foundation for major changes ahead as human communities passed from being food gatherers to food producers.

THE AGRICULTURAL REVOLUTIONS

■ *How did plant and animal domestication set the scene for the emergence of complex societies?*

Around 10,000 years ago global climate changes seem to have induced some societies to enhance their food supplies with domesticated plants and animals. More and more people became food producers over the following millennia. Although hunting and gathering did not disappear, this transition from foraging to food production was one of the great turning points in history because it fostered a rapid increase in population and greatly altered humans' relationship to nature.

Plant Cultivation and Domesticated Animals

Because agriculture arose in combination with new kinds of stone tools, archaeologists called this period the **Neolithic**, or New Stone Age, and the rise of agriculture the *Neolithic Revolution*. While archeologists were first alerted to the beginning of a food production revolution by the presence of new, specialized tools for agriculture, such as polished stone heads to work the soil and stone mortars to pulverize grain, the name *Neolithic Revolution* can be misleading: first, stone tools were not its essential component, and second, it was not a single event but occurred in a series of transformations in different parts of the world that likely began when forager bands, returning year after year to the same seasonal camps, deliberately scattered the seeds of desirable plants in locations where they would thrive and discouraged the growth of competing plants by clearing them away. By 8000 B.C.E. wheat and barley had been domesticated in the Middle East; sorghum in Africa; and rice in China (possibly as early as 10,000 B.C.E). By about 5000 B.C.E. the inhabitants of the American continents, who first arrived around 18,000 B.C.E. were domesticating maize (mayz) (corn) in Mexico, manioc in Brazil and Panama, and beans and squash in Mesoamerica. Thus a better term is **Agricultural Revolutions**, which emphasizes that the central change was in food production and that agriculture arose independently in many places.

In most cases agriculture included the domestication of animals—dogs at first to help hunters track game, and later sheep, goats, cattle, donkeys, humped-back Zebu (ZEE-boo), and water buffalo from the Middle East and northern Africa to India and China. In the Americas, domesticated llamas provided transportation and wool, while guinea pigs, dogs, and turkeys furnished meat. Varieties of domesticated animals spread from one region to another. Once cattle became tame enough to be yoked to plows, they became essential to grain production.

Neolithic The period of the Stone Age associated with the ancient Agricultural Revolution(s).

Agricultural Revolutions The change from food gathering to food production that occurred between ca. 8000 and 2000 B.C.E. Also known as the Neolithic Revolution.

In addition, animal droppings provided valuable fertilizer.

In the more arid parts of Africa and western and Central Asia, **pastoralism**, a way of life dependent on large herds of small and large stock, predominated. As the Sahara approached its maximum dryness around 2500 B.C.E., pastoralists replaced farmers, who migrated southward (see Chapter 8). Moving their herds to new pastures and watering places throughout the year made pastoralists almost as mobile as foragers and discouraged accumulation of bulky possessions and construction of substantial dwellings. Early herders probably relied more heavily on milk than on meat, since killing animals reduced their herds. During wet seasons, they may also have done some hasty crop cultivation or bartered meat and skins for plant foods with nearby farming communities.

Why did the Agricultural Revolutions occur? Some theories assume that growing crops had obvious advantages, such as the promise of a secure food supply. However, most experts believe that climate change drove people to abandon hunting and gathering in favor of agriculture or pastoralism. With the end of the Great Ice Age between 6000 and 2000 B.C.E., the temperate lands became exceptionally warm. This is the same time when people in many parts of the world adopted agriculture. The precise nature of the crisis probably varied. In the Middle East, shortages of wild food caused by dryness or overhunting may have stimulated food production. Elsewhere, a warmer, wetter climate could turn grasslands into forests, reducing supplies of game and wild grains.

In many drier parts of the world, where wild food remained abundant, people did not take up agriculture. The inhabitants of Australia relied exclusively on foraging until recent centuries, as did some peoples on other continents. Amerindians in the arid grasslands from Alaska to the Gulf of Mexico hunted bison, and salmon-fishing sustained groups in the Pacific Northwest. Abundant supplies of fish, shellfish, and aquatic animals permitted food gatherers east of the Mississippi River to thrive. In the equatorial rain forest and in the southern part of Africa, conditions favored retention of the older ways.

Whatever the causes, the gradual adoption of food production transformed most parts of the world.

A hundred thousand years ago, world population, mostly living in the temperate and tropical regions of Africa and Eurasia, did not exceed 2 million. The population may have fallen even lower during the last glacial epoch, between 32,000 and 13,000 years ago. Agriculture supported a gradual population increase, perhaps to 10 million by 5000 B.C.E., and then mushroomed to between 50 and 100 million by 1000 B.C.E.[1]

Life in Neolithic Communities

Evidence that an ecological crisis may have triggered the transition to food production has prompted a reexamination of the assumption that farmers enjoyed better lives than foragers. Early farmers probably had to work much harder and for much longer periods than food gatherers. Long days spent clearing and cultivating land yielded meager harvests. Guarding herds from predators, guiding them to fresh pastures, and tending to their needs imposed similar burdens.

There were other problems as well. Although early farmers were less likely to starve, their diet was less varied and nutritious than that of foragers. Skeletal remains show that Neolithic farmers were shorter on average than earlier foragers. Death from contagious diseases ravaged farming settlements, which were contaminated by human waste, infested by disease-bearing vermin and insects, and inhabited by domestic animals—especially pigs and cattle—whose diseases could infect people.

However, a dependable supply of food that could be stored between harvests to see people through the nonproductive seasons, droughts, and other calamities proved decisive in the long run. Over several millennia, farmers came to outnumber nonfarmers, and in most cases, farmers seem to have displaced foragers by gradual infiltration rather than by conquest. The families who chose farming settled permanently near their fields. As they did in forager bands,

---

[1] Colin McEvedy and Richard Jones, *Atlas of World Population History* (New York: Penguin Books, 1978), 13–15.

---

pastoralism A way of life dependent on moving large herds of small and large stock to new pastures and watering places throughout the year.

kinship and marriage bound farming communities together.

The religions of foragers tended to center on sacred groves, springs, and wild animals. In contrast, the rituals of farmers often centered on the Earth Mother. Pastoralists tended to worship the all-powerful (and usually male) sky-god. Assemblages of **megaliths** ("big stones") seem to relate to religious beliefs. Stonehenge, a famous megalithic site in England constructed about 2000 B.C.E., marked the position of the sun and other celestial bodies at key points in the year.

Most early farmers lived in small villages, but in some parts of the world a few villages grew into towns, which served as centers of trade and specialized crafts. One early town in the Middle East that has been extensively excavated is Çatal Hüyük (cha-TAHL hoo-YOOK) in central Turkey. The ruins of Çatal Hüyük date to between 7000 and 5000 B.C.E. and cover 32 acres (13 hectares). Its residents lived in mud-brick rooms with elaborate decorations. Çatal Hüyük had no defensive wall. Instead, the outer walls of its houses formed a continuous barrier without doors or large windows. Residents entered their house by means of ladders through holes in the roof.

Long-distance trade at Çatal Hüyük featured obsidian, a hard volcanic rock that craftspeople made into tools, weapons, mirrors, and ornaments. Other residents made fine pottery, wove baskets and woolen cloth, made stone and shell beads, and worked leather and wood. House sizes varied, but there is no evidence of a dominant class or centralized political structure. Wall paintings, remarkably similar to earlier cave paintings, reveal the continuing importance of hunting. Scenes depict men and women adorned with leopard skins. Men were buried with weapons rather than farming tools, and wild foods—acorns, wild grains, and game animals—still featured prominently in the residents' diet. But fields around the town produced crops of barley and wheat and vegetables. Domesticated pigs were kept along with goats and sheep.

Çatal Hüyük had one religious shrine for every two houses. Many rooms contain depictions of horned wild bulls, female breasts, goddesses, leopards, and handprints. Rituals involved burning grains, legumes (LEG-yooms), and meat but not sacrificing live animals. Statues of plump female deities far outnumber statues of male deities, suggesting that the inhabitants primarily venerated a goddess of fertility. According to the site's principal excavator, "it seems extremely likely that the cult of the goddess was administered mainly by women."[2]

Metalworking became an important specialized occupation in the late Neolithic period. At Çatal Hüyük objects of copper and lead—metals that occur naturally in fairly pure form—date to about 6400 B.C.E. Silver and gold also appear at early dates in various parts of the world. Because of their rarity and softness, those metals did not replace stone tools and weapons. The discovery of decorative and ceremonial objects of metal in graves suggests they were symbols of status and power.

Towns, specialized crafts, and religious shrines forced farmers to produce extra food for nonfarmers like priests and artisans. The building of permanent houses, walls, and towers, not to mention megalithic monuments, also called for added labor. Stonehenge, for example, took 30,000 person-hours to build. Whether these tasks were performed freely or coerced is unknown.

---

[2] James Mellaart, *Çatal Hüyük: A Neolithic Town in Anatolia* (New York: McGraw-Hill, 1967), 202.

SECTION REVIEW

- Around 10,000 years ago humans began to cultivate plants, selecting for those with the highest nutritional yield, and to domesticate animals. These Agricultural Revolutions arose in various parts of the world.

- Climate change at the end of the last Ice Age is probably the major reason for the switch from food gathering to food production.

- The lives of farmers are, in many respects, harder and more hazardous than those of hunter-gatherers, but the more secure food supply made possible by agriculture led to a great increase in human population.

- In some places small agricultural villages developed into towns that were centers of trade and home to sophisticated craftspeople and people in other specialized professions. Farmers had to produce surpluses to feed nonfarming specialists.

megaliths Structures and complexes of very large stones constructed for ceremonial and religious purposes in Neolithic times.

Neolithic Goddess Many versions of a well-nourished and pregnant female figure were found at Çatal Hüyük. Here she is supported by twin leopards whose tails curve over her shoulders. To those who inhabited the city some 8,000 years ago, the figure likely represented fertility and power over nature. The Art Archive/ Museum of Anatolian Civilisations Ankara/Gianni Dagli Orti

MESOPOTAMIA

■ *How did Mesopotamian civilization emerge, and what technologies promoted its advancement?*

Mesopotamia means "land between the rivers" in Greek. The name reflects the centrality of the Tigris (TIE-gris) and Euphrates (you-FRAY-teez) Rivers to the way of life in this region. Mesopotamia lies mostly within modern Iraq. To the north and east, an arc of mountains extends from northern Syria and southeastern Anatolia to the Zagros (ZAG-rohs) Mountains, which separate the plain from the Iranian Plateau. This is an alluvial plain—a flat, fertile expanse built up over many millennia by silt that the

rivers deposited. The Syrian and Arabian deserts lie to the west and southwest, the Persian Gulf to the southeast.

Floods in this plain, caused by snow melting in the northern mountains, could be sudden and violent. They could ruin crops and change the course of rivers, cutting off fields and towns from water and communication. In this environment, the people of ancient Mesopotamia saw themselves at the mercy of gods who embodied the forces of nature. Because of the unpredictable floods and a hot, dry climate where evaporation of flood drainage leeched toxic salt into the soil, Mesopotamia came late to farming, approximately in 5000 B.C.E. But shortly after 3000 B.C.E. the Mesopotamians had constructed an irrigation system to control the supply of water from the Tigris and Euphrates. This struggle against nature is reflected in the Babylonian myths (**Babylon** was the most important city in southern Mesopotamia). The myths say that human beings were created by Marduk, the chief god of Babylon, from the bloody defeat of Tiamat (TIE-ah-mut), a female figure who personified the salt sea.

"Civilization" The Mesopotamians, like other peoples throughout history, equated civilization with their own way of life, but *civilization* is an ambiguous concept, and the charge that a particular group is "uncivilized" has been used throughout human history to justify many distressing acts. Thus it is important to explain the rise of complex societies in Mesopotamia and Egypt from approximately 3500 to 1500 B.C.E. (see Map 1.1). (China, developing slightly later, is discussed in Chapter 3.)

Our starting point roughly coincides with the origins of writing, allowing us to observe aspects of human experience not revealed by archaeological evidence alone. The people living in Mesopotamia at the start of the "historical period"—the period for which we

Babylon The largest and most important city in Mesopotamia. It achieved particular eminence as the capital of the Amorite king Hammurabi in the eighteenth century B.C.E.

Map 1.1 River-Valley Civilizations, 3500–1500 B.C.E. The earliest complex societies arose in the floodplains of large rivers: in the fourth millennium B.C.E. in the valley of the Tigris and Euphrates Rivers in Mesopotamia and the Nile River in Egypt, in the third millennium B.C.E. in the valley of the Indus River in Pakistan, and in the second millennium B.C.E. in the valley of the Yellow River in China. © Cengage Learning

Chronology

	Mesopotamia	Egypt
3500 B.C.E.		3100–2575 B.C.E. Early Dynastic
3000 B.C.E.	3000–2350 B.C.E. Early Dynastic (Sumerian)	
2500 B.C.E.		2575–2134 B.C.E. Old Kingdom
	2350–2230 B.C.E. Akkadian (Semitic)	2134–2040 B.C.E. First Intermediate Period
2000 B.C.E.	2112–2004 B.C.E. Third Dynasty of Ur (Sumerian)	2040–1640 B.C.E. Middle Kingdom
	1900–1600 B.C.E. Old Babylonian (Semitic)	1640–1532 B.C.E. Second Intermediate Period
1500 B.C.E.		1532–1070 B.C.E. New Kingdom

have written evidence—were the **Sumerians**. Archaeological evidence places them in southern Mesopotamia by 5000 B.C.E. and perhaps even earlier. Writing first appeared in Mesopotamia before 3300 B.C.E. According to one plausible theory, it may have originated to keep track of property, and it used a system known as **cuneiform**, which is Latin for "wedge-shaped" because of the wedge-shaped impressions created from pressing the point of a reed into a moist clay tablet.

The *Epic of Gilgamesh*, whose roots date to before 2000 B.C.E., defines *civilization* as the people of ancient Mesopotamia understood it. Gilgamesh, an early king (who may be depicted on the sculpture shown here), sends a temple prostitute to tame Enkidu (EN-kee-doo), a wild man who lives like an animal in the grasslands. Using her sexual charms to win Enkidu's trust, the temple prostitute tells him:

> Come with me to the city, to Uruk (OO-rook), to the temple of Anu and the goddess Ishtar . . . to Uruk, where the processions are and music, let us go together through the dancing to the palace hall where Gilgamesh presides.[3]

She clothes Enkidu and teaches him to eat cooked food, drink beer, and bathe and oil his body. Her words and actions signal the principal traits of civilized life in ancient Mesopotamia.

Scholars define **civilization** as having certain political, social, economic, and technological traits: (1) cities as administrative centers, (2) a political system based on control of a defined territory rather than kinship connections, (3) many people engaged in specialized, non-food-producing activities, (4) status distinctions based largely on accumulation of substantial wealth by some groups, (5) monumental building, (6) a system for keeping permanent records, (7) long-distance trade, and (8) major advances in science and the arts.

Cities, Kings, and Religion

The *Epic of Gilgamesh* shows both the ambition of kings and their value to the community. Gilgamesh, who is probably based on a historical king of Uruk, stirs resentment by demanding sexual favors

The Art Archive/Alamy

Gilgamesh Strangling a Lion This eighth-century B.C.E. sculpture of a king, possibly Gilgamesh, from the palace of the Assyrian king Sargon II, represents the magical power and omnipotence of kingship. The Gilgamesh story was still popular in Mesopotamia twenty centuries after the king of Uruk's lifetime.

from new brides, but the community relies on his immense strength, wisdom, and courage. In his quest of everlasting glory, Gilgamesh walls the city magnificently, stamping his name on every brick. His journey

Sumerians The people who dominated southern Mesopotamia through the end of the third millennium B.C.E.

cuneiform A system of writing in which wedge-shaped symbols represented words or syllables. It originated in Mesopotamia and was used initially for Sumerian and Akkadian but later was adapted to represent other languages of western Asia. Literacy was confined to a relatively small group of administrators and scribes.

civilization An ambiguous term often used to denote more complex societies but sometimes used by anthropologists to describe any group of people sharing a set of cultural traits.

---

[3] David Ferry, *Gilgamesh: A New Rendering in English Verse* (New York: Noonday Press, 1992).

to the faraway Cedar Mountains reflects the king's role in accessing valuable resources.

Mesopotamians opened new land to agriculture by building and maintaining their irrigation networks. Successful construction and maintenance of these irrigation systems required leaders who were able to organize large numbers of people to work together. Other projects called for similar coordination: harvesting, sheep shearing, building fortification walls and large public buildings, and warfare. Scholars have long believed that the earliest cities and complex societies arose in southern Mesopotamia as a result of the need to organize labor, especially for the creation and maintenance of irrigation channels. However, recent archaeological discoveries in northern Mesopotamia, where agriculture first developed in this part of the world and was sustained by rainfall, are suggesting a more complicated picture, as a number of sites in northeast Syria appear to have developed urban centers, bureaucracy, and other elements of social complexity at roughly the same time.

Most cities evolved from villages. When a successful village grew, small satellite villages developed nearby and eventually merged with the main village to form an urban center. Mesopotamian cities controlled the agricultural land and collected crop surpluses from villages in their vicinity. In return, the city provided rural districts with military protection against raiders and a market where villagers could acquire manufactured goods. Many early Mesopotamian city dwellers went out each day to labor in nearby fields. Others specialized in pottery, artwork, weapons, tools, and other crafts forged out of metal. The term **city-state** refers to a self-governing urban center and the agricultural territories it controls.

Little is known about the political systems of early Mesopotamian city-states. The two centers of power seen in written records are the temple and the palace of the king. The temples owned extensive agricultural lands, and head priests managed their wealth and played prominent political and economic roles in early communities. Temples contained the shrine of the chief deity, chapels for lesser deities, and offices and housing for priests and temple staff. The compound focused on the **ziggurat** (ZIG-uh-rat), a multistory, mud-brick, pyramid-shaped tower. Scholars are still debating the ziggurat's function and

meaning. Gods were anthropomorphic (an-thru-po-MORE-fik)—like humans in forms and conduct—and the temple would have been considered the god's residence. Priests tried to anticipate the gods' needs and appease them, with the high priest performing the central acts in the rituals. Certain priests entertained the gods with music, others exorcised evil spirits, and still others interpreted dreams and divined the future by examining the organs of sacrificed animals, reading patterns in rising incense smoke, or casting dice. Priests passed their office to their sons.

It is unknown whether common people had much access to temple buildings and how religious practices and belief affected their everyday lives, but the survival of many **amulets** (small charms meant to protect the bearer from evil) suggests a widespread belief in magic. Elite and common folk would have come together for the great festivals, such as the twelve-day New Year's festival held at harvest each spring where the Babylonian Creation Epic would have been read.

In the third millennium B.C.E., Sumerian documents show the emergence of the *lugal* (LOO-gahl), or "big man"—we would call him a king. The location of the temple in the heart of the city and the less prominent siting of the king's palace symbolize the later emergence of royalty. A plausible theory maintains that certain men chosen by the community to lead the armies in time of war extended their authority in peacetime. Some Mesopotamian kings claimed divinity, but this concept did not take root. Normally, the king portrayed himself as the deity's earthly representative and saw to the upkeep and building of temples and the proper performance of ritual. The king's power grew at the expense of the priests, and priests and temples gradually became dependent on the pal-

---

city-state A small independent state consisting of an urban center and the surrounding agricultural territory. A characteristic political form in early Mesopotamia, Archaic and Classical Greece, Phoenicia, and early Italy.

ziggurat A massive pyramidal stepped tower made of mud bricks. It is associated with religious complexes in ancient Mesopotamian cities, but its function is unknown.

amulet Small charm meant to protect the bearer from evil. Found frequently in archaeological excavations in Mesopotamia and Egypt, amulets reflect the religious practices of the common people.

ace. Other royal responsibilities included maintaining city walls and defenses, extending and repairing irrigation channels, guarding property rights, warding off outside attackers, and establishing justice. Although the lugal's position was not hereditary, it often passed from a father to a capable son.

Sargon (SAHR-gone), ruler of the city of Akkad (AH-kahd) around 2350 B.C.E., was the first to unite many cities under one king and capital. By razing the walls of conquered cities and installing governors backed by garrisons of Akkadian troops, Sargon, and the four family members who succeeded him, established a reign that lasted over 120 years. They gave land to soldiers to ensure their loyalty. For reasons that remain obscure, the Akkadian state fell around 2230 B.C.E.

The Sumerian language and culture became dominant again in the cities of the southern plain under the Third Dynasty of Ur (2112–2004 B.C.E.). Through campaigns of conquest and marriage alliances, this dynasty of five kings flourished for a century, maintaining tight control through a rapidly expanding bureaucracy of administrators and obsessive record keeping. Messengers and well-maintained road stations enabled rapid communication, and an official calendar, standardized weights and measures, and uniform writing practices increased the efficiency of the central administration.

The Third Dynasty of Ur built a great wall 125 miles (201 kilometers) long to protect against nomadic Amorites (AM-uh-rite), but the Amorites toppled the dynasty and founded a new city at Babylon, not far from Akkad. Toward the end of a long reign, **Hammurabi** (HAM-uh-rah-bee) (r. 1792–1750 B.C.E.) launched a series of aggressive military campaigns, and Babylon became the capital of what historians call the "Old Babylonian" state, which stretched beyond Sumer and Akkad into the north and northwest from 1900 to 1600 B.C.E. Hammurabi's Law Code, inscribed on a polished black stone pillar, reflects social divisions that may also have been valid at other times. Society was divided into three classes: (1) the free, landowning class, largely living in the cities, which included royalty, high-ranking officials, warriors, priests, merchants, and some artisans and shopkeepers; (2) the class of dependent farmers and artisans, whose legal attachment to royal, temple, or private estates made them the primary rural workforce; and (3) the class of slaves, primarily employed in domestic service. Penalties for crimes prescribed in the Law Code depended on the class of the offender, with the most severe punishments reserved for the lower orders.

Trade and Mesopotamian Society

Conquest gave some Mesopotamian city-states access to vital resources. Trade offered an alternative, and long-distance commerce flourished in most periods. Evidence of seagoing vessels appears as early as the fifth millennium B.C.E. Wood, metals, and stone came from foreign lands in exchange for wool, cloth, barley, and vegetable oil. Cedar forests in Lebanon and Syria yielded wood, Anatolia yielded silver, Egypt gold, and the eastern Mediterranean and Oman (on the Arabian peninsula) copper. Tin, which in alloy with copper made bronze, came from Afghanistan (in southern Central Asia), and chlorite, a greenish, easily carved stone, from the Iranian plateau. Jewelers and stone-carvers used black diorite from the Persian Gulf, blue lapis lazuli (LAP-is LAZ-uh-lee) from Afghanistan, and reddish carnelian (kahr-NEEL-yuhn) from Pakistan. In the third millennium B.C.E., merchants worked for the palace or temple and exchanged surpluses from the royal or temple farmlands for raw materials and luxury goods. Coined money played no role, but fixed weights of precious metal, primarily silver, or measures of grain could be exchanged for the calculated value. In the second millennium B.C.E., merchants became more independent and merchant guilds gained influence.

In the Old Babylonian period, as the class of people who were not dependent on the temple or palace grew in numbers and importance, the amount of land and other property in private hands increased, and the hiring of free laborers became more common. But we know little about the daily lives of ordinary Mesopotamians, especially those in villages or on

Hammurabi Amorite ruler of Babylon (r. 1792–1750 B.C.E.). He conquered many city-states in southern and northern Mesopotamia and is best known for a code of laws, inscribed on a black stone pillar, illustrating the principles to be used in legal cases.

large estates in the countryside, because they left few archaeological or written remains. Slaves, dependent workers, and hired laborers were all compensated with commodities such as food and oil in quantities proportional to their age, gender, and tasks. Slavery was not as fundamental to the economy as it would be in the later societies of Greece and Rome (see Chapters 4 and 5). Many slaves came from mountain tribes, either captured in war or sold by slave traders. Others were people unable to pay their debts. Normally slaves were not chained, but they were identified by a distinctive hairstyle; if given their freedom, a barber shaved off the telltale mark.

It is likewise difficult to discover much about the experiences of women. The written sources were produced by male **scribes**—trained professionals who applied their reading and writing skills to tasks of administration—and for the most part reflect elite male activities. Anthropologists theorize that women lost social standing and freedoms in societies where agriculture superseded hunting and gathering because women no longer provided most of the community's food. Food production in Mesopotamia depended on the heavy physical labor that fell to men of plowing, harvesting, and digging irrigation channels. Since food surpluses permitted families to have more children, bearing and rearing children became the primary occupation of many women, preventing them from acquiring the specialized skills of the scribe or artisan. Women could own property, maintain control of their dowry (a sum of money given by the woman's father to support her in her husband's household), and even engage in trade. Some worked outside the household in textile factories and breweries or as prostitutes, tavern keepers, bakers, or fortunetellers. Non-elite women who stayed at home helped with farming, planted vegetable gardens, cooked, cleaned, fetched water, tended the household fire, and wove baskets and textiles.

The standing of women seems to have declined further in the second millennium B.C.E., perhaps because of the rise of an urbanized middle class and an increase in private wealth. The laws favored the rights of husbands. Although Mesopotamian society was generally monogamous, a man could take a second wife if the first gave him no children, and in later Mesopotamian history kings and wealthy men had

several wives. Marriage alliances arranged between families made women into instruments for preserving and increasing family wealth. Alternatively, a family might decide to avoid a daughter's marriage—and the resulting loss of a dowry—by dedicating her to the temple service of a deity as a "god's bride." Later constraints on women's lives in the region, such as largely confining themselves to the home and wearing veils in public (see Chapter 9), may have originated in the second millennium B.C.E.

Technology and Science

The term *technology*, from the Greek word *techne*, meaning "skill" or "specialized knowledge," normally refers to the tools and machines that humans use to manipulate the physical world. Many scholars now use the term more broadly for any specialized knowledge used to transform the natural environment and human society. Writing was one such form of early technology.

Careful observation of the skies and advances in mathematics that used a number-system expressed as fractions or multiples of 60 (in contrast to our base-10 system; this is the origin of the seconds and minutes we use in calculating time today) made the Mesopotamians sophisticated practitioners of astronomy. Priests compiled lists of omens or unusual sightings on earth and in the heavens, together with a record of the events that coincided with them. They consulted these texts at critical times, for they believed that the recurrence of such phenomena could provide clues to future developments. The underlying premise was that the elements of the material universe, from the microscopic to the macrocosmic, were interconnected in mysterious but undeniable ways.

Clay, Mesopotamia's most abundant resource, went into the making of mud bricks. Whether dried in the sun or baked in an oven for greater durability, these constituted the main building material. Reed mats, laid between the mud-brick layers of ziggurats, served the same engineering purpose as girders in

scribe In the governments of many ancient societies, a professional position reserved for men who had undergone the lengthy training required to be able to read and write using cuneiform, hieroglyphics, or other early, cumbersome writing systems.

modern high-rise construction. The abundance of good clay also made pottery the most common material for dishes, storage vessels, and oil lamps (see Material Culture: Lamps and Candles). By 4000 B.C.E. the potter's wheel, spun by hands and feet, made possible rapid manufacture in precise and complex shapes.

Other technologies that enabled the Mesopotamians to meet the challenges of their physical environment included wheeled carts and sled-like platforms dragged by cattle to transport goods. In northern Mesopotamia, donkeys were the chief pack animals for overland caravans before the advent of the camel around 1200 B.C.E. (see Chapter 8). Evidence of boats used in river and sea trade appears as early as the fifth millennium B.C.E.

The Mesopotamians had to import metals, but they also became skilled in metallurgy, refining ores containing copper and alloying them with arsenic or tin to make **bronze**. Craftsmen poured molten bronze into molds to produce tools and weapons. The cooled and hardened bronze took a sharper edge than stone, was less likely to break, and was more easily repaired. Stone implements remained in use among poor people, who could not afford bronze.

Early military forces were nonprofessional militias of able-bodied men called up for short periods when needed. The powerful states of the later third and second millennia B.C.E. built up armies of well-trained and well-paid full-time soldiers. In the early

second millennium B.C.E. horses appeared in western Asia, and the horse-drawn chariot came into vogue. Infantry found themselves at the mercy of swift chariots carrying a driver and an archer who could easily run them down. Using increasingly effective siege machinery, Mesopotamian soldiers could climb over, undermine, or knock down the walls protecting the cities of their enemies.

EGYPT

■ *What role did the environment and religion play in the evolution of Egyptian civilization?*

No place exhibits the impact of the natural environment on the history and culture of a society better than ancient Egypt. Though located at the intersection of Asia and Africa, Egypt was less a crossroads than an isolated land protected by surrounding barriers of desert and a harborless, marshy seacoast. Whereas Mesopotamia was open to migration or invasion and was dependent on imported resources, Egypt's natural isolation and material self-sufficiency fostered a unique culture that for long periods had relatively little to do with other civilizations.

The Land of Egypt: "Gift of the Nile"

The world's longest river, the Nile flows northward from Lake Victoria and several large tributaries in the highlands of tropical Africa, carving a narrow valley between a chain of hills on either side until it reaches the Mediterranean Sea (see Map 1.2). Though bordered mostly by desert, the banks of the river support lush vegetation. About 100 miles (160 kilometers) from the Mediterranean, the river divides into channels to form a triangular delta. Most of Egypt's population lives on the twisting, green ribbon of land along the river or in the Nile Delta. Bleak deserts of mountains, rocks, and dunes occupy the rest of the country. The ancient Egyptians distinguished between the low-lying, life-sustaining "Black

SECTION REVIEW

- Mesopotamia developed in the plain of the unpredictable Tigris and Euphrates Rivers, and Mesopotamian gods embodied the often-violent forces of nature.

- The first people to develop a complex society that produced written records were the Sumerians.

- Mesopotamia was home to a coalition of city-states that grew out of villages and controlled rural territory.

- At the expense of the priesthood, kings assumed responsibility for administrative, legal, and military activities.

- The urban civilization of Mesopotamia developed a high degree of social division, a hierarchy in which women steadily lost standing.

- The Mesopotamians developed a wide range of technologies, the most important of which was writing.

bronze An alloy of copper with a small amount of tin (or sometimes arsenic), which is harder and more durable than copper alone. The term *Bronze Age* is applied to the era—the dates of which vary in different parts of the world—when bronze was the primary metal for tools and weapons.

Material Culture

Lamps and Candles

It is hard to imagine today how dark the world was after the sun went down throughout most of human history. The glow of a fire did not extend far. Nor were torches easy to make or long-lasting. A stick wrapped with oil-soaked cloth at one end does make an effective torch, but humans were in need of light long before they figured out how to make cloth. As for flammable oil, vegetable oils extracted from the seeds of olive or palm trees, or from plants like flax, lettuce, and corn, became abundant only with the spread of plant domestication in the Neolithic period. Prior to that, animal fat or tallow could be used, though it had the disadvantage of smelling like meat.

The Agricultural Revolutions made available not only vegetable oils but also pottery, and later metal, vessels that could be used as lamps. A fireproof vessel would be filled with oil, and a wick would be placed so that one end was immersed in the oil and the other open to the air. The oil would saturate the wick, and a flame touched to the wick would vaporize a small amount of oil and ignite the resultant gas. A poor wick might sputter, smoke, or go out. The pith, or inner porous core of plants of the rush family, could be used as wicks in rush lamps, or the oil-soaked pith stiffened by part of the outer skin of the rush could be stood upright and lit like slender candles in rush lights.

Aside from the pith of rushes, wicks were usually made of string or a sliver of wood. Since a wick of greater diameter produces a larger flame, braiding was used to make a thicker string. Of all natural fibers, cotton makes the best wicks because of its absorbency. Different varieties of cotton were native to India and pre-Columbian America, but cotton became a major crop in the Middle East only in the early Islamic period of the eighth century C.E. Christian Europe knew cotton only as an expensive import until the twelfth century, when a cotton industry was founded in northern Italy. Access to superior wicks contributed to an increase in European candle use.

Waxes differ from oils in being solid at room temperature. Molding wax around a wick produces a candle. Beeswax provided an ideal material for odorless candles and was in use for lighting as early as ancient Egyptian times. However, beeswax was scarce and expensive. Some premodern trade routes, such as those going south to the

Ancient Lamp Vessel *This 2,500-year-old oil lamp from Megiddo in Israel has grooves for two wicks. It is made of bronze, a valuable metal. Pottery lamps were much cheaper and show up abundantly in ancient archaeological sites.*

Erich Lessing/Art Resource, NY

Middle East along the rivers of Russia, featured beeswax as a major product. Beeswax candles came to play a prominent and often symbolic role in Christian, Jewish, and Buddhist religious rituals. Mosques, on the other hand, were traditionally lit by oil lamps.

Though whaling was practiced in certain coastal regions in prehistoric times, the extraction of whale oil on an industrial scale began in the sixteenth century and grew rapidly over the next three hundred years. Oil extracted from the whale's fat, or blubber, was widely used for lamps. Of even greater value was a wax called spermaceti that was made from an oily substance in the heads of sperm whales. A large whale might yield three tons of spermaceti. It burned without odor in candles and became the standard for candle making until the discovery of paraffin, a wax made from petroleum, in 1830. Paraffin generally replaced spermaceti as the preferred wax for candles.

The small flames of oil lamps and candles did not produce much illumination. *Candela* is the name of the unit of light intensity that became increasingly precise over the course of the nineteenth and twentieth centuries. It is intended to represent the light produced by a single candle, though many technical specifications, such as the color of the light, make it only an approximation. An even rougher approximation equates 120 candelas with the illumination provided by a 100-watt light bulb. This last approximation suggests how little light a single lamp or candle could provide in premodern times for reading, sewing, or doing any kind of fine work after sundown.

QUESTIONS FOR ANALYSIS

1. How would the provision of artificial light affect patterns of life with the change of seasons?
2. What human activities, such as storytelling, might have been enhanced by a lack of light?
3. How did gradual adoption of gaslights (1792) and the electric light bulb (1879) change people's lives?

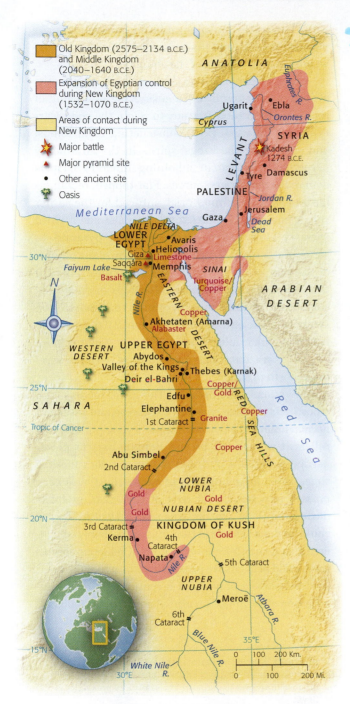

Map 1.2 Ancient Egypt The Nile River, flowing south to north, carved out of the surrounding desert a narrow green valley that became heavily settled in antiquity.

© Cengage Learning

Land" of dark soil and the elevated, deadly "Red Land" of the desert. The fifth-century B.C.E. Greek traveler Herodotus (he-RAH-duh-tuhs) called Egypt the "gift of the Nile."

The river was the main means of travel and communication, with the most important cities located upstream away from the Mediterranean. Because the river flows from south to north, the Egyptians called the southern part of the country "Upper Egypt" and the northern delta "Lower Egypt." The First Cataract of the Nile, the northernmost of a series of impassable rocks and rapids below Aswan (AS-wahn) (about 500 miles [800 kilometers] south of the Mediterranean), formed Egypt's southern boundary in most periods, but Egyptian control sometimes extended farther south into what was called "Kush" (later Nubia, today part of southern Egypt and northern Sudan). The Egyptians also settled a chain of large oases west of the river, green and habitable "islands" in the midst of the desert.

While the hot, sunny climate favored agriculture, rain rarely fell south of the delta, and irrigation channels carried water into the valley to increase the area suitable for planting. Unlike the Tigris and Euphrates, the Nile flooded at exactly the right time for grain agriculture. When the waters receded, they left behind a moist, fertile layer of mineral-rich silt in which farmers could easily plant their crops. An Egyptian creation myth featured the emergence of a life-supporting mound of earth from a primeval swamp.

The level of the flood's crest determined the abundance of the next harvest. Too little water left fertile land unirrigated and hence uncultivable, plunging the country into famine. The ebb and flow of successful and failed regimes seems to have been linked to the cycle of floods. Nevertheless, remarkable stability characterized most eras, and Egyptians viewed the universe as an orderly and beneficent place.

Egypt had other resources besides the Nile. Papyrus reeds growing in marshes yielded fibers that made good sails, ropes, and a kind of paper. The wild animals and birds and the abundant river fish attracted hunters and fishermen. Building stone was quarried and floated downstream from southern Egypt. And the state organized armed expeditions and forced labor to exploit copper and turquoise deposits in the Sinai Desert to the east and gold from Nubia to the south.

The farming villages that appeared in Egypt as early as 5500 B.C.E. relied on domesticated plant and animal species that had originated several millennia earlier in western Asia. Egypt's emergence as a focal point of civilization, however, stemmed at least partially from a gradual change in climate from the fifth to the third millennium B.C.E. Before that time, the Sahara, today the world's largest desert, had a relatively mild and wet climate. Its lakes and grasslands supported a variety of plant and animal species as well as populations of hunter-gatherers (see Chapter 8). As the Sahara became a desert, displaced groups migrated into the Nile Valley, where they developed a sedentary way of life.

Divine Kingship

The increasing population called for greater complexity in political organization, including a form of local kingship. Later generations of Egyptians saw the unification of smaller units into a single state by Menes (MEH-neez), a ruler from the south, as a pivotal event. Kings of Egypt bore the title "Ruler of the Two Lands"—Upper and Lower Egypt—and wore two crowns symbolizing the unification of the country. Unlike Mesopotamia, therefore, Egypt was unified early in its history.

Following the practice of Manetho, an Egyptian priest from the third century B.C.E., historians divide Egyptian history into thirty dynasties (sequences of kings from the same family). The rise and fall of dynasties often reflect the dominance of different parts of the country. More generally, scholars refer to the "Old," "Middle," and "New Kingdoms," each a period of centralized political power and brilliant cultural achievement, punctuated by "Intermediate Periods" of political fragmentation and cultural decline. Although experts debate the specific dates for these periods, the chronology reflects current opinion.

The Egyptian state centered on the king, often known by the New Kingdom term **pharaoh**, from an Egyptian phrase meaning "palace." From the Old Kingdom on, if not earlier, Egyptians considered the king to be a god sent to earth to maintain **ma'at** (muh-AHT), the divinely authorized order of the universe. He was the indispensable link between his people and the gods, and his benevolent rule ensured the welfare and prosperity of the country.

So much depended on the kings that their deaths evoked elaborate efforts to ensure the well-being of their spirits on their journey to rejoin the gods. Carrying out funerary rites, constructing royal tombs, and sustaining the kings' spirits in the afterlife by perpetual offerings in adjoining funerary chapels demanded massive resources. Flat-topped, rectangular tombs made of mud brick sufficed for the earlier rulers, but around 2630 B.C.E. Djoser (JO-sur), a Third Dynasty king, constructed a stepped **pyramid**—a series of stone platforms laid one on top of the other—at Saqqara (suh-KAHR-uh), near Memphis. Rulers of the Fourth Dynasty filled in the steps to create the smooth-sided, limestone pyramids that most often symbolize ancient Egypt. Between 2550 and 2490 B.C.E. the pharaohs Khufu (KOO-foo) and Khafre (KAF-ray) erected huge pyramids at Giza, several miles north of Saqqara.

Egyptians accomplished this construction with stone tools (bronze was still expensive and rare) and no machinery other than simple levers, pulleys, and rollers. Calculations of the human muscle power needed to build a pyramid within a ruler's lifetime suggest that large numbers of people must have been pressed into service for part of each year, probably during the flood season, when no agricultural work could be done. The Egyptian masses probably considered this demand for labor a kind of religious service that would help ensure prosperity. The age of the great pyramids lasted only about a century, although construction of pyramids on a smaller scale continued.

pharaoh The central figure in the ancient Egyptian state. Believed to be an earthly manifestation of the gods, he used his absolute power to maintain the safety and prosperity of Egypt.

ma'at Egyptian term for the concept of divinely created and maintained order in the universe. The divine ruler was the earthly guarantor of this order.

pyramid A large, triangular stone monument, used in Egypt and Nubia as a burial place for the king. The largest pyramids, erected during the Old Kingdom near Memphis, reflect the Egyptian belief that the proper and spectacular burial of the divine ruler would guarantee the continued prosperity of the land.

Pyramids of Menkaure, Khafre, and Khufu at Giza, ca. 2500 B.C.E. With a width of 755 feet (230 meters) and a height of 480 feet (146 meters), the Great Pyramid of Khufu is the largest stone structure ever built. The construction of these massive edifices depended on relatively simple techniques of stonecutting, transport (the stones were floated downriver on boats and rolled to the site on sledges), and lifting (the stones were dragged up the face of the pyramid on mud-brick ramps). However, the surveying and engineering skills required to level the platform, lay out the measurements, and securely position the blocks were very sophisticated and have withstood the test of time.

Michele Burgess/SuperStock

Administration and Communication

Ruling dynasties usually placed their capitals in the area of their original power base. **Memphis**, near today's Cairo at the apex of the Nile Delta, held this central position during the Old Kingdom. **Thebes**, far to the south, supplanted it during the Middle and New Kingdom periods (see Map 1.2). A complex bureaucracy kept detailed records of the country's resources. At the village, district, and central government levels, bureaucrats kept track of land, products, and people, extracting as taxes as much as 50 percent of the annual revenues of the country. This income supported the palace, bureaucracy, and army, paid for building and maintaining temples, and made possible great monuments celebrating the king's grandeur. The government maintained a monopoly over key sectors of the economy and controlled long-distance trade. The urban middle-class traders who increasingly managed the commerce of Mesopotamia had no parallel in Egypt.

A writing system had been developed before the beginning of the Early Dynastic period. **Hieroglyphics** (high-ruh-GLIF-iks), the earliest form of this system, featured picture symbols standing for words, syllables, or individual sounds. Hieroglyphic writing long continued to be used on monuments and ornamental inscriptions, but by 2500 B.C.E., administrators and copyists had developed a cursive script, in which the original pictorial nature of the symbol was less apparent, for their everyday needs. The Egyptians used writing for many purposes other than administrative record keeping. Their written literature included tales of adventure and magic, love poetry, religious hymns, and instruction manuals on technical subjects. Scribes in workshops attached to the temples made copies of traditional texts.

Egyptians wrote with ink on a writing material called **papyrus** (puh-PIE-ruhs), made from the stems of the papyrus reed that grew in the Nile marshes. Papyrus makers laid out the stems in a vertical and horizontal grid pattern, moistened them, and then

Memphis The capital of Old Kingdom Egypt, near the head of the Nile Delta. Early rulers were interred in the nearby pyramids.

Thebes Capital city of Egypt and home of the ruling dynasties during the Middle and New Kingdoms. Monarchs were buried across the river in the Valley of the Kings.

hieroglyphics A system of writing in which pictorial symbols represented sounds, syllables, or concepts. It was used for official and monumental inscriptions in ancient Egypt. Because of the long period of study required to master this system, literacy in hieroglyphics was confined to a relatively small group of scribes and administrators.

papyrus A reed that grows along the banks of the Nile River in Egypt. From it was produced a coarse, paperlike writing medium used by the Egyptians and many other peoples in the ancient Mediterranean and Middle East.

pounded them with a soft mallet until they adhered into a sheet of writing material. The plant grew only in Egypt, and papyrus was exported in large quantities throughout the ancient world. The word *paper* comes from Greek and Roman words for papyrus.

Strong monarchs appointed and promoted officials on the basis of ability and accomplishment, giving them grants of land cultivated by dependent peasants. Low-level officials worked in villages and district capitals; high-ranking officials served in the royal capital. During the Old Kingdom, the tombs of officials lay near the monumental tomb of the king so that they could serve him in death as they had in life.

Egyptian history exhibits a recurring tension between the centralizing power of the monarchy and the decentralizing tendencies of the bureaucracy. The shift of officials' tombs from the vicinity of the royal tomb to the home districts where they spent much of their time and exercised power more or less independently signaled the breakdown of centralized power in the late Old Kingdom and First Intermediate Period. Another sign was the tendency of administrative posts to become hereditary. The early monarchs of the Middle Kingdom restored centralized control by reducing the power and prerogatives of the old elite and creating a new class of administrators.

The common observation that Egypt was a land of villages without real cities stems from its capitals being primarily extensions of the palace and central administration. Compared to Mesopotamia, a far larger percentage of Egyptians lived in farming villages, and Egypt's wealth derived to a higher degree from cultivating the land. The towns and cities that did exist unfortunately lie buried beneath modern urban sites, since Egypt has too little land in its cultivable regions to afford abandonment of a large area.

Egypt largely stuck to itself during the Old and Middle Kingdoms, all foreigners being technically regarded as enemies. When necessary, local militia units backed up a small standing army of professional soldiers. Nomadic groups in the eastern and western deserts and Libyans to the northwest posed a nuisance more than a real danger. The king maintained limited contact with other advanced civilizations in the region, and Egypt's interests abroad focused on maintaining access to valuable resources rather than on acquiring territory. Trade with the coastal towns of the Levant (luh-VANT) (modern Israel, the Palestinian territories, Lebanon, and Syria) brought in cedar wood in return for grain, papyrus, and gold.

Egypt's strongest interest involved goods from the south. Nubia had rich sources of gold (Chapter 3 examines the rise in Nubia of a civilization influenced by Egypt but also vital, original, and long-lasting), and the southern course of the Nile offered the easiest passage to sub-Saharan Africa. In the Old Kingdom, Egyptian noblemen led donkey caravans south to trade for gold, incense, and products of tropical Africa such as ivory, ebony, and exotic animals. Forts along the border protected Egypt from attack. In the early second millennium B.C.E. Egyptian forces invaded Nubia, extending the border to the Third Cataract of the Nile and taking possession of the gold fields.

The People of Egypt

The estimated million to a million and a half inhabitants of Egypt included various physical types, ranging from dark-skinned people related to the populations of sub-Saharan Africa to lighter-skinned people akin to the populations of North Africa and western Asia. Though Egypt experienced no migrations or invasions on a scale common in Mesopotamian history, settlers periodically trickled into the Nile Valley and mixed with the local people.

Egypt had less pronounced social divisions than Mesopotamia, where a formal class structure emerged. The king and high-ranking officials enjoyed status, wealth, and power. Below them came lower-level officials, local leaders, priests and other professionals, artisans, and well-to-do farmers. Peasants, at the bottom, constituted the vast majority of the population.

Peasants lived in rural villages and devoted themselves to the seasonally changing tasks of agriculture: plowing, sowing, tending emerging shoots, reaping, threshing, and storing. They maintained irrigation channels, basins, and dikes. Fish and meat from domesticated animals—cattle, sheep, goats, and poultry—supplemented a diet based on wheat or barley, beer, and vegetables. Villagers shared implements, work animals, and storage facilities and helped one another at peak times in the agricultural cycle and in building projects. They prayed and feasted together at festivals to the local gods. Periodically they had to contribute labor to state projects. If taxation or compulsory service was too great a burden, flight into the desert was the only escape.

This account of village life depends on bits and pieces of archaeological and literary evidence. Tomb paintings of the elite sometimes depict the lives of common folk. The artists employed conventions to indicate status: obesity for the wealthy and comfortable, baldness and deformity for the working classes. Egyptian poets frequently employed metaphors of farming and hunting, and papyrus documents preserved in the hot, dry sands tell of property transactions and legal disputes among ordinary people. Slavery existed on a limited scale but was of limited economic significance and was softened by humane treatment and the possibility of being freed.

Some information is available about the lives of women of the upper classes, but it is filtered through the brushes and pens of male artists and scribes. Tomb paintings show women of the royal family and elite classes accompanying their husbands and engaging in typical domestic activities. They are depicted with dignity and affection, though they are clearly subordinate to the men. The artistic convention of depicting men with a dark red and women with a yellow flesh tone implies that the elite woman's proper sphere was indoors, away from the searing sun. In the beautiful love poetry of the New Kingdom, lovers address each other in terms of apparent equality and express emotions of romantic love.

Legal documents show that Egyptian women could own property, inherit property from their parents, and will their property to whomever they wished. Marriage, usually monogamous, was not confirmed by any legal or religious ceremony and essentially constituted a decision by a man and woman to establish a household together. Either party could dissolve the relationship, and the divorced woman retained rights over her dowry. At certain times queens and queen-mothers played significant behind-the-scenes roles in the politics of the court, and priestesses sometimes supervised the cults of female deities. In general, the limited evidence suggests that women in ancient Egypt enjoyed greater respect and more legal rights and social freedom than women in Mesopotamia and other ancient societies.

Belief and Knowledge

Egyptian religion was rooted in the landscape of the Nile Valley and the vision of cosmic order that it evoked. The sun rose every day in a clear and cloudless sky, and the river flooded on schedule every year, ensuring a bounteous harvest. Recurrent cycles and periodic renewal seemed a part of the natural world. Egyptians imagined the sky to be a great ocean surrounding the inhabited world. The sun-god Re (ray) traversed its waterway in a boat by day, then returned through the Underworld at night, fighting off the attacks of demonic serpents so that he could be born anew in the morning. In one especially popular story Osiris (oh-SIGH-ris), a god who once ruled Egypt, is slain by his jealous brother Set, who scatters his dismembered remains. Isis, Osiris's sister and wife, finds and reassembles the pieces, while Horus, his son, takes revenge on Set. Restored to life and installed as king of the Underworld, Osiris represents hope for a new life in a world beyond this one.

The king, represented as Horus and as the son of Re, fit into the pattern of the dead returning to life and the sun-god renewing life. As Egypt's chief priest, he intervened with the gods on behalf of his land and people. Egyptian rulers zealously built new temples, refurbished old ones, and made lavish gifts to the gods, at the same time overseeing construction of their own tombs. Thus much of the country's wealth went for religious purposes in a ceaseless effort to win the gods' favor, maintain the continuity of divine kingship, and ensure the renewal of the life-giving forces.

Some deities normally appeared with animal heads; others always took human form. Few myths about the origins and adventures of the gods have survived, but there must have been a rich oral tradition. Many towns had temples for locally prominent deities. When a town became the capital of a ruling dynasty, the chief god of that town became prominent across the land. Thus did Ptah (puh-TAH) of Memphis, Re of Heliopolis (he-lee-OP-uh-lis), and Amon (AH-muhn) of Thebes become gods of all Egypt, serving to unify the country and strengthen the monarchy.

During great festivals, the priests paraded a boat-shaped litter carrying the shrouded statue and cult items of the deity around the town. This brought large numbers of people into contact with the deity in an outpouring of devotion and celebration. Little is known about the day-to-day beliefs and practices of the common people, however. At home, family members made small offerings to Bes, the god of marriage and domestic happiness, to local deities, and to the family's ancestors. They relied on amulets and depictions of demonic figures to protect the bearer and ward off evil forces. In later times Greeks and Romans commented on the Egyptian devotion to magic.

Egyptians believed in the afterlife and prepared extensively for a safe passage and a comfortable existence once they arrived. A common belief was that death was a journey beset with hazards. The Egyptian Book of the Dead, present in many excavated tombs, contained rituals and spells to protect the journeying spirit. The weighing of the deceased's heart in the presence of the judges of the Underworld presented the ultimate challenge—the one that determined whether the person had led a good life and deserved to reach the blessed destination.

Obsession with the afterlife led to great concern about the physical condition of the dead body and led Egyptians to perfect techniques of mummification for preserving it. The idea probably derived from the slow decomposition of bodies buried in hot, dry sand on the edge of the desert, an early practice. The elite classes spent the most on mummification. Vital organs were removed, preserved, and stored in stone jars laid out around the corpse. Body cavities were filled with various packing materials. After immersing the cadaver for long periods in dehydrating and preserving chemicals, Egyptians wrapped it in linen. The **mummy** was then placed in one or more decorated wooden caskets within a tomb.

Building tombs at the edge of the desert left the lowlands free for farming. Pictures and samples of food and objects from everyday life accompanied the mummy to provide whatever he or she might need in the next life. Much of what is now known about ancient Egyptian life comes from examining utilitarian and luxury household objects found in tombs. Small figurines called shawabtis (shuh-WAB-tees) represented the servants whom the deceased might need

SECTION REVIEW

- In the benign environment of the Nile Valley, a unified Egypt emerged from a collection of small kingdoms.
- The ruler was the divine pharaoh responsible for maintaining the cosmic order.
- The state was administered from royal capitals and through a bureaucracy in which scribes kept detailed records in hieroglyphic script.
- Less urban than Mesopotamia, Egypt primarily concerned itself with maintaining the flow of important resources.
- Social divisions in Egypt were less pronounced than in Mesopotamia, slavery was limited, and women enjoyed greater freedom than elsewhere in the ancient world.
- Egyptian religion reflected the predictability of the environment and centered on the afterlife, the inspiration for many of Egypt's important technologies.

or the laborers he might send as substitutes if asked to provide compulsory labor. The elite classes attached chapels to their tombs and left endowments to subsidize the daily attendance of a priest and offerings of foodstuffs to sustain their spirits for all eternity.

The forms of the tomb also reflected wealth and status. Simple pit graves or small mud-brick chambers sufficed for the common people. The privileged classes built larger tombs. Kings erected pyramids and other grand edifices, employing subterfuge to hide the sealed chamber containing the body and treasures, as well as curses and other magical precautions to foil tomb robbers. Rarely did they succeed, however. Archaeologists have seldom discovered an undisturbed royal tomb.

The ancient Egyptians explored many areas of knowledge and developed advantageous technologies. They learned about chemistry through the mummification process, which also provided opportunities to learn about human anatomy, and Egyptian doctors were in demand in courts throughout western Asia. They developed mathematics to measure the dimensions of fields and to calculate the quantity of agricultural produce owed to the state. Through careful observation of the stars they constructed the most

mummy A body preserved by chemical processes or special natural circumstances, often in the belief that the deceased will need it again in the afterlife.

accurate calendar in the world, and they knew that when the star Sirius appeared on the horizon shortly before sunrise, the Nile flood surge was imminent. Pyramids, temple complexes, and other monumental building projects called for great skill in engineering. Long underground passageways were excavated to connect mortuary temples by the river with tombs near the desert's edge. On several occasions Egyptian kings dredged out a canal more than 50 miles (80 kilometers) long in order to join the Nile Valley to the Red Sea and expedite the transport of goods.

CONCLUSION

The first modern humans emerged in Africa and migrated to every corner of the earth. Research suggests that climate change drove these foragers to abandon hunting and gathering and adopt the practices of agriculture and pastoralism. In the warmer era following the Great Ice Age around 9000 B.C.E., populations on every inhabited continent except Australia underwent this great transformation, selecting high-yield strains of plants for cultivation and breeding livestock.

It is no accident that the first civilizations to develop high levels of political centralization, urbanization, and technology were situated in river valleys where rainfall was insufficient for reliable agriculture. Dependent on river water to irrigate the cultivated land that fed their populations, Mesopotamian and Egyptian rulers channeled considerable human resources into the construction and maintenance of canals, dams, and dikes. This effort required the formation of political centers that could organize the necessary labor force.

In both Egypt and Mesopotamia, kingship emerged as the dominant political form. The Egyptian king's divine origins and symbolic association with the forces of renewal made him central to the welfare of the entire country and gave him religious authority superseding the temples and priests. Egyptian monarchs lavished much of the country's wealth on their tombs, believing that a proper burial would ensure the continuity of kingship and the attendant blessings that it brought to the land and people. Mesopotamian rulers, who were not normally regarded as divine but still dominated the religious institutions, built new cities, towering walls, splendid palaces, and religious edifices as lasting testaments to their power.

The unpredictable and violent floods in the Tigris-Euphrates Basin were a constant source of alarm for the people of Mesopotamia. In contrast, the predictable, opportune, and gradual Nile floods were eagerly anticipated events in Egypt. The relationship with nature stamped the worldview of both peoples. Mesopotamians tried to appease their harsh deities so as to survive in a dangerous world. Gilgamesh, the hero of the Mesopotamian epic, is tormented by terrifying visions of the afterlife: disembodied spirits of the dead stumbling around in the darkness of the Underworld for all eternity, eating dust and clay and slaving for the heartless gods of that realm. Egyptians, on the other hand, largely trusted in and nurtured the supernatural powers that, they believed, guaranteed orderliness and prosperity.

Although the populations of Egypt and Mesopotamia were ethnically diverse, both regions experienced a remarkable degree of cultural continuity. New immigrants readily assimilated to the dominant language, belief system, and lifestyles of the civilization. Mesopotamian women's apparent loss of freedom and legal privilege in the second millennium B.C.E. also may have been related to the higher degree of urbanization and class stratification in this society. In contrast, Egyptian pictorial documents, love poems, and legal records indicate respect and greater equality for women in the valley of the Nile.

CHAPTER REVIEW

EARLY HUMANS

■ *In light of scientific advances in our understanding of human origins, what have we learned about our relationship to the earth and other living species?* (page 5)

The theory of evolution, supported by an enormous body of evidence, leads to far-reaching conclusions. Every living species evolved from a common ancestor. Humans are descended from earlier hominid species that evolved in Africa beginning about 7 million years ago. Every modern human descended from communities that evolved in Africa 50,000 years ago, with some groups migrating to the other habitable continents. All human communities are directly related to each other, to all other living species, and to the earth.

THE AGRICULTURAL REVOLUTIONS

■ *How did plant and animal domestication set the scene for the emergence of complex societies?* (page 10)

Domestic plants and animals made it possible for sizable populations to live even in regions that offered little support for foraging groups. As farming became the main source of food, settlement in villages became a normal way of life. In time, this led to complex political structures and the division of labor characteristic of civilized life.

MESOPOTAMIA

■ *How did Mesopotamian civilization emerge, and what technologies promoted its advancement?* (page 13)

The first Mesopotamian people to keep written records were the Sumerians. Some Sumerian towns grew into city-states composed of an urban center that ruled surrounding agricultural land. Priests originally dominated these states, but they gave way to kings who assumed religious, administrative, legal, and military responsibilities. Sharp social divisions were reflected in the class-based penalties of the Law Code of Hammurabi. Mesopotamian gods embodied the uncertain forces of the environment. The people strove to appease them through rites focused on temples maintained by priests. Mesopotamian culture pioneered cuneiform writing, canal irrigation, bronze casting, and monumental architecture.

EGYPT

■ *What role did the environment and religion play in the evolution of Egyptian civilization?* (page 19)

Protected by deserts and coastal marshes and nurtured by the predictable flooding of the Nile River, Egyptian

civilization was relatively self-sufficient and secure. As the Sahara Desert dried and the population in the Nile Valley increased, political organization became more complex, eventually unifying into a single kingdom under a divine king, the pharaoh. Less urban and socially stratified than Mesopotamian society, Egypt relied on peasant farmers with few slaves and a comparatively free female population. Egyptian religion embodied the orderly and benign qualities of the Nile and involved a complex vision of the afterlife. Much wealth went for religious purposes preparing for the afterlife and glorifying the pharaoh. To this end, Egyptians constructed monuments, tombs, and temples and applied their knowledge of chemistry and anatomy to mummification.

Key Terms

culture (p. 5)	Babylon (p. 13)
history (p. 5)	Sumerians (p. 15)
evolution (p. 5)	cuneiform (p. 15)
hominid (p. 6)	civilization (p. 15)
australopithecines (p. 6)	city-state (p. 16)
bipedalism (p. 6)	ziggurat (p. 16)
Great Ice Age (p. 6)	amulet (p. 16)
Homo habilis (p. 6)	Hammurabi (p. 17)
Stone Age (p. 7)	scribe (p. 18)
Paleolithic (p. 7)	bronze (p. 19)
Homo erectus (p. 7)	pharaoh (p. 22)
Homo sapiens (p. 8)	ma'at (p. 22)
foragers (p. 8)	pyramid (p. 22)
Neolithic (p. 10)	Memphis (p. 23)
Agricultural Revolutions (p. 10)	Thebes (p. 23)
	hieroglyphics (p. 23)
pastoralism (p. 11)	papyrus (p. 23)
megaliths (p. 12)	mummy (p. 26)

The Middle East and the Mediterranean

© Cengage Learning

Ancient stories—even when not historically accurate—provide valuable insights into how people thought about their origins and identity. One story concerned the founding of the city of Carthage (KAHR-thuhj) in present-day Tunisia, which for centuries dominated the waters and water-borne commerce of the western Mediterranean. Tradition held that Dido, a member of the royal family of the Phoenician city-state of Tyre (tire) in southern Lebanon, fled with her supporters to the western Mediterranean after her husband was murdered by her brother, the king. On the North African coast the refugees made friendly contact with local people, who offered them as much land as a cow's hide could cover. By cleverly cutting the hide into narrow strips, they marked out a substantial territory for Kart Khadasht, the "New City" (called *Carthago* by their Roman enemies).

This story highlights the spread of cultural patterns from older centers to new regions in the Mediterranean lands and western Asia. Trade, diplomatic contacts, military conquests, and the relocation of large numbers of people spread knowledge, beliefs, practices, and technologies.

By the early first millennium B.C.E. many societies of the region were entering the **Iron Age**. Iron offered advantages over bronze. It was a single metal rather than an alloy, and there were many sources of iron ore. Once the technology had been mastered—iron has to be heated to a higher temperature than bronze, and its hardness depends on the amount of carbon added during the forging process—iron tools were found to have harder, sharper edges than bronze tools.

The first part of this chapter resumes the story of Mesopotamia and Egypt in the second millennium B.C.E.: their relations with neighboring peoples, the development of a prosperous, "cosmopolitan" network of states in the Middle East, and the destruction and decline that set in around 1200 B.C.E. We also look at how the Minoan and Mycenaean civilizations of the Aegean Sea adopted the technologies and cultural patterns of the older Middle Eastern centers and prospered from participation in long-distance trade.

The remainder of the chapter examines three societies from 1000 to 500 B.C.E.: the Assyrians of northern Mesopotamia; the Israelites; and the Phoenicians of Lebanon and their colonies in the western Mediterranean, mainly Carthage.

THE COSMOPOLITAN MIDDLE EAST, 1700–1100 B.C.E.

■ *How did a cosmopolitan civilization develop in the Middle East during the Late Bronze Age, and what forms did it take?*

Both Mesopotamia and Egypt succumbed to outside invaders in the seventeenth century B.C.E. Eventually the outsiders were either ejected or assimilated, and conditions of stability and prosperity were restored. Between 1500 and 1200 B.C.E. large states dominated the Middle East (see Map 2.1), controlling the smaller states and kinship groups as they competed with, and sometimes fought against, one another for control of commodities and trade routes.

Historians have called the Late Bronze Age a "cosmopolitan" era, meaning a time of widely shared cultures and lifestyles. Diplomatic relations and commercial contacts between states fostered the flow of goods and ideas, and elite groups shared similar values and high standards of living. The peasants in the countryside, who constituted the majority of the population, saw some improvement in their standard of living but reaped fewer benefits from the increasing contacts and trade.

Western Asia By 1500 B.C.E. Mesopotamia was divided into two distinct political zones: Babylonia in the south and Assyria in the north (see Map 2.1). The city of Babylon had gained ascendancy under the dynasty of Hammurabi in the eighteenth and seventeenth centuries B.C.E., but Kassite (KAS-ite) people from the Zagros (ZAH-grohs) Mountains to the east had seized power by 1460 B.C.E. Though Kassite names derive from their native language, the Kassites otherwise embraced Babylonian

Iron Age Historians' term for the period during which iron was the primary metal for tools and weapons. The advent of iron technology began at different times in different parts of the world.

Chronology

	Western Asia	Egypt	Syria–Palestine	Mediterranean
2000 B.C.E.	**2000** B.C.E. Horses in use **1700–1200** B.C.E. Hittites dominant in Anatolia	**2040–1640** B.C.E. Middle Kingdom **1640–1532** B.C.E. Hyksos dominate northern Egypt **1532** B.C.E. Beginning of New Kingdom	**1800** B.C.E. Abraham migrates to Canaan	**2000** B.C.E. Rise of Minoan civilization on Crete; early Greeks arrive in Greece **1600** B.C.E. Rise of Mycenaean civilization in Greece
1500 B.C.E.	**1500** B.C.E. Hittites develop iron metallurgy **1460** B.C.E. Kassites assume control of southern Mesopotamia **1200** B.C.E. Destruction of Hittite kingdom	**1470** B.C.E. Queen Hatshepsut dispatches expedition to Punt **1353** B.C.E. Akhenaten launches reforms **1290–1224** B.C.E. Reign of Ramesses the Great **1200–1150** B.C.E. Sea Peoples attack Egypt **1070** B.C.E. End of New Kingdom	**1500** B.C.E. Early "alphabetic" script developed at Ugarit **1250–1200** B.C.E. Israelite occupation of Canaan **1150** B.C.E. Philistines settle southern coast of Israel	**1450** B.C.E. Destruction of Minoan palaces in Crete **1200–1150** B.C.E. Destruction of Mycenaean centers in Greece
1000 B.C.E.	**1000** B.C.E. Iron metallurgy begins **911** B.C.E. Rise of Neo-Assyrian Empire **744–727** B.C.E. Reforms of Tiglathpileser **668–627** B.C.E. Reign of Ashurbanipal **626–539** B.C.E. Neo-Babylonian kingdom	**750** B.C.E. Kings of Kush control Egypt **671** B.C.E. Assyrian conquest of Egypt	**1000** B.C.E. Jerusalem made Israelite capital **969** B.C.E. Hiram of Tyre comes to power **960** B.C.E. Solomon builds First Temple **920** B.C.E. Division into two kingdoms of Israel and Judah **721** B.C.E. Assyrian conquest of northern kingdom **701** B.C.E. Assyrian humiliation of Tyre	**1000** B.C.E. Iron metallurgy **814** B.C.E. Foundation of Carthage
600 B.C.E.	**612** B.C.E. Fall of Assyria		**587** B.C.E. Capture of Jerusalem **515** B.C.E. Deportees from Babylon return to Jerusalem **450** B.C.E. Completion of Hebrew Bible; Hanno the Phoenician explores West Africa	**500–200** B.C.E. Rivalry of Carthaginians, Greeks, and Romans in western Mediterranean

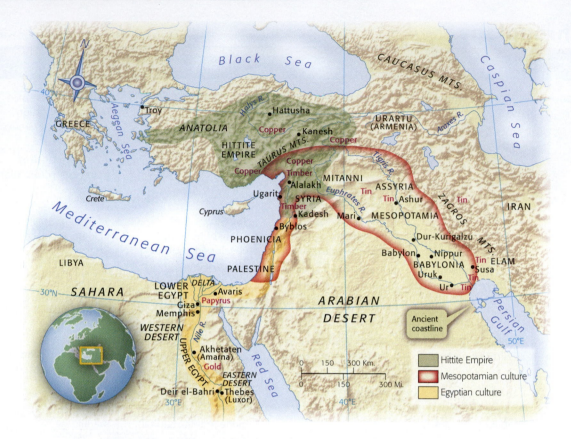

Map 2.1   The Middle East in the Second Millennium B.C.E. Although warfare was not uncommon, treaties, diplomatic missions, and correspondence in Akkadian cuneiform fostered cooperative relationships between states. All were tied together by extensive networks of exchange centering on the trade in metals. Peripheral regions, such as Nubia and the Aegean Sea, were drawn into the web of commerce.
© Cengage Learning

language and culture and intermarried with the native population. During their 250 years in power, the Kassite rulers of Babylonia defended their core area and traded for raw materials, but they did not pursue territorial conquest.

The Assyrians of the north proved more ambitious. As early as the twentieth century B.C.E. the city of Ashur (AH-shoor) on the northern Tigris anchored a busy trade route stretching across the northern plain to the Anatolian Plateau (modern Turkey). Assyrian merchants settled outside the walls of Anatolian cities and exchanged textiles and tin (a component of bronze) for Anatolian silver. In the eighteenth century B.C.E., an Assyrian dynasty briefly controlled the upper Euphrates River near the present-day Syria-Iraq border. The trade routes connecting Mesopota-

mia to Anatolia and the Syria-Palestine coast were key to the power of this "Old Assyrian" kingdom. After 1400 B.C.E. a resurgent "Middle Assyrian" kingdom engaged in campaigns of conquest and economic expansion.

Other ambitious states developed around the Mesopotamian heartland, including Elam (EE-luhm) in southwest Iran and Mitanni (mih-TAH-nee) between the upper Euphrates and Tigris Rivers. Most formidable were the **Hittites** (HIT-ites), who became

Hittites A people from central Anatolia who established an empire in Anatolia and Syria in the Late Bronze Age. With wealth from the trade in metals and military power based on chariot forces, the Hittites vied with New Kingdom Egypt for control of Syria-Palestine before falling to unidentified attackers around 1200 B.C.E.

the foremost power in Anatolia from around 1700 to 1200 B.C.E. From their capital at Hattusha (haht-tush-SHAH), near present-day Ankara (ANG-kuh-ruh) in central Turkey, they deployed the fearsome new technology of horse-drawn war chariots. They exploited Anatolia's rich deposits of copper, silver, and iron to play a key role in international commerce and were the first to develop a technique for making tools and weapons of iron, a process they kept secret because it provided military and economic advantages.

During the second millennium B.C.E. Mesopotamian political and cultural concepts spread across western Asia. Akkadian (uh-KAY-dee-uhn) became the language of diplomacy and correspondence between governments. The Elamites (EE-luh-mites) and Hittites, among others, adapted the cuneiform system to write their own languages. In the Syrian coastal city-state of Ugarit (OO-guh-reet), thirty cuneiform symbols were used to write consonant sounds, an early use of the alphabetic principle and a considerable advance over the hundreds of signs required in conventional writing.

New Kingdom Egypt

After flourishing for nearly four hundred years (see Chapter 1), the Egyptian Middle Kingdom collapsed in the seventeenth century B.C.E. Egypt entered a period of political fragmentation and economic decline. Around 1640 B.C.E. northern Egypt came under foreign rule for the first time at the hands of the Hyksos (HICK-soes), or "Princes of Foreign Lands."

Historians are uncertain who the Hyksos were. Semitic peoples had been migrating from the Levant (present-day Syria, Jordan, Lebanon, Israel, and the Palestinian territories) into the eastern Nile Delta for centuries. In the chaotic conditions of this time, other people may have joined them, establishing control first in the delta and then in the middle of the country. The Hyksos possessed war chariots and composite bows made of wood and horn for greater range, which gave them an advantage over the Egyptians. They intermarried with Egyptians and assimilated to native ways, speaking the Egyptian language and maintaining Egyptian institutions and culture. Nevertheless, unlike in Mesopotamia, the Egyptians continued to regard the Hyksos as "foreigners."

As with the formation of the Middle Kingdom five hundred years earlier, the reunification of Egypt under a native dynasty was accomplished by princes from Thebes. After three decades of warfare, Kamose (KAH-mose) and Ahmose (AH-mose) expelled the Hyksos from Egypt and inaugurated the New Kingdom, which lasted from about 1532 to 1070 B.C.E.

New Kingdom Egypt saw a shift from traditional Egyptian isolationism to aggressive expansion northward into Syria-Palestine and southward into Nubia. Timber, gold, and copper in taxes and tribute (payments from conquered peoples) were the prizes of this expansion. The occupied lands also provided a buffer against foreign attack. In Nubia, Egypt imposed direct control and pressed the native population to adopt Egyptian language and culture. In the Syria-Palestine region, the Egyptians stationed garrisons at strategically placed forts and supported local rulers willing to collaborate.

The New Kingdom was a period of innovation. Egyptian soldiers, administrators, diplomats, and merchants traveled widely, bringing back new fruits and vegetables, new musical instruments, and new technologies, such as an improved potter's wheel and weaver's loom.

At least one woman held the throne of New Kingdom Egypt. When her husband died, Queen **Hatshepsut** (hat-SHEP-soot) claimed the royal title for herself (r. 1473–1458 B.C.E.). In inscriptions she often used the male pronoun for herself, and drawings and sculptures show her wearing the long beard of the ruler of Egypt.

Around 1470 B.C.E. Hatshepsut sent a naval expedition down the Red Sea to the fabled land of Punt (poont), an exotic land that historians believe may have been near the coast of eastern Sudan or Eritrea. Hatshepsut was seeking the source of myrrh (murr), a reddish-brown resin that the Egyptians burned in religious rites and used in medicines and cosmet-

Hatshepsut Queen of Egypt (r. 1473–1458 B.C.E.). She dispatched a naval expedition to Punt (possibly northeast Sudan or Eritrea), the faraway source of myrrh. There is evidence of opposition to a woman as ruler, and after her death her name and image were frequently defaced.

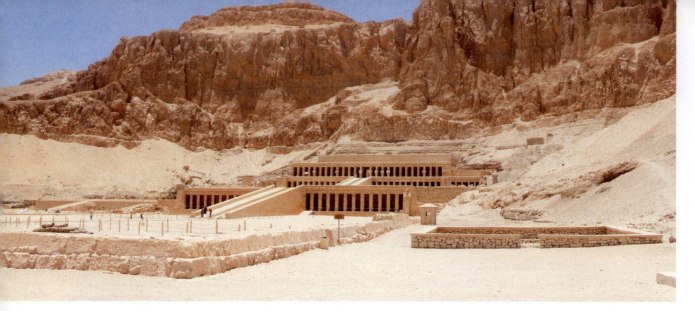

The Mortuary Temple of Queen Hatshepsut at Deir el-Bahri, Egypt, ca. 1460 B.C.E. This beautiful complex of terraces, ramps, and colonnades featured relief sculptures and texts commemorating the famous expedition to Punt. Hatshepsut, facing resistance from traditionalists opposed to a woman ruling Egypt, sought to prove her worth by publicizing the opening of direct contact with the source of highly prized myrrh. EugenZ/Shutterstock.com

ics. When the expedition returned with myrrh and sub-Saharan luxury goods—ebony, ivory, cosmetics, live monkeys, panther skins—Hatshepsut celebrated the achievement in a great public display and in words and pictures on the walls of her mortuary temple at Deir el-Bahri (DARE uhl–BAH-ree). After her death, her image was defaced and her name blotted out wherever it appeared, presumably by officials opposed to a woman ruler.

A century later another untraditional ruler ascended the throne as Amenhotep (ah-muhn-HOE-tep) IV. He soon began to refer to himself as **Akhenaten** (ah-ken-AHT-n) (r. 1353–1335 B.C.E.), meaning "beneficial to the Aten" (AHT-n) (the disk of the sun), and spread his belief in Aten as the supreme deity. He closed the temples of other gods, challenging the age-old supremacy of the chief god Amon (AH-muhn) and the power and influence of his priests.

Some scholars have credited Akhenaten with the invention of monotheism—the belief in one exclusive god. It is likely, however, that Akhenaten was attempting to reassert the superiority of the king over the priests and to renew belief in the king's divinity. Worship of Aten was confined to the royal family: the people of Egypt were pressed to revere the divine ruler.

Akhenaten built a new capital at modern-day Amarna (uh-MAHR-nuh), halfway between Memphis and Thebes (see Map 2.1). He relocated thousands of Egyptians to construct the site and serve the ruling elite. His artists created a new style that broke with the conventions of earlier art: the king, his wife Nefertiti (nef-uhr-TEE-tee), and their daughters were depicted in fluid, natural poses with strangely elongated heads and limbs and swelling abdomens.

Akhenaten's reforms were strongly resented by government officials and priests whose privileges and wealth were linked to the traditional system. After his death the temples were reopened; Amon was reinstated as chief god; the capital was returned to Thebes; and the priests regained their influence. The boy-king Tutankhamun (tuht-uhnk-AH-muhn) (r. 1333–1323 B.C.E.), famous solely because his was the only royal tomb found by archaeologists that had not been pillaged by robbers, reveals both in his name (meaning "beautiful in life is Amon") and in his insignificant reign the ultimate failure of Akhenaten's revolution.

The rulers of a new dynasty, the Ramessides (RAM-ih-sides), returned to the policy of conquest and

Akhenaten Egyptian pharaoh (r. 1353–1335 B.C.E.). He built a new capital at Amarna, fostered a new style of naturalistic art, and created a religious revolution by imposing worship of the sun-disk.

Ramesses II in a War Chariot Attacks Nubian Enemies This is a restoration of a thirteenth century B.C.E. painting on the wall of a temple at Beit el Wali. Other paintings depict the pharaoh attacking Asiatic enemies and making offerings to the high god Amon. www.BibleLandPictures.com/Alamy

expansion that Akhenaten had neglected. **Ramesses II** (RAM-ih-seez)—sometimes called Ramesses the Great—ruled for sixty-six years (r. 1290–1224 B.C.E.) and dominated his age. Living into his nineties, he may have fathered more than a hundred children. Since 1990 archaeologists have been excavating a network of corridors and chambers carved deep into a hillside near Thebes, where many sons of Ramesses were buried.

Commerce and Communication

Early in his reign Ramesses II fought a major battle against the Hittites at Kadesh in northern Syria (1285 B.C.E.). Although Egyptian propaganda boasted of a great victory, the lack of territorial gains suggests that it was essentially a draw. In subsequent years Egyptian and Hittite diplomats negotiated a treaty, which was strengthened by Ramesses' marriage to a Hittite princess. At issue was control of Syria-Palestine, strategically located between the great powers of the Middle East and at the end of the east-west trade route across Asia. The inland cities—such as Mari (MAH-ree) on the upper

Euphrates and Alalakh (UH-luh-luhk) in western Syria—were hubs of international trade. The coastal towns—particularly Ugarit and the Phoenician towns of the Lebanese seaboard—extended commerce to the lands ringing the Mediterranean Sea.

Commerce in metals energized long-distance trade. Assyrian trafficked in silver from Anatolia (above) and Egyptians gratified their passion for Nubian gold (see Chapter 3). Copper came from Anatolia and Cyprus, tin from Afghanistan and possibly the British Isles. Both ores traveled long distances and passed through many hands before reaching their final destinations.

New modes of transportation expedited communications and commerce across great distances and inhospitable landscapes. Horses, domesticated by nomadic peoples in Central Asia, were brought into

Ramesses II A long-lived ruler of New Kingdom Egypt (r. 1290–1224 B.C.E.). He reached an accommodation with the Hittites of Anatolia after a standoff in battle at Kadesh in Syria. He built on a grand scale throughout Egypt.

Mesopotamia through the Zagros Mountains around 2000 B.C.E. and reached Egypt before 1600 B.C.E. The speed of the horse contributed to the creation of large states and empires, enabling soldiers and government agents to cover great distances quickly. Swift, maneuverable horse-drawn chariots became the premier instrument of war.

Sometime after 1500 B.C.E. in western Asia, but not for another thousand years in Egypt, people began to make common use of camels, though the animal was domesticated much earlier in southern Arabia. Their strength made them ideal pack animals, and their ability to go without water made possible travel across barren terrain.

THE AEGEAN WORLD, 2000–1100 B.C.E.

■ *What civilizations emerged in the Aegean world, and what relationship did they have to the older civilizations to the east?*

In this era of far-flung trade and communication, the emergence of the Minoan (mih-NO-uhn) civilization on the island of Crete and the Mycenaean (my-suh-NEE-uhn) civilization of Greece demonstrates the fertilizing influence of older centers on outlying lands and peoples. The landscape of southern Greece and the Aegean islands is rocky and arid, with small plains lying between ranges of hills. The limited arable land was suitable for grains, grapevines, and olive

trees. Flocks of sheep and goats grazed the slopes. Sharply indented coastlines, natural harbors, and small islands within sight of one another made the sea the fastest and least costly mode of travel. Lacking metals and timber, Aegean peoples had to import these commodities from abroad. As a result, the rise, success, and eventual fall of the Minoan and Mycenaean societies were closely tied to their commercial and political relations with other peoples in the region.

Minoan Crete

The **Minoan** civilization that had come into being on the island of Crete by 2000 B.C.E. (see Map 2.1) featured centralized government, monumental building, bronze metallurgy, writing, and record keeping. Archaeologists named this civilization after King Minos, who, in Greek legend, ruled a naval empire in the Aegean and kept the monstrous Minotaur (MIN-uh-tor) (half-man, half-bull) in a mazelike labyrinth built by the ingenious inventor Daedalus (DED-ih-luhs).

The ethnicity of the Minoans is uncertain, and their writing has not been deciphered. But their sprawling palace complexes at Cnossos (NOS-suhs), Phaistos (FIE-stuhs), and Malie (mahl-YAH) and the distribution of Cretan pottery and other artifacts around the Mediterranean and Middle East testify to widespread trading connections. Egyptian, Syrian, and Mesopotamian influences can be seen in the design of the Minoan palaces, but the absence of identifiable representations of Cretan rulers contrasts sharply with the grandiose depictions of kings in the Middle East and suggests a different conception of authority. Also noteworthy are the absence of fortifications at the palace sites and the presence of high-quality indoor plumbing.

Statuettes of women with elaborate headdresses and serpents coiling around their limbs may represent fertility goddesses. Colorful frescoes (paintings done on the moist plaster surfaces of walls) in the palaces portray groups of women in frilly skirts conversing

Minoan Prosperous civilization on the Aegean island of Crete in the second millennium B.C.E. The Minoans engaged in far-flung commerce around the Mediterranean and exerted powerful cultural influences on the early Greeks.

or watching performances as well as young acrobats vaulting over the horns of an onrushing bull, either for sport or as a religious activity. Servants carrying jars and fishermen throwing nets and hooks from their boats suggest a joyful attitude toward work, but this may say more about elite ideals than about the reality of daily toil. Stylized vase paintings depicting plants with swaying leaves and playful octopuses winding their tentacles around the surface of the vase communicate a delight in nature's beauty.

All the Cretan palaces except at Cnossus, along with the houses of the elite and peasants in the countryside, were deliberately destroyed around 1450 B.C.E. Because Mycenaean Greeks took over at Cnossus, most historians regard them as the culprits.

Mycenaean Greece

Most historians believe that speakers of an Indo-European language ancestral to Greek migrated into the Greek peninsula around 2000 B.C.E. Through intermarriage, blending of languages, and melding of cultural practices, the indigenous population and the newcomers created the first Greek culture. For centuries this society remained simple and static. Farmers and shepherds lived in Stone Age conditions, wringing a bare living from the land. But in 1876 a German businessman, Heinrich Schliemann (SHLEE-muhn), intent on proving true the ancient Greek *Iliad* and *Odyssey* epics that spoke of Agamemnon (ag-uh-MEM-non), the king of **Mycenae** (my-SEE-nee), discovered proof of an advanced civilization that lasted from around 1600 to 1150 B.C.E. Schliemann found deep, rectangular **shaft graves** with not only the bodies of men, women, and children but also gold jewelry, ornaments, weapons, and utensils. Clearly, some people had acquired wealth, authority, and the capacity to mobilize human labor. Subsequent excavation uncovered a large palace complex, massive walls, and more shaft graves.

The sudden appearance of Mycenaean culture in mainland Greece is puzzling. There is no evidence of Cretan political control of the mainland, but these early Greeks were clearly influenced by the Minoan palaces, centralized economy, and administrative bureaucracy, as well as the writing system. They adopted Minoan styles of architecture, pottery, and fresco and vase painting. Historians speculate that

trade, piracy, and the booty brought back by mercenaries (soldiers who served for pay in foreign lands) might be responsible.

Excavations revealed other settlements with the same features discovered at Mycenae: a citadel built on a hilltop and surrounded by high, thick walls. The fortified enclosure—made of stones so large that later Greeks believed the one-eyed giant Cyclopes (SIGH-kloe-pees) had lifted them into place—provided refuge for the entire community in time of danger and contained the palace and administrative complex. The large central hall with an open hearth and columned porch was surrounded by courtyards, living quarters for the royal family and their retainers, offices, storerooms, and workshops. Brightly painted scenes of war, the hunt, and daily life, as well as decorative motifs from nature, covered the palace walls.

Additional information is provided by over four thousand baked clay tablets written in a script called **Linear B**. Like its predecessor, the undecipherable Minoan script called Linear A, Linear B uses pictorial signs to represent syllables, but the language is an early form of Greek. Palace administrators kept track of people, animals, and objects in exhaustive detail, listing the number of chariot wheels in storerooms, the rations paid to workers, and the gifts dedicated to various gods. However, individual people—even kings—receive no mention, leaving us largely in the dark about the political and legal system, social structure, gender relations, religious beliefs, or even historical events.

Mycenae Site of a fortified palace complex in southern Greece that controlled a Late Bronze Age kingdom. In ancient epic poems, Mycenae was the base of King Agamemnon, who commanded the Greeks besieging Troy. Contemporary archaeologists call the complex Greek society of the second millennium B.C.E. "Mycenaean."

shaft graves A term used for the burial sites of elite members of Mycenaean Greek society in the mid-second millennium B.C.E. At the bottom of deep shafts lined with stone slabs, the bodies were laid out along with gold and bronze jewelry, implements, weapons, and masks.

Linear B A set of syllabic symbols, derived from the writing system of Minoan Crete, used in the Mycenaean palaces of the Late Bronze Age to write an early form of Greek. It was used primarily for palace records, and the surviving Linear B tablets provide substantial information about the economic organization of Mycenaean society and tantalizing clues about political, social, and religious institutions.

Fresco from the Aegean Island of Thera, ca. 1650 B.C.E. This picture shows the arrival of a fleet in a harbor as people watch from the walls of the town. The Minoan civilization of Crete was famous in legend for its naval power. The fresco reveals the appearance and design of ships in the Bronze Age Aegean. In the seventeenth century B.C.E., the island of Thera was devastated by a massive volcanic explosion, thought by many to be the origin of the myth of Atlantis sinking beneath the sea.

The seafaring skill of Minoans and Mycenaeans encouraged long-distance trade. Commercial vessels depended primarily on sails, and their crews navigated during daylight hours to keep the land in sight and then went ashore at night to eat and sleep. The ships' shallow keels enabled the crews to pull them up onto the beach.

Cretan and Greek pottery and crafted goods are found not only in the Aegean but also in other parts of the Mediterranean and Middle East, sometimes in enough quantity and variety to suggest settlements of Aegean peoples. The oldest artifacts are Minoan; then Minoan and Mycenaean objects are found side by side; and eventually Greek wares replace Cretan goods altogether. This indicates that Cretan mer-

chants pioneered trade routes and were later joined by Mycenaean traders, who supplanted them in the fifteenth century B.C.E.

The many Aegean pots found throughout the region must have once contained such products as wine and olive oil. Other possible exports include textiles, weapons, and other crafted goods, as well as slaves and mercenary soldiers. As for imports, amber (from northern Europe) and ivory carved in Syria have been discovered at Aegean sites, and the large population of southern Greece may have relied on imports of grain. Above all, the Aegean lands needed metals, both gold and the copper and tin needed to make bronze. Sunken ships carrying copper ingots have been found on the floor of the Mediterranean.

Only the elite classes owned metal goods, which may have been symbols of their superior status.

Mycenaeans were tough, warlike, and acquisitive. They traded with those who were strong and took from those who were weak. This way of life led to conflict with the Hittite kings of Anatolia in the fourteenth and thirteenth centuries B.C.E. Documents in the archives at the Hittite capital refer to the king and land of Ahhijawa (uh-key-YAW-wuh), most likely a Hittite rendering of *Achaea* (uh-KEY-uh), a term used for the Greeks. They indicate that relations were sometimes friendly, sometimes strained, and that the people of Ahhijawa took advantage of Hittite preoccupation or weakness. The *Iliad*, which Schliemann had tried to prove true over a century ago, can be seen against this backdrop of Mycenaean belligerence and opportunism, telling a tale of the Achaeans' ten-year siege and eventual destruction of Troy, a city on the fringes of Hittite territory controlling the sea route between the Mediterranean and Black Seas. Archaeology has confirmed a destruction at Troy around 1200 B.C.E.

The Fall of Late Bronze Age Civilizations

Hittite difficulties with Ahhijawa and the Greek attack on Troy foreshadowed the troubles that culminated in the destruction of many of the old centers of the Middle East and Mediterranean around 1200 B.C.E. In this period, for reasons not well understood, large numbers of people were on the move. As migrants swarmed into one region, they displaced other peoples, who then joined the tide of refugees. Around 1200 B.C.E. unidentified invaders destroyed the Hittite capital, Hattusha, and the Hittite kingdom. The tide of destruction moved south into Syria, and the great coastal city of Ugarit was swept away. Egypt managed to beat back two attacks: an assault on the Nile Delta around 1220 B.C.E. by "Libyans and Northerners coming from all lands," and a major invasion by the "Sea Peoples" about thirty years later. Although the Egyptian ruler claimed a great victory, the Philistines (FIH-luh-steen) occupied the coast of Palestine (this is the origin of the name subsequently used for this region), and Egypt soon withdrew. The Egyptians also lost their foothold in Nubia, opening the way for the emergence of the native kingdom centered on Napata (see Chapter 3).

Among the invaders listed in the Egyptian inscriptions are the Ekwesh (ECK-wesh), who could be Achaeans—that is, Greeks. Whether or not the Mycenaeans participated in these or other invasions, their own centers also experienced collapse. The rulers apparently saw trouble coming; at some sites they began to build more extensive fortifications and took steps to guarantee water supplies. But their efforts were in vain. Nearly all the palaces were destroyed in the first half of the twelfth century B.C.E.

Curiously, archaeological records contain no trace of foreign invaders. However, the demise of Mycenaean civilization at roughly the same time as the fall of other regional civilizations suggests that external factors played a role. The position of the Mycenaean ruling class may have depended on the import of vital commodities and the profits from trade, and they may have suffered from the destruction of trading partners and disruption of routes. Competition for limited resources may have led to internal unrest and, ultimately, political collapse.

The end of Mycenaean civilization illustrates the interdependence of the major centers of the Late Bronze Age. The destruction of the palaces ended the domination of the ruling class. The administrative apparatus revealed in the Linear B tablets disappeared, and writing passed out of use along with the

SECTION REVIEW

- Influenced by contact with older cultures, Minoan Crete was the first European civilization to develop complex government and advanced technologies.

- The Minoans participated in extensive long-distance trade, which prompted a blending of foreign and indigenous cultural forms and practices.

- Minoan civilization was deliberately destroyed, perhaps by Mycenaean Greeks.

- In Greece, Mycenaean civilization rose suddenly and developed common patterns of settlement, organization, and technology.

- The Mycenaeans participated in long-distance trade and piracy activities, which likely became the basis of later heroic legends.

- Large migrations precipitated the collapse of many Late Bronze Age civilizations, including the Mycenaean, after which Greece entered a Dark Age.

palace officials who had utilized it. Archaeological studies indicate the depopulation of some regions of Greece and a flow of people to other regions that escaped destruction. The Greek language persisted, and a thousand years later people were still worshiping gods mentioned in the Linear B tablets. People also continued to make the vessels and implements that they were familiar with, although with a marked decline in artistic and technical skill. Mycenaean cultural uniformity gave way to regional variations in shapes, styles, and techniques, reflecting the increased isolation of different Greek areas. The peoples of the region entered a centuries-long "Dark Age" of poverty, isolation, and loss of knowledge.

THE ASSYRIAN EMPIRE, 911–612 B.C.E.

■ *How did the Assyrian Empire rise to power and eventually dominate most of the ancient Middle East?*

New centers emerged in the centuries after 1000 B.C.E. The chief force for change was the powerful and aggressive **Neo-Assyrian Empire** (911–612 B.C.E.). Compared to the flat expanse of Babylonia to the south, the Assyrian homeland in northern Mesopotamia is hillier and has a more temperate climate and greater rainfall. Peasant farmers, accustomed to defending themselves against marauders, provided the foot-soldiers for the ceaseless Neo-Assyrian campaigns: westward across the plain and desert as far as the Mediterranean, north into mountainous Urartu (ur-RAHR-too) (modern Armenia), east across the Zagros range onto the Iranian Plateau, and south along the Tigris River to Babylonia.

These campaigns followed important trade routes and provided immediate booty and the prospect of tribute and taxes. They also secured access to iron and silver and brought the Assyrians control of international commerce. Driven by pride, greed, and religious conviction, the Assyrians defeated the other great kingdoms of the day. At its peak their empire stretched from Anatolia, Syria-Palestine, and Egypt in the west, across Armenia and Mesopotamia, and as far as western Iran. Although historians sometimes apply the term *empire* to earlier regional powers, the Assyrians created a new kind of empire, larger in extent than anything seen before and dedicated to the enrichment of the imperial center at the expense of the subjugated periphery.

The king was literally and symbolically the center of the Assyrian universe. All the land belonged to him, and all the people, even the highest-ranking officials, were his servants. Assyrians believed that the gods chose the king as their earthly representative. Normally the king chose a son as successor, and his choice was confirmed by divine oracles and the Assyrian elite. In the revered ancient city of Ashur the high priest anointed the new king's head with oil and gave him the insignia of kingship: a crown and scepter. The kings also were buried in Ashur.

Messengers and spies brought the king information from every corner of the empire. The king appointed officials, heard complaints, dictated correspondence to an army of scribes, and received foreign envoys. He was the military leader, responsible for planning campaigns, and was often away from the capital commanding operations in the field.

Among other responsibilities, the king supervised the state religion, devoting much time to elaborate public and private rituals and to upkeep of the temples. He consulted the gods through rituals of divination. All actions were carried out in the name of Ashur, the chief god. Military victories were cited as proof of Ashur's superiority over the gods of the conquered peoples.

Relentless government propaganda secured popular support for military campaigns that mostly benefited the king and the nobility. Royal inscriptions posted throughout the empire catalogued recent victories, extolled the unshakeable determination of the king, and promised ruthless punishments to anyone who resisted. Relief sculptures depicting hunts, battles, sieges, executions, and deportations covered the walls of the royal palaces. Looming over most scenes was the king, larger than anyone else, muscular and fierce. Few visitors to the Assyrian court could fail to be awed and intimidated.

Neo-Assyrian Empire An empire extending from western Iran to Syria-Palestine, conquered by the Assyrians of northern Mesopotamia between the tenth and seventh centuries B.C.E. They used force and terror and exploited the wealth and labor of their subjects. They also preserved and continued the cultural and scientific developments of Mesopotamian civilization.

Hulton Archive/Stringer/Getty Images

Wall Relief from the Palace of Sennacherib at Nineveh Against a backdrop of wooded hills representing the landscape of Assyria, workers are hauling a huge stone sculpture from the riverbank to the palace under the watchful eyes of officials and soldiers. They accomplish this task with simple equipment—a lever, a sledge, and thick ropes—and a lot of human muscle power.

Conquest and Control

Superior military organization and technology lay behind Assyria's unprecedented conquests. Early armies consisted of men who served in return for grants of land and peasants and slaves contributed by large landowners. Later, King Tiglathpileser (TIG-lath-pih-LEE-zuhr) (r. 744–727 B.C.E.) created a core army of professional soldiers made up of Assyrians and the most formidable subject peoples. At its peak the Assyrian state could mobilize a half-million troops, including lightly armed bowmen and slingers, armored spearmen, cavalry equipped with bows or spears, and four-man chariots.

Iron weapons and cavalry gave Assyrian soldiers an advantage. However, Assyrian engineers also developed machinery and tactics for besieging fortified towns. They tunneled under the walls, built mobile towers for archers, and applied battering rams to weak points. Couriers and signal fires provided long-distance communication, while a network of spies gathered intelligence.

Terror tactics discouraged resistance and rebellion. Civilians were thrown into fires, prisoners were skinned alive, and the severed heads of defeated rulers hung on city walls, all of which was well publicized. **Mass deportation**—the forced uprooting of entire communities and resettlement elsewhere— broke the spirit of rebellious peoples. Although this tactic had a long history in the ancient Middle East, the Neo-Assyrian monarchs used it on an unprecedented scale, and up to 4 million people may have been relocated. Deportation also shifted human resources from the periphery to the center, where the deportees worked on royal and noble estates, opened new lands for agriculture, and built palaces and cities.

mass deportation The forcible removal and relocation of large numbers of people or entire populations. The mass deportations practiced by the Assyrian and Persian Empires were meant as a terrifying warning of the consequences of rebellion. They also brought skilled and unskilled labor to the imperial center.

The Assyrians never discovered an effective method of governing an empire of such vast distances, varied landscapes, and diverse peoples. Control tended to be tight at the center and in lands closest to the core area, and less so farther away. The Assyrian kings waged many campaigns to reinstate control over territories subdued in previous wars.

Assyrian officials oversaw the collection of tribute and taxes, maintained law and order, raised troops, undertook public works, and provisioned armies and administrators passing through their territory. The expectation of land or shares of booty and taxes, fear of punishment, and oaths of allegiance bound the elite and skilled professionals—priests, diviners, scribes, doctors, and artisans—to the monarch. Provincial governors were subject to frequent inspections by royal overseers.

The Assyrians ruthlessly exploited the wealth and resources of their subjects to fund their military campaigns and administration. Wealth from the periphery was funneled to the center, where the king and nobility grew rich. Triumphant kings expanded the ancestral capital and religious center at Ashur and built magnificent new royal cities encircled by high walls and containing ornate palaces and temples. Dur Sharrukin (DOOR SHAH-roo-keen), the "Fortress of Sargon," was completed in a mere ten years by a massive labor force composed of prisoners of war and Assyrian citizens who owed periodic service to the state.

Nevertheless, the Assyrian Empire was not simply parasitic. There is some evidence of royal investment in provincial infrastructure. The cities and merchant classes thrived on expanded long-distance commerce, and some subject populations were surprisingly loyal to their Assyrian rulers.

Assyrian Society and Culture

Surviving sources primarily shed light on the deeds of kings and elites. Only a little is known about the lives and activities of the millions of Assyrian subjects. The government did not distinguish between native Assyrians and the increasingly large number of immigrants and deportees in the Assyrian homeland. All were referred to as "human beings," entitled to the same legal protections and liable for the same labor and military service.

SECTION REVIEW

- One of the most important civilizations to emerge after the upheavals of the Late Bronze Age was the Neo-Assyrian Empire.

- Led by all-powerful kings, the Assyrians waged campaigns of aggressive expansion.

- The Assyrians' military success rested on superior organization and technology, such as iron weapons, cavalry, and the ability to attack fortifications.

- The Assyrians controlled subject peoples through terror tactics and mass deportations.

- The Assyrian state exploited subject territories, transporting wealth from the periphery to the center of the empire.

- Assyrian scholars preserved and added to the long intellectual and scientific legacy of Mesopotamian civilization.

Over time the inflow of outsiders changed the ethnic makeup of the core area.

The vast majority of subjects worked on the land. The agricultural surpluses they produced allowed substantial numbers of people—the standing army, government officials, religious experts, merchants and artisans—to engage in specialized activities.

Most trade took place at the local level, with individual artisans and small workshops producing pottery, tools, and clothing. The state fostered long-distance trade, since imported luxury goods—metals, fine textiles, dyes, gems, and ivory—brought in substantial customs revenues and pleased the elite. Silver was the basic medium of exchange, weighed out for each transaction in a time before the invention of coins.

Assyrian scholars preserved and built on the achievements of their Mesopotamian predecessors. When archaeologists excavated the palace of Ashurbanipal (ah-shur-BAH-nee-pahl) (r. 668–627 B.C.E.), one of the last Assyrian kings, at Nineveh (NIN-uh-vuh), they discovered more than twenty-five thousand tablets or fragments. The **Library of Ashurbanipal** contained official documents as well as literary and

Library of Ashurbanipal A large collection of writings drawn from the ancient literary, religious, and scientific traditions of Mesopotamia. It was assembled by the seventh-century B.C.E. Assyrian ruler Ashurbanipal. The many tablets unearthed by archaeologists constitute one of the most important sources of present-day knowledge of the long literary tradition of Mesopotamia.

scientific texts. Some were originals that had been brought to the capital; others were copies made at the king's request. The "House of Knowledge" referred to in some documents may have been an academy that attracted learned men to the imperial center. Much of what we know about Mesopotamian art, literature, science, and earlier history comes from discoveries at Assyrian sites.

ISRAEL, 2000–500 B.C.E.

■ *How did the civilization of Israel develop, following both familiar cultural patterns and a unique course of its own?*

The small land of Israel probably appeared insignificant to the Assyrian masters of western Asia, but it would play an important role in world history. Two interconnected dramas played out here between around 2000 and 500 B.C.E. First, a loose collection of nomadic groups engaged in herding and caravan traffic became a sedentary, agricultural people, developed complex political and social institutions, and became integrated into the commercial and diplomatic networks of the Middle East. Second, these people transformed the austere cult of a desert god into the concept of a single, all-powerful, and all-knowing deity, in the process creating ethical and intellectual traditions that underlie the beliefs and values of Judaism, Christianity, and Islam.

The land and people at the heart of this story have gone by various names: Canaan, Israel, Palestine; Hebrews, Israelites, Jews. For the sake of consistency, the people are referred to here as *Israelites*, the land they occupied in antiquity as **Israel**.

Israel is a crossroads linking Anatolia, Egypt, Arabia, and Mesopotamia. Its natural resources are few. The Negev Desert and the vast wasteland of the Sinai (SIE-nie) lie to the south. The Mediterranean coastal plain was in the hands of others, particularly the Philistines, throughout much of this period. Galilee to the north, with its sea of the same name, was a relatively fertile land of grassy hills and small plains. The narrow ribbon of the Jordan River runs down the eastern side of the region into the Dead Sea, so named because its high salt content is toxic to life.

Origins, Exodus, and Settlement

The fundamental source of information about ancient Israel is the collection of writings preserved in the **Hebrew Bible** (called the Old Testament by Christians). The Hebrew Bible brings together several collections of materials that originated with different groups and advocated particular interpretations of past events. Traditions about the Israelites' early history were long transmitted orally. Not until the tenth century B.C.E. were they written down in a script borrowed from the Phoenicians. The text that we have today dates from the fifth century B.C.E., with a few later additions, and reflects the point of view of the priests who controlled the Temple in Jerusalem. The Hebrew language of the Bible reflects the speech of the Israelites until about 500 B.C.E., when it was supplanted by Aramaic. Historians disagree about how accurately this document represents Israelite history. However, it provides a foundation to be used critically and tested against archaeological discoveries.

The history of ancient Israel follows a familiar pattern in the ancient Middle East. Nomadic pastoralists, occupying marginal land between the inhospitable desert and settled agricultural areas, sometimes engaged in trade and sometimes raided the farms and villages of settled peoples, but eventually they settled down to an agricultural way of life and later developed a unified state.

The Hebrew Bible tells the story of Abraham and his descendants. Born in the city of Ur in southern Mesopotamia, Abraham rejected the idol worship of his homeland and migrated with his family and livestock across the Syrian desert. Eventually he arrived in the land of Israel, which had been promised to him and his descendants by the Israelite god, Yahweh.

Israel In antiquity, the land between the eastern shore of the Mediterranean and the Jordan River, occupied by the Israelites from the early second millennium B.C.E. The modern state of Israel was founded in 1948.

Hebrew Bible A collection of sacred books containing diverse materials concerning the origins, experiences, beliefs, and practices of the Israelites. Most of the extant text was compiled by members of the priestly class in the fifth century B.C.E. and reflects the concerns and views of this group.

These "recollections" of the journey of Abraham (who, if he was a real person, probably lived around 1800 B.C.E.) may compress the experiences of generations of pastoralists who migrated from the grazing lands between the upper reaches of the Tigris and Euphrates Rivers to the Mediterranean coastal plain. They camped by a permanent water source in the dry season and drove herds of sheep, cattle, and donkeys to a well-established sequence of grazing areas during the rest of the year. The animals provided them with milk, cheese, meat, and cloth.

The nomadic Israelites and the settled peoples were suspicious of one another. This friction between herders and farmers permeates the story of the innocent shepherd Abel, who was killed by his farmer brother Cain.

Abraham's son Isaac and then his grandson Jacob became the leaders of this migratory group of herders. In the next generation the squabbling sons of Jacob's several wives sold their brother Joseph as a slave to passing merchants heading for Egypt. Through luck and ability Joseph became a high official at the pharaoh's court. Thus he was in a position to help his people when drought struck and forced the Israelites to migrate to Egypt. The sophisticated Egyptians looked down on these rough herders and eventually enslaved them and put them to work on royal building projects.

Several points need to be made about this biblical account. First, the Israelite migration to Egypt and later enslavement may have been connected to the rise and fall of the Hyksos. Second, although surviving Egyptian sources do not refer to Israelite slaves, they do complain about Apiru (uh-PEE-roo), a derogatory term applied to caravan drivers, outcasts, bandits, and other marginal groups. Some scholars believe there may be a connection between the similar-sounding terms *Apiru* and *Hebrew*. Third, the period of alleged Israelite slavery coincided with the ambitious building programs launched by several New Kingdom pharaohs. However, there is little archaeological evidence of an Israelite presence in Egypt.

The Bible further relates that Moses, an Israelite with connections to the Egyptian royal family, led the Israelites out of captivity. The narrative of their departure, the Exodus, is overlaid with folktale motifs, including the ten plagues that Yahweh inflicted on Egypt to persuade the pharaoh to release the Israelites, and the miraculous parting of the waters of the Red Sea that enabled the refugees to escape. Oral tradition may have embellished memories of a real emigration from Egypt followed by years of wandering in the wilderness of Sinai.

During their reported forty years in the desert, the Israelites entered into a "covenant" or pact with their god, Yahweh: they would be his "Chosen People" if they promised to worship him exclusively. This pact was confirmed by tablets that Moses brought down from the top of Mount Sinai, inscribed with the Ten Commandments that set out the basic tenets of Jewish belief and practice. The Commandments prohibited murder, adultery, theft, lying, and envy and demanded respect for parents and rest from work on the Sabbath, the seventh day of the week.

Joshua, Moses's successor, led the Israelites from the east side of the Jordan River into the land of Canaan (KAY-nuhn) (modern Israel and the Palestinian territories), where they attacked and destroyed Canaanite (KAY-nuh-nite) cities. Archaeological evidence confirms the destruction of some Canaanite towns between 1250 and 1200 B.C.E., though not precisely the towns mentioned in the biblical account. Shortly thereafter, lowland sites were resettled and new sites were established in the hills. The material culture of the new settlers was cruder but continued Canaanite patterns.

Most scholars doubt that Canaan was conquered by a unified Israelite army. In a time of widespread disruption, movements of peoples, and decline and destruction of cities throughout this region, it is more likely that Israelite migrants took advantage of the disorder and were joined by other groups and even refugees from the Canaanite cities.

In a pattern common throughout history, the new coalition of peoples invented a common ancestry. The "Children of Israel," as they called themselves, were divided into twelve tribes supposedly descended from the sons of Jacob and Joseph. Each tribe was installed in a different part of the country. Its chief was primarily responsible for mediating disputes and safeguarding the group. Charismatic figures, famed for their daring in war or genius in arbitration, were called "Judges" and enjoyed a special standing that transcended tribal boundaries. The tribes also shared access to a shrine

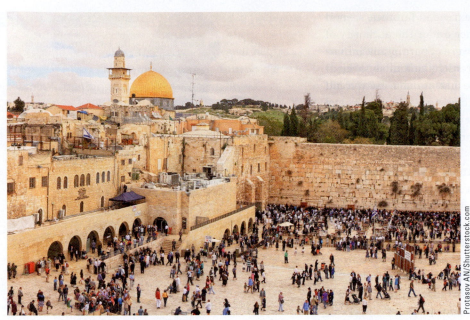

The Western Wall in Jerusalem The sole remaining remnant of King Herod's magnificent Second Temple, the religious center of ancient Judaism. It replaced Solomon's Temple, destroyed in the Babylonian conquest of 586 B.C.E., but was destroyed by the Romans in 70 C.E. in the course of suppressing a revolt in Judaea. The site is also sacred to Islam, with the golden Dome of the Rock in the background.

Protasov AN/Shutterstock.com

in the hill country at Shiloh (SHIE-loe), which housed the Ark of the Covenant, a sacred chest containing the tablets that Yahweh had given Moses.

Rise of the Monarchy

The troubles afflicting the eastern Mediterranean around 1200 B.C.E. also brought the Philistines to the coastal plain of Israel, where they came into frequent conflict with the Israelites. The long-haired strongman Samson, who toppled a Philistine temple, and the shepherd boy David, whose sling felled the towering warrior Goliath, became biblical heroes. A religious leader named Samuel recognized the need for a strong central authority and anointed Saul as the first king of Israel around 1020 B.C.E. When Saul perished in battle, the throne passed to David (r. ca. 1000–960 B.C.E.), who oversaw Israel's transition from tribal confederacy to unified monarchy. He strengthened royal authority by making the captured hill city of Jerusalem his capital. Soon after, David brought the Ark to Jerusalem, making the city the religious as well as political center of the kingdom.

The reign of David's son Solomon (r. ca. 960–920 B.C.E.) marked the high point of the Israelite monarchy. Alliances and trade linked Israel with near and distant lands. Solomon and Hiram, the king of Phoenician Tyre, dispatched a fleet into the Red Sea to bring back gold, ivory, jewels, sandalwood, and exotic animals. The story of the visit to Solomon by the queen of Sheba may be mythical, but it reflects the reality of trade with Saba (SUH-buh) in south Arabia (present-day Yemen) or the Horn of Africa (present-day Somalia). Such wealth supported a lavish court life, a sizable bureaucracy, and an intimidating chariot army that made Israel a regional power. Solomon undertook an ambitious building program employing slaves and the compulsory labor of citizens. To strengthen the link between religious and secular authority, he built the **First Temple** in Jerusalem.

The Temple priests became a powerful and wealthy class, receiving a share of the annual harvest in return for making animal sacrifices to Yahweh. The expansion of Jerusalem, new commercial opportunities, and the increasing prestige of the Temple hierarchy contributed to a growing gap between urban and rural, rich and poor. Fiery prophets, claiming revelation from Yahweh, accused the monarchs and aristocracy of corruption, impiety, and neglect of the poor.

First Temple A monumental sanctuary built in Jerusalem by King Solomon in the tenth century B.C.E. to be the religious center for the Israelite god Yahweh. The Temple priesthood conducted sacrifices, received a tithe or percentage of agricultural revenues, and became economically and politically powerful.

The Israelites lived in extended families, several generations residing together under the authority of the eldest male. Male heirs were of paramount importance, and first-born sons received a double share of the inheritance. If a couple had no son, they could adopt one, or the husband could have a child by the wife's slave attendant. If a man died childless, his brother was expected to marry his widow and sire an heir.

Women provided the family with vital goods and services, but they could not inherit property or initiate divorce. An unfaithful wife could be put to death. Peasant women labored with other family members in agriculture or herding in addition to caring for the house and children. As the society became urbanized, some women worked outside the home as cooks, perfumers, wet nurses (a recent mother hired to suckle another person's child), prostitutes, and singers of laments at funerals. A few women reached positions of power, such as Deborah the Judge, who led troops in battle against the Canaanites. "Wise women" composed sacred texts in poetry and prose. This reality has been obscured, in part by the male bias of the Hebrew Bible, in part because the status of women declined as Israelite society became more urbanized.

Fragmentation and Dispersal

After Solomon's death around 920 B.C.E., resentment over royal demands and the neglect of tribal rights split the monarchy into two kingdoms: Israel in the north, with its capital at Samaria (suh-MAH-ree-yuh); and Judah (JOO-duh) in the southern territory around Jerusalem. The two were sometimes at war, sometimes allied.

This period saw the final formulation of **monotheism**, the belief in Yahweh as the one and only god. Nevertheless, many Israelites were attracted to the ecstatic rituals of the Canaanite storm-god Baal (BAHL) and the fertility goddess Asherah (uh-SHARE-uh). Prophets condemned the adoption of foreign ritual and threatened that Yahweh would punish Israel severely.

The two Israelite kingdoms and other small states in the region laid aside their rivalries to mount a joint resistance to the Neo-Assyrian Empire, but to no avail. In 721 B.C.E. the Assyrians destroyed the northern kingdom of Israel and deported much of its

SECTION REVIEW

- As the Hebrew Bible suggests, the Israelites began as nomadic pastoralists who, after a period of enslavement, settled permanently in Canaan.

- Pressure from hostile Philistines forced the Israelites to adopt a more complex government.

- The resulting monarchy unified the Israelites into the kingdom of Israel, which reached its height under Solomon.

- During the monarchy, the temple priests became a powerful class, and Israelite society became more urban and economically divided.

- Patrilineal extended families became the basic social unit, and the status of women declined.

- After the breakup of Israel, Jewish monotheism reached its final form, successive conquests created the Diaspora, and a distinctive Jewish identity emerged.

population to the east. New settlers were brought in from Syria, Babylon, and Iran, changing the area's ethnic, cultural, and religious character. The kingdom of Judah survived more than a century, sometimes rebelling, sometimes paying tribute to the Assyrians or the Neo-Babylonian kingdom (626–539 B.C.E.) that succeeded them.

When the Neo-Babylonian monarch Nebuchadnezzar (NAB-oo-kuhd-nez-uhr) captured Jerusalem in 587 B.C.E., he destroyed the Temple and deported to Babylon the royal family, the aristocracy, and many skilled workers such as blacksmiths and scribes. The deportees prospered so well in their new home "by the waters of Babylon" that half a century later most of their descendants refused the offer of the Persian monarch Cyrus (see Chapter 3) to return to their homeland. This was the origin of the **Diaspora** (die-ASS-peh-rah)—a Greek word meaning "dispersion" or "scattering." This dispersion outside the homeland of

monotheism Belief in the existence of a single divine entity. Some scholars cite the devotion of the Egyptian pharaoh Akhenaten to Aten (sun-disk) and his suppression of traditional gods as the earliest instance. The Israelite worship of Yahweh developed into an exclusive belief in one god, and this concept passed into Christianity and Islam.

Diaspora Greek word meaning "dispersal," used to describe the communities of a given ethnic group living outside their homeland. Jews, for example, spread from Israel to western Asia and Mediterranean lands in antiquity and today can be found throughout the world.

many Jews—as we may now call these people, since an independent Israel no longer existed—continues to this day. To maintain their religion and culture, the Diaspora communities developed institutions like the synagogue (Greek for "bringing together"), a communal meeting place that served religious, educational, and social functions.

The Babylonian Jews who did make the long trek back to Judah met with a cold reception from the local population. Persevering, they rebuilt the Temple in modest form and edited the Hebrew Bible into roughly its present form.

Exile and loss of political autonomy sharpened Jewish identity. Jews lived by a rigid set of rules. Dietary restrictions forbade the eating of pork and shellfish and mandated that meat and dairy products not be consumed together. Ritual baths were used to achieve spiritual purity. The Jews venerated the Sabbath (Saturday, the seventh day of the week) by refraining from work and from fighting, following the example of Yahweh, who, according to the Bible, rested on the seventh day after creating the world. These strictures and others, including a ban on marrying non-Jews, tended to isolate the Jews from other peoples, but they also fostered a powerful sense of community.

PHOENICIA AND THE MEDITERRANEAN, 1200–500 B.C.E.

■ *How did the Phoenicians rise to commercial dominance over much of the Mediterranean world?*

While the Israelites were forging a united kingdom, the people who occupied the Mediterranean coast to the north were developing their own distinctive **Phoenician** (fi-NEE-shun) civilization. Historians generally used this Greek word instead of *Can'ani*—Canaanites—the word they used for themselves.

The Phoenician City-States

Many Canaanite settlements were destroyed during the violent upheavals and mass migrations around 1200 B.C.E. discussed earlier. Aramaeans (ah-ruh-MAY-uhn)—nomadic pastoralists like the early Israelites—migrated into the interior portions of Syria while Israelites and Philistines gained domination farther south.

By 1100 B.C.E. Canaanite territory had shrunk to a narrow strip of Lebanon between the mountains and the sea. New political forms and seaborne commerce provided the key to Canaanite survival. Sometime after 1000 B.C.E. the Canaanites encountered the Greeks, who referred to them as *Phoinikes*, or Phoenicians. The term may mean "red men" and refer to the color of their skin, or it may refer to the precious purple dye they extracted from the murex snail (see Environment and Technology: Ancient Textiles and Dyes).

Rivers and rocky spurs sliced the Lebanese coastal plain into a series of small city-states, chief among them Byblos (BIB-loss), Sidon (SIE-duhn), and Tyre. Trading raw materials (cedar and pine, metals, incense, papyrus), foodstuffs (wine, spices, salted fish), and crafted luxury goods (textiles, carved ivory, glass) brought wealth and influence to the Phoenician city-states.

Expansion into the Mediterranean

Before 1000 B.C.E. Byblos was the most important Phoenician city-state. The English word *bible* comes from the Greek *biblion*, meaning "book written on papyrus from Byblos." The Greeks recognized the Phoenicians as the inventors of the alphabet, which used about two dozen symbols, each representing a sound. (The Greeks later added symbols for vowel sounds—see Chapter 4.) Little Phoenician writing survives, however, probably because scribes used perishable papyrus. As a result, little is known about the internal affairs of the Phoenician cities beyond the names of some kings.

After 1000 B.C.E. Tyre surpassed Byblos. Located on an offshore island, Tyre was practically impregnable. It had two harbors—one facing north, the other south—that were connected by a canal. The city boasted a large marketplace, a magnificent palace complex with treasury and archives, and temples to the gods Melqart (MEL-kahrt) and Astarte (uh-STAHR-tee). Some of its

Phoenicians Canaanites living on the coast of modern Lebanon and Syria in the first millennium B.C.E. From major cities such as Tyre and Sidon, Phoenician merchants and sailors explored the Mediterranean, engaged in widespread commerce, and founded Carthage and other colonies in the western Mediterranean.

Ancient Textiles and Dyes

Throughout human history the production of textiles—cloth for clothing, blankets, carpets, and coverings of various sorts—required an expenditure of human labor second only to the work necessary to provide food. Nevertheless, textile production in antiquity has left few archaeological traces. The plant fibers and animal hair used for cloth quickly decompose except in rare circumstances. Some textile remains have been found in the hot, dry conditions of Egypt, the cool, arid Andes of South America, and the peat bogs of northern Europe. But most of our knowledge of ancient textiles depends on the discovery of equipment used in textile production—such as spindles, loom weights, and dyeing vats—and on pictorial representations and descriptions in texts.

Cloth production usually has been the work of women for a simple but important reason: responsibility for child rearing limits women's ability to participate in other activities but does not consume all their time and energy. In many societies textile production has been complementary to child-rearing activities, for it can be done in the home, is relatively safe, does not require great concentration, and can be interrupted without consequence. The growing and harvesting of plants such as cotton or flax (from which linen is made) and the shearing of wool from sheep and, in the Andes, llamas are outdoor activities, but the subsequent stages of production can be carried out inside the home. The basic methods of textile production did not change much from early antiquity until the late eighteenth century C.E., when the fabrication of textiles was transferred to mills and mass production began.

When textile production has been considered "women's work," most of the output has been for household consumption. However, women weavers in Peru developed new raw materials, new techniques, and new decorative motifs around three thousand years ago. They began to use the wool of llamas and alpacas in addition to cotton. Three women worked side by side and passed the weft from hand to hand in order to produce a fabric of greater width. Women weavers also introduced embroidery and decorated garments with new religious motifs, such as the jaguar-god. Their high-quality textiles were given as tribute to the elite and were used to trade for luxury goods.

More typically, men dominated commercial production. In ancient Phoenicia, fine textiles with bright, permanent colors became a major export product. Most prized was the red-purple known as Tyrian purple because Tyre was the major source. Persian and Hellenistic kings wore robes dyed this color, and a white toga with a purple border was the sign of a Roman senator.

The production of Tyrian purple was an exceedingly laborious process. The spiny dye-murex snail lives on the sandy Mediterranean bottom at depths ranging from 30 to 500 feet (10 to 150 meters). Nine thousand snails were needed to produce 1 gram (0.035 ounce) of dye. The dye was made from a colorless liquid in the snail's hypobranchial gland. The gland sacs were removed, crushed, soaked with salt, and exposed to sunlight and air for some days; then they were subject to controlled boiling and heating.

Huge mounds of broken shells on the Phoenician coast are testimony to the ancient industry. The snail may have been rendered nearly extinct at many locations, and some scholars speculate that Phoenician colonization in the Mediterranean was motivated in part by the search for new sources of snails.

Felt decoration depicting a fenix/Hermitage, St. Petersburg, Russia/De Agostini Picture Library/A. Dagli Orti/The Bridgeman Art Library

Scythian Felt Cloth from Pazyryk, ca. 500 B.C.E. *Found in a subterranean tomb in Siberia, the textile was preserved by the permafrost. It depicts a winged figure with a human upper body and antlers.*

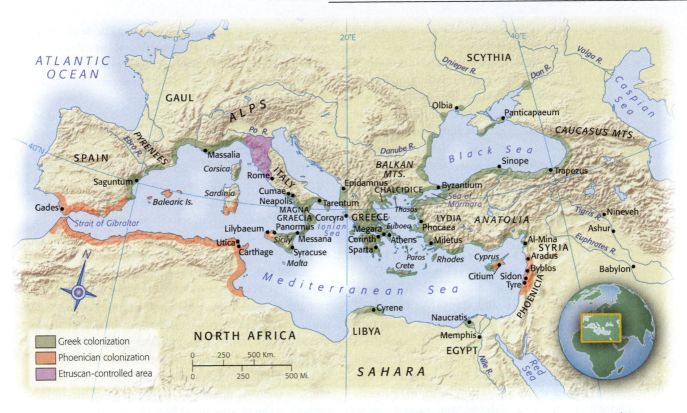

Map 2.2 Colonization of the Mediterranean In the ninth century B.C.E., the Phoenicians of Lebanon began to explore and colonize parts of the western Mediterranean, including the coast of North Africa, southern and eastern Spain, and the islands of Sicily and Sardinia. The Phoenicians were primarily interested in access to valuable raw materials and trading opportunities. © Cengage Learning

thirty thousand inhabitants lived in suburbs on the mainland. Its one weakness was its dependence on the mainland for food and fresh water.

After 900 B.C.E. Tyre turned its attention westward, establishing colonies on Cyprus, a copper-rich island 100 miles (161 kilometers) from the Syrian coast (see Map 2.2). By 700 B.C.E. a string of settlements in the western Mediterranean formed a "Phoenician triangle" composed of the North African coast from western Libya to Morocco; the south and southeast coast of Spain, including Gades (GAH-days) (modern Cadiz [kuh-DEEZ]) on the Strait of Gibraltar, controlling passage between the Mediterranean and the Atlantic Ocean; and the islands of Sardinia, Sicily, and Malta off the coast of Italy (see Map 2.2). Many settlements were situated on promontories or offshore islands in imitation of Tyre. The Phoenician trading network spanned the entire Mediterranean.

Frequent and destructive Assyrian invasions of Syria-Palestine and the lack of arable land to feed a swelling population probably motivated Tyrian expansion. Overseas settlement provided an outlet for excess population, new sources of trade goods, and new trading partners. Tyre maintained its autonomy until 701 B.C.E. by paying tribute to the Assyrian kings. In that year it finally fell to an Assyrian army that stripped it of much of its territory and population, allowing Sidon to become the leading city in Phoenicia.

Carthage's Commercial Empire

Thanks to Greek and Roman reports about their wars, historians know more about **Carthage** and the other Phoenician

Carthage City located in present-day Tunisia, founded by Phoenicians around 800 B.C.E. It became a major commercial center and naval power in the western Mediterranean until defeated by Rome in the third century B.C.E.

colonies than they do about the Phoenician home-land. For example, the account of the origins of Carthage that begins this chapter comes from Roman sources but probably is based on a Carthaginian original. Archaeological excavation has roughly confirmed the city's traditional foundation date of 814 B.C.E. The new settlement grew rapidly and soon dominated other Phoenician colonies in the west.

Located just outside the present-day city of Tunis in Tunisia, on a promontory jutting into the Mediterranean, Carthage stretched between the original hilltop citadel and a double harbor. The inner harbor could accommodate 220 warships. A watchtower allowed surveillance of the surrounding area, and high walls made it impossible to see in from the outside. The outer commercial harbor was filled with docks for merchant ships and shipyards. In case of attack, the harbor could be closed off by a huge iron chain.

Government offices ringed a large central square where magistrates heard legal cases outdoors. The inner city was a maze of narrow, winding streets, multistory apartment buildings, and sacred enclosures. Farther out lay a sprawling suburban district where the wealthy built spacious villas amid fields and vegetable gardens. This entire urban complex was enclosed by a wall 22 miles (35 kilometers) in length. At the most critical point—the 2-1/2-mile-wide (4-kilometer) isthmus connecting the promontory to the mainland—the wall was over 40 feet (13 meters) high and 30 feet (10 meters) thick and had high watchtowers.

With a population of roughly 400,000, Carthage was one of the largest cities in the world by 500 B.C.E. The population was ethnically diverse, including people of Phoenician stock, indigenous peoples ancestral to modern-day Berbers, and immigrants from other Mediterranean lands and sub-Saharan Africa. The Phoenicians readily intermarried with other peoples.

Each year two "judges" were elected from upper-class families to serve as heads of state and carry out administrative and judicial functions. The real seat of power was the Senate, where members of the leading merchant families, who sat for life, directed the affairs of the state. An inner circle of thirty or so

senators made the crucial decisions. The leadership occasionally convened an Assembly of the citizens to elect public officials or vote on important issues, particularly when they were divided or wanted to stir up popular enthusiasm for some venture.

There is little evidence at Carthage of the kind of social and political unrest that plagued Greece and Rome. A merchant aristocracy (unlike an aristocracy of birth) was not a closed group, and a climate of economic and social mobility allowed newly successful families and individuals to push their way into the circle of influential citizens. The ruling class also made sure that everyone benefited from the riches of empire.

Carthaginian power rested on its navy, which dominated the western Mediterranean for centuries. Phoenician towns provided a network of friendly ports. The Carthaginian fleet consisted of fast, maneuverable galleys (oared warships). Each bore a sturdy, pointed ram in front that could pierce the hull of an enemy vessel below the water line, while marines (soldiers aboard a ship) fired weapons. Innovations in the placement of benches and oars eventually made room for as many as 170 rowers.

Carthaginian foreign policy, reflecting the economic interests of the dominant merchant class, focused on protecting the sea lanes, gaining access to raw materials, and fostering trade. Foreign merchants were free to sail to Carthage to market their goods, but if they tried to operate elsewhere on their own, they risked having their ships sunk by the Carthaginian navy. Treaties between Carthage and other states included formal recognition of this maritime commercial monopoly.

The archaeological record provides few clues about the commodities traded by the Carthaginians. These may have included perishable goods—foodstuffs, textiles, animal skins, slaves—and raw metals whose Carthaginian origin would not be evident. Carthaginian ships carried goods manufactured elsewhere, and products brought to Carthage by foreign traders were re-exported.

There is also evidence for trade with sub-Saharan Africa. Hanno (HA-noe), a Carthaginian captain of the fifth century B.C.E., claimed to have sailed through the Strait of Gibraltar into the Atlantic Ocean

The Tophet of Carthage Here, from the seventh to second centuries B.C.E., the cremated bodies of sacrificed children were buried. Archaeological excavation has confirmed the claim in ancient sources that the Carthaginians sacrificed children to their gods at times of crisis. Stone markers, decorated with magical signs and symbols of divinities as well as family names, were placed over ceramic urns containing the ashes and charred bones of one or more infants or, occasionally, older children.

Werner Forman Archive/Glow Images

and to have explored the West African coast (see Map 2.2). Other Carthaginians explored the Atlantic coast of Spain and France and secured control of an important source of tin in the "Tin Islands," probably Cornwall in southwestern England.

War and Religion

Carthage did not directly rule a large territory. A belt of fertile land in northeastern Tunisia, owned by Carthaginians but worked by native peasants and imported slaves, provided a secure food supply. Beyond this core area the Carthaginians ruled most of their "empire" indirectly and allowed other Phoenician communities in the western Mediterranean to remain independent. These communities looked to Carthage for military protection and followed its lead in foreign policy. Only Sardinia and southern Spain came under the control of a Carthaginian governor and garrison, presumably to safeguard their resources.

Trade may explain the unusual fact that citizens were not required to serve in the army: they were of more value as traders and sailors. Another sign that war was not the primary business of the state was the separation of military command from civilian government. Generals were chosen by the Senate and kept in office for as long as they were needed. Since the indigenous North African population was not politically or militarily well organized, Carthage had little to fear close to home. When Carthage was drawn into a series of wars with the Greeks and Romans from the fifth through third centuries B.C.E., it relied on mercenaries from the most warlike peoples in its dominions or from neighboring areas. These well-paid mercenaries were under the command of Carthaginian officers.

Like the deities of Mesopotamia (see Chapter 1), the Carthaginian gods—chief among them Baal Hammon (BAHL ha-MOHN), a male storm-god, and Tanit (TAH-nit), a female fertility figure—were powerful and capricious entities. Roman sources report that members of the Carthaginian elite would sacrifice their own male children in times of crisis. Excavations at Carthage and other western Phoenician towns have turned up *tophets* (TOE-fet)—walled enclosures with thousands of small, sealed urns containing the burned bones of children. Originally practiced by the upper classes, child sacrifice became more common and involved broader elements of the population after 400 B.C.E.

SECTION REVIEW

- Following the upheavals around 1200 B.C.E., Canaanite communities on the coast of Lebanon adopted the city-state political form and turned to seaborne commerce for survival.

- A string of settlements expanded Phoenician control of the Mediterranean, forming a "Phoenician triangle" from the coasts of North Africa and Spain to the islands off the coast of Italy.

- Carthage, founded a little before 800 B.C.E., became the dominant city-state of the Phoenician coalition and through its naval prowess enforced a Carthaginian commercial monopoly in the western Mediterranean.

- The religion of the Carthaginians, which included the sacrifice of children in times of crisis, was perceived as different and despicable by their Greek and Roman rivals.

Plutarch (PLOO-tawrk), a Greek who lived around 100 C.E., long after the demise of Carthage, wrote the following on the basis of earlier sources:

> The Carthaginians are a hard and gloomy people, submissive to their rulers and harsh to their subjects, running to extremes of cowardice in times of fear and of cruelty in times of anger; they keep obstinately to their decisions, are austere, and care little for amusement or the graces of life.[1]

We should not take the hostile opinions of Greek and Roman sources at face value. Still, it is clear that the Carthaginians were perceived as different and that cultural barriers, leading to misunderstanding and prejudice, played a significant role in ongoing conflicts. The struggle between Carthage and Rome for control of the western Mediterranean was especially protracted and bloody (see Chapter 5).

FAILURE AND TRANSFORMATION, 750–550 B.C.E.

■ *What factors prompted the transformation of the ancient Middle East between 750 and 550 B.C.E.?*

The extension of Assyrian power over the entire Middle East had enormous consequences for all the

[1] Plutarch, *Moralia*, 799 D, trans. B. H. Warmington, *Carthage* (Harmondsworth, England: Penguin, 1960), 163.

peoples of the region and caused the stories of Mesopotamia, Israel, and Phoenicia to converge. In 721 B.C.E. the Assyrians destroyed the northern kingdom of Israel, and for over a century the southern kingdom of Judah faced relentless pressure. Assyrian threats spurred the Phoenicians to colonize and exploit the western Mediterranean. Even Egypt, for so long impregnable behind its desert barriers, fell to Assyrian invaders in the mid-seventh century B.C.E.

Closer to the Assyrian homeland, the southern plains of Sumer and Akkad, the birthplace of Mesopotamian civilization, were reduced to a protectorate, while Babylon was alternately razed and rebuilt by Assyrian kings. Urartu and Elam, Assyria's great power rivals, were destroyed. By 650 B.C.E. Assyria stood supreme in western Asia. But the arms race with Urartu, the frequent expensive campaigns, and the protection of lengthy borders sapped Assyrian resources. Brutality and exploitation aroused the hatred of conquered peoples. At the same time, changes in the ethnic composition of the army and the population of the homeland had reduced popular support for the Assyrian state.

Two new political entities spearheaded resistance to Assyria. First, Babylonia had been revived by the Neo-Babylonian, or Chaldaean (chal-DEE-uhn), dynasty (the Chaldaeans had infiltrated southern Mesopotamia around 1000 B.C.E.). Second, the Medes (MEED), an Iranian people, were extending their kingdom on the Iranian Plateau in the seventh century B.C.E. The two powers launched a series of attacks on the Assyrian homeland that destroyed the chief cities by 612 B.C.E.

The rapidity of the Assyrian fall was stunning, and the destruction systematically carried out by the vic-

SECTION REVIEW

- The Assyrians transformed the Middle East, conquering Egypt, Israel, Urartu, and Elam.

- Yet the Assyrians' empire was overextended and their conquests weakened them. With the help of the Medes, the Chaldaeans overthrew the Assyrians and established a Neo-Babylonian kingdom.

- Babylon, rebuilt by the Chaldaeans, became the greatest city in the world in the sixth century B.C.E.

tors led to the depopulation of northern Mesopotamia. The Medes took over the Assyrian homeland and the northern plain as far as eastern Anatolia, but most of the territory of the old empire fell to the **Neo-Babylonian kingdom** (626–539 B.C.E.), thanks to the energetic campaigns of kings Nabopolassar (NAB-oh-poe-lass-uhr) (r. 625–605 B.C.E.) and Nebuchadnezzar (NEB-uh-kuh-nez-uhr) (r. 604–562 B.C.E.). Babylonia underwent a cultural renaissance, pursuing mathematics, astronomy, and astrology, resurrecting old cults and festivals, rebuilding temples, and ultimately becoming the greatest metropolis of the sixth-century B.C.E. world.

or even city-states like those of Phoenicia and Carthage that lived from trade rather than tribute. These small states and societies were vulnerable to attack by larger, more powerful neighbors, and sometimes they succumbed. Yet just as often, they survived or reappeared. The other kind of kingdom was the great and powerful Assyrian Empire, which used advanced military tactics and weapons, and sheer brutality, to conquer and exploit an area of unprecedented size and diversity. The far-reaching expansion and the subsequent rapid fall of the Assyrian Empire were the most important factors in the transformation of the ancient Middle East.

CONCLUSION

The Late Bronze Age in the Middle East was a "cosmopolitan" era of shared lifestyles and technologies. Besides the already ancient river-valley kingdoms, the period from 2000 to 500 B.C.E. saw two kinds of societies emerge in the Middle East and the Mediterranean world. One was small kingdoms like Israel and Minoan Crete

Neo-Babylonian kingdom Under the Chaldaeans (nomadic kinship groups that settled in southern Mesopotamia in the early first millennium B.C.E.), Babylon again became a major political and cultural center in the seventh and sixth centuries B.C.E. After participating in the destruction of Assyrian power, the monarchs Nabopolassar and Nebuchadnezzar took over the southern portion of the Assyrian domains.

CHAPTER REVIEW

THE COSMOPOLITAN MIDDLE EAST, 1700–1100 B.C.E.

■ *How did a cosmopolitan civilization develop in the Middle East during the Late Bronze Age, and what forms did it take?* (page 30)

Historians have called the Late Bronze Age a "cosmopolitan" era, meaning a time of widely shared cultures and lifestyles. The cultural patterns that originated in the river-valley civilizations of Egypt and Mesopotamia persisted into this era. Peoples such as the Amorites, Kassites, and Chaldaeans, who migrated into the Tigris-Euphrates plain, adopted its language, religious beliefs, political and social institutions, and forms of artistic expression. Similarly, the Hyksos, who migrated into

the Nile Delta and controlled much of Egypt for a time, adopted the ancient ways of Egypt. When the founders of the New Kingdom finally ended Hyksos domination, they reinstituted the united monarchy and the religious and cultural traditions of earlier eras.

THE AEGEAN WORLD, 2000–1100 B.C.E.

■ *What civilizations emerged in the Aegean world, and what relationship did they have to the older civilizations to the east?* (page 36)

The Late Bronze Age expansion of commerce and communication stimulated the emergence of new civilizations, including those of the Minoans and Mycenaean

Greeks in the Aegean Sea. These civilizations borrowed heavily from the technologies and cultural practices of Mesopotamia and Egypt, creating dynamic syntheses of imported and indigenous elements. Cretan art and architecture display the wide range of cultural influences from the Minoans' extensive trading contacts, as well as the unique forms of Minoan civilization. The Mycenaean Greeks built their own civilization under the influence of Minoan Crete, and their palaces served as centers for crafts, trade, and administrative record keeping. Trade brought the Mycenaeans, like the Minoans, into steady contact with older eastern civilizations.

THE ASSYRIAN EMPIRE, 911–612 B.C.E.

■ *How did the Assyrian Empire rise to power and eventually dominate most of the ancient Middle East?* (page 40)

Ultimately, the very interdependence of the societies of the Middle East and eastern Mediterranean made them vulnerable to the destructions and disorder of the decades around 1200 B.C.E. The entire region slipped into a "Dark Age" of isolation, stagnation, and decline that lasted several centuries. The early centuries after 1000 B.C.E. saw a resurgence of political organization and international commerce, as well as the spread of technologies and ideas. The Neo-Assyrian Empire, the great power of the time, represented a continuation of the Mesopotamian tradition, though the center of empire moved to the north. The king wielded supreme authority in all areas, and state propaganda presented him as all-powerful and victorious. The Assyrians won control of their empire through superior organization and military technology and maintained it through terror and mass deportation of subject peoples. Assyrian social structure mirrored that of earlier Mesopotamian cultures, with most people working the land. Assyrian scholarship built on earlier traditions, and Ashurbanipal's library collected the literary and scientific heritage of Mesopotamia.

ISRAEL, 2000–500 B.C.E.

■ *How did the civilization of Israel develop, following both familiar cultural patterns and a unique course of its own?* (page 43)

Our main textual source of information about the Israelites, the Hebrew Bible, must be reconciled with archaeological findings. It recounts that the Israelites began as nomadic pastoralists who wandered from Mesopotamia to the Mediterranean coastal plain and then to Egypt, where they suffered enslavement. During the Exodus, Yahweh and the Israelites entered into a covenant. The Israelites then settled permanently in Canaan, where they coalesced into a political federation, the "Children of Israel." Conflict with the Philistines forced them to adopt a more complex political structure. The resulting monarchy reached its height under Solomon, during whose reign the Temple priests rose to prominence and Israelite society grew more urban and economically stratified. After Solomon's death the kingdom divided into Israel and Judah, and the monotheism that Judaism would bequeath to the world reached its final form. While the long, slow evolution of the Israelites from wandering groups of herders to an agriculturally based monarchy followed a pattern common in ancient western Asia, the religious and ethical concepts that they formulated were unique and have had a powerful impact on world history.

PHOENICIA AND THE MEDITERRANEAN, 1200–500 B.C.E.

■ *How did the Phoenicians rise to commercial dominance over much of the Mediterranean world?* (page 47)

After the upheavals of the Late Bronze Age, the Phoenician city-states along the coast of Lebanon flourished. Under pressure from the Neo-Assyrian Empire, the Phoenicians, with Tyre in the lead, began spreading westward into the Mediterranean. Carthage became the most important city outside the Phoenician homeland.

Ruled by leading merchant families, it extended its commercial empire throughout the western Mediterranean, maintaining power through naval superiority.

FAILURE AND TRANSFORMATION, 750–550 B.C.E.

■ *What factors prompted the transformation of the ancient Middle East between 750 and 550 B.C.E.?* (page 52)

In their drive for empire, the Assyrians destroyed many older states and, directly or indirectly, displaced large numbers of people. Their brutality, as well as the population shifts that resulted from their deportations, undercut support for their state. The Chaldaeans and Medes led resistance to Assyrian rule, and the empire swiftly collapsed. This conquest led to the depopulation of northern Mesopotamia.

Key Terms

Iron Age (p. 30)

Hittites (p. 32)

Hatshepsut (p. 33)

Akhenaten (p. 34)

Ramesses II (p. 35)

Minoan (p. 36)

Mycenae (p. 37)

shaft graves (p. 37)

Linear B (p. 37)

Neo-Assyrian Empire (p. 40)

mass deportation (p. 41)

Library of Ashurbanipal (p. 42)

Israel (p. 43)

Hebrew Bible (p. 43)

First Temple (p. 45)

monotheism (p. 46)

Diaspora (p. 46)

Phoenicians (p. 47)

Carthage (p. 49)

Neo-Babylonian kingdom (p. 53)

New Civilizations in East Asia, Africa, and Europe

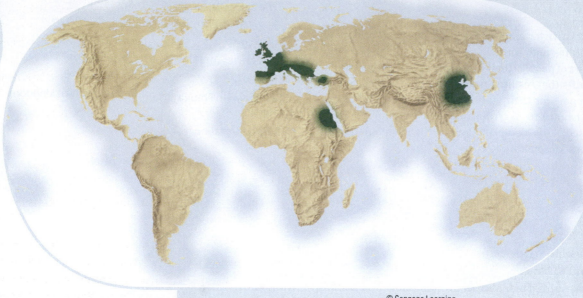

© Cengage Learning

CHAPTER PREVIEW

EARLY CHINA, 2000–221 B.C.E.
- How did early Chinese rulers use religion to justify and strengthen their power?

NUBIA, 2300 B.C.E.–350 C.E.
- How did the technological and cultural influences of Egypt affect the formation of Nubia?

PASTORAL NOMADS OF THE EURASIAN STEPPES, 1000–100 B.C.E.
- How was the rise of steppe nomadism dependent on interactions with settled agricultural peoples, and what new challenges did the nomads pose to farming societies?

CELTIC EUROPE, 1000–50 B.C.E.
- What were the causes behind the spread of Celtic peoples across much of continental Europe and the later retreat of Celtic cultures to the western edge of the continent?

Conclusion

DIVERSITY & DOMINANCE: Human Nature and Good Government in the *Analects* of Confucius and the Legalist Writings of Han Fei

Around 2200 B.C.E. an Egyptian official named Harkhuf (HAHR-koof), who lived at Aswan (AS-wahn) on the southern boundary of Egypt, set out on his fourth trek to a place called Yam, far to the south in the land that later came to be called Nubia. He brought gifts from the Egyptian pharaoh for the ruler of Yam, and he returned home with three hundred donkeyloads of incense, ebony, ivory, and other exotic products. Despite the diplomatic fiction of exchanging gifts, we should probably consider Harkhuf a trader; and the prize of his trip was so special that the eight-year-old boy pharaoh, Pepi II, could not contain his excitement. He wrote:

> Come north to the residence at once! Hurry and bring with you this pygmy whom you brought from the land of the horizon-dwellers live, hale, and healthy, for the dances of the god, to gladden the heart, to delight the heart of king Neferkare [Pepi] who lives forever! When he goes down with you into the ship, get worthy men to be around him on deck, lest he fall into the water! When he lies down at night, get worthy men to lie around him in his tent. Inspect ten times at night! My majesty desires to see this pygmy more than the gifts of the mine-land and of Punt![1]

Scholars identify Yam with Kerma, later the capital of the kingdom of Nubia, on the upper Nile in modern Sudan. For Egyptians, Nubia was a wild and dangerous place. But it was developing a more complex political organization that fostered trade with Egypt and tropical regions farther south (where pygmies would have lived).

In this chapter we bring into the picture parts of the world outside the largely self-sufficient older river-valley civilizations of Mesopotamia and Egypt and the newer Mediterranean civilizations that were shaped by networks of long-distance trade. The societies examined in this chapter emerged later in East Asia, sub-Saharan Africa, the Eurasian steppes, and continental Europe.

---

[1] Quoted in Miriam Lichtheim, ed., *Ancient Egyptian Literature: A Book of Readings* (Berkeley: University of California Press, 1978).

In the second millennium B.C.E. a civilization based on irrigation agriculture arose in the valley of the Yellow River and its tributaries in northern China. In the same epoch, in Nubia (southern Egypt and northern Sudan), the first complex society in tropical Africa continued to develop from the roots observed earlier by Harkhuf. The first millennium B.C.E. witnessed the rise of a new kind of nomadism on the Eurasian steppes and the spread of Celtic peoples across much of continental Europe. These societies had no contact with one another and represent a variety of responses to environmental and historical circumstances. However, they have certain features in common and collectively point to a distinct stage in the development of human societies.

EARLY CHINA, 2000–221 B.C.E.

■ *How did early Chinese rulers use religion to justify and strengthen their power?*

On the eastern edge of the vast Eurasian landmass, Neolithic cultures developed as early as 8000 B.C.E., and a more complex civilization evolved in the second and first millennia B.C.E. Under the Shang and Zhou dynasties, many of the institutions and values of classical Chinese civilization emerged and spread south and west. As elsewhere, the rise of cities, specialization of labor, bureaucratic government, writing, and other advanced technologies depended on intensive agriculture along a great river system—the Yellow River (Huang He [hwahng-HUH]) and its tributaries.

Geography and Resources   With mountains and deserts to the west and north making overland travel difficult and slow (see Map 3.1), the great river systems of eastern China—the Yellow and the Yangzi (yang-zuh) Rivers and their tributaries—provide the main axes of east-west movement. In the eastern river valleys dense populations practiced intensive agriculture; on the steppe lands of Mongolia, the deserts and oases of Xinjiang (shin-jyahng), and the high plateau of Tibet, sparser populations lived largely by herding. Within the eastern agricultural zone, the north and the south have strikingly different environments. Monsoons drench southern China with heavy rainfall in the summer,

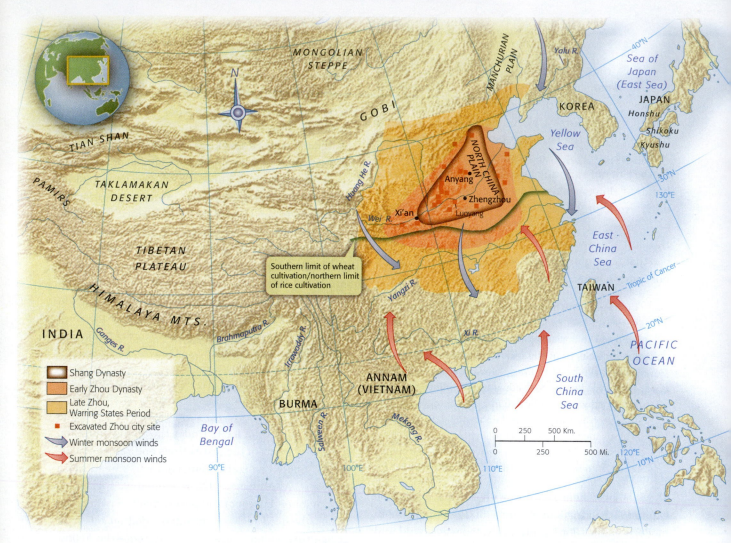

Map 3.1 China in the Shang and Zhou Periods, 1750–221 B.C.E. The Shang dynasty arose in the second millennium B.C.E. in the floodplain of the Yellow River. While southern China benefits from the monsoon rains, northern China depends on irrigation. As population increased, the Han Chinese migrated from their eastern homeland to other parts of China, carrying with them their technologies and cultural practices. Other ethnic groups predominated in more outlying regions, and the nomadic peoples of the northwest constantly challenged Chinese authority. © Cengage Learning

the most beneficial time for agriculture. Rainfall is more erratic in northern China. As in Mesopotamia, where civilization developed in relatively unfriendly environments, China's early history unfolded in the demanding environment of the northern plains. By the third century C.E., however, the gradual flow of population toward the warmer southern lands caused the political and intellectual center to move south.

Since prehistoric times, winds blowing from Central Asia had deposited a yellowish-brown dust called **loess** (less) on the North China Plain, creating an

abundance of potentially productive land (this dust suspended in the water gives the Yellow River its distinctive hue and name). The thick soil was extremely fertile and soft enough to be worked with wooden digging sticks. However, in some areas, forests had to be cleared; more importantly, recurrent floods on the Yellow River necessitated earthen dikes and overflow

loess A fine, light silt deposited by wind and water. It constitutes the fertile soil of the Yellow River Valley in northern China.

Chronology

	China	Eurasian Steppes	Celtic Europe	Nubia
8000 B.C.E.	**8000–2000 B.C.E.** Neolithic cultures			**4500 B.C.E.** Early agriculture in Nubia
2500 B.C.E.				**2200 B.C.E.** Harkhuf's expeditions to Yam
2000 B.C.E.	**2000 B.C.E.** Bronze metallurgy **1750–1045 B.C.E.** Shang dynasty			**1750 B.C.E.** Rise of kingdom of Kush based on Kerma
1500 B.C.E.				**1500 B.C.E.** Egyptian conquest of Nubia
1000 B.C.E.	**1045–221 B.C.E.** Zhou dynasty **600 B.C.E.** Iron metallurgy	**1000 B.C.E.** Initial development of pastoral nomadism **700 B.C.E.** Scythians drive out Cimmerians and settle area north of Black Sea	**1000 B.C.E.** Origin of Celtic culture in central Europe **1000 B.C.E.** Celtic elites trade for Mediterranean goods	**1000 B.C.E.** Decline of Egyptian control in Nubia **750 B.C.E.** Rise of kingdom based on Napata **712–660 B.C.E.** Nubian kings rule Egypt
500 B.C.E.	**551–479 B.C.E.** Life of Confucius **221–206 B.C.E.** Legalism becomes philosophy of Qin Empire	**440 B.C.E.** Greek historian Herodotus reports on nomadic Scythians **ca. 300 B.C.E.** Ruler of Chinese state of Zhao equips troops like nomad horsemen **100 B.C.E.** Chinese historian Sima Qian describes Xiongnu nomads	**500–300 B.C.E.** Migrations across Europe **390 B.C.E.** Celts sack Rome	**300 B.C.E.–350 C.E.** Kingdom of Meroë

channels. In this landscape, agriculture demanded the coordinated efforts of large groups of people. To cope with the periodic droughts, catch basins (reservoirs) were dug to store river water and rainfall. As the population grew, people built retaining walls to partition the hillsides into flat arable terraces.

Shang Period Bronze Vessel Vessels such as this large wine jar were used in rituals by the Shang ruling class to make contact with their ancestors. As both the source and the proof of the elite's authority, these vessels were often buried in Shang tombs. The complex shapes and elaborate decorations testify to the artisans' skill. Covered ritual 'Fang-yi' wine vessel with 'Tao-tie' motif, Shang Dynasty (cast bronze with grey patina), Chinese School, (12th century B.C.)/Arthur M. Sackler Museum, Harvard University Art Museums, USA/Bequest of Grenville L. Winthrop/The Bridgeman Art Library

The staple crops in the northern region were millet, a grain indigenous to China, and wheat, originally from the Middle East. Rice required a warmer climate and prospered in the south. The cultivation of rice in the Yangzi River Valley and the south required a great outlay of labor. Rice paddies—the fields where rice is grown—must be flat and surrounded by irrigation channels to bring or drain water according to

precise schedules. Seedlings sprout in a nursery and are transplanted one by one to the paddy, which is then flooded. Flooding eliminates weeds and rival plants and supports microscopic organisms that keep the soil fertile. When the crop is ripe, the paddy is drained; the rice stalks are harvested with a sickle; and the edible kernels are separated out. The reward for this effort is a harvest that can feed more people per cultivated acre than any other grain, which explains why the south eventually became more populous than the north.

Archaeological evidence shows that the Neolithic population of China grew millet, raised pigs and chickens, and used stone tools. They made pottery on a wheel and fired it in high-temperature kilns. They also pioneered silk production, first raising silkworms on mulberry trees, then unraveling their cocoon filaments to spin into thread. Lacking stone, they built walls by hammering soil inside temporary wooden frames until it became hard as cement. By 2000 B.C.E. they had begun casting bronze (roughly a thousand years after the Middle East Bronze Age).

Legends say that the ancient dynasty of the Xia (shah) ruled the core region of the Yellow River Valley. Some archeologists identify the Xia with the Neolithic Longshan cultural complex in the centuries before and after 2000 B.C.E. However, history proper begins with the rise of the **Shang** (shahng) clans, which coincides with the earliest written records.

The Shang Period, 1750–1045 B.C.E.

The Shang originated in the part of the Yellow River Valley that lies in the present-day province of Henan (heh-nahn). After 1750 B.C.E., they extended their control north into Mongolia, west as far as Gansu (gahn-soo), and south to the Yangzi River Valley. The warrior aristocracy that dominated Shang society reveled in warfare, hunting (for recreation and to fine-tune battle skills), exchanging gifts, and feasting.

Shang The dominant people in the earliest Chinese dynasty for which we have written records (ca. 1750–1045 B.C.E.).

The king ruled the core area of the Shang state directly, while aristocrats served as generals, ambassadors, and supervisors of public projects. Other members of the royal family and high-ranking nobility governed outlying provinces. The most distant regions were governed by native rulers who swore allegiance to the Shang king. The king was often on the road, traveling to the courts of his subordinates to reinforce their loyalty.

Frequent military campaigns, often against the nomadic people who occupied the steppe and desert regions to the north and west, occupied the warrior class and yielded considerable plunder. Prisoners of war taken in these campaigns served as slaves in the Shang capital.

The Shang kingdom had several capitals, the last and most important near modern Anyang (ahn-yahng) (see Map 3.1). Shang cities were centers of political control and religion. Surrounded by massive walls of pounded earth, they contained palaces, administrative buildings, storehouses, royal tombs, shrines of gods and ancestors, and housing for aristocrats. Commoners lived in agricultural villages outside these centers. Urban street grids aligned with the north star and gates opening to the cardinal directions demonstrate an ongoing Chinese concern with feng shui (fung shway), the spatial orientation of buildings according to a sense of cosmic order.

Writing was the key to effective administration. Pictograms (pictures representing objects and concepts) and phonetic symbols representing the sounds of syllables were combined to form a complex system of hundreds of signs. Only a small educated elite had the time to master this system. Despite substantial changes through the ages, the fundamental principles of the Chinese system still endure. As a result, people speaking languages that sound quite different, such as Mandarin and Cantonese, can read and understand the same text.

Shang ideology glorified the king as the intermediary between the people and Heaven. Shang religion also revered and made sacrifices to male ancestors, who were believed to be intensely interested in the fortunes of their descendants. Burials of kings entailed sacrifices, not only of animals but also of humans, including noble officials of the court, women, servants, soldiers, and prisoners of war.

Before taking any action, the Shang rulers used divination to determine the will of Heaven.

Bronze weapons and ritual vessels symbolized authority and nobility, and Shang tombs contain many such objects. The relatively modest tomb of one queen yielded 450 bronze articles (ritual vessels, bells, weapons, and mirrors)—remarkable because copper and tin, the principal ingredients of bronze, were not plentiful in northern China. (Also found in the same tomb were numerous objects of jade, bone, ivory, and stone, seven thousand cowrie shells, sixteen sacrificed men, women, and children, and six dogs!)

Finding and mining deposits of copper and tin, transporting the refined metal to the capital, and crafting these beautifully wrought weapons and vessels constituted a major Shang enterprise. Bronzesmiths working in foundries outside the main cities also made chariot fittings and musical instruments. Stylized depictions of real and imaginary animals were a favorite decorative theme.

Far-reaching networks of trade brought to the Shang jade, ivory, and mother of pearl (a hard, shiny substance from the interior of mollusk shells) used for jewelry, carved figurines, and decorative inlays. Some evidence suggests that Shang China may have exchanged goods and ideas with distant Mesopotamia. The horse-drawn chariot, which the Shang adopted from nomads of the northwest, became a formidable instrument of war.

The Zhou Period, 1045–221 B.C.E.

Shang domination of central and northern China lasted more than six centuries. In the eleventh century B.C.E. the last Shang king was defeated by Wu, the ruler of **Zhou** (joe), a dependent state in the Wei (way) River Valley. The Zhou line of kings (ca. 1027–221 B.C.E.) was the longest lasting and most revered of all dynasties in Chinese history. The Zhou preserved the essentials of Shang culture and added new elements of ideology and technology.

> **Zhou** The people and dynasty that took over the dominant position in north China from the Shang and created the concept of the Mandate of Heaven to justify their rule. The Zhou era, particularly the vigorous early period (1045–771 B.C.E.), was remembered in Chinese tradition as a time of prosperity and benevolent rule.

To justify their seizure of power to the restive remnants of Shang clans, the early Zhou monarchs styled themselves "Sons of Heaven," and their rule was called the **Mandate of Heaven**. According to the new theory advanced by their propagandists, the supreme deity, known as Heaven, would support the king as long as he served as a wise, principled, and energetic guardian of the people. Prosperity and stability proved divine favor, but royal misbehavior, a fault attributed to the last Shang ruler, could forfeit Heaven's mandate. Corruption, violence, and insurrection were signs of divine displeasure.

The Zhou kings continued some of the Shang rituals, but there was a marked decline in the practice of divination and in extravagant sacrifices and burials. The priestly power of the ruling class, the only ones who had been able to make contact with the spirits of ancestors during the Shang period, faded away. The resulting separation of religion and government made way for the development of important philosophical and mystical systems. The bronze vessels that had been sacred implements in the Shang period now became family treasures.

The early period of Zhou rule, the eleventh through ninth centuries B.C.E., is sometimes called the Western Zhou era because of the location of the capitals in the western part of the kingdom. These centuries saw the development of a sophisticated administrative apparatus. The Zhou built a series of capital cities with pounded-earth foundations and walls. The major buildings all faced south, in keeping with the feng shui principles of harmonious relationship with the terrain, the forces of wind, water, and sunlight, and the invisible energy perceived to be flowing through the natural world. All government officials, including the king, were supposed to be models of morality, fairness, and concern for the welfare of the people.

Like the Shang, the Zhou regime was decentralized. Members and allies of the royal family ruled more than a hundred largely autonomous territories. Elaborate court ceremonials, embellished by music and dance, impressed on observers the glory of Zhou rule and reinforced the bonds of obligation between rulers and ruled.

Around 800 B.C.E. Zhou power began to wane. Ambitious local rulers operated ever more independently and waged war on one another, while nomadic peoples attacked the northwest frontiers (see Map 3.1). In 771 B.C.E. members of the Zhou lineage relocated to a new, more secure, eastern capital near Luoyang (LWOE-yahng), initiating the five-hundred-year Eastern Zhou era. There they continued to hold the royal title and receive at least nominal homage from the local rulers, the real power brokers of the age. Historians conventionally divide this period of political fragmentation, shifting centers of power, and fierce competition among numerous small states into the Spring and Autumn Period (771–481 B.C.E.), after a collection of chronicles that give annual entries for those two seasons, and the Warring States Period (from 480 to the unification of China in 221 B.C.E.).

Numerous competing kingdoms meant numerous capital cities, some of which became quite large. To the north, long walls of pounded earth were constructed, the ancestors of the Great Wall of China, to protect the kingdoms from each other and from nomads. Chinese armies adopted the nomad practice of putting fighters on horseback. The northwest nomads were probably also the source of the iron-working skills that led to iron replacing bronze as the primary metal for tools and weapons around 600 B.C.E. Bureaucracies in many states expanded their functions, composing law codes, collecting taxes directly, imposing monetary standards, and managing large-scale public works projects.

Eventually this activity led to a philosophy called **Legalism**, which argued that maintaining the

Mandate of Heaven   Chinese religious and political ideology developed by the Zhou, according to which it was the prerogative of Heaven, the chief deity, to grant power to the ruler of China and to take away that power if the ruler failed to conduct himself justly and in the best interests of his subjects.

Legalism   In China, a political philosophy that emphasized the unruliness of human nature and justified state coercion and control. The ruling class invoked it to validate the authoritarian nature of the regime and its profligate expenditure of subjects' lives and labor. It was later superseded by a more benevolent Confucian doctrine of governmental moderation.

wealth and power of the state justified an authoritarian political control. Legalists maintained that human nature is essentially wicked and that people behave properly only if compelled by strict laws and harsh punishments. They believed that every aspect of human society ought to be controlled and personal freedom sacrificed for the good of the state.

Confucianism, Daoism, and Chinese Society

Bureaucratic government superseded aristocratic rule in some of the major Zhou states. To maintain their influence, aristocrats sought a new role as advisers to the rulers. Kongzi (kohng-zuh) (551–479 B.C.E.)—known in the West by the Latin form of his name, **Confucius**—lived through the political flux and social change of this anxious time. Coming from one of the smaller states, he had not been particularly successful in obtaining administrative posts. However, his doctrine of duty and public service, initially aimed at fellow aristocrats, was to become a central influence in Chinese thought.

Many elements in Confucius's teaching had roots in earlier Chinese belief, including folk religion and the rites of the Zhou royal family, such as the veneration of ancestors and elders and worship of the deity Heaven. Confucius drew a parallel between the family and the state. Just as the family is a hierarchy, with the father at its top, sons next, then wives and daughters in order of age, so too the state is a hierarchy, with the ruler at the top, the public officials as the sons, and the common people as the women.

Confucius took a traditional term for the feelings between family members, *ren* (ruhn) and expanded it into a universal ideal of benevolence toward all humanity, which he believed was the foundation of moral government. Government exists, he said, to serve the people, and the administrator or ruler gains respect and authority by displaying fairness and integrity. Confucian teachings emphasized benevolence, avoidance of violence, justice, rationalism, loyalty, and dignity.

Though Confucius had little influence in his own time, his later follower Mencius (Mengzi, 371–289 B.C.E.), who opposed despotism and argued against the authoritarian ideology of the Legalists, made the master's teachings much better known (see Diversity and Dominance: Human Nature and Good Government in the *Analects* of Confucius and the Legalist Writings of Han Fei). Confucianism eventually became the dominant political philosophy and the core of the educational system for government officials.

The Warring States Period also saw the rise of the school of thought known as Daoism. If Confucianism emphasized social engagement, its great rival, **Daoism (DOW-ism)**, urged withdrawal from the empty formalities, rigid hierarchy, and distractions of Chinese society. According to tradition, Laozi (low-zuh), the originator of Daoism (believed to have lived in the sixth century B.C.E., though some scholars doubt his existence), sought to stop the warfare of the age by urging humanity to follow the *Dao*, or "path." Daoists accepted the world as they found it, adhering to the "path" of nature and avoiding useless struggles. They avoided violence if at all possible and took the minimal action necessary for a task; rather than fight the current of a stream, a wise man allows the onrushing waters to pass around him. This passivity arose from the Daoist's sense that the world was always changing and lacked any absolute morality or meaning. In the end, Daoists believed, all that matters is the individual's fundamental understanding of the "path."

The original Daoist philosophy was greatly expanded in subsequent centuries to incorporate popular beliefs, magic, and mysticism. Daoism represented an important stream of thought throughout Chinese history. By idealizing individuals who find their own "path" to right conduct, it offered an alternative to the Confucian emphasis on hierarchy and duty and to the Legalists' approval of force.

Confucius Western name for the Chinese philosopher Kongzi (551–479 B.C.E.). His doctrine of duty and public service had a great influence on subsequent Chinese thought and served as a code of conduct for government officials.

Daoism Chinese school of thought, originating in the Warring States Period with Laozi. Daoism offered an alternative to the Confucian emphasis on hierarchy and duty, emphasizing instead understanding the "path" of nature.

Human Nature and Good Government in the *Analects* of Confucius and the Legalist Writings of Han Fei

Although monarchy (the rule of one man) was the standard form of government in ancient China and was rarely challenged, political theorists and philosophers thought a great deal about the qualities of the ideal ruler, his relationship to his subjects, and the means by which he controlled them. These considerations about how to govern people were inevitably molded by fundamental assumptions about the nature of human beings. In the Warring States Period, as the major states struggled desperately with one another for survival and expansion, such discussions took on a special urgency, and the Confucians and Legalists came to represent two powerful, and largely contradictory, points of view.

The Analects are a collection of sayings of Confucius, probably compiled and written down several generations after he lived, though some elements may have been added even later. They cover a wide range of matters, including ethics, government, education, music, and rituals. Taken as a whole, they are a guide to living an honorable, virtuous, useful, and satisfying life. While subject to reinterpretation according to the circumstances of the times, Confucian principles have had a great influence on Chinese values and behavior ever since.

Han Fei (280–233 b.c.e.), who was, ironically, at one time the student of a Confucian teacher, became a Legalist writer and political adviser to the ruler of the ambitious state of Qin (chin), who emerged from the same Wei River Valley as the Zhou and succeeded the Zhou as China's ruling class (see Chapter 5). The Qin dynasty was the first to put into practice Legalist political methods. Eventually Han Fei lost out in a power struggle at court and was forced to kill himself.

The following selections illuminate the profound disagreements between Confucians and Legalists over the essential nature of human beings and how the ruler should conduct himself in order to most effectively govern his subjects and protect his kingdom.

Confucius

4:5 Confucius said: "Riches and honors are what all men desire. But if they cannot be attained in accordance with the *dao* [the path] they should not be kept. Poverty and low status are what all men hate. But if they cannot be avoided while staying in accordance with the *dao*, you should not avoid them. If a Superior Man departs from *ren* [humaneness], how can he be worthy of that name? A Superior Man never leaves *ren* for even the time of a single meal. In moments of haste he acts according to it. In times of difficulty or confusion he acts according to it."

16:8 Confucius said: "The Superior Man stands in awe of three things: (1) He is in awe of the decree of Heaven. (2) He is in awe of great men. (3) He is in awe of the words of the sages. The inferior man does not know the decree of Heaven; takes great men lightly and laughs at the words of the sages."

4:14 Confucius said: "I don't worry about not having a good position; I worry about the means I use to gain position. I don't worry about being unknown; I seek to be known in the right way."

7:15 Confucius said: "I can live with coarse rice to eat, water for drink and my arm as a pillow and still be happy. Wealth and honors that one possesses in the midst of injustice are like floating clouds."

13:6 Confucius said: "When you have gotten your own life straightened out, things will go well without your giving orders. But if your own life isn't straightened out, even if you give orders, no one will follow them."

12:2 Zhonggong asked about the meaning of *ren*. The Master said: "Go out of your home as if you were receiving an important guest. Employ the people as if you were assisting at a great ceremony. What you don't want done to yourself, don't do to others. Live in your town without stirring up resentments, and live in your household without stirring up resentments."

1:5 Confucius said: "If you would govern a state of a thousand chariots (a small-to-middle-size state), you must pay strict attention to business, be true to your word, be economical in expenditure and love the people. You should use them according to the seasons."

2:3 Confucius said: "If you govern the people legalistically and control them by punishment, they will avoid crime, but have no personal sense of shame. If you govern them by means of virtue and control them with propriety, they will gain their own sense of shame, and thus correct themselves."

12:7 Zigong asked about government. The Master said, "Enough food, enough weapons and the confidence of the people." Zigong said, "Suppose you had no alternative but to give up one of these three, which one would ►

be let go of first?" The Master said, "Weapons." Zigong said, "What if you had to give up one of the remaining two, which one would it be?" The Master said, "Food. From ancient times, death has come to all men, but a people without confidence in its rulers will not stand."

12:19 Ji Kang Zi asked Confucius about government saying: "Suppose I were to kill the unjust, in order to advance the just. Would that be all right?" Confucius replied: "In doing government, what is the need of killing? If you desire good, the people will be good. The nature of the Superior Man is like the wind, the nature of the inferior man is like the grass. When the wind blows over the grass, it always bends."

2:19 The Duke of Ai asked: "How can I make the people follow me?" Confucius replied: "Advance the upright and set aside the crooked, and the people will follow you. Advance the crooked and set aside the upright, and the people will not follow you."

2:20 Ji Kang Zi asked: "How can I make the people reverent and loyal, so they will work positively for me?" Confucius said, "Approach them with dignity, and they will be reverent. Be filial and compassionate and they will be loyal. Promote the able and teach the incompetent, and they will work positively for you."

Han Fei

Past and present have different customs; new and old adopt different measures. To try to use the ways of a generous and lenient government to rule the people of a critical age is like trying to drive a runaway horse without using reins or whips. This is the misfortune that ignorance invites. . . .

Humaneness [*ren*] may make one shed tears and be reluctant to apply penalties, but law makes it clear that such penalties must be applied. The ancient kings allowed law to be supreme and did not give in to their tearful longings. Hence it is obvious that humaneness cannot be used to achieve order in the state. . . .

The best rewards are those that are generous and predictable, so that the people may profit by them. The best penalties are those that are severe and inescapable, so that the people will fear them. The best laws are those that are uniform and inflexible, so that the people can understand them. . . .

Hardly ten men of true integrity and good faith can be found today, and yet the offices of the state number in the hundreds. . . . Therefore the way of the enlightened ruler is to unify the laws instead of seeking for wise men, to lay down firm policies instead of longing for men of good faith. . . .

When a sage rules the state, he does not depend on people's doing good of themselves; he sees to it that they are not allowed to do what is bad. If he depends on people's doing good of themselves, then within his borders he can count fewer than ten instances of success. But if he sees to it that they are not allowed to do what is bad, then the whole state can be brought to a uniform level of order. Those who rule must employ measures that will be effective with the majority and discard those that will be effective with only a few. Therefore they devote themselves not to virtue but to law. . . .

When the Confucians of the present time counsel rulers, they do not praise those measures that will bring order today, but talk only of the achievements of the men who brought order in the past. . . . No ruler with proper standards will tolerate them. Therefore the enlightened ruler works with facts and discards useless theories. He does not talk about deeds of humaneness and rightness, and he does not listen to the words of scholars. . . .

Nowadays, those who do not understand how to govern invariably say, "You must win the hearts of the people!" . . . The reason you cannot rely on the wisdom of the people is that they have the minds of little children. If the child's head is not shaved, its sores will spread; and if its boil is not lanced, it will become sicker than ever . . . for it does not understand that the little pain it suffers now will bring great benefit later. . . .

Now, the ruler presses the people to till the land and open up new pastures so as to increase their means of livelihood, and yet they consider him harsh; he draws up a penal code and makes the punishments more severe in order to put a stop to evil, and yet the people consider him stern. . . . He makes certain that everyone within his borders understands warfare and sees to it that there are no private exemptions from military service; he unites the strength of the state and fights fiercely in order to take its enemies captive, and yet the people consider him violent. . . . [These] types of undertaking all ensure order and safety to the state, and yet the people do not have sense enough to rejoice in them.

QUESTIONS FOR ANALYSIS

1. What do Confucius and Han Fei believe about the nature of human beings? Are they intrinsically good and well-behaved, or bad and prone to misbehave?

2. What are the qualities of an ideal ruler for Confucius and Han Fei?

3. By what means can the ruler influence his subjects in Confucian thought? How should the ruler compel obedience in the people in Legalist thought?

4. What do Confucians and Legalists think about the value of the past as a model for the present?

5. Why might Confucius's passionate concern for ethical behavior on the part of officials and rulers arise at a time when the size and power of governments were growing?

Sources: Confucius selections from "The Analects of Confucius," translated by A. Charles Muller, from http://www.acmuller.net/con-dao/analects.html. Reprinted by permission of Charles Muller. Passages from "The Five Vermin" from Han Fei Tzu, translated by Burton Watson. Copyright © 1964 Columbia University Press. Reprinted with permission of the publisher.

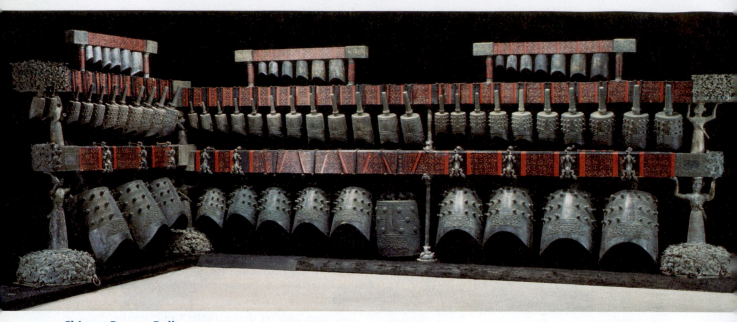

Chinese Bronze Bells   This set of 65 bells was discovered in the tomb of Marquis Yi, the ruler of one of the warring states in the 5th century B.C.E. Bells in different sizes were central components of ancient Chinese "orchestras." In the Eastern Zhou era, each state had its own distinctive set of instruments, an assertion of independence and local pride.   Asian Art & Archaeology, Inc./Corbis

Social organization also changed in this period. The kinship structures of the Shang and early Zhou periods, based on the clan (a relatively large group of related families), gave way to the three-generation family of grandparents, parents, and children as the fundamental social unit. Only men could conduct rituals and make offerings to the ancestors, though women could help maintain the household's ancestral shrines. Fathers held authority over women and children, arranged marriages for their offspring, and could sell the labor of family members. A man was limited to one wife but was permitted additional sexual partners, who had the lower status of concubines. The elite classes used marriage to create political alliances, and it was common for the groom's family to offer a substantial "bride-gift," a proof of the wealth and standing of his family, to the family of the prospective bride. A man whose wife died had a duty to remarry in order to produce male heirs to keep alive the cult of the ancestors, whereas women were discouraged from remarrying.

These differences in male and female activities were explained by the concept of **yin** and **yang**, the complementary nature of male and female roles in the natural order. The male principle (yang) was equated with the sun: active, bright, and shining; the female principle (yin) corresponded to the moon: passive, shaded, and reflective. Female gentleness balanced male toughness, female endurance and need for completion balanced male action and initiative, and female supportiveness balanced male leadership. In its earliest form, the theory considered yin and yang as equal and alternately dominant, like day and night, creating balance in the world. However, as a result of the changing role of women in the Zhou period and the pervasive influence of Confucian ideology, the male principle came to be seen as superior to the female.

yin/yang In Chinese belief, complementary factors that help to maintain the equilibrium of the world. Yang is associated with masculine, light, and active qualities; yin with feminine, dark, and passive qualities.

SECTION REVIEW

- Neolithic farming communities grew in the Yellow and Yangzi River Valleys and adapted to the very different environments in each.

- The Shang dynasty emerged in the Yellow River Valley and grew to encompass parts of the Yangzi River Valley.

- Shang technologies included pictographic writing, bronze work, and artifacts related to royal divination, male ancestor worship, and the power of the warrior aristocracy.

- The first king of the Zhou dynasty defeated the Shang, claiming the Mandate of Heaven as justification for this victory.

- Like the Shang, the Zhou state was decentralized, and it devolved into a collection of independent and hostile states.

- Legalism became the major political philosophy, but Confucianism and Daoism also emerged and established most of the basic principles of Chinese culture.

NUBIA, 2300 B.C.E.–350 C.E.

■ *How did the technological and cultural influences of Egypt affect the formation of Nubia?*

Since the first century B.C.E. the name *Nubia* has been applied to a 1,000-mile (1,600-kilometer) stretch of the Nile Valley lying between Aswan and Khartoum (kahr-TOOM) and straddling the southern part of the modern nation of Egypt and the northern part of Sudan. The ancient Egyptians called it *Tasety*, meaning "Land of the Bow," after the favorite weapon of the warriors. Nubia is the only trade corridor and continuously inhabited stretch of territory connecting sub-Saharan Africa (the lands south of the Sahara Desert) with North Africa. It was richly endowed with natural resources such as gold, copper, and semiprecious stones.

Egypt's quest for Nubian gold helps explain the early rise of a civilization with a complex political organization, social stratification, metallurgy, monumental building, and writing. However, most scholars today have moved away from the traditional view that Nubian civilization derived from Egypt and emphasize the mutually beneficial interactions between the two lands and the growing evidence that Nubian culture drew on influences from sub-Saharan Africa.

Early Cultures and Egyptian Domination, 2300–1100 B.C.E.

The central geographical feature of Nubia, as of Egypt, is the Nile River. The Nubian segment of the Nile flows through a landscape of rocky desert, grassland, and fertile plain. In a torrid climate with minimal rainfall, agriculture depended on river irrigation. Six cataracts, barriers formed by large boulders and rapids, obstructed boat traffic. Boats operating between the cataracts and caravans skirting the river made travel possible.

In the fifth millennium B.C.E., bands of people in northern Nubia made the transition from seminomadic hunting and gathering to a settled life based on grain agriculture and cattle herding. The majority of the population came to live in agricultural villages alongside the river. Even before 3000 B.C.E. Egyptian craftsmen worked in ivory and in ebony wood that must have come from tropical Africa by way of Nubia.

As we saw with the journey of Harkhuf at the beginning of this chapter, Nubia enters the Egyptian historical record around 2300 B.C.E. in accounts of trade missions. At that time Aswan, just north of the First Cataract, was the southern limit of Egyptian control. Egyptian noblemen stationed there led donkey caravans south in search of gold, incense, ebony, ivory, slaves, and exotic animals from tropical Africa. This was dangerous work, requiring delicate negotiations with local Nubian chiefs to secure protection, but it brought substantial rewards to those who succeeded.

During the Middle Kingdom (ca. 2040–1640 B.C.E.), Egypt adopted a more aggressive stance toward Nubia. Egyptian rulers sought to control the gold mines in the desert east of the Nile and to cut out the Nubian middlemen who drove up the cost of luxury goods from the tropics. A string of mud-brick forts on islands and riverbanks south of the Second Cataract was built to protect Egypt's southern frontier and regulate the flow of commerce. These Egyptian garrisons were sufficiently intimidating that relations with the indigenous population of northern Nubia, while intermittent, were generally peaceful.

Farther south, where the Nile makes a great U-shaped turn in a fertile plain, a more complex political entity was evolving from the chiefdoms of the third millennium B.C.E. The Egyptians gave the name **Kush** to the kingdom whose capital was located at Kerma, one of the earliest urbanized centers in tropical Africa. Beginning around 1750 B.C.E. the kings of Kush marshaled a labor force to build monumental walls and structures of mud brick. Royal burials containing dozens and even hundreds of sacrificed servants and wives, along with sumptuous objects, testify to the wealth and power of the rulers of Kush and suggest a belief in some sort of afterlife. Kushite craftsmen showed skill in metalworking, whether for weapons or jewelry, and their pottery surpassed anything produced in Egypt.

During the expansionist New Kingdom (ca. 1532–1070 B.C.E.) the Egyptians penetrated more deeply into Nubia (see Chapter 2). They destroyed Kush and its capital and extended their frontier to the Fourth Cataract. A high-ranking Egyptian official called "Overseer of Southern Lands" or "King's Son of Kush" ruled Nubia from a new administrative center at Napata (nah-PAH-tuh), near Gebel Barkal (JEB-uhl BAHR-kahl), the "Holy Mountain," believed to be the home of a local god. Egypt exploited the gold mines of Nubia to help buttress its commerce with other lands. Fatalities were high among native workers in the brutal desert climate, and the army had to ward off attacks from desert nomads.

Five hundred years of Egyptian domination in Nubia left many marks. The Egyptian government imposed Egyptian culture on the native population. To guarantee the good behavior of their relatives in Nubia, children from elite families were brought to the Egyptian royal court; to absorb Egyptian language, culture, and religion, which they later carried home with them. Other Nubians served Egyptians as archers; the manufactured goods that they brought back to Nubia have been found in their graves. The Nubians built Egyptian-style towns and erected stone temples to Egyptian gods, particularly Amon. The frequent depiction of Amon with the head of a ram may reflect a blending of the chief Egyptian god with a Nubian ram deity.

The Kingdom of Meroë, 800 B.C.E.–350 C.E.

Egypt's weakness after 1200 B.C.E. led to the collapse of its authority in Nubia, and in the eighth century B.C.E. a powerful new native kingdom emerged in southern Nubia. Its history can be divided into two parts. During the early period, between the eighth and fourth centuries B.C.E., Napata, the former Egyptian headquarters, was the primary center. During the later period, from the fourth century B.C.E. to the fourth century C.E., the center was farther south, at **Meroë** (MER-oh-ee), near the Sixth Cataract.

For half a century, from around 712 to 660 B.C.E., the kings of Nubia ruled all of Egypt as the Twenty-fifth Dynasty. They conducted themselves in the age-old manner of Egyptian rulers, using Egyptian titles, costumes, and burial customs. However, they kept their Nubian names and were depicted with physical features suggesting peoples of sub-Saharan Africa. Building on a monumental scale for the first time in centuries and reinvigorating Egyptian art, architecture, and religion, they inaugurated an artistic and cultural renaissance. The Nubian kings resided at Memphis, the Old Kingdom capital, while Thebes, the New Kingdom capital, was the residence of a celibate female member of the king's family who was titled "God's Wife of Amon."

The Nubian dynasty made a disastrous mistake in 701 B.C.E. when it offered help to local rulers in Syria-Palestine who were struggling against the Assyrian Empire. The Assyrians retaliated by invading Egypt and driving the Nubian monarchs back to their southern domain by 660 B.C.E. Napata again became the chief royal residence and religious center of the kingdom. However, Egyptian cultural influences remained strong. Court documents continued to be written in Egyptian hieroglyphs, and the mummified remains of the rulers were buried in modestly sized sandstone pyramids along with hundreds of shawabti (shuh-WAB-tee) figurines.

Kush An Egyptian name for Nubia, the region alongside the Nile River south of Egypt, where an indigenous kingdom with its own distinctive institutions and cultural traditions arose beginning in the early second millennium B.C.E.

Meroë Capital of a flourishing kingdom in southern Nubia from the fourth century B.C.E. to the fourth century C.E. In this period Nubian culture shows more independence from Egypt and the influence of sub-Saharan Africa.

Gebel Barkal The "Holy Mountain" of Nubia, located in northern Sudan at a great bend in the Nile near the Fourth Cataract. At its base sat the ancient city of Napata, first the capital of the New Kingdom Egyptian occupying forces, then of the independent state of Kush from the eighth to fourth centuries B.C.E. Several pillars survive from the temple of Amon, as well as a number of small burial pyramids. KENNETH GARRETT/National Geographic Stock

By the end of the fourth century B.C.E. the center of gravity had shifted south to Meroë, perhaps because Meroë was better situated for agriculture and trade, the economic mainstays of the Nubian kingdom. As a result, sub-Saharan cultural patterns gradually replaced Egyptian ones. Egyptian hieroglyphs gave way to a new set of symbols, still essentially undeciphered, for writing the Meroitic language. People continued to worship Amon as well as Isis, an Egyptian goddess connected to fertility and sexuality, but those deities had to share the stage with Nubian deities like the lion-god Apedemak. Meroitic art combined Egyptian, Greco-Roman, and indigenous traditions.

Women of the royal family played an important role in Meroitic politics, another reflection of the influence of sub-Saharan Africa. The Nubians employed a matrilineal system in which the king was succeeded by the son of his sister. Nubian queens sometimes ruled by themselves and sometimes in partnership with their husbands. Greek, Roman, and biblical sources refer to a queen of Nubia named Candace. Since these sources relate to different times,

Candace was probably a title rather than a proper name. At least seven queens ruled between 284 B.C.E. to 115 C.E. They are depicted in scenes reserved for male rulers in Egyptian imagery, smiting enemies in battle and being suckled by the mother-goddess Isis. Roman sources marvel at the fierce resistance put up by a one-eyed warrior-queen.

Meroë was a huge city for its time, more than a square mile in area, and it overlooked fertile grasslands and dominated converging trade routes. Great reservoirs were dug to catch precious rainfall. The city was a major center for iron smelting (after 1000 B.C.E. iron had replaced bronze as the primary metal for tools and weapons). The Temple of Amon was approached by an avenue of stone rams, and the enclosed "Royal City" was filled with palaces, temples, and administrative buildings. In 2002 archaeologists using a magnetometer to detect structures buried in the sand discovered a large palace, which they plan to excavate.

Meroë collapsed in the early fourth century C.E., overrun by nomads from the western desert who had become more mobile because of the arrival of the

69

SECTION REVIEW

- Fertile and rich in natural resources, Nubia became an important source of raw materials in Egypt.

- Egyptian cultural influence moved deeper into Nubia as the Middle and New Kingdoms extended Egyptian authority farther south.

- The rich Nubian kingdom of Kush fell to the New Kingdom, but after five hundred years a Nubian dynasty rose and took control of Egypt itself for a short time.

- After the fall of this dynasty, Meroë assumed control of southern Nubia, which was dominated by sub-Saharan cultural practices.

- Meroë was a large and powerful city in its prime, but it was already weak by the time it fell to nomadic invaders.

camel in North Africa. However, Meroë had already been weakened when profitable commerce with the Roman Empire was diverted to the Red Sea and to the rising kingdom of Aksum (AHK-soom) in present-day Ethiopia (see Chapter 8).

PASTORAL NOMADS OF THE EURASIAN STEPPES, 1000–100 B.C.E.

■ *How was the rise of steppe nomadism dependent on interactions with settled agricultural peoples, and what new challenges did the nomads pose to farming societies?*

For most of human history people were foraging **nomads** ("wanderers" in Greek) who moved from one temporary encampment to another, mostly as a strategy for feeding themselves. But with the Agricultural Revolutions humans began to settle in one place, build permanent homes, acquire more possessions, and create more complex societies (see Chapter 1).

The domestication of herd animals, such as sheep, goats, and cattle, made a new kind of nomadism possible. People lived off the products of their animals, consuming the meat, milk and other dairy products, clothing themselves with hair and hides, and utilizing animal manure to fuel fires. We have already seen several examples of nomadic peoples: the Amorites who migrated into southern Mesopotamia and assimilated with the peoples there to eventually found Baby-

lon (see Chapter 1); the Aramaeans, whose language, Aramaic, became widespread in Syria-Palestine; and the early Israelites, whose migratory lifestyle was recorded in the Hebrew Bible (see Chapter 2). Many scholars believe that the proto-Indo-Europeans, speakers of the language or languages ancestral to the large family of Indo-European languages found across much of Europe and Asia, were nomadic herders who migrated from an original homeland north of the Black and Caspian Seas. They are believed to have first domesticated horses, which enhanced their ability to herd other animals (see Chapter 2).

Steppe Nomads

Our concern here is with a new kind of pastoral nomadism that arose across the vast Eurasian **Steppes** (a word of Russian origin)—a treeless ecological zone of grass-and-shrub-covered plains that extend from Hungary in eastern Europe across Ukraine and southern Russia, Central Asia, Mongolia, and southern Siberia. In the first millennium B.C.E. the peoples who occupied these relatively arid lands did not wander randomly but rather drove their herds to familiar encampments appropriate to their needs in different seasons, being careful not to overexploit pastures and water sources so that they could be used when they returned. There were, no doubt, significant ethnic and linguistic differences among these peoples, who operated within certain territorial bounds worked out with other groups. They became horse-riding warriors who under normal circumstances were as prone to fight each other as to raid the lands and possessions of the farmers in neighboring areas. In fact, the success of their way of life depended on a symbiotic interaction with settled agricultural peoples, often by trading animal products (live animals, meat, hides, wool, cheese) for agricultural products and manufactured goods (metalwork and textiles), and sometimes by raiding and stealing. These various tribes shared many features of technology, culture,

nomads People without permanent, fixed places of residence, whose way of life and means of subsistence require them to periodically migrate, often with their herds of domesticated animals, to a familiar series of temporary seasonal encampments.

steppe An ecological region of grass- and shrub-covered plains that is treeless and too arid for agriculture.

Ria Novosti/Alamy

Scythian Gold Pectoral This gold pectoral (decorative item worn over the breast), found in Ukraine and dating to the fourth century B.C.E., displays the beauty and quality of craftsmanship of Scythian art. The lower register shows griffins attacking a horse, while two men with quivers examine a fleece shirt in the upper register.

and political and social organization, due, in large part, to their mobility and the speed with which objects and ideas could move across this open landscape. Indeed, the steppe was the conduit by which products, such as wheat, and technologies, including bronze and iron metalworking, chariots, and cavalry warfare, traveled from western and Central Asia to East Asia.

The Scythians

While the origins of pastoral nomadism on the steppes are shrouded in the mists of prehistory, archaeological information and the accounts of literate ancient peoples tell us something about them. The first Greek historian, Herodotus, writing in 440 B.C.E., claims that the nomadic Cimmerians, driven out of their northern homelands by another nomadic people, the **Scythians**, invaded Anatolia (modern Turkey) in the seventh century B.C.E. These Cimmerians are also mentioned in Assyrian records. The Greeks used the term *Scythian* broadly, lumping together various peoples who spoke similar languages and lived north and east of their Aegean homeland (in present-day Ukraine and southern Russia). These peoples,

however, would not have regarded themselves as belonging to the same ethnic group.

Herodotus traveled in the region where Greeks had established colonies around the coasts of the Black Sea and derived information from Greek traders who traveled far inland and Scythian natives who interacted with the Greeks. He depicts the fundamental quality of the Scythians as people without cities or permanent homes, who migrate together with their herds of sheep, goats, and cattle and their prized horses. Scythians belonged to kinship groups ruled by kings. They and their families lived in carts that were also used to transport their few possessions. Herodotus also makes clear that there were different groups of Scythians practicing somewhat different ways of life. Besides the purely nomadic groups, there were others that engaged in a mixed pastoral and agricultural economy, and some groups (perhaps influenced by the nearby Greek settlers) were settled agriculturalists, evidence of the important interdependency of nomadic pastoralists with agricultural peoples.

Herodotus also describes the Scythians as exceedingly warlike and savage—their chief god equated with the Greek god of war, Ares—who are said to drink the blood of their enemies, cut off their heads as trophies, and make goblets out of their skulls, napkins and coats from their skins. In religious practices the Scythians had no images of the gods, no shrines and no altars, and employed a sacrificial ritual quite different from that of the Greeks that sometimes included human sacrifice. When their kings died, they were accompanied in the grave by murdered servants, guards, and horses. Herodotus's comparatively lengthy account of the Scythian barbarians suggests he may have wanted to emphasize how different they were as a way of "reflecting" what was characteristically Greek.

While likely taking pleasure in relating his story at the expense of the powerful Persians, Herodotus shows how these exceedingly mobile nomads drew the Persian king Darius ever further into unknown Scythian territory, their lack of permanent settlements and cultivated fields presenting no obvious targets for the

Scythians Term used by the ancient Greeks for the nomadic peoples living on the steppe north of the Black and Caspian Seas.

Persians to attack and hold hostage. They practiced a "scorched earth" policy of burning the grass and destroying the wells, and they clearly felt no shame in retreat. The Persian king realized that the Scythians were toying with him when, as the armies were finally drawn up for battle, a hare darted across an open space and all the Scythians took off in pursuit of it. As Herodotus tells the story, it was all Darius could do to make a successful escape home with part of his army. Herodotus may have misunderstood Darius's real purpose—to drive the Scythians far from Persian-controlled lands—but he nevertheless illustrated brilliantly the unique difficulties that nomads presented to even powerful ancient states and empires, many of whom found it cheaper to just buy off the nomads by giving them "gifts" in return for not attacking.

China and the Nomads

Chinese accounts of the peoples of the eastern side of the Eurasian Steppes, also known as Inner Asia, usually match those of the Greeks and Romans. As the Chinese states of the Spring and Autumn and Warring States Periods came under increasing pressure from swift-moving, horse-borne warriors, they began to build walls along their northern frontiers to keep the raiders out, and in the late fourth century B.C.E. the forward-thinking ruler of the state of Zhao took the unprecedented step of outfitting some of his troops with trousers and mounting them on horseback.

Our fullest Chinese account of the northern nomads comes from Sima Qian (ca. 100 B.C.E.), who in many ways corresponds to Herodotus as "the father of history" in East Asia. Like Herodotus, he may have been using his description of the lifestyle of the Xiongnu (SHONG-noo) nomads to highlight characteristic aspects of Chinese civilization. Sima Qian served at the court and had access to archival records and earlier historical texts. He also traveled on official business among the barbarians. He reports that the Xiongnu had no cities, no fixed dwellings, no agriculture, and no writing. They migrated with their herds to pastures and sources of water. They were trained as warriors from an early age, and for this reason the young and fit were given preference over the old and useless. Although tough and warlike by nature, they felt no shame in retreating. Their armies lacked discipline and order, and they largely fought for their own personal gain. They swooped in like birds and vanished just as quickly, cutting off the heads of their vanquished enemies. Human sacrifice was part of their royal funerals. In Sima Qian's account, a former Chinese official who has defected to the nomads points out that, unlike the Chinese, their lives were simple and unencumbered by excessive rules, rituals, or bureaucracy. Here, again, we should note that because the Xiongnu either controlled or were allied to groups that practiced agriculture, they had access to items they could not produce themselves. Many scholars believe that the Xiongnu and several other nomadic peoples on the East Asian steppe spoke Turkish languages, while the Yuezhi, (YOUAY-jee) located further west, spoke an Indo-European language.

In addition to information we can cull from ancient texts like those of Herodotus and Sima Qian, we also have information from archaeological excavation of the large burial mounds of the elite, and in a number of cases the permafrost of Siberia, which has preserved materials, such as textiles, that normally do not survive in the archaeological record. The art of the nomads—mainly golden jewelry and horse fittings and colorful carpets and other textiles—is beautiful to the modern eye, with its emphasis on animals, real and fantastic, often shown in combat, in twisting, interlocked poses that conform gracefully to the surface on which they are displayed.

As we will see in subsequent chapters, the relatively small, fractious tribes of steppe nomads were, at the least, a constant nuisance to the sedentary agricultural peoples living to the south of them. However, from time to time they united in great confederacies under charismatic leaders, and then they presented a serious military threat. The Han Chinese emperors would be at war for centuries with the Xiongnu; the Parthians would take over Iran and much of Mesopotamia and become Rome's only great-power rival (see Chapter 5); the Late Roman Empire would be hard-pressed by Avars and Huns; and in the medieval period the Mongols and several Turkish peoples would overrun most of Asia (see Chapter 12).

While nomadism has become increasingly rare, it has been estimated that 30 to 40 million people still practice this ancient way of life, primarily in Central Asia and the West African Sahel region.

- Humans were all nomadic until the Agricultural Revolutions, and the domestication of animals led to the rise of pastoral nomadism.

- After 1000 B.C.E. pastoral nomads dominated the vast Eurasian steppelands. They still needed goods produced by farming peoples, which they obtained by trading or raiding.

- Our information about the ancient steppe nomads comes primarily from archaeology and the accounts of Greek, Roman, and Chinese texts.

- The toughness and mobility of nomadic peoples posed a challenge to states and empires, and in certain periods nomads united to become major threats.

CELTIC EUROPE, 1000–50 B.C.E.

■ *What were the causes behind the spread of Celtic peoples across much of continental Europe and the later retreat of Celtic cultures to the western edge of the continent?*

The southern peninsulas of Europe—present-day Spain, Italy, and Greece—share in the mild climate of all the Mediterranean lands and are separated from "continental" Europe to the north by high mountains (the Pyrenees and Alps). Consequently, the history of southern Europe in antiquity is primarily connected to that of the Middle East, at least until the Roman conquests north of the Alps (see Chapters 4 and 5).

Continental Europe (including the modern nations of France, Germany, Switzerland, Austria, the Czech Republic, Slovakia, Hungary, Poland, and Romania) was more forested but was well suited to agriculture and herding. It contained broad plains with good soil and had a temperate climate with cold winters, warm summers, and ample rainfall. Large, navigable rivers (the Rhone, Rhine, and Danube) facilitated travel and the exploitation of natural resources like timber and metals.

Humans had lived in this part of Europe for many thousands of years, but their lack of a writing system limits our knowledge of the earliest inhabitants. Around 500 B.C.E., Celtic peoples spread across a substantial portion of Europe, and by coming into contact with the literate societies of the Mediterranean, entered the historical record. Information about the early **Celts** (kelts) comes from the archaeological

record, Greek and Roman authors, and the Celtic oral traditions of Wales and Ireland that were written down during the European Middle Ages.

The Spread of the Celts

The term *Celtic* refers to a branch of the Indo-European family of languages found throughout Europe and in western and southern Asia. Scholars link the Celtic language group to archaeological remains first appearing in parts of present-day Germany, Austria, and the Czech Republic after 1000 B.C.E. Celtic elites were trading with Mediterranean societies for craft goods and wine. This contact may have stimulated the new styles of Celtic manufacture and art that appeared at this time.

These new cultural features coincided with Celtic migrations to many parts of Europe. The motives behind these population movements, their precise timing, and the manner in which they were carried out are not well understood, but probably included pressure from Germanic peoples still farther east who would eventually displace them. Celts occupied nearly all of France and much of Britain and Ireland, and they merged with indigenous peoples to create the Celtiberian culture of northern Spain. Other Celtic groups overran northern Italy in the fifth century B.C.E., sacking Rome in 390; raided central Greece; and settled in central Anatolia (modern Turkey). By 300 B.C.E. Celtic peoples were spread across Europe north of the Alps, from present-day Hungary to Spain and Ireland.

Although these widely diffused Celtic groups shared elements of language and culture, there was no Celtic "nation." Instead they were divided into hundreds of small, loosely organized kinship groups. Traditional depictions of Celtic society come largely from the observations of Greek and Roman writers. However, current scholarship focuses on the differences as much as the similarities among Celtic peoples. It is unlikely that the ancient Celts ever identified themselves as belonging to anything akin to our modern conception of "Celtic civilization."

The Greeks and Romans remarked particularly on the appearance of male Celts—their burly

Celts Peoples sharing common linguistic and cultural features that originated in Central Europe in the first half of the first millennium B.C.E.

size, long red hair (which they often made stiff and upright by applying a cement-like solution of lime), shaggy mustaches, and loud, deep voices. Trousers (usually an indication of horse-riding peoples) and twisted gold neck collars were similarly distinctive, but not as unusual as the terrifying warriors who fought naked and collected the skulls of defeated enemies. The surviving accounts describe the Celts as wildly fond of war, courageous, childishly impulsive and emotional, and fond of boasting and exaggeration, yet quick-witted and eager to learn.

Celtic Society

The Roman general Gaius Julius Caesar, who conquered Gaul (present-day France) between 58 and 51 B.C.E. (see Chapter 5) penned the greatest source of information about Celtic society. Many Celtic groups in Gaul had once been ruled by kings, but by 60 B.C.E they periodically chose public officials, perhaps under Greek and Roman influence. Their society was divided into an elite class of warriors, professional groups of priests and bards (singers of poems about glorious deeds of the past), and commoners. The warriors owned land and flocks of cattle and sheep and monopolized both wealth and power, while the common people labored on their land. The Celts built houses (usually round in Britain, rectangular in France) out of wattle and daub—a wooden framework filled in with clay and straw—with thatched straw roofs. Several such houses belonging to related families might be surrounded by a wooden fence for protection.

The warriors of Welsh and Irish legend reflect a stage of political and social development less complex than that of the Celts in Gaul. They raided one another's flocks, reveled in drunken feasts, and engaged in contests of strength and wit. At banquets warriors would fight to the death just to claim the choicest cut of the meat, the "hero's portion."

Druids, the Celtic priests in Gaul and Britain, formed a well-organized fraternity that performed religious, judicial, and educational functions. Trainees spent years memorizing prayers, secret rituals, legal precedents, and other traditions. The priesthood was the one Celtic institution that crossed tribal lines. The Druids sometimes headed off warfare between feuding groups and served as judges in cases involving Celts from different groups. In the first cen-

The Gundestrup Cauldron This silver vessel was found in a peat bog in Denmark, but it must have come from elsewhere. It is usually dated to the second or first century B.C.E. On the inside right are Celtic warriors on horse and on foot, with lozenge-shaped shields and long battle-horns. On the inside left is a horned deity, possibly Cernunnos. Universal History Archive/Getty Images

tury C.E. the Roman government attempted to stamp out the Druids, probably because of concern that they might serve as a rallying point for Celtic opposition to Roman rule and also because of their involvement in human sacrifices.

The Celts supported large populations by tilling the heavy but fertile soils of continental Europe, and their metallurgical skills probably surpassed those of the Mediterranean peoples. Celts living on the Atlantic shore of France built sturdy oceangoing boats, and they developed extensive trade networks along Europe's large, navigable rivers. One lucrative commodity was tin, which Celtic traders from southwest England brought to Greek buyers in southern France. By the first century B.C.E. some hill-forts were evolving into urban centers.

Women's lives were focused on child rearing, food production, and some crafts. Their situation was superior to that of women in the Middle East

Druids The class of religious experts who conducted rituals and preserved sacred lore among some ancient Celtic peoples.

and in the Greek and Roman Mediterranean. Greek and Roman sources depict Celtic women as strong and proud. Welsh and Irish tales portray self-assured women who sit at banquets with their husbands, engage in witty conversation, and provide ingenious solutions to vexing problems. Marriage was a partnership to which both parties contributed property, and each had the right to inherit the estate if the other died. Celtic women also had greater freedom in their sexual relations than did their southern counterparts.

Tombs of elite women have yielded rich collections of clothing, jewelry, and furniture for use in the next world. Daughters of the elite were married to leading members of other tribes to create alliances. When the Romans invaded Celtic Britain in the first century C.E., they sometimes were opposed by Celtic tribes headed by queens, although some experts see this as an abnormal circumstance created by the Roman invasion itself.

Belief and Knowledge

Historians know the names of more than four hundred Celtic gods and goddesses, mostly associated with particular localities or kinship groups. More widely revered deities included Lug (loog), the god of light, crafts, and inventions; the horse-goddess Epona (eh-POH-nuh); and the horned god Cernunnos (KURN-you-nuhs). "The Mothers," three goddesses depicted together holding symbols of abundance, probably played a part in a fertility cult. Halloween and May Day preserve the ancient Celtic holidays of Samhain (SAH-win) and Beltaine (BEHL-tayn), respectively, which took place at key moments in the agricultural cycle.

The early Celts did not build temples, but instead worshiped wherever they felt the presence of divinity—at springs, groves, and hilltops. At the sources of the Seine and Marne Rivers in France, archaeologists have found huge caches of Celtic wooden statues thrown into the water by worshipers.

Wagons filled with extensive grave goods show up in elite burials, suggesting a belief in some sort of afterlife. In Irish and Welsh legends, heroes and gods pass back and forth between the natural and supernatural worlds much more readily than in the mythology of other cultures, and magical occurrences are

SECTION REVIEW

- From central and eastern Europe, Celtic peoples spread across the continent.
- These peoples shared language and culture but no single state.
- Although Celtic societies varied in complexity, they all shared the institutions of the Druid priesthood, practiced agriculture, and developed sophisticated technologies.
- Celtic women enjoyed relatively high status, and some even led warriors against Roman invaders.
- Celtic religion involved a vast array of deities and some sort of afterlife.
- Celtic culture declined under Roman rule, and the Germanic migrations pushed it to the western margin of Europe.

commonplace. Celtic priests set forth a doctrine of reincarnation—the rebirth of the soul in a new body.

The evolution of Celtic society in Spain, southern Britain, France, and parts of central Europe slowed after the Roman conquests from the second century B.C.E. to the first century C.E. The peoples in these lands largely assimilated Roman ways (see Chapter 5). From the third century C.E. on, Germanic invaders from the east diminished the Celts still further. Only on the western fringes of the European continent—in Brittany (northwest France), Wales, Scotland, and Ireland—did Celtic peoples maintain their language, art, and culture into modern times.

CONCLUSION

The civilizations of early China, Nubia, the Eurasian Steppes, and the Celts emerged in very different ecological contexts in widely separated parts of the Eastern Hemisphere, and the patterns of organization, technology, behavior, and belief that they developed were, in large part, responses to the challenges and opportunities of those environments.

In the North China Plain, as in the river-valley civilizations of Mesopotamia and Egypt, the presence of great, flood-prone rivers and the lack of dependable rainfall led to the formation of powerful institutions capable of organizing large numbers of people to dig and maintain irrigation channels and build dikes. An authoritarian central government has been a recurring feature of Chinese history, beginning with the Shang monarchy and the warrior elite.

In Nubia, the initial impetus for the formation of a strong state was the need for protection from desert nomads and from the Egyptian rulers who coveted Nubian gold and other resources. Control of these resources and of the trade route between sub-Saharan Africa and the north, as well as the agricultural surplus to feed administrators and specialists in the urban centers, made the rulers and elites of Kerma, Napata, and Meroë wealthy and formidable.

Pastoral nomads found ways to exploit the challenging environment of the Eurasian Steppes. The very nature of their lifestyle, based on migrating with their herds of domesticated animals to seasonal camping grounds, meant that they had no permanent settlements and maintained small, kinship-based groups. Thus, under normal circumstances, their political organization was relatively simple. However, in moments of crisis, or when a charismatic military leader came to the fore, they could unite in formidable confederacies.

The Celtic peoples of continental Europe never developed a strong state. They occupied fertile lands with adequate rainfall for agriculture, grazing territory for flocks, and timber for fuel and construction. Kinship groups dominated by warrior elites and controlling compact territories were the usual form of organization.

CHAPTER REVIEW

EARLY CHINA, 2000–221 B.C.E.
How did early Chinese rulers use religion to justify and strengthen their power? (page 57)

Throughout history, elites have used religion to bolster their position. The Shang rulers of China were indispensable intermediaries between their kingdom and powerful and protective ancestors and gods. Bronze vessels were used to make offerings to ancestral spirits, and royal and elite families were buried in elaborate tombs that were intended to serve the occupant in the afterlife. Their Zhou successors developed the concept of the ruler as divine Son of Heaven who ruled in accord with the Mandate of Heaven.

NUBIA, 2300 B.C.E.–350 C.E.
How did the technological and cultural influences of Egypt affect the formation of Nubia? (page 67)

The civilization that developed in Nubia was powerfully influenced by its interactions with the more complex and technologically advanced neighboring society in Egypt. Nubia was engaged in trade with Egypt for most of its history, and Egyptians often sought to connect and dominate the gold trade. In the New Kingdom period, the Egyptian government imposed Egyptian culture, language, and religion on the native population, and Nubian architecture came to be based on Egyptian models. In the eighth century B.C.E. the kingdom of Meroë emerged and Nubia controlled all of Egypt for half a century. While they kept their Nubian names, the rulers imitated the style of Egyptian rulers and retained many Egyptian traditions. By the fourth century, power shifted south to Meroë and sub-Saharan African cultural influences replaced Egyptian ones.

PASTORAL NOMADS OF THE EURASIAN STEPPES, 1000–100 B.C.E.
How was the rise of steppe nomadism dependent on interactions with settled agricultural peoples, and what new challenges did the nomads pose to farming societies? (page 70)

The economy of the steppe nomads depended on the agricultural products and manufactured goods (metalwork and textiles) they could trade for animal products (live animals, meat, hides, wool, cheese). These horse-riding warriors were described as exceedingly brutal and warlike and were also known to raid agricultural settlements for the products they wanted. In this regard they were at the very least a nuisance to farming communities. However, their mobility and speed brought objects, ideas, and technologies—such as wheat, bronze and iron metalworking, chariots, and cavalry warfare—all the way from western and Central Asia to East Asia.

CELTIC EUROPE, 1000–50 B.C.E.

What were the causes behind the spread of Celtic peoples across much of continental Europe and the later retreat of Celtic cultures to the western edge of the continent? (page 73)

The Celtic peoples migrated into Europe from the east, probably because of pressure from Germanic peoples who would eventually displace them. The Celtic elites of central Europe initially traded for luxury goods with the Mediterranean, and when they began to expand into lands to the west and south after 500 B.C.E. they came into even closer contact with the Mediterranean peoples. Eventually, many Celtic groups were incorporated into the Roman Empire. Druids, the Celtic priests in Gaul and Britain, performed religious and other functions. Rather than constructing temples, the Celts worshiped hundreds of gods and goddesses in natural surroundings, where they felt the presence of divinity. By the first century C.E. the Romans had conquered parts of Europe and assimilated many Celts to their ways.

Key Terms

loess (p. 58)
Shang (p. 60)
Zhou (p. 61)
Mandate of Heaven (p. 62)
Legalism (p. 62)
Confucius (p. 63)
Daoism (p. 63)
yin/yang (p. 66)
Kush (p. 68)
Meroë (p. 68)
nomads (p. 70)
steppe (p. 70)
Scythians (p. 71)
Celts (p. 73)
Druids (p. 74)

Animal Domestication

Because the earliest domestication of plants and animals took place long before the existence of written records, we cannot be sure how and when humans first learned to plant crops and make use of tamed animals. Historians usually link the two processes as part of an Agricultural Revolution, but they were not necessarily connected.

The domestication of plants is much better understood than the domestication of animals. Foraging bands of humans primarily lived on wild seeds, fruits, and tubers. Eventually some humans tried planting seeds and tubers, favoring varieties that they particularly liked, and a variety that may have been rare in the wild became more common. When such a variety suited human needs, usually by having more food value or being easier to grow or process, people stopped collecting the wild types and relied on farming and further developing their new domestic type.

In the case of animals, the basis of selection to suit human needs is less apparent. Experts looking at ancient bones and images interpret changes in hair color, horn shape, and other visible features as indicators of domestication. But these visible changes did not generally serve human purposes. It is usually assumed that animals were domesticated for their meat, but even this is questionable. Dogs, which may have become domestic tens of thousands of years before any other species, were not eaten in most cultures, and cats, which became domestic much later, were eaten even less often. As for the uses most commonly associated with domestic animals, some of the most important, such as milking cows, shearing sheep, and harnessing oxen and horses to pull plows and vehicles, first appeared thousands of years after domestication.

Cattle, sheep, and goats became domestic around ten thousand years ago in the Middle East and North Africa. Coincidentally, wheat and barley were being domesticated at roughly the same time in the same general area. This is the main reason historians generally conclude that plant and animal domestication are closely related. Yet other major meat animals, such as chickens, which originated as jungle fowl in Southeast Asia, and pigs, which probably became domestic separately in several parts of North Africa, Europe, and Asia, have no agreed-upon association with early plant domestication. Nor is plant domestication connected with the horses and camels that became domestic in western Asia and the donkeys that became domestic in the Sahara region around six thousand years ago. Moreover, though the wild forebears of these species were probably eaten, the domestic forms were usually not used for meat.

In the Middle East humans may have originally kept wild sheep, goats, and cattle for food, though wild cattle were large and dangerous and must have been hard to control. It is questionable whether, in the earliest stages, keeping these animals captive for food would have been more productive than hunting. It is even more questionable whether the humans who kept animals for this purpose had any reason to anticipate that life in captivity would cause them to become domestic.

Human motivations for domesticating animals can be better assessed after a consideration of the physical changes involved in going from wild to domestic. Genetically transmitted tameness, defined as the ability to live with and accept handling by humans, lies at the core of the domestication process. In separate experiments with wild rats and foxes in the twentieth century, scientists found that wild individuals with strong fight-or-flight tendencies reproduce poorly in captivity, whereas individuals with the lowest adrenaline levels have the most offspring in captivity. In the wild, the same low level of excitability would have made these individuals vulnerable to predators and kept their reproduction rate down. However, early humans probably preferred the animals that seemed the tamest and destroyed those that were most wild. In the rat and fox experiments, after twenty generations or so, the surviving animals were born with much smaller adrenal glands and greatly reduced fight-or-flight reactions. Since adrenaline production normally increases in the transition to adulthood, many of the low-adrenaline animals also retained juvenile characteristics, such as floppy ears and pushed-in snouts, both indicators of domestication.

Historians disagree about whether animal domestication was a deliberate process or the unanticipated outcome of keeping animals for other purposes. Some assume that domestication was an understood and reproducible process. Others argue that, since a twenty-generation time span for wild cattle and other large quadrupeds would have amounted to several human lifetimes, it is unlikely that the people who ended up with domestic cattle had any recollection of how the process started. This would also rule out the possibility that people who had unwittingly domesticated one species would have attempted to repeat the process with other species, since they did not know what they and their ancestors had done to produce genetically transmitted tameness.

Historians who assume that domestication was an understood and reproducible process tend to conclude that humans domesticated every species that could be domesticated. This is unlikely. Twentieth-century efforts to domesticate bison, eland, and elk have not fully succeeded, but they have generally not been maintained for as long as twenty generations. Rats and foxes have more rapid reproduction rates, and the experiments with them succeeded.

Animal domestication is probably best studied on a case-by-case basis as an unintended result of other processes. In some instances, sacrifice probably played a key role. Religious traditions of animal sacrifice rarely utilize, and sometimes prohibit, the ritual killing of wild animals. It is reasonable to suppose that the practice of capturing wild animals and holding them for sacrifice eventually led to the appearance of genetically transmitted tameness as an unplanned result.

Horses and camels were domesticated relatively late, and most likely not for meat consumption. The societies within which these animals first appeared as domestic species already had domestic sheep, goats, and cattle for meat, and they used oxen to carry loads and pull plows and carts. Horses, camels, and later reindeer may represent successful experiments with substituting one draft animal for another, with genetically transmitted tameness an unexpected consequence of separating animals trained for riding or pulling carts from their wilder kin.

Once human societies had developed the full range of uses of domestic animals—meat, eggs, milk, fiber, labor, transport—the likelihood of domesticating more species diminished. In the absence of concrete knowledge of how domestication had occurred, it was usually easier for people to move domestic livestock to new locations than to attempt to develop new domestic species. Domestic animals accompanied human groups wherever they ventured, and this practice triggered enormous environmental changes as domestic animals, and their human keepers, competed with wild species for food and living space.

Part Two

The Formation of New Cultural Communities, from 1500 B.C.E.

© Cengage Learning

	1000 B.C.E.	800 B.C.E.	600 B.C.E.
AMERICAS	**1200–400** Olmec civilization in Mesoamerica		
		900–250 Chavín civilization in Peru	Gold metallurgy in Chavín **500** •
EUROPE	**1000** Iron metallurgy		Celts spread across Europe **500** •
		800–500 Archaic period in Greece	Roman Republic **507** •
			477–404 Athenian Empire and democracy
AFRICA		• **814** Carthage founded	Hanno of Carthage explores West African coast **465** •
	Rise of Nubian kingdom at Napata **800** •	**712–660** Nubian domination of Egypt	
MIDDLE EAST	**1000** David establishes Jerusalem as capital of Israel	Babylonian conquest of Jerusalem **587** •	
	911–612 Neo-Assyrian Empire		**522–486** Darius I rules Persian Empire
ASIA AND OCEANIA	**1000** Aryans settle Ganges Plain	Iron metallurgy in China **600** •	**563–483** Life of the Buddha
	1027–221 Zhou kingdom in China		**551–479** Life of Confucius

From 1000 B.C.E. to 400 C.E., important changes occurred in the ways of life established in the river-valley civilizations in the two previous millennia, and the scale of human institutions and activities increased. On the shores of the Mediterranean and in Iran, India, and Southeast Asia, new centers arose in lands watered by rainfall and worked by a free peasantry. These societies developed new patterns of political and social organization and economic activity, and they moved in new intellectual, artistic, and spiritual directions.

The rulers of the empires of this era constructed extensive networks of roads and promoted urbanization. These measures brought more rapid communication, trade over greater distances, and the broad diffusion of religious ideas, artistic styles, and technologies. Large cultural zones unified by common traditions emerged—Iranian, Hellenistic, Roman, Hindu, and Chinese—and exercised substantial influence on subsequent ages.

The expansion of agriculture and trade and improvements in technology led to population increases, the spread of cities, and the growth of a comfortable middle class. In many places iron replaced bronze as the preferred metal for weapons, tools, and utensils, and metals were available to more people than in the preceding age. People using iron tools cleared extensive forests around the Mediterranean, in India, and in eastern China. Iron weapons gave an advantage to the armies of Greece, Rome, and imperial China.

New systems of writing, more easily and rapidly learned, moved the preservation and transmission of knowledge out of the control of specialists and gave birth to new ways of thinking, new genres of literature, and new types of scientific endeavor.

In the Western Hemisphere, the development of urban, agricultural civilizations in the Andes, the Yucatán lowlands, and the central plateau of Mexico, first noted among the Olmec of Mesoamerica and the Chavín culture of Peru, climaxed in the Maya and Andean cultures. These cultural exchanges and interactions were counterparts to changes in Eurasia and Africa during the same era.

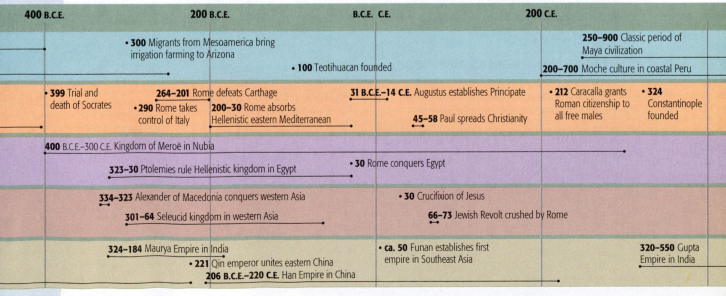

400 B.C.E.	200 B.C.E.	B.C.E. C.E.	200 C.E.
	•300 Migrants from Mesoamerica bring irrigation farming to Arizona		**250–900** Classic period of Maya civilization
	•100 Teotihuacan founded		**200–700** Moche culture in coastal Peru
•399 Trial and death of Socrates	**264–201** Rome defeats Carthage	**31 B.C.E.–14 C.E.** Augustus establishes Principate	**•212** Caracalla grants Roman citizenship to all free males	**•324** Constantinople founded
	•290 Rome takes control of Italy	**200–30** Rome absorbs Hellenistic eastern Mediterranean	**45–58** Paul spreads Christianity	
400 B.C.E.–300 C.E. Kingdom of Meroë in Nubia			
	323–30 Ptolemies rule Hellenistic kingdom in Egypt	**•30** Rome conquers Egypt	
	334–323 Alexander of Macedonia conquers western Asia	**•30** Crucifixion of Jesus	
	301–64 Seleucid kingdom in western Asia	**66–73** Jewish Revolt crushed by Rome	
	324–184 Maurya Empire in India	**•ca. 50** Funan establishes first empire in Southeast Asia	**320–550** Gupta Empire in India
	•221 Qin emperor unites eastern China		
	206 B.C.E.–220 C.E. Han Empire in China		

Greece and Iran

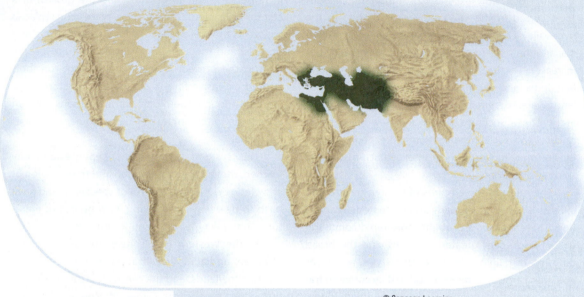

© Cengage Learning

The Greek historian Herodotus (heh-ROD-uh-tuhs) (ca. 485–425 B.C.E.) relates that the Persian king Darius (duh-RIE-us) I, whose empire stretched from eastern Europe to northwest India, questioned some Greek and Indian sages. Under what circumstances, he asked the Greeks, would they eat their deceased fathers' bodies? The Greeks, who practiced cremation, recoiled in revulsion. Darius then asked the Indians whether they would ever burn the bodies of their dead parents. This similarly repelled them because they practiced ritual eating of the bodies of the dead. Herodotus argues from this that every group of people regards its own practices as "natural" and superior. This story reminds us that ancient sources such as Herodotus's writings are sometimes accurate, as Herodotus is about Greek funerary customs, and sometimes wildly inaccurate, as are his views on Indian rituals.

The story also reminds us that the Persian Empire and the Hellenistic Greek kingdoms that succeeded it brought together peoples and cultural systems from Europe, Africa, and Asia that previously had little direct contact with one another. This cross-cultural interaction both alarmed and stimulated the peoples involved, in some instances giving rise to new cultural synthesis.

This chapter recounts the experience of the Persians and Greeks in the first millennium B.C.E. Historians traditionally consider the rivalry of Greeks and Persians the first act of an age-long drama: the clash of East and West, of fundamentally different ways of life destined to collide. Ironically, Greeks and Persians had more in common than they realized. They spoke related languages belonging to the Indo-European family, and they inherited similar cultural traits, forms of social organization, and religious outlooks from their shared past.

ANCIENT IRAN, 1000–500 B.C.E.

■ *How did the Persian Empire rise from its Iranian homeland and succeed in controlling vast territories and diverse cultures?*

Iran, the "land of the Aryans," links western Asia with southern and Central Asia. In the sixth century B.C.E.

the Persians of southwest Iran created the largest empire the world had yet seen. Heirs to the Assyrian and Babylonian imperial tradition, they introduced distinctly Iranian elements and developed new forms of political and economic organization.

Scant written evidence from within the Persian Empire forces us to rely on works by Greeks—ignorant outsiders at best, usually hostile, and interested primarily in events that affected themselves. This leaves us largely uninformed about developments in the central and eastern portions of the Persian Empire, though archaeology and close analysis of the few writings from within the empire can supplement and help correct the Greek perspective.

Geography and Resources

Iran is bounded by the Zagros (ZUHG-roes) Mountains on the west, the Caucasus (KAW-kuh-suhs) Mountains and Caspian Sea to the northwest and north, and the mountains of Afghanistan (ancient Arachosia) and the desert of Baluchistan (buh-loo-chi-STAN) (ancient Gedrosia) on the east and southeast. The southern limit is a barren seacoast on the Persian Gulf and Indian Ocean. The northeast lies open to attacks or population movements from Central Asia.

Winter precipitation in the mountains feeds streams that either flow away from the central plateau into rivers that drain into seas or flow into the plateau and terminate in salt lakes and deserts. Husbanding water is the key to survival in Iran's arid interior. Lacking a great river like the Nile, Indus, or Tigris-Euphrates, ancient Iran had a sparse population, most numerous in the moister north and west and decreasing toward the arid south and east. The Great Salt Desert, covering much of eastern Iran and Baluchistan, did not support life. Mountain barriers separated scattered settlements on the southern coastal plains from the interior plateau.

Wheat and barley grown during the comparatively wet winter season were the most common crops. However, by 800 B.C.E. Iranian farmers had worked out techniques for digging underground irrigation channels that prevented evaporation and used gravity to deliver water from the subsurface water table in the foothills of the mountains to fields in otherwise uncultivable desert. Constructing these channels and the vertical shafts that gave access to them demanded cooperative labor, but since each village had its own channel, the large-scale, government-sponsored irrigation projects typical of Mesopotamia were probably not required. This factor favored the rise of local aristocracies capable of defending their lands.

The mountains yielded copper, tin, iron, gold, and silver, all exploited on a limited scale in antiquity, as well as wood for fuel, construction, and crafts, the hillsides being more heavily wooded than they are now. Export goods consisted largely of metals and products from further east carried across Iran by traders.

The Rise of the Persian Empire

The term *Iranians* as used for premodern history describes a group of peoples speaking related languages and sharing certain cultural characteristics that lived in a broad swath of territory between the Zagros Mountains and Central Asia, with some groups as far east as northwest China. One group, the Medes (*Mada* in Iranian),* gained political dominance in northwestern Iran in the late second millenium B.C.E, influenced in part by the ancient centers in Mesopotamia and Urartu (modern Armenia and northeast Turkey). The Medes played a major role in destroying the Assyrian Empire in the late seventh century B.C.E. and extended their control westward across Assyria into Anatolia (modern Turkey). They also projected power southeastward into the land of the Elamites, which was increasingly identified with an immigrant Iranian people known as the Persians (*Parsa*).

The Persian rulers, called Achaemenids (a-KEY-muh-nid) because they traced their lineage back to an ancestor named Achaemenes, cemented relations with the Median court through marriage. **Cyrus** (*Kurush*), the son of a Persian chieftain and a Median princess, united the Persian tribes and overthrew the Median monarch around 550 B.C.E. The differences between these two peoples being slight—notably in dialect and costume—Cyrus placed both Medes and

Persians in positions of responsibility and retained the framework of Median rule. The Greeks could not readily tell them apart and may not have recorded their history accurately.

Patriarchal family organization among the Medes and Persians, like that of the Greeks, Romans, and most other Indo-European peoples, gave the male head of the household authority over family members. The warrior class dominated the other two social and occupational classes, the priests and peasants. Noble warriors, the most illustrious being the king, owned land and took pleasure in hunting, fighting, and feasting. The priests, or magi (*magush*), supervised sacrifices and other rituals. Village-based farmers and shepherds made up the third class.

Over the course of two decades the energetic Cyrus (r. 550–530 B.C.E.) redrew the map of western Asia. In 546 B.C.E. he won a cavalry battle outside Sardis, the capital of Lydia in western Anatolia, reportedly because the smell of his camels caused a panic among his opponents' horses. All Anatolia, including the Greek city-states on the western coast, came under Persian control. In 539 B.C.E. he swept into southern Mesopotamia, where the Neo-Babylonian dynasty had ruled since the collapse of Assyrian power (see Chapter 2). Disaffected elements within Babylon surrendered the city to Cyrus. Cyrus respected the Babylonian priesthood and had his son crowned king in accordance with local traditions.

Cyrus died in 530 B.C.E. while campaigning against nomadic Iranians in the northeast. His son Cambyses (kam-BIE-sees) (*Kambujiya*, r. 530–522 B.C.E.) set his sights on Egypt. Defeating the Egyptians in bloody battle, the Persians sent exploratory expeditions south to Nubia and west to Libya. Greek sources depict Cambyses as a cruel and impious madman, but contemporary Egyptian documents reflect a practical outlook. Like his father, he cultivated local priests and notables and respected their traditions.

> **Cyrus** Founder of the Achaemenid Persian Empire. Between 550 and 530 B.C.E. he conquered Media, Lydia, and Babylon. Revered in the traditions of both Iran and the subject peoples, he employed Persians and Medes in his administration and respected the institutions and beliefs of subject peoples.

---

* Familiar Greek names of Iranian groups and individuals are followed by the original Iranian names in parentheses.

Chronology

	Greece and the Hellenistic World	Persian Empire
1500 B.C.E.	1150–800 B.C.E. Greece's "Dark Age"	
1000 B.C.E.		ca. 1000 B.C.E. Persians settle in southwest Iran
800 B.C.E.	ca. 800 B.C.E. Greek seafaring resumes	
500 B.C.E.		550–530 B.C.E. Reign of Cyrus
		480–479 B.C.E. Xerxes invades Greece
400 B.C.E.	431–404 B.C.E. Peloponnesian War	
300 B.C.E.		334–323 B.C.E. Alexander the Great defeats Persia
100 B.C.E.	30 B.C.E. Rome annexes Egypt	

When Cambyses died in 522 B.C.E., **Darius I** (duh-RIE-uhs) (*Darayavaush*), seized the throne, crushing challengers with skill, energy, and ruthlessness. The Medes now played lesser roles; most important posts went to leading Persian nobles. Darius (r. 522–486 B.C.E.) extended Persian control eastward to the Indus Valley and westward into Europe, bridging the Danube River and chasing the nomadic Scythian (SITH-ee-uhn) peoples north of the Black Sea. In maritime matters, Darius dispatched a fleet to explore the route from the Indus Delta to the Red Sea and completed a canal linking the Red Sea with the Nile.

Imperial Organization and Ideology

Each of the empire's twenty provinces, stretching from eastern Europe to Pakistan, was placed under a Persian **satrap** (SAY-trap), or governor, usually a relative or connection by marriage. The satrap's court mirrored the royal court on a smaller scale. Governorships frequently became hereditary, so that satraps' families lived in the province governed by their head, acquired knowledge about local conditions, and formed connections with the local elite. The farther a province was from the empire's center, the more autonomy the satrap had, since slow communications made contact with the royal center difficult.

Darius prescribed how much precious metal each province owed annually, and the satrap collected and sent it. Some went for necessary expenditures, but most was hoarded. This practice increasingly took precious metal out of circulation, forcing up the price of gold and silver and making it hard for provinces to meet their quotas. Evidence from Babylonia shows increasing taxes and official corruption and a corresponding economic decline by the fourth century B.C.E.

Royal roads, well maintained and patrolled, connected outlying provinces to the imperial center. Way stations sheltered important travelers and couriers, and garrisons controlled movement at strategic points: mountain passes, river crossings, and important urban centers. The ancient Elamite capital of Susa, in southwest Iran, served as the imperial administrative center, the destination for Greeks and others with requests and messages for the king.

Darius I Third ruler of the Persian Empire (r. 521–486 B.C.E.). He crushed the widespread initial resistance to his rule and gave major government posts to Persians rather than to Medes. He established a system of provinces and tribute, began construction of Persepolis, and expanded Persian control in the east (Pakistan) and west (northern Greece).

satrap The governor of a province in the Achaemenid Persian Empire, often a relative of the king. He was responsible for protection of the province and for forwarding tribute to the central administration. Satraps in outlying provinces enjoyed considerable autonomy.

It took at least three months to make the journey to Susa. For Greek ambassadors, the time spent travelling, waiting for an audience, and returning home could take a year or more.

The king lived and traveled with numerous wives and children. Information about the royal women comes from foreign sources and is thus suspect. The Book of Esther in the Hebrew Bible tells how King Ahasuerus (uh-HAZZ-yoo-ear-uhs) (Xerxes [ZERK-sees] to the Greeks) picked the Jewish woman Esther as a wife, putting her in a position to save the Jewish people from a plot to massacre them. Greek sources depict royal women as pawns in power struggles and as intriguers, poisoning rival wives and plotting their sons' paths to the throne.

The king's entourage also included (1) the sons of Persian aristocrats, who were educated at court and also served as hostages for their parents' loyalty; (2) noblemen who attended the king when not on other assignments; (3) administrative officers; (4) the royal bodyguard; and (5) courtiers and slaves. Long gone were the simple days when the king hunted and caroused with his warrior companions. Inspired by Mesopotamian conceptions of monarchy, the Persian king became an aloof figure of majesty and splendor: "The Great King, King of Kings, King in Persia, King of Countries." He referred to everyone, even the Persian nobility, as "my slaves," and anyone who approached him had to bow down before him.

The king owned vast tracts of land throughout the empire, some of which he gave to his supporters. Donations called "bow land," "horse land," and "chariot land" in Babylonian documents obliged the recipient to provide military service. The *paradayadam* (meaning "walled enclosure"—the term has come into English as *paradise*), consisting of gardens or orchards belonging to the king or high nobility, symbolized the prosperity of the king and his servants.

Traditions remembered Darius as issuing the "laws of the King," appointing royal judges throughout the empire, and encouraging the codification of the laws of subject peoples. As master of a decentralized empire, he allowed each people their own traditions and ordinances.

Sometimes the kings returned to **Persepolis** (per-SEH-poe-lis) (*Parsa*), a ceremonial capital in the Persian homeland in southwest Iran that had been founded by Darius and completed by his son Xerxes (Ahasueras to the Hebrews). The palaces, audience halls, treasury buildings, and barracks built on an artificial platform extending from a mountainside took inspiration from Mesopotamia, where the Assyrian kings had created fortress-cities to advertise their power.

Texts found in Persepolis and inscribed in Elamite cuneiform on baked clay tablets show government officials distributing food and other goods to workers of various nationalities, some of them prisoners of war working on construction projects, irrigation networks, or royal estates. Women received less than men of equivalent status, but pregnant women and new mothers received more. Skilled workers of either sex received more than the unskilled.

The relief sculptures on the foundations, walls, and stairwells at Persepolis feature representatives of the peoples of the empire—recognizable by distinctive hairstyles, beards, dress, hats, and footwear—bringing gifts to the king. These images do not depict a real ceremony but rather advertise the vast extent, abundant resources, and cooperative spirit of the empire. One scene shows erect subjects effortlessly shouldering a giant platform bearing Darius's throne. Similar scenes from the Assyrian Empire show the subjects staggering under the weight. Persepolis probably served as a setting of New Year's festivals, coronations, marriages, and funerals. Tombs cut into the cliffs at nearby Naqsh-i Rustam (NUHK-shee ROOS-tuhm) sheltered the remains of Darius and his successors.

Several dozen inscriptions cut into cliff faces provide perspectives on the imperial ideology. At Naqsh-i Rustam, for example, Darius claims:

> Ahuramazda (ah-HOOR-uh-MAZZ-duh) [the chief deity], when he saw this earth in commotion, thereafter bestowed it upon me, made me king. . . . By the favor of Ahuramazda I put it down in its place. . . . I am of such a sort that I am a friend to right, I am not a friend to wrong. It is not my desire that the weak

Persepolis A complex of palaces, reception halls, and treasury buildings erected by the Persian kings Darius I and Xerxes in the Persian homeland. It is believed that the New Year's festival was celebrated here, as well as the coronations, weddings, and funerals of the Persian kings, who were buried in cliff-tombs nearby.

Sculpted Images on a Stairwell at Persepolis, ca. 500 B.C.E. Persepolis, in the Persian homeland, was built by Darius I and his son Xerxes, and it was used for ceremonies of special importance to the Persian king and people—coronations, royal weddings, funerals, and the New Year's Festival. Relief images like these on the stone foundations, walls, and stairways, representing members of the court and embassies bringing gifts, broadcast a vision of the grandeur and harmony of the Persian Empire.

man should have wrong done to him by the mighty; nor is that my desire, that the mighty man should have wrong done to him by the weak.[1]

Darius's inscriptions also show that the Persians honored promises and telling the truth. Several inscriptions castigate evildoers as followers of "The Lie."

Since the religion of **Zoroastrianism** (zo-ro-ASS-tree-uh-niz-um) recognized Ahuramazda as god, it seems certain that Darius and his successors were Zoroastrians. Questions surround the origins of this religion. Worshipers believe that Zarathustra (Zoroaster in Greek) wrote hymns called *Gathas*, the dialect and physical setting of which indicate an origin in northern Afghanistan. Scholarly guesses place Zarathustra's life sometime between 1700 and 500 B.C.E. According to Zarathustra, Ahuramazda, "the wise lord," created the world. Angra Mainyu (ANG-ruh MINE-yoo), "the hostile spirit," and a host of demons threaten it. In this dualist universe, the struggle between good and evil plays out for 12,000 years. At the end of time, good will prevail, and the world will return to the pure state of creation. In the meantime, humanity participates in this cosmic struggle, and individuals reap rewards or torments in the afterlife according to their actions.

The Persians also drew on pre-Zoroastrian moral and metaphysical concepts. Alive to the beauties of nature, they venerated water, which they kept pure, and fire, which burned continuously at altars. Bodily purity, a matter of intense concern, ceased with death. Zoroastrians exposed corpses to carrion-eating birds and the elements to avoid sullying the earth through burial or fire through cremation. Some earlier gods, such as Mithra, a sun-deity and defender of oaths and compacts, retained divine status despite Zarathustra's focus on one god.

Zoroastrianism preached belief in one supreme deity, maintained high ethical standards, and

---

[1] Quoted in Roland G. Kent, *Old Persian: Grammar, Texts, Lexicon*, 2nd ed. (New Haven, CT: American Oriental Society, 1953), 138, 140.

Zoroastrianism A religion originating in ancient Iran that became the official religion of the Achaemenids. It centered on a single benevolent deity, Ahuramazda, who engaged in a struggle with demonic forces before prevailing and restoring a pristine world. It emphasized truth-telling, purity, and reverence for nature.

SECTION REVIEW

- Early Iranians developed complex societies that enabled them to carry settled agriculture from mountain valleys to the less hospitable plains.

- The Medes instituted a complex political order and, after helping to destroy the Assyrian Empire, subdued the Persians.

- Under Cyrus, the Persians overthrew the Medes, and the two cultures merged.

- Cyrus and his successors expanded the empire, respecting the local traditions of conquered peoples.

- The empire reached its fullest extent under Darius I, who created its basic administrative structure and imperial ideology.

- The religion of the empire was Zoroastrianism, which may have influenced Judaism and Christianity.

promised salvation. Expanding with the advance of the Persian Empire, it may have exerted influence on Judaism and thus, indirectly, on Christianity. God and the Devil, Heaven and Hell, reward and punishment, the Messiah and the End of Time: all appear in this belief system. Yet the Islamic conquest of Iran in the seventh century C.E. (see Chapter 9) triggered the faith's decline, and only tiny communities still survive in Iran. Some larger communities, called Parsees, live in South Asia.

THE RISE OF THE GREEKS, 1000–500 B.C.E.

■ *What were the most distinctive elements of Greek civilization, and how and why did they evolve in the Archaic and Classical periods?*

The cultural features that emerged in resource-poor Greece in the first millennium B.C.E. depended on access to foreign markets and sources of raw materials. Greek merchants and mercenaries brought home not only raw materials and crafted goods but also ideas. Population pressure, poverty, war, and political crisis prompted Greeks to venture throughout the Mediterranean and western Asia, carrying with them their language and culture and exerting influence on other societies. Greek identity and interest in geography, ethnography, and history grew from experience with non-Greek practices and beliefs, as well as from a two-century-long rivalry with the Persian Empire.

Geography and Resources

Bounded by the Atlantic, the Alps, the Syrian Desert, and the Sahara, the lands of the Mediterranean climatic zone share seasonal weather patterns and many plants and animals. In summer a stalled weather front near the entrance of the Mediterranean holds up storms from the Atlantic and allows winds from the Sahara to flow over the region. In winter, the front dissolves and ocean storms roll in, bringing waves, wind, and cold. Such similarities facilitated migration within the zone, since people did not have to change familiar practices and occupations.

Greek civilization arose on the Greek mainland, the Aegean islands, and the western coast of Anatolia. As we saw in Chapter 2, small plains between low mountain ranges characterize southern Greece, a land with no navigable rivers. The islands dotting the Aegean, inhabited from early times, made sailing from Greece to Ionia (western Anatolia) comparatively easy. From about 1000 B.C.E. Greeks began to settle Ionia, where rivers with broad, fertile plains made for a comfortable life. These coastal Greeks maintained closer contact with Greeks across the Aegean than with the peoples of Anatolia's rugged interior. The sea served as a connector, not a barrier.

Mainland farmers depended on rainfall to water their crops. In the south, limited land, thin topsoil, and sparse rainfall supported only small populations. Farmers planted the plains with barley, which is hardier than wheat, and the edge of the plain with olive trees. Grapevines grew on the terraced lower slopes of the foothills. Sheep and goats grazed the hillsides. Northern Greece, with more rainfall and broader plains, supported herds of cattle and horses. Resources included abundant building stone and fine marble but few metal deposits or forests.

The difficulty and expense of overland transport, the availability of good anchorages, and the need to import metals, timber, and grain drew the Greeks to the sea. They obtained timber from the northern Aegean, gold and iron from Anatolia, copper from Cyprus, tin from the western Mediterranean, and grain from the Black Sea, Egypt, and Sicily. Though never comfortable with "the wine-dark sea," as Homer called it, the Greeks relied on it, their small, frail ships hugging the coastline or island-hopping where possible.

The Emergence of the Polis

After the destruction of the Mycenaean palace-states (see Chapter 2), Greece lapsed into a "Dark Age" (ca. 1150–800 B.C.E.), a time of depopulation, poverty, and backwardness that left few traces in the archaeological record. Decline of trade and lack of access to resources lay behind the poverty of the Dark Age. Within Greece, regional distinctiveness in pottery and crafts indicates declining interconnections.

By reestablishing contact between the Aegean and the Middle East, Phoenician traders (see Chapter 2) gave Greek civilization a push that inaugurated the Archaic period of Greek history (ca. 800–480 B.C.E.). Greek seafarers reappeared in the Mediterranean waters looking for raw materials, trade opportunities, and fertile farmland.

Lifelike human and animal figures and imaginative mythical beasts on painted Greek pottery signal new ideas from the east, as does the adoption of an alphabetical writing system of Phoenician inspiration. Cuneiform or hieroglyphics, systems in which several hundred symbols stood for syllables rather than letters, took years of training and remained the preserve of an elite scribal class. By contrast, the alphabetic symbols made literacy easy to acquire.

First used for economic purposes or for preserving oral poetry, the Greek alphabet facilitated new forms of literature, law codes, religious dedications, and epitaphs. Yet Greek culture continued to center on storytelling, rituals, and performances. Theatrical drama, philosophical dialogues, and political and courtroom oratory demonstrate the dynamic interaction of speaking and writing.

Population grew rapidly during the Archaic period, as we know from a five- to sevenfold increase in cemeteries around Athens during the eighth century B.C.E. On the previously uncultivated margins of the plains, herding gave way to intensive farming. This increasing population and prosperity stimulated the importation of food and raw materials, a merging of villages into urban centers, and specialization of labor. Freed from farming and rising surpluses, some people developed skills in crafts, commerce, and religion.

The Greek **polis** (POE-lis), or city-state, ranging in size from a few thousand souls to several hundred thousand in the case of Athens, consisted of an urban center and the surrounding countryside. Typically, a fortified hilltop, the *acropolis* (uh-KRAW-poe-lis) ("top of the city"), offered refuge in emergencies, with the town spread around its base. In the open area around government buildings and markets, called an *agora* (ah-go-RAH) ("gathering place"), citizens debated the decisions of leaders and organized for war. Walls surrounded the urban center; but population growth prompted construction beyond them. Food came from surrounding farms, though many who lived within the walls worked nearby fields. Unlike the dependent rural workers of Mesopotamia, Greek farmers enjoyed full citizenship.

By the early seventh century B.C.E., frequent city-state conflicts had led to a new kind of warfare based on **hoplites** (HAWP-lite)—heavily armored infantrymen who fought in close formation. Protected by helmet, breastplate, and leg guards, each hoplite brandished a thrusting spear while guarding his left side and the right side of the hoplite beside him with a round shield, keeping a sword in reserve. Victory depended on maintaining one's battle line while breaking open the enemy's. The losers suffered most of their casualties while fleeing.

Private citizens, mostly farmers called up for brief periods rather than professional soldiers, served as hoplites. Courage to stand one's ground counted for more than strength for bearing weapons and armor. When an army approached, the farmers of the polis under attack mustered to defend their land and buildings. The clash of hoplite lines resulted in quick decision. Battles rarely lasted more than a few hours, with the survivors promptly returning home to their farms.

---

polis The Greek term for a city-state, an urban center and the agricultural territory under its control. It was the characteristic form of political organization in southern and central Greece in the Archaic and Classical periods. Of the hundreds of city-states in the Mediterranean and Black Sea regions settled by Greeks, some were oligarchic, others democratic, depending on the powers delegated to the Council and the Assembly.

hoplite A heavily armored Greek infantryman of the Archaic and Classical periods who fought in the close-packed phalanx formation. Hoplite armies—militias composed of middle- and upper-class citizens supplying their own equipment—were for centuries superior to all other military forces.

As population growth strained the agricultural resources of the small plains, many city-states sent excess population abroad to establish independent colonies. Sometimes people were chosen by lot to be colonists and forbidden to return on pain of death. At other times people in search of adventure or an escape from poverty volunteered. Colonists sought the approval of the god Apollo at his sanctuary at Delphi and then departed by sea carrying a fire from the communal hearth of the mother-city, a symbol of the kinship and religious ties that would connect the two communities. The "founder," a prominent member of the mother-city, chose a hill or other natural refuge, assigned parcels of land, and drafted laws. Sometimes colonists intermarried with local inhabitants; alternatively, they drove them away or reduced them to semiservility.

From the mid-eighth through mid-sixth centuries B.C.E., colonists spread Greek culture to the northern Aegean area, the Libyan coast of North Africa, and around the Black Sea, with southern Italy and Sicily becoming heavily Greek. Establishing new homes, farms, and communities posed many challenges, but the similarity in climate and ecology helped the Greek settlers transplant their way of life.

Greeks called themselves *Hellenes* (HELL-leans) (*Graeci* is what the Romans later called them) to distinguish themselves from *barbaroi* (literally "non-Greek speakers," whence the English word *barbarian*). Interaction with new peoples and exposure to their cultures made the Greeks aware of their unity of language, religion, and lifestyle. It also introduced them to new ideas and technologies. Developments in the colonial world traveled back to the Greek homeland: urban planning, forms of political organization, and new intellectual currents.

Coinage, invented in the early sixth century B.C.E. in Lydia (western Anatolia), spread throughout the Greek world and beyond. Scarcity, durability, divisibility, and ease of use made silver, gold, bronze, and copper appropriate for minting into metal pieces of state-guaranteed weight and purity. (Societies in other parts of the world used items with similar qualities, including beads, hard-shelled beans, and cowrie shells.) Coinage made weighing quantities of metal obsolete and fostered quicker trading transactions, better record keeping, and easier wealth storage.

Trade grew, as did the total wealth of communities, but different weight standards used by different states often confused exchanges of currencies.

Colonization relieved pressures within Archaic Greek communities but did not eliminate political instability. At some point, the Dark Age kings depicted in Homer's *Iliad* and *Odyssey* were superseded by councils representing noble families that derived their wealth and power from landownership. The peasants who farmed these lands kept only a portion of their harvest. Debt-slaves, people who lost their freedom when they could not repay money or seed borrowed from the lord, also worked the land. Free peasants owned small farms and joined urban-based craftsmen and merchants as part of a "middle class."

In the mid-seventh and sixth centuries B.C.E., **tyrants**—individuals who seized power in violation of normal political institutions—gained control of many city-states. Often disgruntled aristocrats with middle-class backing, they appealed to hoplite soldiers, whose numbers increased with growing prosperity and lower prices for weaponry, and granted these supporters political rights.

Some tyrants passed their positions on to sons, but communities eventually expelled the tyrant families and opted for oligarchy (OLL-ih-gahr-key), in which a group of the wealthiest men held power, or **democracy**, in which all free adult males shared power. This broadening of the political system was made possible by the absence of a professional military class.

Even before they invaded the Greek peninsula at the end of the third millennium B.C.E., the Greeks worshiped several sky-gods, such as Zeus, who sent storms and lightning, and Poseidon, who was master

tyrant The term the Greeks used to describe someone who seized and held power in violation of the normal procedures and traditions of the community. Tyrants appeared in many Greek city-states in the seventh and sixth centuries B.C.E., often taking advantage of the disaffection of the emerging middle class and, by weakening the old elite, unwittingly contributing to the evolution of democracy.

democracy System of government in which all "citizens" (however defined) have equal political and legal rights, privileges, and protections, as in the Greek city-state of Athens in the fifth and fourth centuries B.C.E.

Vase Painting Depicting a Sacrifice to the God Apollo, ca. 440 B.C.E. For the Greeks, who believed in a multitude of gods who looked and behaved like humans, the central act of worship was the sacrifice, the ritualized offering of a gift. Sacrifice created a relationship between the human worshiper and the deity and raised expectations that the god would bestow favors in return. Here we see a number of male devotees, wearing their finest clothing and garlands in their hair, near a sacred outdoor altar and statue of Apollo. The god is shown at the far right, standing on a pedestal and holding his characteristic bow and laurel branch. The first worshiper offers the god bones wrapped in fat. All of the worshipers will feast on the meat carried by the boy. Bildarchiv Preussischer Kulturbesitz/Art Resource, NY

of the sea and earthquakes. These deities were given personalities by Homer's *Iliad* and *Odyssey*, heroic epics that were memorized by schoolboys and recited by performers. The gods are portrayed as anthropomorphic (an-throh-poh-MORE-fik), or humanlike in appearance (though taller, more beautiful, and more powerful, with a supernatural radiance), with humanlike emotions of love, anger, and jealousy. But unlike humans, they are immortal.

State religious ceremonies conferred civic identity. **Sacrifice**, the central ritual, took place at altars in front of the temples where the gods were thought to reside. Gifts as humble as a small cake or a cup of wine poured on the ground accompanied prayers for favor and protection. In grander sacrifices, people would kill one or more animals, smear the altar with its blood, and burn parts of its body so that the aroma would ascend to the gods.

Oracles situated at sacred sites responded to human pleas for information, advice, or prediction. At Delphi in central Greece, the most honored site, the god Apollo spoke through his priestesses, the Pythia (PITH-ee-uh), whose obscure utterances were interpreted by the male priests who administered the sanctuary. There were also fertility cults that were usually based on female deities and appealed to the agricultural majority of the population, but our dependence on literary texts that express the values of an educated urban elite limits our knowledge of them.

New Intellectual Currents

Prosperity, new technologies, and social and political development led to innovations in intellectual outlook and artistic outlook, including a growing emphasis on the individual. In early Greek communities, the family enveloped the individual, and land belonged collectively to the family, including ancestors and descendants. Ripped from this communal network and forced to resettle elsewhere, colonists became models of individualism, as did the tyrant who seized power for himself alone.

> **sacrifice** A gift given to a deity, often with the aim of creating a relationship, gaining favor, and obligating the god to provide some benefit to the sacrificer, sometimes in order to sustain the deity and thereby guarantee the continuing vitality of the natural world.

This valuing of the uniqueness, talents, and rights of the individual was a form of humanism, which remains a central tenet of Western civilization.

In the new lyric poetry, short verses deal with personal subjects drawn from the poet's experience. Archilochus (ahr-KIL-uh-kuhs), a soldier and poet living in the first half of the seventh century B.C.E., wrote:

> Some barbarian is waving my shield, since I was obliged to leave that perfectly good piece of equipment behind under a bush. But I got away, so what does it matter? Let the shield go; I can buy another one equally good.[2]

Here Archilochus pokes fun at the heroic ideal that scorned soldiers who ran from the enemy. In challenging traditional values and expressing personal feelings, lyric poets pointed toward the modern Western conception of poetry.

In religion, thinkers now known as pre-Socratic philosophers called into question Homer's representations of the gods. Xenophanes (zeh-NOFF-eh-nees), living in the sixth century B.C.E., protested:

> But if cattle and horses or lions had hands, or were able to draw with their hands and do the works that men can do, horses would draw the forms of the gods like horses, and cattle like cattle, and they would make their bodies such as they each had themselves.[3]

The term *pre-Socratic* refers to philosophers before Plato, a student of Socrates, who in the later fifth century B.C.E. shifted the focus of philosophy to ethical questions. They rejected traditional explanations of the origins and nature of the world and sought more rational answers. How was the world created? What is it made of? Why does it change? Some postulated that earth, air, fire, and water, the primal elements, combine or dissolve to form the substances found in nature. One taught that microscopic atoms (from a Greek word meaning "indivisible") move through the void of space, colliding randomly and combining in various ways to form the natural world—an intuition that resembles modern atomic theory. Most pre-Socratics came from Ionia and southern Italy, where Greeks lived close to non-Greeks. Encountering peoples with different ideas may have stimulated some of their thoughts.

Also in Ionia in the sixth century B.C.E., men later referred to as logographers (loe-GOG-ruff-er) ("writers of prose accounts") gathered information on ethnography (the physical characteristics and cultural practices of a people), Mediterranean geography, the foundation of cities, and the origins of famous families. They called their accumulation of information *historia*, "investigation/research." The most famous of these works, the *Historia* by **Herodotus** (ca. 485–425 B.C.E.) from Halicarnassus in southwest Anatolia, contains geographic and ethnographic reports, legends, and marvels in its early parts and later focuses on the Persian-Greek wars of the previous generation. Herodotus opens his work as follows:

> I, Herodotus of Halicarnassus, am here setting forth my history, that time may not draw the color from what man has brought into being, nor those great and wonderful deeds, manifested by both Greeks and barbarians, fail of their report, and, together with all this, the reason why they fought one another.[4]

His search for causes reveals the thinking of a true historian. Thus did *historia* begin to narrow and acquire the modern meaning of *history*, with Herodotus gaining the nickname *Father of History*.

Athens and Sparta

Athens and Sparta, the preeminent city-states of the late Archaic and Classical periods, differed in character despite environmental and cultural similarities. The Spartans' ancestors migrated into the

---

[2] Richmond Lattimore, *Greek Lyrics*, 2d ed. (Chicago: University of Chicago Press, 1960), 2.

[3] G. S. Kirk and J. E. Raven, *The Presocratic Philosophers: A Critical History with a Selection of Texts* (Cambridge, England: Cambridge University Press, 1957), 169.

[4] Herodotus, *The History*, trans. David Grene (Chicago: University of Chicago Press, 1988), 33. (Herodotus 1.1)

Herodotus Heir to the technique of *historia* ("investigation/research") developed by Greeks in the late Archaic period. He came from a Greek community in Anatolia and traveled extensively, collecting information in western Asia and the Mediterranean lands. He traced the antecedents and chronicled the wars between the Greek city-states and the Persian Empire, thus originating the Western tradition of historical writing.

Peloponnese (PELL-uh-puh-neze), the southernmost part of Greece, around 1000 B.C.E. Their community resembled others until the seventh century B.C.E., when the population increases and shortage of farmland that affected all communities prompted them to react differently. Instead of sending out colonies, the Spartans invaded the fertile plain of Messenia to the west. The resulting takeover, aided perhaps by hoplite tactics, saw the Messenians reduced to the status of helots (HELL-ut), the most abused and exploited population on the Greek mainland.

The Spartan state quickly turned into a military camp, always prepared for a helot uprising. The state divided Messenia and Laconia, the Spartan homeland, into several thousand lots, each assigned to a Spartan citizen. Helots worked the land and turned over a part of their harvest to their Spartan masters. Freed from farming, the Spartans devoted their lives to military affairs.

The Spartan army outclassed all others because it did not rely on militias summoned only during crises. The Spartans paid a price, however. Taken from their families and put into barracks at age seven, boys underwent a severe regime of discipline, beatings, and deprivation. The demands of the state consumed a Spartan male's whole life.

The economic, political, and cultural revival of the Archaic Greek world passed Sparta by: no poets or artists, no precious metals or coinage, no commerce or other activities that could introduce inequality. The fifth-century B.C.E. Athenian historian Thucydides (thoo-SID-ih-dees) remarked that in his day Sparta looked like a large village and that no future observer of the site would be able to guess its power.

Other Greeks admired the Spartans' courage, commitment, and martial skills but abhorred their arrogance, ignorance, and cruelty. The Spartan Council of Elders and two kings, who commanded in battle, practiced a cautious and isolationist foreign policy. Reluctant to venture far for fear of a helot uprising, they worked for peace through the Peloponnesian League, a system of alliances with their neighbors.

Athens, by comparison, possessed an unusually large and populous territory: the fertile plains of Attica with their groves of olive trees. By the fifth

century B.C.E., Athens numbered approximately 300,000 people. Villages and a few larger towns dotted the peninsula where the urban center stood beside the sheer-sided Acropolis some 5 miles (8 kilometers) from the sea.

In 594 B.C.E., to avoid civil war, the Athenians conferred lawgiving powers on Solon, an aristocrat with ties to the merchant community. Solon divided the citizens into four classes based on the annual yield of their farms. The top three classes could hold state offices. The lowest class, with little or no property, held no offices but could participate in meetings of the Assembly. Although a far cry from democracy, this linkage between rights, privileges, and wealth broke the power of a dominant cluster of aristocratic families and favored social and political mobility. By abolishing debt slavery, Solon also guaranteed the freedom of Athenian citizens.

Despite Solon's efforts, in 546 B.C.E., an aristocrat named Pisistratus (pie-SIS-truh-tuhs) seized power. Because most Athenians still lived in villages, identified primarily with a district, and accepted the leadership of landlords who lived in sturdy manor houses, Pisistratus turned to the urban population for support. He undertook building projects, including a Temple of Athena on the Acropolis, and instituted or expanded popular urban festivals: the City Dionysia (die-ul-NIZ-eeuh), later famous for dramatic performances, and the Panathenaea (pan-ath-un-NEE-uh), a religious procession combined with athletic and poetic competitions.

With Spartan assistance, the Athenians expelled Pisistratus's sons, who had inherited his position. In the 460s and 450s B.C.E. **Pericles** (PER-eh-kleez) led a democratic movement to transfer all power to popular organs of government: the Assembly, the Council of 500, and the People's Courts. Henceforward, Athenians of moderate or slender means could hold office and participate in politics. Selected by lot for even the highest positions, officials now received pay for their

Pericles Aristocratic leader who guided the Athenian state through the transformation to full participatory democracy for all male citizens, supervised construction of the Acropolis, and pursued a policy of imperial expansion that led to the Peloponnesian War. He formulated a strategy of attrition but died from the plague early in the war.

SECTION REVIEW

- Geographical and environmental barriers turned Greeks to the sea.
- Under Phoenician influence, the Greeks built a new civilization centered on the polis.
- Overseas colonization extended Greek culture, but it did not relieve political instability.
- State religious ceremonies solidified civic identity.
- New forms of intellectual inquiry and artistic production emerged.
- Evolving along divergent paths, Athens and Sparta became the preeminent city-states.

services and so could afford to leave their other occupations. Some key offices—managing public money, commanding military forces—were filled by elections that took into account the candidates' abilities.

The Assembly of all citizens held open debates several times a month in which anyone could speak to the issues of the day. Members of the Council of 500 took turns presiding and representing the Athenian state. Through effective political organizing, Pericles dominated Athenian politics from 461 B.C.E. until his death in 429 B.C.E.

Athens's economic position paralleled its political evolution. From the time of Pisistratus, Athenian pottery became increasingly prominent throughout the Mediterranean. These pots often contained olive oil, Athens's chief export, but elegant painted vases were also luxury commodities in themselves. Trade-related increases in the size and prosperity of the middle class help explain the growth of Athenian democracy.

THE STRUGGLE OF PERSIA AND GREECE, 546–323 B.C.E.

■ *How did the Persian Wars and their aftermath affect the politics and culture of ancient Greece and Iran?*

In the fifth and fourth centuries B.C.E., Greek life was dominated by the Persian-Greek wars. Although the Persians probably considered developments farther east more important, in the end, the encounters of Greeks and Persians profoundly affected the history of the eastern Mediterranean and western Asia.

Early Encounters

Cyrus's conquest of Lydia in 546 B.C.E. led to the subjugation of the Ionian Greek cities. Some groups and individuals collaborated with the Persian government, but in 499 B.C.E. Greeks and other subject peoples on the western frontier staged the Ionian Revolt. The Persians needed five years and a massive infusion of troops and resources to stamp out the insurrection.

The failed revolt led to the **Persian Wars**: two Persian attacks on Greece in the early fifth century B.C.E. In 490 B.C.E. Darius dispatched a naval fleet to punish Eretria (er-EH-tree-uh) and Athens, two mainland Greek states allied with the Ionian rebels. Disloyal citizens betrayed Eretria to the Persians, who marched the survivors off to exile. In this, as in many other things, Persians copied their Assyrian predecessors, although they did not boast of mass deportations. Athens would probably have suffered a similar fate if its hoplites had not defeated the lighter-armed Persian troops in a sharp engagement at Marathon, 26 miles (42 kilometers) from Athens.

After Xerxes (*Khshayarsha*, r. 486–465 B.C.E.) succeeded his father in 486 B.C.E., he gathered a huge invasion force, including contingents from all over the Persian Empire and a large fleet. Crossing the Hellespont (the narrow strait separating Europe and Asia) and traversing Thrace, the Persian throng descended into central and southern Greece. Xerxes sent messengers ahead demanding of the city-states "earth and water"—tokens of submission.

Many city-states complied. But in southern Greece the Spartans formed an alliance that historians call the Hellenic League. At the pass of Thermopylae (thuhr-MOP-uh-lee) in central Greece, three hundred Spartans and their king fought to the last man to buy time for their fellows to escape. The Persians sacked Athens, but the outnumbered Athenians

Persian Wars Conflicts between Greek city-states and the Persian Empire, ranging from the Ionian Revolt (499–494 B.C.E.) through Darius's punitive expedition that failed at Marathon (490 B.C.E.) and the defeat of Xerxes's massive invasion of Greece by the Spartan-led Hellenic League (480–479 B.C.E.). This first major setback for Persian arms launched the Greeks into their period of greatest cultural productivity. Herodotus chronicled these events in the first "history" in the Western tradition.

lured the Persian navy into narrow waters at Salamis (SAH-lah-miss), where, despite their numbers, they could not maneuver. The Persians lost their advantage, and the Athenians administered a devastating defeat. A rout of the Persian army at Plataea (pluh-TEE-uh) the following spring relieved the immediate threat.

Athens's stubborn refusal to submit and the effectiveness of the Athenian navy earned the city great respect. Naval strategies dominated the next phase of the war, which was designed to liberate Greek states still under Persian control. This focus gave Athens priority over land-based, isolationist Sparta. The Delian (DEE-lih-yuhn) League, formed in 477 B.C.E., brought the Greek states together. In less than twenty years, League forces led by Athenian generals swept the Persians from the waters of the eastern Mediterranean and freed all Greek communities except those in distant Cyprus.

The Height of Athenian Power

Scholars date the Classical period of Greek history (480–323 B.C.E.) to this defense of the Greek homeland. Ironically, Athens exploited its crucial role in these events to become an imperial power. Some Greek allies contributed money instead of troops, and the Athenians used the money to strengthen their navy. They treated other members of the Delian League as subjects and demanded annual contributions. States attempting to leave the League were brought back by force, stripped of their defenses, and subordinated to Athens.

Athenian naval technology transformed Greek warfare and brought power and wealth to Athens itself. Unlike commercial sailing ships, which over time had developed a stabler and more capacious round-bodied design, slender military vessels relied on large numbers of rowers. Having little deck room or storage space, these ships hugged the coastline and put ashore nightly to replenish food supplies and let the crew sleep. Fifty-oared ships had dominated naval warfare until the late sixth century B.C.E. when sleek, fast **triremes** (TRY-reems), powered by 170 rowers, brought an end to crude engagements in which warriors cleared the enemy's decks with spears and arrows before boarding and fighting hand to hand. Approximately 115 by 18 feet (35 by 6 meters) in size,

Replica of Ancient Greek Trireme Greek warships had a metal-tipped ram in front to pierce the hulls of enemy vessels and a pair of steering rudders in the rear. Though equipped with masts and sails, in battle these warships were propelled by 170 rowers. This modern, full-size replica, manned by international volunteer crews, is helping scholars to determine attainable speeds and maneuvering techniques. Replica of the trireme 'Olympia' at sea (photo)/Private Collection/Ancient Art and Architecture Collection Ltd./Mike Andrews/The Bridgeman Art Library

the trireme positioned rowers on three levels with oars of different lengths to avoid interference. The fragile vessels could achieve up to 7 knots in short bursts. Athenian crews, by constant practice, became the best in the eastern Mediterranean. They disabled enemy vessels by sheering off their oars, smashing their hulls below the water line with an iron-tipped prow, or forcing collisions by running around them in ever-tightening circles.

The primacy of the fleet contributed to a democratic system in which each male citizen had, at least in principle, an equal voice. The middle or upper class produced hoplites, who bought their own armor and weapons. Rowers came from the lower classes, but they insisted on full rights as protectors of the community.

Athenian maritime power reached farther than any citizen militia. Victors in Greek wars seldom occupied enemy lands permanently (the exception being Sparta's takeover of Messenia). Booty with

trireme Greek and Phoenician warship of the fifth and fourth centuries B.C.E. It was sleek and light, powered by 170 oars arranged in three vertical tiers. Manned by skilled sailors, it was capable of short bursts of speed and complex maneuvers.

minor adjustments to boundary lines sufficed. But Athens could exert continual domination and readily did so to promote commerce. Athens's port, Piraeus (pih-RAY-uhs), became the most important commercial center in the eastern Mediterranean.

Annual dues from subject states subsidized the increasingly expensive Athenian democracy and paid the construction costs of the Parthenon, a majestic temple to Athena on the Acropolis. The Athenian leader Pericles gained extraordinary popularity by hiring many Athenians to construct and decorate this and other monuments. When political enemies protested Pericles's use of Delian League funds for construction, he replied: "They [Athens's subjects] do not give us a single horse, nor a soldier, nor a ship. All they supply is money. It is no more than fair that after Athens has been equipped with all she needs to carry on the war, she should apply the surplus to public works, which, once completed, will bring her glory for all time."[5]

The proceeds of empire indirectly subsidized the festivals at which the dramatic tragedies of Aeschylus (ESS-kuh-luss), Sophocles, and Euripedes (yer-RIP-uh-deez) and the comedies of Aristophanes (ar-uh-STOFF-uh-neez) were performed. The brightest and most creative artists and thinkers flocked to Athens. Traveling teachers called Sophists ("wise men") provided instruction in logic and public speaking to fee-paying pupils. The new discipline of rhetoric—the crafting of attractive and persuasive arguments—gave those with training and quick wits a great advantage in politics and the courts. Greeks became connoisseurs of oratory, eagerly listening for each innovation yet so aware of the power of words that *sophist* came to mean one who uses cleverness to manipulate reality.

These new intellectual currents came together in 399 B.C.E. when the philosopher **Socrates** (ca. 470–399 B.C.E.) went on trial charged with corrupting the youth of Athens and not believing in the city's gods. A sculptor by trade, Socrates spent his time conversing with young men who enjoyed hearing him deflate the pretensions of those who thought themselves wise. He wryly commented that he knew one more thing than everyone else: that he knew nothing.

At his trial, Socrates easily disposed of the actual charges: he was a deeply religious man, and the families of the young men he associated with supported him. He argued that the real basis of the prosecution was twofold: (1) blame for attempts by several of his aristocratic students to overthrow the Athenian democracy, and (2) blame for the controversial teachings of the Sophists, which many believed undermined morality and religious tradition. In Athenian trials, juries of hundreds of citizens decided guilt and punishment, often spurred by emotion more than legal principles. Convicted by a close vote, Socrates maintained his innocence and said he should be rewarded for his services instead. This statement led the jury to condemn him to death by drinking hemlock. Socrates's disciples considered him a martyr, and smart young men like Plato withdrew from public life and dedicated themselves to philosophical pursuits.

Socrates himself wrote nothing, preferring to converse with people he met in the street. His student Plato (ca. 428–347 B.C.E.), who learned from books and habitually wrote down his thoughts, may represent the first truly literate generation. On the outskirts of Athens, Plato founded the Academy, a school where young men could pursue higher education. Yet even Plato reflected the oral nature of his upbringing by writing dialogues—an oral form—in which his protagonist, Socrates, uses the "Socratic method" of question and answer to reach a deeper understanding of values such as justice, excellence, and wisdom. Plato refused to write down the most advanced teachings of the Academy. Higher reality, he believed, appeared only in pale reflection in the sensible world and could be grasped only by "initiates" who had completed the earlier stages.

Socrates Athenian philosopher (ca. 470–399 B.C.E.) who shifted the emphasis of philosophical investigation from questions of natural science to ethics and human behavior. He attracted young disciples from elite families but made enemies by revealing the ignorance and pretensions of others, culminating in his trial and execution by the Athenian state.

---

[5] Plutarch, *Pericles* 12, trans. Ian Scott-Kilvert, *The Rise and Fall of Athens: Nine Greek Lives by Plutarch* (Harmondsworth: Penguin Books, 1960), 178.

Inequality in Classical Greece

The Athenian democracy that historically underlies modern traditions of democracy included only a small percentage of Attica's population: true citizens—free adult males of pure Athenian ancestry. Excluding women, children, slaves, and foreigners, this group amounted to 30,000 or 40,000 people out approximately 300,000. Equally exclusive practices probably existed in less well-known Greek democracies.

Slaves, mostly foreigners, constituted perhaps one-third of the population of Attica in the fifth and fourth centuries B.C.E. The average Athenian family owned at least one slave. Slaves ran the shop or worked the farm while the master attended meetings of the Assembly or served on one of the boards overseeing the day-to-day activities of the state. As "living pieces of property," slaves did any work, submitted to any sexual acts, and suffered any punishments their owners ordained, though some communities prohibited arbitrarily killing slaves. Overall, Greece saw few of the extremes of cruelty and abuse inflicted on slaves in other places and times.

Farms being small, most slaves performed domestic service rather than field labor, often working with the master or mistress on the same tasks. Daily contact fostered relationships between owners and slaves that made it hard for owners to act inhumanely. Still, Greek thinkers justified slavery by arguing that *barbaroi* (non-Greeks) lacked the capacity to reason and thus were better off under Greek owners. The stigma attached to slavery was so great that most Athenians refused to work as wage laborers because following an employer's orders resembled being his slave.

The position of women varied. Spartan women, who were expected to bear and raise strong children, exercised regularly and enjoyed a level of public visibility and outspokenness that shocked other Greeks. At the opposite extreme, Athenians confined and oppressed women. Ironically, the exploitation of women in Athens reflects the high degree of freedom that Athenian men enjoyed in the democratic state.

Inequality marked Athenian marriages. A man of thirty—reasonably educated, a war veteran, and experienced in business and politics—commonly married, after negotiating with her parents, a teenage girl

Vase Painting Depicting Women at an Athenian Fountain House, ca. 520 B.C.E. Paintings on Greek vases provide the most vivid pictorial record of ancient Greek life. The subject matter usually reflects the interests of the aristocratic males who purchased the vases—warfare, athletics, mythology, drinking parties—but sometimes we are given glimpses into the lives of women and the working classes. These women are presumably domestic servants sent to fetch water for the household from the public fountain. The large water jars they are filling are like the one on which this scene is depicted. Scala/Art Resource, NY

with no formal education and minimal training in weaving, cooking, and household management. Coming into the home of a husband she hardly knew, the wife had no political rights and limited legal protection. Given the differences in age, social experience, and authority, the relationship between husband and wife resembled that of father and daughter. The function of marriage was to produce children, preferably male. The ancients were sufficiently ashamed of infanticide—the killing through exposure of

Material Culture

Wine and Beer in the Ancient World

The most prized beverages of ancient peoples were wine and beer. Sediments found in jars excavated at a site in northwest Iran prove that techniques for the manufacture of wine were known as early as the sixth millennium B.C.E. Beer dates back at least as far as the fourth millennium B.C.E. Archaeological excavations have brought to light the equipment used in preparing, transporting, serving, and imbibing these beverages.

In Egypt and Mesopotamia, beer, which was made from wheat or barley by a rather elaborate process, was the staple drink of both the elite and the common people. Women prepared beer for the family in their homes, and breweries produced large quantities for sale. Because the production process left chaff floating on the surface of the liquid, various means were employed to filter out this unwelcome byproduct. Sculptures on Mesopotamian stone reliefs and seals show several drinkers drawing on straws immersed in a large bowl. Archaeologists have found examples of the perforated metal cones that fit over the submerged ends of the straws and filtered the liquid beer drawn through them. It is likely that the sharing of beer from a common vessel by several people had social implications, creating a bond of friendship among the participants. Archaeologists have also found individual beer "mugs" resembling a modern watering can: closed bowls with a perforated spout to filter the chaff and a semicircular channel carrying the liquid into the drinker's mouth.

In Greece, Rome, and other Mediterranean lands, where the climate was suitable for cultivating grape vines, wine was the preferred beverage. Vines were prepared in February and periodically pruned and their unwanted tendrils pinched off. The full-grown grapes were picked in September, then crushed (with a winepress or by people trampling on them) to produce a liquid that was sealed in casks for fermentation. The new vintage was sampled the following February. Exuberant religious festivals marked key moments in the cycle. Initially expensive and therefore confined to the wealthy and for religious ceremonies, in later antiquity wine became available to a wider spectrum of people. Unlike beer, which requires refrigeration, wine can be stored for a long time in sealed containers and thus could be transported and traded across the Mediterranean lands, continental Europe, and western Asia. The usual containers for wine were long, conical pottery jars, which the Greeks called *amphoras*.

The Greeks normally mixed wine with water, and they developed an elaborate array of vessels, made of pottery, metal, and glass, to facilitate mixing, serving, and drinking the precious liquid (see the photo of the silver and bronze wine set). *Kraters* were large mixing bowls into which the wine and water were poured. The *hydria* was used to carry water, and a heater could be used to warm the water when that was desired. Another special vessel could be used to chill the wine by immersion in cold water. Ladles (long-handled spoons) and elegantly narrow vessels with spouts were used to pour the concoction into the drinkers' cups. The most popular shapes for individual drinking vessels were a shallow bowl with two handles, called a *kylix*, and the *kantharos*, a large, deep, two-handled cup. Another popular implement in Greece and western Asia was the *rhyton*, a horn-shaped vessel that tapered into the head and forepaws of an animal with a small hole at the base. The drinker would fill the horn, holding his thumb over the hole until he was ready to drink or pour, then move his thumb and release a thin stream of wine that appeared to be coming out of the animal's mouth.

The drinking equipment belonging to wealthy Greeks was often decorated with representations of the god of wine, Dionysus, holding a kantharos and surrounded by

unwanted children—to say little about it. But it is likely that more girls than boys were abandoned.

The husband spent the day outdoors attending to work or political responsibilities; he dined with male friends at night (see Material Culture: Wine and Beer in the Ancient World). The wife stayed home to cook, clean, raise the children, and supervise the servants. The closest relationship in the family was likely to be between the wife and her slave attendant, a woman of roughly the same age. The servant could be sent on errands. The wife stayed home, except to attend funerals and certain festivals or to make discreet visits to female relatives. Greek men claimed that confinement to the home stifled female promiscuity and prevented illegitimate births that could threaten family property and erode regulation of citizenship

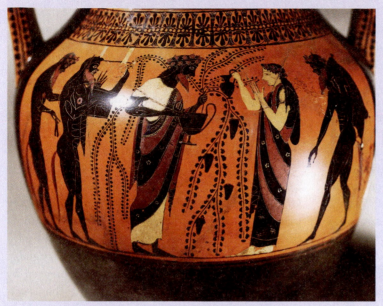

Dionysus in the Vineyard *This Greek vase of the late sixth century B.C.E. depicts Dionysus, the god of wine. Carrying a large kantharos or drinking vessel, he is enveloped by vines carrying bunches of ripe grapes, and accompanied by several Satyrs (mythical creatures combining human features with those of goats or horses) and his human bride Ariadne. Greek drinking paraphernalia often depicted Dionysus and elements of his mythology and cult.* Photo By DEA/G. DAGLI ORTI/ De Agostini/Getty Images

a dense tangle of vines and grape clusters. His entourage included the half-human, half-horse Centaurs and the Maenads, literally "crazy women." These were female worshipers who drank wine and engaged in frenzied dancing until they achieved an ecstatic state and sensed the presence of the god.

Greeks, Romans, and other Mediterranean peoples used wine for more conventional religious ceremonies, pouring libations on the ground or on the altar as an offering to the gods. It was also used on occasion for medical purposes, as a disinfectant and painkiller, or as an ingredient in various medicines. Above all, wine was featured at the banquets and drinking parties that forged and deepened social bonds. In the Greek world, the *symposion* (meaning "drinking together") was held after the meal. The host presided over the affair, making the crucial decision about the proportion of water to wine, suggesting topics of conversation, and trying to keep some semblance of order. There might also be entertainment in the form of musicians, dancers, and acrobats.

In Shang China, magnificent bronze vessels whose surfaces were covered with abstract designs and representations of otherworldly animals were fashioned for use in elaborate ceremonies at ancestral shrines (see photo on page 60). The vessels contained offerings of wine and food for the spirits of the family's ancestors, who were imagined to still need sustenance in the afterlife. The treasured bronze vessels were often buried with their owners so that they could continue to employ them after death. In later periods, as the ancestral sacrifices became less important, beautiful bronze vessels, as well as their ceramic counterparts, became part of the equipment at the banquets of the well-to-do.

QUESTIONS FOR ANALYSIS

1. What social benefits arise from drinking together?
2. How does wine serve religious purposes?
3. What evidence is there that collective drinking was practiced by the privileged social classes?

rights. Athenian law allowed a husband to kill an adulterer caught in the act with his wife.

Without documents written by women, we cannot tell how Athenian women felt about their situation. Women's festivals, such as the Thesmophoria (thes-moe-FOE-ree-uh), provided a rate opportunity for women to get out. During this three-day festival, the women of Athens lived together and managed their own affairs in a great encampment, carrying out mysterious rituals to enhance the fertility of the land. Bold and self-assertive women appeared on the Athenian stage: the defiant Antigone (an-TIG-uh-nee) of Sophocles's play, who buried her brother despite the king's prohibition; and the wives in Aristophanes's comedy *Lysistrata* (lis-us-STRAH-tuh), who withheld sex from their husbands until the men ended a war.

Although imagined by men and probably reflecting a fear of strong women, these characters must partly reflect the playwrights' mothers, sisters, and wives.

To find his intellectual and emotional "equal," men often looked to other men. Bisexuality arose as much from the social structure as from biological inclinations. An older man commonly admired, pursued, and mentored a youth, thus making bisexuality part of the youth's education and initiation into the adult male community. Though commonplace among intellectual groups that loom large in the written sources, the frequency of bisexuality and the confinement of women among the Athenians remains uncertain.

Failure of the City-State and Triumph of the Macedonians

Athens's rise to empire led in 431 B.C.E. to the outbreak of the **Peloponnesian War**, a struggle for survival between Athenian and Spartan alliances that encompassed most of the Greek world. To insulate themselves from attack by land, in midcentury the Athenians had built three long walls connecting the city with the port of Piraeus and the adjacent shoreline. As long as Athens controlled the sea-lanes and could provision itself, a land-based siege could not starve it into submission.

At the start of the war, Pericles broke precedent by refusing to engage the Spartan-led armies that invaded Attica each year, knowing that the enemy hoplites must soon return to their farms. Thus, instead of culminating in a short, decisive battle, the Peloponnesian War dragged on for nearly three decades with great loss of life and resources. It sapped the morale of all Greece and ended only with the defeat of Athens in a naval battle in 404 B.C.E. Because the Persian Empire had bankrolled the construction of ships by the Spartan alliance, Sparta finally was able to take the conflict into Athens's own element, the sea.

The victorious Spartans, who had entered the war championing "the freedom of the Greeks," took over Athens's overseas empire until their increasingly highhanded behavior aroused the opposition of other city-states. Indeed, the fourth century B.C.E. was a time of nearly continuous skirmishing among Greek states. The independent polis that lent glory to Greek culture also fostered rivalries and fears among neighbors.

This lack of unity allowed the Persians to recoup old losses. By the King's Peace of 387 B.C.E., encompassing most of the war-weary Greek states, all of western Asia, including the Ionian Greek communities, went to Persia. The Persian king guaranteed a status quo that kept the Greeks divided and weak until rebellions in Egypt, Cyprus, and Phoenicia, combined with troubles from some western satraps, diverted his attention from thoughts of another Greek invasion.

Meanwhile, in northern Greece Philip II (r. 359–336 B.C.E.) was transforming his previously backward kingdom of Macedonia into the premier military power. (Although southern Greeks had long doubted the "Greekness" of the rough and rowdy Macedonians, modern scholarship considers their language and culture as Greek at base, though influenced by non-Greek neighbors.) Philip improved the traditional hoplite formation and increased its striking power and mobility by equipping soldiers with longer thrusting spears and less armor. Using horses bred in Macedonia's broad grassy plains, he also experimented with coordinating infantry and cavalry. Finally, his engineers developed new siege weapons, including the first catapults—machines using the power of twisted cords that, when relaxed, hurled arrows or stones great distances.

In 338 B.C.E. Philip defeated a southern coalition and established the Confederacy of Corinth to control the Greek city-states. Appointed military commander of all the Greeks, he planned a campaign against Persia and established a bridgehead on the Asiatic side of the Hellespont. These plans may have reflected the advice of Greek thinkers who urged an anti-Persian crusade to unify their quarrelsome countrymen.

An assassin cut short Philip's ambitions in 336 B.C.E. **Alexander** (356–323 B.C.E.), his son and heir, crossed into Asia in 334 B.C.E., vowing revenge for

Peloponnesian War A protracted (431–404 B.C.E.) and costly conflict between the Athenian and Spartan alliance systems that convulsed most of the Greek world. The war was largely a consequence of Athenian imperialism. Possession of a naval empire allowed Athens to fight a war of attrition. Ultimately, Sparta prevailed because of Athenian errors and Persian financial support.

Alexander King of Macedonia in northern Greece. Between 334 and 323 B.C.E. he conquered the Persian Empire, reached the Indus Valley, founded many Greek-style cities, and spread Greek culture across the Middle East. Later known as Alexander the Great.

Xerxes's invasion a century and half earlier. In 331 B.C.E. he defeated the Persians in three pitched battles against the western satraps at the village of Gaugamela (GAW-guh-mee-luh), north of Babylon.

Alexander the Great, as he came to be called, maintained the Persian administration system but replaced Persian officials with Macedonians and Greeks. To control strategic points, he settled wounded and aged ex-soldiers in a series of Greek-style cities, beginning with Alexandria in Egypt. After his victory at Gaugamela, he experimented with leaving cooperative Persian officials in place, also admitting some Persians and other Iranians into his army and court circle. Adopting elements of Persian dress and court ceremonials, he married several Iranian women who had useful royal or aristocratic connections, and he pressed his leading comrades to do the same.

In opting for these unexpected policies, which the Macedonian nobility fiercely resented, Alexander probably acted from both pragmatic and idealistic motives. His Asian campaign began with visions of glory, booty, and revenge. But the farther east he traveled, the more he saw himself as the legitimate successor of the Persian king (a claim facilitated by the death of Darius III). Alexander may have recognized that he had responsibilities to all the peoples who fell under his control and that administering so vast an empire would require the cooperation of local leaders. In this, he was following the example of the Achaemenids.

SECTION REVIEW

- Greek rebellion against Persian domination provoked the Persian Wars.

- During successive Persian invasions, Athens and Sparta led Greek resistance.

- Victory left Athens a naval power with imperial aspirations, and its wealth nourished the great cultural achievements of the Classical period.

- Athenian democracy rested upon several forms of inequality, including the subjugation of women and slaves.

- Rivalry between Sparta and Athens sparked the Peloponnesian War, which destroyed Athens and weakened all the city-states.

- Macedonia then became the dominant power in Greece, conquering city-states and, under Alexander the Great, the Persian Empire.

THE HELLENISTIC SYNTHESIS, 323–30 B.C.E.

■ *How did Greeks and non-Greeks interact and develop new cultural syntheses during the Hellenistic Age?*

Historians call the epoch following Alexander's conquests the **Hellenistic Age** (323–30 B.C.E.) because the lands in northeastern Africa and western Asia that came under Greek rule became "Hellenized"—that is, powerfully influenced by Greek culture. Greeks migrated in large numbers from their overcrowded homeland to serve as a privileged class of soldiers and administrators on the new frontiers, where they replicated the lifestyle of the city-state. This era of large kingdoms, containing ethnically mixed populations, great cities, powerful rulers, pervasive bureaucracies, and vast disparities in wealth, differed profoundly from the Archaic and Classical ages with their small, homogeneous, independent city-states. The Hellenistic world more closely resembled our own in its long-distance trade and communications, new institutions like libraries and universities, new kinds of scholarship and science, and sophisticated tastes in art and literature.

When he died suddenly in 323 B.C.E. at the age of thirty-two, Alexander had no plans for the succession. A half century of chaos followed as the most ambitious and ruthless of his generals struggled to succeed him. When the dust cleared, they had broken the empire into three major kingdoms, each ruled by a Macedonian dynasty: the Seleucid (sih-LOO-sid), Ptolemaic (tawl-uh-MAY-ik), and Antigonid (an-TIG-uh-nid) kingdoms (see Map 4.1). The Antigonids ruled the Macedonian homeland and tried with varying success to extend their control over southern Greece; the Ptolemies ruled Egypt; and the Seleucids inherited the majority of Alexander's conquests in Asia. A rough balance of power prevented any of the three from gaining the upper hand and enabled smaller states to survive by playing off the great powers.

Hellenistic Age Historians' term for the era, usually dated 323–30 B.C.E., in which Greek culture spread across western Asia and northeastern Africa after the conquests of Alexander the Great. The period ended with the fall of the last major Hellenistic kingdom to Rome, but Greek cultural influence persisted until the spread of Islam in the seventh century C.E.

The Seleucids, who ruled the bulk of Alexander's empire, faced the greatest challenges. The Indus Valley and Afghanistan soon split off, and over the course of the third and second centuries B.C.E. Iran fell to the Parthians (see Chapter 8). Thereafter Mesopotamia, Syria, and parts of Anatolia constituted the Seleucid core, with the kings ruling from Antioch (AN-tee-awk) in Syria. Like the Persians before them, they governed many different ethnic groups organized under various political and social forms. In the farming villages, where most of the population resided, the Seleucids maintained an administration modeled on the Persian system. They also continued Alexander's policy of founding Greek-style cities to serve as administrative centers and attract colonists from Greece. The Seleucids desperately needed Greek soldiers, engineers, and administrators.

In Europe, the Antigonid dynasty ruled the Macedonian homeland and parts of northern Greece. Compact and ethnically homogeneous, the Antigonid kingdom experienced little of the hostility that the Seleucid and Ptolemaic rulers faced. Macedonian garrisons gave the Antigonids a toehold in central and southern Greece, and the shadow of Macedonian intervention always threatened the south. The southern states responded by joining confederations, such as the Achaean (uh-KEY-uhn) League in the Peloponnese, in which the member-states maintained local autonomy but pooled resources and military power.

Athens and Sparta stood apart from these confederations. Never abandoning their myth of invincibility, the Spartans made a number of heroic but futile stands against Macedonian armies. Athens, now cherished for the artistic and literary accomplishments of the fifth century B.C.E., pursued a policy of neutrality. The city became a large museum filled with the relics and memories of a glorious past, as well as a university town that attracted the children of the well-to-do from all over the Mediterranean and western Asia.

Egypt Under the Ptolemies

The dynasty of the **Ptolemies** (TAWL-uh-meze) ruled Egypt and sometimes laid claim to Palestine. Since most Egyptians belonged to one ethnic group and lived in villages alongside the Nile, the Ptolemies ruled from **Alexandria**, which was situated near the mouth of the westernmost branch of the Nile and linked Egypt with the Mediterranean world. Memphis and Thebes, the capitals of ancient Egypt, had been located upriver. In the language of the Ptolemaic bureaucracy, Alexandria was technically "beside Egypt" rather than in it, as if to emphasize the gulf between rulers and subjects and the fact that it was not on the Nile River.

Like the Seleucids, the Ptolemies encouraged Greek immigration. In return for collaboration in the military or civil administration, the immigrants received land and a privileged position in the new society. But the Ptolemies did not plant Greek-style cities throughout the Egyptian countryside and made no effort to force the Greek language or customs on the Egyptian population. So separate was the ruling class from the subject population that only the last Ptolemy, Queen Cleopatra (r. 51–30 B.C.E.), who lost her kingdom to Rome, bothered to learn the Egyptian language.

The advent of new masters brought few changes to the Egyptian peasants. Vast revenues poured into the royal treasury from rents (the king owned most of the land), taxes, and royal monopolies on olive oil, salt, papyrus, and other key commodities. Nevertheless, from the early second century B.C.E., native insurrections in the countryside, though quickly stamped out by government forces and Greek and Hellenized settlers, indicate growing resentment of the Greeks' exploitation and arrogance.

Alexandria, the greatest Hellenistic city with a population of nearly half a million, had at its heart the royal compound, containing the palace and administrative buildings. The magnificent Mausoleum of Alexander enshrined Alexander's body, which the first Ptolemy had stolen during its return to Macedonia for burial. He had hoped that the luster of the

Ptolemies The Macedonian dynasty, descended from one of Alexander the Great's officers, that ruled Egypt for three centuries (323–30 B.C.E.). From their magnificent capital at Alexandria on the Mediterranean coast, the Ptolemies largely took over the system created by Egyptian pharaohs to extract the wealth of the land, rewarding Greeks and Hellenized non-Greeks serving in the military and administration.

Alexandria City on the Mediterranean coast of Egypt founded by Alexander. It became the capital of the Hellenistic kingdom of the Ptolemies. It contained the famous Library and the Museum, a center for leading scientific and literary figures. Its merchants engaged in trade with areas bordering the Mediterranean and the Indian Ocean.

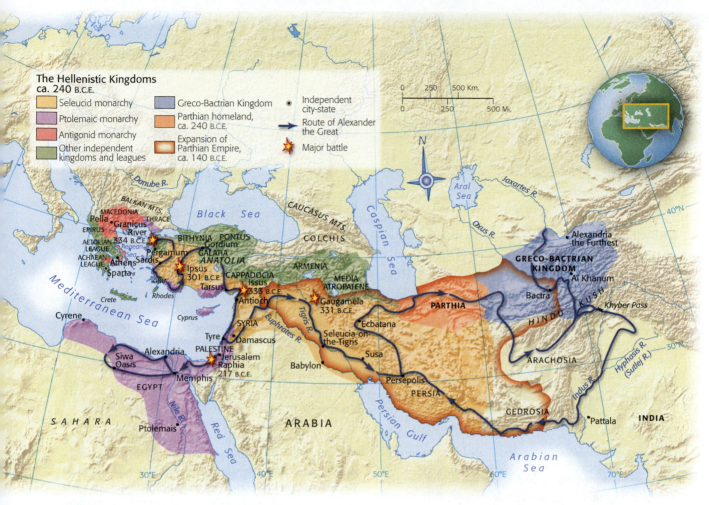

Map 4.1 Hellenistic Civilization After the death of Alexander the Great in 323 B.C.E., his vast empire soon split apart into a number of large and small political entities. A Macedonian dynasty was established on each continent: the Antigonids ruled the Macedonian homeland and tried with varying success to extend their control over southern Greece; the Ptolemies ruled Egypt; and the Seleucids inherited the majority of Alexander's conquests in Asia, though they lost control of the eastern portions because of the rise of the Parthians of Iran in the second century B.C.E. This period saw Greeks migrating in large numbers from their overcrowded homeland to serve as a privileged class of soldiers and administrators on the new frontiers, where they replicated the lifestyle of the city-state. © Cengage Learning

great conqueror, who was declared to be a god, would give him legitimacy as a ruler.

The famed Library of Alexandria had several hundred thousand volumes. The Museum, or "House of the Muses" (divinities who presided over the arts and sciences), supported the work of the great poets, philosophers, doctors, and scientists. A great lighthouse—a multistory tower with a fiery beacon visible at a distance of 30 miles (48 kilometers)—guided seafarers to two harbors serving the commerce of the Mediterranean, the Red Sea, and the Indian Ocean.

Alexandrian Greeks enjoyed citizenship in a polis, complete with Assembly, Council, and officials overseeing local affairs. They took advantage of Greek-style amenities and institutions: public baths and shaded arcades, theaters featuring revivals of ancient plays, and concert halls for musical performances and demonstrations of oratory. Young men of the privileged elite took classes at gymnasiums where athletics and fitness combined with music and literature in the curriculum. Jews had their own civic corporation, government, officials, and courts and

- The death of Alexander the Great and the breakup of his empire inaugurated the Hellenistic Age.

- Large kingdoms were ruled by Macedonian dynasties in which Greek culture was fused with local traditions.

- More Greek city-states retained autonomy through alliances, but Sparta and Athens stood apart and lost power.

- Egypt under the Ptolemies was the most successful Hellenistic state, and its capital Alexandria became the greatest Hellenistic city.

predominated in two of the five main residential districts. The sights, sounds, and smells of Syria, Anatolia, and the Egyptian countryside lent distinctiveness to other quarters.

Hellenistic Societies

In all the Hellenistic states, ambitious members of the indigenous populations learned the Greek language and adopted elements of the Greek lifestyle, because doing so helped them become part of the privileged and wealthy ruling class. Language and customs more than physical traits made a person a Greek. The Hellenistic Age saw a spontaneous synthesis of Greek and indigenous ways. Egyptians migrated to Alexandria, and Greeks and Egyptians intermarried in the villages of the countryside. Greeks living amid the monuments and descendants of the ancient civilizations of Egypt and western Asia learned the mathematical and astronomical wisdom of Mesopotamia, the mortuary rituals of Egypt, and the attractions of foreign religions. With little official planning or blessing and stemming for the most part from the day-to-day experiences of ordinary people, a great multicultural experiment unfolded as Greek and Middle Eastern cultural traits clashed and merged.

CONCLUSION

Greece and Iran represent two ways in which societies with shared Indo-European linguistic and religious roots adapted to different geographical environments and indigenous cultures. Although scholars can easily trace resemblances among gods, customs, and philosophical outlooks in these areas, the people themselves had no sense of kinship with one another. Only briefly, under Alexander the Great, did they come into direct contact in meaningful ways, and the resulting Hellenistic culture touched all three regions.

While some technologies, such as coinage, took hold in all areas and trade flourished, both overland and across the Mediterranean Sea, local circumstances dictated political and social formations. The ancient cultural centers of Egypt and Mesopotamia influenced the Greeks and the Persians.

It is intriguing to compare Greek civilization to ancient China in the Zhou era (see Chapter 3). Too far apart to have had any influence on each other, both reveal striking similarities. Their most innovative developments took place during periods of political fragmentation, rivalry, and warfare—the Archaic and Classical periods of Greek history and the Spring and Autumn and Warring States Periods in China—rather than in the more stable centuries under the Roman and Han emperors (Chapter 5 will compare Rome and early imperial China). Their differences are equally revealing and underlie the ways in which Western and East Asian civilizations have diverged, with implications for our own times.

CHAPTER REVIEW

ANCIENT IRAN, 1000–500 B.C.E.

■ *How did the Persian Empire rise from its Iranian homeland and succeed in controlling vast territories and diverse cultures?* (page 83)

The Medes, who were the first Iranians to build a complex political order, helped destroy the Assyrian Empire. Cyrus then united the Persians and overthrew the Medes, prompting the two similar cultures to blend. Expansion into Mesopotamia, Syria, and Anatolia connected the Persian Empire with older cultural and commercial networks. Under Darius I, the empire reached its fullest extent and basic governmental structure: provinces governed by satraps, tribute money funneled to the center, and a decentralized legal system. An extensive road and post system connected the imperial center with the periphery.

THE RISE OF THE GREEKS, 1000–500 B.C.E.

■ *What were the most distinctive elements of Greek civilization, and how and why did they evolve in the Archaic and Classical periods?* (page 88)

A rugged geography inhibiting overland travel turned the Greeks to the sea. The focus of this Greek civilization was the polis, whose citizens participated in government and defended it as hoplites. Population pressures spurred overseas colonization, which spread Greek culture throughout the Mediterranean world. The late Archaic period saw the emergence of new forms of literary and intellectual endeavor, such as history and philosophical inquiry, that matured in the Classical period.

THE STRUGGLE OF PERSIA AND GREECE, 546–323 B.C.E.

■ *How did the Persian Wars and their aftermath affect the politics and culture of ancient Greece and Iran?* (page 94)

Athens, Sparta, and their allies repulsed Persian invasions on land and at sea. Victory left Athens a naval power with an overseas empire and sufficient wealth from tribute and trade to finance temples on the Acropolis and other cultural achievement in drama and philosophy. Warlike Sparta and artistic, cosmopolitan Athens represented opposite extremes of Greek culture, but rivalry between then exploded into the Peloponnesian War, which shattered Athens and weakened the other city-states. Exploring this weakness, Persia recovered

old losses but encountered Macedonian expansion and ultimate defeat by Alexander the Great.

THE HELLENISTIC SYNTHESIS, 323–30 B.C.E.

■ *How did Greeks and non-Greeks interact and develop new cultural syntheses during the Hellenistic Age?* (page 101)

The death of Alexander the Great ushered in the Hellenistic Age. From his empire his generals carved kingdoms for themselves, founding Macedonian dynasties that presided over an international Greek culture. The Seleucids ruled the largest kingdom, founding Greek-style cities but ruling in the Persian manner. Both they and the Ptolemies encouraged Greek immigration, but in Egypt Greeks remained a class apart and had little to do with native Egyptians. The Antigonids ruled Macedonia, but the southern and central Greek cities resisted them through alliances. Sparta and Athens remained apart, both losing power in the region. Alexandria became the major Hellenistic city, a showcase of the cultural synthesis that marked the age.

Key Terms

Cyrus (p. 84)	Herodotus (p. 92)
Darius I (p. 85)	Pericles (p. 93)
satrap (p. 85)	Persian Wars (p. 94)
Persepolis (p. 86)	trireme (p. 95)
Zoroastrianism (p. 87)	Socrates (p. 96)
polis (p. 89)	Peloponnesian War (p. 100)
hoplite (p. 89)	Alexander (p. 100)
tyrant (p. 90)	Hellenistic Age (p. 101)
democracy (p. 90)	Ptolemies (p. 102)
sacrifice (p. 91)	Alexandria (p. 102)

An Age of Empires: Rome and Han China

© Cengage Learning

According to Chinese sources, in the year 166 C.E. a group of travelers identifying themselves as envoys from Andun, the king of distant Da Qin, arrived at the court of the Chinese emperor Huan, one of the Han dynasty rulers. Andun was Marcus Aurelius Antoninus, the emperor of Rome.

These first known "Romans" to reach China probably hailed from one of Rome's eastern provinces, perhaps Egypt or Syria, and may have stretched the truth in claiming to be official representatives of the Roman emperor. The Chinese officials had had no direct contact with the Roman Empire, however, and so the travelers, probably merchants hoping to trade for highly prized Chinese silk, easily got away with the imposture.

Direct or regular contact between the empires never developed, but the episode reveals that in the early centuries C.E. Rome and China dimly recognized each other's existence across the far-flung trading networks that spanned the Eastern Hemisphere. Both states, moreover, emerged from the last centuries B.C.E. and the first centuries C.E. as a new kind of empire, both qualitatively and quantitatively.

Since neither empire influenced the other, what caused them to arise and flourish at the same time? Some stress supposedly common factors, such as climate change or challenges from Central Asian nomads, but no theory has won the general support of scholars. The Roman Empire encompassed the lands surrounding the Mediterranean Sea and substantial portions of inland Europe and the Middle East. The Han Empire, named for China's ruling family, stretched from the Pacific Ocean to the oases of Central Asia. The largest empires the world had yet seen, they nevertheless managed to centralize control, achieve unprecedented stability and longevity, and assert dominance over the many cultures and peoples within their borders.

ROME'S CREATION OF A MEDITERRANEAN EMPIRE, 753 B.C.E.–330 C.E.

■ *How did Rome create and maintain its vast Mediterranean empire?*

The boot-shaped Italian peninsula, with the large island of Sicily, constitutes a bridge almost linking Europe and North Africa (see Map 5.1). Rome too lay at a crossroads, being situated at the midpoint of the peninsula, about 15 miles (24 kilometers) from its western coast, where a north-south road intersected an east-west river route. The Tiber River on one side and a double ring of seven hills on the other afforded natural protection to the site.

The Apennine Mountains form Italy's spine, separating the eastern and western coastal plains, and the arc of the Alps shields it on the north. Navigable rivers and passes through the Apennines, and even through the snowcapped Alps, eased travel by merchants and armies. The Mediterranean climate afforded a long growing season and favorable conditions for a wide variety of crops. Hillside forests, today largely gone, provided timber for construction and fuel. Iron and other metals came from the region of Etruria in the northwest.

Although hills account for 75 percent of the Italy's land area, the coastal plains and river valleys provide arable land, with fertile volcanic soil capable of supporting a much larger population than Greece. As it expanded within Italy, the Roman state tapped these human resources.

A Republic of Farmers

According to legend, Romulus, cast adrift on the Tiber River as a baby and nursed by a she-wolf, founded Rome in 753 B.C.E. Archaeological research, however, has revealed occupation on the Palestine Hill, one of the city's seven hills, dating to 1000 B.C.E. Several hilltop communities merged shortly before 600 B.C.E., forming an urban nucleus made possible by the draining of a swamp on the site of the future Roman Forum (civic center).

The Latin speech and cultural patterns of the inhabitants of the site resembled those of most of the other peoples of the peninsula. However, tradition remembered Etruscan immigrants (who were linguistically and culturally different from the technologically advanced Romans) arriving in the seventh century B.C.E., and Rome came to pride itself on offering refuge to exiles and outcasts.

Agriculture anchored the economy of early Rome, and land constituted wealth. Landowners brought

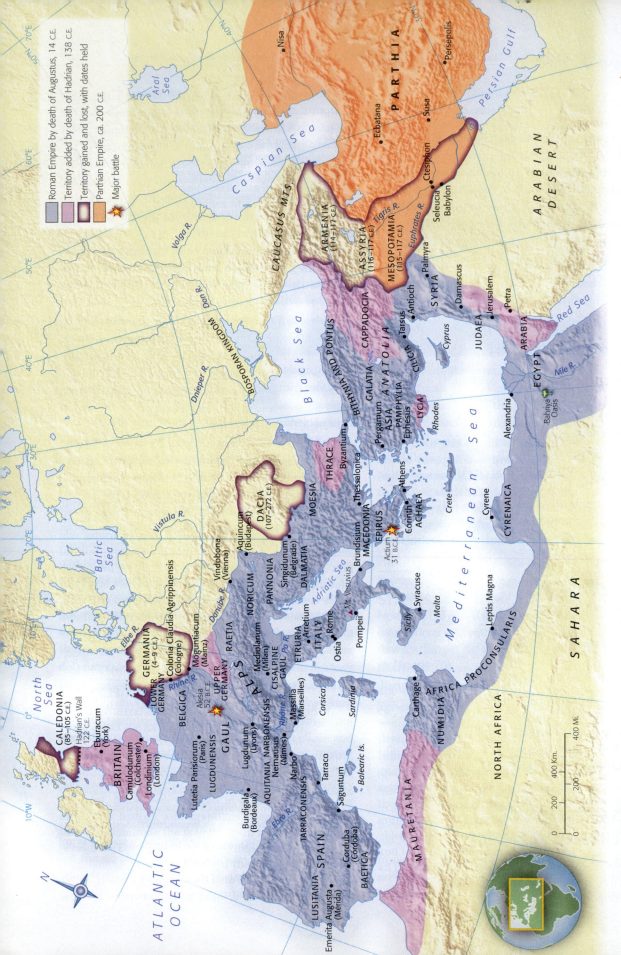

Legend

- Roman Empire by death of Augustus, 14 C.E.
- Territory added by death of Hadrian, 138 C.E.
- Territory gained and lost, with dates held
- Parthian Empire, ca. 200 C.E.
- ★ Major battle

PARTHIA

- Nisa
- Ecbatana
- Susa
- Persepolis

Persian Gulf

Aral Sea

Caspian Sea

Volga R.

Don R.

Dnieper R.

Vistula R.

BOSPORAN KINGDOM

CAUCASUS MTS.

ARMENIA (114–117 C.E.)

ASSYRIA (116–117 C.E.)

MESOPOTAMIA (115–117 C.E.)

Tigris R.

Euphrates R.

- Ctesiphon
- Seleucia
- Babylon

SYRIA

- Palmyra
- Antioch
- Damascus
- Jerusalem
- Petra

ARABIA

ARABIAN DESERT

Red Sea

Nile R.

EGYPT

- Alexandria
- Bahriya Oasis

Black Sea

BITHYNIA AND PONTUS

CAPPADOCIA

GALATIA

ASIA **ANATOLIA**

- Pergamum
- Ephesus
- Tarsus
- Byzantium

PAMPHYLIA

LYCIA

CILICIA

- Cyprus
- Rhodes

JUDEA

Mediterranean Sea

THRACE

MACEDONIA

MOESIA

DACIA (107–272 C.E.)

- Aquincum (Budapest)

PANNONIA

NORICUM

- Vindobona (Vienna)
- Singidunum (Belgrade)

DALMATIA

- Thessalonica
- Athens
- Corinth

ACHAEA

EPIRUS

★ Actium 31 B.C.E.

- Brundisium

Adriatic Sea

- Crete
- Syracuse
- Cyrene

CYRENAICA

Sicily

Malta

- Leptis Magna

AFRICA PROCONSULARIS

SAHARA

NORTH AFRICA

NUMIDIA

- Carthage

MAURETANIA

Mt. Vesuvius

- Pompeii
- Rome
- Ostia
- Arretium

ITALY

ETRURIA

CISALPINE GAUL

- Mediolanum (Milan)

Po R.

ALPS

RAETIA

UPPER GERMANY

★ Alesia 52 B.C.E.

LOWER GERMANY

- Mogontiacum (Mainz)
- Colonia Claudia Agrippinensis (Cologne)

GERMANIA (4–9 C.E.)

Rhine R.

Elbe R.

Danube R.

BELGICA

GAUL

- Lugdunum (Lyons)
- Lutetia Parisiorum (Paris)

LUGDUNENSIS

AQUITANIA

- Burdigala (Bordeaux)

NARBONENSIS

- Nemausus (Nîmes)
- Massilia (Marseilles)
- Narbo
- Tarraco

Corsica

Sardinia

Balearic Is.

TARRACONENSIS

SPAIN

- Saguntum
- Corduba (Córdoba)

BAETICA

LUSITANIA

- Emerita Augusta (Mérida)

Ebro R.

North Sea

CALEDONIA (85–105 C.E.)

Hadrian's Wall 122 C.E.

- Eburacum (York)

BRITAIN

- Camulodunum (Colchester)
- Londinium (London)

Baltic Sea

ATLANTIC OCEAN

Rhône R.

N

0   200   400 Km.
0   200   400 Mi.

Map 5.1 **The Roman Empire** The Roman Empire came to encompass all the lands surrounding the Mediterranean Sea, as well as parts of continental Europe. When Augustus died in 14 C.E., he left instructions to his successors not to expand beyond the limits he had set, but Claudius invaded southern Britain in the mid-first century and the soldier-emperor Trajan added Romania early in the second century. Deserts and seas provided solid natural boundaries, but the long and vulnerable river borders in central and eastern Europe would eventually prove expensive to defend and vulnerable to invasion by Germanic and Central Asian peoples. © Cengage Learning

Chronology

	Rome	China
1000 B.C.E.	1000 B.C.E. First settlement on site of Rome	
500 B.C.E.	507 B.C.E. Establishment of the Republic	480–221 B.C.E. Warring States Period
300 B.C.E.	264–202 B.C.E. Wars against Carthage guarantee Roman control of western Mediterranean	221 B.C.E. Qin emperor unites eastern China
200 B.C.E.	200–146 B.C.E. Wars against Hellenistic kingdoms lead to control of eastern Mediterranean	206 B.C.E. Han dynasty succeeds Qin 140–87 B.C.E. Emperor Wu expands the Han Empire
100 B.C.E.	88–31 B.C.E. Civil wars and failure of the Republic 31 B.C.E.–14 C.E. Augustus establishes the Principate	25 C.E. Han capital transferred from Chang'an to Luoyang
30 C.E.	Between 30 and 36 C.E. Crucifixion of Jesus	
200 C.E.	235–284 C.E. Third-Century Crisis	220 C.E. Fall of Han dynasty
300 C.E.	324 C.E. Constantine moves capital to Constantinople	

social status and political privilege while buttressing fundamental values. Most early Romans cultivated their own small plots of land, but a few families managed to acquire large tracts of land. The heads of these wealthy families served in the Senate, a "Council of Elders" that dominated the politics of the Roman state. Their families constituted the senatorial class. Tradition maintains that seven kings ruled Rome between 753 and 507 B.C.E., Romulus being the first and the tyrannical Tarquinius Superbus the last. In 507 B.C.E. members of the senatorial class, led by Brutus "the Liberator," deposed Tarquinius Superbus and instituted a *res publica*, a "public possession," or republic.

Far from being a democracy, the **Roman Republic**, which lasted from 507 to 31 B.C.E., vested power in several assemblies. Male citizens could attend their sessions, but the votes of the wealthy counted for more than the votes of the poor. The hierarchy of state officials, elected for one year, culminated in two consuls, who presided over the Senate and other assemblies and commanded the army on campaigns.

Technically an advisory council, first to the kings and later to the annually changing Republican officials, the **Roman Senate** increasingly made policy and governed. Senators nominated their sons for public offices and filled senatorial vacancies with former officials. This self-perpetuating body, whose members served for life, brought together the state's wealth, influence, and political and military experience.

Roman families consisted of several generations as well as domestic slaves. The oldest living male, the *paterfamilias*, exercised absolute authority over every family member. This *auctoritas*, enjoyed by important male members of the society as a whole, enabled a man to inspire and demand obedience from his inferiors.

Complex ties of obligation, such as the **patron/ client relationship**, bound together individuals and families. *Clients* sought the help and protection of *patrons*, men of wealth and influence. A senator might have dozens or even hundreds of clients to whom he provided legal advice and representation,

Roman Republic The period from 507 to 31 B.C.E., during which Rome was largely governed by the aristocratic Roman Senate.

Roman Senate A council whose members were the heads of wealthy, landowning families. Originally an advisory body to the early kings, in the era of the Roman Republic the Senate effectively governed the Roman state and the growing empire. Under Senate leadership, Rome conquered an empire of unprecedented extent in the lands surrounding the Mediterranean Sea.

patron/client relationship In ancient Rome, a fundamental social relationship in which the patron—a wealthy and powerful individual—provided legal and economic protection and assistance to clients, men of lesser status and means, and in return the clients supported the political careers and economic interests of their patron.

Statue of a Roman Carrying Busts of His Ancestors, First Century B.C.E. Roman society was extremely conscious of status, and the status of an elite Roman family was determined in large part by the public achievements of ancestors and living members. A visitor to a Roman home found portraits of distinguished ancestors in the entry hall, along with labels listing the offices they held. Portrait heads were carried in funeral processions.

Alinari/Art Resource, NY

under the jurisdiction of the paterfamilias of her husband's family. Unable to own property or represent herself in legal proceedings, she had to depend on a male guardian to advocate her interests.

Despite these limitations, Roman women were less constrained than their Greek counterparts (see Chapter 4). Over time they gained greater personal protection and economic freedom. Some took advantage of a form of marriage that left a woman under the jurisdiction of her father and independent after his death. Many stories involve strong women who greatly influenced their husbands or sons and thereby helped shape Roman history. Roman poets expressed love for women who appeared educated and outspoken, and the careers of the early emperors abound with tales of self-assured and assertive queen-mothers and consorts.

Like other Italian peoples, Romans believed in invisible forces known as *numina*. Vesta, the living, pulsating energy of fire, dwelled in the hearth; Janus guarded the door; and the Penates watched over food stored in the cupboard. Other deities resided in hills, caves, grottoes, and springs. Small offerings of cakes and liquids supplicated the favor of these spirits. Certain gods operated in larger spheres—for example, Jupiter, the god of the sky, and Mars, initially a god of agriculture as well as war.

The Romans strove to maintain the *pax deorum* ("peace of the gods"), a covenant between the gods and the Roman state. Boards of priests drawn from the aristocracy performed sacrifices and other rituals to win the gods' favor. In return, the Roman state counted on the gods for success in its undertakings. When the Romans encountered the Greeks of southern Italy, they equated their major deities with gods from the Greek pantheon, such as Zeus (Jupiter) and Ares (Mars), and took over the myths attached to them.

physical protection, and monetary loans in tough times. In turn, the client followed his patron out to battle, supported him in the political arena, worked on his land, and even contributed to his daughter's dowry. Throngs of clients awaited their patrons in the morning and accompanied them to the Forum for the day's business. Especially large retinues brought great prestige. Middle-class clients of the aristocracy might be patrons of poorer men. Rome thus accepted and institutionalized inequality and made of it a system of mutual benefits and obligations.

Roman women played no public role and hence appear infrequently in sources. Nearly all information pertains to those in the upper classes. In early Rome, a woman never ceased to be a child in the eyes of the law. She started out under the absolute authority of her paterfamilias. When she married, she came

Expansion in Italy and the Mediterranean

The fledgling Roman Republic of 500 B.C.E. did not stand out among the city-states of Latium, a region of central Italy. Three and a half centuries later, Rome commanded a huge empire encompassing virtually all the Mediterranean lands. Expansion began slowly but picked up momentum, peaking in the third and second centuries B.C.E.

Some scholars ascribe Rome's success to the greed and aggressiveness of a people fond of war. Others observe that the structure of the Roman state encouraged recourse to war, because the two consuls had only one year in office in which to gain military glory. The Romans invariably claimed that they were only defending themselves. It is possible that fear drove the Romans to expand their territory, as the vulnerability of new conquests necessitated ever more buffers against attack.

Ongoing friction between the pastoral hill peoples of the Apennines, who depended on herding, and the farmers of the coastal plains sparked Rome's conquest of Italy. In the fifth century B.C.E., Rome achieved leadership within a league of central Italian cities organized for defense against the hill peoples. In the fourth century B.C.E., the Romans occasionally defended the wealthy and sophisticated cities of Campania, the region on the Bay of Naples possessing the richest farmland in the peninsula. By 290 B.C.E., after three wars with the peoples of Samnium in central Italy, the Romans had extended their "protection" over nearly the entire peninsula.

The Romans consolidated their hold over Italy by granting the political, legal, and economic privileges of citizenship to conquered populations. In this, they contrasted with the Greeks, who did not share citizenship with outsiders (see Chapter 4). The Romans co-opted the most influential elements within the conquered communities and made Rome's interests their interests. Rome also demanded that its Italian subjects provide soldiers, thus creating a seemingly inexhaustible reservoir of manpower that bolstered military success. Rome could endure higher casualties than the enemy and prevail by sheer numbers.

Between 264 and 202 B.C.E. Rome fought two protracted wars against the Carthaginians, those energetic descendants of the Phoenicians who had settled in Tunisia and dominated the commerce of the western Mediterranean (see Chapter 2). The Roman state emerged as the master of the western Mediterranean and acquired its first overseas provinces in Sicily, Sardinia, and Spain (see Map 5.1). Between 200 and 146 B.C.E. a series of wars pitted the Roman state against the major Hellenistic kingdoms in the eastern Mediterranean. Reluctant to occupy such distant territories, the Romans withdrew their troops. But when the settlements they imposed failed to take root, a frustrated Roman government took over direct administration of these turbulent lands. The conquest of the Celtic peoples of Gaul (modern France; see Chapter 3) by Rome's most brilliant general, Gaius Julius Caesar, between 59 and 51 B.C.E. led to the first territorial acquisitions in Europe's heartland.

The Romans resisted extending to distant provinces the governing system and privileges of citizenship they employed in Italy. Indigenous elite groups willing to collaborate with Rome enjoyed considerable autonomy, including responsibility for local administration and tax collection. Every year a senator, usually someone who had held high office, served as governor in each province. Accompanied by a surprisingly small retinue of friends and relations who served as advisers and deputies, the governor defended the province against outside attack and internal disruption, oversaw the collection of taxes, and judged legal cases.

Over time, this system proved inadequate. Officials chosen through political connections often lacked competence, and the one-year period of service gave them little time to gain experience. A few governors extorted huge sums of money from the provincial populace. Rome still depended on the institutions and attitudes of a city-state to govern an ever-growing empire.

The Failure of the Republic

The frequent wars and territorial expansion of the third and second centuries B.C.E. set off changes in the Italian landscape. Peasant farmers spent long periods of time away from home on military service, while most of the wealth generated by conquest and empire ended up helping the upper classes purchase Italian land. Investors easily acquired the property of absent soldier-farmers by purchase, deception, or intimidation. The small self-sufficient farms of the Italian countryside, whose peasant owners provided the backbone of the Roman legions (units of 6,000 soldiers), gave way to *latifundia*, literally "broad estates," or ranches.

The new owners had ample space to graze herds of cattle or grow grapes for wine in the place of less profitable wheat. Thus, much of Italy, especially in the cities, became dependent on expensive imported grain. Meanwhile, cheap slave labor provided by war prisoners made it hard for peasants who had lost their farms to find work in the countryside (see Diversity and Dominance: Socioeconomic Mobility, Winners and Losers in Imperial Rome and Han China). They moved to Rome and other cities, but they found no work there either and ended up living in poverty. The growing urban masses, idle and prone to riot, would play a major role in the political struggles of the late Republic.

The decline of peasant farmers in Italy produced a shortage of men who owned the minimum amount of property required for military service. During a war that the Romans fought in North Africa at the end of the second century B.C.E., Gaius Marius—a "new man," as the Romans labeled politically active individuals from outside the traditional ruling class—achieved political prominence by accepting poor, propertyless men into his legions, to whom he promised farms upon retirement from military service. These grateful troops helped Marius get elected to an unprecedented (and illegal) six consulships.

Between 88 and 31 B.C.E., several ambitious individuals—Sulla, Pompey, Julius Caesar, Mark Antony, and Octavian—commanded armies that were more loyal to them than to the state. Their use of Roman troops to increase their personal power led to civil wars between military factions. The generals who seized Rome on several occasions executed their political opponents and exercised dictatorial control.

By 31 B.C.E., however, Julius Caesar's grandnephew and heir, Octavian (63 B.C.E.–14 C.E.), had eliminated all rivals and set about refashioning the Roman system of government while retaining the offices, honors, and social prerogatives of the senatorial class. A dictator in fact, he never called himself king or emperor, claiming merely to be *princeps*, "first among equals"—hence the term **Roman Principate** for the period following the Roman Republic. **Augustus**, a title Octavian received from the Senate, implied prosperity and piety and became the name by which he is known to posterity. Augustus's ruthlessness, patience, and intuitive grasp of psychology enabled him to manipulate each group

in society. When he died in 14 C.E., after forty-five years of carefully veiled rule, scarcely anyone could remember the Republic. During his reign, the empire expanded into Egypt and parts of the Middle East and central Europe, leaving only the southern half of Britain and modern Romania to be added later.

So popular was Augustus that four members of his family succeeded to the position of "emperor" (as we call it) despite serious personal and political shortcomings. After the mid-first century C.E., other families obtained the post. In theory, the Senate affirmed the early emperors; in reality, the armies chose them. By the second century C.E., the so-called Good Emperors instituted a new mechanism of succession: each designated as his successor a mature man of proven ability whom he adopted as his son and with whom he shared offices and privileges.

Augustus had allied himself with the **equites** (EH-kwee-tays), the class of well-to-do Italian merchants and landowners second in wealth and social status only to the senatorial class. These competent and self-assured individuals became the core of a new civil service. At last Rome had an administrative bureaucracy capable of managing a large empire with considerable honesty, consistency, and efficiency.

An Urban Empire

Calling the Roman Empire of the first three centuries C.E. an "urban" empire does not mean that most people lived in cities and towns. Perhaps 80 percent of the 50 to 60 million people lived in agricultural villages or isolated farms. The network of towns and

---

Roman Principate A term used to characterize Roman government in the first three centuries C.E., based on the ambiguous title *princeps* ("first citizen") adopted by Augustus to conceal his military dictatorship.

Augustus Honorific name of Octavian, founder of the Roman Principate, the military dictatorship that replaced the failing rule of the Roman Senate. After defeating all rivals, between 31 B.C.E. and 14 C.E. he laid the groundwork for several centuries of stability and prosperity in the Roman Empire.

equites In ancient Italy, prosperous landowners second in wealth and status to the senatorial aristocracy. The Roman emperors allied with this group to counterbalance the influence of the old aristocracy and used the equites to staff the imperial civil service.

Scene from Trajan's Column, Rome, ca. 113 C.E. The Roman emperor Trajan erected a marble column 125 feet (38 meters) in height to commemorate his triumphant campaign in Dacia (modern Romania). The relief carving, which snakes around the column for 656 feet (200 meters), illustrates numerous episodes of the conquest and provides a detailed pictorial record of the equipment and practices of the Roman army in the field. This panel depicts soldiers building a fort.

cities served as administrative centers, however, with corresponding benefits for the urban populace.

Numerous towns had several thousand inhabitants. A handful of major cities—Alexandria in Egypt, Antioch in Syria, and Carthage—had populations of several hundred thousand. Rome itself had approximately a million residents. The largest cities put huge strains on the government's technical ability to provide food and remove sewage.

In Rome, the upper classes lived in elegant hillside townhouses. The house centered around an *atrium*, a rectangular courtyard with an open skylight that let in light and rainwater for drinking and washing. A dining room for dinner and drinking parties, an interior garden, a kitchen, and perhaps a private bath surrounded the atrium, with bedrooms on the upper level. Pebble mosaics on the floors and frescoes of mythological scenes or outdoor vistas on the wall and ceilings gave a sense of openness in the absence of windows. Many aristocrats owned a number of villas in the countryside as retreats from the pressures of city life.

The poor inhabited crowded slums in the low-lying parts of the city. Damp, dark, and smelly, with few furnishings, these wooden tenements suffered from frequent fires. Fortunately, Romans could spend the day outdoors for most of the year.

Socioeconomic Mobility, Winners and Losers in Imperial Rome and Han China

Throughout human history, most people have been born into societies in which there was little opportunity or likelihood that they could significantly improve their social or economic circumstances. However, in complex and urbanized civilizations like imperial Rome or Han China, economic advancement—which is, then, generally linked to a higher social status—is more achievable for various reasons, including conditions of peace and stability favorable to commerce brought by the imperial power, the construction of roads over which goods can be conveyed, increased wealth and higher standards of living for many, the presence of large numbers of potential customers in urban centers, and innovative technologies for producing high-quality products. However, two further points need to be made. First, in situations of open economic competition, there are losers as well as winners. And, second, the existence of new forms of wealth and its acquisition by new groups of people tends to destabilize and threaten traditional institutions and values. We are fortunate in having texts from early imperial Rome and Han China that illustrate these processes from the vantage point of "the losers."

Juvenal wrote poetic satires of Roman society in the late first and early second centuries C.E. Of course satire, by its very nature, exaggerates, but to be effective and funny it has to be based on something real. The main speaker in Juvenal's *Third Satire* is a friend of the poet named Umbricius, who has decided to abandon the ever more dangerous and frustrating city of Rome for a quieter town on the Bay of Naples.

. . .'There is no room in the city
for respectable skills,' he said, 'and no reward for one's efforts.

Today my means are less than yesterday; come tomorrow,
the little left will be further reduced. . .
What can I do in Rome? I can't tell lies; if a book
is bad I cannot praise it and beg for a copy; the stars
in their courses mean nothing to me; I'm neither willing nor
    able
to promise a father's death; I've never studied the innards
of frogs; I leave it to others to carry instructions and presents
to a young bride from her lover; none will get help from me
in a theft; that's why I never appear on a governor's staff;. . .
Who, these days, inspires affection except an accomplice –
one whose conscience boils and seethes with unspeakable
    secrets?. . .
I shan't mince words. My fellow Romans, I cannot put up with
    a city of Greeks. . .
They make for the Esquiline, or the willow's Hill, intent on
    becoming
the vital organs and eventual masters of our leading houses.
Nimble wits, a reckless nerve, and a ready tongue. . .
What of the fact that the nation excels in flattery, praising
the talk of an ignorant patron, the looks of one who is ugly. . .
the whole country's a play. You chuckle, he shakes with a
    louder
guffaw; he weeps if he spots a tear in the eye of his patron,
yet he feels no grief; on a winter's day if you ask for a brazier,
he dons a wrap; if you say 'I'm warm,' he starts to perspire.
So we aren't on equal terms; he always has the advantage
who night and day alike is able to take his expression
from another's face, to throw up his hands and cheer if his
    patron
produces an echoing belch or pees in a good straight line. . .
There's no room here for any Roman. . .
That same man, moreover, provides a cause and occasion
for universal amusement if his cloak is ripped and muddy,
if his toga is a little stained, and one of his shoes gapes open. . .
Of all that luckless poverty involves, nothing is harsher
than the fact that it makes people funny.' ➤

Umbricius complains about the difficulty that educated, middle-class Romans like Juvenal and himself have in finding gainful employment and making a decent living. They cannot compete with the swarms of "Greeks"—by which he means people from the Greek-speaking Eastern Mediterranean, which would include Greeks proper, Syrians, and Egyptians—who are such accomplished actors, flatterers, and liars that they ingratiate themselves with the rich and powerful and get all the good jobs and contracts. The real Romans, who have too much dignity to stoop to this level, are left on the outside looking in. As they descend into poverty in a city in which the cost of lodging, food, and everything else is exorbitantly high, they are scorned and humiliated.

We see in this poem a resurgence of long-standing Roman prejudice toward the Greeks. Ironically, the presence of so many Easterners at Rome was a product of the empire, both because large numbers of prisoners of war initially serving as slaves in Italy gained their freedom and Roman citizenship, and because the capital city was a magnet attracting the most able and ambitious people in the empire to come to Rome to make their fortune.

A striking Han Chinese parallel to Juvenal's *Third Satire* can be found in an essay on friendship written by Wang Fu. He lived in the first half of the second century C.E. and never obtained an official post, leading him to complain that the system was not operating with fairness.

People compete to flatter and to get close to those who are wealthy and prominent. . . People are also quick to snub those who are poor and humble. . . If a person makes friends with the rich and prominent, he will gain the benefits of influential recommendations for advancement in office and the advantages of generous presents and other emoluments. But if he makes friends with the poor and humble, he will lose money either from giving them handouts or from unrepaid loans. . . This is the reason that crafty, calculating individuals can worm their way up the official ladder while ordinary scholars slip ever more into obscurity. Unless the realm has a brilliant ruler, there may be no one to discern this. . . Alas! The gentlemen of today speak nobly but act basely. Their words are upright, but their hearts are false. Their actions do not reflect their words, and their words are out of harmony with their thoughts. . . In their lofty speeches they refer to virtuous and righteous persons as being worthy. But when they actually recommend people for office, they consider only such requirements as influence and prominence. If a man is just an obscure scholar, even if he possesses the virtue of Yan Hui and Min Ziqian, even if he is modest and diligent, even if he has the ability of Yi Yin and Lu Shang, even if he is filled with the most devoted compassion for the people, he is clearly not going to be employed in this world.

As Wang Fu sees it, men of ambition focused all their attention on cultivating the rich and powerful in order to get the recommendations that led to official appointments, and in the process they ignored their real friends, whereas men of talent who could not or would not play this game were overlooked and scorned for their poverty. While appointment to public office was supposed to be meritocratic, based, first, on knowledge of the classic Confucian texts as determined by an exam and then by performance in office, Wang Fu's essay makes clear that what mattered most was connections to powerful people and the recommendations those people made to their peers in the government.

QUESTIONS FOR ANALYSIS

1. What kinds of abilities lead to success in imperial Rome and China?
2. Are the authors of these two texts just whining because they have had little success, or are they justified in claiming that the situation is unfair?
3. How are the new circumstances of increased socioeconomic mobility damaging traditional institutions and values?

Sources: First selection [translated by Niall Rudd, *Juvenal, The Satires* (Oxford 1992)]. Second selection [translated by Lily Hwa, in Patricia Buckley Ebrey (ed.), *Chinese Civilization, A Sourcebook*, 2nd ed. (The Free Press, 1993)]

Roman Shop Selling Food and Drink The bustling town of Pompeii on the Bay of Naples was buried in ash by the eruption of Mt. Vesuvius in 79 C.E. Archaeologists have unearthed the streets, stores, and houses of this typical Roman town. Shops such as this sold hot food and drink served from clay vessels set into the counter. Shelves and niches behind the counter contained other items. In the background can be seen a well-paved street and a public fountain where the inhabitants could fetch water.

Other cities and towns, including the ramshackle settlements that sprang up beside frontier forts, mirrored the capital city in political organization, physical layout, and appearance. A town council and two annually elected officials drawn from prosperous members of the community maintained law and order and collected both urban and rural taxes. In return for the privilege of running local affairs and in appreciation for the state's protection of their wealth and position, this "municipal aristocracy" served Rome loyally. In striving to imitate Roman senators, they lavishly endowed their communities with attractive elements of Roman urban life: a forum, government buildings, temples, gardens, baths, theaters, amphitheaters, and games and public entertainments of all sorts. These amenities made the situation of the urban poor superior to that of the rural poor. Poor

people in a city could pass time at the baths, seek refuge from the elements under the colonnades, and attend the games.

Hard work and drudgery marked life in the countryside, relieved only by occasional festival days and the everyday pleasures of sex, family, and conversation. Rural people had to fend for themselves in dealing with bandits, wild animals, and other hazards. People outside urban centers had little direct contact with the government beyond occasional run-ins with bullying soldiers and the dreaded arrival of the tax collector.

The concentration of ownership reversed temporarily during the civil wars that ended the Republic; it resumed under the emperors. But the end of new conquests reduced the number of slaves and forced landowners to find new labor. Landlords turned to tenant farmers, whom they allowed to live on and cultivate plots of land in return for a portion of their crops. The landowners themselves still lived in the cities and hired foremen to manage their estates. Thus wealth based on rural productivity became concentrated in the cities.

In the *pax Romana* ("Roman peace"), the safety and stability guaranteed by Roman might, commerce flourished, allowing some urban dwellers to become rich from manufacture and trade. Meat and vegetables were usually exchanged locally because transportation was costly and many products spoiled quickly. The city of Rome, however, depended on grain shipments from Sicily, North Africa, and Egypt to feed its huge population. Special naval squadrons performed this task.

Some exporters dealt in glass, metalwork, delicate pottery, and other fine manufactured products. The centers of production, first located in Italy, moved into the provinces as knowledge of the necessary skills spread. Roman armies on the frontiers provided a large market, and their presence promoted the prosperity of border provinces. Other merchants traded in luxury items from beyond the empire's boundaries, especially Chinese silks, Indian spices, and Arabian incense. The tax revenues of rich provinces like Gaul (France) and Egypt flowed to Rome to support the emperor and the central government, and to the frontier provinces to subsidize the armies.

While Hellenism dominated the eastern Mediterranean (see Chapter 4), **Romanization**, the spread of the Latin language and Roman way of life, proved an enduring consequence of empire among the diverse peoples in the western provinces. As the language of the conquerors spread among the common people as well as the elite, it became the basis for Portuguese, Spanish, French, Italian, and Romanian. However, in frontier areas along the Rhine and Danube Rivers, where Roman control was tenuous and migration by Germanic peoples was changing the ethnic balance by the third century C.E., Latin made only limited headway.

The Roman government did not force Romanization. The inhabitants of the provinces themselves chose Latin and adopted cultural practices like wearing a *toga* (the traditional cloak worn by Roman male citizens). Making this choice brought advantages,

as learning English and wearing Western clothing do today. Latin facilitated dealings with the Roman administration and helped merchants get contracts to supply the military. Many also must have been drawn by the aura of success surrounding the language and culture of a people who had created so vast an empire.

As towns sprang up and acquired the Roman urban amenities, they attracted ambitious members of the indigenous populations. The empire gradually and reluctantly extended Roman citizenship, with its attendant privileges, legal protections, and certain tax exemptions, to people living outside Italy. Completing a twenty-six-year term of service in the native military units that backed up the Roman legions earned soldiers citizenship that could pass to their descendants. Emperors granted citizenship to individuals or entire communities as a reward for service. Then in 212 C.E. the emperor Caracalla granted citizenship to all free, adult, male inhabitants of the empire.

The gradual extension of citizenship mirrored the empire's transformation from an Italian dominion over the Mediterranean lands into a commonwealth of peoples. As early as the first century C.E., some of the leading literary and intellectual figures came from the provinces. By the second century even the emperors hailed from Spain, Gaul, and North Africa.

The Rise of Christianity

The Jewish homeland of Judaea (see Chapter 2), roughly equivalent to present-day Israel, came under direct Roman rule in 6 C.E. Over the next half century, the insensitivity of the Roman governors to the Jewish belief in one god increased tension with the inhabitants. Various kinds of opposition to Roman rule

pax Romana Literally, "Roman peace," it connoted the stability and prosperity that Roman rule brought to the lands of the Roman Empire in the first two centuries C.E. The movement of people and trade goods along Roman roads and safe seas allowed for the spread of cultural practices, technologies, and religious ideas.

Romanization The process by which the Latin language and Roman culture became dominant in the western provinces. Indigenous peoples in the provinces often chose to Romanize because of the political and economic advantages that it brought, as well as the allure of Roman success.

sprang up. Many Jews anticipated the arrival of the Messiah, the "Anointed One," presumed to be a military leader who would liberate the Jewish people and drive the Romans out.

It is in this context that we must see the career of **Jesus**, a young carpenter from the Galilee region in northern Israel. In place of what he considered excessive concern with money and power among Jewish leaders and perfunctory religious observance by mainstream Jews, Jesus prescribed a return to the personal faith and spirituality of an earlier age. He eventually attracted the attention of the Jewish authorities in Jerusalem, who regarded popular reformers as potential troublemakers. Sometime between 30 and 36 C.E. they turned him over to the Roman governor, Pontius Pilate. Jesus was imprisoned, condemned, and executed by crucifixion, a punishment usually reserved for common criminals. His followers, the Apostles, subsequently sought to spread his teachings and their belief that he had been resurrected (returned from death to life) among their fellow Jews.

Paul, a Jew from the Greek city of Tarsus in southeast Anatolia, converted to the new creed and between 45 and 58 C.E. devoted himself to spreading the word. Traveling throughout Syria-Palestine, Anatolia, and Greece, he found most Jews unwilling to accept his claim that Jesus was the Messiah and had ushered in a new age. Frustrated, Paul redirected his efforts to non-Jews (sometimes called *gentiles*) who were also experiencing a spiritual hunger. He set up a string of Christian (from the Greek name *christos*, meaning "anointed one," given to Jesus by his followers) communities in the eastern Mediterranean.

Paul's career exemplifies the cosmopolitan nature of the Roman Empire in this era. Speaking both Greek and Aramaic, he moved comfortably between the Greco-Roman and Jewish worlds. He used Roman roads, depended on the peace guaranteed by Roman arms, called on his Roman citizenship to protect him from local authorities, and moved from city to city in his quest for converts.

In 66 C.E., tensions in Roman Judaea erupted in a revolt that lasted until 73. The Jerusalem-based Christian community, which focused on converting Jews, fell victim to the Roman reconquest. This cleared the field for Paul's non-Jewish converts, and Christianity began to diverge more and more from its Jewish roots. The sect grew slowly but steadily. Many early converts came from disenfranchised groups: women, slaves, and the urban poor. They hoped to receive the respect not accorded them in the larger society and to obtain positions of responsibility when the early Christian communities elected them leaders. However, as the religious movement grew and prospered, it developed a hierarchy of priests and bishops and engaged in bitter disputes over theological doctrine (see Chapter 10).

As monotheists forbidden to worship other gods, early Christians met persecution from Roman officials, who often took their refusal to worship the emperor as a sign of disloyalty. Nevertheless, occasional government attempts at suppression and mob attacks did not keep converts from joining the Christian movement. By the late third century C.E. adherents to Christianity were a sizable minority within the empire and included many educated and prosperous people holding local and imperial posts.

During the Greek Classical period, a number of "mystery" cults had gained popularity by claiming to provide secret information about the nature of life and death and promising a blessed afterlife to their adherents. In the Hellenistic and Roman periods, belief systems making similar promises arose in the eastern Mediterranean and spread throughout the Greco-Roman lands, responding to a spiritual and intellectual hunger not satisfied by paganism. These included the cults of the mother-goddess Cybele in Anatolia, the Egyptian goddess Isis, and the Iranian sun-god Mithra. As we shall see, the ultimate victory

Jesus A Jew from Galilee in northern Israel who sought to reform Jewish beliefs and practices. He was executed as a revolutionary by the Romans. Hailed as the Messiah and son of God by his followers, he became the central figure in Christianity, a belief system that developed in the centuries after his death.

Paul A Jew from the Greek city of Tarsus in Anatolia, he initially persecuted the followers of Jesus but, after receiving a revelation on the road to Syrian Damascus, became a Christian. Taking advantage of his Hellenized background and Roman citizenship, he traveled throughout Syria-Palestine, Anatolia, and Greece, preaching the new religion and establishing churches. Finding his greatest success among pagans ("gentiles"), he began the process by which Christianity separated from Judaism.

Roman Aqueduct near Tarragona, Spain The growth of towns and cities challenged Roman officials to provide an adequate supply of water. Aqueducts channeled water from a source, sometimes many miles away, to an urban complex, using only the force of gravity. To bring an aqueduct from high ground into the city, Roman engineers designed long, continuous rows of arches that maintained a steady downhill slope. Scholars sometimes can roughly estimate the population of an ancient city by calculating the amount of water that was available to it. Lenar Musin/Shutterstock.com

of Christianity over these rivals arose from historical circumstances as much as from spiritual appeal.

Technology and Transformation

The relative safety of travel brought by Roman arms and engineering helped the early Christians to spread their faith. Surviving remnants of roads, fortification walls, aqueducts, and buildings testify to the Romans' engineering expertise. In peacetime, army engineers built bridges, siege works, and ballistic weapons. Romans also pioneered the use of arches for the even distribution of weight without the use of thick supporting walls. **Aqueducts**—long elevated or underground conduits—used gravity to bring water from its source to urban centers. Another invention was concrete—a mixture of lime powder, sand, and water—that could be poured into molds to create vast vaulted and domed interior spaces, unlike the rectilinear pillar-and-post construction of the Greeks and Egyptians.

Defending borders that stretched for thousands of miles posed a great administrative challenge. In a document released after his death, Augustus advised against expanding the empire because of the costs of administration and defensive strategy. Mountains,

> **aqueduct** A conduit, either elevated or underground, that used gravity to carry water from a source to a location—usually a city—that needed it. The Romans built many aqueducts in a period of substantial urbanization.

119

deserts, and seas protected the empire at most points. But the lengthy Rhine/Danube frontier in Germany and central Europe was vulnerable and thus had to be guarded by forts whose relatively small garrisons were not always up to the task of repelling raiders. On more desolate frontiers in Britain and North Africa, the Romans built long walls to keep out the peoples who lived beyond.

Most of Rome's neighbors lacked sufficient technology and military organization to pose a serious threat. The one exception lay on the eastern frontier, where the Parthian kingdom controlled the lands that are today Iran and Iraq (see Chapter 4). Rome and Parthia fought exhaustingly for centuries, with neither side gaining significant territory.

The Roman state prospered for two and a half centuries after Augustus stabilized the political situation and instituted a program of reforms. But in the third century C.E. cracks in the edifice became visible. Historians call the period from 235 to 284 C.E. the **third-century crisis**, a time when political, military, and economic problems nearly destroyed the empire. Rulers changed frequently, as twenty or more men claimed the office of emperor during this period. Most reigned for only a few months or years before being overthrown by a rival or killed by their own troops. Germanic peoples on the Rhine/Danube frontier took advantage of the disorders to raid deep into the empire. For the first time in centuries, Roman cities built protective walls. Some regions, feeling a lack of imperial protection, turned to anyone who promised to put their interests first.

Political and military emergencies devastated the empire's economy. Buying the loyalty of the army and paying to defend the increasingly permeable frontiers drained the treasury. The resultant demands for more tax revenues from the provinces, as well as the interruption of commerce by fighting, eroded urban prosperity. Shortsighted emperors, desperate for cash, secretly reduced the amount of precious metal in Roman coins and pocketed the excess. But the public quickly caught on, and the devalued coinage became less and less acceptable in the marketplace. Indeed, the empire reverted to a barter economy, which curtailed large-scale and long-distance commerce even more.

The municipal aristocracy, once the empire's most vital and public-spirited class, suffered heav-

ily. As town councilors, its members had to make up shortfalls in taxes owed to the state. As the decline in trade eroded their wealth, many evaded their civic duties and even went into hiding. At the same time, population shifted out of the cities and into the countryside, as my people sought employment and protection from both raiders and government officials on the estates of wealthy and powerful country landowners.

Just when things looked bleakest, one man pulled the empire back from the brink. Diocletian, like several other emperors, hailed from one of the eastern European provinces most vulnerable to invasion. Of humble origins, he rose through the ranks of the army and gained power in 284. He was so successful that he ruled for more than twenty years and died in bed.

To halt inflation (the process by which prices rise as money loses value), Diocletian issued an edict specifying the maximum prices for various commodities and services. To ensure an adequate labor supply in vital services, he froze people in their professions and made them train their sons to succeed them. This unprecedented regulation of prices and vocations had unforeseen consequences. A "black market" arose among buyers and sellers who chose to ignore the price controls. More broadly, many imperial citizens began to see the government as an oppressive entity that no longer deserved their loyalty.

When Diocletian resigned in 305, the old divisiveness reemerged as various claimants battled for the throne. The eventual winner was a general named **Constantine** (r. 306–337), who reunited the empire under his sole rule. In 312, Constantine won a key battle at the Milvian Bridge over the Tiber River near Rome. He later claimed that before the battle, he had seen in the sky a cross (the sign of the Christian God) superimposed on the sun. Believing that the Christian God had helped him achieve the victory, Con-

third-century crisis Historians' term for the political, military, and economic turmoil that beset the Roman Empire during much of the third century C.E.: frequent changes of ruler, civil wars, barbarian invasions, decline of urban centers, and near-destruction of long-distance commerce and the monetary economy. After 284 C.E. Diocletian restored order by making fundamental changes.

Constantine Roman emperor (r. 312–337). After reuniting the Roman Empire, he moved the capital to Constantinople and made Christianity a favored religion.

stantine converted to Christianity. Throughout his reign, he supported the Christian church, although he tolerated other beliefs as well. Historians disagree about whether Constantine's conversion resulted from spiritual motives or from a pragmatic desire to unify the empire under a single religion. Regardless of the reason, large numbers of people now converted because they saw that Christians had advantages over non-Christians in seeking offices and favors.

Constantine also transferred the capital in 324 from Rome to Byzantium, an ancient Greek city on the Bosporus (BAHS-puhr-uhs) strait connecting the Mediterranean and the Black Sea. Renamed Constantinople (cahn-stan-tih-NO-pul) ("City of Constantine"), it represented a concentration of attention on the threatened imperial borders in eastern Europe (see Map 5.1). The cities and middle class of the eastern provinces had withstood the third-century crisis better than those in the west. In addition, more educated people and more Christians were living in the east (see Chapter 10).

Some see the conversion of Constantine and the transfer of the imperial capital as events marking the end of Roman history. But many of the important changes that culminated during Constantine's reign had their roots in the previous two centuries, and the Roman Empire as a whole survived for at least another century. Moreover, the eastern, or Byzantine, portion of it (discussed in Chapter 10) survived Constantine by more than a thousand years. Nevertheless, the Roman Empire of the fourth century differed fundamentally from what had existed before, a fact that justifies seeing Constantine's reign as the beginning of a new epoch in the West.

THE ORIGINS OF IMPERIAL CHINA, 221 B.C.E.–220 C.E.

■ *How did imperial China evolve under the Qin and Han dynasties?*

A fragmentation seemingly dictated by geography characterized the early history of China (see Chapter 3). The Shang (ca. 1750–1045 B.C.E.) and Western Zhou (1045–771 B.C.E.) wielded authority over a relatively compact zone in northeastern China. The last few centuries of nominal Zhou rule—the Warring States Period—saw rivalry among a group of small states, a situation reminiscent of the contemporary Greek city-states (see Chapter 4). As in Greece, competition and conflict fostered many elements of a national culture.

In the second half of the third century B.C.E. the Qin (chin) state of the Wei (way) River Valley conquered its rivals and created China's first empire (221–206 B.C.E.). But it barely survived the death of its founder, Shi Huangdi (shih wahng-dee). Power passed to a new dynasty, the Han, which ruled China from 206 B.C.E. to 220 C.E. (see Map 5.2). The imperial tradition of political and cultural unity thus begun lasted into the twentieth century and still has meaning for China today.

Resources and People

China, an imperial state controlling lands of great diversity in topography, climate, plant and animal life, and human population, faced greater obstacles to long-distance communication and a uniform way of life than did the Roman Empire. Rome's territories were roughly similar in climate and agriculture, but Rome benefited from an internal sea—the Mediterranean—that facilitated rapid and inexpensive transport. Different resources, technologies, institutions, and values made the Chinese empire possible.

Agriculture produced the wealth and taxes that supported the institutions of imperial China. The main tax, a percentage of the annual harvest,

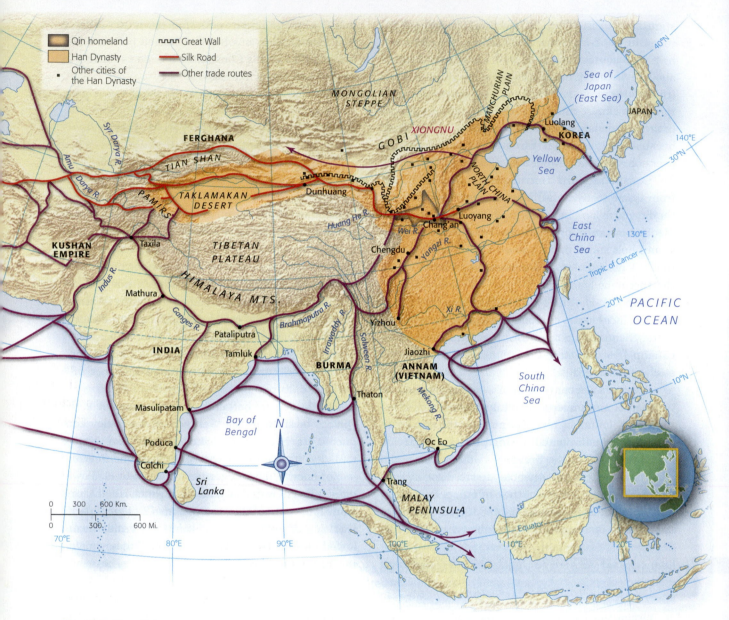

Map 5.2 Han China The Qin and Han rulers of northeast China extended their control over all of eastern China and extensive territories to the west. A series of walls in the north and northwest, built to check the incursions of nomadic peoples from the steppes, were joined together to form the ancestor of the present-day Great Wall of China. An extensive network of roads connecting towns, cities, and frontier forts promoted rapid communication and facilitated trade. The Silk Road carried China's most treasured products to Central, South, and West Asia and the Mediterranean lands.
© Cengage Learning

funded government activities ranging from the luxurious lifestyle of the royal court to the military garrisons on the frontiers. The imperial capitals, first Chang'an (chang-ahn) (modern Xi'an [shee-ahn]), and later Luoyang (LWOE-yang), housed large populations that had to be fed. As intensive agriculture

spread in the Yangzi River Valley, the need to transport southern crops to the north spurred the construction of canals to connect the Yangzi with the Yellow River. The government also stored surplus grain during prosperous times for sale at reasonable prices during shortages.

To assess its labor resources, the government periodically conducted a census. Results survive for the years 2 C.E. and 140 C.E. The earlier survey indicates approximately 12 million households and 60 million people; the later, not quite 10 million households and 49 million people. Then as now, the vast majority of the population lived in the eastern river-valley regions that supported intensive agriculture. By early Han times, the demographic center in the Yellow River Valley and North China Plain had begun to shift south to the Yangzi River Valley.

In the intervals between seasonal agricultural tasks, able-bodied men donated one month of labor to public building projects—palaces, temples, fortifications, and roads—or to transporting goods, excavating and maintaining canals, cultivating imperial estates, or mining. The state also required two years of military service. On the frontiers, conscripted young Chinese men built walls and forts, kept an eye on barbarian neighbors, fought when necessary, and grew crops to support themselves. Registers of land and households enabled imperial officials to keep track of money and services due. Like the Romans, the Chinese governments depended on a large population of free peasants to contribute taxes and services to the state.

Throughout the Han dynasty, the Han Chinese gradually expanded into the territory of other ethnic groups. Population growth in the core regions and a shortage of good lands spurred the pioneers onward. Sometimes the government organized new settlements at strategic sites and on the frontiers. Neighboring kingdoms also invited Chinese settlers so they could exploit their skills and learn their technologies.

Han people preferred regions suitable to the agriculture they had practiced in the eastern river valleys. On the northern frontier, they pushed back nomadic populations. They also expanded into the tropical forests of southern China and settled in the western oases. Places not suitable for their preferred kind of agriculture, particularly the steppe and deserts, did not attract them.

Hierarchy, Obedience, and Belief

The Han Chinese brought with them their social organization, values, language, and other cultural practices. The Chinese family, the basic social unit, included not only the living generation but also the ancestors. The Chinese believed their ancestors maintained an ongoing interest in the fortunes of the family and therefore consulted, appeased, and venerated them to maintain their favor. Viewed as a living, self-renewing organism, the family required sons to perpetuate itself and ensure the immortality offered by the ancestor cult.

The doctrine of Confucius (Kongzi), which had its origins in the sixth century B.C.E. (see Chapter 3), became a fundamental source of values in the imperial period. Confucianism considered hierarchy a natural social phenomenon and assigned tasks and rules of conduct to each person. Absolute authority rested with the father, who presided over the rituals that linked living family members to the ancestors. Each person had a place and responsibilities based on gender, age, and relationship to other family members, and people saw themselves as part of an interdependent unit rather than as individual agents. The same concepts operated in society as a whole. Peasants, soldiers, administrators, and rulers all made distinctive contributions to the welfare of society. Confucianism optimistically maintained that education, imitation of role models, and self-improvement could guide people to the right path. Because the state mirrored the family, the basic family values of loyalty, obedience to authority, respect for elders and ancestors, and concern for honor and appropriate conduct carried over into the relationships between individuals and the state.

Contemporary written sources say little about the experience of women. Confucian ethics stressed the impropriety of women participating in public life. Traditional wisdom about appropriate female conduct appears in a story of the mother of the Confucian philosopher Mencius (Mengzi):

> A woman's duties are to cook the five grains, heat the wine, look after her parents-in-law, make clothes, and that is all! . . . [She] has no ambition to manage affairs outside the house. . . . She must follow the "three submissions." When she is young, she must submit to her parents. After her marriage, she must submit to her husband. When she is widowed, she must submit to her son.[1]

[1] Patricia Buckley Ebrey, ed., *Chinese Civilization and Society: A Sourcebook* (New York: Free Press, 1981), 33–34.

Asian Art & Archaeology, Inc./CORBIS

This ideal, perpetuated by males of the upper classes who composed most of the surviving texts, placed women under considerable pressure to conform. Women of the lower classes, less affected by Confucian ways of thinking, may have been less constrained than their more "privileged" counterparts.

After her parents arranged her marriage, a young bride went to live with her husband's family, who saw her as a stranger until she proved herself. Ability and force of personality (as well as the capacity to produce sons) could make a difference, but dissension between the wife and her mother-in-law and sisters-in-law grew out of their competition for influence with husbands, sons, and brothers and for a larger share of the economic resources held in common by the family.

Like the early Romans, the Chinese believed that divinity resided within nature rather than outside or above it. They worshiped and tried to appease the forces of nature. The state maintained shrines to the lords of rain, winds, and soil, as well as to certain great rivers and high mountains. Gathering at mounds or altars dedicated to local earth spirits, people sacrificed sheep and pigs and beat drums to promote fertility. Unusual natural phenomena like eclipses or heavy rains prompted them to tie a red cord around the sacred spot, symbolically restraining the deity. A belief that supernatural forces, bringing good and evil fortune, flowed through the landscape led experts in *feng shui*, "earth divination," to determine the most favorable location and orientation for buildings and graves. The faithful adapted their lives to the complex rhythms of nature.

Most people believed in ghosts and spirits. Some sought potions that would impart immortality. The desire to cheat death included taking life-enhancing drugs or building ostentatious tombs, flanked by towers or covered by mounds of earth, and filling them with what they believed they would need for a blessed afterlife. The objects in these tombs provide a wealth of knowledge about Han society.

Silk Burial Banner from Mawangdui This banner was placed on the coffin containing the mummified body of Lady Dai, wife of the ruler of a dependent kingdom in southern China, in the mid-second century B.C.E. The lower and upper portions depict the Underworld and Heaven, while the middle register shows the deceased and her family offering sacrifices to help her soul ascend to Heaven.

The First Chinese Empire

From the mid-third century B.C.E., the state of **Qin** began to methodically conquer the other "warring states" of China, and by 221 B.C.E. it had united the northern plain and the Yangzi River Valley under one rule. After defeating the last of his rivals in 221 B.C.E., the ruthless and energetic young king gave himself a title that symbolized the creation of the first Chinese empire—**Shi Huangdi**, or "First Emperor." The name *China* is probably derived from *Qin* (pronounced "chin").

The new regime sought to eliminate rival centers of authority. Its first target was the landowning aristocracy of the conquered states, already weakened by centuries of interstate rivalry. It abolished primogeniture—the right of the eldest son to inherit all the landed property—requiring estates to be broken up and passed on to several heirs. It also weakened the system that created aristocratic wealth by abolishing slavery and establishing a free peasantry. Slaves and peasant serfs, who previously worked the lands for the aristocracy and owed landlords a substantial portion of their harvest, now owed taxes and labor, as well as military service, to the state.

In place of the aristocracy, Shi Huangdi created a centrally controlled administrative structure with district officials who owed their appointments to the king and who were watched over by his agents. The Qin government's commitment to standardization helped create a unified Chinese civilization. A code of law, in force throughout the empire, applied punishments evenhandedly to all members of society. The Qin also imposed standardized weights and measures, a single coinage, a common system of writing, and even a specified axle-length for carts so that they would create a single set of ruts in the road.

Thousands of miles of roads, comparable in scale to the roads of the Roman Empire, connected the parts of the empire and helped move Qin armies quickly. The Qin also built canals to connect the northern and southern river systems, at first for military purposes but eventually for transporting commercial goods as well. The 20-mile-long (32.2-kilometer-long) Magic Canal, which ingeniously linked two rivers that flowed in opposite directions with strong currents, is still in use. The frontier walls of the old states were gradually combined into a continuous barricade, the precursor of the Great Wall, which protected cultivated lands from raids by northern steppe nomads (see Chapter 3), although a recent study suggests that its primary function was to take in newly captured territory where large numbers of Chinese peasants could be dispatched and ordered to begin cultivation.[2]

Mobilizing manpower for irrigation and flood control, military service, road and wall construction, and the building of a monumental tomb for the ruler taught the king's administrators organizational skills and strengthened their hand against the nobles. But such projects also required that the Qin government relocate large numbers of people and institute an oppressive program of forced labor and military service.

Li Si (luh suh), the prime minister, persuaded Shi Huangdi that Confucian scholars were subverting the goals of the regime with appeals to the past that demanded benevolent and nonviolent conduct from rulers. A crackdown ensued in which Confucian books were burned and scholars brutally executed. The Qin ruler favored instead a philosophy known as Legalism (see Chapter 3), a system of discipline and obedience maintained through the rigid application of rewards and punishments. Its major proponent, Li Si himself, considered the will of the ruler supreme.

The recent discovery of a manual of Qin laws used by an administrator, with prescriptions less extreme than expected, suggests that the sins of the Qin may have been exaggerated by later sources. Nevertheless, rebellions ended the dynasty after the death of Shi Huangdi and attest to both the resentment of the aristocracy and the anger of the commoners. The regime

[2] Nicola Di Cosmo, *Ancient China and Its Enemies: The Rise of Nomadic Power in East Asian History* (Cambridge: Cambridge University Press, 2002), 155–158.

Qin A people and state in the Wei River Valley of eastern China that conquered rival states and created the first Chinese empire (221–206 B.C.E.). The Qin ruler, Shi Huangdi, standardized many features of Chinese society and ruthlessly marshaled subjects for military and construction projects, engendering hostility that led to the fall of his dynasty shortly after his death. The Qin framework was largely taken over by the succeeding Han dynasty.

Shi Huangdi Founder of the short-lived Qin dynasty and creator of the Chinese Empire (r. 221–210 B.C.E.). He is remembered for his ruthless conquests of rival states, standardization of practices, and forcible organization of labor for military and engineering tasks. His tomb, with its army of life-size terracotta soldiers, has been partially excavated.

Digital Vision/Getty Images

Terracotta Soldiers from the Tomb of Shi Huangdi, "First Emperor" of China, Late Third Century B.C.E. Near the monumental tomb that he built for himself, the First Emperor filled a huge underground chamber with more than seven thousand life-size baked-clay statues of soldiers. The terra-cotta army was unearthed in the 1970s.

had lasted only fifteen years, but the achievements of the Qin—the unification of China and the creation of a Chinese style of civilization—would endure.

The Long Reign of the Han

When the dust cleared, Liu Bang (le-oo bahng), possibly a peasant by background, established a new dynasty, the **Han** (206 B.C.E.–220 C.E.). Rejecting the excesses and mistakes of the Qin, he restored the institutions of a venerable past. Though he retained much of the administrative structure and Legalist ideology put in place by the Qin, he also revised Confucianism to address the circumstances of a large, centralized political entity and to temper the Qin Legalist methods. This Confucianism emphasized the benevolence of government and the appropriateness of particular rituals and behaviors in a manifestly hierarchical society. The Han administration became the standard for later ages, and the Chinese people today refer to themselves ethnically as Han.

As in the Zhou monarchy (see Chapter 3), people thought that the emperor, the "Son of Heaven," enjoyed the Mandate of Heaven, wielding authority like a father in a family and linking the living generations with the ancestors. The emperor brought the support of the powerful imperial ancestors and guaranteed the harmonious interactions of Heaven and earth. More than his Roman counterpart, he was regarded as a divinity on earth. His word was law. Failure to govern well, however, could lose him the backing of Heaven. Given the belief that events in Heaven, the natural world, and human society corresponded, floods, droughts, and earthquakes could be seen as both the consequences and symptoms of an ethical failure and mismanagement. Natural disasters, and

> **Han** A term used to designate (1) the ethnic Chinese people who originated in the Yellow River Valley and spread throughout regions of China suitable for agriculture and (2) the dynasty of emperors who ruled from 206 B.C.E. to 220 C.E.

the misery that ensued, could spawn revolution. If the revolution was successful, Heaven was seen to have withdrawn its support from an unworthy ruler.

After eighty years of imperial consolidation, Emperor Wu (r. 140–87 B.C.E.) launched a period of military expansion south into Fujian, Guangdong, and present-day North Vietnam, north into Manchuria and present-day North Korea, and west into Inner Mongolia and Xinjiang (SHIN-jyahng). Extending his control into the northwest, Emperor Wu laid the foundations for the so-called Silk Road (see Chapter 8), the series of trade routes that connected China, via Inner and Central Asia, to India, the Middle East, and the Mediterranean. As the name suggests, silk was the most important trade commodity linking the peoples of the Eastern Hemisphere. A Chinese text claims that Emperor Wu sent agents to the "Southern Sea," which may refer to India or Southeast Asia, to acquire prized Roman glass, indicating the reach of China in maritime trade routes as well as the overland Silk Road. However, controlling the routes and territories proved expensive, so Wu's successors curtailed further expansion.

The Han Empire endured, with a brief interruption, for more than four hundred years. People lived in various milieus—cities, rural villages and farms, or military camps on the frontiers. **Chang'an**, in the Wei River Valley, the strategic region from which the Zhou and Qin dynasties had emerged, served as the capital from 200 B.C.E. to 25 C.E.—the period of the Early, or Western, Han. From 25 to 220 C.E., the Later, or Eastern, Han established its base in the more centrally located Luoyang.

Protected by a ring of hills but with ready access to the fertile plain, Chang'an was surrounded by a wall of pounded earth and brick 15 miles (24 kilometers) in circumference. In 2 C.E. its population was 246,000. Contemporaries described it as a bustling place, filled with courtiers, officials, soldiers, merchants, craftsmen, and foreign visitors. Broad thoroughfares running north and south intersected with others running east and west. High walls protected and restricted access to the imperial palaces, administrative offices, barracks, and storehouses. Temples and marketplaces were scattered about the civic center. Chang'an became a model of urban planning, its main features imitated in cities and towns throughout China (it is estimated that between 10 and 30 percent of the population lived in urban centers).

Han literature describes the appearance of the capitals and the activities taking place in the palace complexes, public areas, and residential streets. Moralizing writers criticized the excesses of the elite. Living in multistory houses, wearing fine silks, traveling in ornate horse-drawn carriages, well-to-do officials and merchants devoted their leisure time to art and literature, occult religious practices, elegant banquets, and various entertainments—music and dance, juggling and acrobatics, dog and horse races, and cock and tiger fights. In stark contrast, the common people inhabited a sprawling warren of alleys, living in dwellings packed "as closely as the teeth of a comb."

Secluded within the palace compound, surrounded by his many wives and children, servants, courtiers, and officials, the emperor presided over an unceasing round of pomp and ritual emphasizing the worship of Heaven and imperial ancestors, as well as the practical business of government. When the emperor died, his chief widow chose his heir from the male members of the ruling clan, thus making the royal compound a hive of intrigue.

A prime minister, a civil service director, and nine ministers charged with military, economic, legal, and religious responsibilities ran the central government. As in imperial Rome, Han officials depended on local officials for the day-to-day administration of the vast empire, allying themselves with the **gentry**, a class just below the aristocracy of moderately prosperous landowners. They were usually men with education and expertise, resembling the Roman *equites* favored by Augustus. Wealthy merchant families, however, were viewed with suspicion and accused of greedily driving up prices and living off the work of others. During hard times, advisers to the emperors

Chang'an City in the Wei River Valley in eastern China. It became the capital of the early Han Empire. Its main features were imitated in the cities and towns that sprang up throughout the Han Empire.

gentry In China, the class of prosperous families, next in wealth below the rural aristocrats, from which the emperors drew their administrative personnel. Respected for their education and expertise, these officials became a privileged group and made the government more efficient and responsive than in the past.

blamed merchants for China's economic ills and proposed banning them and their children from holding government posts.

The new gentry class, with imperial support, adopted a version of Confucianism that provided a system for training officials to be intellectually capable and morally worthy of their roles and set forth a code of conduct for measuring their performance. Chinese tradition speaks of an imperial university located outside Chang'an and said to have thirty thousand students, as well as provincial centers of learning. From these centers, students entered government service. Exempt from taxes and compulsory military or labor services, they led comfortable lives by the standards of the time. While the granting of government jobs on the basis of performance on the exams theoretically should have given everyone an equal chance, in reality the sons of the gentry had distinct advantages because they received better training in Confucian classics. The Han period was rich in intellectual developments, thanks to the relative prosperity of the era, the growth of urban centers, and state support of scholars. Gradually, the gentry became a new aristocracy of sorts, and scholar-officials became a self-perpetuating, privileged class.

Daoism, which originated in the Warring States Period (see Chapter 3), took deeper root among the common people in the Han period. With its emphasis on the *Dao*, or "path," of nature, its valuing of harmony with the cycles and patterns of the natural world, and its search for enlightenment through solitary contemplation and physical and mental discipline rather than education, Daoism called into question age-old beliefs and values and rejected the hierarchy and rules of Confucianism. It urged passive acceptance of the disorder of the world, denial of ambition, contentment with simple pleasures, and trust in one's own instincts.

Technology and Trade

Chinese tradition, which seems to recognize the importance of technology for the success and spread of Chinese civilization, credits the legendary first five emperors with the introduction of major new technologies.

The advent of bronze tools around 1500 B.C.E. helped open land for agriculture on the North China Plain. A millennium later, iron arrived, and the Chinese took full advantage of this technology. Chinese metalworkers used more advanced techniques than metalworkers elsewhere in the world. Whereas Roman blacksmiths produced wrought-iron tools and weapons by hammering heated iron, the Chinese mastered the technique of liquefying iron and pouring it into molds. The resulting cast-iron and steel tools and weapons had higher carbon content and were harder and more durable.

In the succeeding centuries, improvements in crossbows and cavalry helped the Chinese military to beat off the attacks of nomads (see Chapter 3). The watermill, which harnessed the power of running water to turn a grindstone, appeared in China long before it did in Europe. The horse collar and breast strap harnessing, which did not constrict the horse's breathing, also allowed horses in China to pull heavier loads than European horses could.

The Han rulers continued the Qin road-building program. Besides using the roads to move troops and supplies, the government created a network of official couriers—a postal service—using horses, boats, and even footpaths, with food and shelter provided at relay stations. Canal construction also continued, and river navigation improved.

Silk dominated China's export trade. Silk cocoons are secreted into the leaves of mulberry trees by silkworms. The Chinese understood this and kept it a closely guarded secret, which gave them a monopoly on the manufacture of silk. Carried through the Central Asian oases to the Middle East, India, and the Mediterranean, and passing through the hands of middlemen who added their own fees to the price, this beautiful textile may have increased in value a hundred-fold by the end of its journey. Controlling the Silk Road and its profits justified periodic military campaigns into Inner Asia and the installation there of garrisons and Chinese colonies (see Chapter 8).

The Decline of the Han Empire

For the Han, as for the Romans, maintaining frontier security, particularly in the north and northwest, posed a serious challenge. In the end, non-Chinese people raiding across the frontier or moving into imperial territory proved a major factor in bringing the empire down.

Gold Belt Buckle, Xiongnu, Second Century B.C.E. The Xiongnu, herders in the lands north of China, shared the artistic conventions of nomadic peoples across the steppes of Asia and eastern Europe, such as this fluid, twisting representation of the animals on which they depended for their livelihood. Shi Huangdi's military incursion into their pasturelands in the late third century B.C.E. catalyzed the formation of the Xiongnu Confederacy, whose horse-riding warriors challenged the Chinese for centuries. The Metropolitan Museum of Art. Image source/Art Resource, NY

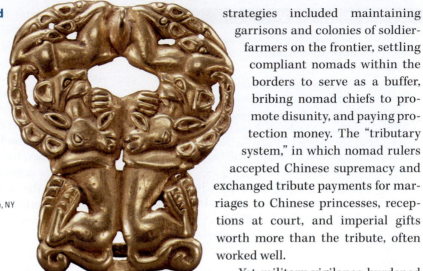

strategies included maintaining garrisons and colonies of soldier-farmers on the frontier, settling compliant nomads within the borders to serve as a buffer, bribing nomad chiefs to promote disunity, and paying protection money. The "tributary system," in which nomad rulers accepted Chinese supremacy and exchanged tribute payments for marriages to Chinese princesses, receptions at court, and imperial gifts worth more than the tribute, often worked well.

Yet military vigilance burdened Han finances and made the economic troubles of later Han times worse. Despite attempts at major reforms to address economic problems, including giving surplus land to landless peasants, some members of the Han family and other elements of the elite resisted their loss of status and property, and the imperial court was weakened. By the end of the first century B.C.E. nobles and successful merchants again acquired control of huge estates, and many peasants sought their protection against the exactions of the imperial government. The Han government was forced to give up conscription, and instead had to pay foreign soldiers and officers—who were not always loyal—to defend its borders. This trend spread over the next two centuries. Poems in the first century C.E. complain of corrupt officials, unchecked attacks by barbarians, uprisings of desperate and hungry peasants, the spread of banditry, widespread poverty, and despair. The dynasty survived till 220 C.E., when the Han king was forced to abdicate, and China entered a period of political fragmentation and economic and cultural regression that lasted until the rise of the Sui (sway) and Tang (thang) dynasties in the late sixth and seventh centuries C.E., a story that we take up in Chapter 11.

Pastoralists and farmers had always exchanged goods on the frontier, but the different ways of life of farmers, who usually accepted Han rule, and herders who preferred their own kings, gave rise to conflict (see Chapter 3). Sometimes herders resorted to raiding agricultural communities, and for centuries the Chinese kingdoms struggled with these tough, horse-riding warriors, building long walls along the frontier to keep them away from vulnerable farmlands. Shortly before the Qin unification of China, several states had begun to train soldiers on horseback to contend with the mobile nomads.

Shi Huangdi sent a large force to drive the nomads far north. His generals succeeded momentarily, extending Chinese territory beyond the great northern loop of the Yellow River. But Shi Huangdi's attack on the nomads had an unanticipated consequence. The threat to their way of life created by the Chinese invasion drove the normally fragmented and quarreling nomad groups to unite in a great confederacy. In the Han period, this **Xiongnu** (SHE-OONG-noo) Confederacy of Turkic peoples threatened the empire. Frequent wars cost lives and resources and gave rise to insulting stereotypes on both sides. The settled Chinese thought of nomads as "barbarians"—rough and uncivilized—much as the Romans viewed the Germanic peoples on their own frontiers.

Access to good horses and pastureland became a state priority in the war against the Xiongnu. Other

Xiongnu A confederation of nomadic peoples living beyond the northwest frontier of ancient China. Chinese rulers tried a variety of defenses and stratagems to ward off these "barbarians," as they called them, and finally succeeded in dispersing the Xiongnu in the first century C.E.

SECTION REVIEW

- Imperial China rested on a foundation of agriculture, and periodic censuses ensured a ready supply of labor for public works.

- The extended family was the basic social unit, and Confucianism provided the value system.

- The Qin established the first empire and a unified Chinese civilization, subordinating the individual to the state to standardize everything from laws to writing—a standardization that contributed to the accomplishment of massive public works.

- Under the Han dynasty, the empire grew, the Confucian scholar-official rose to prominence, and Daoism gained more popularity with common people.

- The Qin and Han periods saw technological advancement, steady urbanization, and expansion of the silk trade.

- The burden of defense against nomadic invaders weakened the empire, which collapsed because of several factors, ushering in a period of fragmentation.

CONCLUSION

Agriculture was the fundamental economic activity and source of government revenues in both Roman and Chinese civilization. Both empires depended initially on a free peasantry—sturdy farmers who could be pressed into military service or other forms of compulsory labor. Conflicts over who owned the land and how it was used caused political and social turmoil in both places. Roman and Chinese autocratic rulers secured their positions by breaking the power of old aristocratic families, seizing their excess land, and giving it to small farmers and to themselves. Later, when wealthy noblemen again gained control of vast estates worked by dependent tenant farmers, the authority of the state eroded.

From ethnically homogeneous cores, both empires spread into territories with diverse ecosystems, populations, and ways of life. The cultural unity that resulted has persisted, at least in part, to the present day. Military conquest paved the way, but Italian and Han settlers, outstripping the resources of their core areas, moved into new regions, bringing their languages, beliefs, customs, and technologies. Conquered peoples were also attracted to the culture and success of the ruler nation. To administer far-flung territories and large populations, both empires delegated considerable autonomy to local officials based in the cities and towns. Administrators were drawn from educated and capable members of a prosperous middle class.

Roads built to expedite the movement of troops became the highways of commerce and culture. Urban networks provided local administrative bases, furthering commerce and radiating imperial culture to the countryside. While a large majority of the population lived in the country, city dwellers enjoyed the advantages of empire. Rome and Chang'an provided models for outlying cities. Travelers could find in outlying regions the same types and styles of buildings and public spaces that they knew from the capital.

Similar problems of defense—long borders located far from the capital and aggressive neighbors—prompted both empires to build walls and chains of forts to protect against incursions. Frontier defense was so costly that it eventually eroded both empires' prosperity. As governments demanded more taxes and services from the civilian population, they lost the loyalty of the people, many of whom sought protection on the estates of powerful landowners. The Roman and Han governments eventually came to rely on soldiers hired from the same "barbarian" peoples confronting them on the frontiers. As the empires became weaker, the borders were overrun and the central governments collapsed. Ironically, the triumphant immigrant groups respected the imperial culture so deeply that they strove to maintain it once they were in power.

Though the empires failed in similar fashion, the long-term consequences differed. In China the imperial model revived in subsequent eras, but the lands of the Roman Empire never reunified. One reason is that the two cultures had different attitudes toward the individual and the state. In China individuals were deeply embedded in families with precisely defined hierarchies, unquestioning obedience, and solemn rituals of deference to elders and ancestors. Respect for authority was deep-seated. Confucianism, which sanctified family hierarchy and provided a code of conduct for public officials, preceded the imperial system. The cultural base could adapt with little change to diverse political circumstances. The Roman family also respected hierarchy and obedience, but it was not the organizational model of the Roman state. Confucianism had no Roman equivalent to orient society when the state collapsed.

Moreover, opportunities for economic and social mobility were greater in the Roman Empire than in ancient China. Whereas the merchant class in China was frequently disparaged and constrained by the government, the absence of government interference in the Roman Empire resulted in greater economic mobility and a thriving and influential middle class in the towns and cities. The Roman army also differed from the Chinese, the former being composed of professional soldiers who increasingly gained privileges and took part in political conflict, and the latter relying on draftees who served for two years and remained on the margins of power struggles.

Although Roman emperors tried to create an ideology to bolster their position, Republican traditions and Christianity's insistence on monotheism negated the Roman emperor's pretensions to divinity. The dynastic principle never took root, and the cult of the emperor had little spiritual content. Thus, in the lands that had once constituted the western part of the Roman Empire, there was no compelling basis for reviving the position of emperor and the territorial claims of empire in later ages. In contrast, the Chinese believed that the emperor was the divine Son of Heaven and drew authority from the power of the royal ancestors.

CHAPTER REVIEW

ROME'S CREATION OF A MEDITERRANEAN EMPIRE, 753 B.C.E.–330 C.E.

■ *How did Rome create and maintain its vast Mediterranean empire?* (page 107)

The Romans were successful empire builders because of their superior military organization and training and a series of very capable generals. They co-opted the ruling elites and brought peace and prosperity to the peoples of the lands they annexed. Yet Rome's military success led to social and economic disruption and acute political struggles. Out of this crisis emerged the Principate, which persevered for several centuries. The emperors developed more effective administrative techniques, and local elites embraced Roman culture.

THE ORIGINS OF IMPERIAL CHINA, 221 B.C.E.–220 C.E.

■ *How did imperial China evolve under the Qin and Han dynasties?* (page 121)

In China, the "First Emperor" established the Qin Empire and put key elements of a unified Chinese civilization in place. The preceding Shang and Zhou states, though not empires, had controlled the North China Plain and developed the concept of the Mandate of Heaven, a claim to divine backing for the ruler as the Son of Heaven. Furthermore, the Legalist political philosophy justified authoritarian measures. But the harshness of the new order generated resistance that soon brought down the Qin, and its Han successors built a durable imperial regime on a moderated version of Qin structures that incorporated Confucian principles.

Key Terms

Roman Republic (p. 109)

Roman Senate (p. 109)

patron/client relationship (p. 109)

Roman Principate (p. 112)

Augustus (p. 112)

equites (p. 112)

pax Romana (p. 117)

Romanization (p. 117)

Jesus (p. 118)

Paul (p. 118)

aqueduct (p. 119)

third-century crisis (p. 120)

Constantine (p. 120)

Qin (p. 125)

Shi Huangdi (p. 125)

Han (p. 126)

Chang'an (p. 127)

gentry (p. 127)

Xiongnu (p. 129)

India and Southeast Asia

© Cengage Learning

In the Bhagavad-Gita (BUH-guh-vahd GEE-tuh), the most renowned Indian sacred text, the legendary warrior Arjuna (AHR-joo-nuh) rides out in his chariot to the open space between two armies preparing for battle. Torn between his social duty to fight for his family's claim to the throne and his conscience, which balks at the prospect of killing relatives, friends, and former teachers in the enemy camp, Arjuna slumps down in his chariot and refuses to fight. But his driver, the god Krishna (KRISH-nuh) in disguise, persuades him, in a carefully structured dialogue, both of the necessity to fulfill his duty as a warrior and of the proper frame of mind for performing these acts. In the climactic moment of the dialogue Krishna endows Arjuna with a "divine eye" and permits him to see the true appearance of God:

> It was a multiform, wondrous vision,
> with countless mouths and eyes
> and celestial ornaments,
> Everywhere was boundless divinity
> containing all astonishing things,
> wearing divine garlands and garments,
> anointed with divine perfume.
> If the light of a thousand suns
> were to rise in the sky at once,
> it would be like the light
> of that great spirit.
> Arjuna saw all the universe
> in its many ways and parts,
> standing as one in the body
> of the god of gods.[1]

In all of world literature, this is one of the most compelling attempts to depict the nature of deity. Graphic images emphasize the vastness, diversity, and multiplicity of the god, but in the end we learn that Krishna is the organizing principle behind all creation, that behind diversity and multiplicity lies a higher unity.

This is an apt metaphor for Indian civilization. The enormous variety of the Indian landscape is mirrored in the patchwork of ethnic and linguistic groups that occupy it, the political fragmentation that has marked most of Indian history, the elaborate hierarchy of social groups into which the Indian population is divided, and the thousands of deities who are worshiped at innumerable holy places that dot the subcontinent. Yet, in the end, one can speak of an Indian civilization united by shared views and values.

This chapter surveys the history of South and Southeast Asia from approximately 1500 B.C.E. to 1025 C.E., highlighting the evolution of features that define Indian civilization. Considerable attention is given to Indian religious conceptions, due both to religion's profound role in shaping Indian society and the sources of information available to historians. For reasons that will be explained below, writing came late to India, and ancient Indians did not develop the same kind of historical consciousness as other peoples of antiquity and took little interest in recording specific historical events.

THE INDUS VALLEY CIVILIZATION

■ *What does material evidence tell us about the Indus Valley civilization and the most likely reason for its collapse?*

Civilization developed almost as early in South Asia as in Mesopotamia and Egypt (see Chapter 2). Just as each Middle Eastern civilization centered on a great river valley, so civilization in the Indian subcontinent originated on the fertile floodplain of the Indus River, where farming created the food surplus essential to urbanized society.

Natural Environment

A plain of more than 1 million acres (400,000 hectares) stretches between the mountains of western Pakistan and the Thar (tahr) Desert to the east in Sind (sinned), the central portion of the Indus Valley (see Map 6.1). Silt carried downstream and deposited on the land by the Indus River over many centuries has elevated the riverbed and its banks above the level of the plain. Twice a year, the river overflows and inundates surrounding land as far as 10 miles (16 kilometers) distant. Snowmelt from the Pamir (pah-MEER) and Himalaya (him-uh-LAY-uh) Mountains

---

[1] Barbara Stoler Miller, *The Bhagavad-Gita: Krishna's Counsel in Time of War* (New York: Bantam, 1986), 98–99.

feeds the floods in March and April. In August, the monsoons bring rains from the southwest that cause a second flood. Though extremely dry for the rest of the year, Sind's floods make two crops a year possible. In ancient times, the Hakra (HAK-ruh) River (sometimes referred to as the Saraswati), which has since dried up, ran parallel to the Indus about 25 miles (40 kilometers) to the east and supplied water to a second cultivable area.

Adjacent regions shared distinctive cultural traits with this core area. In Punjab (literally "five waters"), to the northeast, five rivers converge to form the main course of the Indus. Closer to the northern mountains, the Punjab receives more rainfall but less floodwater than Sind. Culturally similar settlements extend from the Punjab as far east as Delhi (DEL-ee) in northwest India. Settlement also extended south through the Indus delta in southern Sind down into India's hook-shaped Kathiawar (kah-tee-uh-WAHR) Peninsula, an area of alluvial plains and coastal marshes. The Indus Valley civilization, as scholars labeled this area of cultural homogeneity when they first discovered it ninety years ago, covered an area roughly equivalent to modern France.

Material Culture   Although archaeologists have located several hundred communities that flourished from approximately 2600 to 1900 B.C.E., the remains of two urban sites known by the modern names **Harappa** and **Mohenjo-Daro** (moe-hen-joe–DAHR-oh) best typify the Indus Valley civilization. Unfortunately, the high water table at these sites makes excavation of the earliest levels of settlement nearly impossible.

Scholars once believed that the people who created this civilization spoke Dravidian (dru-VID-ee-uhn) languages related to those spoken today in southern India. Invaders from the northwest speaking Indo-European languages, they thought, conquered these people around 1500 B.C.E., causing some of them to migrate to the southeast. Skeletal evidence, however, indicates that the population of the Indus Valley has remained stable from ancient ties to the present. Settled agriculture in this region seems to date back to at least 5000 B.C.E.

The writing system of the Indus Valley people contained more than four hundred signs to represent syllables and words. Archeologists have recovered thousands of inscribed seal stones and copper tablets. The inscriptions are so brief, however, that no one has yet deciphered them, though some scholars believe they represent an early Dravidian language.

Harappa, 3.5 miles (5.6 kilometers) in circumference, may have housed a population of 35,000, and Mohenjo-Daro several times that. These cities show marked similarities in planning and construction: high, thick, encircling walls of brick; streets laid out in a rectangular grid; and covered drainpipes that carried away waste. The consistent width of streets and length of city blocks, and the uniformity of the mud bricks used in construction, suggest a strong central authority, located possibly in the citadel—an elevated, enclosed compound containing large buildings. Scholars think the well-ventilated structures near the citadel stored grain for use and for export. The presence of barracks may point to some regimentation of skilled artisans.

Though it is presumed that these urban centers controlled the surrounding farmlands, different centers may have served different functions, which might account for their locations. Mohenjo-Daro seems to dominate the great floodplain of the Indus. Harappa, which is nearly 500 miles (800 kilometers) to the north, sits in the zone where farmlands give way to pasturelands. No settlements have been found west of Harappa, which may have served as a gateway for copper, tin, precious stones, and other resources from the northwest. Coastal towns in the south engaged in seaborne trade with the Persian Gulf, as well as in fishing and gathering highly prized seashells. Although published accounts of the Indus Valley civilizations tend to treat Mohenjo-Daro and Harappa, the most extensively excavated sites, as the norm, most people surely lived in smaller settlements, which exhibit the same artifacts and the same standardization of styles and shapes as the large cities.

Harappa *Site of one of the great cities of the Indus Valley civilization of the third millennium B.C.E. It was located on the northwest frontier of the zone of cultivation (in modern Pakistan).*

Mohenjo-Daro *Largest of the cities of the Indus Valley civilization, centrally located in the extensive floodplain of the Indus River in contemporary Pakistan.*

Chronology

	India	Southeast Asia
3000 B.C.E.	2600 B.C.E. Beginning of Indus Valley civilization 1900 B.C.E. End of Indus Valley civilization	3000 B.C.E. Malay peoples begin migrating from southern China into mainland Southeast Asia
1500 B.C.E.	ca. 1500 B.C.E. Migration of Indo-European peoples into northwest India	Before 1000 B.C.E. Beginning of migrations from mainland Southeast Asia to islands in Pacific and Indian Oceans
1000 B.C.E.	ca. 1000 B.C.E. Indo-Europeans settle the Ganges Plain	
500 B.C.E.	ca. 500 B.C.E. Beginnings of Buddhism and Jainism 300 B.C.E. Tamil kingdoms 324 B.C.E. Mauryan Empire founded	
1 C.E.	320 C.E. Gupta Empire founded	ca. 50–560 C.E. Funan dominates southern Indochina and the Isthmus of Kra
500 C.E.	606–647 C.E. Reign of Harsha Vardhana	ca. 500 C.E. Trade route develops through Strait of Malacca 683 C.E. Rise of Srivijaya in Sumatra 770–825 C.E. Construction of Borobodur in Java
1000 C.E.		1025 C.E. Decline of Srivijaya

Metal appears more frequently in Indus Valley sites than in Mesopotamia and Egypt. Tools and other useful objects outweigh in importance the decorative objects—jewelry and the like—so often found in those other regions. Whereas metal goods were largely the possessions of elite in the Middle East, in the Indus Valley they belonged to a broad cross-section of the population.

Technologically, the Indus Valley people showed skill in irrigation, used the potter's wheel, and fired bricks in kilns for use in the foundations of large public buildings (sun-dried bricks exposed to floodwaters would have dissolved quickly). Smiths worked with various metals—gold, silver, copper, and tin. The varying ratios of tin to copper in their bronze objects suggest awareness of the hardness of different mixtures. They used less tin, a relatively scarce metal, in objects that did not require maximum hardness, like knives, and more tin in things like axes that had to be harder.

Archaeological finds point to widespread trading contacts. Mountain passes through the northwest granted access to the valuable resources of eastern Iran and Afghanistan, as well as to ore deposits in western India. These resources included metals (such as copper and tin), precious stones (lapis lazuli, jade, and turquoise), building stone, and timber. Rivers provided thoroughfares for transporting goods within the zone of Indus Valley culture.

Inhabitants of the Indus Valley and of Mesopotamia obtained raw materials from some of the same sources. The discovery of Indus Valley seal stones in the Tigris-Euphrates Valley indicates that merchants from the former region may have acted as middlemen in long-distance trade, obtaining raw materials from the northwest and shipping them to the Persian Gulf.

We know little about the political, social, economic, and religious structures of Indus Valley society. Efforts to link artifacts and images to cultural features characteristic of later periods of Indian history, including a sociopolitical institution (a system of hereditary occupational groups, the predominant role of priests), architectural forms (bathing tanks like those later found in Hindu temples, private interior courtyards in houses), and religious beliefs and practices (depictions of gods and sacred animals on seal stones, a cult of the mother-goddess), remain speculative. Further knowledge on these matters awaits additional archaeological finds and the deciphering of the Indus Valley script.

Transformation of the Indus Valley Civilization

The Indus Valley cities were abandoned sometime after 1900 B.C.E. Archaeologists once thought that invaders destroyed them, but they now believe this civilization suffered "systems failure"—a breakdown of the fragile interrelationship of political, social, and economic systems that sustained order and prosperity. The precipitating cause may have been one or more natural disasters, such as an earthquake or massive flooding. Gradual ecological changes may also have played a role as the Hakra river system dried up and salinization (an increase in the amount of salt in the soil, inhibiting plant growth) and erosion increased.

Towns left dry by a change of riverbed, seaports removed from the coast by silt deposited in deltas, and regions suffering loss of fertile soil would have necessitated the relocation of populations and a change in the livelihood of those who remained. The causes, patterns, and pace of change probably varied, with urbanization persisting longer in some areas. The urban centers eventually succumbed, however, and village-based farming and herding took their place. As the interaction between regions lessened, regional variation replaced the standardization of technology and style of the previous era.

Historians can do little more than speculate about the causes behind the changes and the experiences of the people who lived in the Indus Valley around 1900 B.C.E. Two tendencies bear remembering, however. In most cases like this, the majority of the population adjusts to the new circumstances. But members of the political and social elite, who depend on the urban centers and complex political and economic structures, lose the source of their authority and merge with the population as a whole.

FOUNDATIONS OF INDIAN CIVILIZATION

■ *What historical forces led to the development of complex social groupings in ancient India?*

India is called a *subcontinent* because it is a large—roughly 2,000 miles (3,200 kilometers) in both length and breadth—and physically isolated landmass within the continent of Asia. The Himalayas (him-AH-lay-uhs), the world's highest mountains, form a barrier to the north; the Indian Ocean bounds it on the east, south, and west (see Map 6.1). The one frontier easily accessible to invaders and migrating peoples lies to the northwest. But people using this corridor must cross over the mountain barrier of the Hindu Kush (HIHN-doo KOOSH) in Afghanistan and the Thar (tahr) Desert east of the Indus River.

The Indian Subcontinent

This region divides into three topographical zones. The mountainous northern zone takes in the heavily forested foothills and high meadows on the edge of the Hindu Kush and Himalaya ranges. Next come the great basins of the Indus and Ganges (GAHN-jeez) Rivers. Originating in the Himalayas, these rivers flood annually, leaving layers of silt that over time have created large fertile plains. The Vindhya range and the Deccan (de-KAN), an arid, rocky plateau reminiscent of the American Southwest, separate northern India from the third zone, the peninsula proper. The Malabar Coast in the west, the Coromandel Coast in the east with its web of rivers descending from the Deccan, the flatlands of Tamil Nadu on the southern tip of the peninsula, and the island of Sri Lanka often have followed paths of political and cultural development separate from those of northern India.

SECTION REVIEW

- As in Mesopotamia and Egypt, and roughly in the same time period, the wide, fertile Indus Valley supported a large urban civilization.

- Cities like Harappa and Mohenjo-Daro and their artifacts display uniformity of planning and construction and standardization of styles and shapes.

- The Indus Valley people developed sophisticated technologies, including a still-undecipherable writing system.

- Cities exchanged goods with each other and maintained extensive trade contacts with other ancient civilizations.

- The Indus Valley civilization collapsed when the cities were abandoned, probably as a result of natural disasters or environmental changes.

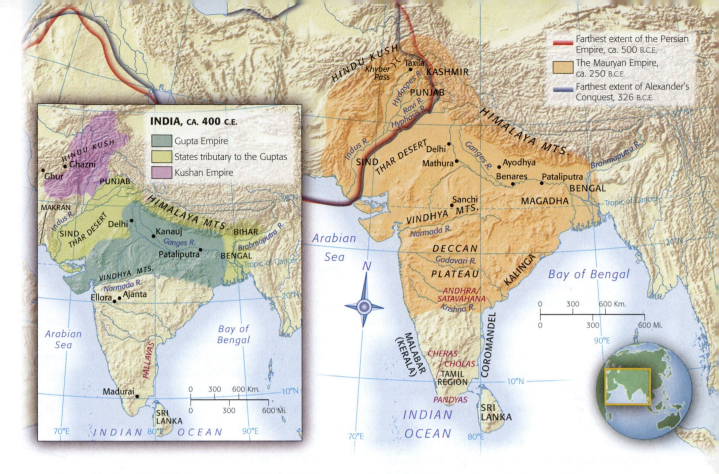

Map 6.1 **Ancient India** Mountains and ocean largely separate the Indian subcontinent from the rest of Asia. Migrations and invasions usually came through the Khyber Pass in the northwest. Seaborne commerce with western Asia, Southeast Asia, and East Asia often flourished. Peoples speaking Indo-European languages migrated into the broad valleys of the Indus and Ganges Rivers in the north. Dravidian-speaking peoples remained the dominant population in the south. The diversity of the Indian landscape, the multiplicity of ethnic groups, and the primary identification of people with their class and caste lie behind the division into many small states that has characterized much of Indian political history.

© Cengage Learning

The mountainous northern rim shelters the subcontinent from cold Siberian winds and gives it a subtropical climate. The **monsoon** (seasonal wind) comes annually when the Indian Ocean lags behind the Asian landmass in heating and cooling with the changing seasons. The temperature difference between water and land acts like a bellows, producing a great wind over the ocean. The southwest monsoon begins in June off the coast of East Africa, picks up moisture from the Indian Ocean, and delivers heavy precipitation to the Ganges Basin and the rainforest belt on India's western coast. The moist, flat Ganges Delta (modern Bengal) favors rice production. Elsewhere, wheat, barley, and millet predominate. Indus Valley farmers, in contrast, see little precipitation and therefore rely on extensive irrigation.

Indian Ocean mariners learned to ride the monsoon winds across open waters from northeast to southwest in January and to make the return voyage in July. Ships ventured across the Arabian Sea to the Persian Gulf, the southern coast of Arabia, and East Africa, and east across the Bay of Bengal to Indochina and Indonesia (see Chapter 8).

monsoon Seasonal winds in the Indian Ocean caused by the differences in temperature between the rapidly heating and cooling landmasses of Africa and Asia and the slowly changing ocean waters. These strong and predictable winds have long been ridden across the open sea by sailors, and the large amounts of rainfall that they deposit on parts of India, Southeast Asia, and China allow for the cultivation of several crops a year.

The Vedic Age, 1500–500 B.C.E.

Many features of later Indian civilization surely date back to the Indus Valley civilization of the third and early second millennia B.C.E. Since the writing from that period remains undeciphered, the earliest textual knowledge about Indian roots comes from the period of 1500–500 B.C.E., called the Vedic Age after the religious texts known as the **Vedas**. While most historians believe that Indo-European-speaking nomads migrated into northwest India at the beginning of the period, others argue for a much earlier Indo-European presence deriving from the spread of agriculture (see Chapter 3).

After the collapse of the Indus Valley civilization, the central authority presumed to have organized large-scale irrigation disappeared and the region became home to bands of Vedic-speaking cattle herders who also engaged in farming. As with other Indo-European peoples—Celts, Greeks, Iranians, Romans—patriarchal traditions made the father dominant in the family just as the king ruled the group as a whole. Warriors boasted of their martial skill and courage, relished combat, feasted on beef, and filled their leisure time with chariot racing and gambling.

After 1000 B.C.E., some groups pushed eastward into the Ganges Plain. Iron tools—harder than bronze and able to hold a sharper edge—allowed settlers to fell trees and work the newly cleared land with ox-drawn plows. The fertile plain, watered by the annual monsoon, sustained two or three crops a year. As in Greece at roughly the same time, the use of iron tools must have led to a population increase.

Stories about this era, not written down until much later but preserved by an oral tradition, speak of rivalry and warfare between two groups: the Aryas, speakers of Vedic Sanskrit and practitioners of the sacrificial religion prescribed in the Vedas; and the Dasas, indigenous speakers of Dravidian languages, whose religion, it is pointedly noted in the Vedas, did not involve sacrifice to or worship of the Vedic gods. Some scholars argue that the real process by which Arya groups became dominant in the north involved the absorption of some Dasas into Arya populations and a merging of elites from both groups. For the most part, however, Aryas pushed the Dasas south into central and southern India, where their descen-

dants still live. Indo-European languages descended from those of the Aryas predominate in northern India today, while Dravidian languages prevail in the south.

The cultural and religious differences between the Aryas and the indigenous peoples contributed to sharp social divisions. A system of **varnas**, literally "colors" but usually translated as "castes," indicated something akin to classes. Individuals belonged by birth to one of four varnas: *Brahmins*, the group comprising priests and scholars; *Kshatriyas* (kshuh-TREE-yuhs), warriors and the king; *Vaishyas* (VIESH-yuhs), all other Aryas; and *Shudras* (SHOOD-ras), non-Aryans who were servants and slaves of the other three varnas. The designation *Shudra* originally may have been reserved for Dasas. Indeed, the term *dasa* came to mean "slave." Eventually a fifth group emerged: the Untouchables. Excluded from the caste system and shunned by the other castes, they worked in demeaning or polluting trades such as tanning, which involved touching dead animals, and sweeping away ashes after cremations.

According to one creation myth, a primordial man named Purusha allowed himself to be sacrificed. From his mouth sprang the varna of Brahmin priests. From his arms came the Kshatriya warriors; from his thighs the Vaishya merchants, artisans, and peasants; and from his feet the Shudra workers.

Within the broad varna divisions, the population further divided into numerous smaller groups, called **jatis**, or *castes*. Each jati had its proper occupation, duties, and rituals. Members of a given jati lived and married within the group and ate only with members

---

Vedas Early Indian sacred "knowledge"—the literal meaning of the term—long preserved and communicated orally by Brahmin priests and eventually written down. These religious texts, including the thousand poetic hymns to various deities contained in the *Rig Veda*, are our main source of information about the Vedic period (ca. 1500–500 B.C.E.).

varna/jati Two categories of social identity of great importance in Indian history. Varnas are the four major social divisions: the Brahmin priest class, the Kshatriya warrior/administrator class, the Vaishya merchant/farmer class, and the Shudra laborer class. Within the system of varnas are many jatis, regional groups of people who have a common occupational sphere and who marry, eat, and generally interact with other members of their group.

of the group. Elaborate rules governed interactions between groups. Members of higher-status groups feared pollution from contacting lower-caste individuals and had to undergo rituals of purification to remove any taint.

The caste system became connected to a belief in reincarnation. Brahmin priests taught that every living creature had an immortal essence: the *atman*, or "self." Separated from the body at death, the atman returned in the body of an insect, an animal, or a human depending on the **karma**, or deeds, of the atman in its previous incarnations. People of exemplary goodness returned in a higher caste. Those who misbehaved fell to a lower caste or even a lower life form. The underlying message ran: You are where you deserve to be, and the only way to improve your lot in the next incarnation is to accept your current station and its attendant duties.

Many of the Vedic deities, mostly male, were associated with the heavens. Indra, like Zeus a god of war and master of the thunderbolt, commanded the greatest devotion and represented the chieftains who led the warriors into battle. Agni, the fire-god, consumed the sacrifice and bridged the spheres of gods and humans. Vedic religion centered on sacrifice, the dedication to a god of a valued possession, often a living creature. The offerings invigorated the gods and thereby sustained their creative powers and promoted stability in the world.

Brahmin priests alone knew the rituals and prayers. The *Rig Veda*, a collection of more than a thousand poetic hymns to various deities, and the *Brahmanas*, detailed prose descriptions and explanations of ritual procedures, all in the Sanskrit language of the Arya upper classes, passed orally from one generation of priests to the next. Writing did not spread in India until the Gupta period (320–550 C.E.), possibly because the Brahmins opposed its introduction. The priests' "knowledge" (the term *veda* means just that) earned them rewards for officiating at sacrifices and gave them social and political power as the intermediaries between gods and humans.

As elsewhere in the ancient world, the lives of Indian women left few traces. Limited evidence indicates that in the Vedic period women studied sacred lore, composed religious hymns, and participated in sacrifices. They could own property and usually did not marry until their middle or late teens. A number of strong and resourceful women appear in the *Mahabharata* epic (discussed later in this chapter). In the *Ramayana* epic, on the other hand, we see the familiar motif of the hero Rama rescuing his wife Sita after she has been abducted.

The internal divisions of Indian society, the complex hierarchy of groups, and the claims of some to superior virtue and purity provided each individual with a clear identity and role and offered the benefits of group solidarity and support. Sometimes groups even upgraded their status within the system, which was not entirely static and provided a mechanism for releasing social tensions. Many of these features have persisted into modern times.

Challenges to the Old Order: Jainism and Buddhism

After 700 B.C.E. reactions against Brahmin power and privilege emerged. People who objected to the rigid social hierarchy could always retreat to the forest that covered much of ancient India. Never far away, these wild places symbolized freedom from societal constraints. Individuals who wandered in the forest sometimes attracted followers. Questioning priestly power and the necessity of sacrifices, they offered alternate paths to salvation: individual pursuit of insight into the nature of the self and the universe through physical and mental discipline (*yoga*), which included dietary restrictions and meditation. They taught that by distancing oneself from desire for the things of this world, one could achieve **moksha**, or liberation, a "deep, dreamless sleep" that released one from the endless reincarnations through union with the divine force of the universe. The

karma In Indian tradition, the residue of deeds performed in past and present lives that adheres to a "spirit" and determines what form it will assume in its next life cycle. The doctrines of karma and reincarnation were used by the elite in ancient India to encourage people to accept their social position and do their duty.

moksha The Hindu concept of the spirit's "liberation" from the endless cycle of rebirths. There are various avenues—such as physical discipline, meditation, and acts of devotion to the gods—by which the spirit can distance itself from desire for the things of this world and be merged with the divine force that animates the universe.

Carved Stone Gateway Leading to the Great Stupa at Sanchi Pilgrims traveled long distances to visit stupas, mounds containing relics of the Buddha. The complex at Sanchi, in central India, was begun by Ashoka in the third century B.C.E., though the gates probably date to the first century C.E. This relief shows a royal procession bringing the remains of the Buddha to the city of Kushinagara.

Upanishads (ooh-PAH-nee-shad), which continue the explanations of ritual begun in the *Brahmanas*, also reflect this questioning of Vedic religion.

Jainism (JINE-iz-uhm) and Buddhism challenged not only Vedic ritualism but also the authority of the Vedic priests. Jainism took its name from the teacher Mahavira (540–468 B.C.E.), known to his followers as Jina, "the Conqueror." Mahavira respected the life force so much that he commanded strict nonviolence. Jains wore masks to avoid inadvertently inhaling small insects and brushed off the seat before sitting down. Some practiced extreme asceticism by embracing nudity and eventually starving themselves to death. Less zealous Jains engaged in commerce in cities, since agricultural work inevitably involved killing.

Buddhism, a far more successful movement, stemmed from the life of Siddhartha Gautama (563–483 B.C.E.), known as the **Buddha**, "the Enlightened One," about whom myriad legends have arisen. From a Kshatriya family in what is now Nepal, he enjoyed the princely lifestyle to which he had been born until

Buddha An Indian prince named Siddhartha Gautama, who renounced his wealth and social position. After becoming "enlightened" (the meaning of *Buddha*), he enunciated the principles of Buddhism. This doctrine evolved and spread throughout India and to Southeast, East, and Central Asia.

he experienced a change of heart and gave up family and privilege to become a wandering ascetic. After six years, he decided that asceticism was no more likely to produce spiritual insight than his earlier luxurious life, so he opened a "Middle Path." Sitting under a tree in a deer park near Benares on the Ganges River, he gained a sudden and profound insight, which he set forth as "Four Noble Truths": (1) life is suffering; (2) suffering arises from desire; (3) the solution to suffering lies in curbing desire; and (4) desire can be curbed if a person follows the "Eightfold Path" of right views, aspirations, speech, conduct, livelihood, effort, mindfulness, and meditation. Rising up, the Buddha preached his First Sermon, a central text of Buddhism, and set into motion the "Wheel of the Law." He soon attracted followers, some of whom took vows of celibacy, nonviolence, and poverty.

At first, Buddhism centered on the individual, denying the usefulness of the gods to a person seeking enlightenment. What mattered was living moderately to minimize desire and suffering and searching for spiritual truth through self-discipline and meditation. One should seek *nirvana*, literally "snuffing out the flame," a release from the cycle of reincarnations and enjoyment of perpetual tranquility. Whereas the *Upanishad* tradition emphasized the eternal survival of the atman, the "self" or nonmaterial essence of the individual, Buddhism regarded the individual as a composite of features such as breath and wind, but without a soul.

At his death, Buddha left no final instructions, urging his disciples to "be their own lamp." As his followers spread his philosophy throughout India and into Central, Southeast, and East Asia, its wide appeal subverted its individualistic and atheistic underpinnings, and Buddhist monasteries with hierarchies of monks and nuns came into being. Worshipers erected *stupas* (STOO-puh) (large earthen mounds symbolizing the universe) over relics of the cremated founder and other holy men and walked around them in a clockwise direction. Believers began to worship the Buddha himself as a god. Many Buddhists also revered *bodhisattvas* (boe-dih-SUT-vuhs), men and women who had achieved enlightenment and were on the threshold of nirvana but chose rebirth into mortal bodies to help others along the path to salvation.

Early representations show the Buddha only indirectly, through symbols such as his footprints, begging bowl, or the tree under which he achieved enlightenment, as if to emphasize his achievement of a state of nonexistence. From the second century C.E., however, statues of the Buddha and bodhisattvas proliferated, sculpted in styles that showed the influence of the Greek settlements established in Bactria (modern Afghanistan) by Alexander the Great.

A schism emerged within Buddhism. Devotees of **Mahayana** (mah-huh-YAH-nuh) ("Great Vehicle") **Buddhism** embraced the popular new features. Practitioners of **Theravada** (there-uh-VAH-duh) ("Teachings of the Elders") **Buddhism** followed most of the original teachings of the founder.

The Rise of Hinduism

Challenged by the new religious movements, Vedic religion evolved by the fourth century C.E. into **Hinduism**, the dominant religion in South Asia today. (The term *Hinduism* originated with Islamic invaders in the eleventh century C.E. as a label for the diverse practices they encountered: "what the Indians do.") Though based on the Vedic religion of northern India, Hinduism incorporated Dravidian cultural elements from the south, such as intense devotion to a deity and the prominence of goddesses.

Brahmin priests survived the transition with their social status and influence intact, but sacrifice lost its central place. Opportunities for individual worshipers to have direct contact with deities increased. Hinduism emphasized the worshiper's personal devotion to a particular deity, usually Vishnu

Mahayana Buddhism "Great Vehicle" branch of Buddhism followed in China, Japan, and Central Asia. The focus is on reverence for Buddha and for bodhisattvas, enlightened persons who have postponed nirvana to help others attain enlightenment.

Theravada Buddhism "Way of the Elders" branch of Buddhism followed in Sri Lanka and much of Southeast Asia. Theravada remains close to the original principles set forth by the Buddha; it downplays the importance of gods and emphasizes austerity and the individual's search for enlightenment.

Hinduism A general term for a wide variety of beliefs and ritual practices that have developed in the Indian subcontinent since antiquity. Hinduism has roots in ancient Vedic, Buddhist, and south Indian religious concepts and practices. It spread along the trade routes to Southeast Asia.

Jeremy Richards/Shutterstock.com

Hindu Temple at Khajuraho This sandstone temple of the Hindu deity Shiva, representing the celestial mountain of the gods, was erected at Khajuraho, in central India, around 1000 C.E., but it reflects the architectural symbolism of Hindu temples developed in the Gupta period. Worshipers made their way through several rooms to the image of the deity, located in the innermost "womb-chamber" directly beneath the tallest tower.

(VIHSH-noo) or Shiva (SHEE-vuh), or Devi (DEH-vee) ("the Goddess"). The goddess is of Dravidian origin, and her incorporation into the cult shows how Arya and indigenous cultures fused to form Hindu civilization. Vishnu, who has a clear Arya pedigree, remains more popular in northern India, and Shiva is dominant in the south. These deities appear in many guises, bear various cult names, and give rise to a complex symbolism of stories, companion animals, birds, and objects.

Vishnu, the preserver, benevolently helps his devotees in time of need. Hindus believe that whenever demonic forces threaten the cosmic order, an *avatara*, or incarnation of Vishnu, appears on the earth. His avatars include the legendary hero Rama, the cowherd-god Krishna, and the Buddha (a clear attempt to co-opt the rival religion's founder). Shiva, who lives in ascetic isolation on Mount Kailasa in the

Himalayas, represents a cyclical process of creation and destruction that is symbolized in statues showing him dancing. Devi can manifest herself as a full-bodied mother-goddess representing fertility and procreation, as Shiva's loving wife Parvati, or as the frightening deity who, under the name Kali or Durga, lets loose violence and destruction.

The multiplicity of gods (330 million according to one tradition), sects, and local practices within Hinduism reflects the ethnic, linguistic, and cultural diversity of India. Yet within this variety, there is unity. A worshiper's devotion to one god or goddess does not entail denial of the other main deities or the host of lesser divinities and spirits. Ultimately, all are manifestations of a single divine force pervading the universe. The underlying unity appears in the way various manifestations of Devi represent different female potentials, as well as in composite statues—

Borromeo/Art Resource, NY

Vishnu Rescuing the Earth Goddess, Fifth Century C.E. This sculpture, carved into the rock wall of a cave at Udayagiri in eastern India, depicts Vishnu in his incarnation as a boar rescuing the Earth Goddess from the vast ocean. As the god treads triumphantly on a subdued snake demon and the joyful goddess clings to his snout, a chorus of gods and sages applaud the miracle.

half Shiva, half Vishnu—signifying complementary aspects of one cosmic principle.

Hindus may approach god and obtain divine favor through special knowledge of sacred truths, mental and physical discipline, or extraordinary devotion to the deity. Worship centers on the temples, which range from humble shrines to richly decorated stone edifices built under royal patronage. Statues beckon the deity to take up temporary residence within the image and be available to eager worshipers. *Puja*, or service to the deity, can include bathing, clothing, or feeding the statue. Glimpsing the divine image conveys blessings.

Sacred places where a worshiper can directly sense and benefit from the divine power dot the Indian subcontinent. Mystery and sanctity surround certain mountains, caves, trees, plants, and rocks. *Tirthayatra*, the term for pilgrimage site, means "journey to a river crossing," illustrating the association of Hindu places with flowing water. The Ganges River is especially sacred. Millions of worshipers travel each year to bathe and receive the restorative and purifying power of its waters. Pilgrimages to shrines foster contact and the exchange of ideas among people from different parts of India, helping to create a broad Hindu identity and the concept of India as a single civilization.

Religious duties depend on social standing and gender as well as stage of life. Young men from the three highest classes (Brahmin, Kshatriya, and Vaishya) undergo ritual rebirth through the ceremony of the sacred thread, marking attainment of manhood and readiness to receive religious knowledge. The life cycle then passes through four stages: (1) student of the sacred texts, (2) married householder with children and material goods, (3) forest dweller meditating on the meaning of existence after the birth of his grandchildren, and (4) wandering ascetic awaiting death. The person living such a life fulfills first his duties to society and then his duties to himself, leaving him disconnected from the world and prepared for moksha (liberation).

SECTION REVIEW

- The Indian subcontinent is divided by a variety of natural barriers and as a whole is isolated from the rest of Asia except for the northwest.

- Indian seafarers used the monsoons to travel to the Middle East, East Africa, and Southeast Asia.

- During the Vedic Age, the Aryas migrated into northern India, and their conquest of the Dasas introduced the caste system.

- Brahmin priests presided over the Vedic religion and led ritual sacrifices.

- Jainism and Buddhism, which stressed more individual approaches, rose to challenge Brahmin power.

- In response, Vedic religion transformed into Hinduism.

Hinduism responded to the needs of people for personal deities with whom they could establish direct connections. The austerity of early Buddhism, its denial of the importance of gods, and its demand that individuals find their own path to enlightenment may have required too much of ordinary people. What eventually made Mahayana Buddhism popular—gods, saints, and myths—also made it more easily absorbed into the vast social and cultural fabric of Hinduism.

INDIAN IMPERIAL EXPANSION AND COLLAPSE

■ *In the face of powerful forces that tended to keep India fragmented, how did the Mauryan Empire of the fourth to second centuries B.C.E. and the Gupta Empire of the fourth to sixth centuries C.E. succeed in unifying much of India?*

Political unity has rarely lasted in India. The varied terrain—mountains, foothills, plains, forests, steppes, deserts—favors different forms of organization and economic activity. Peoples occupying topographically diverse zones may also differ in language and cultural practices. Caste and family have generated the strongest feelings of personal identity, allegiance to a higher political authority being a secondary concern. Nevertheless, two empires arose in the Ganges Plain: the Mauryan (MORE-yuhn) Empire of the fourth to second centuries B.C.E. and the Gupta (GOOP-tuh) Empire of the fourth to sixth centuries C.E.

The Mauryan Empire, 324–184 B.C.E.

Among the many kinship groups and independent states that dotted the north Indian landscape, the kingdom of Magadha, in the modern state of Bihar, began to play an influential role around 600 B.C.E. thanks to wealth based on agriculture, iron mines, and strategic location astride the trade routes of the eastern Ganges Basin. In the late fourth century B.C.E. Chandragupta Maurya (MORE-yuh), a man of Vaishya or Shudra origins, took control of Magadha and founded the **Mauryan Empire**. Greek tradition claimed that Alexander the Great met an Indian native named "Sandracotus," an apparent corruption of "Chandragupta," when his armies reached the Punjab (northern Pakistan) in 326 B.C.E., implying that he might have served as a role model for the new ruler.

Greek rule in the Punjab collapsed after Alexander's death, allowing Chandragupta (r. 324–301 B.C.E.) and his successors Bindusara (r. 301–273 B.C.E.) and Ashoka (r. 273–232 B.C.E.) to extend Mauryan control over the entire subcontinent except its southern tip.

Tradition holds that Kautilya, a crafty elderly Brahmin, guided Chandragupta and wrote a treatise on government, the *Arthashastra* (ahr-thuh-SHAHS-truh). Although recent studies have shown that the existing form of the *Arthashastra* dates only to the third century C.E., its core text may well go back to Kautilya. This pragmatic guide to political success advocates the so-called *mandala* (man-DAH-luh) (circle) theory of foreign policy: "My enemy's enemy is my friend." It also presents schemes for enforcing and increasing the collection of tax revenues and prescribes the use of spies to keep watch on one's subjects.

A quarter of all agricultural output went in taxes to support the Mauryan government. Relatives and associates of the king governed districts based on

Mauryan Empire The first state to unify most of the Indian subcontinent. It was founded by Chandragupta Maurya in 324 B.C.E. and survived until 184 B.C.E. From its capital at Pataliputra in the Ganges Valley it grew wealthy from taxes on agriculture, iron mining, and control of trade routes.

ethnic boundaries. The imperial army—with infantry, cavalry, and elephant divisions—secured central authority, which also controlled mining, shipbuilding, and arms making. Standard coinage fostered support for the government and promoted trade.

The Mauryan kings ruled Pataliputra (modern Patna), where five tributaries join the Ganges. Descriptions by foreign visitors testify to the international connections of the Indian monarchs. Surrounded by a timber wall and moat, the city extended along the river for 8 miles (13 kilometers). Six governing committees oversaw manufacturing, trade, sales, taxes, the welfare of foreigners, and the registration of births and deaths.

Ashoka, Chandragupta's grandson, began his reign by extending the boundaries of the empire. After killing, wounding, or deporting thousands of people during his conquest of Kalinga (modern Orissa, a coastal region southeast of Magadha), remorse overcame him and he converted to Buddhism, thereafter preaching nonviolence, morality, moderation, and religious tolerance in both government and private life.

Ashoka publicized this program through edicts inscribed on great rocks and polished sandstone, the earliest decipherable Indian texts:

> For . . . many hundreds of years the sacrificial slaughter of animals, violence toward creatures, unfilial conduct toward kinsmen, and improper conduct toward Brahmins and ascetics have increased. Now with the practice of morality by King [Ashoka], the sound of war drums has become the call to morality. . . . You [government officials] are appointed to rule over thousands of human beings in the expectation that you will win the affection of all men. All men are my children. Just as I desire that my children will fare well and be happy in this world and the next, I desire the same for all men. . . . King [Ashoka] . . . desires that there should be the growth of the essential spirit of morality or holiness among all sects. . . . There should not be glorification of one's own sect and denunciation of the sect of others for little or no reason. For all the sects are worthy of reverence for one reason or another.[2]

Despite his commitment to employ peaceful means whenever possible, Ashoka reminded potential transgressors that "the king, remorseful as he is, has the strength to punish the wrongdoers who do not repent."

Commerce and Culture in an Era of Political Fragmentation

The Mauryan Empire prospered for a time after Ashoka's death in 232 B.C.E. Then, weakened by dynastic disputes, it collapsed under attacks in the northwest in 184 B.C.E. Five hundred years passed before another state succeeded in extending control over northern India. In the meantime, settlers descended from troops left in northern Afghanistan by Alexander the Great established the Greco-Bactrian kingdom (180–50 B.C.E.), and two nomadic groups from Central Asia followed them, set off by the pressure of Han Chinese forces on the Xiongnu (see Chapter 5). The Shakas, an Iranian people, were dominant from 50 B.C.E. to 50 C.E., followed by the Kushans (KOO-shahn) (50 to 240 C.E.), originally from Xinjiang in northwest China. At its height the Kushan kingdom controlled much of present-day Uzbekistan, Afghanistan, Pakistan, and northwest India, fostering trade through both the overland Silk Road and Indian Ocean seaports (see Chapter 8). The eastern Ganges region reverted to the patchwork of small principalities that had characterized the Mauryan era.

Despite the political fragmentation, however, economic, cultural, and intellectual development continued. The roads and towns of the Mauryas fostered commerce within the subcontinent, while land and sea routes linked India to China, Southeast Asia, Central Asia, the Middle East, East Africa, and the lands of the Mediterranean. Guilds of merchants and artisans regulated the lives of their members and had an important voice in local affairs. They supported culture and endowed the religious sects, particularly Buddhism and Jainism, with temples and monuments.

---

[2] B. G. Gokhale, *Asoka Maurya* (New York: Twayne, 1966), 152–153, 156–157, 160.

Ashoka Third ruler of the Mauryan Empire in India (r. 273–232 B.C.E.). He converted to Buddhism and broadcast his precepts on inscribed stones and pillars, the earliest surviving Indian writing.

During the last centuries B.C.E. and first centuries C.E. the two greatest Indian epics, the *Ramayana* (ruh-MAH-yuh-nuh) and the *Mahabharata* (muh-huh-BAH-ruh-tuh), based on centuries-old oral predecessors, achieved their final form. They place the events they describe in the distant past, but their proud kings, beautiful queens, family wars, heroic conduct, and chivalric values seem to reflect the late Vedic period, when Aryan warrior societies moved onto the Ganges Plain.

The *Ramayana* relates the exploits of Rama, a heroic prince who came to be considered an incarnation of Vishnu. When the chief of the demons kidnaps his wife, Sita, he destroys the demons with the help of his brother and a troop of monkeys. The vast **Mahabharata**—eight times the length of the Greek *Iliad* and *Odyssey* combined—tells how two sets of cousins, the Pandavas and Kauravas, quarreled over succession to the throne and fought a cataclysmic battle at Kurukshetra. The battle is so destructive on both sides that Yudhishthira, the eldest of the Pandava brothers and their leader, accepts the fruits of victory only reluctantly.

The **Bhagavad-Gita** is a self-contained (and perhaps originally separate) episode set in the battle. The hero Arjuna shrinks from fighting his kinsmen until his charioteer, the god Krishna, tutors him on the necessity of fulfilling his duty as a warrior. Death means nothing in a universe of endless reincarnation. The Bhagavad-Gita resolves the tension in Indian civilization between duty to society and duty to one's own soul. Dutiful action taken without regard for personal benefits serves society and may earn release from the cycle of rebirths.

Science and technology flourished in this era as well. Indian doctors applied herbal remedies and served in the courts of western and southern Asia. Panini (late fourth century B.C.E.) undertook a detailed analysis of Sanskrit, which arrested its natural development and turned it into a formal, literary language. Prakrits—popular dialects—emerged to become the ancestors of the modern languages of northern and central India.

Historians of southern India consider the period from the third century B.C.E. to the third century C.E. dominated by three often feuding **Tamil kingdoms**— of Cholas, Pandyas, and Cheras—a "classical" period for Tamil art and literature. Under the patronage of the Pandya kings and guided by an academy of five hundred authors, Tamil writers composed grammatical treatises, collections of ethical proverbs, epics, and short poems about love, war, wealth, and the beauty of nature while performers excelled in music, dance, and drama.

The Gupta Empire, 320–550 C.E.

Like its Mauryan predecessor, the **Gupta Empire** grew from the kingdom of Magadha and had its capital at Pataliputra. Its founder called himself Chandra Gupta (r. 320–335), borrowing the name of the Mauryan founder. Though they never controlled as much land as the Mauryans, the Gupta monarchs took the title "Great King of Kings."

Trade, agriculture, and iron mining brought prosperity to the Guptas as they had to the Mauryans, and the kings followed similar methods of taxation and administration. In addition to a 25 percent tax on agriculture, users of the irrigation network paid fees, and some commodities were subject to special taxes. The state maintained monopolies over mining and production, exploited state-owned farmlands, and required subjects to work a specified number of days on maintaining roads, wells, and irrigation works.

The Gupta administration and intelligence network were smaller and less pervasive than those of the Mauryans. A powerful army maintained tight control of the empire's core, but provincial governors had a free hand, which they sometimes used to exploit the populace. Governorships often passed from father to

---

Mahabharata A vast epic chronicling the events leading up to a cataclysmic battle between related kinship groups in early India. It includes the Bhagavad-Gita.

Bhagavad-Gita The most important work of Indian sacred literature, a dialogue between the great warrior Arjuna and the god Krishna on duty and the fate of the spirit.

Tamil kingdoms The kingdoms of southern India, inhabited primarily by speakers of Dravidian languages, which developed in partial isolation, and somewhat differently, from the Arya north. They produced epics, poetry, and performance arts. Elements of Tamil religious beliefs were merged into the Hindu synthesis.

Gupta Empire A powerful Indian state based, like its Mauryan predecessor, on a capital at Pataliputra in the Ganges Valley. It controlled most of the Indian subcontinent through a combination of military force and its prestige as a center of sophisticated culture.

son within high-ranking military or administrative families. The most distant areas, controlled by kinship groups or subordinate kings, made annual donations of tribute. Garrisons stationed at frontier points kept trade routes open and ensured the collection of customs duties.

A constant round of solemn rituals, dramatic ceremonies, and cultural events in Pataliputra demonstrated to visitors from remote areas the benefits of belonging to the empire. Modern historians call such a regime a **theater-state**. Rulers and subjects in the Gupta theater-state had an economic relationship. The former accumulated luxury goods and profits from trade and redistributed them to dependents through gifts and other means. Subordinate princes gained prestige by emulating the center and maintained close ties through visits, gifts, and marriages with all the Gupta family. Gupta patronage also supported the Indian mathematicians, who invented the concept of zero and developed the Arabic numerals and place-value notations (see Environment and Technology: Indian Mathematics).

The moist climate of the Ganges Plain does not favor the preservation of buildings and artifacts, so archaeology has little to say about the Gupta era. However, a Chinese Buddhist monk named Faxian (fah-shee-en), who made a pilgrimage to the homeland of his faith around 400 C.E., penned a description of the Gupta kingdom:

> The cities and towns of this country are the greatest of all in the Middle Kingdom. The inhabitants are rich and prosperous, and vie with one another in the practice of benevolence and righteousness. . . . The heads of the Vaishya families in them establish in the cities houses for dispensing charity and medicines. All the poor and destitute in the country, orphans, widowers, and childless men, maimed people, and cripples, and all who are diseased, go to those houses, and are provided with every kind of help.[3]

At this time, the civil disabilities of women, which had always existed as custom, hardened into law with the emergence of books like *The Law of Manu*. Indian women lost the right to own or inherit property, and girls married at an increasingly early age, sometimes at six or seven. The husband could thus ensure his wife's virginity and, by bringing her up in his own household, could train her to suit his purposes. As in Confucian China, a woman owed obedience to her father, then her husband, and finally her sons (see Chapter 3). In certain parts of India, a practice called *sati* (suh-TEE) required a widow to cremate herself on her husband's funeral pyre. Widows who refused to follow this custom could not remarry and suffered social rejection.

Entering a Jainist or Buddhist religious community offered some women an escape from male control. Women from powerful families and courtesans trained in poetry and music, as well as sexual technique, sometimes enjoyed high social standing and gave money for Buddhist stupas and other shrines.

The Gupta monarchs sought sanctity through reviving Vedic practices, and Brahmin priests regained influence. Yet the kings also patronized Buddhist and Jain endeavors. Buddhist monasteries with hundreds or even thousands of monks and nuns in residence flourished in the cities. Northern India drew Buddhist pilgrims from Southeast and East Asia to the birthplace of their faith.

The classic form of the Hindu temple, which evolved during the Gupta era, symbolizes the sacred mountain or palace where the gods of mythology reside. Sitting atop a raised platform surmounted by high towers, it mirrors the order of the universe. From an exterior courtyard, worshipers approached the central shrine containing the statue of the deity. In rich temples, painted or sculpted gods and mythical events covered the walls. Frescoes and statues also adorned cave temples carved into cliffs.

The vibrant commerce of the period of fragmentation continued under the Guptas. Coins served as a medium of exchange, and artisan guilds influenced the economic, political, and religious life of towns. The Guptas sought control of the ports on

---

[3] James Legge, *The Travels of Fa-hien: Fa-hien's Record of Buddhistic Kingdoms* (Delhi: Oriental Publishers, 1971), 77–79.

theater-state Historians' term for a state that acquires prestige and power by developing attractive cultural forms and staging elaborate public ceremonies (as well as redistributing valuable resources) to attract and bind subjects to the center. Examples include the Gupta Empire in India and Srivijaya in Southeast Asia.

environment & technology

Indian Mathematics

The so-called Arabic numerals used in most parts of the world today were developed in India. The Indian system of place-value notation was far more efficient than the unwieldy numerical systems of Egyptians, Greeks, and Romans, and the invention of zero was a profound intellectual achievement. This system is used even more widely than the alphabet derived from the Phoenicians (see Chapter 2) and is, in one sense, the only truly global language.

In its fully developed form the Indian method of arithmetic notation employed a base-ten system. It had separate columns for ones, tens, hundreds, and so forth, as well as a zero sign to indicate the absence of units in a given column. This system makes possible the economical expression of even very large numbers. It also allows for the performance of calculations not possible in a system like the numerals of the Romans, where any real calculation had to be done mentally or on a counting board.

A series of early Indian inscriptions using the numerals from 1 to 9 are deeds of property given to religious institutions by kings or other wealthy individuals. They were incised in the Sanskrit language on copper plates. The earliest known example has a date equivalent to 595 C.E. A sign for zero is attested by the eighth century, but textual evidence leads to the inference that a place-value system and the zero concept were already known in the fifth century.

This Indian system spread to the Middle East, Southeast Asia, and East Asia by the seventh century. Other peoples quickly recognized its capabilities and adopted it, sometimes using indigenous symbols. Europe received the new technology somewhat later. Gerbert of Aurillac, a French Christian monk, spent time in Spain between 967 and 970, where he was exposed to the mathematics of the Arabs. A great scholar and teacher who eventually became Pope Sylvester II (r. 999–1003), he spread word of the "Arabic" system in the Christian West.

Knowledge of the Indian system of mathematical notation eventually spread throughout Europe, partly through the use of a mechanical calculating device—an improved version of the Roman counting board, with counters inscribed with variants of the Indian numeral forms. Because the counters could be turned sideways or upside down, at first there was considerable variation in the forms.

Copper Plate with Indian Numerals *This property deed from western India shows an early form of the symbol system for numbers that spread to the Middle East and Europe and today is used all over the world.* Facsimile by Georges Ifrah. Reproduced by permission of Georges Ifrah.

But by the twelfth century they had become standardized into forms close to those in use today. As the capabilities of the place-value system for calculations became clear, the counting board fell into disuse. This led to the adoption of the zero sign—not necessary on the counting board, where a column could be left empty—by the twelfth century. Leonardo Fibonacci, a thirteenth-century C.E. Italian who learned algebra in Muslim North Africa and employed the Arabic numeral system in his mathematical treatise, gave additional impetus to the movement to discard the traditional system of Roman numerals.

Why was this marvelous system of mathematical notation invented in ancient India? The answer may lie in the way its range and versatility correspond to elements of Indian cosmology. The Indians conceived of immense spans of time—trillions of years (far exceeding current scientific estimates of the age of the universe as approximately 14 billion years)—during which innumerable universes like our own were created, existed for a finite time, then were destroyed. In one popular creation myth, Vishnu is slumbering on the coils of a giant serpent at the bottom of the ocean, and worlds are being created and destroyed as he exhales and inhales. In Indian thought our world, like others, has existed for a series of epochs lasting more than 4 million years, yet the period of its existence is but a brief and insignificant moment in the vast sweep of time. The Indians developed a number system that allowed them to express concepts of this magnitude.

- Chandragupta Maurya took control of the kingdom of Magadha and established the Mauryan Empire.
- The collapse of Greek rule in the Punjab enabled Chandragupta and his successors to expand the empire.
- The empire reached its fullest extent under Ashoka, after whose death it disintegrated.
- Economic and cultural activity continued during an era of fragmentation; to the south, Tamil culture entered its classical period.
- Also centered in Magadha, the Gupta Empire was less centralized than the Mauryan, but it thrived on the same economic bases.
- The Guptas revived Vedic practices and presided over both the legal hardening of gender discrimination and the expansion of overseas trade.

the Arabian Sea but lost trade as the Roman Empire weakened. However, trade with Southeast and East Asia increased. Merchants from eastern and southern India voyaged to the Malay (muh-LAY) Peninsula and the islands of Indonesia to exchange cotton cloth, ivory, metalwork, and animals for Chinese silk or Indonesian spices. The overland Silk Road from China brought further trade but was vulnerable to disruption by Central Asian nomads (see Chapter 8).

The Gupta Empire collapsed around 550 C.E. under pressure from nomadic invaders from the steppes of Central Asia (see Chapter 3). In the early seventh century, Harsha Vardhana (r. 606–647 C.E.), the ruler of the region around Delhi, briefly restored imperial power. An account of his region by a courtier named Bana shows him to be a fervent Buddhist, poet, patron of artists, and dynamic warrior. After Harsha's death, northern India reverted to its political fragmentation and remained divided until the Islamic invasions of the eleventh and twelfth centuries (see Chapter 14).

SOUTHEAST ASIA, 50–1025 C.E.

■ *How did the geography of Southeast Asia contribute to its commerce and to the influence of Hinduism and Buddhism?*

Southeast Asia consists of three geographical zones: the Indochina mainland, the Malay Peninsula, and thousands of islands extending on an east-west axis far out into the Pacific Ocean (see Map 6.2). Encompassing a vast area of land and water, this region is now occupied by the countries of Myanmar (myahn-MAH) (Burma), Thailand, Laos, Cambodia, Vietnam, Malaysia, Singapore, Indonesia, Brunei (broo-NIE), and the Philippines. Poised between the ancient centers of China and India, Southeast Asia has been influenced by the cultures of both civilizations. The region first rose to prominence and prosperity because of its intermediate role in the trade exchanges between southern and eastern Asia.

The strategic importance of Southeast Asia is enhanced by the region's natural resources. This is a geologically active zone; the islands are the tops of a chain of volcanoes. Lying along the equator, Southeast Asia has a tropical climate. The temperature hovers around 80 degrees Fahrenheit (30 degrees Celsius), and the monsoon winds provide dependable rainfall throughout the year. Thanks to several growing cycles each year, the region is capable of supporting a large human population. The most fertile agricultural lands lie along the floodplains of the largest silt-bearing rivers or contain rich volcanic soil deposited by ancient eruptions.

Early Civilization

Rain forest covers much of Southeast Asia. As early as 2000 B.C.E. people in this region were clearing land for farming by cutting and burning the vegetation. The cleared land was farmed for several growing seasons. When the soil was exhausted, the farmers abandoned the patch, allowing the forest to reclaim it, while they cleared and cultivated other nearby fields in similar fashion. Rice was the staple food—labor-intensive, but able to support a large population. A number of domesticated plant and animal species spread from Southeast Asia to other regions, including rice, soybeans, sugar cane, yams, bananas, coconuts, chickens, and pigs.

The Malay peoples who became the dominant population in this region were the product of several waves of migration from southern China beginning around 3000 B.C.E. Some indigenous peoples merged with the Malay newcomers; others retreated to remote mountain and forest zones. Subsequently, rising population and disputes within communities

Map 6.2 Southeast Asia Southeast Asia's position between the ancient centers of civilization in India and China had a major impact on its history. In the first millennium C.E. a series of powerful and wealthy states arose in the region by gaining control of major trade routes: first Funan, based in southern Vietnam, Cambodia, and the Malay Peninsula, then Srivijaya on the island of Sumatra, then smaller states on the island of Java. Shifting trade routes led to the rise and fall of the various centers. © Cengage Learning

prompted streams of people to leave the Southeast Asian mainland for the islands. By the first millennium B.C.E. Southeast Asians had developed impressive navigational skills. They knew how to ride the monsoon winds and interpret the patterns of swells, winds, clouds, and bird and sea life. Over a period of several thousand years groups of Malay peoples in large, double outrigger sailing canoes spread out across the Pacific and Indian Oceans—half the circumference of the earth—to settle thousands of islands.

The inhabitants of Southeast Asia clustered along riverbanks or in fertile volcanic plains. Their fields and villages were never far from the rain forest, with its wild animals and numerous plant species. Forest trees provided fruit, wood, and spices, and the shallow waters surrounding the islands teemed with fish. This region was also an early center of metallurgy. Metal-smiths heated copper and tin ore to the right temperature for producing and shaping bronze

implements by using hollow bamboo tubes to funnel oxygen to the furnace.

Northern Indochina, by its geographic proximity, was vulnerable to Chinese pressure and cultural influences, and it was under Chinese political control for a thousand years (111 B.C.E.–939 C.E.). Farther south, larger states emerged in the early centuries C.E. in response to two powerful forces: commerce and Hindu-Buddhist culture. Southeast Asia was situated along the trade routes that merchants used to carry Chinese silk westward to India and the Mediterranean. The movements of nomadic peoples had disrupted the old land route across Central Asia, but in India demand for silk was increasing—both for domestic use and for transshipment to satisfy the fast-growing luxury market in the Roman Empire. Gradually merchants extended this exchange network to include goods from Southeast Asia, such as aromatic woods, resins, and cinnamon, pepper, cloves, nutmeg, and other spices. Southeast Asian centers rose to prominence by serving this trade network and controlling key points.

The other force leading to the rise of larger political entities was the influence of Hindu-Buddhist culture imported from India. Commerce brought Indian merchants and sailors into the ports of Southeast Asia. As Buddhism spread, Southeast Asia became a way station for Indian missionaries and East Asian pilgrims going to and coming from the birthplace of their faith. Shrewd Malay rulers looked to Indian traditions as a rich source of ideas and prestige. They borrowed Sanskrit terms such as *maharaja* (mah-huh-RAH-juh) ("great king"), utilized Indian models of bureaucracy, ceremonial practices, and forms of artistic representation, and employed priests, administrators, and scribes skilled in Sanskrit writing to expedite government business. Their special connection to powerful gods and higher knowledge raised them above their rivals.

The Southeast Asian kingdoms, however, were not just passive recipients of Indian culture. They took what was useful to them and synthesized it with indigenous beliefs, values, and institutions—for example, local concepts of chieftainship, ancestor worship, and forms of oaths. Moreover, they trained their own people in the new ways, so that the bureaucracy contained both foreign experts and native disciples. The whole process amounted to a cultural dialogue between India and Southeast Asia, in which both were active participants.

The first major Southeast Asian center, called **Funan** (FOO-nahn) by Chinese visitors, flourished between the first and sixth centuries C.E. (see Map 6.2). Its capital was at the modern site of Oc-Eo in southern Vietnam. Funan occupied the delta of the Mekong (MAY-kawng) River, a "rice bowl" capable of supporting a large population. The rulers mobilized large numbers of laborers to dig irrigation channels and prevent destructive floods. By extending its control over most of southern Indochina and the Malay Peninsula, Funan was able to dominate the trade route from India to China. The route began in the ports of northeast India, crossed the Bay of Bengal, continued by land over the Isthmus of Kra on the Malay Peninsula, and then crossed the South China Sea (see Map 6.2). Indian merchants found that offloading their goods from ships and carrying them

across the narrow strip of land was safer than making the 1,000-mile (1,600-kilometer) voyage around the Malay Peninsula—a dangerous trip marked by treacherous currents, rocky shoals, and pirates. Once the portage across the isthmus was finished, the merchants needed food and lodging while waiting for the monsoon winds to shift so they could make the last leg of the voyage to China by sea. Funan stockpiled food and provided security for those engaged in this trade—in return for customs duties and other fees.

Chinese observers have left reports of the prosperity and sophistication of Funan, emphasizing the presence of walled cities, palaces, archives, systems of taxation, and state-organized agriculture. Nevertheless, Funan declined in the sixth century. The most likely explanation is that international trade routes changed and Funan no longer held a strategic position.

The Srivijayan Kingdom

By the sixth century a new, all-sea route had developed. Merchants and travelers from south India and Sri Lanka sailed through the Strait of Malacca (between the west side of the Malay Peninsula and the northeast coast of the island of Sumatra) and into the South China Sea. This route presented both human and navigational hazards, but it significantly shortened the traveling time.

A new center of power, **Srivijaya** (shree-vuh-JAH-yuh)—Sanskrit for "Great Conquest"—dominated the new southerly route by 683 C.E. The capital of the Srivijayan kingdom was at modern-day Palembang in southeastern Sumatra, 50 miles (80 kilometers) up the broad and navigable Musi River, with a good natural harbor. The kingdom was well situated to control the southern part of the Malay Peninsula, Sumatra, parts

Funan An early complex society in Southeast Asia between the first and sixth centuries C.E. It was centered in the rich rice-growing region of southern Vietnam, and it controlled the passage of trade across the Malaysian isthmus.

Srivijaya A state based on the Indonesian island of Sumatra between the seventh and eleventh centuries C.E. It amassed wealth and power by a combination of selective adaptation of Indian technologies and concepts, control of the lucrative trade routes between India and China, and skillful showmanship and diplomacy in holding together a disparate realm of inland and coastal territories.

of Java and Borneo, and the Malacca (muh-LAH-kuh) and Sunda straits—vital passageways for shipping (see Map 6.2).

The Srivijayan kingdom gained ascendancy over its rivals and assumed control of the international trade route by fusing four distinct ecological zones into an interdependent network. The core area was the productive agricultural plain along the Musi River. The king and his clerks, judges, and tax collectors controlled this zone directly. Control was less direct over the second zone, the upland regions of Sumatra's interior, with its commercially valuable forest products. Local rulers there were bound to the center by oaths of loyalty, elaborate court ceremonies, and the sharing of profits from trade. The third zone consisted of river ports that had been Srivijaya's main rivals. They were conquered and controlled thanks to an alliance between Srivijaya and neighboring sea nomads, pirates who served as a Srivijayan navy in return for a steady income.

The fourth zone was a fertile "rice bowl" on the central plain of the nearby island of Java—a region so productive, because of its volcanic soil, that it houses and feeds the majority of the population of present-day Indonesia. Srivijayan monarchs maintained alliances, cemented by intermarriage, with several ruling dynasties in this region, and the Srivijayan kings claimed descent from the main Javanese dynasty. These arrangements gave Srivijaya access to large quantities of foodstuffs that people living in the capital and merchants and sailors visiting the various ports needed.

The kings of Srivijaya who constructed and maintained this complex network of social, political, and economic relationships were men of energy and skill. Although their authority depended in part on force, it owed more to diplomatic and even theatrical talents. Like the Gupta monarchy, Srivijaya was a theater-state, securing its preeminence and binding dependents by its sheer splendor and its ability to attract labor, talent, and luxury products. The court was the scene of ceremonies designed to dazzle observers and reinforce an image of wealth, power, and sanctity. Subordinate rulers took oaths of loyalty carrying dire threats of punishment for violations, and in their home locales they imitated the splendid ceremonials of the capital.

The Srivijayan king, drawing upon Buddhist conceptions, presented himself as a bodhisattva, one who has achieved enlightenment and utilizes his precious insights for the betterment of his subjects. The king was believed to have magical powers, controlling powerful forces of fertility associated with the rivers in flood and mediating between the spiritually potent realms of the mountains and the sea. He was also said to be so wealthy that he deposited bricks of gold in the river estuary to appease the local gods, and a hillside near town was covered with silver and gold images of the Buddha. The gold originated in East or West Africa and came to Southeast Asia through trade with the Muslim world (see Chapter 9).

The kings built and patronized Buddhist monasteries and schools. In central Java, local dynasties allied with Srivijaya built magnificent temple complexes to advertise their glory. The most famous of these, **Borobodur** (booh-roe-boe-DOOR), built between 770 and 825 C.E., was the largest human construction in the Southern Hemisphere.

The kings of Srivijaya carried out this marvelous balancing act for centuries. But the system was vulnerable to shifts in the pattern of international trade. Some such change must have contributed to the decline of Srivijaya in the eleventh century, even though the immediate cause was a destructive raid on the capital by forces of the Chola kingdom of southeast India in 1025 C.E.

After the decline of Srivijaya, leadership passed to new, vigorous kingdoms on the eastern end of Java, and the maritime realm of Southeast Asia remained prosperous and connected to international trade networks. Through the ages Europeans remained dimly aware of this region as a source of spices and other luxury items. Some four centuries after the decline of Srivijaya, an Italian navigator serving under the flag of Spain—Christopher Columbus—sailed westward across the Atlantic Ocean, seeking to establish a direct route to the fabled "Indies" from which the spices came.

Borobodur A massive stone monument on the Indonesian island of Java, erected by the Sailendra kings around 800 C.E. The winding ascent through ten levels, decorated with rich relief carving, is a Buddhist allegory for the progressive stages of enlightenment.

Aerial View of the Buddhist Monument at Borobodur, Java The great monument of volcanic stone was more than 300 feet (90 meters) in length and over 100 feet (30 meters) high. Pilgrims made a 3-mile-long (nearly 5-kilometer-long) winding ascent through ten levels intended to represent the ideal Buddhist journey from ignorance to enlightenment. Numerous sculptured reliefs depicting Buddhist legends provide glimpses of daily life in early Java.

SECTION REVIEW

- Climate and resources enabled Southeast Asia to support large human populations.

- Located on the trade and pilgrimage routes between China and India, Southeast Asia came under strong Hindu and Buddhist influence.

- Shrewd rulers used Indian knowledge and personnel to enhance their power and prestige.

- Funan rose to prominence between the first and sixth centuries C.E. by controlling the trade route across the Malay Peninsula.

- The Srivijayan kingdom flourished between the seventh and eleventh centuries C.E. and dominated the new international trade route through the Strait of Malacca.

CONCLUSION

This chapter traces the emergence of complex societies in India and Southeast Asia between the second millennium B.C.E. and the first millennium C.E. Because of migrations, trade, and the spread of belief systems, an Indian style of civilization spread throughout the subcontinent and adjoining regions and eventually made its way to the mainland and island chains of Southeast Asia. In this period were laid cultural foundations that in large measure still endure.

The development and spread of belief systems—Vedism, Buddhism, Jainism, and Hinduism—have a central place in this chapter because nearly all the surviving sources are religious. Ancient Indians held a strikingly different view of time than did their Israelite, Greek, and Chinese contemporaries, and they did not generate historiographic texts. The distinctive Indian conception—of vast epochs in which universes are created and destroyed again and again and the essential spirit of living creatures is reincarnated repeatedly—made the particulars of any brief moment seem relatively insignificant.

Political and social division has been the norm throughout much of the history of India, a consequence of the diversity of the subcontinent and the complex mix of ethnic and linguistic groups inhabiting it. The elaborate structure of classes and castes was a response to this diversity. Strong central governments, such as those of the Mauryan and Gupta kings, rose to dominance by gaining control of resources and important trade routes and developing effective military and administrative institutions. However, the periods of fragmentation and multiple small centers of power seemed as economically and intellectually dynamic as the periods of unity.

Many distinctive social and intellectual features of Indian civilization—the class and caste system, models of kingship and statecraft, and Vedic, Jain, and Buddhist belief systems—originated in the great river valleys of the north, where descendants of Indo-European immigrants predominated. Hinduism embraced elements drawn from the Dravidian cultures of the south as well as from Buddhism. The capacity of the Hindu tradition to assimilate a wide range of popular beliefs facilitated the spread of a common Indian civilization across the subcontinent, although there was considerable variation from one region to another.

Southeast Asia, as a crossroads of trade, was influenced by both China and India. Commerce brought migrants and merchants from both regions to Southeast Asia. As Buddhism spread, Southeast Asia became a way station for Indian missionaries and Chinese pilgrims. Malay rulers looked to Indian traditions as a rich source of ideas and prestige, and they used Indian models of bureaucracy, ceremonial practices, and forms of artistic representation. Thus the Southeast Asian kingdoms synthesized foreign cultural influences with indigenous beliefs, values, and institutions.

CHAPTER REVIEW

THE INDUS VALLEY CIVILIZATION
■ *What does material evidence tell us about the Indus Valley civilization and the most likely reason for its collapse?* (page 133)

The cities of Harappa and Mohenjo-Daro provide evidence of early civilization in the fertile Indus Valley. Both display a striking uniformity of planning and construction, including high brick walls and a rectangular grid of streets. Excavated artifacts exhibit standard shapes and styles, with some evidence indicating trade with resource-rich regions to the north and Mesopotamia in the west. Unfortunately, the writing system of this civilization remains undeciphered. The abandonment of the cities signaled the end of this civilization. The probable cause was "systems failure" resulting from ecological changes in the river valley and along the coast.

FOUNDATIONS OF INDIAN CIVILIZATION
■ *What historical forces led to the development of complex social groupings in ancient India?* (page 136)

Arya kinship groups moving into northwest India after 1500 B.C.E. established a religiously sanctioned class (varna) system of priests, warriors, landowners and merchants, and peasants and laborers. With further subdivisions into castes (jati), this system ordered the

relations among ethnically, linguistically, and culturally diverse populations. Various forms of resistance to the secular and religious domination of the Brahmins arose, including the more egalitarian Buddhist and Jain belief systems. Traditionalists responded to this through Hinduism, which provided people with a number of ways to make a personal connection with the gods.

INDIAN IMPERIAL EXPANSION AND COLLAPSE
■ *In the face of powerful forces that tended to keep India fragmented, how did the Mauryan Empire of the fourth to second centuries B.C.E. and the Gupta Empire of the fourth to sixth centuries C.E. succeed in unifying much of India?* (page 144)

Despite geographical obstacles, religious diversity, and social orientation toward the caste system, the Mauryan (fourth to second centuries B.C.E.) and Gupta (fourth to sixth centuries C.E.) rulers brought most of the subcontinent under their control. Both dynasties exploited the agricultural productivity of the Ganges Plain, monopolized mining and weapons production, built standing armies, and developed complex bureaucracies and networks of spies. These centralizing factors encouraged urban growth, long-distance trade, and new forms of art and literature.

SOUTHEAST ASIA, 50–1025 C.E.

■ *How did the geography of Southeast Asia contribute to its commerce and to the influence of Hinduism and Buddhism?* (page 149)

Southeast Asia, a region rich in resources with a tropical climate favorable for agriculture, generated a lively trade, both locally and with South and East Asia. Geographically situated between the Indian Ocean and the South China Sea, the Malay Peninsula had either to be crossed at its narrowest point or sailed around to connect markets with consumers. South Asian sailors, merchants, and pilgrims brought Hinduism and Buddhism to the region. Kingdoms in southern Indochina, the Malay Peninsula, and Java found their ideas appealing. Malay rulers blended Indian religions with local traditions to produce a distinctive civilization.

Key Terms

Harappa (p. 134)
Mohenjo-Daro (p. 134)
monsoon (p. 137)
Vedas (p. 138)
varna/jati (p. 138)
karma (p. 139)
moksha (p. 139)
Buddha (p. 140)
Mahayana Buddhism (p. 141)
Theravada Buddhism (p. 141)

Hinduism (p. 141)
Mauryan Empire (p. 144)
Ashoka (p. 145)
Mahabharata (p. 146)
Bhagavad-Gita (p. 146)
Tamil kingdoms (p. 146)
Gupta Empire (p. 146)
theater-state (p. 147)
Funan (p. 151)
Srivijaya (p. 151)
Borobodur (p. 152)

Peoples and Civilizations of the Americas

© Cengage Learning

Humans reached the Western Hemisphere through a series of migrations from Asia. Some scholars believe that the first migrations occurred as early as 35,000 to 25,000 B.C.E., but most accept a later date of 20,000 to 13,000 B.C.E. Although some limited contacts with other cultures—for example, with Polynesians—may have occurred later, the peoples in the Western Hemisphere were virtually isolated from the rest of the world for at least 15,000 years. Thus, while technological innovations passed back and forth among the civilizations of Asia, Africa, and Europe, the peoples of the Americas faced the challenges of the natural environment on their own.

As people spread throughout the hemisphere, they encountered environments that ranged from polar extremes to tropical rain forests to towering mountain ranges. In two areas, Mesoamerica (Mexico and northern Central America) and the mountainous Andean region of South America, conditions proved conducive to the emergence of complex societies. Domestication of maize, beans, squash, and sweet potatoes occurred there well before 3000 B.C.E. In the following millennia, technological innovations like metallurgy and a limited trade led to greater social stratification and the beginnings of urbanization in both regions. Cultural elites used their increasing political and religious authority to organize great numbers of laborers for projects such as large-scale irrigation and drainage works, cleared forests, and hillside terracing, thus providing the economic platform for the construction of urban centers.

The Amerindian[1] hereditary elites organized their societies to meet these challenges, even as

their ambitions ignited new conflicts. No single set of political institutions or technologies worked in every environment, and American cultures varied widely. Productive and diversified agriculture and cities that rivaled the Chinese and Roman capitals in size and beauty developed in Mesoamerica and the Andean region of South America. In the rest of the hemisphere, indigenous peoples maintained a wide variety of settlement patterns, political forms, and cultural traditions based on combinations of hunting and agriculture.

FORMATIVE OLMEC AND CHAVÍN CIVILIZATIONS, 1200–200 B.C.E.

■ *How did the Olmec and Chavín civilizations influence later Mesoamerican and Andean civilizations?*

By 1000 B.C.E. the major urban centers of Mesoamerica and the Andes, dominated by monumental structures devoted to religion and the elite, had become civilizations and begun to project their political and cultural power over broad territories. These civilizations, the Olmec of Mesoamerica and the Chavín of the Andes, would persist for more than a thousand years.

The Mesoamerican Olmec, 1200–400 B.C.E.

Mesoamerica is a region of great geographic and climatic diversity. It is extremely active geologically, experiencing both earthquakes and volcanic eruptions. Mountain ranges break the region into microenvironments, including the temperate climates of the Valley of Mexico and the Guatemalan highlands, the tropical forests of the Petén and Gulf of Mexico coast, the rain forest of the southern Yucatán and Belize, and the drier scrub forest of the northern Yucatán (see Map 7.1).

Within each of these ecological niches, Amerindian peoples made use of a wide variety of indigenous plants, including maize, beans, and squash, as well as minerals like obsidian, quartz, and jade. But no animals were domesticated. Eventually, contacts across environmental boundaries led to trade and cultural exchange with emerging centers in the region and ultimately with Central and South America.

[1] Before 1492, the inhabitants of the Western Hemisphere had no single name for themselves, no sense that physical similarities created a shared identity. Identity derived from kin groups, language, cultural practices, and political structures. Conquest and the occupation by Europeans after 1492 imposed on America's original inhabitants a racial consciousness and racial identity. All collective terms for these first American peoples reflect this history. *Indians, Native Americans, Amerindians, First Peoples,* and *Indigenous Peoples* find common usage. This book uses the names of individual cultures and states wherever possible. It tries to reserve *Amerindian* and other terms that suggest transcultural identity and experience for the period after 1492.

Map 7.1 Olmec and Chavín Civilizations The regions of Mesoamerica (most of modern Mexico and Central America) and the Andean highlands of South America have hosted impressive civilizations since early times. The civilizations of the Olmec and Chavín were the originating civilizations of these two regions, providing the foundations of architecture, city planning, and religion. © Cengage Learning

Enhanced trade, increasing agricultural productivity, and rising population led, in turn, to urbanization and the appearance of powerful political and religious elites. Yet even though all Mesoamerican civilizations shared fundamental elements of material culture, technology, religious belief and ritual, political organization, art, architecture, and sports, the region was never unified politically.

The most influential early Mesoamerican civilization was the **Olmec**, flourishing between 1200 and 400 B.C.E. (see Map 7.1). The center of Olmec

civilization was located near the tropical Atlantic coast of what are now the Mexican states of Veracruz and Tabasco. The earliest settlements in the region depended on rich plant diversity and fishing,

> **Olmec** The first Mesoamerican civilization. Between about 1200 and 400 B.C.E., the Olmec people of central Mexico created a vibrant civilization that included intensive agriculture, wide-ranging trade, ceremonial centers, and monumental construction. The Olmec had great cultural influence on later Mesoamerican societies.

Chronology

	Mesoamerica	Northern Peoples	Andean Region
3000 B.C.E.	**Before 3000 B.C.E.** Domestication of maize, beans, and squash		**Before 3000 B.C.E.** Domestication of potato, quinoa, sweet potato, and llama
	Before 2000 B.C.E. Early urbanization	**Before 2000 B.C.E.** Domestication of squash and seed crops like sunflower	**Before 2000 B.C.E.** Early urbanization
2000 B.C.E.	**1200 B.C.E.** Beginning of Olmec civilization		
1000 B.C.E.			**900 B.C.E.** Beginning of Chavín civilization
500 B.C.E.	**400 B.C.E.** End of Olmec civilization **100 B.C.E.** First stage of Teotihuacan temple complex		**200 B.C.E.** End of Chavín civilization
100 C.E.	**250** Maya early classic period begins	**100–400** Hopewell culture in Ohio River Valley	**200** Moche begin to dominate Peruvian coast
500 C.E.			**500–1000** Tiwanaku and Wari control Andean highlands
	750 Teotihuacan destroyed	**700** Beginning of Anasazi culture in Four Corners region	**700** End of Moche domination
	800–900 Maya classic-era cities abandoned	**800** Beginning of Mississippian culture	
	968 Toltec capital of Tula founded		**900** Chimú begins to dominate Peruvian coast
1000 C.E.	**1175** Tula destroyed	**1050–1250** Cahokia reaches peak population	
		1150 Anasazi center of Pueblo Bonito abandoned; other Anasazi centers enter crisis after 1200	**1470s** End of Chimú domination
	Until 1500 Culhuacán and Cholula continue Toltec tradition		
1500 C.E.		**1500** End of Mississippian culture	

but by 3000 B.C.E. the staples of the Mesoamerican diet—maize, beans, and squash—had been domesticated. Manioc, a calorie-rich root crop originating in Brazil, was also grown in the floodplains. The first stage of urbanization was tied to the trade and

use of products like salt, cacao (chocolate beans), potters' clay, and limestone. It is unclear whether Olmec urban centers were rival city-states or were subject to a centralized political authority, but scholars agree that San Lorenzo (1200–900 B.C.E.), with a

Olmec Head Giant heads sculpted from basalt are a widely recognized legacy of Olmec culture. Sixteen heads have been found, the largest approximately 11 feet (3.4 meters) tall. Experts in Olmec archaeology believe the heads are portraits of individual rulers, warriors, or ballplayers. Some were depicted wearing the padded helmet used as protection in the sacred ballgame.

Georg Gerster/Photo Researchers, Inc.

population between 10,000 to 18,000, was the largest and most important Olmec center. San Lorenzo's cultural influence ultimately extended south and west to the Pacific coast of Central America and north to central Mexico. Also founded around 1200 B.C.E., La Venta (LA BEN-tah) became the preeminent Olmec center when San Lorenzo was abandoned or destroyed around 900 B.C.E. After La Venta's collapse around 600 B.C.E., Tres Zapotes (TRACE zah-POE-tace) became the largest Olmec center, although it was much smaller than either of its predecessors.

Little is known about Olmec political structure, but it seems likely that the rise of major urban centers coincided with the appearance of a form of kingship that combined religious and secular roles. San Lorenzo and other Olmec cities served primarily as religious centers, laid out in alignment with the religious observation of the stars (a practice that led to a calendar used to predict seasonal rains and guide planting and harvesting and that likely influenced later innovations of the Maya). The deities of the polytheistic Olmec had both male and female natures.

Human and animal characteristics were blended in the motifs found on ceramics, sculptures, and buildings. Rulers and their close kin came to be associated with the gods through bloodletting ceremonies and human sacrifice and through the staging of elaborate rituals that brought together urban and rural populations. Rulers were especially associated with the jaguar. Priests and shamans who foretold the future and acted as healers claimed the ability to make direct contact with supernatural powers by transforming themselves into powerful animals, such as crocodiles, snakes, and sharks. These transformative powers were also associated with a ballgame played with a solid rubber ball in banked courts located near the center of temple precincts. Versions of this game survived until the arrival of Europeans in the sixteenth century.

The urban elite's power grew with the development of persuasive religious ideologies and compelling religious rituals that helped organize and subordinate neighboring rural populations. As a result, urban centers were dominated by religious architecture, including pyramids, monumental mounds, and raised platforms. Large artificial platforms and mounds of packed earth framed the collective rituals and political activities that brought the rural population to the cities at special times in the year. This massive urban architecture required thousands of laborers recruited from surrounding rural areas. Skilled artisans who lived in or near the urban core decorated the buildings with carvings and sculptures. Olmec artisans also produced exquisite carved jade figurines, necklaces, and ceremonial knives and axes. The diffusion of these Olmec products among distant locations suggests a specialized merchant class that traded for obsidian, jade, and pottery.

The mounting wealth and power of the elite and the growing populations of Olmec cities depended on a bargain struck with the much larger populations of the surrounding countryside. The rural masses provided the labor that constructed the pyramids, platforms, and ball courts of the urban centers as well as the food that sustained urban populations. In exchange, they participated in the awe-inspiring ceremonies that explained human origins or unforeseen natural events and helped guide collective life.

Each major Olmec center was eventually abandoned, its monuments defaced and buried and its buildings destroyed. Archaeologists interpret these events differently; some see them as evidence of internal upheavals or military defeat by neighboring peoples, and others suggest that they were associated with the death of a ruler. Regardless of the causes for Olmec decline, the influence of this civilization endured for centuries. Every subsequent Mesoamerican civilization utilized the rich legacy of Olmec material culture, technology, religious belief and ritual, political organization, art, architecture, and sports.

Early South American Civilization: Chavín, 900–200 B.C.E.

Geography played an important role in the development of human society in the Andes. The region's diverse environments—a mountainous core, arid coastal plain, and dense interior jungles—challenged human populations, encouraging the development of specialized regional production as well as complex social institutions and cultural values that facilitated interregional exchanges and shared labor responsibilities. These adaptations to environmental challenge became enduring features of Andean civilization.

The earliest urban centers in this region were villages of a few hundred people built along the coastal plain or in the foothills near the coast. The abundance of fish and mollusks along the coast of Peru provided a dependable supply of food that helped make the development of early cities possible. The coastal populations traded these products along with decorative shells for maize, other foods, and textiles produced in the foothills. The two regions also exchanged ceremonial practices, religious motifs, and aesthetic ideas. Recent discoveries demonstrate that as early as 2600 B.C.E. the vast site called Caral had developed many of the characteristics now viewed as the hallmarks of later Andean civilization, including ceremonial plazas, pyramids, elevated platforms and mounds, and extensive irrigation works. The scale of public works in Caral suggests a population of thousands and a political structure capable of organizing the production and distribution of maritime and agricultural products over a broad area.

Chavín, one of the most impressive of South America's early urban civilizations (see Map 7.1), inherited many of the cultural and economic characteristics of Caral. The capital city, Chavín de Huantar (cha-BEAN day WAHN-tar), was located at 10,300 feet (3,139 meters) in the eastern range of the Andes north of the modern city of Lima. Between 900 and 200 B.C.E., a period roughly coinciding with Olmec civilization in Mesoamerica, Chavín dominated a densely populated region that included large areas of the Peruvian coastal plains and Andean foothills. Chavín de Huantar's location at the intersection of trade routes connecting the coast with populous mountain valleys and tropical lowlands on the eastern flank of the Andes allowed the city's rulers to control trade

Chavín The first major urban civilization in South America (900–200 B.C.E.). Its capital, Chavín de Huántar, was located high in the Andes Mountains of Peru. Chavín became politically and economically dominant in a densely populated region that included two distinct ecological zones, the Peruvian coastal plain and the Andean foothills.

among these distinct ecological zones and gain an important economic advantage over regional rivals.

Chavín's dominance as a ceremonial and commercial center depended on earlier developments in agriculture and trade, including the introduction of maize cultivation from Mesoamerica. Maize increased the food production of the coast and interior foothills, allowing greater levels of urbanization. As Chavín grew, its trade linked the coast to inland producers of quinoa (a local grain), potatoes, and llamas in the high mountain valleys and, to a lesser extent, the Amazonian production of coca and fruits.

Reciprocal labor obligations that permitted the construction and maintenance of roads, bridges, temples, palaces, and large irrigation and drainage projects, as well as textile production, developed as well. In later times, groups of related families who held land communally and claimed descent from a common ancestor organized these labor obligations. Group members thought of each other as brothers and sisters and were obliged to aid one another, providing a model for the organization of labor and distribution of goods at every level of Andean society.

Llamas, the only domesticated beasts of burden in the Americas, played an important role in the integration of the Andean region. They were first domesticated in the mountainous interior of Peru and were crucial to Chavín's development. Llamas provided meat and wool and helped transport goods. A single driver could control ten to thirty animals, each carrying up to 70 pounds (32 kilograms); a human porter could carry only about 50 pounds (22.5 kilograms). The increased use of llamas to move goods from one ecological zone to another promoted specialization of production and increased trade.

The enormous scale of the capital and the dispersal of Chavín's pottery styles, religious motifs, and architectural forms over a wide area suggest that Chavín imposed some form of political integration and trade dependency on its neighbors that may have relied in part on military force. However, most modern scholars believe that, as in the case of the Olmec civilization, Chavín's influence depended more on the development of an attractive and convincing religious belief system and related rituals. Chavín's most potent religious symbol, a jaguar deity, was dispersed over a broad area, and archaeological

evidence suggests that Chavín de Huantar served as a pilgrimage site.

The architectural signature of Chavín was a large complex of multilevel platforms made of packed earth or rubble and faced with cut stone or adobe (sun-dried brick made of clay and straw). Small buildings used for ritual purposes or as elite residences were built on these platforms. Nearly all the buildings were decorated with relief carvings of serpents, condors, jaguars, or humans. The largest building at Chavín de Huantar measured 250 feet (76 meters) on each side and rose to a height of 50 feet (15 meters). About one-third of its interior was hollow, containing narrow galleries and small rooms that may have housed the remains of royal ancestors.

American metallurgy was first developed in the Andean region. The later introduction of metallurgy in Mesoamerica, like the appearance of maize agriculture in the Andes, suggests sustained contact between the two regions. Archaeological investigations of Chavín de Huantar and smaller centers have revealed remarkable three-dimensional silver, gold, and gold alloy ornaments that represent a clear advance over earlier technologies. Bronze and iron, however, were unknown.

Improvements in both the manufacture and decoration of textiles are also associated with the rise of Chavín. The quality of these products, which were probably used by the elite or in religious rituals, added to the reputation and prestige of the culture and aided in the projection of its power and influence. The most common decorative motif in sculpture, pottery, and textiles was a jaguar-man similar in conception to the Olmec symbol. In both civilizations and in many other cultures in the Americas, this powerful predator provided an enduring image of religious authority and a vehicle through which the gods could act in the world.

Class distinctions also appear to have increased in Chavín. Priests directed religious life, and there is

---

llama A hoofed animal indigenous to the Andes Mountains. It was the only domesticated beast of burden in the Americas before the arrival of Europeans. The use of llamas to transport goods made possible specialized production and trade among people living in different ecological zones and fostered the integration of these zones by Chavín and later Andean states.

SECTION REVIEW

- Well before 3000 B.C.E. newly domesticated plants, new technologies, and trade led to greater social stratification and the beginnings of urbanization in Mesoamerica and the Andean region of South America.

- The Olmec of Mesoamerica (1200–400 B.C.E.) and the Chavín civilization (900–200 B.C.E.) in the Andes each coordinated exchanges of goods between different ecological zones.

- Olmec urban centers were probably ruled by kings, who were associated with deities and represented by highly skilled artisans in monumental head sculptures.

- Chavín utilized llamas, the only domesticated beasts of burden in the hemisphere, developed important technologies, and devised a unifying religious system.

- Ruling elites residing in urban centers staged elaborate religious ceremonies designed to impress subjects and enhance their prestige.

evidence that both local chiefs and a more powerful chief or king dominated Chavín's politics. Excavations of graves reveal that superior-quality textiles as well as gold crowns, breastplates, and jewelry distinguished rulers from commoners.

There is no convincing evidence, like defaced buildings or broken images, that the eclipse of Chavín (unlike the Olmec centers) was associated with conquest or rebellion. However, recent investigations have suggested that increased warfare throughout the region around 200 B.C.E. disrupted Chavín's trade and undermined the authority of the governing elite. Regardless of what caused the collapse of this powerful culture, the technologies, material culture, statecraft, architecture, and urban planning associated with Chavín influenced the Andean region for centuries.

CLASSIC-ERA CULTURE AND SOCIETY IN MESOAMERICA, 200–900

■ *What were the most important shared characteristics of Mesoamerican cultures in the classic period?*

Between 200 and 900 C.E., the peoples of Mesoamerica entered a period of remarkable cultural creativity. Despite differences in language and the absence of regional political integration, Mesoamericans were unified by similarities in material culture, religious beliefs, and social structures forged in the Olmec era. Building on this legacy, the peoples of what is now Central America and south and central Mexico developed new political institutions, made great strides in astronomy and mathematics, and improved agricultural productivity.

Archaeologists call the mix of achievements after 300 C.E. the classic period. Population grew, a greater variety of products were traded over longer distances, social hierarchies became more complex, and great cities served as governing and religious centers. Impressive platforms and pyramids were devoted to religious functions. Large urban populations, divided into classes, served hereditary political and religious elites who also controlled the nearby towns and countryside.

The agricultural foundation of Mesoamerican civilization had been developed centuries earlier. The major agricultural technologies—irrigation, wetland drainage, and hillside terracing—preceded the cities built after 200 C.E. by more than a thousand years. What made the achievements of the classic era possible was the extended reach and power of religious and political leaders. The impressive architecture and great size of Teotihuacan (teh-o-tee-WAH-kahn) and the great Maya cities such as Tikal illustrate both Mesoamerican aesthetic achievements and the development of powerful political institutions.

Teotihuacan

At the height of its power, from 450 to 600 C.E., **Teotihuacan** (100 B.C.E.–750 C.E.), located about 30 miles (48 kilometers) northeast of modern Mexico City, housed between 125,000 and 150,000 inhabitants. The largest city in the Americas, it outshone all but a few contemporary European and Asian cities.

The religious architecture of Teotihuacan included enormous pyramids dedicated to the sun and moon and more than twenty smaller temples devoted to other gods, all of which flanked a central avenue. The god Quetzalcoatl (kate-zahl-CO-ah-tal),

Teotihuacan A powerful city-state in central Mexico (100 B.C.E.–750 C.E.). Its population was about 150,000 at its peak in 600.

The Temple of the Sun The temple of the sun in the background is the largest pyramid in Tenochtitlan. The smaller temple of Quetzalcoatl in foreground displays the serpent images associated with this culture god common to most Mesoamerican civilizations.

G.Dagli Orti/The Art Archive

the feathered serpent, was considered the originator of agriculture and the arts. Like the Olmec, Teotihuacan's population practiced human sacrifice as a sacred duty toward the gods and as a necessity for the well-being of human society. The excavation of the temple of Quetzalcoatl uncovered scores of sacrificial victims.

Teotihuacan's urban population had grown rapidly from the forced relocation of villagers following volcanic eruptions. Nevertheless, more than two-thirds of the city's residents continued to farm, walking from their city homes to their fields. The elite used the city's growing labor resources to expand agriculture by draining swamps, building irrigation works, and cutting terraces into hillsides. They also expanded **chinampas** (chee-NAM-pahs), misleadingly called "floating gardens." These narrow artificial islands, anchored by trees and created by heaping lake muck and waste material on beds of reeds, were crucial in sustaining the growing population because the subsurface irrigation resisted frost and thus permitted year-round agriculture.

The housing of commoners changed as the population grew. Apartment-like stone buildings housed, among other people, the craftspeople who produced

goods for export. Teotihuacan pottery has turned up throughout central Mexico and even in the Maya region of Guatemala. More than 2 percent of the urban population crafted similarly widespread obsidian tools and weapons.

The city's role as a religious center signified divine approval of the increasingly prosperous elite. Members of the elite controlled the state bureaucracy, tax collection, and commerce. Their diet and style of dress reflected their prestige, and they lived in separate aristocratic compounds. Temple and palace murals confirm the central position and great prestige of the priestly class. Pilgrims came to Teotihuacan from far away, and some became permanent residents.

Unlike other classic-period societies, the people of Teotihuacan did not have a single ruler. The deeds of the rulers do not feature in public art, nor were rulers represented by statues as in other Mesoamerican civilizations. Thus historians debate the role of the military at Teotihuacan. Unlike later postclassic

chinampas Raised fields constructed along lakeshores in central Mexico to increase agricultural yields.

civilizations, Teotihuacan was not an imperial state controlled by a military elite, and the absence of walls or other defensive structures before 500 suggests relative peace. However, archaeology points to a powerful military protecting long-distance trade and compelling peasants to hand over their surplus production. Representations of soldiers in typical Teotihuacan dress in the Maya region of Guatemala may indicate that the military were used to expand trade.

The forces that brought about the end of Teotihuacan about 750 remain a mystery, but evidence of weaknesses appears as early as 500, when the urban population declined to about 40,000 and the city began to build defensive walls. Fortifications and pictorial evidence from murals suggest that the city's final decades were violent. Indications of conflict within the ruling elite and of mismanagement of resources have challenged earlier theories of conquest by a nearby rival city or by nomadic peoples from the north. Class conflict and the breakdown of public order may explain the destruction of the most important temples in the city center, the defacing of religious images, and the burning of elite palaces. The eclipse of Teotihuacan reverberated throughout Mexico and into Central America.

The Maya

Contemporary with Teotihuacan, the **Maya** developed a civilization in the region that today includes Guatemala, Honduras, Belize, and southern Mexico. The difficulties of a tropical climate and fragile soils make the cultural and architectural achievements of the Maya all the more remarkable. Although they shared a single culture, they never unified politically. Instead, rival kingdoms led by hereditary rulers competed for dominance (see Map 7.2).

Today, Maya farmers cut down small trees and brush and burn the dead vegetation to fertilize the land. This swidden agriculture produces high yields for a few years, but it exhausts the soil's nutrients, eventually forcing a move to more fertile land. The high population levels of the Maya classic period (250–900 C.E.) required more intensive forms of agriculture. Maya living near the major urban centers achieved high yields by draining swamps and building elevated fields. They used irrigation in areas with long dry seasons and built terraced hillsides in the cooler

Map 7.2 Maya Civilization, 250–1400 C.E. The Maya never created an integrated and unified state. Instead Maya civilization developed as a complex network of independent city-states. © Cengage Learning

highlands. Nearly every household planted a garden to provide condiments and fruits. The Maya also practiced forest management, favoring the growth of useful trees and shrubs and promoting the conservation of deer and other animals hunted for food.

During the classic period, city-states proliferated, the most powerful controlling groups of smaller dependent cities. Religious temples and rituals linked the power of kings to the gods. Unlike earlier sites, these cities had dense central precincts dominated by buildings that were commonly aligned with the movements of the sun and Venus. High pyramids and elaborately decorated palaces, often built on high ground or on constructed mounds, surrounded open plazas, an awesome prospect for the masses drawn in for religious and political rituals.

Maya Mesoamerican civilization concentrated in Mexico's Yucatán Peninsula and in Guatemala and Honduras but never unified into a single empire. Major contributions were in mathematics, astronomy, and development of the calendar.

The Great Plaza at Tikal The impressive architectural and artistic achievements of the classic-era Maya are still visible in the ruins of Tikal, in modern Guatemala. Maya centers provided a dramatic setting for the rituals that dominated public life. Construction of Tikal began before 150 B.C.E.; the city was abandoned about 900 C.E. A ball court and residences for the elite were part of the Great Plaza. Daniel Loncarevic/Shutterstock.com

Bas-reliefs and bright paint covered nearly all public buildings. Common motifs included religious allegories, the genealogies of rulers, and important historical events. Carved altars and stone monoliths arose near major temples. As was true throughout the hemisphere, this rich legacy of monumental architecture was constructed without the aid of wheels—no pulleys, wheelbarrows, or carts—or metal tools. Masses of men and women aided only by levers and stone tools cut and carried construction materials and lifted them into place.

The Maya cosmos consisted of three layers connected along a vertical axis that traced the course of the sun. The earthly arena of human existence came between the heavens, conceptualized as a sky-monster, and a dark underworld. A sacred tree rose through the three layers, its roots in the underworld and its branches in the heavens. The temple precincts of Maya cities physically represented this cosmology: the pyramids as sacred mountains reaching to the heavens and their doorways as portals to the underworld.

Rulers and other members of the elite decorated their bodies with paint and tattoos and wore elaborate costumes of textiles, animal skins, and feathers to project both secular power and divine sanction. Kings communicated directly with the supernatural residents of the other worlds and with deified royal ancestors through bloodletting rituals and hallucinogenic trances. Scenes of rulers drawing blood from lips, ears, and penises are common in frescoes and on painted pottery.

Warfare in particular was infused with religious meaning and elaborate rituals. Scenes of battle and the torture and sacrifice of captives appear frequently. The king, his kinsmen, and other ranking nobles fought personally, with the goal of securing captives rather than territory. Elite captives were nearly always sacrificed; commoners usually became slaves.

Few women directly ruled Maya kingdoms, though women from ruling lineages did play important political and religious roles. The consorts of male rulers participated in bloodletting rituals and in other public ceremonies. Their noble blood helped legitimate their husbands' rule. Though generally patrilineal (tracing descent in the male line), some male rulers traced their lineages from both the male and female lines. Some rulers emphasized the female line if it held higher status. Women were also healers and shamans. In addition, scholars believe that women played a central role in religious rituals of the home. Among the lower classes, women were essential to the management of family life and the household economy, maintaining garden plots and weaving.

Building on Olmec contributions, the Maya developed the calendar, mathematics, and writing. The complexity of their calendric system, with each day marked by three separate dating systems, reflects their interest in time and the cosmos. Like other Mesoamerican peoples, the Maya calendar tracked a ritual cycle (260 days divided into thirteen months of 20 days) as well as a solar calendar (365 days divided into eighteen months of 20 days, plus 5 "unfavorable days" at the end of the year). The concurrence of these two calendars every 52 years was considered especially ominous. Alone among Mesoamerican peoples, the Maya also maintained a continuous "long count" calendar, which began at a fixed date in the past that scholars have identified as 3114 B.C.E., a date probably associated with creation.

The Maya systems of mathematics, which underlay the calendar, incorporated the concept of the zero and place value but had limited notational signs. Maya writing used hieroglyphs that signified whole words or concepts as well as phonetic cues or syllables. Aspects of public life, religious belief, and the biographies of rulers and their ancestors were recorded in bark-paper books, on pottery, and on the stone columns and monumental buildings of the urban centers.

Abandonment or destruction befell many of the major urban centers between 800 and 900, although a small number survived for centuries. In many areas, decades of urban population decline and increased warfare preceded the collapse. Some experts maintain that the destruction of Teotihuacan after 650 disrupted trade, thus undermining the legitimacy of Maya rulers who used trade goods in rituals. Others suggest that the population pressure led to environmental degradation and declining agricultural productivity. This, in turn, might have caused social conflict and warfare as desperate elites sought additional agricultural land through conquest.

THE POSTCLASSIC PERIOD IN MESOAMERICA, 900–1300

■ *What role did warfare play in the postclassic period of Mesoamerica?*

The collapse of Teotihuacan and many of the major Maya centers occurred over more than a century and a half, making the division between classic and postclassic periods somewhat arbitrary. In fact, some important classic-period civilizations survived unscathed, and essential cultural characteristics

SECTION REVIEW

- Between 200 and 900 C.E., Mesoamerican peoples built civilizations with characteristics derived from Olmec culture.

- Their achievements were made possible by the increased power of political and religious leaders.

- Both Teotihuacan and the Maya city-states were supported by intensive agriculture and contained monumental religious architecture.

- Teotihuacan grew into a powerful economic and religious center without a single ruler or powerful military elite.

- The Maya city-states were ruled by kings and elites that practiced ritualized warfare.

- Maya women appear to have enjoyed high status, and both civilizations adopted practices and technologies from their Olmec predecessors.

in religious belief and practice, architecture, urban planning, and social organization carried over to the postclassic period.

Nevertheless, important differences exist. The population of Mesoamerica apparently expanded in the postclassic period, causing an intensification of agricultural practices and increased warfare. Governing elites increased the size of their armies and developed political institutions that facilitated their control of large and culturally diverse territories acquired through conquest.

The Toltecs

Scholars speculate that the **Toltecs** (TOLL-teks) originated as a satellite population protecting the northern frontier of Teotihuacan from nomad raids. After migrating south, they created an important postclassic civilization based on the cultural legacy of Teotihuacan, including the preservation of Teotihuacan religious architecture and rituals and the use of irrigation and terraced hillsides.

The Aztecs and their fifteenth-century contemporaries erroneously believed that the Toltecs were the source of nearly all of Mesoamerica's cultural achievements (see Chapter 15). As one Aztec source declared:

> In truth [the Toltecs] invented all the precious and marvelous things. . . . All that now exists was their discovery. . . . And these Toltecs were very wise; they were thinkers, for they originated the year count, the day count. All their discoveries formed the book for interpreting dreams. . . . And so wise were they [that] they understood the stars which were in the heavens.[2]

Actually, the most important Toltec innovations came from politics and war. Their civilization was dependent on military power, and they created the first conquest state. Their political influence extended from their political capital at Tula (TOO-la), founded in 968 C.E. north of modern Mexico City, to Central America. The violent imagery of their military achievements and religious rituals dominated the Mesoamerican imagination in the late postclassic period. Nearly all the public buildings and temples in

Tula carried scenes of human sacrifice, including the decoration of a prominent ceremonial platform with images of impaled skulls, the **tzompantli** (zohm-PAHNT-lee). The massive architecture of the city center also featured impressive statues of warriors and serpents, colonnaded patios, and numerous temples. At its peak Tula had a population of approximately 60,000.

Like the earlier Teotihuacan, Tula and its subject dependencies had a multiethnic character, hosting distinct culture and language communities. At the height of their power, the Toltecs forged a military alliance with another multiethnic state with historic ties to Teotihuacan, **Culhuacán** (kool-whah-KHAN), located to the south. Together they established networks of tribute and trade throughout the central Mexican region.

Accounts dictated to Catholic priests by native informants during the Spanish conquest do not agree on the demise of the Toltecs. Most sources seem to indicate that two rulers shared power at Tula and that this division of power eventually weakened the Toltec state. Sometime around 1150 C.E. a struggle between elite groups identified with rival religious cults undermined Toltec society. According to Aztec legends, Topiltzin (tow-PEELT-zeen)—one of the two rulers and a priest of the cult of Quetzalcoatl—and his followers bitterly accepted exile in the east. One text relates the following:

> Thereupon he [Topiltzin] looked toward Tula, and then wept. . . . And when he had done these things . . . he went to reach the seacoast. Then he fashioned a raft of serpents. When he had arranged the raft, he placed himself as if it were his boat. Then he set off across the sea.[3]

[3] Quoted in Nigel Davies, The Toltec Heritage: *From the Fall of Tula to the Rise of Tenochtitlán* (Norman: University of Oklahoma Press, 1980), 3.

[2] From the Florentine Codex, quoted in Inga Clendinnen, *Aztecs* (New York: Cambridge University Press, 1991), 213.

Toltecs Powerful postclassic empire in central Mexico (900–1175 C.E.). It influenced much of Mesoamerica. Aztecs claimed ties to this earlier civilization.

tzompantli Images of impaled skulls in scenes of human sacrifice included in the decoration of a prominent public buildings and temples in Tula.

Culhuacán Multiethnic Mesoamerican state south of and historically connected with Teotihuacan.

Tula The capital of the Toltecs was dominated by massive public architecture like these carved stone figures. DEA/G.DAGLI ORTI/Getty Images

Toltec decline set in after 1150. By 1175 internal conflict and northern invaders had wreaked destruction upon the once-dominant city of Tula, triggering a centuries-long process of cultural and political assimilation to produce a new Aztec political order based on the Toltec heritage (see Chapter 15).

Cholula

Located near the Mexican city of Puebla, Cholula developed at about the same time as Teotihuacan. It is situated to serve as an exchange point linking the Maya southeast with the Valley of Mexico and with the Mixtec peoples of the southwest. Like Teotihuacan, it was a major religious center and included one of the largest pyramids of Mesoamerica. As a key trade and religious pilgrimage destination, it had a large culturally and linguistically diverse population, including a large Toltec community. Cholula's original ties to the Toltecs are unclear, but sometime after 1000 C.E. its resident Toltec population appealed for help to Culhuacán. Just as Topiltzin would later try to save Tula, his father, Mixcoatl, went to the aid of Cholula. While the fate of this vulnerable Toltec community is not known, Cholula survived as an

169

SECTION REVIEW

- Postclassic civilizations carried on the basic forms of religious belief and ritual, architecture, city planning, and social organization of their predecessors.

- Mesoamerican populations increased, causing intensified agriculture and warfare.

- The Toltecs built upon Teotihuacan's legacy, creating a powerful empire through military conquest and alliances. Their influence spread across central Mexico.

- The architecture of the Toltec capital Tula was decorated with militaristic themes and images of human sacrifice, indicating the increased violence of the postclassic period.

- After the collapse of Tula in the twelfth century, elements of Toltec culture and political culture survived in Culhuacán and Cholula.

important regional power until the Spanish conquest, thus connecting the legacies of both Teotihuacan and the Toltecs to the rise of the powerful Aztec Empire (see Chapter 15).

NORTHERN PEOPLES

■ *In what ways did Mesoamerica influence the cultural centers in North America?*

Mesoamerica's classic period ended around 900 C.E. By then, settled life and complex social and political structures based on improved agriculture and population growth had appeared in the southwestern desert region of today's United States and in eastern river alleys. Along the Ohio River, Amerindian peoples living in large villages created monumental earthworks, practiced hunting and gathering, and harvested locally domesticated seed crops, such as sunflowers. In both areas, cultivating maize introduced from Mesoamerica required large-scale irrigation projects. However, the two regions evolved different political traditions. The Anasazi (ah-nah-SAH-zee) and their neighbors in the Southwest maintained a relatively egalitarian social structure and a political organization based on kinship and age. The mound builders of the East had hereditary chiefs who wielded both secular and religious authority over the political center and subordinate small towns.

Southwestern Desert Cultures

Immigrants from Mexico brought irrigation agriculture to Arizona around 300 B.C.E. With two harvests per year, population grew and villages appeared. The Hohokam of the Salt and Gila River Valleys show strong Mexican influence, with platform mounds and ball courts similar to those of Mesoamerica. Hohokam pottery, clay figurines, cast copper bells, and turquoise mosaics also reflect this influence. By 1000 C.E. the Hohokam had constructed an elaborate irrigation system that included one canal more than 18 miles (30 kilometers) in length. Hohokam agricultural and ceramic technology gradually spread, but it was the Anasazi to the north who left the most vivid legacy.

Archaeologists use **Anasazi**, a Navajo word meaning "ancient ones," to identify a number of dispersed desert cultures located in the Four Corners region of Arizona, New Mexico, Colorado, and Utah. Between 450 and 750 C.E. the early Anasazi lived in large villages and grew maize, beans, and squash. Their cultural life centered in underground buildings called kivas, which they may have used for weaving cotton and making pottery with geometric patterns. After 900, they began to construct large multistory residential and ritual centers.

Chaco Canyon sheltered one of the largest communities: eight large towns in the canyon itself and more on surrounding mesas, suggesting a regional population of 15,000. Each town contained hundreds of rooms arranged in tiers around a central plaza. At Pueblo Bonito, the largest town, a four-story block of residences and storage spaces contained more than 650 rooms. This town, abandoned in 1150, had thirty-eight kivas, including a great kiva more than 65 feet (19 meters) in diameter.

Social life and craft activities took place in small, open plazas or common rooms. While men were often away from the village hunting, trading, and doing irrigation work, women prepared food and cared for children, as well as shared in agricultural tasks and

Anasazi Important culture of what is now the southwest United States (700–1300 C.E.). Centered on Chaco Canyon in New Mexico and Mesa Verde in Colorado, the Anasazi culture built multistory residences and worshiped in subterranean buildings called kivas.

Mesa Verde Cliff Dwelling Located in southern Colorado, the Anasazi cliff dwellings of the Mesa Verde region hosted a population of about 7,000 in 1250 C.E. The construction of housing complexes and religious buildings in the area's large caves was prompted by increased warfare in the region. Kenneth Murray/Photo Researchers, Inc.

many crafts. Among modern Pueblos, the cultural descendants of the Anasazi, houses and furnishings belong to women's extended families that include their mothers and sisters.

Late in Chaco's development, traders provided turquoise to Toltec-period peoples in northern Mexico to exchange for shell jewelry, copper bells, macaws, and trumpets. More important signs of Mesoamerican influence, such as pyramid-shaped mounds, ball courts, and class distinctions signaled by burials or residences, do not appear at Chaco. It seems more likely that the Chaco Canyon culture developed from earlier societies in the region.

Drought probably forced the abandonment of Chaco Canyon in the twelfth century. Nevertheless, the Anasazi continued in the Four Corners region for more than a century. Anasazi settlements on the Colorado Plateau and in Arizona used large natural caves high above valley floors. Such hard-to-reach locations suggest increased warfare, probably provoked by population pressure on limited arable land. The Pueblo peoples of the Rio Grand Valley and Arizona still live in multistory villages and worship in kivas.

Mound Builders: The Hopewell and Mississippian Cultures

From around 100 C.E. the Hopewell culture spread through the Ohio River Valley. Hopewell people constructed large villages and monumental earthworks. Once established, their influence spread west to Illinois, Michigan, and Wisconsin, east to New York and Ontario, and south to Alabama, Louisiana, Mississippi, and even Florida. For sustenance the

Hopewell people depended on hunting and gathering and a limited agriculture based on domesticated seed crops. Hopewell is an early example of a North American **chiefdom**—a territory with a population as large as 10,000 and rule by a hereditary leader with both religious and secular responsibilities. Chiefs organized periodic rituals of feasting and gift giving that established bonds among diverse kinship groups and guaranteed access to specialized crops and craft goods. They also managed long-distance trade for luxury goods and additional food supplies.

The largest Hopewell towns in the Ohio River Valley served as ceremonial and political centers and had several thousand inhabitants. Large mounds housing elite burials and serving as platforms for temples and the chief's residence dominated these centers. Elite burial vaults contain valuable goods like river pearls and copper jewelry and sometimes include the bodies of women and retainers apparently sacrificed to accompany a dead chief into the afterlife. The abandonment of major Hopewell sites around 400 C.E. has no clear environmental or political explanation.

Hopewell technology and mound building were linked to the development of the Mississippian culture (800–1500 C.E.). Although the dependence on maize, beans, and squash suggests an indirect link to Mesoamerica, the urbanized Mississippian chiefdoms resulted instead from the accumulated effects of small increases in agricultural productivity, the adoption of the bow and arrow, and the expansion of trade networks. The largest towns shared a common urban plan based on a central plaza surrounded by large platform mounds. There, people bartered essential commodities, such as flint used for weapons and tools.

The Mississippian culture culminated in the urban site of Cahokia, located near East St. Louis, Illinois. North America's largest mound, a terraced structure 100 feet (30 meters) high and 1,037 by 790 feet (316 by 241 meters) at the base, stands at its center, an area of elite housing and temples ringed by areas where commoners lived. At its height in about 1200 C.E., Cahokia had a population of about 20,000—as large as the great Maya city of Tikal.

Cahokia controlled surrounding agricultural lands and a large number of secondary towns ruled by subchiefs. One tomb containing more than fifty

SECTION REVIEW

- In parts of North America, agricultural improvements and population growth stimulated the development of complex societies.

- In Chaco Canyon, the Anasazi practiced irrigated agriculture and produced architecture that suggests an egalitarian society.

- Some Chaco Canyon settlements exerted broad territorial influences until changing conditions forced relocation to less accessible sites.

- The Hopewell peoples built large villages with monumental earthworks and organized themselves into hierarchical chiefdoms.

- The Mississippian culture built on these patterns, with great sites such as Cahokia revealing stratified societies.

young women and retainers sacrificed to accompany a ruler after death suggests the exalted position of Cahokia's chiefs. Nothing links the decline and eventual abandonment of Cahokia (1250) to military defeat or civil war, although climate changes and population pressures may have undermined its vitality. Smaller Mississippian centers flourished in the southeastern United States until the arrival of Europeans.

ANDEAN CIVILIZATIONS, 200–1400

■ *How did the Amerindian peoples of the Andean area adapt to their environment and produce socially complex and politically advanced societies?*

Much of the Andean region's mountainous zone seems too high for agriculture and human habitation, and the arid plain of its Pacific coastland poses a difficult challenge to cultivation. To the east of the Andes Mountains, the hot, humid tropical environment of the Amazon headwaters also discouraged the organization of complex societies. Yet the Amerindian peoples of the Andean area developed some of the most socially complex and politically advanced societies of the Western Hemisphere (see Map 7.3).

chiefdom Form of political organization with rule by a hereditary leader who held power over a collection of villages and towns. Less powerful than kingdoms and empires, chiefdoms were based on gift giving and commercial links.

Map 7.3 Andean Civilizations, 200 B.C.E.–1532 C.E. In response to environmental challenges posed by an arid coastal plain and high interior mountain ranges, Andean peoples made complex social and technological adaptations. Irrigation systems, the domestication of the llama, metallurgy, and shared labor obligations helped provide a firm economic foundation for powerful, centralized states.

© Cengage Learning

Legend:
- Moche area of influence, 200–700
- Moche site
- Wari area of influence, 500–1000
- Wari site
- Tiwanaku core area
- Tiwanaku area of influence, 500–1000
- Tiwanaku site
- Chimu area of influence, 900–1470
- Chimu site

Cultural Response to Environmental Challenge

People living in the high mountain valleys and on the dry coastal plains overcame significant environmental challenges through effective organization of labor. The record-keeping system used—a device of knotted colored cords called **khipus** (KEY-pooz)—helped administrations record population counts and tribute obligations. Though more limited than the record keeping followed in Mesoamerica, this system enabled the inhabitants to construct large-scale drainage and irrigation works and to terrace hillsides to control erosion and provide additional farmland, all of which increased agricultural production. People worked collectively on road building, urban construction, and even textile production.

The clan, or **ayllu** (aye-YOU), provided the foundation for Andean achievement. Members of an ayllu held land communally and claimed descent from a common ancestor, though they were not always related in fact. Ayllu members thought of themselves as brothers and sisters with obligations to help one another in tasks beyond the ability of a single household.

When territorial states became ruled by hereditary aristocracies and kings after 1000 B.C.E., these obligations were organized on a larger scale. The **mita** (MEET-ah) system required ayllu members to work the fields and care for the llama and alpaca herds owned by religious establishments, the royal court, and the aristocracy. Each ayllu met a yearly quota of workers for specific tasks. Mita laborers built and maintained roads, bridges, temples, palaces, and large irrigation and drainage projects. They also produced textiles and goods essential to ritual life, such as beer made from maize and coca (dried leaves chewed as a stimulant and now also the source of cocaine).

Jobs divided along gender lines, but the work of men and women was interdependent. Men hunted and served as soldiers and administrators, while women had responsibilities in textile production, agriculture, and the home. One early Spanish commentator remarked:

> [Women] did not just perform domestic tasks, but also [labored] in the fields, in the cultivation of their lands, in building houses, and carrying burdens.... And more than once I heard that while women were carrying those burdens, they would feel labor pains,

khipus System of knotted colored cords used by preliterate Andean peoples to record information.

ayllu Andean lineage group or kin-based community.

mita Andean labor system based on shared obligations to help kinsmen and work on behalf of the ruler and religious organizations.

Moche Warrior The Moche of ancient Peru were among the most accomplished ceramic artists of the Americas. Moche potters produced representations of gods and spirits, scenes of daily life, and portrait vases of important people. This warrior is armed with a mace, shield, and protective helmet. The Trustees of the British Museum/Art Resource, NY

and giving birth, they would go to a place where there was water and wash the baby and themselves. Putting the baby on top of the load they were carrying, they would then continue walking as before they gave birth.[4]

The unique environmental challenges of the Andean region led to distinctive highland and coastal cultures. Here, more than in Mesoamerica, geography influenced regional cultural integration and state formation. Because the region's mountain ranges created a multitude of small ecological areas with specialized resources, each community sought to control a variety of environments to gain access to essential goods. Coastal regions produced maize, fish, and cotton; mountain valleys contributed quinoa, potatoes, and tubers; higher elevations contributed the wool and meat of llamas and alpacas; and the Amazonian region provided coca and fruits. Colonists sent to exploit these ecological niches remained linked to their original region and ayllu by marriage and ritual. Historians commonly refer to this system of controlled exchange across ecological boundaries as vertical integration, or verticality.

Moche

Around 200 C.E., some four centuries after the collapse of Chavín, the **Moche** (MO-che) achieved dominance among the Andean civilizations in the north coastal region of Peru. While they did not establish a centralized state, they did deploy military force, and major urban centers like Cerro Blanco (see Map 7.3) established hegemony over smaller towns and villages. In the major Moche cities, elaborate religious rituals tied hereditary rulers to the gods, creating a potent ideology that was key to Moche expansion.

The Moche cultivated maize, quinoa, beans, manioc, and sweet potatoes with the aid of massive irrigation works. At higher elevations, they produced coca, which was used ritually. Complex network of canals and aqueducts connecting fields with water sources as far away as 75 miles (121 kilometers) depended on mita labor. Large herds of alpacas and llamas transported goods across the region's difficult terrain. Their wool, along with cotton, provided the raw material for textile production, and their meat was an important part of the Moche diet.

Murals and decorated ceramics show Moche society to be stratified and theocratic. Labor organi-

---

[4] Quoted in Irene Silverblatt, *Moon, Sun, and Witches: Gender Ideologies and Class in Inca and Colonial Peru* (Princeton, NJ: Princeton University Press, 1987), 10.

Moche Civilization of north coast of Peru (200–700 C.E.). An important Andean civilization that built extensive irrigation networks as well as impressive urban centers dominated by brick temples.

zations helped to promote class divisions. Wealth and power, along with political control, lay in the hands of priests and military leaders, a situation reinforced by military conquest. The elite lived above the commoners atop large platforms at Moche ceremonial centers. The power of the elite was highly individualized and associated with divine sanction, and they literally looked down on the commoners whose labor supported them. Their rich attire, including tall headdresses and elaborate gold jewelry that covered the lower portion of the face with a gold plate suspended from the nose and gold plugs for ears, confirmed their connections to the gods.

One tomb of a warrior-priest buried in the Lambeyeque Valley contained a treasure that included gold, silver, and copper jewelry, textiles, feather ornaments, and shells (see Diversity and Dominance: Burials as Historical Texts). Two women and three men were executed and then buried with this powerful man in order to serve him in the afterlife.

Commoners lived by subsistence farming and labored for their ayllu and the elite. Agriculture, the care of llama herds, and the household economy involved both men and women. Commoners lived in one-room buildings clustered in the outlying areas of cities and in surrounding agricultural zones.

Moche textiles, ceramics, and metallurgy give evidence of numerous skilled artisans. As in Chavín, women played a major role in textile production, and even elite women devoted time to weaving. Moche craftspeople produced highly individualized portrait vases, ceramics decorated with line drawings representing myths and rituals, and vessels depicting explicit sexual acts. Their metalwork included gold and silver objects devoted to religious and decorative functions or to elite adornment, as well as heavy copper and copper alloy tools for agricultural and military purposes.

The archaeological record makes clear that the rapid decline of major centers coincided with a succession of natural disasters in the sixth century and the rise of a new military power in the Andean highlands. When an earthquake altered the course of the Moche River, major flooding caused serious damage, and a thirty-year drought expanded the area of coastal sand dunes, which then blew sand onto fragile agricultural lands, overwhelming the irrigation sys-

tem. As the land dried, periodic heavy rains caused erosion, which further damaged fields and weakened the economy. Despite massive efforts to keep the irrigation canals open and despite the construction of new urban centers in less vulnerable valleys to the north, Moche civilization never fully recovered. In the eighth century, a new military power, the **Wari** (WAH-ree), put pressure on trade routes linking the coastal region with the highlands and thus contributed to the disappearance of the Moche.

Tiwanaku and Wari

After 500 C.E., Wari and Tiwanaku were the two powerful civilizations that dominated the Andean highlands. The ruins of **Tiwanaku** (tee-wah-NA-coo) (see Map 7.3), stand at nearly 13,000 feet (3,962 meters) near Lake Titicaca in modern Bolivia. Tiwanaku's expansion depended on the adoption of technologies that increased agricultural productivity. Modern excavations provide the outline of vast drainage projects that reclaimed nearly 200,000 acres (80,000 hectares) of rich lakeside marshes for agriculture. This system of raised fields and ditches permitted intensive cultivation similar to that achieved by the use of chinampas in Mesoamerica. Fish and llamas added protein to a diet largely dependent on potatoes and grains. Llamas were also crucial for long-distance trade that brought in maize, coca, tropical fruits, and medicinal plants. The resulting abundance permitted a dense cycle of feasting and religious observance that fueled the rise of a powerful elite.

Tiwanaku's construction featured high-quality stone masonry. Thousands of laborers were mobilized to cut and move the large stones many miles for large terraced pyramids, sunken plazas, walled enclosures, and a reservoir. With copper alloy tools their only metallic resource, Tiwanaku's artisans cut stone so precisely that little mortar was needed to fit the blocks. They also produced gigantic human statuary. Together, these sacred structures, oriented to reflect celestial cycles and distant Andean peaks, provided an awe-inspiring setting for the religious rituals that

Wari Andean civilization culturally linked to Tiwanaku, perhaps beginning as a colony of Tiwanaku.

Tiwanaku Name of capital city and empire centered on the region near Lake Titicaca in modern Bolivia (375–1000 C.E.).

Diversity & Dominance

Burials as Historical Texts

Efforts to reveal the history of the Americas before the arrival of Europeans depend on the work of archaeologists. The burials of rulers and other members of elites can be viewed as historical texts that describe how textiles, precious metals, beautifully decorated ceramics, and other commodities were used to reinforce the political and cultural power of ruling lineages. In public, members of the elite were always surrounded by the most desirable goods and rarest products as well as by elaborate rituals and ceremonies. The effect was to create an aura of godlike power. The material elements of political and cultural power were also integrated into the experience of death and burial as members of the elite were sent into the afterlife.

The first photograph is of an excavated Moche tomb in Sipán, Peru. The Moche (200–ca. 700 C.E.) were one of the most important of the civilizations of the Andean region and masters of metallurgy, ceramics, and textiles. The excavations at Sipán revealed a "warrior-priest" buried with an amazing array of gold ornaments, jewels, textiles, and ceramics. Also buried with him were five human sacrifices: two women, perhaps wives or concubines, two male servants, and a warrior. Three of these victims—the warrior, one woman, and a male servant—are each missing a foot, perhaps cut off to guarantee their continued faithfulness to the deceased ruler in the afterlife.

The second photograph shows the excavation of a classic-era (250–ca. 800 C.E.) Maya burial at Río Azul in Guatemala. After death this elite male was laid out on a carved wooden platform and cotton mattress and his body was painted with decorations. Mourners covered his body in rich textiles and surrounded him with valuable goods. These included a necklace of individual stones carved ➤

© Heinze Plenge/NGS Image Collection

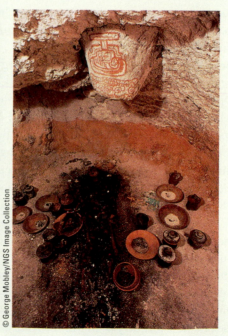

© George Mobley/NGS Image Collection

Burials Reveal Ancient Civilizations *(Left) Around 300 C.E., this Moche warrior-priest was buried amid rich tribute at Sipán in Peru. Also buried were the bodies of retainers or kinsmen probably sacrificed to accompany this powerful man. The body lies with the head on the right and the feet on the left. (Right) Similarly, the burial of a member of the Maya elite at Río Azul in northern Guatemala indicates the care taken to surround the powerful with fine ceramics, jewelry, and other valuable goods.*

in the shape of heads, perhaps a symbol of his prowess in battle, and high-quality ceramics, some filled with foods consumed by the elite like cacao. The careful preparation of the burial chamber had required the work of numerous artisans and laborers, as was the case in the burial of the Moche warrior-priest. In death, as in life, these early American civilizations acknowledged the high status, political power, and religious authority of their elites.

legitimized the elite's domination of society and the city's control of distant territories.

At its height around 800 C.E., Tiwanaku had a population of around 60,000. Its highly stratified society was ruled by a hereditary elite. Most men and women devoted themselves to agriculture and the care of llamas; however, the elite controlled the ayl-lus of the surrounding region, and as their military power grew, they also drafted labor from conquered and incorporated populations. Thousands of skilled artisans expanded and embellished the ceremonial architecture and produced metal goods, textiles, and pottery. Tiwanaku ceramics found in distant places suggest a specialized merchant class. Military

Paulo Afonso/Shutterstock.com

The Ritual Center of Tiwanaku During the Middle Horizon period Tiwanaku was one of the most impressive cities in the Andean region. The ritual center was characterized by beautiful stone construction, sunken plazas, and by large carved stone representations of the gods.

Travel Accounts of Africa and India

The most revealing description of ancient trade in the Indian Ocean and the economic forces shaping the Indian Ocean trading system is found in The Periplus of the Erythraean Sea, *a sailing itinerary (*periplus *in Greek). Composed in the first century* C.E. *by an unknown Greco-Egyptian merchant, it highlights the diversity of peoples and products from the Red Sea to the Bay of Bengal. Historians believe that the descriptions of market towns were based on firsthand experience. The following passages deal with East Africa and the coastal lands of the Indian subcontinent (see Map 8.1).*

Of the designated ports on the Erythraean Sea [Indian Ocean], and the market-towns around it, the first is the Egyptian port of Mussel Harbor. To those sailing down from that place, on the right hand . . . there is Berenice. The harbors of both are at the boundary of Egypt. . . .

On the right-hand coast next below Berenice is the country of the Berbers. Along the shore are the Fish-Eaters, living in scattered caves in the narrow valleys. Further inland are the Berbers, and beyond them the Wild-flesh-Eaters and Calf-Eaters, each tribe governed by its chief . . . .

Below the Calf-Eaters there is a little market-town on the shore . . . called Ptolemais of the Hunts, from which the hunters started for the interior under the dynasty of the Ptolemies. . . . But the place has no harbor and is reached only by small boats. . . .

Beyond this place, the coast trending toward the south, there is the Market and Cape of Spices [and] an abrupt promontory at the very end of the Berber coast toward the east. . . . A sign of an approaching storm . . . is that the deep water becomes more turbid and changes its color. When this happens they all run to a large promontory called Tabae, which offers safe shelter. . . .

Beyond Tabae [lies] . . . another market-town called Opone. . . . [I]n it the greatest quantity of cinnamon is produced . . . and slaves of the better sort, which are brought to Egypt in increasing numbers. . . .

[Ships also come] from the places across this sea, . . . bringing to these . . . market-towns the products of their own places; wheat, rice, clarified butter, sesame oil, cotton cloth . . . and honey from the reed called sacchari [sugar cane]. Some make the voyage especially to these market-towns, and others exchange their cargoes while sailing along the coast. This country is not subject to a King, but each market-town is ruled by its separate chief.

Beyond Opone, the shore trending more toward the south . . . this coast [the Somali region of Azania, or East Africa] is destitute of harbors . . . until the Pyralax islands [Zanzibar]. . . . [A] little to the south of south-west . . . is the island Menuthias [Madagascar], . . . low and wooded, in which there are rivers and many kinds of birds and the mountain-tortoise. There are no wild beasts except the crocodiles; but there they do not attack men. In this place there are sewed boats, and canoes hollowed from single logs. . . .

Two days' sail beyond, there lies the very last market-town of the continent of Azania, which is called Rhapta [Dar es-Salaam]. . . name[d] from the sewed boats (rhapton ploiarion) . . . in which there is ivory in great quantity, and tortoise-shell. Along this coast live men of piratical habits, very great in stature, and under separate chiefs for each place. . . . And these markets of Azania are the very last of the continent. . . .

Now the whole country of India has very many rivers, and very great ebb and flow of the tides. . . . Parts of the dry land are sea, and [parts are]. . . dry where ships were sailing just before; and the rivers, under the inrush of the flood tide, when the whole force of the sea is directed against them, are driven upwards more strongly against their natural current. . . .

The country inland . . . is inhabited by numerous tribes. . . . Above these is the very warlike nation of the Bactrians, who are under their own king. And Alexander, setting out from these parts, penetrated to the Ganges. . . . [T]o the present day ancient drachmae are current in Barygaza, coming from this country, bearing inscriptions in Greek letters, and the devices of those who reigned after Alexander. . . .

Inland from this place and to the east, is the city called Ozene [Ujjain]. . . . [F]rom this place are brought down all things needed for the welfare of the country. . . and many things for our trade: agate and carnelian, Indian muslins. . . .

➤

> There are imported into this market-town wine, Italian preferred, also Laodicean and Arabian; copper, tin, and lead; coral and topaz; thin clothing and inferior sorts of all kinds . . . gold and silver coin, on which there is a profit when exchanged for the money of the country. . . . And for the King there are brought into those places very costly vessels of silver, singing boys, beautiful maidens for the harem, fine wines, thin clothing of the finest weaves, and the choicest ointments. There are exported from these places [spices], ivory, agate and carnelian . . . cotton cloth of all kinds, silk cloth. . . .

[T]he adjoining coast extends in a straight line from north to south. . . . The inland country back from the coast toward the east comprises many desert regions and great mountains; and all kinds of wild beasts—leopards, tigers, elephants, enormous serpents, hyenas, and baboons of many sorts; and many populous nations, as far as the Ganges. . . .

Beyond this, the course trending toward the north, there are many barbarous tribes, among whom are the Cirrhadae, a race of men with flattened noses, very savage; another tribe, the Bargysi; and the Horse-faces and the Long-faces, who are said to be cannibals.

After these, the course turns toward the east again, and . . . [the] Ganges comes into view. . . . [J]ust opposite . . . there is an island in the ocean, the last part of the inhabited world toward the east, under the rising sun itself[,] . . .and it has the best tortoise-shell of all the places on the Erythraean Sea.

After this region under the very north, the sea outside ending in a land called This, there is a very great inland city called Thinae, from which raw silk and silk yarn and silk cloth are brought on foot. . . . But the land of This is not easy of access; few men come from there, and seldom.

The Chinese traveler Xuanzang (600–664) journeyed across Inner Asia to India, making pilgrimage to Buddhist holy places and searching for Sanskrit scriptures to take back to China with him. His descriptions of the places he visited reflect his interests. The following passages come from his description of India.

Towns and Buildings

The towns and villages have inner gates; the walls are wide and high; the streets and lanes are tortuous, and the roads winding. The thoroughfares are dirty and the stalls arranged on both sides of the road with appropriate signs. Butchers, fishers, dancers, executioners, and scavengers, and so on, have their abodes without the city. In coming and going these persons are bound to keep on the left side of the road till they arrive at their homes. Their houses are surrounded by low walls, and form the suburbs. The earth being soft and muddy, the walls of the town are mostly built of brick or tiles. The towers on the walls are constructed of wood or bamboo; the houses have balconies and belvederes, which are made of wood, with a coating of lime or mortar, and covered with tiles. The different buildings have the same form as those in China: rushes, or dry branches, or tiles, or boards are used for covering them. The walls are covered with lime and mud, mixed with cow's dung for purity. At different seasons they scatter flowers about. Such are some of their different customs.

Dress and Appearance

Their clothing is not cut or fashioned; they mostly affect fresh-white garments; they esteem little those of mixed color or ornamented. The men wind their garments round their middle, then gather them under the armpits, and let them fall down across the body, hanging to the right. The robes of the women fall down to the ground; they completely cover their shoulders. They wear a little knot of hair on their crowns, and let the rest of their hair fall loose. Some of the men cut off their moustaches, and have other odd customs. . . . In North India, where the air is cold, they wear short and close-fitting garments. . . . The dress and ornaments worn by the nonbelievers are varied and mixed. Some wear peacocks' feathers; some wear as ornaments necklaces made of skull bones; some have no clothing, but go naked; some wear leaf or bark garments; some pull out their hair and cut off their moustaches; others have bushy whiskers and their hair braided on the top of their heads. The costume is not uniform, and the color, whether red or white, not constant.

QUESTIONS FOR ANALYSIS

1. How do the differing interests of a trader and a religious pilgrim show up in what they report?
2. How do these narratives show the influence of the countries the authors are coming from?
3. Given the different viewpoints of travelers, what is the value of travel accounts as sources for history?

Source: Samuel Beal, *Buddhist Records of the Western World, Translated from the Chinese of Hiuen Tsiang (A.D. 629)* (London: Trubner and Company, 1884; reprint Delhi: Oriental Books Reprint Corporation, 1969), 73–76.

The Sasanid Empire and the Rise of Islam

© Cengage Learning

A technology we take for granted, paper-making, was originally invented in China. After Arab conquests in the seventh century C.E. established an Islamic caliphate stretching from Spain to Central Asia, knowledge of papermaking spread from China to the Middle East. Paper provided a medium that was superior to papyrus and parchment and well suited to a variety of purposes. Maps, miniature paintings, and, of course, books became increasingly common and inexpensive. With cheaper books came bookstores, and one of the most informative manuscripts of the period of the Islamic caliphate is a *Fihrist*, or descriptive catalogue, of the books sold at one bookstore in Baghdad.

Abu al-Faraj Muhammad al-Nadim, a man with good connections at the caliph's court, compiled the catalogue, though his father probably founded the bookstore. Its latest entry dates to ca. 990, al-Nadim's death date. Superbly educated, al-Nadim wrote such well-informed comments on books and authors that his catalogue presents a detailed survey of the intellectual world of Baghdad.

The first of the *Fihrist*'s ten books deals with Arabic language and sacred scriptures: the Quran, the Torah, and the Gospel. The second covers Arabic grammar, and the third writings from people connected with the caliph's court: historians, government officials, singers, jesters, and the ruler's boon companions. *Al-Nadim* means "boon companion," so it is assumed that the author knew this milieu well. After dealing with Arabic poetry, Muslim sects, and Islamic law in Books 3 through 6, he comes to Greek philosophy, science, and medicine in Book 7.

Most things we would find today in a bookstore are relegated to the final three chapters. Book 8 divides into three sections, the first being "Story Tellers and Stories." Here he lists a Persian book called *A Thousand Stories*, which in translation became *The Arabian Nights*. Al-Nadim's version no longer survives; the collection we have today comes from a manuscript written five hundred years later.

Then come books about "Exorcists, Jugglers, and Magicians," followed by "Miscellaneous Subjects and Fables." These include books on "Freckles, Twitching, Moles, and Shoulders," "Horsemanship, Bearing of Arms, the Implements of War," "Veterinary Surgery," "Birds of Prey, Sport with Them and Medical Care of Them," "Interpretation of Dreams," "Perfume," "Cooked Food," "Poisons," and "Amulets and Charms."

Non-Muslim sects and foreign lands—India, Indochina, and China—fill Book 9, leaving Book 10 for a few final notes on philosophers not mentioned previously.

All together, the thousands of titles and authors commented on by al-Nadim provide both a panorama of what interested book buyers in tenth-century Baghdad and a saddening picture of how profound the loss of knowledge has been since that glorious era.

Baghdad Bookstore With the advent of papermaking, manufacturing books became increasingly common and inexpensive. As a result, bookstores also became more common. Notice how books are shelved on their sides in wall cubicles.

akg-images

THE SASANID EMPIRE, 224–651

■ *How did the Sasanid Empire evolve under the influence of east-west trade?*

The rise in the third century of a new Iranian state, the **Sasanid** (SAH-suh-nid) **Empire**, continued the old rivalry between Rome and the Parthians along the Euphrates frontier. However, behind this façade of continuity, a social and economic transformation took place that set the stage for a new and powerful religiopolitical movement: Islam.

Politics and Society

Ardashir, a descendant of an ancestor named Sasan, defeated the Parthians around 224 and established the Sasanid kingdom. The new rulers confronted the Romans, whom later historians frequently refer to as the Byzantines after about 330. The rival empires launched numerous attacks on each other between the 340s and 628, but in times of peace, the empires flourished, allowing goods transported over the Silk Road to enter the Mediterranean.

The Sasanid and Byzantine Empires were alike in maintaining central control of imperial finances and military power. The political hinterlands of the mountains and plateaus of Iran proper were often ruled by the cousins of the shah (king) or by powerful families descending from the pre-Sasanid Parthian nobility. Each empire also found effective ways of integrating frontier peoples as mercenaries or caravaneers. There were differences, however. Despite the dominance of aristocratic families, long-lasting political fragmentation of the medieval European variety (see Chapter 10) did not develop in the Sasanid Empire. Also, although many

nomads lived in the mountain and desert regions, no folk migrations took place comparable to that of the Germanic peoples who defeated Roman armies and established kingdoms in formerly Roman territory from about the third century C.E. on.

Cities were small walled communities that served more as military strong-points than as centers of population and production. Sasanid silver work and silk fabrics testify to the sumptuous lifestyle of the warrior elite. Society revolved around a local aristocracy that lived on rural estates and cultivated the arts of hunting, feasting, and war just like the warriors described in the sagas of ancient kings and heroes sung at their banquets.

The Silk Road brought many new crops to Mesopotamia. Sasanid farmers pioneered in planting cot-

> **Sasanid Empire** Iranian empire, established around 224, with a capital in Ctesiphon, Mesopotamia. The Sasanid emperors established Zoroastrianism as the state religion. Islamic Arab armies overthrew the empire around 651.

Sasanid Silver Plate with Gold Decoration The Sasanid aristocracy, based in the countryside, invested part of its wealth in silver plates and vessels. This image of a Sasanid king hunting on horseback also reflects a favorite aristocratic pastime. Erich Lessing/Art Resource, NY

Chronology

	The Arab Lands	Iran and Central Asia
200		**224–651** Sasanid Empire
	570–632 Life of the Prophet Muhammad	
600	**634** Conquests of Iraq and Syria commence **639–642** Conquest of Egypt by Arabs **656–661** Ali caliph; first civil war **661–750** Umayyad Caliphate rules from Damascus	**Before 1000 B.C.E.** Beginning of migrations from mainland Southeast Asia to islands in Pacific and Indian Oceans
700	**711** Berbers and Arabs invade Spain from North Africa **750** Beginning of Abbasid Caliphate **755** Umayyad state established in Spain **776–809** Caliphate of Harun al-Rashid	**711** Arabs capture Sind in India **747** Abbasid revolt begins in Khurasan
800	**835–892** Abbasid capital moved from Baghdad to Samarra	**875** Independent Samanid state founded in Bukhara
900	**909** Fatimids seize North Africa, found Shi'ite Caliphate **929** Abd al-Rahman III declares himself caliph in Cordoba **945** Shi'ite Buyids take control in Baghdad **969** Fatimids conquer Egypt	**945** Buyids from northern Iran take control of Abbasid Caliphate
1000	**1055** Seljuk Turks take control in Baghdad **1099** First Crusade captures Jerusalem **1171** Fall of Fatimid Egypt **1187** Saladin recaptures Jerusalem **1250** Mamluks control Egypt **1258** Mongols sack Baghdad and end Abbasid Caliphate **1260** Mamluks defeat Mongols at Ain Jalut	**1036** Beginning of Turkish Seljuk rule in Khurasan

ton, sugar cane, rice, citrus trees, eggplants, and other crops adopted from India and China. Although the acreage devoted to new crops increased slowly, these products became important consumption and trade items during the succeeding Islamic period.

Religion and Empire

Religion permeated all aspects of community life. Most subjects of the Byzantine emperors and Sasanid shahs identified themselves first and foremost as members of a religious community. Their schools and law courts were religious, they looked on religious leaders as moral guides in daily life, and most books discussed religious subjects. In some areas, priests represented their flocks even in such secular matters as tax collection. The establishment of the Zoroastrian faith (see Chapter 4) as a state religion similar to Christianity in the Byzantine Empire (see Chapter 10) marked the fresh emergence of religion as an instrument of politics both within and between the empires.

Both Zoroastrianism and Christianity practiced intolerance. A late-third-century inscription in Iran boasts of the persecutions of Christians, Jews, and Buddhists carried out by the Zoroastrian high priest. Yet sizable Christian and Jewish communities remained, especially in Mesopotamia. Similarly, from the fourth century onward, councils of Christian bishops declared many theological beliefs heretical—so unacceptable that they were un-Christian.

Christians became pawns in the political rivalry with the Byzantines and were sometimes persecuted, sometimes patronized, by the Sasanid kings. In 431 a council of bishops called by the Byzantine emperor declared the Nestorian Christians heretics for over-emphasizing the humanness of Christ. The Nestorians believed that human characteristics and divinity coexisted in Jesus and that Mary was not the mother of God, as many other Christians maintained, but the mother of the human Jesus. After the bishops' ruling, the Nestorians sought refuge under the Sasanid shah and eventually extended their missionary activities along the Central Asian trade routes.

A parallel episode within Zoroastrianism transpired in the third century when Mani, preaching a faith theologically derived from Zoroastrianism—a dualistic struggle between Good and Evil—founded a new religion in Mesopotamia: Manichaeism. Although at first Mani enjoyed the favor of the shah, he and many of his followers were martyred in 276. His religion survived and spread widely, particularly along the Silk Road but also into North Africa and Europe. Nestorian missionaries competed with Manichaean missionaries for converts in Central Asia.

The Arabs became enmeshed in this web of religious conflict. Along their Euphrates frontier, the Sasanids subsidized nomadic Arab chieftains to protect their empire from invasion. The Byzantines did the same with Arabs on their Jordanian frontier. The border protectors for the Byzantines adopted a Monophysite theology, which emphasized Christ's divine nature; the allies of the Sasanids, the Nestorian faith. Even in the interior deserts, Semitic polytheism, with its worship of natural forces and celestial bodies, began to encounter the religiopolitical ideas of the Sasanid and Byzantine Empires. These ideas would contribute to the subsequent rise of Islam and a new political empire based on religion.

SECTION REVIEW

- The Sasanids overthrew the Parthians and continued their predecessors' rivalry with Rome.
- Sasanid farmers pioneered the cultivation of Silk Road crops. Sasanid kings made Zoroastrianism the state religion, and other religions, particularly Christianity, experienced both toleration and persecution.
- Diverse religious ideas spread and competed, especially along the Silk Road and in the Arab border areas.

THE ORIGINS OF ISLAM

■ How did the traditions and religious views of pre-Islamic peoples become integrated into the culture shaped by Islam?

The Arabs of 600 C.E. lived exclusively in the Arabian peninsula and on the desert fringes of Syria, Jordan, and Iraq. Outside the Euphrates and Jordanian frontiers where Arabs protected the Sasanid and Byzantine Empires, respectively, Arab pastoralists remained isolated and independent, seldom engaging the attention of the shahs and emperors. It was farther to the south in these interior Arabian lands that the religion of Islam took form.

The Arabian Peninsula Before Muhammad

Throughout history more people living on the Arabian peninsula have subsisted as farmers than as pastoral nomads. Farming villages supported the comparatively dense population of Yemen, where abundant rainfall waters the highlands during the spring monsoon, and small inlets along the southern coast favored fishing and trading communities. But the enormous sea of sand known as the "Empty Quarter" isolated many southern regions from the Arabian interior. In the seventh century, most people in southern Arabia knew more about Africa, India, and the Persian Gulf than about the forbidding interior and the scattered camel- and sheep-herding nomads who lived there.

Caravan trading provided a rare link among peoples. Nomads derived income from providing camels, guides, and safe passage to merchants bringing the primary product of the south, the aromatic resins frankincense and myrrh, to northern customers. Return caravans brought manufactured products from Mesopotamia and Syria.

Nomad dominance of the caravan trade received a boost from the invention of militarily efficient camel saddles. This invention contributed to the rise of Arab-dominated caravan cities and to Arab pastoralists becoming the primary suppliers of animal power throughout the region. By 600 C.E., wheeled vehicles—mostly ox carts and horse-drawn chariots—had all but disappeared from the Middle East, replaced by camels and donkeys.

Mecca, a late-blooming caravan city, occupies a barren mountain valley halfway between Yemen and Syria and somewhat inland from the Red Sea coast. A nomadic kin group known as the Quraysh (koo-RAYSH) settled in Mecca in the fifth century and assumed control of trade. Mecca rapidly achieved a measure of prosperity, partly because it was too far from Byzantine Syria, Sasanid Iraq, and Ethiopian-controlled Yemen for them to attack it.

A cubical shrine with idols inside called the Ka'ba (KAH-buh), a holy well called Zamzam, and a sacred precinct surrounding the two wherein killing was prohibited contributed to the emergence of Mecca as a pilgrimage site. Some Meccans associated the shrine with stories known to Jews and Christians. They regarded Abraham (Ibrahim in Arabic) as the builder of the Ka'ba, and they identified a site outside Mecca as the location where God asked Abraham to sacrifice his son. The son was not Isaac (Ishaq in Arabic), the son of Sarah, but Ishmael (Isma'il in Arabic), the son of Hagar, cited in the Bible as the forefather of the Arabs.

Muhammad in Mecca

Born in Mecca in 570, **Muhammad** grew up an orphan in the house of his uncle. He engaged in trade and married a Quraysh widow named Khadija (kah-DEE-juh), whose caravan interests he superintended. Their son died in childhood, but several daughters survived. Around 610 Muhammad began meditating at night in the mountainous terrain around Mecca. During one night vigil, known to later tradition as the "Night of Power and Excellence," a being whom Muhammad later understood to be the angel Gabriel (Jibra'il in Arabic) spoke to him:

> Proclaim! In the name of your Lord who created. Created man from a clot of congealed blood. Proclaim! And your Lord is the Most Bountiful. He who has taught by the pen. Taught man that which he knew not.[1]

For three years Muhammad shared this and subsequent revelations only with close friends and family. This period culminated in his conviction that he was hearing the words of God (Allah [AH-luh] in Arabic). Khadija, his uncle's son Ali, his friend Abu Bakr

(ah-boo BAK-uhr), and others close to him shared this conviction. The revelations continued until Muhammad's death in 632.

Like most people of the time, including Christians and Jews, the Arabs believed in unseen spirits: gods, demonic *shaitans*, and desert spirits called *jinns* who were thought to possess seers and poets. Therefore, when Muhammad recited his rhymed revelations in public, many people believed he was inspired by an unseen spirit, even if it was not, as Muhammad asserted, the one true god.

Muhammad's earliest revelations called on people to witness that one god had created the universe and everything in it, including themselves. At the end of time, their souls would be judged, their sins balanced against their good deeds. The blameless would go to paradise; the sinful would taste hellfire:

> By the night as it conceals the light;
> By the day as it appears in glory;
> By the mystery of the creation of male and female;
> Verily, the ends ye strive for are diverse.
> So he who gives in charity and fears God,
> And in all sincerity testifies to the best,
> We will indeed make smooth for him the path to Bliss.
> But he who is a greedy miser and thinks himself self-sufficient,
> And gives the lie to the best,
> We will indeed make smooth for him the path to misery.[2]

The revelation called all people to submit to God and accept Muhammad as the last of his messengers. Doing so made one a **Muslim,** meaning one who makes "submission," **Islam**, to the will of God.

[2]Quran. Sura 92, verses 1–10.

Mecca City in western Arabia; birthplace of the Prophet Muhammad and ritual center of the Islamic religion.

Muhammad Arab prophet (570–632 C.E.); founder of religion of Islam.

Muslim An adherent of the Islamic religion; a person who "submits" (in Arabic, *Islam* means "submission") to the will of God.

Islam Religion expounded by the Prophet Muhammad on the basis of his reception of divine revelations, which were collected after his death into the Quran. In the tradition of Judaism and Christianity, and sharing much of their lore, Islam calls on all people to recognize one creator god—Allah—who rewards or punishes believers after death according to how they led their lives.

[1]Quran. Sura 96, verses 1–5.

Because earlier messengers mentioned in the revelations included Noah, Moses, and Jesus, Muhammad's hearers connected his message with Judaism and Christianity, religions they were already familiar with. Yet his revelations charged the Jews and Christians with being negligent in preserving God's revealed word. Thus, even though they identified Abraham/Ibrahim, whom Muslims consider the first Muslim, as the builder of the Ka'ba (which superseded Jerusalem as the focus of Muslim prayer in 624), Muhammad's followers considered his revelation more perfect than the Bible because it had not gone through an editing process.

Some scholars maintain that Muhammad appealed especially to people distressed over wealth replacing kinship as the most important aspect of social relations and over neglect of orphans and other powerless people. Most Muslims, however, put less emphasis on a social message than on the power and beauty of Muhammad's recitations.

Formation of the Umma

Fearing that accepting Muhammad as the sole agent of the one true God would threaten their power and prosperity, Mecca's leaders pressured his kin to disavow him and persecuted the weakest of his followers. Stymied by this hostility, Muhammad and his followers fled Mecca in 622 to take up residence in the agricultural community of **Medina** 215 miles (346 kilometers) to the north. This hijra (HIJ-ruh)—Mohammad's journey from Mecca to Medina—marks the beginning of the Muslim calendar.

Prior to the hijra, Medinan representatives had met with Muhammad and agreed to accept and protect him and his followers because they saw him as an inspired leader who could calm their perpetual feuding. Together, the Meccan migrants and major groups in Medina bound themselves into a single **umma** (UM-muh), a community defined by acceptance of Islam and of Muhammad as the "Messenger of God," his most common title. Partly because three Jewish kin groups chose to retain their own faith, the direction of prayer was changed from Jerusalem toward the Ka'ba in Mecca, now thought of as the "House of God."

Having left their Meccan kin groups, the immigrants in Medina felt vulnerable. During the last decade of his life, Muhammad took active responsibility for

his umma. Fresh revelations provided a framework for regulating social and legal affairs and stirred the Muslims to fight against the still-unbelieving city of Mecca. At various points during the war, Muhammad charged the Jewish kin groups, whom he had initially hoped would recognize him as God's messenger, with disloyalty, and he finally expelled or eliminated them. The sporadic war, largely conducted by raiding and negotiating with desert nomads, sapped Mecca's strength and convinced many Meccans that God favored Muhammad. In 630 Mecca surrendered, and Muhammad and his followers made the pilgrimage to the Ka'ba unhindered.

Muhammad stayed in Medina, which had grown into a bustling city-state. Delegations came to him from all over Arabia and returned home with believers who could teach about Islam and collect alms, or charity for the poor. Muhammad's mission to bring God's message to humanity had brought him unchallenged control of a state that was coming to dominate the Arabian peninsula.

In 632, after a brief illness, Muhammad died. Within twenty-four hours a group of Medinan leaders, along with three of Muhammad's close friends, determined that Abu Bakr, one of the earliest believers and the father of Muhammad's favorite wife A'isha (AH-ee-shah), should succeed him. They called him the *khalifa* (kah-LEE-fuh), or "successor," the English version of which is *caliph*. But calling Abu Bakr a successor did not clarify his powers. Everyone knew that neither Abu Bakr nor anyone else could receive revelations, and they likewise knew that Muhammad's revelations made no provision for succession or for any government purpose beyond maintaining the umma.

Abu Bakr continued and confirmed Muhammad's religious practices, notably the so-called Five Pillars of Islam: (1) avowal that there is only one god and Muhammad is his messenger, (2) prayer five times a day, (3) fasting during the lunar month of Ramadan, (4) paying alms, and (5) making the pilgrimage

Medina City in western Arabia to which the Prophet Muhammad and his followers emigrated in 622 to escape persecution in Mecca.

umma The community of all Muslims. A major innovation against the background of seventh-century Arabia, where traditionally kinship rather than faith had determined membership in a community.

to Mecca at least once during one's lifetime. He also reestablished and expanded Muslim authority over Arabia's communities, some of which had abandoned their allegiance to Medina or followed various would-be prophets. Muslim armies fought hard to confirm the authority of the newborn **caliphate**. In the process, some fighting spilled over into non-Arab areas in Iraq.

Reportedly, Abu Bakr ordered the men who had written down Muhammad's revelations to collect them in a book. Hitherto written haphazardly on pieces of leather or bone, these now became a single document gathered into chapters. Muslims believe the **Quran** (kuh-RAHN), or the Recitation, acquired its final form around the year 650. They see it not as the words of Muhammad but as the unalterable word of God. Theologically, it compares not so much to the Bible, a book written by many hands over many centuries, as to the person of Jesus Christ, whom Christians consider an earthly manifestation of God.

Though united in accepting God's will, the umma soon disagreed over the succession to the caliphate. When rebels assassinated the third caliph, Uthman (ooth-MAHN), in 656 and the assassins nominated Ali, Muhammad's first cousin and the husband of his daughter Fatima, to succeed him, civil war broke out. Ali had been passed over three times previously, even though many people considered him to be the Prophet's natural heir. Those who believed Ali was the Prophet's heir came to be known as **Shi'ites**, after the Arabic term *Shi'at Ali* ("Party of Ali").

When Ali accepted the nomination to be caliph, two of Muhammad's close companions and his favorite wife A'isha challenged him. Ali defeated them in the Battle of the Camel (656), so called because the fighting raged around the camel on which A'isha was seated in an enclosed woman's saddle.

After the battle, the governor of Syria, Mu'awiya (moo-AH-we-yuh), a kinsman of the slain Uthman from the Umayya clan of the Quraysh, renewed the challenge. Inconclusive battle gave way to arbitration. The arbitrators decided that Uthman, whom his assassins considered corrupt, had not deserved death and that Ali had erred in accepting the caliphate. Ali rejected these findings, but before fighting could resume, one of his own supporters killed him for agreeing to the arbitration. Mu'awiya offered Ali's

SECTION REVIEW

- Islam emerged among the nomadic pastoralists and caravan traders of the Arabian peninsula.
- Mecca grew as a caravan city and pilgrimage site identified with Jewish and Christian stories.
- Muhammad experienced revelations that called people to submit to God's will.
- Facing hostility in Mecca, Muhammad and his followers fled to Medina, where they formed the umma.
- As caliph succeeding Muhammad, Abu Bakr confirmed the Five Pillars of Islam and ordered the composition of the Quran.
- Civil war within the umma resulted in the Sunni/Shi'ite division and the foundation of the Umayyad Caliphate.

son Hasan a dignified retirement and thus emerged as caliph in 661.

Mu'awiya chose his own son, Yazid, to succeed him, thereby instituting the **Umayyad** (oo-MY-ad) **Caliphate**. When Hasan's brother Husayn revolted in 680 to reestablish the right of Ali's family to rule, Yazid ordered Husayn and his family killed. Sympathy for Husayn's martyrdom helped transform Shi'ism from a political movement into a religious sect.

Several variations in Shi'ite belief developed, but Shi'ites all agree that Ali was the rightful successor to Muhammad and that God's choice as Imam, leader of the Muslim community, has always been one or another of Ali's descendants. They see the caliphal office as more secular than religious. Because the Shi'ites seldom held power, their religious feelings came to focus on outpourings of sympathy for Husayn and other martyrs and on messianic dreams that one of their Imams would someday triumph.

caliphate Office established in succession to the Prophet Muhammad, to rule the Islamic empire; also the name of that empire.

Quran Book composed of divine revelations made to the Prophet Muhammad between roughly 610 and his death in 632; the sacred text of the religion of Islam.

Shi'ites Muslims belonging to the branch of Islam believing that God vests leadership of the community in a descendant of Muhammad's son-in-law Ali. Shi'ism is the state religion of Iran.

Umayyad Caliphate First hereditary dynasty of Muslim caliphs (661 to 750). From their capital at Damascus, the Umayyads ruled an empire that extended from Spain to India. Overthrown by the Abbasid Caliphate.

Those Muslims who supported the first three caliphs gradually came to be called "People of Tradition and Community"—in Arabic, *Ahl al-Sunna wa'l-Jama'a*, **Sunnis** for short. Sunnis consider the caliphs to be Imams. As for Ali's followers who had abhorred his acceptance of arbitration, they evolved into small and rebellious Kharijite sects (from *kharaja*, meaning "to secede or rebel") claiming righteousness for themselves alone. These three divisions of Islam, the last now quite minor, still survive.

THE RISE AND FALL OF THE CALIPHATE, 632–1258

■ *Was the Baghdad caliphate really the high point of Muslim civilization?*

The Islamic caliphate built on the conquests the Arabs carried out after Muhammad's death gave birth to a dynamic and creative religious society. By the late 800s, however, one piece after another of this huge realm broke away. Yet the idea of a caliphate, however unrealistic, remains today a touchstone of Sunni belief in the unity of the umma.

Sunni Islam never gave a single person the power to define true belief, expel heretics, and discipline clergy. Thus, unlike Christian popes and patriarchs, the caliphs had little basis for reestablishing their universal authority once they lost political and military power.

The Islamic Conquests, 634–711

Arab conquests outside Arabia began under the second caliph, Umar (r. 634–644). Arab armies wrenched Syria (636) and Egypt (639–642) away from the Byzantine Empire and defeated the last Sasanid shah, Yazdigird III (r. 632–651). After a decade-long lull, expansion began again. Tunisia fell and became the governing center from which was organized, in 711, the conquest of Spain by an Arab-led army mostly composed of Berbers from North Africa. In the same year, Sind—the southern Indus Valley in today's Pakistan—succumbed to invaders from Iraq. The Muslim dominion remained roughly stable in size for three centuries until conquest began anew in the eleventh century. India and Anatolia experienced invasions; sub-Saharan Africa and other regions saw Islam expand peacefully by trade and conversion.

Muhammad's close companions, men of political and economic sophistication inspired by his charisma, guided the conquests. The social structure and hardy nature of Arab society lent itself to flexible military operations; and the authority of Medina, reconfirmed during the caliphate of Abu Bakr, ensured obedience.

The decision made during Umar's caliphate to prohibit Arabs from assuming ownership of conquered territory proved important. Umar tied army service, with its regular pay and windfalls of booty, to residence in military camps—two in Iraq (Kufa and Basra), one in Egypt (Fustat), and one in Tunisia (Qairawan). East of Iraq, Arabs settled around small garrison towns at strategic locations and in one large garrison at Marv in present-day Turkmenistan. This policy kept the armies together and ready for action and preserved normal life in the countryside, where some three-fourths of the population lived. Only a tiny proportion of the Syrian, Egyptian, Iranian, and Iraqi populations understood the Arabic language.

The million or so Arabs who participated in the conquests over several generations constituted a small, self-isolated ruling minority living on the taxes paid by a vastly larger non-Arab, non-Muslim subject population. The Arabs had little material incentive to encourage conversion, and there is no evidence of coherent missionary efforts to spread Islam during the conquest period.

The Umayyad and Early Abbasid Caliphates, 661–850

The Umayyad caliphs presided over an Arab realm rather than a religious empire. Ruling from Damascus, their armies consisted almost entirely of Muslim Arabs. Sasanid and Byzantine administrative practices continued in force. Only gradually did the caliphs replace non-Muslim secretaries and tax officials with Muslims and introduce Arabic as the language of government. Distinctively Muslim silver and gold coins introduced at the end

Sunnis Muslims belonging to branch of Islam believing that the community should select its own leadership. The majority religion in most Islamic countries.

of the seventh century symbolized the new order. Henceforward, silver dirhams and gold dinars bearing Arabic religious phrases circulated in monetary exchanges from Morocco to the frontiers of China.

The Umayyad dynasty fell in 750 after a decade of growing unrest. Converts to Islam numbered no more than 10 percent of the indigenous population, but they were still important because of the comparatively small number of Arab warriors. These converts resented Arab social domination. In addition, non-Syrian Arabs envied the Syrian domination of caliphal affairs, and pious Muslims looked askance at the secular and even irreligious behavior of the caliphs. Finally, Shi'ites and Kharijites attacked the Umayyad family's legitimacy as rulers, launching a number of rebellions.

In 747 a rebellion began in Khurasan (kor-uh-SAHN), in what is today northeastern Iran, and overthrew the last Umayyad caliph three years later, though one family member escaped to Spain to found an Umayyad principality there in 755. Many Shi'ites supported the rebellion, thinking they were fighting for the family of Ali. As it turned out, the family of Abbas, one of Muhammad's uncles, controlled the secret organization that coordinated the revolt. Upon victory they established the **Abbasid** (ah-BASS-id) **Caliphate**. Some of the Abbasid caliphs who ruled after 750 befriended their relatives in Ali's family, and one even flirted with transferring the caliphate to them. The Abbasid family, however, held on to the caliphate until 1258, when Mongol invaders killed the last of them in Baghdad (see Chapter 12).

Initially, the Abbasid dynasty made a fine show of leadership and piety. Theology and religious law became preoccupations at court and among a growing community of scholars devoted to interpreting the Quran, collecting the sayings of the Prophet, and compiling Arabic grammar. (In recent years, some Western scholars have maintained that the Quran, the sayings of the Prophet, and the biography of the Prophet were all composed around this time to provide a foundation myth for the regime. This reinterpretation of Islamic origins has not been generally accepted either in the scholarly community or among Muslims.) Some caliphs sponsored ambitious projects to translate great works of Greek, Persian, and Indian thought into Arabic.

With its roots among the semi-Persianized Arabs of Khurasan, the new dynasty gradually adopted the ceremonies and customs of the Sasanid shahs. Government grew increasingly complex in Baghdad, the newly built capital city on the Tigris River. As more non-Arabs converted to Islam, the ruling elite became more cosmopolitan. Greek, Iranian, Central Asian, and African cultural currents met in the capital and gave rise to an abundance of literary works, a process facilitated by the introduction of papermaking from China. Arab poets neglected the traditional odes extolling life in the desert and wrote instead wine songs (despite Islam's prohibition of alcohol) or poems in praise of their patrons.

The translation of Aristotle into Arabic, the founding of the main currents of theology and law, and the splendor of the Abbasid court—reflected in stories of *The Arabian Nights* set in the time of the caliph Harun al-Rashid (hah-ROON al–rah-SHEED) (r. 776–809)—in some respects warrant calling the early Abbasid period a "golden age." Yet the refinement of Baghdad culture only slowly made its way into the provinces. Egypt remained predominantly Christian and Coptic-speaking in the early Abbasid period. Iran never adopted Arabic as a spoken tongue. Most of Berber-speaking North Africa rebelled and freed itself of direct caliphal rule after 740.

Gradual conversion to Islam among the conquered population accelerated in the second quarter of the ninth century. Social discrimination against non-Arab converts gradually faded, and the Arabs themselves—at least those living in cosmopolitan urban settings—lost their previously strong attachment to kinship and ethnic identity.

Political Fragmentation, 850–1050

Abbasid decline became evident in the second half of the ninth century as conversion to Islam accelerated (see Map 9.1). No government ruling so vast an empire could hold power easily. Caravans traveled only 20 miles (32 kilometers) a day, and the couriers of

Abbasid Caliphate Descendants of the Prophet Muhammad's uncle, al-Abbas, the Abbasids overthrew the Umayyad Caliphate and ruled an Islamic empire from their capital in Baghdad (founded 762) from 750 to 1258.

the caliphal post system usually did not exceed 100 miles (160 kilometers) a day. News of frontier revolts took weeks to reach Baghdad. Military responses might take months.

During the first two Islamic centuries, revolts against Muslim rule had been a concern. The Muslim umma had therefore clung together, despite the long distances. But with the growing conversion of the population to Islam, fears that Islamic dominion might be overthrown faded. Once they became the overwhelming majority, Muslims realized that a highly centralized empire did not necessarily serve the interests of all the people.

By the middle of the ninth century, revolts targeting Arab or Muslim domination gave way to movements within the Islamic community concentrating on seizure of territory and formation of principalities. None of the states carved out of the Abbasid Caliphate after that time repudiated or even threatened Islam. They did, however, cut the flow of tax revenues to Baghdad, thereby increasing local prosperity. Increasingly starved for funds by breakaway provinces and by an unexplained fall in revenues from Iraq itself, the caliphate experienced a crisis in the late ninth century. Distrusting generals and troops from outlying areas, the caliphs purchased Turkish slaves, **mamluks (MAM-luke)**, from Central Asia and established them as a standing army. Well trained and hardy, the Turks proved an effective but expensive military force. When the government could not pay them, the mamluks took it on themselves to seat and unseat caliphs, a process made easier by the construction of a new capital at Samarra, north of Baghdad on the Tigris River.

The Turks dominated Samarra without interference from an unruly Baghdad populace that regarded them as rude and highhanded. However, the money and effort that went into the huge city, which was occupied only from 835 to 892, further sapped the caliphs' financial strength and deflected labor from more productive pursuits.

In 945, after several attempts to find a strongman to save it, the Abbasid Caliphate fell under the control of rude mountain warriors from Daylam in northern Iran. Led by the Shi'ite Buyid **(BOO-yid)** family, they conquered western Iran as well as Iraq. Each Buyid commander ruled his own principality. After two centuries of glory, the sun began to set on Baghdad.

The Abbasid caliph remained, but the Buyid princes controlled him. Being Shi'ites, the Buyids had no special reverence for the Sunni caliph. The Shi'ite teachings they followed held that the twelfth and last Imam had disappeared around 873 and would return as a messiah only at the end of time. Thus they had no Shi'ite Imam to defer to and retained the caliph only to help control their predominantly Sunni subjects.

Dynamic growth in outlying provinces paralleled the caliphate's gradual loss of temporal power. In the east in 875, the dynasty of the Samanids **(sah-MAN-id)**, one of several Iranian families to achieve independence, established a glittering court in Bukhara, a major city on the Silk Road (see Map 9.1). Samanid princes patronized literature and learning, but the language they favored was Persian written in Arabic letters. For the first time, a non-Arabic literature rose to challenge the eminence of Arabic within the Islamic world.

In the west, the Berber revolts against Arab rule led to the appearance after 740 of the city-states of Sijilmasa **(sih-jil-MAS-suh)** and Tahert **(TAH-hert)** on the northern fringe of the Sahara. The Kharijite beliefs of these states' rulers interfered with their east-west overland trade and led them to develop the first regular trade across the Sahara Desert. Once traders looked to the desert, they discovered that Berber speakers in the southern Sahara were already carrying salt from the desert into the Sahel region. The northern traders discovered that they could trade salt for gold by providing the southern nomads, who controlled the salt sources but had little use for gold, with more useful products, such as copper and manufactured goods. Sijilmasa and Tahert became wealthy cities, the former minting gold coins that circulated as far away as Egypt and Syria.

The earliest known sub-Saharan beneficiary of the new exchange system was the kingdom of **Ghana (GAH-nuh)**. It first appears in an Arabic text of the late eighth century as the "land of gold." Few details

mamluks Under the Islamic system of military slavery, Turkish military slaves formed an important part of the armed forces of the Abbasid Caliphate of the ninth and tenth centuries. Mamluks eventually founded their own state, ruling Egypt and Syria (1250–1517).

Ghana First known kingdom in sub-Saharan West Africa between the sixth and thirteenth centuries C.E. Also the modern West African country once known as the Gold Coast.

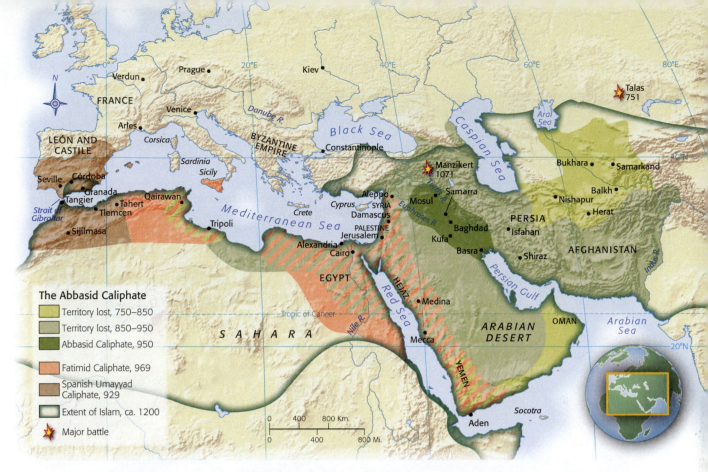

Map 9.1 Rise and Fall of the Abbasid Caliphate Though Abbasid rulers occupied the caliphal seat in Iraq from 750 to 1258, when Mongol armies destroyed Baghdad, real political power waned sharply and steadily after 850. The rival caliphates of the Fatimids (909–1171) and Spanish Umayyads (929–976) were comparatively short-lived. © Cengage Learning

survive about the early years of this realm, which was established by the Soninke (soh-NIN-kay) people and covered parts of Mali, Mauritania, and Senegal, but it prospered until 1076, when it was conquered by nomads from the desert. It was one of the first lands outside the orbit of the caliphate to experience a gradual and peaceful conversion to Islam.

The North African city-states lost their independence after the Fatimid (FAH-tuh-mid) dynasty, whose members claimed (perhaps falsely) to be Shi'ite Imams descended from Ali, established itself in Tunisia in 909. After consolidating their hold on northwest Africa, the Fatimids culminated their rise to power by conquering Egypt in 969. Claiming the title of caliph in a direct challenge to the Abbasids, the Fatimid rulers governed from a palace complex outside the old conquest-era garrison city of Fustat (fuss-TAHT). They named the complex Cairo. For the first time Egypt became a major cultural, intellectual, and

political center of Islam. The abundance of Fatimid gold coinage, now channeled to Egypt from West Africa, made the Fatimids an economic power in the Mediterranean.

Cut off from the rest of the Islamic world by the Strait of Gibraltar and, from 740 onward, by independent city-states in Morocco and Algeria, Umayyad Spain developed a distinctive Islamic culture blending Roman, Germanic, and Jewish traditions with those of the Arabs and Berbers. Historians disagree on how rapidly and completely the Spanish population converted to Islam. If we assume a process similar to that in the eastern regions, it seems likely that the most rapid surge in Islamization occurred in the middle of the tenth century.

As in the east, governing cities symbolized the Islamic presence in al-Andalus, as the Muslims called their Iberian territories. Cordoba, Seville, Toledo, and other cities grew substantially, becoming much larger

Mosque of Ibn Tulun in Fustat Completed in 877, this mosque symbolized Egypt becoming for the first time a quasi-independent province under its governor. The kiosk in the center of the courtyard contains fountains for washing before prayer. Before its restoration in the thirteenth century, the mosque had a spiral minaret and a door to an adjoining governor's palace.

and richer than contemporary cities in neighboring France. Converts to Islam and their descendants, unconverted Arabic-speaking Christians, and Jews joined with the comparatively few descendants of Arab settlers to create new architectural and literary styles. In the countryside, where the Berbers preferred to settle, a fusion of preexisting agricultural technologies with new crops, notably citrus fruits, and irrigation techniques from the east gave Spain the most diverse and sophisticated agricultural economy in Europe.

The rulers of al-Andalus took the title *caliph* only in 929, when Abd al-Rahman (AHB-d al–ruh-MAHN) III (r. 912–961) did so in response to a similar declaration by the newly established (909) Fatimid ruler in Tunisia. By the century's end, however, this caliphate encountered challenges from breakaway movements that eventually splintered al-Andalus into a number of small states. Political decay did not impede cultural growth. Some of the greatest writers and thinkers in Jewish history worked in Muslim Spain in the eleventh and twelfth centuries, sometimes writing in Arabic, sometimes in Hebrew. Judah Halevi (1075–1141) composed exquisite poetry and explored questions of religious philosophy. Maimonides (1135–1204) made a major compilation of Judaic law and expounded on Aristotelian philosophy. At the same time, Islamic thought in Spain attained its loftiest peaks in Ibn Hazm's (994–1064) treatises on love and other subjects, the Aristotelian philosophical writings of Ibn Rushd (IB-uhn RUSHED) (1126–1198, known in Latin as Averroës [uh-VERR-oh-eez]) and Ibn Tufayl (IB-uhn too-FILE) (d. 1185), and the mystic speculations of Ibn al-Arabi (IB-uhn ahl–AH-rah-bee) (1165–1240). Christians, too, shared in the intellectual and cultural dynamism of al-Andalus. Translations from Arabic to Latin made during this period had a profound effect on the later intellectual development of western Europe (see Chapter 10).

Tomb of the Samanids in Bukhara This early-tenth-century structure has the basic layout of a Zoroastrian fire temple: a dome on top of a cube. However, geometric ornamentation in baked brick marks it as an early masterpiece of Islamic architecture. The Samanid family achieved independence as rulers of northeastern Iran and western Central Asia in the tenth century.

The Samanids, Fatimids, and Spanish Umayyads, three of many regional principalities, represent the political diversity and awakening of local awareness that coincided with Abbasid decline. Yet drawing and redrawing political boundaries did not result in the rigid division of the Islamic world into kingdoms. Religious and cultural developments, particularly the rise in cities of a social group of religious scholars known as the **ulama** (oo-leh-MAH)—Arabic for "people with (religious) knowledge"—worked against any permanent division of the Islamic umma.

Assault from Within and Without, 1050–1258

The role played by Turkish mamluks in the decline of Abbasid power established an enduring stereotype of the Turk as a ferocious, unsophisticated warrior. This image gained strength in the 1030s when the Seljuk (sel-JOOK) family established a Turkish Muslim state based on nomadic power. Taking the Arabic title *Sultan*, meaning "power," and the revived Persian title *Shahan-shah*, or King of Kings, the Seljuk ruler Tughril (TUUG-ruhl) Beg created a kingdom that stretched from northern Afghanistan to Baghdad, which he occupied in 1055. After a century under the thumb of the Shi'ite Buyids, the Abbasid caliph breathed easier under the slightly lighter thumb of the Sunni Turks. The Seljuks pressed on into Syria and Anatolia, administering a lethal blow to Byzantine power at the Battle of Manzikert (MANZ-ih-kuhrt) in 1071. The Byzantine army fell back on Constantinople, leaving Anatolia open to Turkish occupation.

Under Turkish rule, which coincided with a severe climatic cooling that reduced harvests in Iran,

ulama Muslim religious scholars. From the ninth century onward, the primary interpreters of Islamic law and the social core of Muslim urban societies.

Iraq, and eastern Anatolia, cities shrank as pastoralists overran their agricultural hinterlands. Irrigation works suffered from lack of maintenance in the unsettled countryside, and tax revenues fell. Quarreling twelfth-century princes fought over cities, but few Turks participated in urban cultural and religious life. The gulf between a religiously based urban society and the culture and personnel of the government deepened. When factional riots broke out between Sunnis and Shi'ites, or between rival schools of Sunni law, rulers generally remained aloof, even as destruction and loss of life mounted.

By the early twelfth century, unrepaired damage from floods, fires, and civil disorder had reduced old Baghdad on the west side of the Tigris to ruins. The withering of Baghdad reflected a broader environmental problem: the collapse of the canal system on which agriculture in the Tigris and Euphrates Valley depended. For millennia a center of world civilization, Mesopotamia underwent substantial population loss and never again regained its geographical importance.

The Turks alone cannot be blamed for the demographic and economic misfortunes of Iran and Iraq. Too-robust urbanization, spurred largely by a boom in Iranian cotton production, resulted in strained food resources when the climate deteriorated after 1000. Baghdad, a city with a torrid climate today, experienced heavy winter snowfalls that killed date trees. The growing practice of paying soldiers and courtiers with land grants led to absentee landlords using agents to collect taxes. These agents gouged villagers to meet their quotas and took little interest in improving production, thus intensifying the agricultural crisis.

Internecine feuding was preoccupying the Seljuk family when the first Christian Crusaders reached the Holy Land and captured Jerusalem in 1099 (see Chapter 10). Though charged with the stuff of romance, the Crusades had little lasting impact on the Islamic lands. The four Crusader principalities of Edessa, Antioch, Tripoli, and Jerusalem simply became pawns in the shifting pattern of politics already in place. Newly arrived knights eagerly attacked the Muslim enemy, whom they called "Saracens" (SAR-uh-suhn); but veteran Crusaders recognized that practicing diplomacy and seeking partners of convenience among rival Muslim princes offered a sounder strategy.

The Muslims finally unified to face the European enemy in the mid-twelfth century. Nur al-Din ibn Zangi (NOOR uhd–DEEN ib-uhn ZAN-gee) established a strong state based in Damascus and sent an army to terminate the Fatimid Caliphate in Egypt. A nephew of the Kurdish commander of that expedition, Salah-al-Din, known in the West as Saladin, took advantage of Nur al-Din's timely death to seize power and unify Egypt and Syria. The Fatimid dynasty fell in 1171. In 1187 Saladin recaptured Jerusalem from the Europeans. He then took the title Khadim al-Haramain (KAH-dim al-ha-ra-MAYN), literally "Servant of the Two Holy Places," meaning Mecca and Medina, in a challenge to the caliph's claim to be the paramount Sunni potentate. Revitalizing the pilgrimage became a core concern for later rulers in Egypt and Syria, particularly after the termination of the Baghdad caliphate in 1258.

Saladin's descendants fought off subsequent Crusades. After one such battle, however, in 1250, Turkish mamluk troops seized control of the government in Cairo, ending Saladin's dynasty. In 1260 these mamluks rode east to confront a new invader. At the Battle of Ain Jalut (ine jah-LOOT) (Spring of Goliath) in Syria, they met and defeated an army of Mongols from Central Asia (see Chapter 12), thus stemming an invasion that had begun several decades before and legitimizing their claim to dominion over Egypt and Syria.

During the ensuing Mamluk period a succession of slave-soldier sultans ruled Egypt and Syria until 1517. Fear of new Mongol attacks receded after 1300, but by then the new ruling system had become fixed. Young Turkish or Circassian slaves, the latter from the eastern end of the Black Sea, were imported from non-Muslim lands, raised in training barracks, and converted to Islam. Owing loyalty to the Mamluk officers who purchased them, they formed a military class that was socially disconnected from the Arabic-speaking native population.

The Mongol invasions, especially their destruction of the Abbasid Caliphate in Baghdad in 1258, shocked the world of Islam. The Mamluk sultan enthroned a relative of the last Baghdad caliph in Cairo, but the Egyptian Abbasids were mere puppets serving Mamluk interests. From Iraq eastward, non-Muslim rule lasted for much of the thirteenth century. Although the Mongols left few ethnic or

- By 711, Arab armies had conquered an empire stretching from Sind in the east to Spain in the west.
- The Umayyad caliphs ruled an ethnic empire; they governed from Damascus using Sasanid and Byzantine administrative methods.
- The Umayyads fell to rebels who established the Abbasid Caliphate at Baghdad, while surviving Umayyads fled to Spain.
- Influenced by Persian culture, the Abbasids presided over significant spiritual, intellectual, and artistic activity.
- Abbasid decline led to fragmentation of the caliphate into independent states, but the Islamic umma remained intact.
- Political divisions continued as successor states to the former caliphate fell, replaced by Seljuk Turk, Crusader, Mamluk, and Mongol states.

linguistic traces in these lands, their initial destruction of cities and slaughter of civilian populations, their diversion of Silk Road trade from Baghdad to more northerly routes ending at Black Sea ports, and their casual disregard, even after conversion to Islam, for Muslim religious life and urban culture hastened currents of change already under way.

ISLAMIC CIVILIZATION

■ *How did regional diversity affect the development of Islamic civilization?*

Though increasingly unsettled in its political dimension and subject to economic disruptions caused by war, the ever-expanding Islamic world underwent a fruitful evolution in law, social structure, and religious expression. Religious conversion and urbanization reinforced each other to create a distinct Islamic civilization. The immense geographical and human diversity of the Muslim lands allowed many "small traditions" to coexist with the developing "great tradition" of Islam.

Law and Dogma

The Shari'a, the law of Islam, provided the foundation of Islamic civilization. Yet aside from certain Quranic verses conveying specific divine ordinances—most pertaining to personal and family matters—Islam had no legal system in the time of Muhammad. Arab custom and the Prophet's own authority offered the only guidance. After Muhammad died, the umma tried to follow his example. This became harder and harder to do, however, as those who knew Muhammad best passed away and many Arabs found themselves living in far-off lands. Non-Arab converts to Islam, who at first tried to follow Arab customs they had little familiarity with, had an even harder time.

Islam slowly developed laws to govern social and religious life. The full sense of Islamic civilization, however, goes well beyond the basic Five Pillars mentioned earlier. Some Muslim thinkers felt that the reasoned consideration of a mature man offered the best resolution of issues not covered by Quranic revelation. Others argued for the sunna, or tradition, of the Prophet as the best guide. To understand that sunna they collected and studied thousands of reports, called **hadith** (hah-DEETH), purporting to convey the precise words or deeds of Muhammad. It became customary to precede each hadith with a chain of oral authorities leading back to the person who had direct acquaintance with the Prophet.

Many hadith dealt with ritual matters, such as how to wash before prayer. Others provided answers to legal questions not covered by Quranic revelation or suggested principles for deciding such matters. By the eleventh century most legal thinkers had accepted the idea that Muhammad's personal behavior provided the best role model and that the hadith constituted the most authoritative basis for law after the Quran itself.

Yet the hadith posed a problem because the tens of thousands of anecdotes included both genuine and invented reports, the latter sometimes politically motivated, as well as stories derived from non-Muslim religious traditions. Only a specialist could hope to separate a sound from a weak tradition. As the hadith grew in importance, so did the branch of learning devoted to their analysis. Scholars discarded thousands for having faulty chains of authority. The most reliable they collected into books that gradually

hadith A tradition relating the words or deeds of the Prophet Muhammad; next to the Quran, the most important basis for Islamic law.

achieved authoritative status. Sunnis placed six books in this category; Shi'ites, four.

As it gradually evolved, the Shari'a embodied a vision of an umma in which all subscribed to the same moral values and political and ethnic distinctions lost importance. Every Muslim ruler was expected to abide by and enforce the religious law. In practice, this expectation often lost out in the hurly-burly of political life. But the Shari'a proved an important basis for an urban lifestyle that varied surprisingly little from Morocco to India.

Converts and Cities

Conversion to Islam, more the outcome of people's learning about the new rulers' religion than an escape from the tax on non-Muslims, as some scholars have suggested, helped spur urbanization. Conversion did not require extensive knowledge of the faith. To become a Muslim, a person simply stated, in the presence of a Muslim: "There is no God but God, and Muhammad is the Messenger of God."

Few converts spoke Arabic, and fewer could read the Quran. Many converts knew no more of the Quran than the verses they memorized for daily prayers. Muhammad had established no priesthood to define and spread the faith. Thus new converts, whether Arab or non-Arab, faced the problem of finding out for themselves what Islam was about and how they should act as Muslims. This meant spending time with Muslims, learning their language, and imitating their practices.

In many areas, conversion involved migrating to an Arab governing center. The alternative, converting to Islam but remaining in one's home community, was difficult because religion had become the main component of social identity in Byzantine and Sasanid times. Converts to Islam thus encountered discrimination if they stayed in their Christian, Jewish, or Zoroastrian communities. Migration both averted discrimination and took advantage of the economic opportunities opened up by tax revenues flowing into the Arab governing centers.

The Arab military settlements of Kufa and Basra in Iraq blossomed into cities and became important centers for Muslim cultural activities. As conversion rapidly spread in the mid-ninth century, urbanization accelerated in other regions, most visibly in

Iran, where most cities previously had been quite small. Nishapur in the northeast grew from fewer than 10,000 pre-Islamic inhabitants to between 100,000 and 200,000 by the year 1000. Other Iranian cities experienced similar growth. In Iraq, Baghdad and Mosul joined Kufa and Basra as major cities. In Syria, Aleppo and Damascus flourished under Muslim rule. Fustat in Egypt developed into Cairo, one of the largest and greatest Islamic cities. The primarily Christian patriarchal cities of Jerusalem, Antioch, and Alexandria, not being Muslim governing centers, shrank and stagnated.

Conversion-related migration meant that cities became heavily Muslim before the countryside did. This reinforced the urban orientation deriving from the fact that Muhammad and his first followers came from the commercial city of Mecca. Mosques in large cities served both as ritual centers and as places for learning and social activities.

Islam colored all aspects of urban social life. Initially the new Muslims imitated Arab dress and customs, particularly favoring plain linen or cotton over the silk brocade of the non-Muslim Iranian elite. In the absence of a central religious authority, local variations developed in the way people practiced Islam and in the hadith they attributed to the Prophet. This gave the rapidly growing religion the flexibility to accommodate many different social situations.

By the tenth century, urban growth was affecting the countryside by expanding the consumer market. Citrus fruits, rice, and sugar cane, introduced by the Sasanids, increased in acreage and spread to new areas. Cotton became a major crop in Iran and elsewhere and stimulated textile production. Irrigation works expanded. Abundant coinage facilitated a flourishing intercity and long-distance trade that provided regular links between isolated districts and integrated the pastoral nomads, who provided pack animals, into the region's economy. Trade encouraged the manufacture of cloth, metal goods, and pottery.

Science and technology also flourished. Building on Hellenistic traditions and their own observations and experience, Muslim doctors and astronomers developed skills and theories far in advance of their European counterparts. Working in Egypt in the eleventh century, the mathematician and physicist Ibn al-Haytham (IB-uhn al–HY-tham) wrote more than a

Women Playing Chess in Muslim Spain As shown in this thirteenth-century miniature, women in their own quarters, without men present, wore whatever clothes and jewels they liked. Notice the henna decorating the hands of the woman in the middle. The woman on the left, probably a slave, plays an oud. Album/Art Resource, NY

hundred works. Among other things, he determined that the Milky Way lies far beyond earth's atmosphere, proved that light travels from a seen object to the eye and not the reverse, and explained why the sun and moon appear larger on the horizon than overhead.

Women and Islam

Seclusion of women and veiling in public already existed in Byzantine and Sasanid times. Women seldom traveled. Those living in rural areas worked in the fields and tended animals, while urban and elite women did not leave their homes without covering themselves (see Material Culture: Head Coverings). Through interpretation of specific verses from the Quran, these practices now became fixtures of Muslim social life. Public roles for women were generally barred, and women who sometimes became literate and studied with relatives did so away from the gaze of unrelated men. Only slave women could perform before unrelated men as musicians and dancers. A misogynistic tone is also sometimes found in Islamic writings. One saying attributed to the Prophet observed: "I was raised up to heaven and saw that most of its denizens were poor people; I was raised into the hellfire and saw that most of its denizens were women."[3]

Nevertheless, Muslim women fared better legally under Islamic law than did Christian and Jewish women under their respective religious codes. While a man could have sexual relations with as many slave concubines as he pleased, and marry as many as four wives, Muslim law put the financial burden of supporting a family exclusively on the husband, who could not legally compel his wife to help out. Women could also remarry if their husbands divorced them, and they received a cash payment upon divorce. Although a man could divorce his wife without stating a cause, a woman could initiate divorce under specified conditions. Women could also practice birth control. They could testify in court, although their testimony counted as half that of a man. They

---

[3]Richard W. Bulliet, *Islam: The View from the Edge* (New York: Columbia University Press, 1994), 87.

Material Culture

Head Coverings

Covering the head is one of the most universal of human cultural characteristics. It is also one of the most common ways of signaling social status. Examples can be drawn from every part of the world, from earliest times down to the modern era. In premodern Chinese society, the color and design of a man's cap indicated his rank as clearly as the insignia on military head coverings does today. In most European societies in the seventeenth and eighteenth centuries, men and frequently women of the higher social orders wore wigs, a practice that still survives in the costume of British judges. Head coverings were particularly important for royalty. From ancient Egypt, where the earliest pharaonic crowns symbolized the union of the northern and southern parts of the Nile Valley, down to the twentieth century and the jewel-studded crown of the shah of Iran, each land developed its own distinctive royal headdress. This also held true for Native American societies in pre-Columbian times and for African and Polynesian societies. In some societies, such as Sasanid Iran and the Ottoman Empire in what is today Turkey, each ruler's crown or turban had a distinctive design that symbolized his rule.

Head coverings have also played significant roles in religion. In orthodox Judaism, for example, men wear hats or skullcaps, and married women wear wigs, as signs of acceptance of God's laws. In Islam, head coverings for women, borrowed from pre-Islamic practice in the Middle East, have become politically controversial in recent years; but prior to the twentieth century it was considered equally improper for a Muslim man to go bareheaded.

Wearing no hat at all was usually a characteristic of slaves or of the poorest elements in society. But it could also signify a deliberate desire to be regarded as humble. Sumerian priests, Buddhist monks and nuns, and certain Sufis in the Muslim world shaved their heads clean. In Europe, early Christian monks and priests shaved the crown of their heads in the Roman Catholic tradition. This form of tonsure competed with and eventually superseded an Irish Catholic practice of shaving the front of the head. Yet head shaving did not always signify humility. Japanese samurai, or warriors, also shaved the front of their heads.

Head coverings for women, as well as wigs and hairdressing styles, sometimes show greater diversity than those for men. This has been particularly true in societies where women of high status mix with men on public occasions. A magnificent wig, hat, or coiffure under these

Muslim Head Coverings *The man standing before a governor in this thirteenth-century miniature painting wears a simple skullcap indicating his low social status. The two attendants* wear turbans, but the governor's turban is built into a high, conical shape. The folds and tails of turbans signified not only rank, but also place of origin. To this day, men from western Afghanistan wear tightly wound white turbans with long tails while men from eastern Afghanistan wear loose colorful turbans. Abu Zayd standing before the governor of Ramba in Baghdad, Arabic miniature, 1237./De Agostini Picture Library/J.E. Bulloz/The Bridgeman Art Library

circumstances might speak as much for the social rank of the woman's husband as for her own.

Given this long history of distinctive head coverings, the abandonment of both men's and women's hats in the second half of the twentieth century marked a major turning point in the history of symbolism. Around the world, the hat-making industry has greatly contracted. Whether one visits China, Egypt, India, France, or Brazil, one finds it difficult to determine the rank or status of most people by looking at what they have on their heads. Heads of government typically pose for group photographs with no hats on at all. Aside from conservative religious groups, the head coverings that remain most often indicate occupations: military, police, construction, athletics, and so on.

The reasons for this change are unclear. The spread of democracy and decline of aristocracy may have contributed to it, but hats have become equally uncommon in dictatorships. A more likely cause is the worldwide role of news photographs, movies, and other pictorial media. The media developed in Europe and the United States tend to take Western customs as normal and exoticize non-Western styles as "native costumes." People everywhere have thus felt pressure to switch to Western styles, including bareheadedness, to fit into the image of the modern world.

QUESTIONS FOR ANALYSIS

1. What might covering the head, or removing a head cover, signify in America today?
2. How desirable is it to be able to distinguish a person's job or social position by looking at his or her head covering?
3. What does wearing a baseball cap convey?

could also go on pilgrimage. In addition, Islamic law guaranteed daughters a share in inheritance equal to half that of a son; the majority of women inherited some amount of money or real estate, and this remained their private property to keep or sell.

In the absence of writings by women about women from this period, the status of women must be deduced from the writings of men. Two episodes involving the Prophet's wife A'isha, the daughter of Abu Bakr, provide examples of how Muslim men appraised women in society. Only eighteen when Muhammad died, A'isha lived for another fifty years. Early reports stress her status as Muhammad's favorite, the only virgin he married and the only wife to see the angel Gabriel. These reports emanate from A'isha herself, who was an abundant source of hadith. As a fourteen-year-old she had become separated from a caravan and rejoined it only after traveling through the night with a man who found her alone in the desert. Gossips accused her of being untrue to the Prophet, but a revelation from God proved her innocence. The second event was her participation in the Battle of the Camel, fought to derail Ali's caliphate. These two episodes came to epitomize what Muslim men feared most about women: sexual infidelity and meddling in politics. Even though the earliest literature dealing with A'isha stresses her position as Muhammad's favorite, his first wife, Khadija, and his daughter, Ali's wife Fatima, eventually surpassed A'isha as ideal women. Both appear as model wives and mothers with no suspicion of sexual irregularity or political manipulation.

As the seclusion of women became commonplace in urban Muslim society, some writers extolled homosexual relationships, partly because a male lover could appear in public or go on a journey. Although Islam deplored homosexuality, one ruler wrote a book advising his son to follow moderation in all things and thus share his affections equally between men and women. Another ruler and his slave-boy became models of perfect love in the verses of mystic poets.

Islam allowed slavery but forbade Muslims from enslaving other Muslims or so-called People of the Book—Jews, Christians, and Zoroastrians, who revered holy books respected by the Muslims. Being enslaved as a prisoner of war constituted an exception. Later centuries saw a constant flow of slaves into Islamic territory from Africa and Central Asia. A hereditary slave society, however, did not develop. Usually slaves converted to Islam, and many masters then freed them as an act of piety. The offspring of slave women and Muslim men were born free.

The Recentering of Islam

Early Islam centered on the caliphate, the political expression of the unity of the umma. No formal organization or hierarchy, however, directed the process of conversion. Thus there emerged a multitude of local Islamic communities so disconnected from each other that numerous competing interpretations of the developing religion arose. Inevitably, the centrality of the caliphate diminished (see Map 9.1). The appearance of rival caliphates in Tunisia and Cordoba accentuated the problem of decentralization. The rise of the ulama as community leaders did not prevent growing fragmentation because the ulama themselves divided into contentious factions. During the twelfth century factionalism began to abate, and new socioreligious institutions, including a revitalized pilgrimage to Mecca, emerged to provide the umma with a different sort of religious center. These new developments stemmed in part from an exodus of religious scholars from Iran in response to economic and political disintegration during the late eleventh and twelfth centuries. The flow of Iranians to the Arab lands and to newly conquered territories in India and Anatolia increased after the Mongol invasion. Immigrant scholars were warmly received. Fully versed in Arabic as well as their native Persian, they brought with them a view of religion developed in Iran's urban centers. A type of religious college, the *madrasa* (MAH-dras-uh), gained sudden popularity outside Iran, where madrasas had been known since the tenth century. Scores of madrasas, many founded by local rulers, appeared throughout the Islamic world. In the fourteenth century, Mecca became a major educational center for the first time since Muhammad's generation.

Iranians also contributed to the growth of mystic groups known as *Sufi* brotherhoods in the twelfth and thirteenth centuries. The doctrines and rituals of certain Sufis spread from city to city, giving rise to the first geographically extensive Islamic religious organizations. Sufi doctrines varied, but a quest for a sense of union with God through rituals and training

Christian Societies Emerge in Europe

© Cengage Learning

In 800, **Charlemagne** (SHAHR-leh-mane) (from Latin *Carolus magnus*, "Charles the Great") was the first in western Europe to bear the title *emperor* in over three hundred years. Rome's decline and Charlemagne's rise marked a shift of focus for Europe—away from the Mediterranean and toward the north and west. As German custom and Christian piety transformed the Roman heritage to create a new civilization, Irish monks preaching in Latin became important intellectual leaders in Germanic lands. The memory of Greek and Roman philosophy faded, and the urban life that had begun in the later days of the Roman Empire declined. Historians originally called this era **medieval**, literally "middle age," because it comes between the era of Greco-Roman civilization and the intellectual, artistic, and economic changes of the Renaissance in the fourteenth century. In fact, many aspects of medieval culture were as rich and creative as those that came earlier and later.

Charlemagne was not the only ruler in Europe to claim the title *emperor*. Another emperor held sway in the Greek-speaking east, where Rome's political and legal heritage continued in the Eastern Roman or **Byzantine Empire**. While western Europeans lived amid the ruins of empire, the Byzantines maintained and reinterpreted Roman traditions. The authority of the Byzantine emperors also blended with the influence of the Christian church in a cultural synthesis that helped shape the emerging kingdom of **Kievan Russia**. Byzantium's centuries-long conflict with Islam helped spur the crusading passion that overtook western Europe in the eleventh century.

The comparison between western and eastern Europe appears paradoxical. Byzantium inherited a robust and self-confident late Roman society and economy, while western Europe could not achieve political unity and suffered severe economic decline. Yet by 1200 western Europe was showing renewed vitality and flexing its military muscles, while Byzantium was showing signs of decline and military weakness. As we explore these different historical paths, we must remember that the emergence of Christian Europe included both developments.

THE BYZANTINE EMPIRE, 600–1200

■ *How did the Byzantine Empire maintain Roman imperial traditions in the east?*

The Byzantine emperors established Christianity as their official religion (see Chapter 5). They also represented a continuation of Roman imperial rule and tradition. Whereas only provincial forms of Roman law survived in the west, Byzantium inherited imperial law intact. Combining the imperial role with political oversight over the Christian church, the emperors made a comfortable transition into the role of all-powerful Christian monarchs. The Byzantine drama, however, played on a steadily shrinking stage. Territorial losses and almost constant military pressure from north and south deprived the empire of long periods of peace.

Church and State

In 324, in the nineteenth year of his reign, the emperor Constantine (r. 306–337) led a procession marking the expanded limits of his new capital: the millennium-old Greek city of Byzantium, located on a long narrow inlet at the entrance of the Bosphorus strait. In the forum of the new Constantinople (cahn-stan-tih-NO-pul), he erected a 120-foot-tall (36-meter-tall) column topped with a statue of Apollo, and he retained the old Roman title *pontifex maximus* (PAHN-tih-fex MAX-ih-mus) (chief priest). Nevertheless, he leaned toward Christianity—historians disagree on when he embraced it fully—and he and his mother studded both his capital and the Christian centers of Jerusalem and Rome with important churches.

Charlemagne King of the Franks (r. 768–814); emperor (r. 800–814). Through a series of military conquests he established the Carolingian Empire, which encompassed all of Gaul and parts of Germany and Italy. Though illiterate himself, he sponsored a brief intellectual revival.

medieval Literally "middle age," a term that historians of Europe use for the period from roughly 500 to 1300, signifying its intermediate point between Greco-Roman antiquity and the Renaissance.

Byzantine Empire Historians' name for the eastern portion of the Roman Empire from the fourth century onward, taken from *Byzantion*, an early name for Constantinople, the Byzantine capital city. The empire fell to the Ottomans in 1453.

Kievan Russia State established at Kiev in Ukraine around 880 by Scandinavian adventurers asserting authority over a mostly Slavic farming population.

Constantine appointed the patriarch of Constantinople and involved himself in doctrinal disputes over which beliefs constituted heresy. In 325 he called hundreds of bishops to a council at Nicaea (nye-SEE-uh) (modern Iznik in northwestern Turkey) to resolve disputes over religious doctrine. The bishops rejected the views of a priest from Alexandria named Arius, who maintained that Jesus was of lesser importance than God the Father. The Arian doctrine enjoyed greatest popularity among the Germanic peoples then migrating along the Danube frontier and into the western Roman lands. An Arian bishop named Ulfilas (ca. 311–383), himself belonging to the Germanic peoples known as Goths,

translated the Bible into Gothic, reportedly using an alphabet of his own devising. This set the Arians apart from Christians, who relied on scriptures written in Latin or Greek.

Following the Arian controversy, disputes over theology and quarrels among the patriarchs of Constantinople, Alexandria, and Antioch continued to tear at the Byzantine Empire. As discussed in Chapter 9, religion permeated society, and the literature of the period shows the widespread concern for religious affairs. A fourth-century bishop reported: "Everything is full of those who are speaking of unintelligible things. . . . I wish to know the price of bread; one answers, "The Father is greater than the Son." I

Map 10.1 The Spread of Christianity By the early eighth century, Christian areas around the southern Mediterranean from northern Syria to northern Spain, accounting for most of the Christian population, had fallen under Muslim rule; the slow process of conversion to Islam had begun. This accentuated the importance of the patriarchs of Constantinople, the popes in Rome, and the later converting regions of northern and eastern Europe. © Cengage Learning

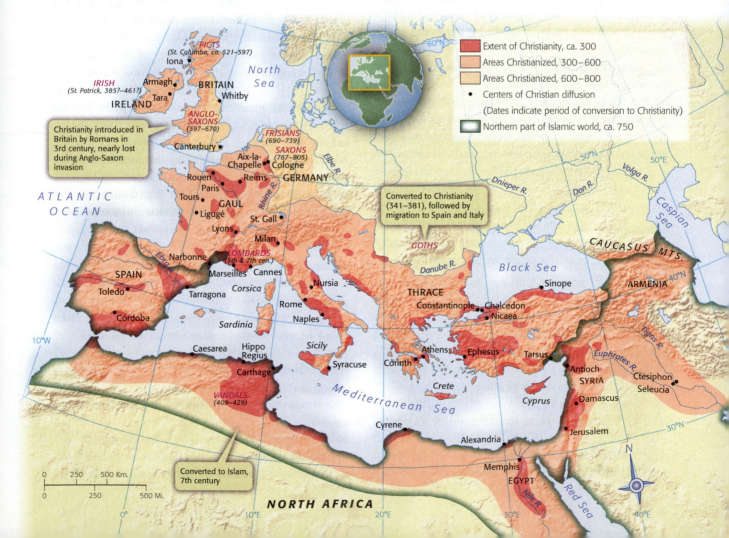

Chronology

	Western Europe	Eastern Europe
600		**634–650** Muslims conquer Byzantine provinces of Syria, Egypt, and Tunisia
	711 Muslim conquest of Spain **732** Battle of Tours	
800	**800** Coronation of Charlemagne **843** Treaty of Verdun divides Carolingian Empire among Charlemagne's grandsons **910** Monastery of Cluny founded **962** Beginning of Holy Roman Empire	**ca. 880** Varangians take control of Kiev **980** Vladimir becomes grand prince of Kievan Russia
1000	**1054** Formal schism between Latin and Orthodox Churches **1066** Normans under William the Conqueror invade England **1076–1078** Climax of investiture controversy **1095** Pope Urban II preaches First Crusade	**1081–1118** Alexius Comnenus rules Byzantine Empire, calls for western military aid against Muslims
1200		**1204** Western knights sack Constantinople in Fourth Crusade

inquire whether my bath is ready; one says, 'The son has been made out of nothing.'"[1]

Early Christians had established communities in many cities (see Map 10.1). The bishops in the four most prominent cities—Jerusalem, Antioch, Alexandria, and Rome—became recognized as patriarchs or paramount leaders, and Constantine made Constantinople a fifth patriarchate (PAY-tree-ar-kayt). Although recognized as important, theologians like St. Augustine (354–430), the bishop of Hippo in North Africa, were not patriarchs.

The patriarchs appointed bishops throughout their regions, and each bishop consecrated priests within his area of jurisdiction, called a *diocese* or *see*. Church rules set by the patriarch or by councils of bishops guided priests in serving ordinary believers. Priests commemorated Christ's sacrifice on the cross in the consumption of wine and a wafer or bread in the Mass, or church service. Church leaders differed on the precise form of other rituals and on which should be considered sacred mysteries, or

sacraments. Before baptism became standardized as a ritual for newborns, for example, it was sometimes postponed until late in life so that the person could benefit from the forgiveness of sin that it conveyed.

One area of disagreement within the church hierarchy centered on Jesus' relationship to God the Father and to the Holy Spirit. The bishops gathered for the Council of Nicaea agreed that, contrary to the Arian view, the three formed a divine Trinity in which three manifestations of god somehow came together. But they did not all understand the Trinity in the same way. They also disagreed on whether Mary was the mother of God or the mother of a human named Jesus. Some Christians thought that images of God or Jesus or Mary, called *icons*, were proper objects to pray before because they stimulated pious thoughts; others, known as *iconoclasts*, or image-breakers, condemned the practice as too much like praying to pagan statues.

In another dispute, Monophysite (muh-NAH-fi-site) (Greek for "one nature") doctrine emphasized the divinity of Jesus Christ and minimized his human characteristics. Finding abhorrent the idea that Christ suffered like an ordinary human on the cross, some Monophysites maintained that another man

---

[1] A.A. Vasiliev, *History of the Byzantine Empire, 324–1435*, vol. 1 (Madison: University of Wisconsin Press, 1978), 79–80.

Byzantine Church from a Twelfth-Century Manuscript
The upper portion shows the church façade and domes. The lower portion shows the interior with a mosaic of Christ enthroned at the altar end. Image Asset Management Ltd./SuperStock

had been substituted for him. Versions of Monophysitism persist to this day in Egyptian, Ethiopian, and Armenian churches.

For some four centuries after 300, disagreements like these led to charges and countercharges of heresy. A heresy was a belief or practice so unacceptable as to be un-Christian. The most severe disagreements resulted in a **schism** (SKIZ-uhm) or formal theological break.

Christianity progressed most rapidly in urban centers. Though the country folk (Latin *pagani*, whence the word *pagan* used as a negative label for polytheists) long retained worship of the old gods, the emperor Julian (r. 361–363) tried in vain to restore the old polytheism as the state cult. When a blind Christian addressed Julian by the pejorative term *apostate*

(renegade from Christianity), the emperor said, "You are blind, and your God will not cure you." To this the Christian replied, "I thank God for my blindness, since it prevents me from beholding your impiety."[2] In 392 the emperor Theodosius banned all pagan ceremonies. The following year he terminated the eleven-hundred-year-old tradition of the Olympic Games, which had originated as religious rites but had become increasingly professionalized in Roman times.

Having a single ruler endowed with supreme legal and religious authority prevented the breakup of the Eastern Empire into petty principalities, despite near-constant border wars. A strong emperor might temporarily recover lost ground, as Justinian (r. 527–565) did in seizing Tunisia from Germanic Vandals and reasserting Byzantine control along the east coast of Italy. To the the north and east, however, various enemies, including the Germanic Goths, the nomadic Huns of Central Asia, and the Sasanids of the Iranian Empire, posed severe threats at different times. Bribes, diplomacy, and occasional military victories usually persuaded the Goths and Huns to settle peacefully or move on and attack western Europe. War with the Sasanids, however, flared up repeatedly for almost three hundred years. Finally, a new enemy appeared from the Arabian peninsula: followers of the Arab prophet Muhammad (see Chapter 9). Between 634 and 650, Arab armies destroyed the Sasanid Empire and captured Byzantine Egypt, Syria, and Tunisia. By the end of the twelfth century at least two-thirds of the Christians in these former Byzantine territories had adopted the Muslim faith.

The loss of such populous and prosperous provinces shook the empire and reduced its power. Although the empire had largely recovered and reorganized militarily by the tenth century, it never regained the lost lands and eventually succumbed to Muslim conquest in 1453. The later Byzantine emperors faced new enemies in the north and south. Following the wave of Germanic migrations, Slavic and Turkish peoples appeared on the northern frontiers

[2] Ibid., 71.

schism A formal split within a religious community.

as part of centuries-long population migrations in Eurasian steppelands. Other Turks led by the Seljuk family became the primary foe in the south.

At the same time, relations with the popes and provinces of western Europe steadily worsened. In the mid-ninth century the patriarchs of Constantinople had challenged the territorial jurisdiction of the peoples of Rome and some of the practices of the Latin Church. These arguments culminated in 1054 in a formal schism between the Latin Church and the Orthodox Church—a break that has been only partially mended.

Society and Urban Life

Imperial authority and urban prosperity in the eastern provinces of the old Roman Empire initially sheltered Byzantium from the economic reverses and population losses suffered from the third century on. However, the territorial losses to Arab invaders coming on the heels of a devastating sixth-century epidemic of bubonic plague, known as "the plague of Justinian," gave Byzantium a taste of decline. Popular narratives of saints' lives show a transition from stories about educated saints hailing from cities to stories about saints who originated as peasants. In many areas, barter replaced money transactions; some cities declined in population and wealth; and the traditional class of local urban notables nearly disappeared.

As the urban elite class shrank, the importance of high-ranking aristocrats at the imperial court and of rural landowners gained importance. Power organized by family began to rival power from class-based officeholding. By the end of the eleventh century, a family-based military aristocracy had emerged. Of Byzantine emperor Alexius Comnenus (uh-LEX-see-uhs kom-NAY-nuhs) (r. 1081–1118) it was said: "He considered himself not a ruler, but a lord, conceiving and calling the empire his own house."[3]

The situation of women changed, too. After the seventh century women increasingly found themselves confined to the home. Some sources indicate that when they went out, they concealed their faces behind veils. Paradoxically, however, from 1028 to 1056 women ruled the Byzantine Empire alongside their husbands. The increase in the seclusion of women resembles simultaneous developments in neighboring Islamic countries, but a firm linkage between them has yet to be found.

Economically, the Byzantine emperors continued the Late Roman practice of setting prices, organizing grain shipments to the capital, and monopolizing luxury goods like Tyrian purple cloth. Such government intervention may have slowed technological development and economic innovation. In the countryside, Byzantine farmers continued to use slow oxcarts and light scratch plows, which were efficient for many, but not all, soil types, long after farmers in western Europe had begun to adopt more efficient techniques.

Because Byzantium's Roman inheritance remained so much more intact than western Europe's, few people recognized the slow deterioration. Gradually, however, pilgrims and visitors from the west saw the reality beyond the awe-inspiring, incense-filled domes of cathedrals and beneath the glitter and silken garments of the royal court. An eleventh-century French visitor wrote:

> The city itself [Constantinople] is squalid and fetid and in many places harmed by permanent darkness, for the wealthy overshadow the streets with buildings and leave these dirty, dark places to the poor and to travelers; there murders and robberies and other crimes which love the darkness are committed. Moreover, since people live lawlessly in this city, which has . . . almost as many thieves as poor men, a criminal knows neither fear nor shame, because crime is not punished by law and never entirely comes to light. In every respect she exceeds moderation; for, just as she surpasses other cities in wealth, so too, does she surpass them in vice.[4]

A Byzantine contemporary, Anna Comnena, the brilliant daughter of Emperor Alexius Comnenus, expressed the view from the other side. She scornfully described a prominent churchman and philosopher who happened to be from Italy: "Italos . . . was unable with his barbaric, stupid temperament to grasp the profound truths of philosophy; even in the act of learning he utterly rejected the teacher's guiding

---

[3] A. P. Kazhdan and Ann Wharton Epstein, *Change in Byzantine Culture in the Eleventh and Twelfth Centuries* (Berkeley: University of California Press, 1985), 71.

[4] Ibid., 248.

hand, and full of temerity and barbaric folly, [believed] even before study that he excelled all others."[5]

Cultural Achievements

Justinian's collection of Roman laws endured far longer than his restoration of Byzantine rule in Italy and North Africa. At his command a team of seventeen legal scholars made a systematic compilation, in Latin, of a thousand years of Roman legal tradition. The *Corpus Juris Civilis*, or Body of Civil Law, as it has been called since the sixteenth century, consisted of four sections: the laws themselves, a digest for lawyers and judges containing quotations from well-known commentaries, and a student textbook. A collection of recent Justinian decrees not previously collected made up the fourth section added later. In the eleventh century a legal scholar named Irnerius (ca. 1055–ca. 1130) revived the study of this code (see Chapter 13) at the University of Bologna (boe-LOAN-yuh) in Italy, and it subsequently became the basis of most modern European legal systems.

Constantinople's cathedral, the Hagia Sophia (Ah-yah SOH-fee-uh) ("Sacred Wisdom"), also dates in its present form to the reign of Justinian and his influential wife, the empress Theodora. Its great dome became a hallmark of Byzantine architecture. Artistic creativity appeared in the design and ornamentation of other churches and monasteries as well. Byzantine religious art, featuring stiff but arresting images of holy figures against gold backgrounds, strongly influenced painting in western Europe down to the thirteenth century, and Byzantine musical traditions strongly affected the chanting employed in medieval Latin churches.

Other important Byzantine achievements date to the empire's long period of political decline. In the ninth century, two brothers named Cyril and Methodius embarked on a highly successful mission to the Slavs of Moravia (part of the modern Czech Republic). Like the Gothic bishop Ulfilas in the fourth century, they preached in the local language, and their followers perfected a writing system, called Cyrillic (sih-RIL-ik), that came to be used by Slavic Christians adhering to the Orthodox—that is, Byzantine—rite. Their careers also mark the beginning of a competition between

SECTION REVIEW

- With Christianity as a state religion, the Eastern Roman Empire retained its unity and became the Byzantine Empire, continuing the Roman imperial and legal traditions in the east.

- Doctrinal and territorial disputes led to a formal schism that split the Orthodox Church from the Catholic Church in the west.

- Plagues and invasions caused significant cultural and political shifts and decline in the Byzantine Empire.

- The culture of the Byzantine Empire made many important aesthetic contributions to the art of Europe.

- Byzantine missionaries spread their faith and the Cyrillic alphabet into eastern Europe.

the Greek and Latin forms of Christianity for the allegiance of the Slavs. The use today of the Cyrillic alphabet among the Russians and other Slavic peoples of Orthodox Christian faith, and of the Roman alphabet among the Slavic Poles, Czechs, and Croatians, testifies to this competition.

EARLY MEDIEVAL EUROPE, 600–1000

◼ *How did the culture of early medieval Europe develop in the absence of imperial rule?*

The disappearance of the imperial legal framework that had persisted to the final days of the Western Roman Empire (see Chapter 5) and the rise of various kings, nobles, and chieftains changed the legal and political landscape of western Europe. In region after region, the family-based traditions of the Germanic peoples, which often fit local conditions better than previous practices, supplanted the edicts of the Roman emperors (see Map 10.2).

Fear and physical insecurity led communities to seek the protection of local strongmen. In places where looters and pillagers might appear at any moment, a local lord with a castle at which peasants could take refuge counted for more than a distant king. Dependency of weak people on strong people became a hallmark of the post-Roman period in western Europe.

The Time of Insecurity

By 530 the Western Roman Empire had fragmented into a handful of dissimilar kingdoms

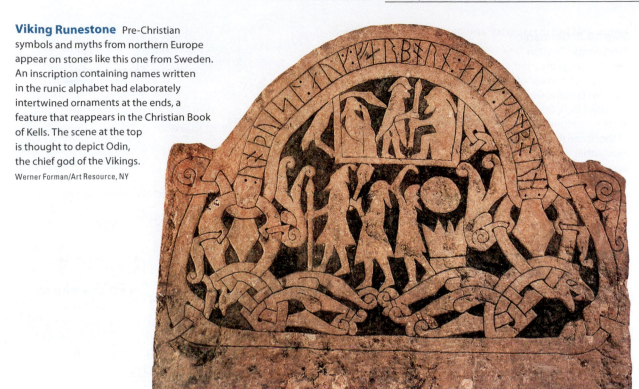

Viking Runestone Pre-Christian symbols and myths from northern Europe appear on stones like this one from Sweden. An inscription containing names written in the runic alphabet had elaborately intertwined ornaments at the ends, a feature that reappears in the Christian Book of Kells. The scene at the top is thought to depict Odin, the chief god of the Vikings.
Werner Forman/Art Resource, NY

under Germanic rulers. The Franks held much of Gaul, the Visigoths ruled Spain, and the Ostrogoths ruled in Italy and present-day Austria and Hungary. By 600 the Lombards had replaced the Ostrogoths in northern Italy, and the Byzantine Empire had regained footholds in the south and around Ravenna along the east coast. The city of Rome lost most of its population and its political importance but retained prominence as the seat of the bishop of Rome. Local noble families competed for control of this position, which over several centuries acquired the title *pope* (supreme cleric) in the Latin-speaking church.

The educated few, most of them Christian priests and monks, spoke and wrote a simplified form of Latin, but the uneducated masses who had lived under Roman rule spoke Romance dialects that eventually became modern Portuguese, Spanish, French, Italian, and Romanian. In the north and east of the Rhine River, where Roman culture had scarcely penetrated, people spoke Germanic and related Scandinavian languages. East of the Elbe River, Slavic speakers formed a third major group. Whatever sense of unity Europe may have experienced under Roman rule gave way to strongly localized identities.

In 711 a frontier raiding party of Muslim Arabs and Berbers crossed the Strait of Gibraltar and defeated the Visigoths in Spain (see Chapter 9). After pushing the remaining Christian chieftains into the northern mountains, the Muslims moved on to France. They occupied much of the southern coast and penetrated as far north as Tours, less than 150 miles (240 kilometers) from the English Channel, before the Frankish leader Charles Martel, Charlemagne's grandfather, stopped their most advanced raiding party in 732 at the Battle of Tours.

Military effectiveness was the key element in the rise of the Carolingian (kah-roe-LIN-gee-uhn) family (from Latin *Carolus*, "Charles"), first as protectors of the Frankish (French) kings, then as kings themselves under Charlemagne's father Pepin (r. 751–768), and finally with Charlemagne as emperor. Charlemagne's Carolingian Empire encompassed all of Gaul and parts of Germany and Italy. When Charlemagne's son Louis the Pious died, the Germanic tradition of splitting property among sons led to the Treaty of Verdun (843), which divided the empire into three parts. French-speaking in the west (France) and middle (Burgundy), and German-speaking in the east (Germany), the three

Map 10.2 Germanic Kingdoms Though German kings asserted authority over most of western Europe, German-speaking peoples were most numerous east of the Rhine River. In most other areas, Celtic languages such as Irish or languages derived from Latin predominated. Though the absolute number of Germanic settlers seems to have been fairly limited, the Germanic Anglo-Saxon tongue increasingly supplanted the Celtic Welsh and Scottish in Britain.

© Cengage Learning

regions never reunited (see Map 10.2). Nevertheless, the Carolingian economic system based on landed wealth and a brief intellectual revival sponsored personally by Charlemagne—himself illiterate—provided a common heritage.

In 793, Viking sea raiders from Scandinavia attacked and plundered an English coastal monastery, the first of hundreds of similar raids. Local sources from France, the British Isles, and Muslim Spain reflect widespread dread of Viking warriors descending from multi-oared, dragon-prowed boats to pillage monasteries, villages, and towns. Versatile Viking vessels could both brave the stormy North Atlantic and maneuver up rivers. By the ninth century raiders from Denmark and Norway were harrying the British and French coasts while Varangians (va-RAN-gee-anz) (Swedes) pursued raiding and trading interests along the rivers of eastern Europe and Russia. In the 800s and 900s Viking captains organized the settlement of Iceland and Greenland, and, around the year 1000, they reached the northern tip

of Newfoundland, which they called *Vinland* ("the land of grapevines").

Vikings long settled on lands they had seized in Normandy (in northwestern France) organized the most important and ambitious expeditions in terms of numbers of men and horses and long-lasting impact. William the Conqueror, the duke of Normandy, invaded England in 1066 and brought Anglo-Saxon domination of the island to an end. Other Normans (from "north men") attacked Muslim Sicily in the 1060s and, after thirty years of fighting, permanently severed it from the Muslim world.

A Self-Sufficient Economy

Archaeology and monastic records reveal a profound economic transformation that accompanied the new Germanic political order. The new rulers cared little for the Romans' urban-based culture, which accordingly shrank in importance. Change was more rapid in some regions than others, but most cities lost population, or even became

Boatbuilding Scene from the Bayeux Tapestry Eleventh-century shipwrights prepare vessels for William of Normandy's invasion of England. Building ships under the orders of Duke William, detail from the Bayeux Tapestry, before 1082 (wool embroidery on linen), French School, (11th century)/ Musee de la Tapisserie, Bayeux, France/With special authorisation of the city of Bayeux/The Bridgeman Art Library

villages. Roman roads fell into disuse and disrepair. Small thatched houses sprang up beside abandoned villas, and marble public buildings became dilapidated. Paying for purchases in coin largely gave way to bartering goods and services. Although trade across the Mediterranean did not entirely stop after the Muslim conquests, archaeological investigations of sunken ships show contact more with North African ports than with Egypt and Syria, and western Europe came to rely on meager local resources.

Roman centralization had channeled the wealth and production of the empire to the capital, which in turn radiated Roman culture to the provinces. As literacy and other aspects of Roman life declined and as Germanic territorial lords replaced Roman governors, Germanic and Celtic cultural traditions became more dominant, and self-sufficient farming estates known as **manors** became centers of agricultural production. The lack of a central government, poor communication, and warfare made unprotected country houses vulnerable to pillaging, so farmers in isolated regions gave their land to large landowners in return for protection. Many became warriors, maintained a force of armed men, or swore allegiance to landowners who had armed forces to protect them.

Depending on local custom, protection ranged from a ditch and wooden stockade to a stone wall surrounding a fortified keep (a stone building). Fortification tended to increase until the twelfth century, when stronger monarchies made it less necessary.

Manor life reflected personal status. A well-appointed manor possessed fields, gardens, grazing lands, fishponds, a mill, a church, workshops for making farm and household implements, and a village where the farmers dependent on the lord of the manor lived. Nobles and their families exercised almost unlimited power over the **serfs**—agricultural workers who belonged to the manor, tilled its fields, and owed other dues and obligations. Serfs could not leave the manor where they were born and attach themselves to another lord. Most peasants in England, France, and western Germany were unfree serfs in the tenth and eleventh centuries. In Bordeaux (bore-DOE), Saxony,

manor In medieval Europe, a large, self-sufficient landholding consisting of the lord's residence (manor house), outbuildings, peasant village, and surrounding land.

serf In medieval Europe, an agricultural laborer legally bound to a lord's property and obligated to perform set services for the lord. In Russia, later, some serfs worked as artisans and in factories; serfdom was not abolished there until 1861.

and a few other regions, free peasantry survived based on the egalitarian social structure of the Germanic peoples during their period of migration. Outright slavery, the mainstay of the Roman economy (see Chapter 5), diminished as more and more peasants became serfs in return for a lord's protection. At the same time, taking prisoners to serve as slaves became less important as an object of warfare.

The average western European of the ninth century was probably better nourished than his or her descendants three hundred years later, when population was increasing and the nobility monopolized the resources of the forests. While nobles ate better than peasants, even the peasant diet of the north was reasonably balanced, featuring beer, lard or butter, and bread made of barley, rye, or wheat, and supplemented by pork from herds of swine fed on forest acorns and beechnuts, and by game from the same forests. The Roman diet based on wheat, wine, and olive oil persisted in the south.

Early Medieval Society in the West

Reversion to a self-sufficient economy limited the freedom and potential for personal achievement of most people, but an emerging class of nobles reaped great benefits. During the Germanic migrations and later among the Vikings of Scandinavia, men regularly answered the call to arms issued by war chiefs, to whom they swore allegiance. All warriors shared in the booty gained from raiding. As settlement enhanced the importance of agricultural tasks, laying down the plow and picking up the sword at the chieftain's call became harder.

Those who continued to join the war parties included a growing number of horsemen. Mounted warriors became the central force of the Carolingian army. At first, fighting from horseback did not make a person either a nobleman or a landowner. By the tenth century, however, nearly constant warfare to protect land rights or support the claims of a lord brought about a gradual transformation in the status of the mounted warrior. At different rates in different areas, landholding became almost inseparable from military service.

The German foes of the Roman legions had equipped themselves with helmets, shields, and swords, spears, or throwing axes. Most fought on foot.

Horsemen, using stirrups first invented by Central Asian pastoralists around the first century C.E., were able to stand in the saddle, lean forward, and absorb the impact when their lances struck the enemy at full gallop. This type of warfare required grain-fed horses that were larger and heavier than the small, grass-fed animals of the Central Asian nomads. Thus agricultural Europe rather than the European steppelands produced the charges of armored knights that by the eleventh century came to dominate the battlefield.

Knights wore an open-faced helmet and a long linen shirt, or hauberk (HAW-berk), studded with small metal disks. A century later, knightly equipment commonly included a visored helmet that covered the head and neck and a hauberk of chain mail. More armor for knight and horse meant a greater financial outlay. Since land was the basis of wealth, a knight needed financial support from land revenues. Accordingly, kings began to reward armed service with grants of land from their own property. Lesser nobles with extensive properties built their own military retinues the same way.

A grant of land in return for a pledge to provide military service was often called a **fief.** At first, kings granted fiefs to their noble followers, known as **vassals,** on a temporary basis. By the tenth century, most fiefs could be inherited as long as the specified military service continued to be provided. Starting in the sixteenth century, it became common to refer to medieval Europe as a "feudal society" (from the Latin *feodum,* meaning land awarded for military service) in which kings and lords gave land to vassals in return for sworn military support.

By analyzing original records, more recent historians have discovered this to be an oversimplification. Relations between landholders and serfs and between lords and vassals differed too much from one place to another to fit together in anything resembling a regular system. The lord of a manor rather than the king provided local governance and justice, and members of the clergy, along with the extensive agricultural lands owned by monasteries and convents, fell under

fief In medieval Europe, land granted in return for a sworn oath to provide specified military service.

vassal In medieval Europe, a sworn supporter of a king or lord committed to rendering specified military service to that king or lord.

Noblewoman Directing Construction of a Church This picture of Berthe, wife of Girat de Roussillon, acting as mistress of the works comes from a tenth-century manuscript that shows a scene from the ninth century. Wheelbarrows rarely appear in medieval building scenes. Copyright Brussels, Royal Library of Belgium

the jurisdiction of the church, further limiting the reach and authority of the monarch.

While practices varied between and within realms, the "typical" medieval realm consisted of lands directly owned by a king or a count and administered by royal officers, with the king's or count's major vassals holding and administering other lands in return for military service. These vassals, in turn, granted land to their own vassals. Kings and lords commanded the service of their vassals for only part of the year. Vassals could hold land from several different lords and owe loyalty to each one. Moreover, the allegiance that a vassal owed to one lord could entail military service to that lord's master in time of need.

Noblewomen became enmeshed in this tangle of obligations as heiresses and as candidates for marriage. A man who married the widow or daughter of a lord with no sons could gain control of that lord's property. Marriage alliances affected entire kingdoms. Noble daughters and sons had little say in marriage matters; issues of land, power, and military service took precedence.

Nevertheless, a noblewomen could own land or administer her husband's estates when he was away at war. Nonnoble women usually worked alongside

their menfolk, performing agricultural tasks such as raking and stacking hay, shearing sheep, and picking vegetables. As artisans, women spun, wove, and sewed clothing. The Bayeux (bay-YUH) Tapestry, a piece of embroidery 230 feet (70 meters) long and 20 inches (51 centimeters) wide depicting William the Conqueror's invasion of England in 1066 (see page 237), was designed and executed entirely by women, though historians do not agree on who those women were.

SECTION REVIEW

- Post-Roman European society was marked by the prevalence of Germanic traditions and the dependency of the weak on the strong.

- The eighth century through the mid-eleventh was a period of great insecurity, with Charlemagne's empire providing short-lived stability.

- After the fall of the empire, technological sophistication and urban life declined, and self-sufficient manors dominated agriculture.

- The mounted warrior elite came to dominate a society shaped by the exchange of rights and obligations.

- Noblewomen were part of the exchange system, while nonnoble women worked alongside men.

THE WESTERN CHURCH

■ *What role did the Western Church play in the politics and culture of Europe?*

Just as eastern European Christians followed the religious guidance of the patriarch of Constantinople, so did the pope wield authority over church affairs in western Europe. And while Orthodox missionaries spread Christianity among the Slavs, Catholic missionaries added territory to Christendom with forays into the British Isles and the lands of the Germans.

In the west Roman nobles lost control of the papacy—the office of the pope—after the tenth century, and it became a more powerful international office. Councils of bishops—which normally set rules called canons to regulate the priests and laypeople under their jurisdiction—became increasingly responsive to papal direction.

Nevertheless, regional disagreements over church regulations, shortages of educated and trained clergy, difficult communications, and political disorder posed formidable obstacles to unifying church standards and practices. Clerics in some parts of western Europe were still issuing prohibitions against the worship of rivers, trees, and mountains as late as the eleventh century. Church problems included lingering polytheism, lax enforcement of prohibitions against priests marrying, nepotism (giving preferment to close kin), and simony (selling ecclesiastical appointments, often to laymen). The persistence of the papacy in asserting its legal jurisdiction over clergy, combating polytheism and heretical beliefs, and calling on secular rulers to recognize the pope's authority constituted a rare force for unity and order in a time of disunity and chaos (see Diversity and Dominance: The Struggle for Christian Morality).

Politics and the Church

The pope needed allies. Although Charlemagne's father Pepin was a strong supporter of the papacy, the relationship between kings and popes was tense, since both thought of themselves as ultimate authorities. In 962 the pope crowned the first "Holy Roman Emperor" (Charlemagne never held this full title). This designation of a secular political authority as the guardian of collective Christian interests proved more apparent then real. Essentially a loose confederation of German princes who named one of their own as emperor, the Holy Roman Empire had little influence west of the Rhine River.

Although the pope crowned the early Holy Roman Emperors, this did not signify political superiority. The law of the church (known as *canon law* because each law was called a *canon*) gave the pope exclusive legal jurisdiction over clergy and church property wherever located. But bishops who held land as vassals owed military support or other services and dues to kings and princes. The secular rulers demanded the power to appoint those bishops because that was the only way to guarantee fulfillment of their duties as vassals. The popes disagreed.

In the eleventh century, this conflict over the control of ecclesiastical appointments came to a head. Hildebrand (HILL-de-brand), an Italian monk, capped a career of reorganizing church finances when the cardinals (a group of senior bishops) meeting in Rome selected him to be Pope Gregory VII in 1073. His personal notion of the papacy (preserved among his letters) represented an extreme position:

§ The pope can be judged by no one;
§ The Roman church has never erred and never will err till the end of time;
§ The pope alone can depose and restore bishops;
§ He alone can call general councils and authorize canon law;
§ He can depose emperors;
§ He can absolve subjects from their allegiance;
§ All princes should kiss his feet.[6]

Such claims antagonized lords and monarchs, who had become accustomed to *investing*—that is, conferring a ring and a staff as symbols of authority on bishops and abbots in their domains. Historians

[6] R. W. Southern, *Western Society and the Church in the Middle Ages* (Harmondsworth, England: Penguin, 1970), 102.

papacy The central administration of the Roman Catholic Church, of which the pope is the head.

Holy Roman Empire Loose federation of mostly German states and principalities, headed by an emperor elected by the princes. It lasted from 962 to 1806.

apply the term **investiture controversy** to the medieval struggle between the church and the lay lords to control ecclesiastical appointments; the term also refers to the broader conflict of popes versus monarchs. When Holy Roman Emperor Henry IV defied Gregory's reforms, Gregory excommunicated him in 1076, thereby cutting him off from church rituals. Stung by the resulting decline in his influence, Henry stood barefoot in the snow for three days outside a castle in northern Italy waiting for Gregory, a guest there, to receive him. Henry's formal act of penance induced Gregory to forgive him and restore him to the church; but the reconciliation, an apparent victory for the pope, proved hollow. In 1078 Gregory deposed Henry but then had to flee from Rome to Salerno, where he died two years later.

A compromise was reached in 1122 at Worms, a town in Germany. In the Concordat of Worms, Emperor Henry V renounced his right to choose bishops and abbots or bestow spiritual symbols upon them. In return, Pope Calixtus II permitted the emperor to invest papally appointed bishops and abbots with any lay rights or obligations before their spiritual consecration. Such compromises did not fully solve the problem, but they reduced tensions between the two sides.

Assertions of royal authority triggered other conflicts as well. Though barely twenty when he became king of England in 1154, Henry II, a great-grandson of William the Conqueror, acted to strengthen the power of the Crown and weaken the nobility. He appointed traveling justices to enforce his laws and made juries, a holdover from traditional Germanic law, into powerful legal instruments. He also established the principle that criminal acts violated the "king's peace" and should be tried and punished in accordance with charges brought by the Crown instead of in response to charges brought by victims.

Henry had a harder time controlling the church. His closest friend and chancellor, or chief administrator, Thomas à Becket (ca. 1118–1170), lived the grand and luxurious life of a courtier. In 1162 Henry persuaded Becket to become a priest and assume the position of archbishop of Canterbury, the highest church office in England. Becket agreed but cautioned that from then on he would act solely in the interest of the church. When Henry sought to try clerics accused of crimes in royal instead of ecclesiastical courts, Archbishop Thomas, now leading an austere and pious life, resisted. In 1170 four of Henry's knights, knowing that the king desired Becket's death, murdered the archbishop in Canterbury Cathedral. Their crime backfired, and an outpouring of sympathy caused Canterbury to become a major pilgrimage center. In 1173 the pope declared the martyred Becket a saint. His authority badly damaged, Henry allowed himself to be publicly whipped twice in penance for the crime.

Henry II's conflict with Thomas à Becket, like the Concordat of Worms, yielded no clear victor. The problem of competing legal traditions made political life in western Europe more complicated than in Byzantium. So-called feudal law, rooted in Germanic custom, gave supreme power to the king. Canon law, based on Roman precedent, visualized a single church with jurisdiction over all of Western Christendom. In the eleventh century Roman imperial law, contained in the *Corpus Juris Civilis*, added a third tradition.

Monasticism

Monasticism featured prominently in the religious life of almost all medieval Christian lands. The origins of group monasticism lay in the eastern lands of the Roman Empire. Pre-Christian practices such as celibacy, continual devotion to prayer, and living apart from society (alone or in small groups) came together in Christian form in Egypt. A hermit named Anthony (ca. 251–356), sometimes called the Father of All Monks, attracted many followers to his life of extreme privation in the Egyptian desert.

Monasticism in western Europe, however, involved groups of monks or nuns living together in organized communities. The person most responsible for introducing this practice in the Latin west was

investiture controversy Dispute between the popes and the Holy Roman Emperors over who held ultimate authority over bishops in imperial lands.

monasticism Living in a religious community apart from secular society and adhering to a rule stipulating chastity, obedience, and poverty. It was a prominent element of medieval Christianity and Buddhism. Monasteries were the primary centers of learning and literacy in medieval Europe.

The Struggle for Christian Morality

Ireland

The medieval church believed that Christians could be absolved of their sins by performing public or private penalties, or acts of humiliation. Priests listened to the believers confess their sins and then set the nature and duration of the penance. Books called penitentials guided the priests by stipulating the appropriate penance for specific sins. These books varied over time and tended to reflect local conditions. One of the earliest is attributed to Saint Patrick, who began his missionary work in Ireland in 432. The selections below deal not just with penalties for sin but also with efforts to impose church discipline on priests.

§ There shall be no wandering cleric in a parish.

§ If any cleric, from sexton [church caretaker] to priest, is seen without a tunic, and does not cover the shame and nakedness of his body; and if his hair is not shaven according to the Roman custom, and if his wife goes about with her head unveiled, he shall be alike despised by laymen and separated from the Church.

§ A monk and a virgin, the one from one place, the other from another, shall not dwell together in the same inn, nor travel in the same carriage from village to village, nor continually hold conversation with each other.

§ It is not permitted to the Church to accept alms from pagans.

§ A Christian who believes that there is a vampire in the world, that is to say, a witch, is to be anathematized [condemned by the Church]; whoever lays that reputation upon a living being, shall not be received into the Church until he revokes with his own voice the crime that he has committed and accordingly does penance with all diligence.

§ A Christian who defrauds anyone with respect to a debt in the manner of the pagans, shall be excommunicated [barred from Christian society] until he pays the debt.

England and Southern Germany

Boniface (ca. 675–754), a widely esteemed bishop of the southern German city of Mainz, began life with the name Winfrid in Anglo-Saxon Britain. After working as a missionary in Frisia in the Netherlands, he devoted the bulk of his life to establishing Christianity and respect for Christian law and morality in southern Germany. His letters reflect his passion for reforming personal behavior along Christian lines.

Boniface to Pope Zacharias, 742

We must confess, our father and lord, that after we learned from messengers that your predecessor in the apostolate [i.e., papacy], Gregory of reverend memory . . . had been set free from the prison of the body and had passed on to God, nothing gave us greater joy or happiness than the knowledge that the Supreme Arbiter had appointed your fatherly clemency to administer the canon law and to govern the Apostolic See. . . .

Some of the ignorant common people, Alemanians, Bavarians, and Franks, hearing that many of the offenses prohibited by us are practiced in the city of Rome imagine that they are allowed by the priests there and reproach us for causing them to incur blame in their own lives. They say that on the first day of January year after year, in the city of Rome and in the neighborhood of St. Peter's church by day or night, they have seen bands of singers parading the streets in pagan fashion, shouting and chanting sacrilegious songs and loading tables with food day and night, while no one in his own house is willing to lend his neighbor fire or tools or any other convenience. They say also that they have seen there women with amulets and bracelets of heathen fashion on their arms and legs, offering them for sale to willing buyers. . . .

Boniface and Other Bishops to King Ethelbald of Mercia (a Saxon Kingdom in England), 746–747

We have heard that you are very liberal in almsgiving, and congratulate you thereon. . . . We have heard also that you repress robbery and wrongdoing, perjury, and rapine with a strong hand, and that you have established peace within your kingdom. . . .

But amidst all this, one evil report as to the manner of life of Your Grace has come to our hearing, which has greatly grieved us and which we would wish were not true. We have learned from many sources that you have never taken to yourself a lawful wife. . . . If you had willed to do this for the sake of chastity and abstinence . . . we should rejoice, for that is not worthy of blame but rather of praise. But if, as many say—but which God forbid!—you have neither taken a lawful spouse nor observed chastity for God's sake but, moved by desire, have defiled your good name before God and man by the crime of adulterous lust, then we are greatly grieved because this is a sin in the sight of God and is the ruin of your fair fame among men.

And now, what is worse, our informants say that these atrocious crimes are committed in convents with holy nuns and virgins consecrated to God, and this, beyond all doubt, doubles the offense. . . .

Northern Germany and Scandinavia

Adam of Bremen's History of the Archbishops of Hamburg-Bremen *consists of four sections. The third is devoted to the Archbishop Adalbert, whose death in 1072 stirred Adam to write. References to classical poets, the lives of saints, and royal documents show that Adam, a churchman, had a solid education and access to many sources, including conversations with kings and nobles.*

This remarkable man [i.e., Archbishop Adalbert] may . . . be extolled with praise of every kind in that he was noble, handsome, wise, eloquent, chaste, temperate. All these qualities he comprised in himself and others besides, such as one is wont to attach to the outer man: that he was rich, that he was successful, that he was glorious, that he was influential. All these things were his in abundance. Moreover, in respect of the mission to the heathen, which is the first duty of the Church at Hamburg, no one so vigorous could ever be found. . . .

As soon as the metropolitan [i.e., Archbishop Adalbert] had entered upon his episcopate, he sent legates to the kings of the north in the interest of friendship. There were also dispersed throughout all Denmark and Norway and Sweden and to the ends of the earth admonitory letters in which he exhorted the bishops and priests living in those parts . . . fearlessly to forward the conversion of the pagans. . . . [One Danish king] forgot the heavenly King as things prospered with him and married a blood relative from Sweden. This mightily displeased the lord archbishop,

who sent legates to the rash king, rebuking him severely for his sin, and who stated finally that if he did not come to his senses, he would have to be cut off with the sword of excommunication. Beside himself with rage, the king then threatened to ravage and destroy the whole diocese of Hamburg. Unperturbed by these threats, our archbishop, reproving and entreating, remained firm, until at length the Danish tyrant was prevailed upon by letters from the pope to give his cousin a bill of divorce. . . .

In Norway . . . King Harold surpassed all the madness of tyrants in his savage wildness. Many churches were destroyed by that man; many Christians were tortured to death by him. But he was a mighty man and renowned for the victories he had previously won in many wars with barbarians in Greece and in the Scythian regions [while assisting the Byzantine empress Zoë fight the Seljuk Turks]. After he came into his fatherland, however, he never ceased from warfare; he was the thunderbolt of the north. . . . And so, as he ruled over many nations, he was odious to all on account of his greed and cruelty. He also gave himself up to the magic arts and, wretched man that he was, did not heed the fact that his most saintly brother [Saint Olaf, one of Harold's predecessors] had eradicated such illusions from the realm and striven even unto death for the adoption of the precepts of Christianity. . . .

Across the Elbe [east of the river Hamburg is on] and in Slavia our affairs were still meeting with great success. For Gottschalk . . . married a daughter of the Danish king and so thoroughly subdued the Slavs that they feared him like a king, offered to pay tribute, and asked for peace with subjection. Under these circumstances our Church at Hamburg enjoyed peace, and Slavia abounded in priests and churches. . . .

QUESTIONS FOR ANALYSIS

1. How are the practices of non-Christians used as good and bad examples for Christians?
2. What limits, if any, do church officials recognize in their role as moral judges?
3. How does the church confront royal authority?

Sources: Excerpts from John T. McNeill and Helena M. Gamer, *Medieval Handbooks of Penance* (New York: Columbia University Press, 1938), 77–78; *The Letters of Saint Boniface*, tr. Ephraim Emerton (New York: Columbia University Press, 2000), 56, 59–60, 103–105; and *History of the Archbishops of Hamburg-Bremen*, tr. Francis J. Tschan (New York: Columbia University Press, 1959 [new ed. 2002]), 114–133.

Benedict of Nursia (ca. 480–547) in Italy. Benedict began his pious career as a hermit in a cave but eventually organized several monasteries, each headed by an abbot. In the seventh century monasteries based on his model spread far beyond Italy. *The Rule of Saint Benedict*, written to govern the monks' behavior, envisions a balanced life of devotion and work, along with obligations of celibacy, poverty, and obedience to the abbot. Those who lived by this or other monastic rules became *regular clergy*, in contrast to *secular clergy*, priests who lived in society instead of in seclusion. The *Rule* of Benedict was the starting point for most forms of western European monastic life and remains in force today in Benedictine monasteries.

Though monks and nuns made up a small percentage of the total population, their secluded way of life reinforced the separation of religious affairs from ordinary politics and economics. Monasteries followed Jesus' axiom to "render unto Caesar what is Caesar's and unto God what is God's" better than the many town-based bishops who behaved like lords.

Monasteries preserved literacy and learning in the early medieval period, although some rulers, like Charlemagne, encouraged scholarship at court. Regular clergy saw copying manuscripts and even writing books as a religious calling, thereby preserving many Roman works that would otherwise have disappeared. The survival of Greek works depended more on Byzantine and Muslim scribes in the east.

Monasteries could plant Christianity in new lands, as Irish monks did in parts of Germany, service the needs of travelers, organize agricultural production on their lands, and raise abandoned infants. Convents provided refuge for widows and other women who lacked male protection or desired a spiritual life. Yet oversight was a problem. A bishop might have authority over an abbot or abbess (head of a convent), but he could not exercise constant vigilance over what went on behind monastery walls.

A reform movement focused on monastic discipline took shape in the Benedictine abbey of Cluny (KLOO-nee) in eastern France. William the Pious, the first duke of Aquitaine, founded Cluny in 910 and freed it of lay authority. A century later the local bishop conferred similar freedom. Cluny's abbots pursued a vigorous campaign, eventually allying with reforming popes like Gregory VII to improve monastic

SECTION REVIEW

- In western Europe, the papacy became the most powerful international institution and thus a source of cultural unity.

- Popes sought secular allies by engaging the support of kings and conferring the title *Holy Roman Emperor*.

- Pope Gregory VII asserted papal primacy and touched off the investiture controversy with the Holy Roman Empire.

- Although the Concordat of Worms partially resolved the controversy, conflicts between secular and papal authority continued.

- Western monasticism originated with Benedict of Nursia, and monasteries and convents became important cultural centers.

- Failing monastic discipline led to the Cluniac and Cistercian reform movements.

discipline and administration. A magnificent new abbey church—with later additions, the largest in the world—symbolized Cluny's preeminence.

At the peak of Cluny's influence, nearly a thousand Benedictine abbeys and priories (lower-level monastic houses) in various countries accepted the authority of its abbot. The Benedictine *Rule* made each monastery independent; but the Cluniac reformers stipulated that every abbot and prior (head of a priory) be appointed by the abbot of Cluny. Monastic reform gained new impetus in the second half of the twelfth century with the rapid rise of the Cistercian order, which emphasized a life of asceticism and poverty.

KIEVAN RUSSIA, 900–1200

■ *What was the significance of the adoption of Orthodox Christianity by Kievan Russia?*

Though Latin and Orthodox Christendom followed different paths in later centuries, which of them would flourish more was not apparent in 900. Many Slavs living in the north eventually accepted the Catholicism of Rome as taught by German missionaries. The Serbs and other southern Slavs took their faith from Constantinople. The conversion of Kievan Russia, farther to the east, shows how economics, politics, and religious life were closely intertwined. The choice of Orthodoxy over Catholicism had important consequences for later European history.

The Rise of the Kievan Empire

The territory between the Black and Caspian Seas in the south and the Baltic and White Seas in the north divides into a series of east-west zones. Frozen tundra in the far north gives way to a cold forest zone, then to a more temperate forest, then to a mix of forest and steppe grasslands, and finally to grassland only. Several navigable rivers, including the Volga, the Dnieper (d-NYEP-er), and the Don, run from north to south across these zones.

Early historical sources reflect repeated linguistic and territorial changes, seemingly under pressure from population migrations. Most of the Germanic peoples, along with some Iranian and west Slavic peoples, migrated into eastern Europe from Ukraine and Russia in Roman times. The peoples who remained behind spoke eastern Slavic languages, except in the far north and south: Finns and related peoples lived in the former region, Turkish-speakers in the latter.

Forest dwellers, farmers, and steppe nomads complemented each other economically. Nomads traded animals for the farmers' grain; and honey, wax, and furs from the forests became important exchange items. Traders could travel east and west by steppe caravan (see Chapter 8), or they could use boats on the rivers to move north and south.

Hoards containing thousands of Byzantine and Islamic coins buried in Poland and on islands in the Baltic Sea where fairs were held attest to the trading activity of Varangians (Swedish Vikings) who sailed across the Baltic and down Russia's rivers. They exchanged forest products and slaves for manufactured goods and coins, which they may have used as jewelry rather than as money, at markets controlled by the Khazar Turks, whose powerful kingdom centered around the mouth of the Volga River.

Historians debate the early meaning of the word *Rus* (from which *Russia* is derived), but at some point it came to refer to Slavic-speaking peoples ruled by Varangians. Unlike western European lords, the Varangian princes and their *druzhina* (military retainers) lived in cities, while the Slavs farmed. The princes occupied themselves with trade and fending off enemies. The Rus of the city of Kiev (KEE-yev),

which was taken over by Varangians around 880, controlled trade on the Dnieper River and dealt more with Byzantium than with the Muslim world because the Dnieper flows into the Black Sea. The Rus of Novgorod (NOHV-goh-rod) played the same role on the Volga. The semilegendary account of the Kievan Rus conversion to Christianity must be seen against this background.

In 980 Vladimir (VLAD-ih-mir) I, a ruler of Novgorod who had fallen from power, returned from exile to Kiev with a band of Varangians and made himself the grand prince of Kievan Russia (see Map 10.3). Though his grandmother Olga had been a Christian, Vladimir built a temple on Kiev's heights and placed there the statues of the six gods his Slavic subjects worshiped. The earliest Russian chronicle reports that Vladimir and his advisers decided against Islam as the official religion because of its ban on alcohol, rejected Judaism (the religion to which the Khazars had converted) because they thought that a truly powerful god would not have let the ancient Jewish kingdom be destroyed, and even spoke with German emissaries advocating Latin Christianity. Why Vladimir chose Orthodox Christianity over the Latin version is not precisely known. The magnificence of Constantinople seems to have been a consideration. After visiting Byzantine churches, his agents reported: "We knew not whether we were in heaven or on earth, for on earth there is no such splendor of [sic] such beauty, and we are at a loss how to describe it. We know only that God dwells there among men, and their service is finer than the ceremonies of other nations."[7]

After choosing a reluctant bride from the Byzantine imperial family, Vladimir converted to Orthodox Christianity, probably in 988, and opened his lands to Orthodox clerics and missionaries. The patriarch of Constantinople appointed a metropolitan (chief bishop) at Kiev to govern ecclesiastical affairs. Churches arose in Kiev, one of them on the ruins of Vladimir's earlier hilltop temple, and writing was introduced, using the Cyrillic alphabet devised earlier for the western Slavs. This extension of Orthodox Christendom northward provided a barrier against the eastward expansion of Latin Christianity. Kiev

---

[7] S. A. Zenkovsky, ed., *Medieval Russia's Epics, Chronicles, and Tales* (New York: New American Library, 1974), 67.

Map 10.3 **Kievan Russia and the Byzantine Empire in the Eleventh Century** By the mid-eleventh century, the princes of Kievan Russia had brought all the eastern Slavs under their rule. The loss of Egypt, Syria, and Tunisia to Arab invaders in the seventh to eighth centuries had turned Byzantium from a far-flung empire into a fairly compact state. From then on the Byzantine rulers looked to the Balkans and Kievan Russia as the primary arena for extending their political and religious influence. © Cengage Learning

became firmly oriented toward trade with Byzantium and turned its back on the Muslim world, though the Volga trade continued through Novgorod.

Struggles within the ruling family and with other enemies, most notably the steppe peoples of the south, marked the later political history of Kievan Russia. But down to the time of the Mongols in the thirteenth century (see Chapter 12), the state remained and served as an instrument for the Christianization of the eastern Slavs.

Society and Culture

In Kievan Russia political power derived from trade rather than from landholding, so the manorial agricultural system of western Europe never developed. Farmers practiced shifting cultivation of their own lands. They would burn a section of forest, then lightly scratch the ash-strewn surface with a plow. When fertility waned, they would move to another section of forest. Poor land and a short growing season in the most northerly latitudes made food scarce. Living on their own estates, the druzhina evolved from infantry into cavalry and focused their efforts more on horse breeding than on agriculture.

Large cities like Kiev and Novgorod may have reached thirty thousand or fifty thousand people—roughly the size of contemporary London or Paris, but far smaller than Constantinople or major Muslim

akg-images/RIA Nowosti

Cathedral of Saint Dmitry in Vladimir Built between 1193 and 1197, this Russian Orthodox cathedral shows Byzantine influence. The three-arch façade, small dome, and symmetrical Greek Cross floor plan strongly resemble features of the Byzantine church shown on page 232.

SECTION REVIEW

- The Kievan state rose from Varangian-ruled cities that controlled river trade in Russia.

- Vladimir of Novgorod took over Kiev and converted to Orthodox Christianity.

- Trade was the basis of political power, farmers practiced shifting agriculture, and warrior retainers evolved into a mounted elite.

- Cities were large by western European standards and served as craft centers.

- Christianity took hold slowly, but the church assumed increasingly active roles in political and economic life.

- Kievan Russia experienced its peak in the twelfth and early thirteenth centuries.

the bones of the deceased in urns. Women continued to use polytheist designs on their clothing and bracelets, and as late as the twelfth century they were still turning to polytheist priests for charms to cure sick children. Traditional Slavic marriage practices involving casual and polygamous relations particularly scandalized the clergy.

Christianity eventually triumphed, and its success led to increasing church engagement in political and economic affairs. In the twelfth century, Christian clergy became involved in government administration, some of them collecting fees and taxes related to trade. Direct and indirect revenue from trade provided the rulers with the money they needed to pay their soldiers. The rule of law also spread as Kievan Russia experienced its peak of culture and prosperity in the century before the Mongol invasion of 1237.

metropolises like Baghdad and Nishapur. Many cities amounted to little more than fortified trading posts. Yet they served as centers for the development of crafts, some, such as glassmaking, based on skills imported from Byzantium. Artisans enjoyed higher status in society than peasant farmers. Construction relied on wood from the forests, although Christianity brought the building of stone cathedrals and churches on the Byzantine model.

Christianity penetrated the general population slowly. Several polytheist uprisings occurred in the eleventh century, particularly in times of famine and passive resistance led some groups to reject Christian burial and persist in cremating the dead and keeping

WESTERN EUROPE REVIVES, 1000–1200

■ *How did Mediterranean trade help revive western Europe?*

Between 1000 and 1200 western Europe slowly emerged from nearly seven centuries of subsistence economy. Population and agricultural production climbed, and a growing food surplus found its way to

Coinage also signaled the upturn in economic activity. In the ninth and tenth centuries most gold coins had come from Muslim lands and the Byzantine Empire. Worth too much for most trading purposes, they seldom reached Germany, France, and England; the widely imitated Carolingian silver penny sufficed. With the economic revival of the twelfth century came the minting of silver coins in Scandinavia, Poland, and other outlying regions. In the following century, Italian cities followed with a new and abundant gold coinage.

THE CRUSADES, 1095–1204

■ *What were the origins and impact of the Crusades?*

Revival coincided with and contributed to the **Crusades**, a series of religiously inspired Christian military campaigns against Muslims in the eastern Mediterranean. Four great expeditions between 1095 and 1204, the last redirected against Constantinople, which the Catholic knights looted, constituted the region's largest military undertakings since the fall of Rome. As a result of the Crusades, noble courts and burgeoning cities in western Europe consumed more goods from the east and later adopted ideas, artistic styles, and industrial processes from the lands of Islam.

The Roots of the Crusades Several social and economic currents of the eleventh century contributed to the Crusades. First, church reformers seeking to soften warlike habits popularized the Truce of God, a movement to limit fighting between Christian lords by specifying times of truce, such as during Lent (the forty days before Easter) and on Sundays. Many knights welcomed a religiously approved alternative to fighting other Christians. Second, ambitious rulers, like the Norman chieftains who invaded England and Sicily, were looking for new lands to conquer. Nobles, particularly younger sons in areas where the oldest son inherited everything, were hungry for land and titles. Third, Italian merchants wanted trading posts in Muslim territory. However, without the rivalry between popes and kings already discussed, and without the desire of the church to demonstrate political authority, the Crusades might never have occurred.

Several factors focused attention on the Holy Land, which had been under Muslim rule for four centuries. **Pilgrimages** played an important role in European religious life. In western Europe, pilgrims traveled under royal protection. Some were actually thieves, beggars, and peddlers, but genuinely pious pilgrims thronged to old churches and sacred relics. Rome and Constantinople were favored destinations, but the most intrepid went to Jerusalem and Antioch to fulfill a vow or to atone for a sin.

Pilgrims who crossed northern Spain to pray at the shrine of Santiago de Compostela learned of Christian kings fighting to dislodge the Muslims to the south. The Umayyad Caliphate in al-Andalus had broken up in the eleventh century, leaving its smaller successor states prey to Christian attacks from the north (see Chapter 9). The word *crusade*, taken from Latin *crux* for "cross," was first used in Spain. Pilgrims returning from Palestine urged both churchmen and nobles to consider the Muslim a proper target for Christian arms. Muslims generally

Crusades (1095–1204) Armed pilgrimages to the Holy Land by Christians determined to recover Jerusalem from Muslim rule. The Crusades brought an end to western Europe's centuries of intellectual and cultural isolation.

pilgrimage Journey to a sacred shrine by Christians seeking to show their piety, fulfill vows, or gain absolution for sins. Other religions also have pilgrimage traditions, such as the Muslim pilgrimage to Mecca and the pilgrimages made by early Chinese Buddhists to India in search of sacred Buddhist writings.

tolerated Christian pilgrims, but after 1071, when the Seljuks defeated the Byzantines at Manzikert (see Chapter 9), security along the pilgrimage route through Anatolia, already none too good, deteriorated further.

Despite the theological differences between the Orthodox and Roman Churches, the Byzantine emperor Alexius Comnenus asked the pope and western European rulers for help against the Muslims. Pope Urban II responded at the Council of Clermont in 1095. He addressed a huge crowd of people gathered in a field and called on them, as Christians, to stop fighting one another and go to the Holy Land to fight Muslims. "God wills it!" exclaimed voices in the crowd. People cut cloth into crosses and sewed them on their shirts to symbolize their willingness to march on Jerusalem. Thus began the First Crusade, though people at the time more often used the word *peregrinatio*, "pilgrimage." Urban promised to free Crusaders who had committed sins from their normal penance, or acts of atonement, the usual reward for peaceful pilgrims to Jerusalem.

The First Crusade captured Jerusalem in 1099 and established four Crusader principalities, the most important being the Latin Kingdom of Jerusalem. The next two expeditions strove with diminishing success to protect these gains. Muslim forces retook Jerusalem in 1187. By the time of the Fourth Crusade in 1204, the original religious ardor had so diminished that the commanders agreed, at the urging of the Venetians, to sack Constantinople first to defray the cost of transporting the army by ship.

The Impact of the Crusades

Exposure to Muslim culture in Spain, Sicily, Mediterranean seaports, and the Crusader principalities awakened Europeans to things lacking in their own lives. Borrowings from Muslim society occurred gradually and are not always easy to date, but Europeans began to produce pasta, paper, sugar, cotton cloth, colored glass, and many other formerly exotic items.

Europeans also learned of Greek philosophical, scientific, and medical writings—and equally important Arab and Iranian works—which were translated into Latin. Some manuscripts came from conquered territory: Sicily, Spain, the Holy Land, and Constantinople. For others, translators worked in parts of Spain still under Muslim rule. Generations passed before all these works were studied and understood, but they eventually transformed the intellectual world of Europe.

Changes in noble lifestyle took place more quickly. Eleanor of Aquitaine (1122?–1204), the most influential woman of the crusading era, accompanied her husband, King Louis VII of France, on the Second Crusade (1147–1149). The Arab influenced court life of her uncle Raymond, who ruled the Crusader principality of Antioch, particularly appealed to her. Once back in France, a lack of male offspring led to an annulment of her royal marriage, and she married Henry of Anjou in 1151. Three years later he inherited the throne of England as Henry II. Eleanor's sons, John and Richard Lion-Heart, famed in romance as the chivalrous foe of Saladin during the Third Crusade (1189–1192), rebelled against their father but eventually succeeded him as kings of England. In Aquitaine, a powerful duchy in southern France, Eleanor maintained her own court for a time. Poet-singers called troubadours enjoyed her favor and made her court a center for music based on the idea of "courtly love," an idealization of feminine beauty and grace that influenced later European ideas of romance. Surviving troubadour melodies show the influence of poetry styles then current in Muslim Spain. The favorite troubadour instrument, moreover, was the lute, a guitarlike instrument with a bulging belly whose design and name (Arabic *al-ud*) came from Muslim Spain.

SECTION REVIEW

- The Crusades coincided with and fueled the western European revival.

- Several religious, political, and economic factors prompted the Crusades, the most immediate of which was the decline of Byzantine power under Seljuk pressure.

- Responding to Byzantine calls for aid, Pope Urban II proclaimed the First Crusade in 1095.

- As a result of the Crusaders, western Europeans gradually absorbed Muslim technological and intellectual achievements.

- Contact with Muslim culture affected the elite most immediately by shaping court life and the troubadour tradition of courtly love.

CONCLUSION

The division of the Roman Empire by Constantine into an eastern and western branch marked Europe from that time on. When the Western Roman Empire collapsed, the Germanic tribes that settled on its territory formed numerous competing kingdoms and principalities. For several centuries, the only unifying factor was the Catholic Church, which provided intellectual and some administrative continuity with the vanished Roman Empire. Secular authorities, however, arose to contest the political authority of the church. Thus, western Europe remained divided among competing states and power centers. After the Viking invasions tapered off in the late tenth century, the economy, culture, and population of western Europe showed a dynamism that spread to areas of northern Europe never reached by the Romans. It also carried over into expansionism against the Muslims of the Holy Land and against Constantinople itself.

Eastern Europe evolved very differently, under the influence of Constantinople. Though it lost many provinces, the Eastern Roman Empire was not overrun by barbarians as the west had been, but retained its imperial structure for another thousand years. Though Christianity replaced all earlier religions as it did in the west, it was in the form of the Orthodox Church, a subordinate branch of the imperial Byzantine government, rather than an independent and competing organization like the Catholic Church in the west. As northeastern Europe (Russia, Ukraine, Belarus) filled in after the viking raiders settled down to trade and build cities, its peoples adopted the Orthodox form of Christianity and with it the subordination of church to state that prevailed in the Byzantine Empire.

CHAPTER REVIEW

THE BYZANTINE EMPIRE, 600–1200

■ *How did the Byzantine Empire maintain Roman imperial traditions in the east?* (page 229)

Divergent ecclesiastical practices paralleled a political separation that dated from the fourth-century division of the roman empire into an eastern portion, the Byzantine Empire ruled from Constantinople, and a western portion that became increasingly fragmented as warlike Germanic peoples assumed more and more control. For the east, the collection and analysis of imperial laws symbolized continuing imperial rule. The emperor also assumed control over the Christian church.

EARLY MEDIEVAL EUROPE, 600–1000

■ *How did the culture of early medieval Europe develop in the absence of imperial rule?* (page 234)

In the west, the heritage of Rome consisted more in the elite use of Latin and the popular rise of Romance languages. The Roman Empire became more and more a shared memory as great buildings decayed into ruins. This memory, however, could be used as a basis of political power, as the rule of Charlemagne demonstrates. After Charlemagne's death, Viking invasions continued to disrupt European life, but their migrations laid the foundations of powerful states in Russia and Normandy. Although some long-distance trade continued, poor infrastructure and the absence of centralized authority led to the rise of a self-sufficient economy based on the manor. The lords and warriors who protected serfs became a mounted military elite that dominated the system of rights and obligations loosely termed "feudalism."

THE WESTERN CHURCH

■ *What role did the Western Church play in the politics and culture of Europe?* (page 240)

Unlike the Eastern Church, where the emperor played a dominating role, the bishops and abbots who spoke for western Christendom sought complete control of both the political and the social realm. They ultimately came into conflict with kings and dukes who resented these claims to power, but the lower ranks of society became increasingly immersed in a Christian culture based on respect for the clergy.

KIEVAN RUSSIA, 900–1200

■ *What was the significance of the adoption of Orthodox Christianity by Kievan Russia?* (page 244)

The Eastern and Western Churches competed in converting the Slavic peoples. The Poles became Roman Catholics, while the Russians established their own Orthodox Church on the Byzantine pattern. Since the rulers of Kiev were of Scandinavian origin like the Norman rulers of northern France, England, and Sicily, there was potentially a basis for continuing interconnections across northern Europe. The decision to follow the Byzantine form of Christianity eliminated that possibility and raised a barrier between Russia and western Europe that lasted for centuries.

WESTERN EUROPE REVIVES, 1000–1200

■ *How did Mediterranean trade help revive western Europe?* (page 247)

Prosperous communes established in major Italian cities, based to some extent on rapid population growth, stimulated an expansion in Mediterranean trade. "Spices" imported from the East were resold in other European markets while Italian merchants opened new trading connections in the Middle East, some of them with Crusader states.

THE CRUSADES, 1095–1204

■ *What were the origins and impact of the Crusades?* (page 250)

A combination of factors including population growth, contests for authority between monarchs and the Catholic church, and a loss of Byzantine territory to Muslims led to a series of military expeditions bent on seizing the Holy Land, and Jerusalem in particular, from the Muslims. The Crusading era led to many changes in European intellectual and cultural life ranging from the stimulus of scientific and philosophical ideas translated from Arabic into Latin; to the adoption of Muslim manufacturing practices, such as glassmaking and papermaking; to the popularization of troubadour poetry and lute playing from Muslim Spain.

Key Terms

Charlemagne (p. 229)
medieval (p. 229)
Byzantine Empire (p. 229)
Kievan Russia (p. 229)
schism (p. 232)
manor (p. 237)
serf (p. 237)
fief (p. 238)
vassal (p. 238)

papacy (p. 240)
Holy Roman Empire (p. 240)
investiture controversy (p. 241)
monasticism (p. 241)
horse collar (p. 248)
Crusades (p. 250)
pilgrimage (p. 250)

Inner and East Asia

© Cengage Learning

The origins of East Asia, characterized by a shared writing system, political ideology, and culture, can be traced to the Sui (sway) and Tang (tahng) Empires. The powerful and expansive Tang Empire (618–907) ended four centuries of rule by short-lived and competing states (see Chapter 5) and became a model for emerging regimes on the Korean Peninsula, in northeast Asia, on the Japanese islands, and, to a certain extent, in continental Southeast Asia. But the formation of East Asia did not occur in isolation. Missionaries from India, along with Chinese pilgrims returning with sacred Sanskrit texts, encouraged the spread of Buddhism. Travelers from India and Persia also brought with them their native religions, artistic aesthetic, popular entertainments, technology, and even cuisine. Nestorian Christian churches and Jewish places of worship existed alongside Buddhist temples and monasteries. A legend credits an uncle of Mohammad with erecting the Red Mosque at Canton in the mid-seventh century. Foreigners worked in the Tang bureaucracy, served in the military, and maintained close ties to the royal family. Many historians characterize the Tang Empire as "cosmopolitan" because of its breadth and diversity, and it left an indelible mark on the Chinese imagination long after it fell. It was succeeded by the Song (soong) Empire. Extraordinarily productive and advanced in terms of technology, economy, and government, the Song Empire was not as globally connected and never approached the Tang's dominance over East Asia.

Other East Asian societies in Japan, Korea, and Vietnam found Confucian values and Chinese culture appealing, but they developed separate social and political institutions and economic systems.

THE SUI AND TANG EMPIRES, 581–755

■ *What was the importance of Inner and Central Asia as a region of interchange during the Tang period?*

The reunification of China took place under the Sui dynasty, father and son rulers who held power from 581 until Turks from Inner Asia (the part of the Eurasian steppe east of the Pamir Mountains) defeated the son in 615. He was assassinated three years later, and the Tang filled the political vacuum.

The small kingdoms of northern China and Inner Asia that had come and gone during the centuries following the fall of the Han Empire had structured themselves around a variety of political ideas and institutions. Some favored the Chinese tradition, with an emperor, a bureaucracy using the Chinese language exclusively, and a Confucian state philosophy (see Chapter 5). Others reflected Tibetan, Turkish, or other regional cultures and depended on Buddhism to legitimate their rule. Throughout the period the relationship between northern China and the deserts and steppe of Inner Asia remained a central focus of political life, a key commercial linkage, and a source of new ideas and practices.

The Sui rulers called their new capital Chang'an in honor of the old Han capital nearby in the Wei (way) River Valley (modern Shaanxi province). Though northern China constituted the Sui heartland, population centers along the Yangzi (yahng-zeh) River in the south grew steadily and pointed to what would be the future direction of Chinese expansion. To facilitate communication and trade with the south, the Sui built the 1,100-mile (1,771-kilometer) **Grand Canal** linking the Yellow River with the Yangzi, and they also constructed irrigation systems in the Yangzi Valley. On their northern frontier, the Sui also improved the Great Wall, the barrier against nomadic incursions that had been gradually constructed by several earlier states.

Sui military ambition, which extended to Korea and Vietnam as well as Inner Asia, required high levels of organization, manpower, and such resources as livestock, wood, iron, and food supplies. The same was true of their massive public works projects. These burdens proved more than the Sui could sustain. Overextension compounded the political dilemma stemming from the military defeat and subsequent assassination of the second Sui emperor. These circumstances opened the way for another strong leader to establish a new state.

Grand Canal The 1,100-mile (1,771-kilometer) waterway linking the Yellow and the Yangzi Rivers. It was begun in the Han period and completed during the Sui Empire.

Horse figures, relief from Emperor T'ai Tsung's tomb in Hsi-An (Shensi), Chinese civilization, 7th century/De Agostini Picture Library/The Bridgeman Art Library

Iron Stirrups   This bas-relief from the tomb of Li Shimin depicts the type of horse on which the Tang armies conquered China and Inner Asia. Saddles with high supports in front and back, breastplates, and cruppers (straps beneath the tail that help keep the saddle in place) point to the importance of high speeds and quick maneuvering. Central and Inner Asian horsemen had iron stirrups available from the time of the Huns (fifth century). Earlier stirrups were of leather or wood. Stirrups could support the weight of shielded and well-armed soldiers rising in the saddle to shoot arrows or use lances.

In 618 the powerful Li family took advantage of Sui disorder to carve out an empire of similar scale and ambition. They adopted the dynastic name Tang (Map 11.1). The brilliant emperor **Li Shimin** (lee shir-meen) (r. 626–649) extended his power primarily westward into Inner Asia. Though he and succeeding rulers of the **Tang Empire** retained many Sui governing practices, they avoided overcentralization by allowing local nobles, gentry, officials, and religious establishments to exercise significant power.

The Tang emperors and nobility descended from the Turkish elites that built small states in northern China after the Han, as well as from Chinese officials and settlers who had moved there. They appreciated the pastoral nomadic culture of Inner Asia (see Chapter 8) as well as Chinese traditions. Some of the most impressive works of Tang art, for example, are large pottery figurines of the horses and two-humped camels used along the Silk Road, brilliantly colored with glazes devised by Chinese potters. Reflecting a similar influence, clothing styles changed in north China, as working people switched from robes to the pants favored by the Turks from Central Asia. Cotton replaced hemp in clothes worn by commoners, and textiles sported Persian and Central Asian designs. In warfare, the Tang combined Chinese weapons—the crossbow and armored infantrymen—with Inner

Li Shimin   One of the founders of the Tang Empire and its second emperor (r. 626–649). He led the expansion of the empire into Inner Asia.

Tang Empire   Empire unifying China and part of Inner Asia (618–907). The Tang emperors presided over a magnificent court at their capital, Chang'an.

Chronology

	Inner Asia	China	Northeast Asia	Japan
200		220–589 China disunited 581–618 Sui unification	313–668 Three Korean kingdoms: Koguryō, Paekche, Silla	
600	751 Battle of Talas River	618 Tang Empire founded 626–649 Li Shimin reign 690–705 Wu Zhao reign 755–763 An Lushan rebellion	668 Silla victory in Korea	645–655 Taika era 710–784 Nara as capital 752 "Eye-Opening" ceremony 794 Heian era
800		840 Suppression of Buddhism 879–881 Huang Chao rebellion 907 End of Tang Empire 960 Song Empire founded	916 Liao Empire founded 918 Koryo founded: Korean Peninsula unified	866–1180 Fujiwara influence
1000			1115 Jin Empire founded	ca. 1000 *The Tale of Genji*
1200		1127–1279 Southern Song period		1185 Kamakura Shogunate founded

Asian expertise in horsemanship and the use of iron stirrups. At their peak, from about 650 to 751, when they were defeated in Central Asia (present-day Kyrgyzstan) by an Arab Muslim army at the Battle of Talas River, the Tang armies were a formidable force.

During the Tang dynasty China also consolidated Chinese trade in the southern coastal region, increasing access to the Indian Ocean. Shipbuilders excelled at compass design and the construction of very large oceangoing vessels. Commercial ships, built to sail from south China to the Philippines and southern Asia, carried twice as much as contemporary vessels in the Mediterranean Sea or the western parts of the Indian Ocean trading system (see Chapter 8). As travel along the Silk Road and to the various ports of the Indian Ocean trading system increased, the economies of the seaports and entrepôts involved in trade became increasingly commercialized, leading to networks of private traders devising new instruments of credit and finance. By about the year 1000 the magnitude of exports from Tang territories, facilitated by China's excellent transportation systems, dwarfed Chinese imports from Europe, West Asia, and South Asia.

Chang'an: Metropolis at the Center of East Asia

Much of the global exchange in China during the Sui and Tang dynasties occurred in the capital Chang'an. Well-maintained roads and water transport connected Chang'an to the coastal towns of south China, most importantly Guangzhou (gwahng-jo) (Canton). As the center of the **tributary system**, which began in

tributary system A system in which, from the time of the Han Empire, countries in East and Southeast Asia not under the direct control of empires based in China nevertheless enrolled as tributary states, acknowledging the superiority of the emperors in China in exchange for trading rights or strategic alliances.

Han times, Chang'an received regular embassies from independent countries who came to acknowledge the Chinese emperor's supremacy by paying tribute (see Chapter 5). Central Asians, Tibetans, Vietnamese, Japanese, and Koreans regularly visited the capital. In the main parts of the city, restaurants, inns, temples, mosques, and street stalls lined the thoroughfares, creating a vigorous commercial world in which material goods and cultural influences mixed. The Tang court promoted polo, a pastime from the steppes, and followed the Inner Asian tradition of allowing noblewomen to compete. Various stringed instruments reached China from the Silk Road, along with Turkish folk melodies. Grape wine from West Asia and tea, sugar, and spices from India and Southeast Asia transformed the Chinese diet. Such changes reflected new economic and trade relationships (see Material Culture: Salt).

More than simply a political and trade center, Chang'an became the premier study-abroad destination in Asia; rulers sent intellectuals to learn statecraft, the techniques of running a government, to bring back to their home governments. Monks from Korea and Japan went to study with Chinese Buddhists and with Indian masters. Visitors brought the most recent ideas home, and Chang'an became the center of a continent-wide system of communication.

During the Tang period, Chang'an and its surrounding suburbs, with a population of nearly 2 million, was the largest metropolitan area in the world at the time. Its sophisticated gridlike layout, with its palace located in the north Pole Star position to reflect the celestial order, was imitated by Korean and Japanese capitals. Most people lived in suburbs that extended beyond the main gates. Many also dwelt in outlying

Map 11.1 The Tang Empire in Inner and Eastern Asia, 750 For over a century the Tang Empire controlled China and a very large part of Inner Asia. The defeat of Tang armies in 751 by a force of Arabs, Turks, and Tibetans at the Talas River in present-day Kyrgyzstan ended Tang westward expansion. To the south the Tang dominated Annam, and Japan and the Silla kingdom in Korea were leading tributary states of the Tang. © Cengage Learning

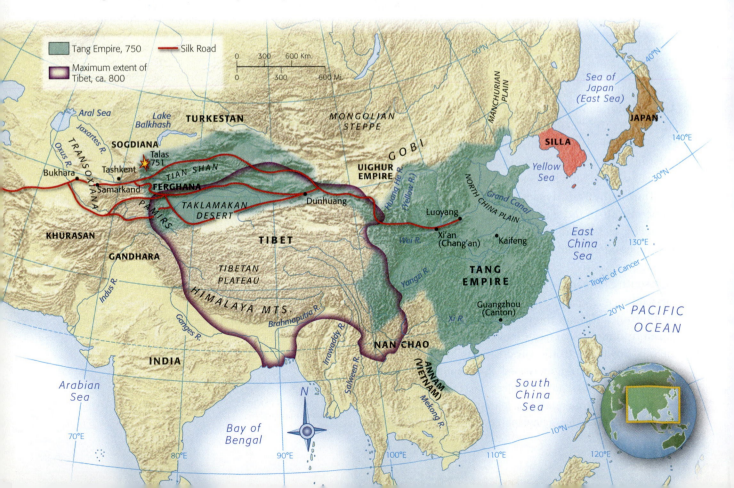

towns that had special responsibilities like maintaining nearby imperial tombs. The diverse population included Asian, Arab, and Persian merchants, who became long-time residents of the city. In Chang'an and other trading centers, foreigners, whether merchants, students, or ambassadors, resided in special compounds enclosed by brick walls and wooden gates that guards locked from curfew (between eight and ten o'clock) till dawn to control crime. By the end of the Tang period, West Asians in Chang'an probably numbered over 100,000. There were so many Iranians living in the city that the government had to set up a special department to handle Iranian-Tang affairs.

Buddhism and the Tang Empire

As the Tang Empire expanded westward, intensified contact with Central Asia and India strengthened Buddhist influence throughout China. Mahayana (mah-HAH-YAH-nah), or "Great Vehicle," Buddhism predominated. Mahayana fostered faith in enlightened beings—bodhisattvas—who postpone nirvana (see Chapter 5) to help others achieve enlightenment. This permitted the absorption of local gods and goddesses into Mahayana sainthood and thereby made conversion more attractive to the common people. Mahayana also encouraged translating Buddhist scripture into local languages, and it accepted religious practices not based on written texts. The adaptability of Mahayana views to different societies and classes of people invigorated travel, language learning, and cultural exchange.

Though Buddhism and Confucianism proved attractive to many different peoples, regional cultures and identities remained strong. At the height of the Tang Empire (between 600 and 751), **Uighur** (WEE-ger) merchants and scribes along the trading routes from Persia to China showed enthusiasm for Buddhist teachings, and Chinese Buddhists on pilgrimage to India advanced contacts between India and **Tibet**. Regular contact and Buddhist influences consolidated the Tang-Tibet relationship. Regional commitments to Tibetan, Uighur, and other languages and writing systems coexisted with the widespread use of written Chinese.

The Tang rulers followed Inner Asian precedents in their political use of Buddhism. State cults based

Panorama Media/AGE Fotostock

Tang Horsewoman   This ceramic tomb figurine from the far northwest, a region populated largely by Turkic speaking peoples, is unusual in being painted rather than glazed. The woman's costume suggests that she is of high rank, but not Chinese. Note the difference between the rider's light, toe-only stirrup and the full iron military stirrup shown on page 256.

on Buddhism had flourished in Inner Asia and north China since the fall of the Han. Some interpretations of Buddhist doctrine accorded kings and emperors the spiritual function of welding humankind into a harmonious Buddhist society. Protecting spirits were to help the ruler govern and prevent harm from coming to his people. Early Tang princes competing for political influence enlisted monastic leaders to pray for them, preach on their behalf, counsel aristocrats to support them, and—perhaps most important—

Uighurs A group of Turkish-speakers who controlled their own centralized empire from 744 to 840 in Mongolia and Central Asia.

Tibet Country centered on the high, mountain-bounded plateau north of India. Tibetan political power occasionally extended farther to the north and west between the seventh and thirteenth centuries.

Material Culture

Salt

Though sodium chloride, or table salt, is one of the world's most abundant chemicals, it's abundance in some areas and scarcity in others has frequently given it an important role in economic history. Here are some examples.

Outcroppings of rock salt known as salt licks play a nutritional role in the lives of many wild mammals. Prehistoric human hunters sought game at these natural animal gathering places, and some scholars believe that human provision of salt played an important role in domesticating some species.

Trade in salt from the southern regions of the Sahara Desert is described as early as the ninth century C.E., but it is probably much older because the Saharan deposits formed an important nutritional source for salt-poor sub-Saharan Africa. The legendary exchange of salt for equivalent quantities of gold symbolizes this commercial importance. Bilma, an oasis town in eastern Niger, still produces salt that is distributed by means of camel caravans trekking across the sand dunes of the Ténére Desert.

In ancient Rome, a strong-smelling sauce known as *garum* became a cooking staple and an important export item. *Garum* was made by crushing cut-up fish, with their entrails, in a small amount of brine. The salt prevented the sauce from spoiling. For common people, using *garum* was a way of avoiding the tax on salt.

Early in the fourteenth century C.E. a Flemish fisherman devised a method of preserving herring, a small fish. After the head and certain internal organs were removed, enzymes from the pancreas began to digest the flesh and make it tender. Then the fish were packed with salt in casks. Salted herring and its raw materials, salt and herring, became mainstays of the commerce of Scotland, northern Germany, and, in particular, the Netherlands. A Dutch proverb maintains that the city of Amsterdam was built on herring casks.

In France, a salt tax known as the *gabelle* became a permanent part of royal revenues in the late fourteenth century C.E. Everyone over the age of eight was forced to buy a minimum amount of salt every week at a price fixed by the government. Most of the salt was produced by evaporating seawater, but inland provinces in the east exploited salt marshes. Popular resentment against the tax contributed to the French Revolution in 1789. A year later the *gabelle* was canceled.

In nineteenth-century China, where the salt tax had been a mainstay of government revenues since the Tang dynasty, brine (saltwater) wells around the western city of Zigong became the basis for one of the country's most prosperous industries. The family-based trusts that

contribute monastic wealth to their war chests. In return, the monasteries received tax exemptions, land privileges, and gifts.

Upheavals and Repression, 750–879

Under the Uighurs, caravan cities like Kashgar and Khotan (see Map 11.1) enjoyed commercial ties with both the Islamic world and China. The location of Tibet also made it a crossroads for trade with China, Southeast Asia, South Asia, and Central Asia. The later years of the Tang Empire saw increasing turmoil as a result of conflict with Tibetans and Turkish Uighurs. One result was a backlash against "foreigners," which to Confucians included Buddhists. The Tang elites came to see Buddhism as undermining the Confucian idea of the family as the model for the state. The Confucian scholar Han Yu (768–824) spoke powerfully for a return to traditional Confucian practices. In "Memorial on the Bone of Buddha" written to the emperor in 819 on the occasion of ceremonies to receive a bone of the Buddha in the imperial palace, he scornfully disparages the Buddha and his followers:

> Now Buddha was a man of the barbarians who did not speak the language of China and wore clothes of a different fashion. His sayings did not concern the ways of our ancient kings, nor did his manner of dress conform to their laws. He understood neither the duties that bind sovereign and subject nor the affections of father and son. If he were still alive today and came to our court by order of his ruler, Your Majesty might condescend to receive him,

extracted the salt from as deep as 3,000 feet were comparable in capital accumulation, management skill, and technological innovation to contemporary European corporations.

In 1930 the British monopoly on salt production in India became the center of a peaceful protest led by Mahatma Gandhi. With seventy-eight followers he marched 240 miles to the seacoast, where the protestors picked up small lumps of salt, thereby breaking the law against private harvesting of salt. Though many were imprisoned, the Salt March became an important model of civil disobedience.

Though salt naturally brings a certain taste to mind, its historic roles relate more to the chemical properties of the salty moisture on the outside of preserved foods. Pieces of pork transform into ham, cucumbers and other vegetables become pickles, and sturgeon eggs become caviar. Since a high concentration of salt kills bacteria, salted foods can be transported and stored for long periods without spoiling or becoming dangerous to eat.

Producing salt from seawater and other sources of brine requires evaporation or boiling. But salt is also available in solid form and can be mined. Cities like Salzburg (literally "Salt Town") in Austria may grow up around salt mines. Underground layers of salt, sometimes hundreds of feet thick, are the residue of dried-up prehistoric seas or oceans. In addition to being processed for consumption, rock salt is used on icy roads. Since saltwater freezes at a lower temperature than fresh water, salt deposited on snow or ice causes melting.

VOLKMAR K. WENTZEL/National Geographic Stock

Camel Caravan Carrying Salt in West Africa *Natural salt deposits, such as those at Bilma in the southern Sahara Desert in Niger, have time and again become the bases for extensive regional and international trade. Transporting the salt can be a challenge, however. Camel transport made salt trading an integral part of the trade between the Saharan region and the agricultural countries of West Africa. In northern Europe the salt springs at Lüneburg near Hamburg, Germany, fed into a maritime trading network throughout the Baltic and North Sea region. Coastal lands could extract salt from seawater by evaporation, though in colder climates, such as Japan, boiling was needed to supplement the power of natural sunlight and heat.*

QUESTIONS FOR ANALYSIS

1. Why did salt become such an important trade product?
2. Why would a tax on salt be easy to administer?
3. How many uses of salt can you think of?

but . . . he would then be escorted to the borders of the state, dismissed, and not allowed to delude the masses. How then, when he has long been dead, could his rotten bones, the foul and unlucky remains of his body, be rightly admitted to the palace? Confucius said, "Respect spiritual beings, while keeping at a distance from them."[1]

Buddhism was also attacked for encouraging women in politics. Wu Zhao (woo jow), a woman who had married into the imperial family, seized control of the government in 690 and declared herself emperor. She based her legitimacy on claiming to be a bodhisattva, an enlightened soul who had chosen to

remain on earth to lead others to salvation. She also favored Buddhists and Daoists over Confucians in her court and government.

Later Confucian writers expressed contempt for Wu Zhao and other powerful women and lamented the influence of women at the Tang court, which had caused "the hearts of fathers and mothers everywhere not to value the birth of boys, but the birth of girls."[2] Confucian elites heaped every possible charge on prominent women who offended them, accusing Emperor Wu of grotesque tortures and murders, including tossing the dismembered but still living bodies of enemies into wine vats and cauldrons.

---

[1] Theodore de Bary, ed., *Sources of Chinese Tradition*, vol. 1, 2d ed. (New York: Columbia University Press, 1999), 584.

[2] Quoted in David Lattimore, "Allusion in T'ang Poetry," in *Perspectives on the T'ang*, ed. Arthur F. Wright and David Twitchett (New Haven, CT: Yale University Press, 1973), 436.

Buddhist Cave Painting at Dunhuang Hundreds of caves dating to the period when Buddhism enjoyed popularity and government favor in China survive in Gansu province, which was beyond the reach of the Tang rulers when they turned against Buddhism. This cave, dated to the period 565–576, depicts the historical Buddha flanked by bodhisattvas. Scenes of the Buddha preaching appear on the wall to the left.

Serious historians dismiss the stories about Wu Zhao as stereotypical characterizations of "evil" rulers. Eunuchs (castrated palace servants) charged by historians with controlling Chang'an and the Tang court and publicly executing rival bureaucrats represent a similar stereotype. In fact Wu seems to have ruled effectively and was not deposed until 705, when extreme old age (eighty-plus) incapacitated her. Nevertheless, traditional Chinese historians commonly describe unorthodox rulers and all-powerful women as evil, and the truth about Wu will never be known.

Even Chinese gentry living in safe and prosperous localities associated Buddhism with social ills. People who worried about "barbarians" ruining their society pointed to Buddhism as evidence of the foreign evil, since it had such strong roots in Inner Asia and Tibet. Because Buddhism shunned earthly ties, monks and nuns severed relations with the secular world in search of enlightenment. They paid no taxes, served in no army. They deprived their families of advantageous marriage alliances and denied

descendants to their ancestors. The Confucian elites saw all this as threatening to the family and to the family estates that underlay the Tang economic and political structure.

By the ninth century, hundreds of thousands of people had entered tax-exempt Buddhist institutions. In 840 the government moved to crush the monasteries, whose tax exemption had allowed them to accumulate land, serfs, and precious objects, often as gifts. Within five years 4,600 temples had been destroyed. Now an enormous amount of land and 150,000 workers were returned to the tax rolls.

Buddhist centers like the cave monasteries at Dunhuang were protected by local warlords loyal to Buddhist rulers in Inner Asia. Nevertheless, China's cultural heritage suffered a great loss in the dissolution of the monasteries. Some sculptures and grottoes survived only in defaced form. Wooden temples and façades sheltering great stone carvings burned to the ground. Monasteries became legal again in later times, but Buddhism never recovered the influence of early Tang times.

The End of the Tang Empire, 879–907

The campaigns of expansion in the seventh century had left the empire dependent on local military commanders and a complex tax collection system. Reverses like the Battle of the Talas River in 751, where Arabs halted Chinese expansion into Central Asia, led to military demoralization and underfunding. In 755 An Lushan, a Tang general on the northeast frontier, led about 200,000 soldiers in rebellion. The emperor fled Chang'an and executed his favorite concubine, Yang Guifei (yahng gway-fay), who was rumored to be An Lushan's lover. (Another woman reviled by Confucians for her influence in government, she was blamed for the outbreak of the An Lushan rebellion.) The rebellion lasted for eight years and resulted in new powers for the provincial military governors who helped suppress it. Even so, Chang'an never recovered, symbolizing Tang's waning influence over satellite states in Korea and Japan.

A disgruntled member of the gentry, Huang Chao (wang show), led the most devastating uprising between 879 and 881. Despite his ruthless treatment of the villages he controlled, his rebellion attracted poor farmers and tenants who could not protect themselves from local bosses and oppressive landlords, or who simply did not know where else to turn in the deepening chaos. The new hatred of "barbarians" spurred the rebels to murder thousands of foreign residents in Canton and Beijing (bay-jeeng).

Local warlords finally wiped out the rebels, but Tang society did not find peace. Refugees, migrant workers, and homeless people became common sights. Residents of northern China fled to the southern frontiers as groups from Inner Asia moved into localities in the north. Though Tang emperors continued in Chang'an until a warlord terminated their line in 907, they never regained power after Huang Chao's rebellion.

CHINA AND ITS RIVALS

■ *What were the effects of the fracturing of power in Inner Asia and China?*

In the aftermath of the Tang, three new states emerged and competed to inherit its legacy (see Map 11.2). The Liao (lee-OW) Empire of the Khitan (kee-THAN) people, pastoral nomads related to the Mongols living on the northeastern frontier, established their rule in the north. They centered their government on several cities, but the emperors preferred life in nomad encampments. In western China, the Minyak people (cousins of the Tibetans) established a state they called "Tanggut" (1038–1227) (TAHNG-gut) to show their connection with the fallen empire. The third state, the Chinese-speaking **Song Empire**, came into being in 960 in central China.

These states embodied the political ambitions of peoples with different religious and philosophical systems—Mahayana Buddhism among the Liao, Tibetan Buddhism among the Tangguts, and Confucianism among the Song. Cut off from Inner Asia, the Song used advanced seafaring and sailing technologies to forge maritime connections with other states in East, West, and Southeast Asia. The Song elite shared the late Tang dislike of "barbaric" or "foreign" influences as they tried to cope with multiple enemies that heavily taxed their military capacities. Meanwhile, Korea, Japan, and some Southeast Asian states strengthened political and cultural ties with China.

SECTION REVIEW

- After the period of disunity following the fall of the Han, China was united under the Sui, followed by the Tang with its founder Li Shimin.

- Tang culture was based on both Chinese tradition and Inner Asian nomadic culture and war expertise.

- Trade led to the spread of Buddhism, prosperity, and a cosmopolitan legacy in the arts and lifestyle of the Tang Empire.

- Uighur and Tibetan turmoil created political problems for the Tang Empire that steadily weakened it.

- In China, this turmoil resulted in a backlash against foreign and female cultural influences and especially Buddhism, as Tang elites led a neo-Confucian reaction.

- The Tang fell due to a combination of destabilizing forces.

Song Empire Empire in central and southern China (960–1126) while the Liao people controlled the north. Empire in southern China (1127–1279; the "Southern Song") while the Jin people controlled the north. Distinguished for its advances in technology, medicine, astronomy, and mathematics.

The Liao and Jin Challenge

The Liao Empire of the Khitan people extended from Siberia to Inner Asia. Variations on the Khitan name became the name for China in these distant regions: "Kitai" for the Mongols, "Khitai" for the Russians, and "Cathay" for Italian merchants like Marco Polo who reported on China in Europe.

The Liao rulers prided themselves on their pastoral traditions as horse and cattle breeders, the continuing source of their military might, and they made no attempt to create a single elite culture. They encouraged Chinese elites to use their own language, study their own classics, and see the emperor through Confucian eyes; and they encouraged other peoples to use their own languages and see the emperor as a champion of Buddhism or as a nomadic chieftain. On balance, Buddhism far outweighed Confucianism in this and other northern states, where rulers depended on their roles as bodhisattvas or as Buddhist kings to legitimate power. Liao rule lasted from 916 to 1125.

The Liao was the most powerful empire at the time, with the largest army in East Asia. Superb horsemen and archers, the Khitans also challenged the Song with siege machines from China and Central Asia. A truce concluded in 1005 required the Song emperor to pay the Liao great quantities of cash and silk annually. A century later, the Song tired of paying tribute and secretly allied with the Jurchens of northeastern Asia, who also resented Liao rule. In 1115 the Jurchens first destroyed the Liao capital in Mongolia and proclaimed their own empire, the Jin (see Map 11.2), and then turned on the Song.

The Jurchens grew rice, millet, and wheat, but they also spent a good deal of time hunting, fishing, and tending livestock. Using Khitan military arts and political organization, they became formidable enemies in an all-out campaign against the Song in 1127. They laid siege to the Song capital, Kaifeng (kie-fuhng), and captured the Song emperor. Within a few years the Song withdrew south of the Yellow River and established a new capital at Hangzhou (hahng-jo), leaving central as well as northern China in Jurchen control. Annual payments to the Jin Empire staved off further warfare. Historians generally refer to this period as the "Southern Song" (1127–1279).

Song Industries

The Southern Song came closer to initiating an industrial revolution than any other premodern state. Many Song advances in technology, medicine, astronomy, and mathematics had come to China in Tang times, sometimes from very distant places. Song officials, scholars, and businessmen had the motivation and resources to adapt this Tang lore to meet their military, agricultural, and administrative needs.

Song mathematicians introduced the use of fractions, first employing them to describe the phases of the moon. From lunar observations, Song astronomers constructed a very precise calendar and, alone among the world's astronomers, noted the explosion of the Crab Nebula in 1054. Song inventors drew on their knowledge of celestial coordinates, particularly the Pole Star, to refine compass design. The magnetic compass, an earlier Chinese invention, shrank in size and gained a fixed pivot point for the needle. With a protective glass cover, the compass now became suitable for seafaring, a use first recorded in 1090.

Development of the seaworthy compass coincided with new techniques in building China's main oceangoing ship, the **junk**. A stern-mounted rudder improved the steering of the large ship in rough seas, and watertight bulkheads helped keep it afloat in emergencies. The shipwrights of the Persian Gulf soon copied these features in their ship designs.

Because they needed iron and steel to make weapons for their army of 1.25 million men, the Song rulers fought their northern rivals for control of mines in north China. Production of coal and iron soared. By the end of the eleventh century cast iron production reached about 125,000 tons (113,700 metric tons) annually, putting it on a par with the output of eighteenth-century Britain. Engineers became skilled at high-temperature metallurgy using enormous bellows, often driven by water wheels, to superheat the molten ore. Military engineers used iron to buttress defensive works because it was impervious to fire or concussion, and armorers mass-produced body

junk A very large flatbottom sailing ship produced in the Tang, Song, and Ming Empires, specially designed for long-distance commercial travel.

armor. Iron construction also appeared in bridges and small buildings. Mass-production techniques for bronze and ceramics in use in China for nearly two thousand years were adapted to iron casting and assembly.

To counter cavalry assaults, the Song experimented with **gunpowder**, which they initially used to propel clusters of flaming arrows. During the wars against the Jurchens in the 1100s the Song introduced a new and terrifying weapon. Shells launched from Song fortifications exploded in the midst of the enemy, blowing out iron shrapnel and dismembering men and horses. However, the short range of these shells limited them to defensive uses.

Economy and Society in Song China

In a warlike era, Song elite culture idealized civil pursuits, and civilians outranked military men socially. Private academies, designed to train young men for the official examinations, became influential in culture and politics. New interpretations of Confucian teachings became so important and influential that the term **neo-Confucianism** is used for Song and later versions of Confucian thought.

Zhu Xi (jew she) (1130–1200), the most important early neo-Confucian thinker, reacted to the many centuries during which Buddhism and Daoism had overshadowed the precepts of Confucius. He and others worked out a systematic approach to cosmology that focused on the central conception that human nature is moral, rational, and essentially good. To combat the Buddhist dismissal of worldly affairs as a transitory distraction, they reemphasized individual moral and social responsibility. Their human ideal was the sage, a person who could preserve mental stability and serenity while dealing conscientiously with troubling social problems. Whereas earlier Confucian thinkers had written about sage kings and political leaders, the neo-Confucians espoused the spiritual idea of universal sagehood, a state that could be achieved through proper study of the new Confucian principles and cosmology.

Popular Buddhist sects also persisted during the Song, demonstrating that anti-Buddhist feelings were

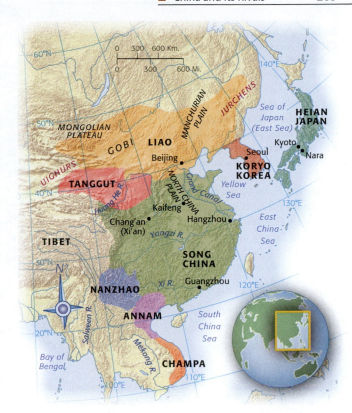

Map 11.2 Liao and Song Empires, ca. 1100 The states of Liao in the north and Song in the south generally ceased open hostilities after a treaty in 1005 stabilized the border and imposed an annual payment on Song China. © Cengage Learning

not as ferocious as Confucian polemics against Buddhism might suggest. Some Buddhists elaborated on Tang-era folk practices derived from India and Tibet. The best known, Chan Buddhism (known as **Zen** in Japan and as Son in Korea), asserted that mental discipline alone could win salvation.

gunpowder A mixture of saltpeter, sulfur, and charcoal, in various proportions. The formula, brought to China in the 400s or 500s, was first used to make fumigators to keep away insect pests and evil spirits. In later centuries it was used to make explosives and grenades and to propel cannonballs, shot, and bullets.

neo-Confucianism Term used to describe new approaches to understanding classic Confucian texts that became the basic ruling philosophy of China from the Song period to the twentieth century.

Zen The Japanese word for a branch of Mahayana Buddhism based on highly disciplined meditation. It is known in Sanskrit as *dhyana*, in Chinese as *chan*, and in Korean as *son*.

Su Song's Astronomical Clock This gigantic clock built at Kaifeng between 1088 and 1092 combined mathematics, astronomy, and calendar-making with skillful engineering. The team overseen by Su Song placed an armillary sphere on the observation platform and linked it with chains to the water-driven central mechanism shown in the cutaway view. The water wheel also rotated the Buddha statues in the multistory pagoda the spectators are looking at. Other devices displayed the time of the day, the month, and the year.

From Joseph Needham's *Science and Civilization in China*, Vol 4. After the original diagram in Su Song's treatise Xinyi Xiangfayao, 1092.

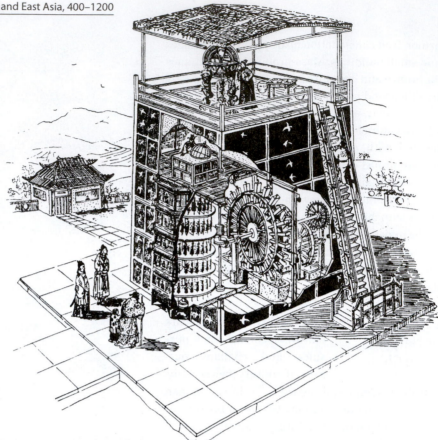

Meditation, a key Chan practice, was employed by Confucians as well as Buddhists. It afforded prospective officials relief from studying for civil service examinations, which continued into the Song from the Tang period. Unlike the ancient Han policy of hiring and promoting on the basis of recommendations, Song-style examinations involved a large bureaucracy. Test questions, which changed each time the examinations were given, often related to economic management or foreign policy even though they were always based on Confucian classics.

Hereditary class distinctions meant less than they had in Tang times, when noble lineages played a greater role in the structure of power. The new system recruited the most talented men, whatever their origin. Yet men from wealthy families enjoyed an advantage, for preparation for the tests consumed so much time that peasant boys could rarely compete. Success in the examinations brought good marriage prospects, the chance for a high salary, and enormous prestige. Failure could bankrupt a family and ruin

a man both socially and psychologically. This put great pressure on candidates, who spent days writing essays in tiny, dim, airless examination cells.

For some, preparation became easier thanks to a technical change from woodblock to an early form of **movable type**, which made printing cheaper. To promote its ideological goals, the Song government authorized the mass production of test preparation books in the years before 1000. Although a man had to be literate to read the preparation books and basic education was still rare, a growing number of candidates without noble, gentry, or elite backgrounds entered the Song bureaucracy.

movable type Type in which each individual character is cast on a separate piece of metal. It replaced woodblock printing, allowing for the arrangement of individual letters and other characters on a page, rather than requiring the carving of entire pages at a time. It may have been invented in Korea in the thirteenth century.

Song River Transport
This seventeenth-century painting shows the emperor Huizong (r. 1100–1126), in red, supervising the ceremonial transfer of pierced stones and a tree. The purpose of their transfer is unknown. Note the differences between the workshop at lower left and the residence at lower right where women, children, and even a pet dog are enjoying life outside the enclosed courtyard.

The availability of printed books changed country life as well, since landlords gained access to expert advice on planting and irrigation techniques, harvesting, tree cultivation, threshing, and weaving. Landlords frequently gathered their tenants and workers to show them illustrated texts on the crafts of farming and explain their meaning. New agricultural land was developed south of the Yangtze River, and iron implements such as plows and rakes, first used in the Tang era, were adapted to southern wet-rice cultivation. The growing profitability of agriculture interested ambitious members of the gentry. Still a frontier for Chinese settlers under the Tang,

the south saw increasing concentration of land in the hands of a few wealthy families. In the process, the indigenous inhabitants of the region retreated into the mountains or southward toward Vietnam.

During the 1100s the total population of the Chinese territories, spurred by prosperity, rose above 100 million. The leading Song cities were still among the largest cities in the world. Health and crowding posed problems in the Song capitals. Multistory wooden apartment houses fronted on narrow streets—sometimes only 4 or 5 feet (1.2 to 1.5 meters) wide—that were clogged by peddlers or families spending time outdoors. The crush of people called for new

Female Musicians   A group of entertainers from a Song period copy of a lost Tang painting titled "Night Revels of Han Xizai." The emperor ordered the painter to document the lifestyle of a man who preferred music, dance, and poetry to accepting appointment as Prime Minister. The mood of genteel indulgence appealed to Song era elites. Chinese women were not veiled, but foot-binding became common under the Song. The Night Revelry of Han Xizai, by Gu Hongzhong the court painter sent by his suspicious monarch to spy on Han and to make a record of Han's licentious behaviour/Werner Forman Archive/The Bridgeman Art Library

techniques in waste management, water supply, and firefighting. In Hangzhou engineers diverted the nearby river to flow through the city, flushing away waste and disease. Arab and European travelers who had firsthand experience with the Song capital, and who were sensitive to urban conditions in their own societies, expressed amazement at Hangzhou's amenities: restaurants, parks, bookstores, wine shops, tea houses, theaters, and other entertainments.

The idea of credit, originating in the robust long-distance trade of the Tang period, spread widely under the Song. Intercity or interregional credit—what the Song called "flying money"—depended on the acceptance of guarantees that the paper could be redeemed for coinage at another location. The public accepted the practice because credit networks tended

to be managed by families, so that brothers and cousins were usually honoring each other's certificates.

"Flying money" certificates differed from government-issued paper money, which the Song pioneered. In some years, military expenditures consumed 80 percent of the government budget. The state responded to this financial pressure by distributing paper money. But this made inflation so severe that by the beginning of the 1100s paper money was trading for only 1 percent of its face value. Eventually the government withdrew paper money and instead imposed new taxes, sold monopolies, and offered financial incentives to merchants.

Hard-pressed for the revenue needed to maintain the army, canals, roads, waterworks, and other state functions, the government finally resorted to tax farming, selling the rights to tax collection to private individuals. Tax farmers made their profit by collecting the maximum amount and sending an agreed-upon smaller sum to the government. This meant exorbitant rates for taxable services, such as tolls, and much heavier tax burdens on the common people.

Rapid economic growth undermined the remaining government monopolies and the traditional strict regulation of business. Now merchants and artisans as well as gentry and officials could make fortunes. With land no longer the only source of wealth, the traditional social hierarchy common to an agricultural economy weakened, while cities, commerce, consumption, and the use of money and credit boomed. Urban life reflected the elite's growing taste for fine fabrics, porcelain, exotic foods, large houses, and exquisite paintings and books.

Along with the revival of Confucianism that began under the Tang and intensified under the Song, women experienced subordination, legal disenfranchisement, and social restriction. Merchants spent long periods away from home, and many maintained several wives in different locations. They often depended on wives to manage their homes and even their businesses in their absence. Although women took on responsibility for the management of their husbands' property, their own property rights suffered legal erosion. Under Song law, a woman's property automatically passed to her husband, and women could not remarry if their husbands divorced them or died.

As the subordination of women proved compatible with Confucianism, it became fashionable to educate girls just enough to read simplified versions of Confucian philosophy that emphasized the lowly role of women. Literacy made these young women more desirable as companions for the sons of gentry or noble families and as mothers in lower-ranking families aspiring to improve their status. The poet Li Qingzhao (lee CHING-jow) (1083–1141) acknowledged and made fun of her unusual status as a highly celebrated female writer:

Although I've studied poetry for thirty years
I try to keep my mouth shut and avoid reputation.
Now who is this nosy gentleman talking about my poetry

Like Yang Ching-chih (yahng SHING-she)
Who spoke of Hsiang Ssu (sang sue) everywhere he went.[3]

(Her reference is to a hermit poet of the ninth century who was continually and extravagantly praised by a court official.)

Female footbinding first appeared among slave dancers at the Tang court, but it did not become widespread until the Song period. The bindings forced the toes under and toward the heel, so that the bones eventually broke and the woman could not walk on her own. In noble and gentry families, footbinding began between ages five and seven. In less wealthy families, girls worked until they were older, so footbinding began only in a girl's teens.

Many literate men condemned the maiming of innocent girls and the general uselessness of footbinding. Nevertheless, bound feet became a status symbol. By 1200 a woman with unbound feet had become undesirable in elite circles, and mothers of elite status, or aspiring to such status, almost without exception bound their daughters' feet. They knew that girls with unbound feet faced rejection. Working women and the indigenous peoples of the south, where northern practices took a longer time to penetrate, did not practice footbinding. Consequently they enjoyed considerably more mobility and economic independence than did elite Chinese women.

---

[3] Quoted at "Women's Early Music, Art, Poetry," http://music.acu.edu/www/iawm/pages/reference/tzusongs.html.

SECTION REVIEW

- Several rival states replaced the fallen Tang Empire, and the close relations between Central Asia and East Asia ended.

- The Liao and Jin Empires encouraged culturally diverse societies and confronted Song China with formidable military threats.

- The Song Empire of central and southern China built upon Tang achievements in technology and science and promoted civil ideals.

- Under the Song, print culture developed, urban populations rose, commercial activity grew through innovation, and women were subordinated to men.

NEW KINGDOMS IN EAST ASIA

■ *To what extent do shared practices justify thinking of East Asia as a unified cultural region in the post-Tang era?*

The best possibilities for expanding the Confucian worldview of the Song lay with newly emerging kingdoms to the east and south. Korea, Japan, and Vietnam, like Song China, devoted great effort to the cultivation of rice, a practice that fit well with Confucian social ideas. Tending the young rice plants, irrigating the rice paddies, and managing the harvest required coordination among many village and kin groups and rewarded hierarchy, obedience, and self-discipline. Confucianism also justified using agricultural profits to support the education, safety, and comfort of the literate elite. In each of these new kingdoms Song civilization melded with indigenous cultural and historical traditions to create a distinctive synthesis.

Chinese Influences

Korea, Japan, and Vietnam had first centralized power under ruling houses in the early Tang period, and their state ideologies continued to resemble that of the early Tang, when Buddhism and Confucianism seemed compatible. Government offices went to noble families and did not depend on passing examinations on Confucian texts. Landowning and agriculture remained the major sources of income, and landowners faced no challenges from a merchant class or urban elite.

Nevertheless, learned men prized literacy in classical Chinese and a good knowledge of Confucian texts. Though formal education was available to only a small number of people, the ruling and landholding elites sought to instill Confucian ideals of hierarchy and harmony among the general population.

Korea

Our first knowledge of Korea, Japan, and Vietnam comes from early Chinese officials and travelers. When the Qin Empire established its first colony in the Korean peninsula in the third century B.C.E., Chinese bureaucrats began documenting Korean history and customs. Han writers noted the horse breeding, strong hereditary elites, and **shamanism** (belief in the ability of certain individuals to contact ancestors and the invisible spirit world) of Korea's small kingdoms. But Korea quickly absorbed Confucianism and Buddhism.

Mountainous in the east and north, Korea was heavily forested until modern times. The land that can be cultivated (less than 20 percent) lies mostly in the south, where a warm climate and monsoon rains support two crops per year. Population movements from Manchuria, Mongolia, and Siberia in the north and toward Japan in the east spread languages that were very different from Chinese but distantly related to the Turkish tongues of Inner Asia .

In the early 500s the dominant landholding families made inherited status—the "bone ranks"—permanent in Silla (SILL-ah or SHILL-ah), a kingdom in the southeast of the peninsula. In the early 660s Silla defeated the southwestern kingdom of Paekche, which had played a major role as a maritime power in transmitting Chinese culture to Japan. Then in 668 the northern Koguryŏ kingdom came to an end after prolonged conflict with the Sui and Tang. Koguryŏ was so influential in Northeast Asia that the Liao and Jin Empires, and subsequent Korean kingdoms, claimed to inherit its legacy.

Supported by the Tang, Silla took control of much of the Korean peninsula. The Silla rulers imitated Tang government and examined officials on the Confucian classics. They also sent Buddhist monks to China. But the intellectual exchange was not one-directional: writings by the monk Wonhyo known as the "Korean Commentary" greatly influenced Buddhism in China. The fall of the Tang in the early 900s coincided with Silla's collapse and enabled the ruling house of **Koryo** (KAW-ree-oh), from which the modern name *Korea* derives, to rule a united peninsula for the next three centuries. Threatened constantly by the Liao and then the Jin in northern China, Koryo maintained amicable relations with Song China in the south. The Koryo

shamanism The practice of identifying special individuals (shamans) who will interact with spirits for the benefit of the community. Characteristic of the Korean kingdoms of the early medieval period and of early societies of Central Asia.

Koryo Korean kingdom founded in 918 and destroyed by a Mongol invasion in 1259.

Silla Warrior This ewer—the projection in front is the pour spout—reflects Korea's early use of cavalry. Horses were probably introduced to Japan by way of Korea.

kings supported Buddhism and made superb printed editions of Buddhist texts.

The oldest surviving woodblock print in Chinese characters comes from Korea in the middle 700s. Commonly used during the Tang period, woodblock printing required great technical skill. A calligrapher would write the text on thin paper, which would then be pasted upside down on a block of wood. Once wetted, the characters showed through from the back, and an artisan would carve away the wooden surface surrounding each character. A fresh block had to be carved for each printed page. Korean artisans developed their own advances in printing. By Song times, Korean experiments with movable type had reached China, where further improvements led to metal or porcelain type from which texts could be cheaply printed.

Japan

Japan consists of four main islands and many smaller ones stretching in an arc from as far south as Georgia to as far north as Maine. The nearest point of contact with

the Asian mainland lies 100 miles away in southern Korea. In early times Japan was even more heavily forested than Korea, with only 11 percent of its land area suitable for cultivation. Mild winters and monsoon rains supported the earliest population centers on the coastlands of the Inland Sea between Honshu and Shikoku Islands. The first rulers to extend their power broadly in the fourth and fifth centuries C.E. were based in the Yamato River Basin on the Kinai Plain at the eastern end of the sea.

The first Chinese description of Japan, dating from the fourth century, tells of an island at the eastern edge of the world that is divided into hundreds of small communities, with the largest one, called Yamatai, ruled over by a shamaness named Himiko or Pimiko. The location of the early Yamatai kingdom remains a source of debate, but archaeological finds point to frequent interaction with China and Korea. In the mid-600s these rulers, acting on knowledge gained from Korean contacts and embassies to Chang'an sent by five different kings, implemented the Taika (TIE-kah) and other reforms, giving the Yamato regime the key features of Tang government. A legal code, an official variety of Confucianism, and an official reverence for Buddhism blended with the local recognition of indigenous and immigrant chieftains as territorial administrators. Within a century, a centralized government with a complex system of law had emerged, as attested by a massive history in the Confucian style.

Women from the aristocracy became royal consorts and thereby linked their kinsmen with the royal court. At the death of her husband in 592, Suiko, a woman from the immigrant aristocratic family of Soga, became empress. She occupied the throne until 628, enjoying a longer reign than any other ruler down to the nineteenth century. Asuka, her capital, saw a flowering of Buddhist art, and her nephew Shotoku opened relations with Sui China and is credited with promulgating a "Constitution" in 604 that had lasting influence on Japan's governing philosophy.

The Japanese mastered and improved on several Chinese skills. They copied Chinese building techniques so well that Nara (NAH-rah) and Kyoto, Japan's early capitals, provide invaluable evidence of the wooden architecture long since vanished from China. During the eighth century Japan in some ways surpassed China in Buddhist studies. In 752 dignitaries from all over Mahayana Buddhist Asia gathered at the enormous Todaiji temple, near Nara, to celebrate the "eye-opening" of the "Great Buddha" statue.

Though the Japanese adopted Chinese building styles and some street plans, Japanese cities were built without walls. One reason was that central Japan was not plagued by constant warfare. Also, the Confucian Mandate of Heaven, which justified dynastic changes, played no role in legitimating Japanese government. The *tenno*, or "heavenly sovereign"—often called "emperor" in English—belonged to a family believed to have ruled Japan since the beginning of history. The dynasty never changed. A prime minister and the leaders of the native religion, in later times called Shinto, the "way of the gods," exercised real control.

By 750 the government in the capital city Nara had reached its zenith. Roads reached out to provincial capitals, and the rulers pushed their rice-growing culture into the territory of the related Hayato people

of southern Kyushu and into northeastern Honshu, where the Emishi, a non-Japanese indigenous population, practiced slash-and-burn agriculture.

In 794 the central government moved to Kyoto, usually called by its ancient name, Heian (hay-ahn). Though power became decentralized toward the end, legally centralized government lasted there until 1185. During this time members of the **Fujiwara** (foo-jee-WAH-rah) clan—a family of priests, bureaucrats, and warriors who had succeeded the Soga clan in influence from 866 to 1180—controlled power and protected the emperor. Fujiwara dominance favored men of Confucian learning over the generally illiterate warriors. Noblemen of the Fujiwara period read the Chinese classics and appreciated painting and poetry.

Gradually the Fujiwara nobles began to entrust responsibility for local government, policing, and tax collection to their warriors, known as *samurai*, literally "one who serves." Though often of humble origins, a small number of warriors had achieved wealth and power by the late 1000s. By the middle 1100s the nobility had lost control, and civil war between rival warrior clans engulfed the capital.

Like other East Asian states influenced by Confucianism, the elite families of Fujiwara Japan did not encourage education for women. The hero of the celebrated Japanese novel about Fujiwara court culture, *The Tale of Genji*, written around the year 1000 and often regarded as the world's first novel, remarks: "Women should have a general knowledge of several subjects, but it gives a bad impression if they show themselves to be attached to a particular branch of learning."[4] However, within the marriage politics of the day, having interesting and talented women helped the Fujiwara monopolize the monarch's attention on their own women rather than those of other families.

Fujiwara noblewomen lived in near-total isolation, generally spending their time on cultural pursuits and the study of Buddhism. To communi-

[4] Quoted in Ivan Morris, *The World of the Shining Prince: Court Life in Ancient Japan* (New York: Penguin Books, 1979), 221–222.

Fujiwara Aristocratic family that dominated the Japanese imperial court between the ninth and twelfth centuries.

cate with their families or among themselves, they depended on writing. The simplified syllabic script that they used represented the Japanese language in its fully inflected form (the Chinese classical script used by Fujiwara men could not do so). Sei Shonagon (SAY SHOH-nah-gohn), a lady attending one of the royal consorts, composed her *Pillow Book* between 996 and 1021. Most likely named for being kept by the author's pillow so she could jot down occasional thoughts, this famous work begins:

> Spring is best at dawn as gradually the hilltops lighten, while the light grows brighter until there are purple-tinged clouds trailing through the sky.
>
> Summer is best at night. That goes without saying when there is a full moon. But when fireflies flit here and there in a dark sky, that too is wonderful. It is even wonderful when it is raining.[5]

Military clans acquired increasing importance during the period 1156–1185, and warfare between rival families culminated in the establishment of the **Kamakura** (kah-mah-KOO-rah) **Shogunate** in eastern Honshu, far from the old religious and political center at Kyoto. The standing of the Fujiwara family fell as nobles and the emperor hurried to accommodate the new warlords. *The Tale of the Heike*, an anonymously composed thirteenth-century epic account of the clan war, reflects a Buddhist appreciation of the impermanence of worldly things, a view that became common among the new warrior class. This class eventually absorbed some of the Fujiwara aristocratic values, but the monopoly of power by a non-military civil elite had come to an end.

Vietnam

Not until Tang times did the relationship between Vietnam and China become close enough for economic and cultural interchange to play an important role. Occupying the coastal regions east of the mountainous spine of mainland Southeast Asia, Vietnam's economic and political life centered on two fertile river valleys, the Red River in the north and the Mekong (may-KONG) in the south. The rice-based agriculture of Vietnam

---

[5] Quoted in Ivan Morris, trans., *The Pillow Book of Sei Shonagon* (New York: Columbia University Press, 1991), section 1.

SECTION REVIEW

- Korea, Japan, and Vietnam adapted Chinese cultural and political models, including the Tang blend of Confucianism and Buddhism.
- In all three cultures, landowning and agriculture remained the principal source of wealth.

made the region well suited for integration with southern China. In both regions the wet climate and hilly terrain demanded expertise in irrigation.

Early Vietnamese peoples may have preceded the Chinese in using draft animals in farming and working with metal. But in Tang and Song times the elites of "Annam" (ahn-nahm)—as the Chinese called early Vietnam—adopted Confucian bureaucratic training, Mahayana Buddhism, and other aspects of Chinese culture. Annamese elites continued to rule in the Tang style after that dynasty's fall. Annam assumed the name *Dai Viet* (die vee-yet) in 936 and maintained good relations with Song China as an independent country.

Champa, located in what is now southern Vietnam, rivaled the Dai Viet state. The cultures of India and the Malay Peninsula strongly influenced Champa through maritime networks of trade and communication. During the Tang period, Champa fought with Dai Viet, but both kingdoms cooperated with the less threatening Song. Among the tribute gifts brought to the Song court by Champa emissaries was **Champa rice** (originally from India). Chinese farmers soon made use of this fast-maturing variety to improve their yields of the essential crop.

Vietnam shared the general Confucian interest in hierarchy, but attitudes toward women, like those in Korea and Japan, differed from the Chinese model. None of the societies adopted footbinding. In Korea strong family alliances that functioned like political and economic organizations allowed women a role in

Kamakura Shogunate The first of Japan's decentralized military governments (1185–1333).

Champa rice Quick-maturing rice that can allow two harvests in one growing season. Originally introduced into Champa from India, it was later sent to China as a tribute gift by the Champa state.

negotiating and disposing of property. Before the adoption of Confucianism, Annamese women had enjoyed higher status than women in China, perhaps because both women and men participated in wet-rice cultivation. The Trung sisters of Vietnam, who lived in the second century C.E. and led local farmers in resistance against the Han Empire, still serve as national symbols in Vietnam and as local heroes in southern China.

CONCLUSION

The Tang Empire put into place a solid system of travel, trade, and communications that allowed cultural and economic influences to move quickly from Central Asia to Japan. Diversity within the empire produced great wealth and new ideas. In northern and Central Asia, these refinements included state ideologies based on Buddhism, bureaucratic practices based on Chinese traditions, and military techniques combining nomadic horsemanship and strategies with Chinese armaments and weapons. As a result of China's great size, ancient culture, and advanced technology, smaller states of East Asia such as Vietnam, Korea, and Japan modeled their political and cultural life on China. But tensions among rival groups weakened the political structure and led to great violence and misery.

Though smaller than its predecessor, the Song Empire showed great productivity, circulating goods and money throughout East Asia and stimulating the economies of neighbors. In Song China, the spread of Tang technological knowledge resulted in major advances in technology and industry, increased productivity in agriculture, and deeper exploration of ideas relating to time, cosmology, and mathematics. Song China dominated military technology and engineering, privatized commerce, and used movable type to promote its ideological goals. The brilliant achievements of the Song period came from mutually reinforcing developments in economy and technology.

Korea, Japan, and Vietnam developed distinct social, economic, and political systems. Buddhism became the preferred religion in all three regions, but Chinese influences, largely deriving from a universal esteem for Confucian thought and writings, put down deep roots. In the absence of a land border with China, Japan retained greater political independence than Korea and Vietnam. All of these societies made advances in agricultural technology and productivity and raised their literacy rates as printing spread. The culture of Japan's imperial center reached a high level of perfection, but the political system was ultimately based on a warrior aristocracy.

CHAPTER REVIEW

THE SUI AND TANG EMPIRES, 581–755
■ *What was the importance of Inner and Central Asia as a region of interchange during the Tang period?* (page 255)

Though the Tang emperors presided over one of the most celebrated periods in Chinese history, they were of Turkish descent and made extensive use of the military and cultural practices of Inner Asian nomads. Silk Road trade flourished under the Tang, and the new popularity of Buddhism entering China from the northwest gateway greatly affected Chinese culture. Nevertheless, most Tang officials came from long-established aristocratic Chinese families.

CHINA AND ITS RIVALS
■ *What were the effects of the fracturing of power in Inner Asia and China?* (page 263)

After the Tang fell, warlords of different ethnic identities fought for control of northern China. The southward flight of people across the Yangzi River led to the formation of power centers well removed from the northwest frontier. The Song dynasty brought political and economic prominence to southern China. But in Korea and Vietnam, the collapse of the Tang encouraged local independence. Chinese culture continued to be admired and imitated, but the new ruling families rejected the Chinese bureaucratic structure even while recognizing that China provided the greatest market for their trade, particularly under the robust economic conditions of the Southern Song.

NEW KINGDOMS IN EAST ASIA

■ *To what extent do shared practices justify thinking of East Asia as a unified cultural region in the post-Tang era?* (page 269)

A reverence for Confucian classics spread from China to all neighboring lands and formed the core of elite education. Buddhism also spread at both the elite and popular levels. However, neither played as strong a political role as Islam did in the Middle East or Christianity in Europe. As a consequence, East Asia emerged during this period as a region with strong cultural links but without a common philosophical or religious tradition of rulership.

Key Terms

Grand Canal (p. 255)

Li Shimin (p. 256)

Tang Empire (p. 256)

tributary system (p. 257)

Uighurs (p. 259)

Tibet (p. 259)

Song Empire (p. 263)

junk (p. 264)

gunpowder (p. 265)

neo-Confucianism (p. 265)

Zen (p. 265)

movable type (p. 266)

shamanism (p. 270)

Koryo (p. 270)

Fujiwara (p. 272)

Kamakura Shogunate (p. 273)

Champa rice (p. 273)

Religious Conversion

Religious conversion has two meanings that often get confused. The term can refer to the inner transformation an individual may feel on joining a new religious community or becoming revitalized in his or her religious belief. Conversions of this sort are often sudden and deeply emotional. In historical terms, they may be important when they transform the lives of prominent individuals.

In its other meaning, religious conversion refers to a change in the religious identity of an entire population, or a large portion of a population. This generally occurs slowly and is hard to trace in historical documents. As a result, historians have sometimes used superficial indicators to trace the spread of a religion. Doing so can result in misleading conclusions, such as considering the spread of the Islamic faith to be the result of forced conversion by Arab conquerors, or taking the routes traveled by Christian or Buddhist missionaries as evidence that the people they encountered adopted their spiritual message, or assuming that a king or chieftain's adherence to a new religion immediately resulted in a religious change among subjects or followers.

In addition to being difficult to document, religious conversion in the broad societal sense has followed different patterns according to changing circumstances of time and place. Historians have devised several models to explain the different conversion patterns. According to one model, while religious labels in a society change quickly, such as through mass baptism, devotional practices remain largely the same. Evidence for this model can be found in the continuation of old religious customs among people who identify themselves as belonging to a new religion. Another model sees religious change as primarily a function of economic benefit or escape from persecution. Taking this approach makes it difficult to explain the endurance of certain religious communities in the face of hardship and discrimination. Nevertheless, most historians pay attention to economic advantage in their assessments of mass conversion. A third model associates a society's religious conversion with its desire to adopt a more sophisticated way of life, by shifting, for example, from a religion that does not use written texts to one that does.

One final conceptual approach to explaining the process of mass religious change draws on the quantitative models of innovation diffusion that were originally developed to analyze the spread of new technologies in the twentieth century. According to this approach, new ideas, whether in the material or religious realm, depend on the spread of information. A few early adopters—missionaries, pilgrims, or conquerors, perhaps—spread word of the new faith to the people they come in contact with, some of whom follow their example and convert. Those converts in turn spread the word to others, and a chain reaction picks up speed in what might be called a bandwagon effect. The period of bandwagon conversion tapers off when the number of people who have not yet been offered an opportunity to convert diminishes. The entire process can be graphed as a logistic or S-shaped curve. Figure 1, the graph of conversion to Islam in Iran based on changes from Persian (non-Islamic) to Arabic (Islamic) names in family genealogies, shows such a curve over a period of almost four centuries.

In societies that were largely illiterate, like those in which Buddhism, Christianity, and Islam slowly achieved spiritual dominance, information spread primarily by word of mouth. The proponents of the new religious views did not always speak the same language as the people they hoped to bring into the faith. Under these circumstances, significant conversion—that is, conversion that involved some understanding of the new religion, as opposed to forced baptism or imposed mouthing of a profession of faith—must surely have started with fairly small numbers.

Language was crucial. Chinese pilgrims undertook lengthy travels to visit early Buddhist sites in India. There they acquired Sanskrit texts, which they translated into Chinese. These translations became the core texts of Chinese Buddhism. In early Christendom, the presence of bilingual (Greek-Aramaic) Jewish communities in the eastern parts of the Roman Empire facilitated the early spread of the religion beyond its Aramaic-speaking homeland. By contrast, Arabic, the language of Islam, was spoken only in the Arabian peninsula and the desert borderlands that extended northwards from Arabia between Syria, Jordan, and Iraq. This initial impediment to the spread of knowledge about Islam dissolved only when intermarriage with non-Muslim, non-Arab women, many of them taken captive and distributed as booty during the conquests, produced bilingual offspring. Bilingual preachers of the Christian faith were similarly needed in the Celtic, Germanic, and Slavic language areas of western and eastern Europe.

This slow process of information diffusion, which varied from region to region, made changing demands on religious leaders and institutions. When a faith was professed primarily by a ruler, his army, and his dependants, religious leaders gave the highest priority to servicing the needs of the ruling minority and perhaps discrediting, denigrating, or exterminating the practices of the majority. Once a few centuries had passed and the new faith had become the religion of the great majority of the population, religious leaders turned to establishing popular institutions and reaching out to the common people. Historical interpretation can benefit from knowing where a society is in a long-term process of conversion.

These various models reinforce the importance of distinguishing between emotional individual conversion experiences and broad changes in a society's religious identity. New converts are commonly thought of as especially zealous in their faith, and that description is often apt in instances of individual conversion experiences. It is less appropriate, however, to broader episodes of conversion. In a conversion wave that starts slowly, builds momentum in the bandwagon phase, and then tapers off, the first individuals to convert are likely to be more spiritually motivated than those who join the movement toward its end. Religious growth depends on making the faith as attractive to late converts as to ecstatic early converts.

Figure 1 Conversion to Islam in Iran

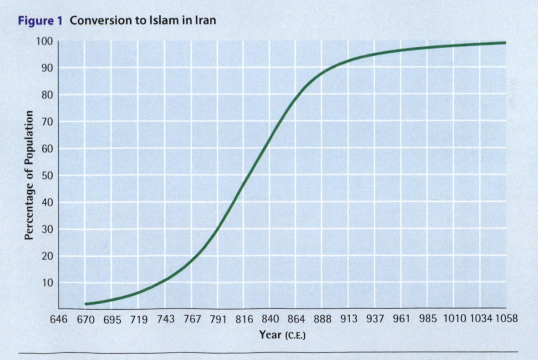

Source: Richard W. Bulliet, *Conversion to Islam in the Medieval Period*, Cambridge, MA: Harvard University Press, 1979, 23. Copyright © 1979 by the President and Fellows of Harvard College.

Part Four

Interregional Patterns of Culture and Contact, 1200–1550

ARCTIC OCEAN

NORTH AMERICA
- Cahokia

EUROPE
- Moscow
- Rome
- Portugal
- Spain
Constantinople
Anatolia
- Baghdad
Iran
Egypt
MIDDLE EAST
Morocco

ASIA
- Samarkand
- Beijing
- China
- Korea
- Japan
- Delhi
- Goa
- India

NORTH ATLANTIC OCEAN

- Hawaii
- Tenochtitlan
Mesoamerica

AFRICA
- Mali
- Benin
- Ethiopia
Kongo
- Great Zimbabwe

PACIFIC OCEAN

SOUTH ATLANTIC OCEAN

INDIAN OCEAN

PACIFIC OCEAN

SOUTH AMERICA
- Cuzco

AUSTRALIA
- New Zealand

Malacca

0 1000 2000 3000 Km.
0 1000 2000 3000 Mi.

© Cengage Learning

	1200	1250	1300	1350
AMERICAS	• **1200** Population of Cahokia reaches 30,000 **1200–1300** Collapse of Anasazi centers			• **1325** Aztecs found Tenochtitlan
EUROPE	• **1215** Magna Carta • **1240** Mongol conquest of Russia		• **1300** First clocks • **1286** Champagne fairs begin to promote regional trade	**1337–1453** Hundred Years War • **1347** Black Death
AFRICA	Kingdom of Benin founded **ca. 1250** • **1240–1500** Mali Empire		• **1270** Solomonic dynasty founded in Ethiopia	• **1324–1325** Mansa Musa's pilgrimage to Mecca brings Islamic learning to Mali
MIDDLE EAST	• **1221** Mongols attack Iran	• **1260** Mamluks defeat Mongols at Ain Jalut • **1258** Mongols take Baghdad, end Abbasid Caliphate	• **1300** Emergence of Ottomans in Anatolia **1295–1304** Rule of Muslim Il-khan Ghazan	
ASIA AND OCEANIA	• **1200** Polynesians settle New Zealand • **1206** Delhi Sultanate founded in India **1206–1227** Reign of Genghis Khan	Polynesians settle Hawaii **1300** • **1274, 1281** Mongol attacks on Japan **1265–1294** Reign of Khubilai Khan		• **1336** Ashikaga Shogunate founded Yuan Empire in China **1279–1368** Ming Empire founded in China **1368** •

Part IV begins with the Mongol conquests under Chinggis Khan, whose empire made Mongolia the center of an administrative and trading system linking Europe, the Middle East, Russia, and East Asia. Overland trade along the Silk Road peaked under the Mongols. Some lands flourished; others groaned under tax burdens and physical devastation.

Societies that escaped conquest also felt the Mongol impact. Around the eastern Mediterranean coast and in eastern Europe, Southeast Asia, and Japan, fear of Mongol attack stimulated defense planning and accelerated processes of urbanization, technological development, and political centralization.

By 1500, Mongol dominance had waned. Eurasia's overland trade faded, and merchants, soldiers, and explorers took to the seas. From China, the admiral Zheng He made state-sponsored long-distance voyages under a new Ming Empire that were spectacular but without long-term results. Meanwhile, Africans explored the Atlantic, and Polynesians colonized the central and eastern Pacific in the 1300s and 1400s. By 1500 Christopher Columbus had reached the Americas; within twenty-five years a Portuguese ship would sail around the world.

The overland routes of Eurasia had generated massive wealth in East Asia and a growing hunger for commerce in Europe. These factors similarly spurred the development of maritime trade. The Ming expanded Chinese influence in Southeast Asia. The Ottomans overthrew the Byzantine Empire and became a major factor in Mediterranean and Black Sea trade, and Christian monarchs in Spain and Portugal, victorious over Muslim enemies, also lay the foundations for new overseas empires. Exposure to the achievements, wealth, and resources of the Americas, sub-Saharan Africa, and Asia guaranteed the further expansion of European exploration and maritime power. Meanwhile in the Western Hemisphere the Aztecs and Inkas were establishing the large Amerindian empires that were destined to clash with invading Europeans.

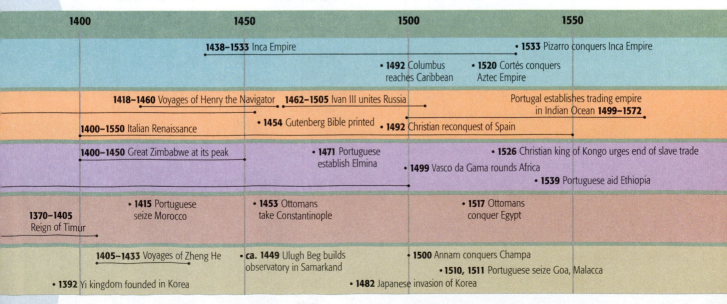

1400	1450	1500	1550
	1438–1533 Inca Empire		• **1533** Pizarro conquers Inca Empire
		• **1492** Columbus reaches Caribbean	• **1520** Cortés conquers Aztec Empire
	1418–1460 Voyages of Henry the Navigator	**1462–1505** Ivan III unites Russia	Portugal establishes trading empire in Indian Ocean **1499–1572**
1400–1550 Italian Renaissance	• **1454** Gutenberg Bible printed	• **1492** Christian reconquest of Spain	
1400–1450 Great Zimbabwe at its peak	• **1471** Portuguese establish Elmina	• **1499** Vasco da Gama rounds Africa	• **1526** Christian king of Kongo urges end of slave trade
			• **1539** Portuguese aid Ethiopia
1370–1405 Reign of Timur	• **1415** Portuguese seize Morocco	• **1453** Ottomans take Constantinople	• **1517** Ottomans conquer Egypt
1405–1433 Voyages of Zheng He	• **ca. 1449** Ulugh Beg builds observatory in Samarkand	• **1500** Annam conquers Champa	
• **1392** Yi kingdom founded in Korea		• **1510, 1511** Portuguese seize Goa, Malacca	
		• **1482** Japanese invasion of Korea	

Mongol Eurasia and Its Aftermath

© Cengage Learning

When Temüjin (TEM-uh-jin) was a boy, a rival group murdered his father. Temüjin's mother tried to shelter him, but she could not find a safe haven, so at fifteen Temüjin sought refuge with the leader of the Keraits (keh-rates), a warring confederation whose people spoke Turkish and respected both Christianity and Buddhism. Temüjin learned the importance of religious tolerance, the necessity of dealing harshly with enemies, and the variety of Inner Asia's cultural and economic traditions.

In 1206 the **Mongols** and their allies acknowledged Temüjin as **Chinggis Khan** (CHING-iz KAHN) (sometimes known as Genghis), or supreme leader. His advisers spoke many languages and belonged to different religions. His deathbed speech, which cannot be literally true even though a contemporary recorded it, captures the strategy behind Mongol success: "If you want to retain your possessions and conquer your enemies, you must make your subjects submit willingly and unite your diverse energies to a single end."[1] By implementing this strategy, Chinggis Khan became the most famous conqueror in history, initiating an expansion of Mongol dominion that by 1250 stretched from Poland to northern China.

European and Asian sources of the time vilified the Mongols as agents of death, suffering, and conflagration, a still-common viewpoint based on reliable accounts of horrible massacres. However, scholars today stress the positive developments that transpired under Mongol rule. The tremendous extent of the Mongol Empire promoted the movement of people and ideas from one end of Eurasia to the other. Trade routes improved, markets expanded, and the demand for products grew. Trade on the Silk Road, which had declined with the fall of the Tang Empire (see Chapter 11), revived.

Between 1218 and about 1350 in western Eurasia and down to 1368 in China, the Mongols focused on specific economic and strategic interests, usually permitting local cultures to survive and develop. In some regions, local reactions to Mongol domination sowed seeds of regional and ethnic identity that blossomed in the period of Mongol decline. Regions as widely separated as Russia, Iran, China, Korea, and Japan benefited from the Mongol stimulation of economic and cultural exchange and also found in their opposition to the Mongols new bases for political consolidation and affirmation of cultural difference.

THE RISE OF THE MONGOLS, 1200–1260

■ *What accounts for the magnitude and speed of the Mongol conquests?*

The Mongol Empire owed much of its success to the cultural institutions and political traditions of the Eurasian steppes and deserts. The pastoral way of life known as nomadism (see Chapter 3) gives rise to imperial expansion only occasionally, and historians disagree about what triggers these episodes. In the case of the Mongols, the personal contributions of Chinggis Khan and his successors remains uncertain.

Mongol Nomadism

The pastoral nomads of the Eurasian Steppes played an on-again, off-again role in European, Middle Eastern, and Chinese history for hundreds of years before the rise of the Mongols (see Chapter 8). The Mongol way of life probably did not differ materially from that of those earlier peoples (see Diversity and Dominance: Observations of Mongol Life). Traditional accounts maintain that the Mongols put their infants on goats to accustom them to riding in preparation for their migratory lifestyle. Like earlier pastoral nomads of the steppes, Mongols moved with their flocks and herds. Powerful families ratified the decisions of the leader, the *khan*, in a public decision-making process

[1]Quotation adapted from Desmond Martin, *Chingis Khan and His Conquest of North China* (Baltimore: The John Hopkins Press, 1950), 303.

Mongols A people of this name is mentioned as early as the records of the Tang Empire, living as nomads in northern Eurasia. After 1206 they established an enormous empire under Chinggis Khan, linking western and eastern Eurasia.

Chinggis Khan The title of Temüjin when he ruled the Mongols (1206–1227). It means the "oceanic" or "universal leader." Chinggis Khan was the founder of the Mongol Empire.

that brought together the many voices of independent individual Mongols and their families. Yet people who disagreed with a decision could strike out on their own. Even during military campaigns, warriors moved with their families and possessions.

Menial work in camps fell to slaves—either prisoners of war or people who sought refuge in slavery to escape starvation. Weak groups secured land rights and protection from strong groups by providing them with slaves, livestock, weapons, silk, or cash. More powerful groups, such as Chinggis Khan's extended family and descendants, lived almost entirely off tribute, so they spent less time and fewer resources on herding and more on warfare designed to secure greater tribute.

Leading families combined resources and solidified intergroup alliances through arranged marriages and acts of allegiance, a process that helped generate political federations. Marriages were arranged in childhood—in Temüjin's case, at the age of eight—and children thus became pawns of diplomacy. Women from prestigious families could wield power in negotiation and management, though they ran the risk of assassination or execution just like men.

The wives and mothers of Mongol rulers traditionally managed state affairs during the interregnum between a ruler's death and the selection of a successor. Princes and heads of ministries treated such regents with great deference and obeyed their commands without question. Since a female regent could not herself succeed to the position of khan, her political machinations usually focused on gaining the succession for a son or other male relative. Families often included believers in two or more religions, most commonly Buddhism, Christianity, or Islam. Virtually all Mongols observed the practices of traditional shamanism, rituals in which special individuals visited and influenced the supernatural world. Whatever their faith, the Mongols believed in world rulership by a khan who, with the aid of his shamans, could speak to and for an ultimate god, represented as Sky or Heaven. This universal ruler transcended particular cultures and dominated them all.

The Mongol Conquests, 1215–1283

Shortly after his acclamation in 1206, Chinggis initiated two decades of Mongol aggression. By 1209 he had cowed the Tanggut (TAHNG-gut) rulers of northwest China, and in 1215 he captured the Jin capital of Yanjing, today known as Beijing (bay-jeeng). He turned westward in 1219 with an invasion of Khwarezm (kaw-REZM), a state east of the Caspian Sea that included much of Iran. After 1221, when most of Iran had fallen, Chinggis left the command of most campaigns to subordinate generals.

Ögödei (ERG-uh-day), Chinggis's son, became the Great Khan in 1227 after his father's death. He completed the destruction of the Tanggut and the Jin and put their territories under Mongol governors. By 1234 he controlled most of northern China and was threatening the Southern Song (see Chapter 11). Two years later Chinggis's grandson Batu (BAH-too) (d. 1255) attacked Russian territories, took control of the towns along the Volga (VOHL-gah) River, and conquered Kievan Russia, Moscow, Poland, and Hungary in a five-year campaign. Only the death of Ögödei in 1241, which caused a suspension of campaigning, saved Europe from invasion. With Chinggis's grandson Güyük (gi-yik) installed as the new Great Khan, the conquests resumed. In the Middle East a Mongol army sacked Baghdad in 1258 and executed the last Abbasid caliph (see Chapter 9).

Chinggis Khan's original objective had probably been collecting tribute, but the success of the Mongol conquests created a new situation. Ögödei unquestionably sought to rule a united empire based at his capital, Karakorum (kah-rah-KOR-um), but after his death family unity began to unravel. The Golden Horde in Russia, the Chagatai (JAH-guh-die) lands in Central Asia, and the Il-khans in Iran were subordinate domains (see Map 12.1); but when Khubilai (KOO-bih-lie) declared himself Great Khan in 1265, the descendants of Chinggis's son Chagatai (d. 1242) and other branches of the family refused to accept him. As Karakorum was destroyed in the ensuing fighting, Khubilai transferred his court to the old Jin capital now renamed Beijing. In 1271 he declared himself founder of the **Yuan Empire**.

Chagatai's descendants continued to dominate Central Asia and enjoyed close relations with the region's Turkish-speaking nomads. This, plus a continuing hatred of Khubilai, contributed to Central

Yuan Empire Empire created in China and Siberia by Khubilai Khan.

Chronology

	Mongolia and China	Central Asia and Middle East	Russia	Korea, Japan, and Southeast Asia
1200	**1206** Temüjin chosen Chinggis Khan of the Mongols	**1219–1223** Invasion of Iran		
	1234 North China seized		**1236** Russia invaded	
		1258 Mongols sack Baghdad		**1258** Mongols conquer Koryo
	1271 Founding of Yuan Empire			
	1279 Southern Song attacked			**1274, 1281** Mongols attack Japan
1300				**1333–1338** End of shogunate
		ca. 1350 Plague in Egypt	**1346** Plague in Kaffa	
	1368 Ming Empire founded			**1392** Korean Choson kingdom
1400		**1453** Ottomans capture Constantinople	**1462–1505** Ivan III tsar	

Asia becoming an independent Mongol center and to the spread of Islam there.

After the Yuan destroyed the Southern Song (see Chapter 11) in 1279, Mongol troops attacked Annam—now northern Vietnam—and in 1283 invaded the kingdom of Champa in southern Vietnam. When the initially successful Mongols suffered a defeat, Khubilai was so infuriated that he postponed an invasion of Japan to focus on the Vietnamese kingdoms. In 1287, the Vietnamese troops, under the command of Tran Hung Dao, Vietnam's most famous military hero, defeated the Mongol forces in a final battle. A plan to invade Java by sea also failed, as did two invasions of Japan in 1274 and 1281.

The Mongols seldom outnumbered their enemies, but they were extraordinary riders and utilized superior bows. The Central Asian bow, made by laminating layers of wood, leather, and bone, could shoot one-third farther (and was correspondingly more difficult to pull) than the bows used by sedentary enemies. Rarely did an archer expend all of the five dozen arrows in his quiver. As the battle opened, arrows shot from a distance decimated enemy marksmen. Then the Mongols charged the enemy's infantry to fight with sword, lance, javelin, and mace. The Mongol cavalry met its match only at the Battle of Ain Jalut (ine jah-LOOT), where an under-strength force confronted Turkish-speaking mamluks whose war techniques matched their own (see Chapter 9).

The Mongols also fired flaming arrows and hurled enormous projectiles—sometimes flaming—from catapults. The original catapults, built on portable Chinese models, had short range and poor accuracy. But during western campaigns in Central Asia, the Mongols encountered a design that was half again as powerful and used it to hammer the cities of Iran and Iraq. Cities that resisted faced slaughter. The terror of certain death was spread by the annihilation of Balkh (bahlk) (in present-day northern Afghanistan) and other cities. Surrender was the only option. Each conquered area contributed men to the "Mongol" armies; in the Middle East, a few Mongol officers commanded armies of recently recruited Turks and Iranians.

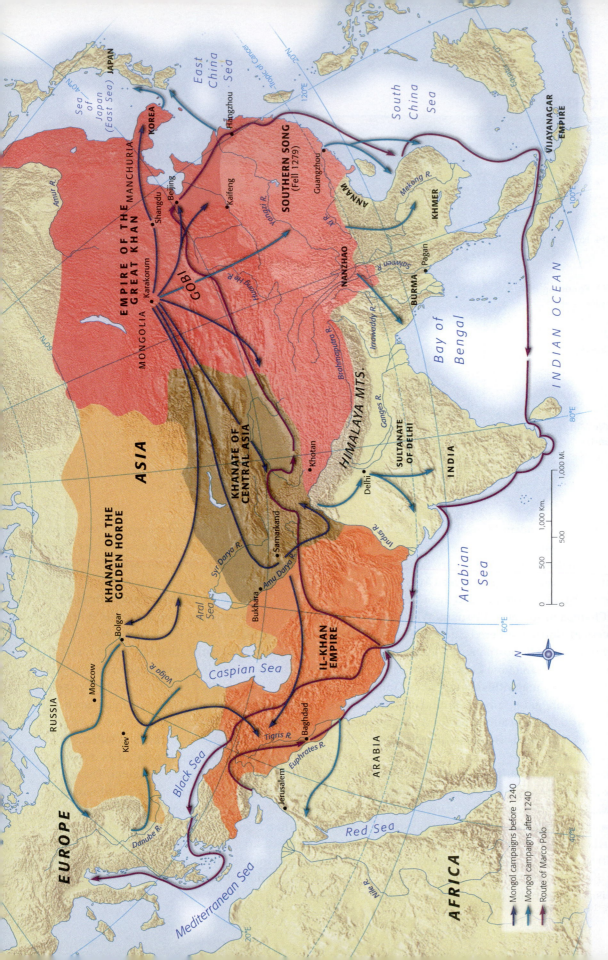

Map 12.1 The Mongol Domains in Eurasia in 1300 After the death of Chinggis Khan in 1227, his empire was divided among his sons and grandsons. Son Ögödei succeeded Chinggis as Great Khan. Grandson Khubilai expanded the domain of the Great Khan into southern China by 1279. Grandson Hülegü was the first Il-khan in the Middle East. Grandson Batu founded the Khanate of the Golden Horde in southern Russia. Son Chagatai ruled the Chagatai Khanate in Central Asia. © Cengage Learning

Mongol campaigns before 1240
Mongol campaigns after 1240
Route of Marco Polo

Overland Trade and Disease

Commercial integration under Mongol rule affected all parts of the empire. Like earlier nomad elites, Mongol nobles had the exclusive right to wear silk, almost all of which came from China. New styles and huge quantities of silk flowed westward to feed the luxury trade in the Middle East and Europe, and artistic motifs from Japan and Tibet reached as far as England and Morocco. Porcelain, another eastern luxury, became important in trade and strongly influenced later tastes in the Islamic world.

Merchants encountered ambassadors, scholars, and missionaries over the long routes to the Mongol courts. Some of the resulting travel literature, like the account of the Venetian Marco Polo (mar-koe POE-loe) (1254–1324), freely mixed the fantastic with the factual. Stories of immense wealth stimulated a European ambition to find easier routes to Asia.

Exchange also spread disease. In the mid-thirteenth century, flea-infested marmots and other rodents became infected and passed their disease to dogs and people. Though other diseases contributed to the mortality of the resulting pandemic, **bubonic plague**, which probably originated in Central Asia, was certainly involved. An earlier theory that southern China was the point of origin seems unlikely as unusually cold Chinese winters from 1344 to 1353 would have impeded the reproduction of fleas. Plague incapacitated the Mongol army during its assault on the city of Kaffa (KAH-fah) in Crimea (cry-MEE-ah) in 1346. They withdrew, but the plague remained. From Kaffa diseased rats carried the fleas to Europe and Egypt by ship (see Chapter 13).

Typhus, influenza, and smallpox traveled the same route. Thus peaceful trade created the "great pandemic" of 1347–1352 and caused deaths far in excess of what the Mongol armies inflicted. Epidemics were exacerbated, however, by the Mongol destruction of dams, irrigation channels, farmland, and crops. By cutting down the trees that helped keep the desert at bay, the Mongols turned large portions of China into the prairie plateaus of the steppe.

> **bubonic plague** A bacterial disease of fleas that can be transmitted by flea bites to rodents and humans; humans in late stages of the illness can spread the bacteria by coughing. Because of its very high mortality rate and the difficulty of preventing its spread, major outbreaks have created crises in many parts of the world.

Passport The Mongol Empire facilitated the movement of products, merchants, and diplomats over long distances. Travelers frequently encountered new languages, laws, and customs. The *paisa* (from a Chinese word for "card" or "sign"), with its inscription in Mongolian, proclaimed that the traveler had the ruler's permission to travel through the region. Europeans later adopted the practice, thus making the *paisa* the ancestor of modern passports. The Metropolitan Museum of Art/Image source/Art Resource, NY

SECTION REVIEW

- The society of the nomadic Mongols functioned through kinship and tribute ties, in which women often played important roles.

- Chinggis Khan began the Mongol conquest to win tribute from Eurasian kingdoms.

- His successors turned to territorial rule, yet internal politics split the empire into smaller states in China and Central Asia.

- The Mongols won territory through superior battle tactics and integrated it into a vast overland commercial network.

- That network allowed the bubonic plague and other diseases to spread across Asia into Europe.

Diversity & Dominance

Observations of Mongol Life

The Mongols, despite the power, geographical extent, and durability of their empire, are known mainly from the observations made by non-Mongols who either traveled in their territory or worked for them. The following passages come from three such authors.

William of Rubruck, a Franciscan friar, journeyed to the court of the Great Khan Mönke in 1253–1255 after living for some period of time in Crusader territory in the Middle East. He carried a letter from the French king, Louis IX (ruled 1226–1270), asking that the friar and a companion be allowed to stay with the Mongols, preach Christianity, and comfort German prisoners. William never made contact with the Germans, but his highly personal observations on Mongol life fascinated European readers.

The dwelling in which they sleep is based on a hoop of interlaced branches, and its supports are made of branches, converging at the top around a smaller hoop, from which projects a neck like a chimney. They cover it with white felt: quite often they also smear the felt with chalk or white clay and ground bones to make it gleam whiter, or sometimes they blacken it. . . . These dwellings are constructed to such a size as to be on occasion thirty feet across: I myself once measured a breadth of twenty feet between the wheeltracks of a wagon, and when the dwelling was on the wagon it protruded beyond the wheels by at least five feet on either side. . . .

The married women make themselves very fine wagons. . . . One rich Mo'al [i.e., Mongol] or Tartar has easily a hundred or two hundred such wagons with chests. Baatu has twenty-six wives, each of whom has a large dwelling, not counting the other, smaller ones placed behind the large one, which are chambers, as it were, where the maids live: to each of these dwellings belong a good two hundred wagons. When they unload the dwellings, the chief wife pitches her residence at the westernmost end, and the others follow according to rank. . . . Hence the court of one wealthy Mo'al will have the appearance of a large town, though there will be very few males in it. . . .

The History of the World-Conqueror by the Iranian historian 'Ata-Malik Juvaini, who worked for the Mongols in Iran, was written in elegant Persian during the 1250s. It combines a glorification of the Mongol rulers with an unflinching picture of the cruelties and devastation inflicted by their conquests.

He [i.e., Chinggis Khan] paid great attention to the chase and used to say that the hunting of wild beasts was a proper occupation for the commanders of armies; and that instruction and training therein was incumbent on warriors and men-at-arms. . . . Whenever the Khan sets out on the great hunt (which takes place at the beginning of the winter season), he issues orders that the troops stationed around his headquarters and in the neighborhood . . . shall make preparation for the chase. . . .

The right wing, left wing and center of the army are drawn up and entrusted to the great emirs; and they set out together with the Royal Ladies and the concubines, as well as provisions of food and drink. For a month, or two, or three they form a hunting ring and drive the game slowly and gradually before them, taking care lest any escape from the ring. . . . Finally . . . the troops come to a halt all around the ring, standing shoulder to shoulder. The ring is now filled with the cries and commotion of every manner of game and the roaring and tumult of every kind of ferocious beast. . . .

When the ring has been so much contracted that the wild beasts are unable to stir, first the Khan rides in together with some of his retinue; then after he has wearied of the sport, they dismount upon high ground in the center . . . to watch the princes likewise entering the ring, and after them, in due order, the noyans [chiefs], the commanders and the troops. Several days pass in this manner; then, when nothing is left of the game but a few wounded and emaciated stragglers, old men and greybeards humbly approach the Khan, offer up prayers for his well-being and intercede for the lives of the remaining animals asking that they be suffered to depart to someplace nearer to grass and water. . . . ➤

> Now war—with its killing, counting of the slain and sparing of the survivors—is after the same fashion, and indeed analogous in every detail, because all that is left in the neighborhood of the battlefield are a few broken-down wretches.

I n 1330 Hu Szu-hui, a physician of Chinese-Turkish family background, presented the Yuan emperor with a manual entitled Proper and Essential Things for the Emperor's Food and Drink. His work reflects both the meat-heavy diet of the steppes and traditional Chinese concern with good nutrition.

Foods That Cure Various Illnesses [60 entries]

Donkey's Head Gruel

It cures apoplexy-vertigo, debility of hand and foot, annoying pain of extremities, and trouble in speaking:

Black donkey's head (one; remove hair and wash clean), black pepper (two measures), tsaoko cardamom (two measures). Cook ingredients until overcooked. Add the five spices in fermented black bean juice. Flavor with the spices. Flavor evenly. Eat on an empty stomach.

Fox Meat Gruel

It cures infantile convulsion, epilepsy, spiritual confusion, indistinct speech, and inappropriate singing and laughing:

Fox meat. (The quantity does not matter. Include organ meat.) [To] ingredient add the five spices according to the regular method. Cook until overcooked. When done eat on an empty stomach.

Bear Meat Gruel

It cures the various winds, foot numbness-insensitivity, and five flaccidities, tendon and muscle spasms:

Bear meat (one measure). [To] ingredient add the five spices in fermented black beans. [Add] onions and sauce. Cook. When done eat on an empty stomach.

Sheep's Stomach Gruel

It cures the various apoplexies:

Sheep's stomach (one; wash clean), non-glutinous rice (two measures), green onions (several), salted fruits, Chinese flower pepper (remove the closed up corns, roast to bring out the juice; 30 corns), sprouting ginger (two measures and a half cut up finely). Combine the six ingredients evenly and put inside the sheep's stomach. Cook until overcooked. When done, flavor with the five spices. Eat on an empty stomach.

Foodstuffs That Mutually Conflict [55 entries]

Horse meat cannot be eaten together with granary rice.

Sheep's liver cannot be eaten together with pepper. It wounds the heart.

Hare meat cannot be eaten together with ginger.

Beef cannot be eaten together with chestnuts.

Mare's milk cannot be eaten together with fish hash. It produces obstruction of the bowels.

Venison cannot be eaten together with catfish.

Beef stomach cannot be eaten together with dog meat.

Quail meat cannot be eaten together with pork. The face will turn black.

Pheasant eggs cannot be eaten together with onions. It produces vermin.

Lettuce cannot be eaten together with cream.

Ground mustard cannot be eaten together with hare meat. It produces sores.

QUESTIONS FOR ANALYSIS

1. How does the subject matter of these passages reveal the different viewpoints of a European, an Iranian, and a Chinese?
2. What in these passages might indicate whether the Mongols were Muslims, Christians, Buddhists, or Confucians?
3. Why would you expect the observations of a traveler to be more or less valuable as historical sources than those of someone who served a Mongol ruler?

Sources: From The Mission of Friar William of Rubruck. His Journey to the Court of the Great Khan Mönke 1253–1255, translated by Peter Jackson, pp. 73–74. Copyright ©1990. From Ata-Malik Juvani's The History of the World Conqueror, translated by Andrew Boyle, pp. 27–29, Cambridge, Mass.: Harvard University Press, Copyright © 1958 by Manchester University Press. Paul D. Buell and Eugene N. Anderson, A Soup for the Qan, 2000, pp. 428–429, 438–440.

THE MONGOLS AND ISLAM, 1260–1500

■ *How did Mongol expansion and Islam affect each other?*

From the perspective of Mongol imperial history, political rivalries determined which branches of the family adopted Islam and which did not. From the standpoint of Islamic history, however, recovery from the devastation that culminated in the destruction of the Abbasid Caliphate in Baghdad in 1258 attests to the vitality of the faith and the ability of Muslims to overcome adversity. Within fifty years of its darkest hour, Islam reemerged as a potent ideological and political force.

Mongol Rivalry   By 1260 the **Il-khan** (IL-con) state, established by Chinggis's grandson Hülegü, controlled Iran, Azerbaijan, Mesopotamia, and parts of Armenia. North of the Caspian Sea the Mongols who had conquered southern Russia established the capital of their Khanate of the **Golden Horde** (also called the Kipchak [KIP-chahk] Khanate) at Sarai (sah-RYE) on the Volga River. Like the Il-khans, they ruled an indigenous Muslim population, mostly Turkish-speaking.

Some members of the Mongol imperial family professed Islam before the Mongol assault on the Middle East, and Turkish Muslims served the family in various capacities. Hülegü himself, though a Buddhist, had a trusted Shi'ite adviser and granted privileges to the Shi'ites. However, the Mongols under Hülegü's command came only slowly to Islam.

Islamic doctrines clashed with Mongol ways. Muslims abhorred the Mongols' worship of Buddhist and shamanist idols. Furthermore, Mongol law specified slaughtering animals without spilling blood, which involved opening the chest and stopping the heart. This horrified Muslims, who were forbidden to consume blood and slaughtered animals by slitting their throats and draining the blood.

Islam became a point of inter-Mongol tension when Batu's successor as leader of the Golden Horde declared himself a Muslim. He swore to avenge the murder of the Abbasid caliph and laid claim to the Caucasus—the mountains between the Black and Caspian Seas—which the Il-khans also claimed.

Some European leaders believed that if they helped the non-Muslim Il-khans repel the Golden Horde from the Caucasus, the Il-khans would help them relieve Muslim pressure on the Crusader principalities in Syria, Lebanon, and Palestine (see Chapter 9). This resulted in a brief correspondence between the Il-khan court and Pope Nicholas IV (r. 1288–1292) and a diplomatic mission that sent two Christian Turks to western Europe as Il-khan ambassadors in the late 1200s. The Golden Horde responded by seeking an alliance with the Muslim mamluks in Egypt (see Chapter 9) against both the Crusaders and the Il-khans. Before the Europeans' diplomatic efforts could bear fruit, a new Il-khan ruler, Ghazan (haz-ZAHN) (1271–1304), declared himself a Muslim in 1295. Conflicting indications of Sunni and Shi'ite affiliation, such as divergent coin inscriptions, indicate that Ghazan had a casual attitude toward theological matters. It is similarly unclear whether the Muslim Turkish nomads who served in his army were Shi'ite or Sunni.

Islam and the State   The Il-khans gradually came to appreciate the traditional urban culture of the Muslim territories they ruled. Nevertheless, they used tax farming to extract maximum wealth from their subjects. The government sold tax-collecting contracts to small partnerships, mostly consisting of merchants who might also finance caravans, small industries, or military expeditions. Whoever offered to collect the most revenue for the government won the contracts. They could use whatever methods they chose and keep anything over the contracted amount.

Tax farming initially lowered administrative costs; but over the long term, the extortions of the tax farmers drove many landowners into debt and servitude. Agricultural productivity declined, making it hard to supply the army. So the government resorted

Il-khan A "secondary" or "peripheral" khan based in Persia. The Il-khans' khanate was founded by Hülegü, a grandson of Chinggis Khan, and was based at Tabriz in the Iranian province of Azerbaijan. It controlled much of Iran and Iraq.

Golden Horde Mongol khanate founded by Chinggis Khan's grandson Batu. It was based in southern Russia and quickly adopted both the Turkish language and Islam. Also known as the Kipchak Horde.

Tomb of Timur in Samarkand The turquoise tiles that cover the dome are typical of Timurid architectural decoration. Timur's family ornamented his capital with an enormous mosque, three large religious colleges facing one another on three sides of an open plaza, and a lane of brilliantly tiled Timurid family tombs in the midst of a cemetery. Timur brought craftsmen to Samarkand from the lands he conquered to build these magnificent structures.

to taking land to grow its own grain. Like property held by religious trusts, this land paid no taxes. Thus the tax base shrank even as the demands of the army and the Mongol nobility continued to grow.

Ghazan faced many economic problems. Citing Islam's humane values, he promised to reduce taxes, but the need for revenue kept the decrease from becoming permanent. The Chinese practice of printing paper money had been tried unsuccessfully by a predecessor. Now it was tried again. This time the experiment pushed the economy into a depression that lasted beyond the end of the Il-khan state in 1349. Mongol nobles competed among themselves for the decreasing revenues, and fighting among Mongol factions destabilized the government.

While the Golden Horde and the Il-khan Empire quarreled, a new power was emerging in the Central Asian Khanate of Chagatai (see Map 12.1). The leader

Timur (TEE-moor), known to Europeans as Tamerlane, maneuvered himself into command of the Chagatai forces and launched campaigns into western Eurasia, apparently seeing himself as a new Chinggis Khan. By ethnic background he was a Turk with only an in-law relationship to the family of the Mongol conqueror. This prevented him from assuming the title *khan*, but not from sacking the Muslim sultanate of Delhi in northern India in 1398 or defeating the sultan of the rising Ottoman Empire in Anatolia in 1402. He was reportedly preparing to march on China when he died in 1405. However, Timur's descendants could not hold the empire together.

Culture and Science in Islamic Eurasia

The Il-khans and Timurids (descendants of Timur) presided over a brilliant cultural flowering in Iran, Afghanistan, and Central Asia based on blending Iranian and Chinese artistic trends and cultural practices. The dominant cultural tendencies were Muslim, however. Timur died before he could reunite Iran and China, but by transplanting Middle Eastern scholars, artists, and craftsmen to his capital, Samarkand, he fostered the cultural achievements of his descendants.

The historian Juvaini (joo-VINE-nee) (d. 1283), who recorded Chinggis Khan's deathbed speech, came from the city of Balkh, which the Mongols had devastated in 1221. His family switched their allegiance to the Mongols, and both Juvaini and his older brother assumed high government posts. The Il-khan Hülegü, seeking to immortalize and justify his conquests, enthusiastically supported Juvaini's writing of the first comprehensive narrative of Chinggis Khan's empire.

Juvaini combined a florid style with historical objectivity, often criticizing the Mongols. This approach served as an inspiration to **Rashid al-Din** (ra-SHEED ad-DEEN), Ghazan's prime minister, when he attempted the first history of the world. Rashid

Timur Member of a prominent family of the Mongols' Chagatai Khanate, Timur through conquest gained control over much of Central Asia and Iran. He consolidated the status of Sunni Islam as orthodox, and his descendants, the Timurids, maintained his empire for nearly a century and founded the Mughal Empire in India.

Rashid al-Din Adviser to the Il-khan ruler Ghazan, who converted to Islam on Rashid's advice.

Robert Harding Picture Library Ltd/Alamy

al-Din's work included the earliest known general history of Europe, derived from conversations with European monks, and a detailed description of China based on information from an important Chinese Muslim official stationed in Iran. The miniature paintings that accompanied some copies of Rashid al-Din's work included depictions of European and Chinese people and events and reflected the artistic traditions of both cultures. The Chinese compositional techniques helped inaugurate the greatest period of Islamic miniature painting under the Timurids. Rashid al-Din traveled widely and collaborated with administrators from other parts of the far-flung Mongol dominions. His idea that government should be in accord with the moral principles of the majority of the population buttressed Ghazan's adherence to Islam.

Under the Timurids, the tradition of the Il-khan historians continued. After conquering Damascus, Timur himself met there with the greatest historian of the age, Ibn Khaldun (ee-bin hal-DOON) (1332–1406), a Tunisian. In a scene reminiscent of Ghazan's answering Rashid al-Din's questions on the history of the Mongols, Timur and Ibn Khaldun exchanged historical, philosophical, and geographical viewpoints. Like Chinggis, Timur saw himself as a world conqueror. At their capitals of Samarkand and Herat (in western Afghanistan), later Timurid rulers sponsored historical writing in both Persian and Chagatai Turkish.

A Shi'ite scholar named **Nasir al-Din Tusi** (nah-SEER ad-DEEN TOO-si) represents the beginning of Mongol interest in the scientific traditions of the Muslim lands. Nasir al-Din may have joined the entourage of Hülegü during a campaign in 1256 against the Assassins, a Shi'ite religious sect derived from the Fatimid dynasty in Egypt and at odds with his more mainstream Shi'ite views (see Chapter 9). Nasir al-Din wrote on history, poetry, ethics, and religion, but he made his most outstanding contributions in mathematics and cosmology. Following Omar Khayyam (oh-mar kie-YAM) (1038?–1131), a poet and mathematician of the Seljuk (SEL-jook) period, he laid new foundations for algebra and trigonometry. Some followers working at an observatory built for Nasir al-Din at Maragheh (mah-RAH-gah), near the Il-khan capital of Tabriz, used the new mathematical techniques to reach a better understanding of celestial orbits.

Observational astronomy and calendar making had engaged the interest of earlier Central Asian rulers, particularly the Uighurs (WEE-ger) and the Seljuks. Under the Il-khans, the astronomers of Maragheh excelled in predicting eclipses, and astrolabes, armillary spheres, three-dimensional quadrants, and other instruments acquired new precision.

These techniques spread worldwide. The remarkably accurate eclipse predictions and tables prepared by Il-khan and Timurid astronomers reached the hostile Mamluk lands in Arabic translation. Byzantine monks took them to Constantinople and translated them into Greek, Christian scholars working in Muslim Spain rendered them into Latin, and in India the sultan of Delhi ordered Sanskrit versions of them. Following one of these routes, the mathematical tables and geometric models of lunar motion devised by one of Nasir al-Din's students somehow became known to Nicholas Copernicus (1473–1543), a Polish monk and astronomer (see Chapter 13). Copernicus adopted this lunar model as his own, virtually without revision, and then proposed it as the proper model for planetary movement as well—but with the planets circling the sun.

The interest in astronomy led to the building of observatories. The Great Khan Khubilai (discussed later in this chapter) summoned a team of Iranians to Beijing to build an observatory for him. Timur's grandson Ulugh Beg (oo-loog bek) (1394–1449), whose avocation was astronomy, constructed a great observatory in Samarkand and actively participated in compiling observational tables that were later translated into Latin and used by European astronomers.

A further advance made under Ulugh Beg came from the mathematician Ghiyas al-Din Jamshid al-Kashi (gee-YASS ad-DIN jam-SHEED al-KAH-shee), who noted that Chinese astronomers had long used one ten-thousandth of a day as a unit in calculating the occurrence of a new moon. This seems to have inspired him to employ decimal notation, by which quantities less than one could be represented by a

Nasir al-Din Tusi Persian mathematician and cosmologist whose academy near Tabriz provided a model for heavenly motions that helped to inspire the Copernican model of the solar system.

SECTION REVIEW

- For the Mongols of the Il-khan and Golden Horde states, Islam became a matter of political rivalry.
- In the Il-khan state Islamic values struggled with economic needs, and the resulting unrest left it open to invasions by Golden Horde Mongols.
- At the same time, Timur took control of the Chagatai territory and began his own imperial conquests.
- Under the Il-khans and Timurids, Iran and Central Asia experienced a flowering of Islamic culture.
- These rulers fostered great achievements in historical writing, literature, art, mathematics, and astronomy.

marker to show place. Al-Kashi's proposed value for *pi* (π) was far more precise than any previously calculated. This innovation arrived in Europe by way of Constantinople, where a Greek translation of al-Kashi's work appeared in the fifteenth century.

REGIONAL RESPONSES IN WESTERN EURASIA

■ *What benefits resulted from the integration of Eurasia into the Mongol Empire?*

Safe, reliable overland trade benefited Mongol ruling centers and commercial cities along the Silk Road. But the countryside, ravaged by conquest, sporadic violence, and heavy taxes, suffered terribly. As Mongol control weakened, regional forces in Russia, eastern Europe, and Anatolia reasserted themselves. Sometimes this meant collaborating with the Mongols; at other times it meant using local ethnic or religious traditions to resist or roll back Mongol influence.

Russia and Rule from Afar

The Golden Horde, a later term for the state established by Chinggis's grandson Batu before 1236, started as a unified state but gradually lost unity as some districts crystallized into smaller khanates. The White Horde, for instance, ruled much of southeastern Russia in the fifteenth century, and the Crimean khanate on the northern shore of the Black Sea succumbed to Russian power only in 1783.

East-west routes across the steppe and north-south routes along the rivers of Russia and Ukraine (you-CRANE) conferred importance on certain trading entrepôts, as they had under Kievan Russia (see Chapter 10). The Golden Horde capital was (Old) Sarai, just north of where the Volga flows into the Caspian Sea (see Map 12.1). The Mongols ruled their Russian domains to the north and east from afar. To facilitate control, they granted privileges to the Orthodox Church, which then helped reconcile the Russian people to their distant masters.

The politics of language played a role in subsequent history. Old Church Slavonic, an ecclesiastical language, revived; but Russian steadily acquired greater importance and eventually became the dominant written language. Russian scholars shunned Byzantine Greek, previously the main written tongue, even after the Golden Horde permitted renewed contacts with Constantinople. The Golden Horde enlisted Russian princes to act as their agents, primarily as tax collectors and census takers.

The flow of silver and gold into Mongol hands starved the local economy of precious metal. Like the Il-khans, the Golden Horde attempted to introduce paper money as a response to the currency shortage. The unsuccessful experiment left such a vivid memory that the Russian word for money (*denga* [DENG-ah]) comes from the Mongolian word for the stamp (*tamga* [TAHM-gah]) used to create paper currency. In reality, commerce depended more on direct exchange of goods than on currency transactions.

Alexander Nevskii (nih-EFF-skee) (ca. 1220–1263), the prince of Novgorod, persuaded some fellow princes to submit to the Mongols. In return, the Mongols favored both Novgorod and the emerging town of Moscow, ruled by Alexander's son Daniel. As these towns eclipsed devastated Kiev as political, cultural, and economic centers, they drew people northward to open new agricultural land far from the Mongol steppes. Decentralization continued in the 1300s, with Moscow only very gradually becoming Russia's dominant political center.

In appraising the Mongol era, some historians stress Mongol destructiveness and brutality in tax collecting. Ukraine, a fertile and well-populated region in

Alexander Nevskii Prince of Novgorod (r. 1236–1263). He submitted to the invading Mongols in 1240 and received recognition as the leader of the Russian princes under the Golden Horde.

the late Kievan period (1000–1230), suffered severe population loss from these sources. Isolated from developments to the west, Russia and parts of eastern Europe are portrayed as suffering under the "Mongol yoke."

Other historians point out that even before the Mongols struck, Kiev had declined economically and ceased to mint coins. Yet the Russian territories regularly paid the heavy Mongol taxes in silver, indicating both economic surpluses and an ability to convert goods into cash. The burdensome taxes stemmed less from the Mongols than from their tax collectors, Russian princes who often exempted their own lands and shifted the load to the peasants.

As for Russia's cultural isolation, skeptics observe that before the Mongol invasion, the powerful and constructive role played by the Orthodox Church oriented Russia primarily toward Byzantium (see Chapter 10). Although this situation did not eliminate contacts with western Europe, repeated wars with the expanding Catholic principality of Lithuania on Russia's western border discouraged extensive relations.

The traditional structure of local government survived Mongol rule, as did the Russian princely families, who continued to battle among themselves for dominance. The Mongols merely added a new player to those struggles. Ivan (ee-VAHN) III, the prince of Moscow (r. 1462–1505), established himself as an autocratic ruler in the late 1400s. Before Ivan, the title **tsar** (from *caesar*), of Byzantine origin, applied only to foreign rulers, whether the emperors of Byzantium or the Turkish khans of the steppe. Ivan's use of the title probably represents an effort to establish a basis for legitimate rule with the decline of the Golden Horde and the disappearance of the Byzantine Empire.

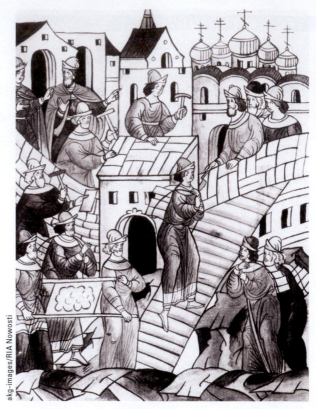

akg-images/RIA Nowosti

Transformation of the Kremlin Like other northern Europeans, the Russians preferred to build in wood, which was easy to handle and comfortable to live in. But they fortified important political centers with stone ramparts. In the 1300s, the city of Moscow emerged as a new capital, and its old wooden palace, the Kremlin, was gradually transformed into a stone structure.

New States in Eastern Europe and Anatolia

Anatolia and parts of Europe responded dynamically to the Mongol challenges. Raised in Sicily, the Holy Roman Emperor Frederick II (r. 1212–1250) appreciated Muslim culture and did not recoil from negotiating with Muslims. When the pope threatened to excommunicate him unless he waged a crusade, Frederick nominally regained Jerusalem through a flimsy treaty with the Mamluk sultan in Egypt. Dissatisfied, the pope continued to quarrel with the emperor, leaving Hungary, Poland, and Lithuania to deal with the Mongol onslaught on their own. Many princes capitulated and went to (Old) Sarai to offer their submission to Batu.

However, the Teutonic (two-TOHN-ik) Knights resisted. These German-speaking warriors sought to Christianize the pagan populations of northern Europe and colonize their territories with German settlers. They also fought against other Christians. To protect Slav territory, Alexander Nevskii joined the Mongols in fighting the Teutonic Knights and their Finnish allies. The latter suffered a catastrophe in 1242, when many broke through an icy northern lake and drowned. This event destroyed the power of the Knights, and the northern Crusades virtually ceased.

tsar (czar) From Latin *caesar*, this Russian title for a monarch was first used in reference to a Russian ruler by Ivan III (r. 1462–1505).

The "Mongol" armies encountered by the Europeans consisted mostly of Turks, Chinese, Iranians, a few Europeans, and at least one Englishman, who went to crusade in the Middle East but joined the Mongols and served in Hungary. But most commanders were Mongol.

Initial wild theories describing the Mongols as coming from Hell or from caves where Alexander the Great confined monsters gradually yielded to a more sophisticated understanding as European embassies to Mongol courts returned with reliable intelligence. In some quarters terror gave way to appreciation. Europeans learned about diplomatic passports, coal mining, movable type, high-temperature metallurgy, higher mathematics, gunpowder, and, in the fourteenth century, the casting and use of bronze cannon. Yet with the outbreak of bubonic plague in the late 1340s, the memory of Mongol terror helped ignite religious speculation that God might again be punishing the Christians (see Chapter 13).

In the fourteenth century several regions, most notably Lithuania (lith-oo-WAY-nee-ah), escaped the Mongol grip. When Russia fell to the Mongols, Lithuania had experienced an unprecedented centralization and military strengthening. Like Alexander Nevskii, the Lithuanian leaders maintained their independence by cooperating with the Mongols. In the late 1300s Lithuania capitalized on its privileged position to dominate Poland and ended the Teutonic Knights' hope of regaining power.

In the Balkans independent kingdoms separated themselves from the chaos of the Byzantine Empire and thrived amidst the political uncertainties of the Mongol period. The Serbian king Stephen Dushan (ca. 1308–1355) proved the most effective leader. Seizing power from his father in 1331, he took advantage of Byzantine weakness to turn the archbishop of Serbia into an independent patriarch. In 1346 the patriarch crowned him "tsar and autocrat of the Serbs, Greeks, Bulgarians, and Albanians," a title that fairly represents the wide extent of his rule. As in the case of Timur, however, his kingdom declined after his death in 1355 and disappeared entirely after a defeat by the Ottomans at the battle of Kosovo in 1389.

The Turkish nomads whose descendants established the **Ottoman Empire** came to Anatolia in the same wave of Turkish migrations as the Seljuks (see

SECTION REVIEW

- Mongol conquest devastated Kievan Russia, but the Russian language acquired greater importance, and many Russian traditions survived.

- Mongol conquest prompted decentralization of Russian power away from Kiev, but the Golden Horde's decline set the stage for the rise of the Russian autocracy.

- The decline of Mongol power and Byzantine weakness enabled the rise of Lithuania and Serbia in eastern Europe and of the Ottoman Empire in Anatolia.

Chapter 9). Though Il-khan influence was strong in eastern Anatolia, a number of small Turkish principalities emerged in the west. The Ottoman principality was situated in the northwest, close to the Sea of Marmara. This location not only put the Ottomans in a position to cross into Europe and take part in the dynastic struggles of the declining Byzantine state, but it also attracted Muslim religious warriors who wished to do battle with Christians on the frontiers. The defeat of the Ottoman sultan by Timur in 1402 was only a temporary setback. In 1453 Sultan Mehmet II captured Constantinople and brought the Byzantine Empire to an end.

The Ottoman sultans, like the rulers of Russia, Lithuania, and Serbia, seized opportunities that arose with the decay of Mongol power. The powerful states they created put strong emphasis on religious and linguistic identity, factors that the Mongols themselves did not stress. As we shall see, Mongol rule stimulated similar reactions in the lands of East and Southeast Asia.

MONGOL DOMINATION IN CHINA, 1271–1368

■ *How did Mongol rule in China foster cultural and scientific exchange?*

After conquering northern China in the 1230s, Great Khan Ögödei told a Confucian adviser that he

Ottoman Empire Islamic state founded by Osman in northwestern Anatolia around 1300. After the fall of the Byzantine Empire, the Ottoman Empire was based at Istanbul (formerly Constantinople) from 1453 to 1922. It encompassed lands in the Middle East, North Africa, the Caucasus, and eastern Europe.

planned to turn the heavily populated North China Plain into a pasture for livestock. The adviser reacted calmly but argued that taxing the cities and villages would bring greater wealth. The Great Khan agreed, but he imposed an oppressive tax-farming system instead of the fixed-rate method traditional to China.

The Chinese suffered under this system during the early years, but the Yuan Empire, established by Chinggis Khan's grandson Khubilai in 1271, also brought benefits: secure trade routes, exchange of experts between eastern and western Eurasia, and transmission of information, ideas, and skills.

The Yuan Empire, 1271–1368

The Yuan sought a fruitful synthesis of the Mongol and Chinese traditions. **Khubilai Khan** gave his oldest son a Chinese name and had Confucians participate in the boy's education. In public announcements and the crafting of laws, he took Confucian conventions into consideration, while Buddhist and Daoist leaders who visited the Great Khan came away believing that they had all but convinced him of their beliefs.

Buddhist priests from Tibet called **lamas** (LAH-mah) became popular with some Mongol rulers. Their idea of a militant universal ruler bringing the whole world under control of the Buddha and thus pushing it nearer to salvation mirrored an ancient Inner Asian idea of universal rulership.

Beijing, the Yuan capital, became the center of cultural and economic life. Karakorum had been geographically remote, but Beijing served as the eastern terminus of caravan routes that began near Tabriz, the Il-khan capital, and (Old) Sarai, the Golden Horde capital. A horseback courier system utilizing hundreds of stations maintained communications along routes that were generally safe for travelers. Ambassadors and merchants arriving in Beijing found a city that was much more Chinese in character than Karakorum had been.

Called Great Capital (Dadu) or City of the Khan (khan-balikh [kahn-BAL-ik], Marco Polo's "Cambaluc"), Khubilai's capital included the Forbidden City, a closed imperial complex with wide streets and a network of linked lakes and artificial islands. In summer, Khubilai practiced riding and shooting at a palace and park in Inner Mongolia. This was Shangdu (shahng-DOO), the "Xanadu" (ZAH-nah-doo) with its "stately pleasure dome" celebrated by the English poet Samuel Taylor Coleridge.

Before the Mongols reunited the country, three separate states with different languages, writing systems, forms of government, and elite cultures competed in China (see Chapter 11). The Tanggut and Jin Empires controlled the north, and the Southern Song controlled most of the area south of the Yellow River. The Great Khans destroyed all three, encouraging the restoration or preservation of many features of Chinese government and society and organizing China into provinces where the appointment of provincial governors systematized control in all parts of the country.

The Mongol-ruled Yuan state was cosmopolitan, attracting many non-Chinese who helped the Mongols govern China. By law, Mongols ranked highest. Below them came Central Asians and Middle Easterners, then northern Chinese, and finally southern Chinese. This ranking reflected a hierarchy of functions. The Mongols were the empire's warriors, the Central Asians and Middle Easterners its census takers and tax collectors. The northern Chinese outranked the southern Chinese because they came under Mongol control almost two generations earlier.

Confucian culture was still promoted in the Yuan Empire. Chinese "Confucians" (under the Yuan, a formal and hereditary status) were reactionary: they fared poorly in securing government appointments, and they also disparaged the merchants in China, many of whom were from the Middle East or Central Asia, as well as physicians, who took Muslim and Hellenistic approaches to medicine. Nevertheless, Confucian education, dress, and rituals were adopted all the way to the newly acquired Yunnan (YOON-nahn), where Sayyid Ajall Shams al-Din (SAY-id a-JELL Shams ad-DEEN), a Muslim governor from Central Asia, was creating a vibrant trade between Tibet, Burma, the Vietnamese kingdoms, and China.

Khubilai Khan Last of the Mongol Great Khans (r. 1260–1294) and founder of the Yuan Empire.

lama In Tibetan Buddhism, a teacher.

Beijing China's northern capital, first used as an imperial capital in 906 and now the capital of the People's Republic of China.

The reintegration of East Asia (though not Japan) with the overland Eurasian trade, which had lapsed with the fall of the Tang (see Chapter 11), stimulated the urban economies. Many cities prospered: in north China by being on the caravan routes; in the interior by being on the Grand Canal; and along the coast by participation in maritime grain shipments from south China. With merchants a privileged group and so few government posts open to the old Chinese elite, many families that had previously spent fortunes on educating sons for government service now went into commerce. Corporations—investor groups that behaved as single commercial and legal units and shared the risk of doing business—handled most economic activities, starting with financing caravans and expanding into tax farming and lending money to the Mongol aristocracy. Central Asians and Middle Easterners headed most corporations in the early Yuan period; but as Chinese bought shares, many acquired mixed membership, or even complete Chinese ownership.

Many gentry families moved from their traditional homes in the country into the city. City life increasingly catered to the tastes of merchants instead of scholars. Specialized shops selling clothing, grape wine, furniture, and religiously butchered meats became common. Teahouses offered sing-song girls, drum singers, operas, and other entertainments previously considered coarse. Writers published works in the style of everyday speech. And the increasing influence of the northern, Mongolian-influenced Chinese language, often called Mandarin in the West, resulted in lasting linguistic change.

Cottage industries linked to the urban economies dotted the countryside, where 90 percent of the people lived. Some villages cultivated mulberry trees and cotton using dams, water wheels, and irrigation systems patterned in part on Middle Eastern models. Treatises on planting, harvesting, threshing, and butchering were published. One technological innovator, Huang Dao Po (hwahng DOW poh), brought knowledge of cotton growing, spinning, and weaving from her native Hainan Island to the fertile Yangzi Delta.

But the agricultural base had been damaged by war, overtaxation, and the passage of armies and could not satisfy the financial needs of the Mongol aristocracy. The countryside did poorly during the Yuan period. Initially, the Mongol princes evicted many farmers and subjected the rest to brutal tax collection. By the time the Yuan shifted to lighter taxes and encouragement of farming at the end of the 1200s, it was too late. Servitude or homelessness had overtaken many farmers, and neglect of dams and dikes caused disastrous flooding, particularly on the Yellow River.

Following earlier precedent, the imperial government made up the financial shortfall with paper money. But people doubted the value of the notes, which were unsecured. Copper coinage partially offset the failure of the paper currency. During the Song, exports of copper to Japan, where the metal was scarce, had caused a severe shortage in China, leading to a rise in the value of copper in relation to silver. By cutting off trade with Japan, the Mongols stabilized the value of copper coins.

According to Song records from before the Mongol conquest and the Ming census taken after their overthrow—each, of course, subject to inaccuracy or exaggeration—China's population may have shrunk by 40 percent during eighty years of Mongol rule, with many localities in northern China losing up to five-sixths of their inhabitants. Scholars have suggested several causes: prolonged warfare, rural distress causing people to resort to female infanticide, epidemics, a southward flight of refugees, and flooding on the Yellow River. The last helps explain why losses in the north exceeded those in the south and why the population along the Yangzi River markedly increased.

The Fall of the Yuan Empire

In the 1340s strife broke out among the Mongol princes. Within twenty years farmer rebellions and inter-Mongol feuds engulfed the land. Amidst the chaos, a charismatic Chinese leader, Zhu Yuanzhang (JOO yuwen-JAHNG), mounted a campaign that destroyed the Yuan Empire and brought China under control of his new empire, the Ming, in 1368. Many Mongols—as well as the Muslims, Jews, and Christians who had come with them—remained in China. Most of their descendants took Chinese names and became part of the diverse cultural world of China.

Many other Mongols, however, who had never moved out of their home territories in Mongolia, now

SECTION REVIEW

- The Great Khans reunified China, expanded its borders, and fostered a synthesis of ideas and cultural traditions.

- Khubilai Khan made Beijing the capital of the Yuan Empire and presided over a social hierarchy with Mongols at the top and southern Chinese at the bottom.

- Mongol rule systematized government, but cities benefited more from Mongol policies than did the countryside.

- Mongol-protected trade routes encouraged a steady exchange of scientific and cultural ideas.

- China's population shrank as a result of Mongol conquest and rule.

- Internal strife weakened the Yuan Empire, which fell to the Ming in 1368, but many Mongols remained in China.

welcomed back refugees from the Yuan collapse. Though Turkish peoples were becoming predominant in the steppe regions in the west, including territories still ruled by descendants of Chinggis Khan, Mongols continued to predominate in Inner Asia, the steppe regions bordering on Mongolia. Some Mongol groups adopted Islam; others favored Tibetan Buddhism. But religious affiliation proved less important than Mongol identity in fostering a renewed sense of unity.

The Ming thus fell short of dominating all the Mongols. The Mongols of Inner Asia paid tribute to the extent that doing so facilitated their trade. Other Mongols, however, remained a continuing threat on the northern Ming frontier.

THE EARLY MING EMPIRE, 1368–1500

■ *In what ways did the Ming Empire continue or discontinue Mongol practices?*

Historians of China, like historians of Russia and Iran, divide over the overall impact of the Mongol era. Since the **Ming Empire** reestablished many practices that are seen as purely Chinese, it receives praise from people who ascribe central importance to Chinese traditions. On the other hand, historians who look upon the Mongol era as a pivotal historical moment when communication across the vast interior of Eurasia served to bring east and west together

sometimes see the inward-looking Ming as less productive than the Yuan.

Ming China on a Mongol Foundation

Zhu Yuanzhang, a former monk, soldier, and bandit, had watched his parents and other family members die of famine and disease, conditions he blamed on Mongol misrule. During the Yuan Empire's chaotic last decades, he vanquished rival rebels and assumed imperial power under the name Hongwu (r. 1368–1398).

Hongwu moved the capital to Nanjing (nahn-JING) ("southern capital") on the Yangzi River, turning away from the Mongols' Beijing ("northern capital"; see Map 12.2). Though Zhu Yuanzhang the rebel had espoused a radical Buddhist belief in a coming age of salvation, once in power he used Confucianism to depict the emperor as the champion of civilization and virtue.

Hongwu choked off relations with Central Asia and the Middle East and imposed strict limits on imports and foreign visitors. Silver replaced paper money for tax payments and commerce. These practices, illustrative of an anti-Mongol ideology, proved as economically unwise as some of the Yuan economic policies and did not last. Eventually, the Ming government came to resemble the Yuan. Ming rulers retained the provincial structure and continued to observe the hereditary professional categories of the Yuan period. Muslims made calendars and astronomical calculations at a new observatory at Nanjing, a replica of Khubilai's at Beijing. The Mongol calendar continued in use.

Continuities with the Yuan became more evident after an imperial prince seized power through a coup d'état to rule as the emperor **Yongle** (yoong-LAW) (r. 1403–1424). He returned the capital to Beijing,

Ming Empire Empire based in China that Zhu Yuanzhang established after the overthrow of the Yuan Empire. The Ming emperor Yongle sponsored the building of the Forbidden City and the voyages of Zheng He. The later years of the Ming saw a slowdown in technological development and economic decline.

Yongle The third emperor of the Ming Empire (r. 1403–1424). He sponsored the building of the Forbidden City, a huge encyclopedia project, the expeditions of Zheng He, and the reopening of China's borders to trade and travel.

Map 12.2 The Ming Empire and Its Allies, 1368–1500 The Ming Empire controlled China but had a hostile relationship with peoples in Mongolia and Inner Asia who had been under the rule of the Mongol Yuan emperors. Mongol attempts at conquest by sea were continued by the Ming mariner Zheng He. Between 1405 and 1433 he sailed to Southeast Asia and then beyond, to India, the Persian Gulf, and East Africa. © Cengage Learning

enlarging and improving Khubilai's Forbidden City, which now acquired its present features: moats, orange-red outer walls, golden roofs, and marble bridges. Yongle intended this combination fortress, religious site, bureaucratic center, and imperial residential park to overshadow Nanjing, and it survives today as China's most imposing traditional architectural complex.

Yongle also restored commercial links with the Middle East. Because hostile Mongols still controlled much of the caravan route, Yongle explored maritime connections. In Southeast Asia, Annam became a Ming province as the early emperors continued

the Mongol program of aggression. This focus on the southern frontier helped inspire the naval expeditions of the trusted imperial eunuch **Zheng He** (JEHNG HUH) from 1405 to 1433.

A Muslim eunuch whose father and grandfather had made the pilgrimage to Mecca, Zheng He had a good knowledge of the Middle East; and his religion

Zheng He An imperial eunuch and Muslim, entrusted by the Ming emperor Yongle with a series of state voyages that took his gigantic ships through the Indian Ocean, from Southeast Asia to Africa.

eased relations with the states of the Indian subcontinent, where he directed his first three voyages. Subsequent expeditions reached Hormuz on the Persian Gulf, sailed the southern coast of Arabia and the Horn of Africa (modern Somalia), and possibly reached as far south as the Strait of Madagascar.

On early voyages Zheng He visited long-established Chinese merchant communities in Southeast Asia to cement their allegiance to the Ming Empire and collect taxes. When a community on the island of Sumatra resisted, he slaughtered the men to set an example. The expeditions added some fifty new tributary states to the Ming imperial universe, but trade did not increase as dramatically. Sporadic embassies reached Beijing from rulers in India, the Middle East, Africa, and Southeast Asia. During one visit the ruler of Brunei (broo-NYE) died and received a grand burial at the Chinese capital. The expeditions stopped in the 1430s after the deaths of Yongle and Zheng He.

Why did the Chinese not develop seafaring for commercial and military gain? Contemporaries considered the voyages a personal project of Yongle, an upstart ruler who had always sought to prove his worthiness. Building the Forbidden City in Beijing and sponsoring gigantic encyclopedia projects might be taken to reflect a similar character. Yongle may also have been emulating Khubilai Khan's sea expeditions against Japan and Southeast Asia. This would fit with the rumor spread by Yongle's political enemies that he was actually a Mongol.

A less speculative approach starts with the fact that the new commercial opportunities fell short of expectations, despite bringing foreign nations into the Ming orbit. In the meantime, Japanese coastal piracy intensified, and Mongol threats in the north and west grew. The human and financial demands of fortifying the north, redesigning and strengthening Beijing, and outfitting campaigns against the Mongols ultimately took priority over the quest for maritime empire.

Technology and Population

The Ming government limited mining, partly to maintain the value of metal coins and partly to tax the industry. As a consequence, metal implements became more expensive for farmers. Techniques for making the high-quality bronze and steel used for weapons also declined, and Japan quickly surpassed China in the production of extremely high-quality swords.

After the death of Emperor Yongle in 1424, shipbuilding skills deteriorated, and few advances occurred in printing, timekeeping, and agricultural technology. Agricultural production peaked around the mid-1400s and remained level for more than a century. New weaving techniques did appear, but technological development in this field had peaked by 1500.

Reactivation of the examination system for recruiting government officials (see Chapter 11) drew large numbers of ambitious men into a renewed study of the Confucian classics. This change reduced the vitality of commerce, where they had previously been employed, just as population growth was creating a labor surplus. Records indicating a growth from 60 million at the end of the Yuan period in 1368 to nearly 100 million by 1400 may not be entirely reliable, but rapid population growth encouraged the production of staples—wheat, millet, and barley in the north and rice in the south—at the expense of commercial crops such as cotton that had stimulated many technological innovations under the Song. Staple crops yielded lower profits, which further discouraged capital improvements. New foods, such as sweet potatoes from the Western Hemisphere, became available but were little adopted. Population growth in southern and central China caused deforestation and raised the price of wood.

Against the Mongol horsemen in the north the Ming used scattershot mortars, explosive canisters, and a few cannon from contacts with the Middle East and later with Europeans. But shipyards and ports shut down to avoid Japanese pirates and prevent Chinese from migrating to Southeast Asia. Fearing a loss of technological secrets, the government also censored the chapters on gunpowder and guns in early Ming encyclopedias. Korea and Japan moved ahead of China—Japan in steel and Korea in the design and production of firearms and ships, in printing techniques, and in the sciences of weather prediction and calendar making. The desire to tap the wealthy Ming market spurred some of these advances.

The Ming Achievement

In the late 1300s and the 1400s the wealth and consumerism of the early Ming stimulated high achievement in literature, the decorative arts, and painting. The plain writing of the Yuan period had produced some of the world's earliest novels. This genre flourished under the Ming: in *Water Margin*, which originated in the raucous drum-song performances loosely related to Chinese opera, and in *Romance of the Three Kingdoms*, which describes the attempts of an upright but doomed war leader and his followers to restore the Han Empire of ancient times and resist the power of the cynical but brilliant villain. *Romance of the Three Kingdoms* and *Water Margin* express the militant but joyous pro-China sentiment of the early Ming era and remain among the most appreciated Chinese fictional works.

Probably the best-known product of Ming technological advance was porcelain. The imperial ceramic works at Jingdezhen (JING-deh-JUHN) experimented with new production techniques and new ways of organizing workers and dividing up jobs. "Ming ware," a blue-on-white style developed in the 1400s from Indian, Central Asian, and Middle Eastern motifs, became especially prized. Other Ming goods in high demand included furniture, lacquered screens, and silk, all of which found ready markets in Southeast Asia and the Pacific, India, the Middle East, and East Africa.

CENTRALIZATION AND MILITARISM IN EAST ASIA, 1200–1500

■ *What are some of the similarities and differences in how Korea and Japan responded to the Mongol threat?*

Korea, Japan, and Annam, the other major states of East Asia, were all affected by confrontation with the Mongols, but with differing results. Japan and Annam escaped Mongol conquest, becoming more effective and expansive regimes with enhanced commitments to independence. Korea revitalized interest in its own language and history. Though the Mongols conquered Korea after a difficult war that resulted in much Korean suffering, members of the Korean elite associated closely with the Yuan Empire. After the fall of the Yuan, merchants continued the international connections established in the Mongol period, while Korean armies consolidated a new kingdom and fended off pirates.

Korea from the Mongols to the Choson Dynasty, 1231–1500

Korea had been the answer to the Mongols' search for coastal areas from which to launch naval expeditions and choke off the sea trade of their adversaries. When the Mongols attacked in 1231, the Choe family assumed the role of military commander and protector of the Koryo (KAW-ree-oh) king (not unlike the shoguns of Japan). The Choe's refusal to sue for peace, or emerge from their capital on Kanghwa Island to drive the Mongols from the Korean peninsula, led to widespread misery among the populace and frustration among military men and nobles alike. The last of the Choe commanders was killed by his underlings in 1258. Soon afterward the king surrendered to the Mongols and became a subject monarch by linking his family to the Great Khan by marriage.

By the mid-1300s the Koryo kings were of mostly Mongol descent and favored Mongol dress, customs, and language. The kings, their families, and their entourages often traveled between China and Korea, thus exposing Korea to the philosophical and artistic styles of Yuan China: neo-Confucianism, Chan Buddhism (called Son in Korea), and celadon (light green) pottery.

Mongol control broke down centuries of comparative isolation. Cotton was introduced in southern Korea; gunpowder came into use; and the art of calendar making stimulated astronomical observation and mathematics. Avenues of advancement opened for Korean scholars willing to learn Mongolian, landowners willing to open their lands to falconry and grazing, and merchants servicing the new royal exchanges with Beijing. These developments contributed to the rise of a new landed and educated class.

When the Yuan Empire fell in 1368, the Koryo ruling family remained loyal to the Mongols until a rebellious general, Yi Songgye (YEE SONG-gye), forced it to recognize the new Ming Empire. In 1392, Yi Songgye established a new kingdom called **Choson (Cho-sun)** with a capital in Seoul and sought to reestablish a distinctive Korean identity. Like Russia and Ming China, the Choson regime publicly rejected the period of Mongol domination. Yet the Choson government continued to employ Mongol-style land surveys, taxation in kind, and military garrison techniques.

Like the Ming emperors, the Choson kings revived the study of the Confucian classics, an activity that required knowledge of Chinese and showed the dedication of the state to learning. This revival may have led to a key technological breakthrough in printing technology. Koreans had begun using Chinese woodblock printing in the 700s. This technology worked well in China, where a large number of buyers wanted copies of a comparatively small number of texts. But in Korea, the comparatively few literate men had interests in a wide range of texts. Movable wooden or ceramic type appeared in Korea in the early thirteenth century and may have been invented there. But the texts were frequently inaccurate and difficult to read. In the 1400s Choson printers, working directly with the king, developed a reliable device to anchor the pieces of type to the printing plate: they replaced the old beeswax adhesive with solid copper frames. This innovation improved the legibility of the printed page, and high-volume, accurate production became possible. Combined with the phonetic *han'gul* (HAHN-goor) writing system, this printing technology laid the foundation for a high literacy rate in Korea.

Choson publications told readers how to produce and use fertilizer, transplant rice seedlings, and engineer reservoirs. Building on Eurasian knowledge imported by the Mongols and introduced under the Koryo, Choson scholars developed a meteorological science of their own. They invented or redesigned instruments to measure wind speed and rainfall and perfected a calendar based on minute comparisons of the Chinese and Islamic systems.

In agriculture, farmers expanded the cultivation of cash crops, the reverse of what was happening in Ming China. Cotton, the primary crop, enjoyed such high value that the state accepted it for tax payments.

SSPL/The Image Works

Movable Type The improvement of cast bronze tiles, each showing a single character, eliminated the need to cast or carve whole pages. Individual tiles—the ones shown are Korean—could be moved from page frame to page frame and gave an even and pleasing appearance. All parts of East Asia eventually adopted this form of printing for cheap, popular books. In the mid-1400s Korea also experimented with a fully phonetic form of writing, which in combination with movable type allowed Koreans unprecedented levels of literacy and access to printed works.

The Choson army used cotton uniforms, and cotton became the favored fabric of the Korean elite. With cotton gins and spinning wheels powered by water, Korea advanced more rapidly than China in mechanization and began to export considerable amounts of cotton to China and Japan.

Although both the Yuan and the Ming withheld the formula for gunpowder from the Korean government, Korean officials acquired the information by subterfuge. By the later 1300s they had mounted

Choson The Choson dynasty ruled Korea from the fall of the Koryo kingdom to the colonization of Korea by Japan.

Defending Japan Japanese warriors board Mongol warships with swords to prevent the landing of the invasion force in 1281.

The Granger Collection, New York

cannon on ships that patrolled against pirates and used gunpowder-driven arrow launchers against enemy personnel and the rigging of enemy ships. Combined with skills in armoring ships, these techniques made the small Choson navy a formidable defense force.

Political Transformation in Japan, 1274–1500

Having secured Korea, the Mongols looked toward Japan, a target they could easily reach from Korea. Their first 30,000-man invasion force in 1274 included Mongol cavalry and archers and sailors from Korea and northeastern Asia. Its weaponry included light catapults and incendiary and explosive projectiles of Chinese manufacture. The Mongol forces landed successfully and decimated the Japanese cavalry, but a great storm on Hakata (HAH-kah-tah) Bay on the north side of Kyushu (KYOO-shoo) Island prevented the establishment of a beachhead and forced the Mongols to sail back to Korea.

The invasion hastened social and political changes that were already under way. Under the Kamakura (kah-mah-KOO-rah) Shogunate established in 1185—a different powerful family actually exercised control—the shogun, or military leader, distributed land and privileges to his followers. In return they paid him tribute and supplied him with soldiers. This stable, but decentralized, system depended on balancing the power of regional warlords. Lords in

the north and east of Japan's main island were remote from those in the south and west. Beyond devotion to the emperor and the shogun, little united them until the terrifying Mongol threat materialized.

After the return of his fleet, Khubilai sent envoys to Japan demanding submission. Japanese leaders executed them and prepared for war. The shogun took steps to centralize his military government, effectively increasing the influence of warlords from the south and west of Honshu (Japan's main island) and from the island of Kyushu, where invasion seemed most likely.

Military planners studied Mongol tactics and retrained and outfitted Japanese warriors for defense against advanced weaponry. Farm laborers drafted from all over the country constructed defensive fortifications. This effort demanded, for the first time, a national system to move resources toward western points rather than toward the imperial or shogunal centers to the east.

The Mongols attacked again in 1281. They brought 140,000 warriors, including many non-Mongols, as well as thousands of horses, in hundreds of ships. However, the wall the Japanese had built to cut off Hakata Bay from the mainland deprived the Mongol forces of a reliable landing point. Japanese swordsmen rowed out and boarded the Mongol ships lingering offshore. Their superb steel swords shocked the invaders. After a prolonged standoff, a typhoon struck and sank perhaps half of the Mongol ships. An epidemic decimated the remaining Mongol troops. What was left of them sailed away, never again to harass Japan. Religious institutions later claimed that their prayers for help brought a "divine wind"— *kamikaze* (kah-me-kah-zay)—that drove away the Mongols.

Nevertheless, the Mongol threat continued to influence Japanese development. Prior to his death in 1294, Khubilai had in mind a third invasion. His successors did not carry through with it, but the shoguns did not know that the Mongols had given up. They rebuilt coastal defenses well into the fourteenth century, helping to consolidate the social position of Japan's warrior elite and stimulating the development of a national infrastructure for trade and communication. But the Kamakura Shogunate, based on regionally collected and regionally dispersed revenues, suffered financial strain in trying to pay for centralized road and defense systems.

Between 1333 and 1338 the emperor Go-Daigo broke the centuries-old tradition of imperial seclusion and aloofness from government and tried to reclaim power from the shoguns. This ignited a civil war that destroyed the Kamakura system. In 1338, with the Mongol threat waning, the **Ashikaga** (ah-shee-KAH-gah) **Shogunate** took control at the imperial center of Kyoto.

Provincial warlords enjoyed renewed independence. Around their imposing castles, they sponsored the development of market towns, religious institutions, and schools. The application of technologies imported in earlier periods, including water wheels, improved plows, and Champa rice, increased agricultural productivity. Growing wealth and relative peace stimulated artistic creativity, mostly reflecting Zen Buddhist beliefs held by the warrior elite. In the simple elegance of architecture and gardens, in the ritual of the tea ceremony, and in the eerie, stylized performances of the Noh theater and the contemplative landscapes of artists, the aesthetic code of Zen became established in the Ashikaga era.

Despite the technological advancement, artistic productivity, and rapid urbanization of this period, competition among warlords and their followers led to regional wars. By the later 1400s these conflicts resulted in the near destruction of the warlords. The great Onin War in 1477 left Kyoto devastated and the Ashikaga Shogunate a central government in name only. Ambitious but low-ranking warriors, some with links to trade with the continent, began to scramble for control of the provinces.

After the fall of the Yuan in 1368, Japan resumed overseas trade, exporting raw materials and swords, as well as folding fans, invented in Japan during the period of isolation. Japan's primary imports from China were books and porcelain. The volatile political environment in Japan gave rise to partnerships between warlords and local merchants. All worked to strengthen their own towns and treasuries through overseas commerce or, sometimes, through piracy.

The Emergence of Vietnam, 1200–1500

Before the first Mongol attack in 1257, the states of Annam (the Chinese name for northern Vietnam) and Champa (southern Vietnam) had clashed frequently. Annam (called Dai Viet in Vietnamese in this period) looked toward China and had once been subject to the Tang. Chinese political ideas, social philosophies, dress, religion, and language heavily influenced its official culture. Champa related more closely to the trading networks of the Indian Ocean; its official culture was strongly influenced by Indian religion, language, architecture, and dress.

Champa's relationship with China depended in part on how close its enemy, Annam, was to China at any particular time. During the Song period Annam was neither formally subject to China nor particularly threatening to Champa militarily, so Champa inaugurated a trade and tribute relationship with China that spread fast-ripening Champa rice throughout East Asia.

The Mongols exacted tribute from both Annam and Champa until the fall of the Yuan Empire in 1368. However, because Mongol political and military ambitions were mostly focused elsewhere, they had

kamikaze The "divine wind," which the Japanese credited with blowing Mongol invaders away from their shores in 1281.

Ashikaga Shogunate The second of Japan's military governments headed by a shogun (a military ruler). Sometimes called the Muromachi Shogunate.

Noh Drama Performance

This slow, rhythmic, chanted form of drama appealed to the military elite with its stories of warriors, women, gods, and demons. The minimal stage is normally bare except for a painting at the rear of a pine tree, symbolizing the means by which deities descend to earth. The actors wear masks and lavish costumes. Four instrumentalists playing flutes and three types of drums punctuate the chanting.

Scenes of urban life under the 'Bakufu' government from a performance of Noh Drama, Tosa School, 1800, Japanese, (detail from six-fold screen, see 67712), (colour woodblock print). Private Collection/Photo © Bonhams, London, UK/The Bridgeman Art Library

minimal impact on Vietnam's politics and culture. The two Vietnamese kingdoms soon resumed their warfare. When Annam moved its army to reinforce its southern border, Ming troops occupied the capital, Hanoi, and installed a puppet government. Almost thirty years elapsed before Annam regained independence and resumed a tributary status. By then the Ming were turning to meet Mongol challenges to their north. In a series of ruthless campaigns, Annam terminated Champa's independence, and by 1500 the ancestor of the modern state of Vietnam, still called Annam, had been born.

The new state still relied on Confucian bureaucratic government and an examination system, but some practices differed from those in China. The Vietnamese legal code, for example, preserved group landowning and decision making within the villages, as well as women's property rights. Both developments probably had roots in an early rural culture based on the growing of rice in wet paddies; by this time the Annamese considered them distinctive features of their own culture.

CONCLUSION

The Mongols were the most successful warriors the world had ever seen. In less than a hundred years, they had conquered an empire that covered half of Eurasia and reached from Poland to Vietnam. And yet half a century later, their empire had broken apart and they had lost most of what they had gained. Why were their conquests so short-lived compared with those of the Romans or the Arabs?

SECTION REVIEW

- Mongol conquest devastated Korea, but Mongol rule opened it to new ideas and technologies.

- The Choson dynasty succeeded the Koryo dynasty and fostered local identity while encouraging economic expansion and technological innovation.

- In Japan, the Mongol threat forced military and organizational innovations, but the expense of these defenses weakened the Kamakura Shogunate.

- Go-Daigo's failed attempt to reassert imperial power resulted in the rise of the Ashikaga Shogunate.

- The warring states of Vietnam avoided Mongol conquest but paid tribute to the Yuan Empire.

- After the Ming withdrawal, Annam conquered Champa, establishing a unified state on both Confucian and local practices.

The Mongols, though ferocious warriors, were too few in number to manage a huge empire, and so they turned to the peoples they had conquered—Chinese, Persians, Turks, and Arabs—to carry out the tasks of administration. They were famous for tolerating many religions and cultures among the people who accepted their rule, but they had no common religion or ideology upon which to build a lasting political culture. Some Mongols converted to Islam, others converted to Buddhism, and still others became Chinese in language and culture. As the Mongol armies were widely scattered, subject peoples whose cultures had never been erased by the Mongols reasserted themselves politically and militarily.

Once Mongol rule was in place, travel across the breadth of Eurasia became safer and easier than it had ever been before or was to be for centuries. Trade flourished, and ideas and technologies spread widely. Yet with trade came the plague, which decimated all the regions that the Mongols occupied. Instead of a Roman or Arab legacy of culture, administration, and religion, subject peoples remembered the Mongols for the violence and brutality of their conquest. However, the reality or threat of Mongol attack and domination encouraged centralization of government, improvement of military techniques, and renewed stress on local cultural identity. Thus, in retrospect, despite its traditional association with death and destruction, the Mongol period appears as a watershed, establishing new connections between widespread parts of Eurasia and leading to the development of strong, assertive, and culturally creative regional states.

CHAPTER REVIEW

THE RISE OF THE MONGOLS, 1200–1260

■ *What accounts for the magnitude and speed of the Mongol conquests?* (page 281)

Nomadic mobility and endurance, expertise in military technology, and systematic army organization made the armies of Chinggis Khan all but invincible. While the Mongols did not usually outnumber their enemies, they were experts on horseback and used superior bows. Turkish pastoral peoples who suffered defeat often enrolled in the Mongol ranks, thus magnifying the power of the Mongols themselves.

THE MONGOLS AND ISLAM, 1260–1500

■ *How did Mongol expansion and Islam affect each other?* (page 288)

As rivalries mounted between the Il-khan and the Golden Horde states, Islam became a point of contention. Rulers who converted to Islam were initially lax in their observance and affiliations. The Il-khans came to value urban Muslim culture, but their merciless taxation policies contributed to a weakness that allowed the Golden Horde to make inroads on Il-khan territory. Meanwhile, Timur rose to power in Chagatai territory and undertook wide-ranging conquests. The Il-khans, Timur, and his successors presided over a flowering of Islamic culture that drew upon Iranian and Chinese cultural elements to contribute notable achievements in historical writing, art, mathematics, and astronomy.

REGIONAL RESPONSES IN WESTERN EURASIA

■ *What benefits resulted from the integration of Eurasia into the Mongol Empire?* (page 291)

The Great Khans attracted emissaries and traders from all over Eurasia to their court, revitalizing the Silk Road. Cultural contact between east and west had greater long-term impact than the Mongols' political power. Muslim astronomers and calendar makers found a welcome reception in China, and Chinese artistic styles became popular in Iran. Mongol occupation, or the threat of Mongol conquest, also helped non-Mongol political leaders galvanize popular support for local state building.

MONGOL DOMINATION IN CHINA, 1271–1368

■ *How did Mongol rule in China foster cultural and scientific exchange?* (page 293)

In China, Yuan rule reestablished connections with Inner Asia that had earlier benefited Tang rule (see Chapter 11). The empire rewarded administrative and military skills more than ethnic or linguistic identity. Muslims from Central Asia brought astronomical expertise to China just as Chinese administrators brought their techniques to Iran. Beijing, the Yuan capital, developed a dynamic cultural scene that produced some of the first Chinese novels. Yet the period also produced war casualties, spread of disease, and migration to southern China.

THE EARLY MING EMPIRE, 1368–1500

■ *In what ways did the Ming Empire continue or discontinue Mongol practices?* (page 296)

The Ming overthrew the Yuan and reaffirmed Chinese ethnicity as a basis for rule. Leaving Beijing, they located their capital in the south and relied on study of the Confucian classics and the examination system for choosing imperial officials. Nevertheless, Mongols still served in the army, and after a time Beijing again became the capital. Though some Yuan administrative practices continued, contact and trade with Inner Asia dwindled because of political disunity in the old Mongol core area.

CENTRALIZATION AND MILITARISM IN EAST ASIA, 1200–1500

■ *What are some of the similarities and differences in how Korea and Japan responded to the Mongol threat?* (page 299)

The conquered Korean rulers remained loyal to the Yuan and benefited from new technologies and administrative techniques. When the Yuan fell, however, a Korean dynasty emerged that stressed non-Mongol ethnicity and reviled the earlier Mongol domination, even while retaining many of the innovations of that period.

After twice repelling Mongol invasions, Japan remained highly militarized. Paradoxically, regional warlords embraced cultural innovations, many of Chinese inspiration, that subsequently became central to Japanese identity. Zen Buddhism, Noh drama, and the ritual of the tea ceremony united the Japanese elite even as the warlords, with their samurai armies, seized control from the ineffective imperial government.

Key Terms

Mongols (p. 281)

Chinggis Khan (p. 281)

Yuan Empire (p. 282)

bubonic plague (p. 285)

Il-khan (p. 288)

Golden Horde (p. 288)

Timur (p. 289)

Rashid al-Din (p. 289)

Nasir al-Din Tusi (p. 290)

Alexander Nevskii (p. 291)

tsar (p. 292)

Ottoman Empire (p. 293)

Khubilai Khan (p. 294)

lama (p. 294)

Beijing (p. 294)

Ming Empire (p. 296)

Yongle (p. 296)

Zheng He (p. 297)

Choson (p. 300)

kamikaze (p. 302)

Ashikaga Shogunate (p. 302)

Europe East and West

© Cengage Learning

In the summer of 1454, a year after the Ottoman Sultan captured the Greek Christian city of Constantinople, Aeneas Sylvius Piccolomini (uh-NEE-uhs SIL-vee-uhs pee-kuh-lo-MEE-nee), destined in four years to become pope, expressed doubts as to whether anyone could persuade the rulers of Christian Europe to take up a new crusade against the Muslims: "Christendom has no head whom all will obey—neither the pope nor the emperor receives his due."

The Christian states thought more of fighting each other. French and English armies had been battling for over a century. The German emperor presided over dozens of states but did not really control them, and the numerous kingdoms and principalities of Spain and Italy could not unite. The Catholic rulers of Hungary, Poland, and Lithuania, on the front line against the Muslim Ottomans, seemed very far away from the western monarchs. With only slight exaggeration, Aeneas Sylvius moaned, "Every city has its own king, and there are as many princes as there are households." He attributed this lack of unity to European preoccupation with personal welfare and material gain, which had increased during the previous century after a devastating plague had carried off a third of Europe's population.

Yet despite all these divisions, disasters, and wars, historians now see the period from 1200 to 1500 (Europe's late Middle Ages) as a time of unusual progress. Prosperous cities adorned with splendid architecture, institutions of higher learning, and cultural achievements counterbalanced the avarice and greed that Aeneas Sylvius lamented. Frequent wars caused havoc and destruction, but they also promoted the development of military technology and more unified monarchies.

Although their Muslim and Byzantine neighbors commonly called Catholic Europeans "Franks," they ordinarily referred to themselves as "Latins," underscoring their allegiance to the Roman church and the Latin language used in its rituals.

RURAL GROWTH AND CRISIS

■ *How well did inhabitants of western Europe, rich and poor, urban and rural, deal with their natural environment?*

Between 1200 and 1500, the European mainland brought more land under cultivation using new farming techniques and made greater use of machinery and mechanical forms of energy. Yet for the nine out of ten people who lived in the countryside, hard labor brought meager returns, and famine, epidemics, and war struck often. After the devastation of the Black Death between 1347 and 1351, social changes speeded up by peasant revolts released many persons from serfdom and brought some improvements to rural life. By contrast, eastern Europe, a region of vast open spaces and sparse population, saw serfdom increase, as nobles, faced with a labor shortage, forced farm workers to till their lands.

Peasants, Population, and Plague

In 1200, most western Europeans lived as serfs tilling the soil on large estates owned by the nobility and the church (see Chapter 10). They owed their lord both a share of their harvests and numerous labor services. These obligations combined with inefficient farming practices meant that peasants received meager returns for their hard work. Even with numerous religious holidays, peasants labored some fifty-four hours a week, more than half the time in support of the local nobility. Each noble family, housed in its stone castle, required the labor of fifteen to thirty peasant families living in one-room thatched cottages containing little furniture and no luxuries.

Scenes of rural life show both men and women at work in the fields, but equality of labor did not mean equality at home. In the peasant's hut as elsewhere in medieval Europe, women were subordinate to men. The influential theologian Thomas Aquinas (uh-KWY-nuhs) (1225–1274) spoke for his age when he argued that although both men and women were theoretically created in God's image, "the image of God is found in man, and not in woman: for man is the beginning and end of woman; as God is the beginning and end of every creature."[1]

Rural poverty resulted partly from rapid population growth. In 1200, China's population may have exceeded Europe's by two to one; by 1300, the population of each was about 80 million. China's population fell because of the Mongol conquest (see Chapter 12), while Europe's doubled between 1100 and 1340. Some historians believe the reviving economy stimulated the increase. Others argue that severe epidemics were few, and warmer-than-usual European temperatures after 950, referred to as the Medieval Warm Period by climate historians, reduced mortality from starvation and exposure.

More people required more productive farming and new agricultural settlements. One widespread new technique, the **three-field system**, replaced the custom of leaving half the land fallow (uncultivated) every year to regain its fertility. Farmers grew crops on two-thirds of their land each year, alternating wheat and rye with oats, barley, or legumes. The third field was left fallow. The oats restored nitrogen to the depleted soil and produced feed for plow horses. In much of Europe, however, farmers continued to let half of their land lie fallow and use oxen (less efficient but cheaper than horses) to pull their plows.

Population growth also encouraged new agricultural settlements. In the twelfth and thirteenth centuries, large numbers of Germans migrated into the fertile lands east of the Elbe River from the Baltic Sea in the north to Transylvania (part of modern Romania) in the south. The Order of Teutonic Knights, founded in the Holy Land but given a (temporary) European base of operations by the king of Hungary in 1211, slaughtered or drove away native inhabitants who had not yet adopted Christianity (see Chapter 12). During the thirteenth century, they conquered, resettled, and administered a vast area along the Baltic that later became Prussia (see Map 13.1).

> **three-field system** A rotational system for agriculture in which two fields grow food crops and one lies fallow. It gradually replaced the two-field system in medieval Europe.

Kharbine-Tapabor/The Art Archive at Art Resource, NY

Rural French Peasants Many scenes of peasant life in winter are visible in this small painting by the Flemish Limbourg brothers from the 1410s. Above the snow-covered beehives one man chops firewood, while another drives a donkey loaded with firewood to a little village. At the lower right a woman, blowing on her frozen fingers, heads past the huddled sheep and hungry birds to join other women warming themselves in the cottage (whose outer wall the artists have cut away).

Draining swamps and clearing forests also brought new land under cultivation. But as population rose, even lands with poor soil or those vulnerable to flooding, frost, or drought were farmed. Average crop yields fell accordingly after 1250, and more people lived at the edge of starvation. According to one historian, "By 1300, almost every child born in western Europe faced the probability of extreme hunger at least once or twice during his expected 30 to 35 years of life."[2] One unusually cold spell at the end of the Medieval Warm Period produced the Great

[1] Quoted in Marina Warner, *Alone of All Her Sex: The Myth and Cult of the Virgin Mary* (New York: Random House, 1983), 179.

[2] Harry Miskimin, *The Economy of the Early Renaissance, 1300–1460* (Englewood Cliffs, NJ: Prentice Hall, 1969), 26–27.

Chronology

	Technology and Environment	Culture	Politics and Society
1200	**1200s** Widespread use of crossbows and windmills	**1209** Franciscan Friars **1216** Dominican Friars **1225–1274** Philosopher-monk Thomas Aquinas	**1200s** Champagne fairs flourish **1204** Fourth Crusade **1211** Teutonic Knights in Hungary **1215** Magna Carta issued
	1250 Growing deforestation		
1300		**1300–1500** Rise of universities **1313–1375** Giovanni Boccaccio, humanist writer	
	1315–1317 Great Famine		**1337** Start of Hundred Years' War
	1347–1351 Black Death	**ca. 1390–1441** Jan van Eyck, painter	**1381** Wat Tyler's Rebellion
1400	**1400s** Cannon and hand-held firearms in use		**1415** Portuguese take Ceuta **1431** Joan of Arc burned **1453** End of Hundred Years' War; Ottomans take Constantinople
	1454 Gutenberg Bible	**1452–1519** Leonardo da Vinci, artist	
		1492 Expulsion of Jews from Spain	**1492** Fall of Muslim state of Granada

Famine of 1315–1317, which affected much of Europe north of the Alps.

The **Black Death** reversed the population growth. Victims developed boils the size of eggs in their groins and armpits, black blotches on their skin, foul body odors, and severe pain. In most cases, death came within a few days. This terrible plague—bubonic plague was the primary form of the Black Death—had been carried from Inner Asia by fleas infesting the fur of certain rats and had moved westward with the Mongol armies (see Chapter 12). In 1346, the Mongols attacked the city of Kaffa (KAH-fah) on the Black Sea; a year later, Genoese (JEN-oh-eez) traders in Kaffa carried the disease to Italy and southern France. For two years, the Black Death spread across Europe, in some places carrying off two-thirds of the population. Town officials closed their gates to people from infected areas and burned the victims' possessions but could not halt the advance of the disease. Even if

medieval doctors had understood its source, eliminating the rats that thrived on urban refuse would have been difficult. Average losses in western Europe amounted to one in three.

The plague brought home to people how sudden and unexpected death could be. Some people became more religious, giving money to the church or lashing themselves with iron-tipped whips to atone for their sins. Others chose reckless enjoyment, spending their money on fancy clothes, feasts, and drinking.

Periodic returns of plague made recovery from population losses slow and uneven. Europe's population in 1400 equaled that in 1200. Not until after 1500 did it rise above its preplague level.

> **Black Death** An outbreak of bubonic plague that spread across Asia, North Africa, and Europe in the mid-fourteenth century, carrying off vast numbers of persons.

Map 13.1 Europe in 1453 This year marked the end of the Hundred Years' War between France and England and the fall of the Byzantine capital city of Constantinople to the Ottoman Empire. Muslim advances into southeastern Europe were offset by the Latin Christian reconquests of Islamic holdings in southern Italy and the Iberian Peninsula and by the conversion of Lithuania. © Cengage Learning

Spread of Latin Christendom

- In 1000 C.E.
- Added 1000–1200
- Lost 1000–1200 (Regained 1200–1500)
- Added 1200–1500
- Lost 1200–1500
- English holdings, 1360
- Boundary of the Holy Roman Empire

0   150   300 Mi.
0   150   300 Km.

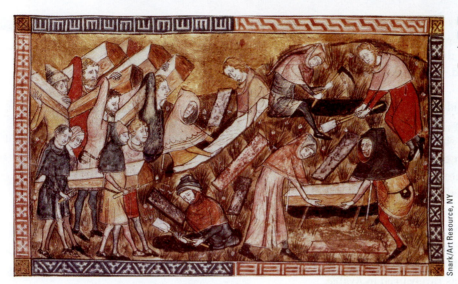

Burying Victims of the Black Death This scene from Tournai, Flanders, captures the magnitude of the plague.

Snark/Art Resource, NY

Social Rebellion

In addition to its demographic and psychological effects, the Black Death triggered social changes in western Europe. Workers who survived demanded higher pay for their services. When authorities tried to freeze wages at the old levels, peasants rose up against wealthy nobles and churchmen. During a widespread revolt in France in 1358, known as the *Jacquerie*, peasants looted castles and killed dozens of persons. In a large revolt in England in 1381 led by Wat Tyler, an estimated 50,000 peasants and craftsmen invaded London, calling for an end to serfdom and obligations to landowners and murdering the archbishop of Canterbury and other officials. Authorities put down these rebellions with great bloodshed and cruelty, but they could not stave off the higher wages and other social changes the rebels demanded.

Serfdom practically disappeared in western Europe as peasants bought their freedom or ran away. Some English landowners who could no longer hire enough fieldworkers began pasturing sheep for their wool. Others grew crops that required less care or made greater use of draft animals and labor-saving tools. Because the plague had not killed livestock and game, survivors had abundant meat and leather. Thus, the welfare of the rural masses generally improved after the Black Death, though the gap between rich and poor remained wide.

In urban areas, employers raised wages to attract workers. Guilds (discussed later in this chapter) shortened the period of apprenticeship. Competition within crafts also became more common. Although the overall economy shrank with the decline in population, per capita production actually rose.

Mills and Mines

Mining, primarily in Germany and east-central Europe, and metalworking and craft mechanization everywhere expanded so greatly in the centuries before 1500 that some historians speak of an "industrial revolution" in medieval Europe. This is too strong a term, but the landscape fairly bristled with mechanical devices. Mills powered by water or wind ground grain, sawed logs, crushed olives, operated bellows, and pounded linen rags for making paper.

Watermills multiplied at a faster rate than the population. In 1086, 5,600 watermills flanked England's many rivers. After 1200, mills spread rapidly across the European mainland. By the early fourteenth century, entrepreneurs had crammed 68 watermills into a 1-mile (1.61-kilometer) section of the Seine (sen) River in Paris. Undershot wheels that depended on the river flowing beneath them were less efficient than overshot wheels where water channeled to fall over the top of the wheel combined the force of gravity with the water's current. Windmills multiplied in comparatively dry lands like Spain and in northern Europe, where water wheels froze in winter.

Designs for watermills dated back to Roman times, and the Islamic world, which inherited Hellenistic technologies, knew of, but failed to develop, both water wheels and windmills. European-style heavy investment in water or wind power made no sense in Muslim lands, where single animals typically operated mills and irrigation devices, because grazing on arid and semiarid wastes made animal power from oxen and camels virtually free. In Europe, by contrast, where grain crops fed both humans and animals, population growth increased the cost of animal energy, particularly of horsepower. One result was that the family name *Miller* became very important in European languages but was rarely used in Arabic, Persian, Turkish.

Owners invested heavily in building mills, but since nature furnished the energy to run them for free, they returned great profits. While individuals or monasteries constructed some mills, most were built by groups of investors. Rich millers often aroused the jealousy of their neighbors. In his *Canterbury Tales*, the English poet Geoffrey Chaucer (ca. 1340–1400) captured their unsavory reputation by portraying a miller as "a master-hand at stealing grain" by pushing down on the balance scale with his thumb.[3]

Waterpower aided the great expansion of iron making. Water powered the stamping mills that pulverized iron ore, the lifting devices that drained water from deep mines, and the bellows (first documented in the West in 1323) that raised temperatures to the point where liquid iron could be poured into molds. Blast furnaces producing high-quality iron are documented from 1380.

In addition to iron mines in many countries, new silver, lead, and copper mines in Austria and Hungary supplied metal for coins, church bells, cannon, and statues. Techniques of deep mining developed in central Europe spread west in the latter part of the fifteenth century. A building boom stimulated stone quarrying in France during the eleventh, twelfth, and thirteenth centuries.

---

[3]Quotations here and later in the chapter are from Geoffrey Chaucer, *The Canterbury Tales*, trans. Nevill Coghill (New York: Penguin Books, 1952), 25, 29, 32.

SECTION REVIEW

- Population growth stimulated improved farming methods and agricultural expansion, but peasant life did not significantly improve.
- Famine and the Black Death reversed the population growth and resulted in social change throughout Europe.
- Improved mill designs and other technology stimulated further industrial growth, which, in turn, changed the landscape.

Industrial growth and urban sprawl changed the landscape. Quarries and mines scarred the hillsides, and dams and canals altered the flow of rivers. Increasingly from 1250 onward forests were cleared for farmland, as well as for ship and building timber and for use in leather tanning, iron smelting, and glassmaking. A single iron furnace could consume all the trees within five-eighths of a mile (1 kilometer) in just forty days. Although some powerful landowners established hunting preserves and those forests were protected, many of Europe's once-dense forests were lost. Urban tanneries, slaughterhouse runoff, and human waste polluted streams. England's Parliament enacted the first recorded antipollution law in 1388, but enforcement proved difficult. More lightly populated, central and eastern Europe experienced less environmental degradation.

URBAN REVIVAL

■ *What social and economic factors led to the growth of cities in late medieval Europe?*

In the tenth century, no town on the European mainland could compete in size, wealth, or comfort with the cities of Byzantium and Islam. Yet by the later Middle Ages, the Mediterranean, Baltic, and Atlantic coasts boasted wealthy port cities, as did some major rivers draining into these seas. Some Byzantine and Muslim cities still exceeded those of the West in size, but not in commercial, cultural, and administrative dynamism, as marked by impressive new churches, guild halls, and residences.

Trading Cities

Most urban growth after 1200 resulted from manufacturing and trade, both between cities and their hinterlands and over long distances. Northern Italy particularly benefited from maritime trade with the port cities of the eastern Mediterranean and, through them, the markets of the Indian Ocean and East Asia. In northern Europe, commercial cities in the county of Flanders (roughly today's Belgium) and around the Baltic Sea profited from regional networks and from overland and sea routes to the Mediterranean.

A Venetian-inspired assault in 1204 against the city of Constantinople, misleadingly named the "Fourth Crusade," temporarily eliminated Byzantine control of the waterway between the Mediterranean and the Black Sea and thereby allowed Venice to seize Crete and expand its trading colonies around the Black Sea. Another boon to Italian trade came from the westward expansion of the Mongol Empire, which opened trade routes from the Mediterranean to China (see Chapter 12).

When Mongol decline interrupted the caravan trade in the fourteenth century, Venetian merchants purchased eastern silks and spices brought by other middlemen to Constantinople, Damascus, and Cairo. Three times a year, Venice dispatched convoys of two or three galleys, with sixty oarsmen each, capable of bringing back 2,000 tons of goods.

The sea trade of Genoa on northern Italy's west coast probably equaled that of Venice. Genoese merchants established colonies in the western and eastern Mediterranean and around the Black Sea. In northern Europe, an association of trading cities known as the **Hanseatic** (han-see-AT-ik) **League** traded extensively in the Baltic, including the coasts of Prussia, newly conquered by German knights. Their merchants ranged eastward to Novgorod in Russia and westward across the North Sea to London.

In the late thirteenth century, Genoese galleys from the Mediterranean and Hanseatic ships from the Baltic were converging on the trading and manufacturing cities in Flanders. Artisans in the Flemish towns of Bruges (broozh), Ghent (gent [hard *g* as in *get*]), and Ypres (EE-pruh) transformed raw wool from England into a fine cloth that was softer and smoother than the coarse "homespuns" from simple

Flemish Weaver (engraving), English School, (19th century)/Private Collection/© Look and Learn/The Bridgeman Art Library

506.—Flemish Weaver. (From a Print of 1568.)

Flemish Weavers, Ypres The spread of textile weaving gave employment to many people in the Netherlands. The city of Ypres in Flanders (now northern Belgium) was an important textile center in the thirteenth century. This drawing from a fourteenth-century manuscript shows a man and a woman weaving cloth on a horizontal loom.

village looms. Dyed in vivid hues, these Flemish textiles appealed to wealthy Europeans, who also appreciated fine textiles from Asia.

Along the overland route connecting Flanders and northern Italy, important trading fairs developed in the Champagne (sham-PAIN) region of Burgundy. The Champagne fairs began as regional markets, exchanging manufactured goods, livestock, and farm produce once or twice a year. When the king of France gained control of Champagne at the end of the twelfth century, royal guarantees of safe conduct to merchants

Hanseatic League An economic and defensive alliance of the free towns in northern Germany, founded about 1241 and most powerful in the fourteenth century.

turned these markets into international fairs that were important for currency exchange and other financial transactions. A century later, fifteen Italian cities had permanent consulates in Champagne to represent the interests of their citizens. During the fourteenth century, the large volume of trade made it cheaper to ship Flemish woolens to Italy by sea than to pack them overland on animal backs. Champagne's fairs consequently lost some international trade, but they remained important as regional markets.

In the late thirteenth century, the English monarchy raised taxes on exports of raw wool, making cloth manufacture in England more profitable than in Flanders. Flemish specialists crossed the English Channel and introduced the spinning wheel, perhaps invented in India, and other devices to England. Annual raw wool exports fell from 35,000 sacks of wool at the beginning of the fourteenth century to 8,000 in the mid-fifteenth century, while English wool cloth production rose from 4,000 pieces just before 1350 to 54,000 a century later.

Florence also replaced Flemish imports with its own woolens industry financed by local banking families. In 1338, Florence manufactured 80,000 pieces of cloth, while importing only 10,000. Elsewhere in northern Italy a new industry appeared to manufacture cotton cloth, which had previously been imported across the Mediterranean. These changes in the textile industry show how competition promoted the spread of manufacturing and encouraged new specialties. Other Italian industries that grew on the basis of techniques borrowed from the Muslim world were papermaking, glassblowing, ceramics, and sugar refining.

In the fifteenth century, Venice surpassed its European rivals in the volume of its trade in the Mediterranean as well as across the Alps into central Europe. Its craftspeople manufactured luxury goods once obtainable only from eastern sources, including cotton and sugar grown with slave labor on the islands of Crete, Cyprus, and Sicily. This industry later became the model for the slave-based sugar economy of the New World (see Chapter 15). Exports of Italian and northern European woolens to the eastern Mediterranean also rose. In the space of a few centuries, western European cities had used the eastern trade to increase their prosperity and then reduce their dependence on eastern goods.

Civic Life   Most northern Italian and German cities were independent states, much like the port cities of the Indian Ocean Basin (see Chapter 14). Other European cities held royal charters exempting them from the authority of local nobles. Their autonomy enabled them to adapt to changing market conditions more quickly than cities controlled by imperial authorities, as in China and the Islamic world. Since anyone who lived in a chartered city for over a year could claim freedom, urban life promoted social mobility.

Europe's Jews mostly lived in cities. Spain had the largest communities because of the tolerance of earlier Muslim rulers, but there were also sizable populations as far east as Magdeburg in Prussia. Commercial cities generally welcomed Jews with manufacturing and business skills. Despite official protection by certain Christian princes and kings, however, Jews endured violent religious persecutions or expulsions in times of crisis, such as during the Black Death (see Diversity and Dominance: Persecution and Protection of Jews, 1272–1349). In 1492, the Spanish monarchs expelled all Jews in the name of religious and ethnic purity. Only the papal city of Rome left its Jews undisturbed throughout the centuries before 1500.

Within most towns and cities, powerful associations known as guilds dominated civic life. **Guilds** brought together craft specialists, such as silversmiths or merchants working in a particular trade, to regulate business practices and set prices. Guilds also trained apprentices and promoted members' interests with the city government. By denying membership to outsiders and Jews, guilds protected the interests of families that already belonged to them. They also perpetuated male dominance of most skilled jobs.

Nevertheless, in a few places, women could join guilds either on their own or as the wives, widows, or daughters of male guild members. Large numbers of poor women also toiled in nonguild jobs in urban textile industries and in the food and beverage trades, generally receiving lower wages than men.

guild In medieval Europe, an association of men (rarely women), such as merchants, artisans, or professors, who worked in a particular trade and banded together to promote their economic and political interests. Guilds were also important in other societies, such as the Ottoman and Safavid Empires.

Some women advanced socially through marriage to wealthy men. One of Chaucer's *Canterbury Tales* concerns a woman from Bath, a city in southern England, who became wealthy by marrying a succession of old men for their money (and then two other husbands for love), "aside from other company in youth." She was also a skilled weaver, Chaucer says: "In making cloth she showed so great a bent, / She bettered those of Ypres and of Ghent."

By the fifteenth century, a new class of wealthy merchant-bankers was operating on a vast scale and specializing in money changing and loans and making investments on behalf of other parties. Merchants great and small used their services. They also handled the financial transactions of ecclesiastical and secular officials and arranged for the transmission to the pope of funds known as Peter's pence, a collection taken up annually in every church in western Europe. Princes and kings supported their wars and lavish courts with credit. Some merchant-bankers even developed their own news services, gathering information on any topic that could affect business.

Florentine financiers offered checking accounts, organized private shareholding companies (the forerunners of modern corporations), and improved bookkeeping techniques. In the fifteenth century, the Medici (MED-ih-chee) family of Florence operated banks in Italy, Flanders, and London. Medicis also controlled the government of Florence and commissioned art works. The Fuggers (FOOG-uhrz) of Augsburg, who had ten times the Medici bank's lending capital, topped Europe's banking fraternity by 1500. Beginning as cloth merchants under Jacob "the Rich" (1459–1525), the family's many activities included trade in Hungarian copper, essential for casting cannon.

Since Latin Christians generally considered charging interest (usury) sinful, Jews predominated in moneylending. Christian bankers devised ways to get around the condemnation of usury. Some borrowers repaid loans in a different currency at a rate of exchange favorable to the lender. Others added to their repayment a "gift" for the lender. For example, in 1501, church officials agreed to repay a Fugger loan of 6,000 gold ducats in five months along with a "gift" of 400 ducats, which would have amounted to an effective interest rate of 16 percent except that the church failed to repay the loan on time.

SECTION REVIEW

- After 1200, most cities grew through manufacture and trade, particularly those of northern Italy, Flanders, and the Baltic coast.

- Expanding trade and technological innovation ultimately reduced Europe's dependence on eastern goods.

- Cities fostered social mobility, but civic life was dominated by guilds, wealthy merchants, and bankers.

- Most urban residents lived in squalor without the public amenities of old Roman and Islamic cities.

- Gothic cathedrals became signs of special civic pride and prestige in European cities.

Yet most residents of European cities suffered in poverty, ill-health, and squalor. European cities generally lacked such amenities as the public baths and water supply systems that had existed in Roman times and still survived in Islamic lands.

Gothic Cathedrals

Master builders and stone masons counted among the skilled people in greatest demand. Though cities competed with one another in the magnificence of their guild halls and town halls, **Gothic cathedrals**, first appearing about 1140 in France, cost the most and brought the greatest prestige. The pointed, or Gothic, arch, replacing the older round, or Romanesque, arch, signaled the new design. External (flying) buttresses stabilizing the high, thin, stone columns below the arches constituted another distinctive feature. This design enabled master builders to push the Gothic cathedrals to great heights and fill the outside walls between the arches with giant windows depicting religious scenes in brilliantly colored stained glass. During the next four centuries, interior heights soared ever higher and walls became dazzling curtains of stained glass.

The men who designed and built the cathedrals had little or no formal education and limited understanding of the mathematical principles of civil engineering. Masons could miscalculate, causing parts

Gothic cathedrals Large churches originating in twelfth-century France; built in an architectural style featuring pointed arches, tall vaults and spires, flying buttresses, and large stained-glass windows.

Diversity & Dominance

Persecution and Protection of Jews, 1272–1349

Because they did not belong to the dominant Latin Christian faith, Jews suffered from periodic discrimination and persecution. For the most part, religious and secular authorities tried to curb such anti-Semitism. Jews, after all, were useful citizens who worshiped the same God as their Christian neighbors. Still, it was hard to know where to draw the line between justifiable and unjustifiable discrimination. The famous reviser of Catholic theology, St. Thomas Aquinas, made one such distinction in his Summa Theologica with regard to attempts at forced conversion.

Now, the practice of the Church never held that the children of Jews should be baptized against the will of their parents. . . .

There are two reasons for this position. One stems from danger to faith. For, if children without the use of reason were to receive baptism, then after reaching maturity they could easily be persuaded by their parents to relinquish what they had received in ignorance. This would tend to do harm to the faith.

The second reason is that it is opposed to natural justice . . . it [is] a matter of natural right that a son, before he has the use of reason, is under the care of his father. Hence, it would be against natural justice . . . for anything to be arranged for him against the will of his parents.

The hostility toward the Jews that Aquinas opposed was much in the air, for in 1272 Pope Gregory X issued several decrees of protection for the legal rights of Jews.

Since it occasionally happens that some Christians lose their Christian children, the Jews are accused by their enemies of secretly carrying off and killing these same Christian children, and of making sacrifices of the heart and blood of these very children. It happens, too, that the parents of these children, or some other Christian enemies of these Jews, secretly hide these very children in order that they may be able to injure these Jews, and in order that they may be able to extort from them a certain amount of money by redeeming them from their straits.

And most falsely do these Christians claim that the Jews have secretly and furtively carried away these children and killed them, and that the Jews offer sacrifice from the heart and the blood of these children, since their law in this matter precisely and expressly forbids Jews to sacrifice, eat, or drink the blood, or eat the flesh of animals having claws. This has been demonstrated many times at our court by Jews converted to the Christian faith: nevertheless very many Jews are often seized and detained unjustly because of this.

We decree, therefore, that Christians need not be obeyed against Jews in such a case or situation of this type, and we order that Jews seized under such a silly pretext be freed from imprisonment, and that they shall not be arrested henceforth on such a miserable pretext, unless—which we do not believe—they be caught in the commission of the crime. We decree that no Christian shall stir up anything against them, but that they should be maintained in that status and position in which they were from the time of our predecessors, from antiquity till now.

We decree, in order to stop the wickedness and avarice of bad men, that no one shall dare to devastate or to destroy a cemetery of the Jews or to dig up human bodies for the sake of getting money [by holding them for ransom]. Moreover, if anyone, after having known the content of this decree, should—which we hope will not happen—attempt audaciously to act contrary to it, then let him suffer punishment in his rank and position, or let him be ➤

punished by the penalty of excommunication, unless he makes amends for his boldness by proper recompense. Moreover, we wish that only those Jews who have not attempted to contrive anything toward the destruction of the Christian faith be fortified by the support of such protection. . . .

Despite such decrees, violence against Jews might burst out when fears and emotions were running high. This selection is from the official chronicles of the upper-Rhineland towns.

In the year 1349 there occurred the greatest epidemic that ever happened. . . . [S]o many people perished that it would be horrible to describe. The pope at Avignon stopped all sessions of court, locked himself in a room, allowed no one to approach him and had a fire burning before him all the time. And from what this epidemic came, all wise teachers and physicians could only say that it was God's will. . . . [I]t is estimated about sixteen thousand people died.

In the matter of this plague the Jews throughout the world were reviled and accused in all lands of having caused it through the poison which they are said to have put into the water and the wells—that is what they were accused of—and for this reason the Jews were burnt all the way from the Mediterranean into Germany, but not in Avignon, for the pope protected them there.

Nevertheless they tortured a number of Jews in Berne and Zofingen who admitted they had put poison into many wells, and they found the poison in the wells. Thereupon they burnt the Jews in many towns and wrote of this affair to Strasbourg, Freibourg, and Basel in order that they too should burn their Jews. . . . The deputies of the city of Strasbourg . . . said that they knew no evil of [the Jews]. . . . [But] a great indignation and clamor against the deputies from Strasbourg [caused] the Bishop and the lords and

the Imperial Cities . . . to do away with the Jews. The result was that they were burnt in many cities, and wherever they were expelled they were caught by the peasants and stabbed to death or drowned. . . .

On Saturday—that was St. Valentine's Day—they burnt the Jews on a wooden platform in their cemetery. . . . And everything that was owed to the Jews was cancelled, and the Jews had to surrender all pledges and notes that they had taken for debts. The council, however, took the cash that the Jews possessed and divided it among the working-men proportionately. The money was indeed the thing that killed the Jews. If they had been poor and if the feudal lords had not been in debt to them, they would not have been burnt.

QUESTIONS FOR ANALYSIS

1. Why do Aquinas and Pope Gregory oppose prejudicial actions against Jews?
2. Why did prejudice increase at the time of the Black Death?
3. What factors account for the differences between the views of Christian leaders and the Christian masses?

Sources: First selection source is Pocket Books, a division of Simon & Schuster, Inc., and the Vernon & Janet Bourke Living Trust from *The Pocket Aquinas*, edited with translations by Vernon G. Bourke. Copyright © 1960 by Washington Square Press. Copyright renewed © 1988 by Simon & Schuster, Inc. Second and third selections from Jacob R. Marcus, ed., *The Jew in the Medieval World: A Source Book, 315–1791* (Cincinnati: Union of American Hebrew Congregations, 1938), 152–154, 45–47. Reprinted with permission of the Hebrew Union College Press, Cincinnati.

of the cathedrals to collapse. The record-high choir vault of Beauvais Cathedral, for instance—154 feet (47 meters) in height—came tumbling down in 1284. But with experience, success rose from the rubble of their mistakes. The cathedral spire in Strasbourg reached 466 feet (142 meters)—as high as a forty-story building. Such heights were unsurpassed until the nineteenth century.

LEARNING, LITERATURE, AND THE RENAISSANCE

◼ *What factors were responsible for the promotion of learning and the arts in Europe?*

Throughout the Middle Ages, people in western Europe lived amid reminders of the achievements of the Romans. They wrote and worshiped in a version of their language, traveled their roads, and obeyed some of their laws. The vestments and robes of popes, kings, and emperors followed the designs of Roman officials. Yet the learning of Greco-Roman antiquity virtually disappeared outside of Byzantium and the Muslim world.

A small revival of learning at the court of Charlemagne in the ninth century was followed by a larger renaissance (rebirth) in the twelfth century in which cities became centers of intellectual and artistic life. The universities established across the Latin countries of Europe after 1200 contributed to this cultural revival. Then in the mid-fourteenth century, the pace of intellectual and artistic life quickened in what is often called the **Renaissance**, which began in northern Italy and later spread to northern and eastern Europe. Some Italian authors saw the Italian Renaissance as a sharp break with an age of darkness.

Universities and Scholarship

Before 1100, Byzantine and Islamic scholarship generally surpassed scholarship in western Europe. When Latin Christians wrested southern Italy from the Byzantines and Sicily and Toledo from the Muslims in the eleventh century, they acquired many manuscripts of Greek and Arabic works. These included works by Plato and Aristotle (AR-ih-stah-tahl) and Greek treatises on medicine, mathematics, and geography, as well as scientific and philosophical writings by Muslim writers. Latin translations of the Iranian philosopher Ibn Sina (IB-uhn SEE-nah) (980–1037), known in the West as Avicenna (av-uh-SEN-uh), had great influence because of their sophisticated blend of Aristotelian and Islamic philosophy. Jewish scholars contributed significantly to the translation and explication of Arabic and other manuscripts.

The thirteenth century saw the foundation of two new religious orders, the Dominicans (1216) and the Franciscans (1209). Living according to a rule but not confined to monasteries, these friars (brothers) brought preaching to the common people and carried the Christian message abroad as missionaries. Some of their most talented members taught in the independent colleges that arose after 1200. Though some aspects of these institutions may derive from institutions of higher Islamic learning called *madrasas* that proliferated after 1100 (see Chapter 10), the Latin countries of Europe innovated the idea of **universities** as degree-granting corporations imparting both religious and nonreligious learning.

Between 1300 and 1500, sixty universities, from St. Andrews in Scotland to Krakow and Prague in eastern Europe, joined the twenty established before that time. Students banded together to start some of them; guilds of professors founded others. Teaching guilds, like craft guilds, set standards for the profession, trained apprentices and masters, and defended their professional interests.

Universities set curricula and instituted final examinations for degrees. Students who passed the exams that ended their apprenticeship received a "license" to teach, while those who completed longer training and defended a masterwork of scholarship became "masters" and "doctors." The University of Paris gradually absorbed the city's various colleges,

Renaissance (European) A period of intense artistic and intellectual activity, said to be a "rebirth" of Greco-Roman culture. Usually divided into an Italian Renaissance, from roughly the mid-fourteenth to mid-fifteenth century, and a Northern (trans-Alpine) Renaissance, from roughly the early fifteenth to early seventeenth century.

universities Degree-granting institutions of higher learning. Those that appeared in the countries of western Europe from about 1200 onward became the model of all modern universities.

but the colleges of Oxford and Cambridge remained independent, self-governing organizations.

Since all universities used Latin, students and masters moved freely across political and linguistic borders, seeking the courses and professors they wanted. Some universities offered specialized training. Legal training centered on Bologna in Italy (buh-LOHN-yuh); Montpellier in southern France and Salerno in Sicily focused on medicine; Paris and Oxford excelled in theology.

Some topics, such as astronomy, were studied outside the university. Both Greek and Arabic traditions presumed that the planets traced circular orbits around the earth, the circle being a perfect geometrical figure. Celestial observations did not always fit this presumption, however. Fifteenth-century astronomers in both Europe and the lands of Islam theorized explanations for the observational deviations. At the very end of the fifteenth century, the Polish-German astronomer Nicolaus Copernicus (co-PER-ni-cus), basing his ideas mainly on the Greek Ptolemy but also aware of more recent writings in Arabic, hit on the idea of planets orbiting the sun instead of the earth. His work, finally published as he lay dying of a stroke in 1543, would pose a challenge to the church's assumption that the earth was the center of God's universe.

Though the new learning sometimes raised inconvenient questions, students aspiring to ecclesiastical careers, and their professors, conferred special prominence on theology, seen as the "queen of the sciences" encompassing all true knowledge. Hence, thirteenth-century theologians sought to reconcile the rediscovered philosophical works of Aristotle and the commentaries of Avicenna with the Bible's revealed truth. These efforts to synthesize reason and faith were known as **scholasticism** (skoh-LAS-tih-sizm).

Thomas Aquinas wrote the most notable scholastic work, the *Summa Theologica* (SOOM-uh thee-uh-LOH-jih-kuh), between 1267 and 1273. Although his exposition of Christian belief organized on Aristotelian principles came to be accepted as a masterly demonstration of the reasonableness of Christianity, scholasticism upset many traditional thinkers. Some church authorities tried to ban Aristotle from the curriculum. However, the considerable freedom of medieval universities from both secular and religious authorities enabled the new ideas to prevail over the fears of church administrators.

Humanists and Printers

This period also saw important literary contributions. The Italian Dante Alighieri (DAHN-tay ah-lee-GYEH-ree) (1265–1321) completed a long, elegant poem, the *Divine Comedy*, shortly before his death. This supreme expression of medieval preoccupations tells the allegorical story of Dante's journey through the nine circles of Hell and the seven terraces of Purgatory, followed by his entry into Paradise. The Roman poet Virgil guides him through Hell and Purgatory; Beatrice, a woman he had loved from afar since childhood and whose death inspired the poem, guides him to Paradise.

The *Divine Comedy* foreshadows the literary fashions of the later Italian Renaissance. Like Dante, later Italian writers made use of Greco-Roman classical themes and mythology and sometimes courted a broader audience by writing not in Latin but in their local language (Dante used the vernacular spoken in Tuscany [TUS-kuh-nee]).

The poet Geoffrey Chaucer, many of whose works show the influence of Dante, wrote in vernacular English. The *Canterbury Tales*, a lengthy poem written in the last dozen years of his life, contains often humorous and earthy tales told by fictional pilgrims on their way to the shrine of Thomas à Becket in Canterbury (see Chapter 10). They present a vivid cross-section of medieval people and attitudes.

Dante influenced a literary movement of the humanists that began in his native Florence in the mid-fourteenth century. The term refers to their interest in grammar, rhetoric, poetry, history, and moral philosophy (ethics)—subjects known collectively as the humanities, an ancient discipline. With the brash exaggeration characteristic of new intellectual fashions, humanist writers like the poet Francesco Petrarch

---

scholasticism A philosophical and theological system, associated with Thomas Aquinas, devised to reconcile Aristotelian philosophy and Roman Catholic theology in the thirteenth century.

humanists (Renaissance) European scholars, writers, and teachers associated with the study of the humanities (grammar, rhetoric, poetry, history, languages, and moral philosophy), influential in the fifteenth century and later.

Dante's *Divine Comedy* This fifteenth-century painting by Domenico di Michelino shows Dante holding a copy of the *Divine Comedy*. Hell is depicted to the poet's right and the terraces of Purgatory behind him, surmounted by the earthly and heavenly Paradise. The city of Florence, with its recently completed cathedral, appears to Dante's left.

(fran-CHES-koh PAY-trahrk) (1304–1374) and the poet and storyteller Giovanni Boccaccio (jo-VAH-nee boh-KAH-chee-oh) (1313–1375) proclaimed a revival of a Greco-Roman tradition they felt had for centuries lain buried under the rubble of post-Roman decay.

This idea of a rebirth of learning dismisses too readily the monastic and university scholars who for centuries had been recovering all sorts of Greco-Roman learning, as well as writers like Dante (whom the humanists revered), who anticipated humanist interests by a generation. Yet the humanists had a great impact as educators, advisers, and reformers. Their greatest influence came in reforming secondary education. They introduced a curriculum centered on the languages and literature of Greco-Roman antiquity, which they felt provided intellectual discipline, moral lessons, and refined tastes. This curriculum dominated European secondary schools well into the twentieth century.

Many humanists tried to duplicate the elegance of classical Latin and (to a lesser extent) Greek, which they revered as the pinnacle of learning, beauty, and wisdom. Boccaccio gained fame with his vernacular writings, which resemble Dante's, and especially for the *Decameron*, an earthy work that has much in common with Chaucer's boisterous tales. Under Petrarch's influence, however, Boccaccio turned to writing in classical Latin.

As humanist scholars mastered Latin and Greek, they turned their language skills to restoring the original texts of Greco-Roman writers and of the Bible. By comparing different manuscripts, they eliminated errors introduced by generations of copyists. To aid in this task, Pope Nicholas V (r. 1447–1455) created the Vatican Library, buying scrolls of Greco-Roman writings and paying to have accurate copies and translations made. Working independently, the Dutch scholar Erasmus (uh-RAZ-muhs) of Rotterdam

A French Printshop, 1537 A workman operates the "press," quite literally a screw device that presses the paper to the inked type. Other employees examine the printed sheets, each of which holds four pages. When folded and sewn together, the sheets make a book. The man on the right is selecting pieces of type from a compartmented box and placing them in a frame for printing.

The Art Archive

(ca. 1466–1536) produced a critical edition of the New Testament in Greek. Erasmus corrected many errors and mistranslations in the Latin text that had been in general use throughout the Middle Ages.

The influence of the humanists grew as the new technology of printing made their critical editions of ancient texts, literary works, and moral guides more available. The Chinese and the Arabs used carved woodblocks for printing, and block-printed playing cards circulated in Europe before 1450, but after that date three European improvements revolutionized printing: (1) movable pieces of type consisting of individual letters, independently invented in Korea (see Chapter 12), (2) walnut oil-based ink suitable for printing on paper without smearing, and (3) the

printing press, a mechanical device that pressed sheets of paper onto inked type.

Johann Gutenberg (yoh-HAHN GOO-ten-burg) (ca. 1394–1468) of Mainz led the way. The Gutenberg Bible of 1454, the first book in the West printed from movable type, exhibited a beauty and craftsmanship testifying to the printer's years of experimentation. Humanists worked closely with the printers, who spread the new techniques to Italy and France. Erasmus did editing and proofreading for the Venetian

printing press A mechanical device for transferring text or graphics from a woodblock or type to paper using ink. Presses using movable type first appeared in Europe in about 1450.

scholar-printer Aldo Manuzio (1449–1515), whose press published many critical editions of classical Latin and Greek texts.

By 1500, at least 10 million printed volumes flowed from presses in 238 European towns, launching a revolution that affected students, scholars, and a growing literate population. These readers consumed unorthodox political and religious tracts along with ancient texts.

Renaissance Artists

Although the artists of the fourteenth and fifteenth centuries continued to depict biblical subjects, the Greco-Roman revival led some, especially in Italy, to portray ancient deities and myths. Another popular trend involved scenes of daily life.

Neither theme was entirely new, however. Renaissance art, like Renaissance scholarship, owed a debt to earlier generations. Italian painters of the fifteenth century credited the Florentine painter Giotto (JAW-toh) (ca. 1267–1337) with single-handedly reviving the "lost art of painting." In religious scenes, Giotto replaced the stiff, staring figures of the Byzantine style, which were intended to overawe viewers, with more natural and human portraits with whose depictions of grief and love viewers could identify. Rather than floating on backgrounds of gold leaf, his saints inhabit earthly landscapes. North of the Alps, the Flemish painter Jan van Eyck (yahn vahn IKE) (ca. 1390–1441) mixed his pigments with linseed oil in place of the usual egg yolk. Oil paints dried more slowly and gave pictures a superior luster. Italian painters quickly copied van Eyck's technique, though his own masterfully realistic paintings on religious and domestic themes remained distinctive.

Leonardo da Vinci (lay-own-AHR-doh dah-VIN-chee) (1452–1519) used oil paints for his *Mona Lisa*. Renaissance artists like Leonardo worked in many media, including bronze sculptures and frescos (painting on wet plaster) like *The Last Supper*. Leonardo's notebooks also contain imaginative designs for airplanes, submarines, and tanks. His younger contemporary Michelangelo (my-kuhl-AN-juh-low) (1472–1564) painted frescoes of biblical scenes on the ceiling of the Sistine Chapel in the Vatican, sculpted

statues of David and Moses, and designed the dome for a new Saint Peter's Basilica in Rome.

The patronage of wealthy and educated merchants and prelates underlay the artistic blossoming in the cities of northern Italy and Flanders. The Florentine banker Cosimo de' Medici (1389–1464) and his grandson Lorenzo (1449–1492), known as "the Magnificent," spent immense sums on paintings, sculpture, and public buildings. In Rome, the papacy (PAY-puh-see) launched a building program that culminated in the construction of the new Saint Peter's Basilica and a residence for the pope.

These scholarly and artistic achievements exemplify the innovation and striving for excellence of the late Middle Ages. The new literary themes and artistic styles of this period had lasting influence on Western culture. But the innovations in the organization of universities, in printing, and in scientific thought had wider implications, for they were later adopted by cultures all over the world.

POLITICAL AND MILITARY TRANSFORMATIONS

■ *What social, political, and military developments contributed to the rise of European nations in this period?*

Stronger and more unified states and armies developed in Europe in parallel with the economic and cultural revivals. Crusades against Muslim states brought consolidation to Spain and Portugal. In Italy and Germany, however, political power remained in the hands of small states and loose alliances. Farther to the east, Lithuania, dynastically linked to Poland, became one of Europe's largest states while Hungary confronted the Ottoman Empire.

Monarchs, Nobles, and the Church

Thirteenth-century states continued early medieval state structures (see Chapter 10). Hereditary monarchs topped the political pyramid, but modest treasuries and the rights of nobles and the church limited their powers. Powerful noblemen who controlled vast estates had an important voice in matters of state. The church guarded closely its traditional rights and independence. Towns, too, had acquired rights and privileges. Towns in Flanders, the Hanseatic League, and Italy approached independence from royal interference. In theory the ruler's noble vassals owed military service in time of war. In practice, vassals sought to limit the monarch's power.

In the year 1200, knights still formed the backbone of European armies, but improved crossbows could shoot metal-tipped arrows with enough force to pierce helmets and light body armor. Professional crossbowmen, hired for wages, became increasingly common and much feared. Indeed, a church council in 1139 outlawed the crossbow—ineffectively—as being too deadly for use against Christians. The arrival in Europe of firearms based on the Chinese invention of gunpowder (see Chapter 12) further transformed the medieval army, first on the Ottoman frontier and then further west.

The church also resisted royal control. In 1302, the outraged Pope Boniface VIII (r. 1294–1303) asserted that divine law made the papacy superior to "every human creature," including monarchs. King Philip "the Fair" of France (r. 1285–1314) responded by sending an army to arrest the pope, a chastisement that hastened Pope Boniface's death. Philip then engineered the election of a French pope, who established a new papal residence at Avignon (ah-vee-NYON) in southern France in 1309.

A succession of French-dominated popes residing in Avignon improved church discipline but at the price of compromising papal neutrality. The **Great Western Schism** between 1378 and 1415 saw rival papal claimants at Avignon and Rome vying for Christian loyalties. The papacy eventually regained its independence and returned to Rome, but the long crisis broke the pope's ability to challenge the rising power of monarchs like Philip.

The English monarchy wielded more centralized power as a result of consolidation that took place after the Norman conquest of 1066. Between 1200 and 1400, the Anglo-Norman kings incorporated Wales and reasserted control over most of Ireland. Nevertheless, under King John (r. 1199–1216), royal power suffered a severe setback. Forced to acknowledge the pope as his overlord in 1213, he lost his bid to reassert claims to Aquitaine in southern France the following year and then yielded to his nobles by signing the Magna Carta in 1215. This "Great Charter" affirmed that monarchs were subject to established law, confirmed the independence of the church and the city of London, and guaranteed the nobles' hereditary rights.

The Hundred Years' War

The conflict between the king of France and his vassals known as the **Hundred Years' War** (1337–1453) grew out of a marriage alliance between Princess Isabella of France and King Edward II of England (r. 1307–1327). Because Edward was a vassal who had inherited French lands from his Norman ancestors, the marriage should have ensured his loyalty. However, when the French royal line produced no other sons, Isabella's son, King Edward III of England (r. 1327–1377), laid claim to the French throne in 1337.

Early in the war, hired Italian crossbowmen reinforced the French cavalry, but the English longbow proved superior. Adopted from the Welsh, the 6-foot (1.8-meter) longbow could shoot farther and more rapidly than the crossbow. Its arrows could not pierce armor, but concentrated volleys found gaps in

Great Western Schism A division in the Latin (Western) Christian Church between 1378 and 1415, when rival claimants to the papacy existed in Rome and Avignon.

Hundred Years' War (1337–1453) Series of campaigns over control of the throne of France, involving English and French royal families and French noble families.

the knights' defenses or struck their less-protected horses. Heavier and more encompassing armor provided a defense but limited a knight's movements. Once pulled off his steed by a foot soldier armed with a pike (hooked pole), he could not get up.

Later in the Hundred Years' War, firearms gained prominence. The first cannon scared the horses with smoke and noise but did little damage. As they grew larger, however, they proved effective in battering the walls of castles and towns. The first artillery use against the French, at the Battle of Agincourt (1415), gave the English an important victory.

Faced with a young French peasant woman called Joan of Arc, subsequent English gains stalled. Acting, she believed, on God's instructions, she put on armor and rallied the French troops to defeat the English in 1429. Shortly afterward, she fell into English hands; she was tried by English churchmen and burned at the stake as a witch in 1431.

In the final battles, French cannon demolished the walls of once-secure castles held by the English and their allies. Armies now depended less on knights and more on bowmen, pikemen, musketeers, and artillerymen.

The war proved a watershed in the rise of **new monarchies** in France and England, centralized states with fixed "national" boundaries and stronger representative institutions. English monarchs after 1453 consolidated control over territory within the British Isles, though the Scots defended their independence. The French monarchs also turned to consolidating control over powerful noble families in Burgundy and Brittany.

The new monarchies needed a way to finance their full-time armies. Some nobles agreed to money payments in place of military service and to additional taxes in time of war. For example, in 1439 and 1445, Charles VII of France (r. 1422–1461) successfully levied a new tax on his vassals' land. This not only paid the costs of the war with England but also gave the monarchy a financial base for the next 350 years.

Merchants' taxes also provided revenues. Taxes on the English wool trade, begun by King Edward III, paid most of the costs of the Hundred Years' War. Some rulers taxed Jewish merchants or extorted large contributions from wealthy towns. Individual merchants sometimes curried royal favor with loans. The fifteenth-century French merchant Jacques Coeur (cur) gained many social and financial benefits for himself and his family by lending money to French courtiers, but his debtors accused him of murder and had his fortune confiscated.

In the west, the church provided a third source of revenue through voluntary contributions to support a war. English and French monarchs won the right to appoint important church officials in their realms in the fifteenth century. In the east, religion became increasingly a political issue as Catholic Lithuania fought a series of wars with Orthodox Russia with little regard for which faith the common people adhered to.

The shift in power to the monarchs and away from the nobility and the church did not deprive nobles of their social position and roles as government officials and military officers. Moreover, the kings of England and France in 1500 had to deal with representative institutions that had not existed in 1200. The English Parliament proved a permanent check on royal power: the House of Lords contained the great nobles and church officials; the House of Commons represented the towns and the leading citizens of the counties. In France, the Estates General, a similar but less effective representative body, represented the church, the nobles, and the towns.

Iberian Unification

Spain and Portugal's **reconquest of Iberia** from Muslim rule expanded the boundaries of Latin Christianity. The knights who pushed the borders of their kingdoms southward furthered both Christianity and their own interests. The spoils of victory included irrigated farmland, rich cities, and ports on

new monarchies Historians' term for the monarchies in France, England, and Spain from 1450 to 1600. The centralization of royal power was increasing within more or less fixed territorial limits.

reconquest of Iberia Beginning in the eleventh century, military campaigns by various Iberian Christian states to recapture territory taken by Muslims. In 1492 the last Muslim ruler was defeated, and Spain and Portugal emerged as united kingdoms.

the Mediterranean Sea and Atlantic Ocean. Serving God, growing rich, and living off the labor of others became a way of life for the Iberian nobility.

The reconquest took several centuries. Toledo fell and became a Christian outpost in 1085. In 1147 English Crusaders bound for the Holy Land helped take Lisbon, which then displaced the older city of Oporto (meaning "the port"), from which Portugal took its name, as both capital and the kingdom's leading city. After a Christian victory in 1212 broke the back of Muslim power, the reconquest accelerated. Within decades, Portuguese and Castilian forces captured the prosperous cities of Cordova (1236) and Seville (1248) and drove the Muslims from the southwestern region known as Algarve (ahl-GAHRV) ("the west" in Arabic). Only the small kingdom of Granada hugging the Mediterranean coast remained in Muslim hands.

By incorporating Algarve in 1249, Portugal attained its modern territorial limits. After a pause to colonize, forcibly Christianize, and consolidate this land, Portugal took the crusade to North Africa. In 1415, Portuguese knights seized the port of Ceuta (say-OO-tuh) in Morocco, where they learned more about the Saharan caravan trade in gold and slaves. During the next few decades, Portuguese mariners sailed down the Atlantic coast of Africa seeking rumored African Christian allies and access to this trade (see Chapter 15).

Elsewhere in Iberia, the reconquest continued. Princess Isabella of Castile married Prince Ferdinand of Aragon in 1469. A decade later, when they inherited their respective thrones, the two kingdoms united to become Spain. Their conquest of Granada in 1492 secured the final piece of Muslim territory for the new kingdom.

Ferdinand and Isabella sponsored the first voyage of Christopher Columbus in 1492 (see Chapter 15). In a third momentous event of that year, the monarchs expelled the Jews from their kingdoms. Attempts to convert or expel the remaining Muslims led to a revolt at the end of 1499 that lasted until 1501. The Spanish rulers expelled the last Muslims in 1502. Portugal expelled the Jews in 1496, including 100,000 refugees from Spain. For some time afterward the Spanish Inquisition, a tribunal established by the two monarchs, exerted itself in identifying and punishing

SECTION REVIEW

- Between 1200 and 1500, monarchs, nobles, and the church struggled over political power.
- Tensions between the French monarchy and the papacy resulted in the Great Western Schism.
- In England, royal power was checked by the papacy and nobility, the latter imposing the Magna Carta on King John.
- The Hundred Years' War between the French monarchy and its vassals introduced new military technologies.
- The war also stimulated the rise of the new centralized monarchies of England and France.
- Spain and Portugal continued the reconquest of Muslim Iberia, a process completed by Ferdinand and Isabella even as the Muslim Ottomans expanded their rule in the east.

Jews, called *Marranos*, and Muslims, called *Moriscos*, who had nominally converted to Christianity but secretly retained their old, forbidden faiths.

The Ottoman Frontier

As Islam receded in the west, it advanced in the east as the Ottoman Empire (see Chapter 12) inflicted defeat after defeat on the Christian Balkan kingdoms. The Ottoman military was balanced between cavalry archers, primarily Turks, and slave infantrymen armed with hand-held firearms.

Slave soldiery had a long history in Islamic lands (see Chapter 9), but the conquest of the Balkans in the late fourteenth century gave the Ottomans access to a new military resource: Christian prisoners of war enslaved and converted to Islam. These "new troops," called *yeni cheri* in Turkish and *Janissaries* (JAN-i-say-ree) in English, gave the Ottomans unusual military flexibility. Not coming from a nomadic background like the Turks, they readily accepted the idea of fighting on foot and learning to use guns, which at that time were still too heavy and awkward for a horseman to load and fire. The Janissaries lived in barracks and trained all year round.

The process of selection for Janissary training changed early in the fifteenth century. The new system, called the *devshirme*, imposed a regular levy of male children on Christian villages in the Balkans. Selected children were placed with Turkish families to learn their language and then sent to Istanbul for instruction in Islam, military training, and, for the most talented, opportunities to become senior military commanders and heads of government departments. The Christian European contest between nobles, monarchs, and church authorities scarcely existed in the Ottoman realm.

CONCLUSION

For seven hundred years after the fall of Rome, western Europe was impoverished economically and culturally compared to the Roman Empire at its height, but also and more importantly, compared to the Byzantine Empire, to the Muslim empires, and to China and India during the same period. At the same time that the Ottomans were expanding their borders in the East, division, disasters, and wars characterized the "Latins" of Europe. Farming techniques were inefficient and farming communities near starvation. But from this unlikely place emerged a new more powerful and prosperous Europe, with kingdoms and their borders forerunners of modern nation-states.

Technological innovation and learning transformed Europe. Crossbows, then gunpowder technology from China, changed the nature of warfare. New wind and water mills substituted inanimate energy for human and animal labor. Farmers increased their yields by planting more of their land and using horses in place of oxen. Commercial expansion, mines, and deforestation took a toll on the land, but the growth of cities, guilds, and banking changed the economy of Europe. Europe became an amalgam of trading cities where now even the textile trade, once an Eastern specialty, surpassed that of the East.

The universities of the later Middle Ages multiplied across Europe, spreading Muslim and classical Greco-Roman knowledge through the common Latin language and invigorating an interest in humanism. The printing press brought learning and literature to more people, and the courts and the church patronized artists, writers, and musicians and built beautiful new buildings. Though the Black Death had decimated the population and set the economy back many decades, by 1500 Europe had rebounded and was preparing to expand beyond the oceans.

CHAPTER REVIEW

RURAL GROWTH AND CRISIS

■ *How well did inhabitants of western Europe, rich and poor, urban and rural, deal with their natural environment?* (page 307)

Ecologically, the peoples of western Europe harnessed the power of wind and water and mined and refined their mineral wealth at the cost of localized pollution and deforestation. However, the inability to improve food production and distribution in response to population growth created a demographic crisis that climaxed with the Black Death, which devastated Europe in the mid-fourteenth century.

URBAN REVIVAL

■ *What social and economic factors led to the growth of cities in late medieval Europe?* (page 312)

Politically, basic features of the modern European state began to emerge. Frequent wars caused kingdoms of moderate size to develop exceptional military strength. The ruling class saw economic strength as the twin of political power and promoted commercial activities such as trade, manufacturing, and finance in the cities, the profits of which they taxed.

LEARNING, LITERATURE, AND THE RENAISSANCE

■ *What factors were responsible for the promotion of learning and the arts in Europe?* (page 318)

Culturally, autonomous universities and printing supported the advance of knowledge though merchant cities also produced a class of literate and leisured individuals. Art and architecture reached unsurpassed peaks in the Renaissance with major innovations in visual styles and building techniques. Late medieval society also displayed a fundamental fascination with luxury goods and manufacturing techniques, many of them acquired from the Muslim world and adapted to a more prosperous and sophisticated consumer society.

POLITICAL AND MILITARY TRANSFORMATIONS

■ *What social, political, and military developments contributed to the rise of European nations in this period?* (page 322)

Many of the tools that western Europe would use to challenge Eastern supremacy—printing, firearms, and navigational devices—originally came from the East. However, western European success depended as much on strong motives for expansion. From the eleventh century onward, population pressure, religious zeal, economic enterprise, and intellectual curiosity drove an expansion of territory and resources that took the Crusaders to the Holy Land, merchants to the eastern Mediterranean and Black Seas, the English into Wales and Ireland, German settlers across the Elbe River, and Iberian Christians into the Muslim south. The early voyages into the Atlantic, discussed in Chapter 15, extended these activities.

Key Terms

three-field system (p. 308)

Black Death (p. 309)

Hanseatic League (p. 313)

guild (p. 314)

Gothic cathedrals (p. 315)

Renaissance (European) (p. 318)

universities (p. 318)

scholasticism (p. 319)

humanists (Renaissance) (p. 319)

printing press (p. 321)

Great Western Schism (p. 323)

Hundred Years' War (p. 323)

new monarchies (p. 324)

reconquest of Iberia (p. 324)

Southern Empires, Southern Seas

© Cengage Learning

CHAPTER PREVIEW

TROPICAL AFRICA AND ASIA
■ *How did environmental differences shape cultural differences in tropical Africa and Asia?*

NEW ISLAMIC EMPIRES
■ *Under what circumstances did the first Islamic empires arise in Africa and India?*

INDIAN OCEAN TRADE
■ *How did cultural and ecological differences promote trade, and in turn how did trade and other contacts promote state growth and the spread of Islam?*

SOCIAL AND CULTURAL CHANGE
■ *What social and cultural changes are reflected in the history of peoples living in tropical Africa and Asia during this period?*

THE WESTERN HEMISPHERE
■ *What were the key differences between the societies of Africa and Asia and the empires of the Aztecs and Inkas?*

Conclusion

ENVIRONMENT & TECHNOLOGY:
The Indian Ocean Dhow

Sultan Abu Bakr (a-BOO BAK-uhr) customarily offered hospitality to distinguished visitors to his city of Mogadishu, an Indian Ocean port on the northeast coast of Africa. In 1331, he provided food and lodging for Muhammad ibn Abdullah **Ibn Battuta** (IB-uhn ba-TOO-tuh) (1304–1369), a young Muslim scholar from Morocco who had set out to explore the Islamic world. With a pilgrimage to Mecca and travel throughout the Middle East behind him, Ibn Battuta was touring the trading cities of the Red Sea and East Africa. Subsequent travels took him to Central Asia and India, China and Southeast Asia, Muslim Spain, and sub-Saharan West Africa. Recounting some 75,000 miles (120,000 kilometers) of travel over twenty-nine years, Ibn Battuta's journal provides invaluable information on these lands.

Hospitality being considered a noble virtue among Muslims, regardless of physical and cultural differences, the reception at Mogadishu mirrored that at other cities. Ibn Battuta noted that Sultan Abu Bakr had skin darker than his own and spoke a different native language (Somali), but as brothers in faith, they prayed together at Friday services, where the sultan greeted his foreign guest in Arabic, the common language of the Islamic world: "You are heartily welcome, and you have honored our land and given us pleasure." When Sultan Abu Bakr and his jurists heard and decided cases after the mosque service, they used the religious law familiar in all Muslim lands.

Islam aside, the most basic links among the diverse peoples of Africa and southern Asia derived from the tropical environment itself. A network of overland and maritime routes joined their territories, providing avenues for the spread of beliefs, technologies, and goods. Ibn Battuta sailed with merchants down the coast of East Africa and joined trading caravans across the Sahara from Morocco to West Africa. His path to India followed overland trade routes, and a merchant ship carried him on to China.

Maritime routes would also prove critical in connecting the Old World to the Western Hemisphere and its unique agricultural products from diverse high-altitude tropical microclimates. Working with simple stone tools, the Aztecs and Inka created remarkable monuments and urban centers and a vast trading network—without the use of horses or camels. Virtually isolated from the rest of the world, these empires were the culmination of long historical developments in Mesoamerica and the Andes.

TROPICAL AFRICA AND ASIA

■ *How did environmental differences shape cultural differences in tropical Africa and Asia?*

The tropical regions of Africa and Asia shared environmental similarities but differed markedly in their interactions with other parts of the world (see Chapter 8). The western regions of Africa were semi-isolated by the Atlantic Ocean and Sahara Desert, while Africa's east coast was in maritime contact with the lands bordering the Indian Ocean. Overland routes through Afghanistan to the Middle East and Central Asia affected India and in turn influenced developments in both mainland and island Southeast Asia.

The Tropical Environment in Africa and Asia

Because of the angle of the earth's axis, the sun's rays warm the **tropics** year-round. The equator marks the center of the tropical zone, and the Tropic of Cancer and Tropic of Capricorn its outer limits. Africa lies almost entirely within the tropics, as do southern Arabia, most of India, and both mainland and island Southeast Asia. In the Western Hemisphere (discussed later in this chapter) the regions that produced the earliest civilizations, Mesoamerica and the Andes and Pacific coast of South America, also lay in the tropics.

Lacking the hot and cold seasons of temperate lands, the rainy and dry seasons of the Afro-Asian tropics derive from atmospheric patterns across the surrounding oceans. Winds flow away from areas

Ibn Battuta Moroccan Muslim scholar, the most widely traveled individual of his time. He wrote a detailed account of his visits to Islamic lands from China to Spain and the western Sudan.

tropics Equatorial region between the Tropic of Cancer and the Tropic of Capricorn. It is characterized by generally warm or hot temperatures year-round, though much variation exists due to altitude and other factors. Temperate zones north and south of the tropics generally have a winter season.

of high atmospheric pressure toward areas of low pressure. The earth's rotation causes these winds to move in a clockwise direction (anticyclone) north of the equator and a counterclockwise direction south of the equator. Thus a permanent high-pressure air mass over the South Atlantic delivers heavy rainfall to the western coast of Africa during much of the year. However, in December and January, large high-pressure zones over northern Africa and Arabia produce a southward movement of dry air that limits the inland penetration of the moist ocean winds.

In the lands around the Indian Ocean, the rainy and dry seasons reflect the influence of alternating winds known as **monsoons.** A gigantic high-pressure zone over the Himalaya (him-AH-la-yuh) Mountains peaks from December to March, producing southern Asia's dry season by forcing strong southward and westward air movements (the northeast monsoon) in the western Indian Ocean. Between April and August, a low-pressure zone over India reverses the process by drawing moist oceanic air from the south and west (the southwest monsoon) and brings southern Asia the heavy rains of its wet season, called the monsoon season.

Areas with the heaviest rainfall—the broad belt along the equator in coastal West Africa and West-Central Africa, parts of coastal India, and Southeast Asia—have dense rain forests. Lighter rains produce other forest patterns. The English word *jungle* comes from an Indian word for the tangled undergrowth in the forests that once covered most of tropical India.

Some other parts of the tropics rarely see rain at all. The world's largest desert, the Sahara, stretches across northern Africa and continues eastward across Arabia, southern Iran, Pakistan, and northwest India. Another desert occupies southwestern Africa. Tropical India and Africa fall mostly between the deserts and rain forests and experience moderate rainy seasons. These lands range from fairly wet woodlands to the much drier grasslands characteristic of much of East Africa.

Altitude produces other climatic variations. Thin atmospheres at high altitudes hold less heat than atmospheres at lower elevations. Snow covers some of the volcanic peaks of eastern Africa all or part of the year. The snowcapped Himalayas that form India's northern frontier rise so high that they block cold air from moving south, giving northern India a more tropical climate than its latitude would suggest. The plateaus of inland Africa and the Deccan (DEK-uhn) Plateau of central India also enjoy cooler temperatures than the coastal plains.

Human Ecosystems

A careful observer touring the tropics in 1200 would have noticed how different societies used the plants, animals, and other resources of their physical environments. Some peoples continued to rely primarily on hunting, fishing, and gathering and lived in small, mobile groups. For Pygmy (PIG-mee) hunters in the dense forests of Central Africa, small size permitted pursuit of prey through dense undergrowth. Hunting also prevailed among some inland groups in Borneo, New Guinea, and the Philippines.

A Portuguese expedition led by Vasco da Gama visited the arid coast of southwestern Africa in 1497 and saw there a healthy group of people feeding themselves on "the flesh of seals, whales, and gazelles, and the roots of wild plants." Fishing, which was common along all the major lakes and rivers as well as in the oceans, could be combined with farming or with ocean trade, particularly in Southeast Asia.

Depending on what a particular ecosystem can support, the density of population can also vary greatly. Herding provided sustenance in areas too arid for agriculture. Pastoralists consumed milk and sometimes blood from their herds but did not eat a lot of meat since their animals were of greater value to them alive than dead. The deserts of northern Africa and Arabia had small populations that ranged widely with their camels, goats, and donkeys. Some, like the Tuareg (TWAH-reg) of the western Sahara, proved invaluable as caravan guides because of their intimate knowledge of the desert. Along the Sahara's southern edge the cattle-herding Fulani (foo-LAH-nee) gradually extended their range until by 1500

> **monsoon** Seasonal winds in the Indian Ocean caused by the differences in temperature between the rapidly heating and cooling landmasses of Africa and Asia and the slowly changing ocean waters. These strong and predictable winds have long been ridden across the open sea by sailors, and the large amounts of rainfall that they deposit on parts of India, Southeast Asia, and China allow for the cultivation of several crops a year.

Chronology

	Tropical Africa	Tropical Asia	Western Hemisphere
1200	**1230s** Mali Empire founded **1270** Solomonic dynasty in Ethiopia founded	**1206** Delhi Sultanate founded in India **1298** Delhi Sultanate annexes Gujarat	
1300	**1324–1325** Mansa Musa's pilgrimage to Mecca	**1398** Timur sacks Delhi; Delhi Sultanate declines	**1300** Aztec capital Tenochtitlan founded
1400	**1400s** Great Zimbabwe at its peak **1433** Tuareg retake Timbuktu; Mali declines	**1430s** Inka expansion begins	
1500		**1500** Port of Malacca at its peak	**1500–1525** Inka conquer Ecuador **1502** Moctezuma II crowned Aztec ruler

they had spread throughout the western and central Sudan. Other cattle herders lived on either side of the Nile in Sudan and in Somalia.

Pastoral groups in India were fewer and located mostly in the Himalayas or the deserts of the northwest. In contrast, South and Southeast Asia's wet climate favored intensive cultivation, and high yields supported dense populations. In 1200, over 100 million people lived in South and Southeast Asia, more than four-fifths of them on the fertile Indian mainland—a little less than the population of China, nearly double the population of Europe, and triple the population in all of Africa.

Rice cultivation dominated in the fertile Ganges Plain of northeast India, mainland Southeast Asia, and southern China. In drier areas, farmers grew grains—wheat, sorghum, and millet—and legumes such as peas and beans whose ripening cycles matched the pattern of the rainy and dry seasons. Tree crops, such as kola nuts in West Africa, coconuts in Southeast Asia, and bananas everywhere, made major contributions to the diet, as did the root crops characteristic of rain forest clearings.

The spread of farming, including the movement to Africa of Indo-Malayan bananas and root crops like yams and cocoyams, also known as taro, did not necessarily change the natural environment. In most of sub-Saharan Africa and much of Southeast Asia, extensive rather than intensive cultivation prevailed. Instead of enriching fields with manure and vegetable compost so they could be cultivated year after year, farmers abandoned fields when the natural fertility of the soil fell and cleared new fields. Ashes from the brush, grasses, and tree limbs they cut down and burned boosted the new fields' fertility. Shifting to new land every few years made efficient use of labor in areas with comparatively poor soils and abundant space.

Water Systems and Irrigation

In the inland delta of the Niger River in West Africa, naturally fertilizing annual floods enabled farmers to grow rice for sale to the trading cities along the Niger bend. However, in India and Southeast Asia, many tropical farmers had to bring water to their crops. Conserving some of the monsoon rainfall for use during the dry season helped in Vietnam, Java, Malaya, and Burma (now Myanmar), which had terraced hillsides with special water-control systems for growing rice. Villagers in southeast India built stone and earthen dams across rivers to store water for gradual release through elaborate irrigation canals. Similar dam and canal systems supplied water farther north.

As had been true since the first river-valley civilizations (see Chapter 1), governments built and controlled the largest irrigation systems. The **Delhi** (DEL-ee) **Sultanate** (1206–1526) in northern India developed extensive new water-control systems. One large reservoir had fields of sugar cane, cucumbers, and melons planted along its rim as the water level fell during the dry season. Irrigation canals built in the Ganges Plain in the fourteenth century remained unsurpassed for five hundred years. Such systems made it possible to grow crops throughout the year.

Since the tenth century, the island of Ceylon (ancient Serandip; modern Sri Lanka [sree LAHNG-kuh]) off India's southern tip possessed the world's greatest concentration of irrigation reservoirs and canals. These facilities supported a large Sinhalese-speaking (sin-huh-LEEZ) kingdom in arid northern Ceylon. In Southeast Asia, another impressive system of reservoirs and canals served Cambodia's capital city, Angkor (ANG-kor).

Eventually both these systems deteriorated. Between 1250 and 1400, the irrigation complex in Ceylon fell into ruin when invaders from south India disrupted the Sinhalese government. As a result, malaria spread by mosquitoes breeding in the irrigation canals ravaged the population. In the fifteenth century, the great Cambodian system fell into ruin when the government that maintained it collapsed. Neither system was ever rebuilt. The vulnerability of complex irrigation systems built by powerful governments contrasts with village-based irrigation systems. Invasion and natural calamity might damage the latter, but they usually bounced back because they depended on local initiative and simpler technologies.

Mineral Resources

Between 1200 and 1500, as the rain forests of coastal West Africa and Southeast Asia opened up for farming, ironworking provided the hoes, axes, and knives farmers used to clear and cultivate their fields. Iron also supplied spear and arrow points, needles, and nails. Indian armorers became known for forging strong and beautiful swords. In Africa, many

Nigel Pavitt/Getty Images

East African Pastoralists Herding large and small livestock has long been a way of life in drier parts of the tropics.

people attributed magical powers to iron smelters and blacksmiths.

The Copperbelt of southeastern Africa came into prominence during the fourteenth and fifteenth centuries. Smelters cast the metal into large X-shaped ingots (metal castings) that local coppersmiths worked into wire and decorative objects. A mining town in the western Sudan visited by Ibn Battuta produced two sizes of copper bars that served as currency in place of coins. Coppersmiths in the West African city of Ife (now in southern Nigeria) cast highly realistic copper and brass (an alloy of copper and zinc) statues and heads that now rank as masterpieces of world art. They utilized the "lost-wax" method, in which molten metal melts a thin layer of wax sandwiched between clay forms, replacing the "lost" wax with hard metal.

African gold moved in quantity across the Sahara and into the Indian Ocean and Red Sea trades. Some came from streambeds along the upper Niger River and in modern Ghana (GAH-nuh). Far to the south, beyond the Zambezi (zam-BEE-zee) River (in modern Zimbabwe [zim-BAHB-way]), archaeologists have discovered thousands of mineshafts, dating from 1200, that were sunk up to 100 feet (30 meters) into the ground to get at gold ores. In northern India, panning

Delhi Sultanate Centralized Indian empire of varying extent, created by Muslim invaders.

SECTION REVIEW

- The environment of tropical Africa and Asia is governed by wind patterns across oceans and the resulting rainfall.

- Deserts and rain forests mark the extreme climate variations in these regions, while mountain ranges produce further variations.

- Depending on the regional environment, people fed themselves mainly through hunting and gathering, herding, or farming.

- In West Africa, India, and Southeast Asia, human societies depended on river and irrigation systems of varying complexity.

- Iron, copper, and gold were central to the local economies and long-distance trade systems of tropical Africa and Asia.

for gold remained important in the streams descending from the mountains, but India's gold and silver mines seem to have been exhausted by this period. Thus, Indians imported considerable quantities of gold for jewelry and temple decoration from Iran and the Ottoman Empire, as well as from Southeast Asia and Africa.

NEW ISLAMIC EMPIRES

■ *Under what circumstances did the first Islamic empires arise in Africa and India?*

Despite the Mongol destruction of the Baghdad caliphate in 1258 (see Chapter 12), Islam continued to spread. In fact, the territorial expansion of Islam between 1200 and 1500 exceeded the Arab conquests of the seventh century. The Ottoman conquests in Europe extended Muslim domains in the Mediterranean heartland, but most of the expansion took place in the Muslim south in Africa, South Asia, and Southeast Asia.

The empires of Mali in West Africa and Delhi in northern India formed the largest and richest tropical states during Islam's second period of expansion. Both utilized administrative and military systems introduced from the Islamic heartland. **Mali**, an indigenous African dynasty that rose in the 1230s, grew out of the peaceful influence of Muslim merchants and scholars, while the Delhi Sultanate was founded and ruled by invading Turkish and Afghan Muslims.

Mali in the Western Sudan

Muslim rule in North Africa beginning in the seventh century (see Chapter 9) greatly stimulated trade across the Sahara. In the centuries that followed, the faith of Muhammad spread slowly to the lands south of the desert, which the Arabs called the *bilad al-sudan* (bih-LAD uhs-soo-DAN), "land of the blacks."

Muslim Berbers invading out of the desert in 1076 caused the collapse of Ghana, the empire that preceded Mali in the western Sudan (see Chapter 9). Takrur (TAHK-roor), a kingdom on the Atlantic coast whose king had become the first sub-Saharan ruler to adopt Islam in the 1030s, allied with the invaders but remained a small state when the Berbers' interests in Morocco and Spain drew their attention away from the sub-Saharan region. Farther east, a truce that had endured since 652 between Christian Nubia along the Nile and Muslim Egypt fell apart in the thirteenth century as the Mamluks of Cairo made repeated attacks (see Chapter 9). The small Christian kingdoms weakened and fell over the next two centuries, but Christian Ethiopia successfully withstood Muslim advances. In general, however, Islam's spread south of the Sahara followed a pattern of gradual and peaceful conversion. The expansion of commercial contacts in the western Sudan and on the East African coast greatly promoted the conversion process.

Shortly after 1200, Takrur expanded under King Sumanguru (soo-muhn-GOO-roo), only to suffer a major defeat some thirty years later at the hands of Sundiata (soon-JAH-tuh), the upstart leader of the Malinke (muh-LING-kay) people. Though both leaders professed Islam, Malinke legends recall their battles as clashes between powerful magicians, suggesting how much old and new beliefs mingled. Sumanguru could reportedly appear and disappear at will, assume dozens of shapes, and catch arrows in midflight. Sundiata defeated Sumanguru's much larger forces through superior military maneuvers and by wounding his adversary with a special arrow that robbed him of his magical powers. Other victories followed, and the Mali Empire was born (see Map 14.1).

Mali Empire created by indigenous Muslims in western Sudan of West Africa from the thirteenth to fifteenth century. It was famous for its role in the trans-Saharan gold trade.

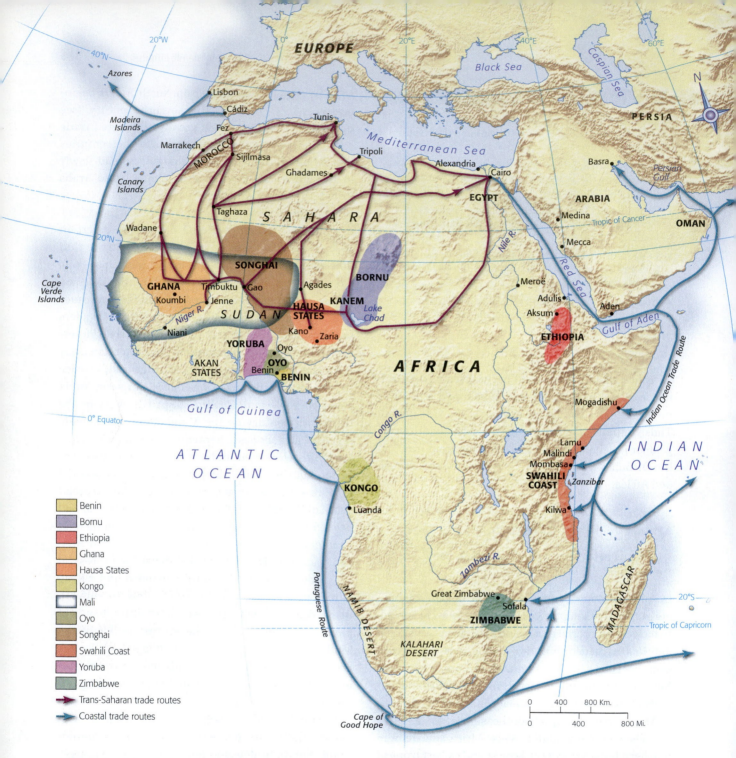

Map 14.1 Africa, 1200–1500 Many African states had beneficial links to the trade that crossed the Sahara and the Indian Ocean. Before 1500, sub-Saharan Africa's external ties were primarily with the Islamic world. © Cengage Learning

Sundiata's empire depended on a well-developed agricultural base and control of the regional and trans-Saharan trade routes, as had Ghana before it. Mali, however, controlled a greater area than Ghana, including not only the core trading area of the upper Niger but also the gold fields of the Niger headwaters to the southwest. Moreover, its rulers fostered the spread of Islam among the empire's political and

Djinguere Ber Mosque in Timbuktu Built almost entirely of earth and organic materials, this fourteenth-century mosque can accommodate 2,000 worshipers. Mansa Kankan Musa, the most famous ruler of the Empire of Mali, is said to have paid Abu Ishaq al-Sahili, a native of Granada in Muslim Spain, 200 kilograms of gold for designing this masterful combination of Islamic and African traditions. Nik Wheeler/Corbis

trading elites. Control of the gold and copper trades and contacts with North African Muslim traders gave Mali unprecedented prosperity.

Under the ruler **Mansa Kankan Musa** (MAHN-suh KAHN-kahn MOO-suh) (r. 1312–1337), the empire's reputation for wealth spread far and wide. Mansa Musa's pilgrimage to Mecca in 1324–1325 fulfilled his personal duty as a Muslim and at the same time put on display his exceptional wealth. He traveled with a large entourage. Besides his senior wife and five hundred of her ladies in waiting and their slaves, one account says there were also sixty thousand porters and a vast caravan of camels carrying supplies and provisions. For purchases and gifts, he brought along eighty packages of gold, each weighing 122 ounces (3.8 kilograms). In addition, five hundred slaves each carried a golden staff. Mansa Musa dispersed so many gifts when he passed through Cairo that the value of gold was depressed for years.

Two centuries after its founding, Mali began to disintegrate. Mansa Musa was succeeded by Mansa Suleiman (r. 1341–1360), but his successors could not prevent rebellions breaking out among the diverse peoples subjected to Malinke rule, while other groups attacked from without. The desert Tuareg retook their city of Timbuktu (tim-buk-TOO) in 1433. By 1500, the rulers of Mali had dominion over little more than the Malinke heartland.

The cities of the upper Niger survived Mali's collapse, but some trade and intellectual life moved east to the central Sudan. Shortly after 1450, several Hausa city-states officially adopted Islam, becoming famous for cotton textiles and leatherworking. The central Sudanic state of Kanem-Bornu (KAH-nuhm–BOR-noo)

> **Mansa Kankan Musa** Ruler of Mali (r. 1312–1337). His pilgrimage through Egypt to Mecca in 1324–1325 established the empire's reputation for wealth in the Mediterranean world.

also expanded in the late fifteenth century from the ancient kingdom of Kanem, whose rulers had accepted Islam in about 1085. At its peak around 1250, Kanem had absorbed the state of Bornu south and west of Lake Chad and gained control of routes crossing the central Sahara. As Kanem-Bornu's armies conquered new territories, they also spread the rule of Islam.

The Delhi Sultanate in India

Beginning in the early eleventh century, the divided states of northwest India, having long ago lost the defensive unity of the Gupta Empire (see Chapter 6), fell prey to raids by the powerful sultan Mahmud (mah-MOOD) based in Ghazna, Afghanistan. From 1206 to 1526, repeated campaigns by successive rulers led to a series of Afghan and Turkish dynasties ruling from the city of Delhi. One partisan Muslim chronicler wrote: "The city [Delhi] and its vicinity was freed from idols and idol-worship, and in the sanctuaries of the images of the [Hindu] Gods, mosques were raised by the worshippers of one God."[1] Turkish adventurers from Central Asia flocked to join the invading armies and overwhelmed the small Indian states, which were often at war with one another.

Between 1206 and 1236, the Muslim invaders extended their rule over the Hindu princes and chiefs in much of northern India. Sultan Iltutmish (il-TOOT-mish) (r. 1211–1236) consolidated the conquest in a series of military expeditions that made his realm the largest in India (see Map 14.2). The caliph in Baghdad, soon to be killed by the Mongols, officially recognized the Delhi Sultanate as a Muslim realm. Incorporating north India into the Islamic world marked the beginning of the invaders' transformation from brutal conquerors to somewhat more benign rulers. Though doctrinally opposed to idol worship, Muslim commanders granted the Hindus freedom from persecution in return for paying the *jizya*, a tax required of Jews and Christians.

Iltutmish astonished his ministers by passing over his weak and pleasure-seeking sons and designating as his heir his beloved and talented daughter Raziya (RAH-zee-uh). He reportedly said, "My sons

are devoted to the pleasures of youth: no one of them is qualified to be king. . . . There is no one more competent to guide the State than my daughter." Her brother, who was given to riding his elephant through the bazaar and showering the crowds with coins, ruled ineptly for seven months before the ministers relented and put Raziya on the throne. A chronicler who knew her explained why this able ruler lasted less than four years (r. 1236–1240):

> Sultan Raziya was a great monarch. She was wise, just, and generous, a benefactor to her kingdom, a dispenser of justice, the protector of her subjects, and the leader of her armies. She was endowed with all the qualities befitting a king, but she was not born of the right sex, and so in the estimation of men all these virtues were worthless. May God have mercy upon her![2]

Doing her best to prove herself a proper king, Raziya dressed like a man and led her troops atop an elephant. In the end, however, the Turkish chiefs imprisoned her; she escaped but was killed by a robber soon afterward.

After a half century of stagnation and rebellion, the ruthless but efficient policies of Sultan Ala-ud-din Khalji (uh-LAH–uh–DEEN KAL-jee) (r. 1296–1316) increased control over the empire's outlying provinces. Successful frontier raids and high taxes filled his treasury, wage and price controls in Delhi kept down the cost of maintaining a large army, and a network of spies stifled intrigue. When a Mongol threat from Central Asia eased, Ala-ud-din's forces marched southward, capturing the rich trading state of **Gujarat** (goo-juh-RAHT) in 1298 and then briefly seizing the southern tip of the Indian peninsula.

Sultan Muhammad ibn Tughluq (TOOG-look) (r. 1325–1351) enlarged the sultanate to its greatest extent at the expense of the independent Indian states but balanced his aggression with religious toleration. He even attended Hindu religious festivals. However, his successor, Firuz Shah (fuh-ROOZ shah) (r. 1351–1388), alienated powerful Hindus by taxing

---

[1]Hasan Nizami, Taju-l Ma-asir, in Henry M. Elliot, *The History of India as Told by Its Own Historians*, ed. John Dowson (London: Trübner and Co., 1869–1871), 2:219.

[2]Minhaju-s Siraj, Tabakat-i Nasiri, in ibid., 2:332–333.

Gujarat Region of western India famous for trade and manufacturing; the inhabitants are called Gujaratis.

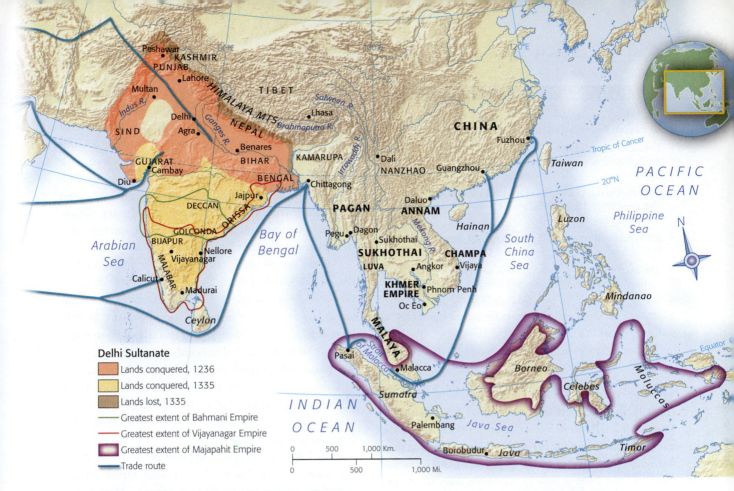

Map 14.2 **South and Southeast Asia, 1200–1500** The rise of new empires and the expansion of maritime trade reshaped the lives of many tropical Asians. © Cengage Learning

the Brahmin elite. Muslim chroniclers praised him for constructing forty mosques, thirty colleges, and a hundred hospitals.

A small minority in a giant land, the Delhi sultans relied on force to keep their subjects submissive, on military reprisals to put down rebellion, and on pillage and high taxes to sustain the ruling elite in luxury and power. The sultanate never escaped the disadvantage of foreign origins and alien religious identity, but some sultans did incorporate a few Hindus into their administrations, and some members of the Muslim elite married women from prominent Hindu families, though the brides had to convert to Islam.

Personal and religious rivalries within the Muslim elite, along with Hindu discontent, threatened the Delhi Sultanate whenever it showed weakness and finally hastened its end. In the mid-fourteenth century, Muslim nobles challenged the sultan's dominion and established the independent Bahmani (bah-MAHN-ee) kingdom (1347–1482) on the Deccan Plateau. Defending against the southward push of Bahmani armies, the Hindu states of south India united to form the Vijayanagar (vee-JAY-yah-nah-GAR) Empire (1336–1565), which at its height controlled rich trading ports on both coasts of south India and held Ceylon as a tributary state.

Hindu Vijayanagar and the Muslim Bahmani state turned a blind eye to religious differences when doing so favored their interests. Bahmani rulers sought to balance Muslim domination by incorporating Hindu leaders into the government, marrying Hindu wives, and appointing Brahmins to high offices. Vijayanagar rulers hired Muslim horsemen and archers to strengthen their military forces and formed an alliance with the Muslim-ruled state of Gujarat.

By 1351, when all of south India had cast off Delhi's rule, much of north India rose in rebellion. In the east, Bengal broke away from the sultanate in 1338. In the west, Gujarat regained its independence by 1390.

SECTION REVIEW

- Islam spread into western sub-Saharan Africa usually by peaceful conversion through trading contacts.

- Founded by Sundiata, Mali depended on agriculture and control of trade routes, and Islam spread among its elites.

- Mali reached its height under Mansa Kankan Musa but declined after the death of his successor, and power shifted eastward.

- Muslim invaders from Afghanistan conquered much of Hindu northern India to establish the Delhi Sultanate.

- The sultanate grew to encompass most of India; the sultans ruled through force, pillage, and heavy taxation.

- Though efficient, the sultanate suffered from internal struggles and fell under pressure from rival states and invaders.

The weakening of Delhi's central authority tempted fresh Mongol interest in the area. In 1398, the Turko-Mongol leader Timur (see Chapter 12) captured the city of Delhi. When his armies withdrew the next year with vast quantities of loot and tens of thousands of captives, the largest city in southern Asia lay empty and in ruins. The Delhi Sultanate never recovered.

For all its shortcomings, the Delhi Sultanate triggered the development of centralized political authority in India. Prime ministers and provincial governors serving under the sultans established a bureaucracy, improved food production, promoted trade, and put in circulation a common coinage. Despite the many conflicts that Muslim conquest and rule provoked, Islam gradually acquired a permanent place in South Asia.

INDIAN OCEAN TRADE

■ *How did cultural and ecological differences promote trade, and in turn how did trade and other contacts promote state growth and the spread of Islam?*

When the collapse of the Mongol Empire in the fourteenth century disrupted overland routes across Central Asia, the Indian Ocean assumed greater strategic importance in tying together the peoples of Eurasia and Africa. Between 1200 and 1500, the volume of trade in the Indian Ocean increased. The Indian Ocean routes also facilitated the spread of Islam.

Monsoon Mariners

The prosperity of Islamic and Mongol empires in Asia, cities in Europe, and new kingdoms in Africa and Southeast Asia stimulated and contributed to the vitality of the Indian Ocean network. The demand for luxuries—precious metals and jewels, rare spices, fine textiles, and other manufactures—rose. Larger ships made shipments of bulk cargoes of ordinary cotton textiles, pepper, food grains (rice, wheat, barley), timber, horses, and other goods profitable.

Some goods were transported from one end of this trading network to the other, but few ships or crews made a complete circuit. Instead, the Indian Ocean trade divided into two legs: from the Middle East across the Arabian Sea to India and from India across the Bay of Bengal to Southeast Asia.

Shipyards in ports on the Malabar Coast (southwestern India) and in the Persian Gulf built large numbers of **dhows** (dow), the characteristic cargo and passenger ships of the Arabian Sea. They grew from an average capacity of 100 tons in 1200 to 400 tons in 1500. On a typical expedition, a dhow might sail west from India to Arabia and Africa on the northeast monsoon winds (December to March) and return on the southwest monsoons (April to August). Small dhows kept the coast in sight. Relying on the stars to guide them, skilled pilots steered large vessels by the quicker route straight across the water. A large dhow could sail from the Red Sea to mainland Southeast Asia in two to four months, but few did so. Eastbound cargoes and passengers from dhows reaching India were likely to be transferred to junks, which dominated the eastern half of the Indian Ocean and the South China Sea (see Environment and Technology: The Indian Ocean Dhow).

Junks, the largest, most technologically advanced, and most seaworthy vessels of the time, appeared first in China and spread with Chinese influence overseas. Enormous nails held together hulls of heavy spruce or fir planks, in contrast with dhows, whose planks were sewn together with palm fiber. Below the deck, watertight compartments minimized flooding in case of damage to the ship's hull. The largest junks reportedly had twelve sails made of bamboo strips woven into

dhows Characteristic cargo and passenger ships of the Arabian Sea.

The Indian Ocean Dhow

The sailing vessels that crossed the Indian Ocean shared the diversity of that trading area. The name by which we know them, *dhow*, comes from the Swahili language of the East African coast. The planks of teak from which their hulls were constructed were hewn from the tropical forests of south India and Southeast Asia. Their pilots, who navigated by stars at night, employed techniques that Arabs had used to find their way across the desert. Some pilots used a magnetic compass, which originated in China.

Dhows came in various sizes and designs, but all had two distinctive features in common. The first was hull construction. The hulls of dhows consisted of planks that were sewn together, not nailed. Cord made of fiber from the husk of coconuts or other materials was passed through rows of holes drilled in the planks. Because cord is weaker than nails, outsiders considered this shipbuilding technique strange. Marco Polo fancifully suggested that it indicated sailors' fear that large ocean magnets would pull any nails out of their ships. Better explanations observe that pliant sewn hulls were cheaper to build than rigid nailed hulls and were less likely to be damaged if the ships ran aground on coral reefs.

The second distinctive feature of dhows was their sails made of palm leaves or cloth. Sails that were either triangular (lateen) or had a very short leading edge were suspended from tall masts and could be turned to catch the wind.

Dhow *This modern model shows the vessel's main features.*

Sewn hulls and lateen sails had appeared centuries earlier, but two innovations appeared between 1200 and 1500. First, a rudder positioned at the stern (rear end) of the ship replaced the large side oar that formerly had controlled steering. Second, shipbuilders increased the size of dhows to accommodate bulkier cargoes.

mats and carried a crew of a thousand men, including four hundred soldiers. A large junk might accommodate a hundred passenger cabins and a cargo of over 1,000 tons. Junks dominated China's foreign shipping to Southeast Asia and India, but the Chinese did not control all of the junks that plied these waters. During the fifteenth century, similar vessels came out of Bengal and Southeast Asia.

Decentralized and cooperative commercial interests, rather than political authorities, connected the several regions that participated in the Indian Ocean trade. The **Swahili** (swah-HEE-lee) **Coast**

supplied ivory, wood, and gold from inland areas of Africa. Ports around the Arabian peninsula supplied horses, incense, and manufactured goods from the Mediterranean region. Merchants in the cities of coastal India received goods from east and west, sold some locally, passed others along, and added Indian goods to the trade. The Strait of Malacca (meh-LAK-eh), between the eastern end of the Indian Ocean and

Swahili Coast East African shores of the Indian Ocean between the Horn of Africa and the Zambezi River; from the Arabic *sawahil*, meaning "shores."

the South China Sea, provided a meeting point for trade from Southeast Asia, China, and the Indian Ocean. In each region, certain ports functioned as giant emporia, consolidating goods from smaller ports and inland areas for transport across the seas.

Africa: The Swahili Coast and Zimbabwe

Trade expanded steadily along the East African coast from about 1250, giving rise to between thirty and forty separate city-states by 1500. After 1200, masonry buildings as much as four stories high replaced mud and thatch dwellings, and archaeological finds include Chinese porcelain, imported glass beads, and other exotic goods. Coastal and island peoples shared a common culture and a language built on African grammar and vocabulary but incorporating many Arabic and Persian terms and written in Arabic script. In time, these people became known as "Swahili," from the Arabic word *sawahil* (suh-WAH-hil), meaning "shores."

What attracted the Arab and Iranian merchants whom oral traditions associate with the Swahili Coast's commercial expansion? By the late fifteenth century, the major port of Kilwa, described by Ibn Battuta as "one of the most beautiful and well-constructed towns in the world," was annually exporting a ton of gold mined by inland Africans much farther south. Much of it came from or passed through a powerful state on the plateau south of the Zambezi River. At its peak in about 1400, its capital city, now known as **Great Zimbabwe**, occupied 193 acres (78 hectares) and had some eighteen thousand inhabitants.

Between about 1250 and 1450, local African craftsmen built stone structures for Great Zimbabwe's rulers, priests, and wealthy citizens. The largest structure, an enclosure the size and shape of a large football stadium with walls of unmortared stone 17 feet (5 meters) thick and 32 feet (10 meters) high, served as the king's court. A large conical stone tower was among the many buildings inside the walls.

As in Mali, mixed farming and cattle herding provided the economic basis of the Great Zimbabwe state, but long-distance trade brought added wealth. Trade began regionally with copper ingots from the upper Zambezi Valley, salt, and local manufactures. Gold exports to the coast expanded in the fourteenth

and fifteenth centuries and brought Zimbabwe to its peak. However, historians suspect that the city's residents depleted nearby forests for firewood while their cattle overgrazed surrounding grasslands. The resulting ecological crisis hastened the empire's decline in the fifteenth century.

The city of **Aden** (A[as in hat]-den) near the southwestern tip of the Arabian peninsula had a double advantage in the Indian Ocean trade. Monsoon winds brought enough rainfall to supply drinking water to a large population and grow grain for export, and its location made it a convenient stopover for trade with India, the Persian Gulf, East Africa, and Egypt. Aden's merchants dealt in cotton cloth and beads from India; spices from Southeast Asia; horses from Arabia and Ethiopia; pearls from the Red Sea; manufactured luxuries from Cairo; slaves, gold, and ivory from Ethiopia; and grain, opium, and dyes from Aden's own hinterland.

Common commercial interests generally promoted good relations among the different religions and cultures of this region. For example, in the mid-thirteenth century, a wealthy Jew from Aden named Yosef settled in Christian Ethiopia, where he acted as an adviser. South Arabia had been trading with neighboring parts of Africa since before the time of King Solomon of Israel. The dynasty that ruled Ethiopia after 1270 boasted (legendary) descent from Solomon and the Queen of Sheba from across the Red Sea. Ethiopia's Solomonic dynasty greatly increased trade through the Red Sea port of Zeila (ZAY-luh), including trade in slaves, amber, and animal pelts, which went to Aden and on to other destinations.

Friction sometimes arose, however. In the late fifteenth century, Ethiopia's territorial expansion and efforts to increase control over the trade provoked conflicts with Muslims who ruled the coastal states of the Red Sea.

Great Zimbabwe City, now in ruins (in the modern African country of Zimbabwe), whose many stone structures were built between about 1250 and 1450, when it was a trading center and the capital of a large state.

Aden Port city in the modern south Arabian country of Yemen. It has been a major trading center in the Indian Ocean since ancient times.

Royal Enclosure, Great Zimbabwe Inside these oval stone walls the rulers of the trading state of Great Zimbabwe lived. Forced to enter the enclosure through a narrow corridor between two high walls, visitors were meant to be awestruck.

Embassy Photo/Visual Connection Archive

India: Gujarat and the Malabar Coast

The state of Gujarat in western India prospered from the expanding trade of the Arabian Sea and the rise of the Delhi Sultanate. Blessed with a rich agricultural hinterland and a long coastline, Gujarat attracted new trade after the Mongol destruction of Baghdad in 1258 disrupted the northern land routes. Despite the violence of its forced incorporation into the Delhi Sultanate in 1298, Gujarat prospered from increased commercial interaction with Delhi's ruling class. Independent again after 1390, the Muslim rulers of Gujarat extended their control over neighboring Hindu states and regained their preeminent position in the Indian Ocean trade.

Gujaratis exported cotton textiles and indigo to the Middle East and Europe in return for gold and silver. They also shipped cotton cloth, carnelian beads, and foodstuffs to the Swahili Coast in exchange for ebony, slaves, ivory, and gold. During the fifteenth century, Gujarat's trade zone expanded eastward to the Strait of Malacca. There Gujarati merchants helped spread the Islamic faith among East Indian

traders, some of whom even imported specially carved gravestones from Gujarat.

Unlike Kilwa and Aden, Gujarat manufactured goods for trade. According to the thirteenth-century Venetian traveler Marco Polo, Gujarat's leatherworkers dressed enough skins in a year to fill several ships to Arabia and other places. They made sleeping mats for export to the Middle East "in red and blue leather, exquisitely inlaid with figures of birds and beasts, and skillfully embroidered with gold and silver wire," as well as leather cushions embroidered in gold.

Later observers compared the Gujarati city of Cambay (modern name Khambhat) with cities in Flanders and northern Italy (see Chapter 13) in the scale, craftsmanship, and diversity of its textile industries. Cotton, linen, and silk cloth, along with carpets and quilts, found a large market in Europe, Africa, the Middle East, and Southeast Asia. Cambay also produced polished gemstones, gold jewelry, carved ivory, stone beads, and both pearls and mother of pearl. At the height of its prosperity in the fifteenth century, its well-laid-out streets and open places boasted fine stone houses with tiled roofs. Although Muslim residents controlled most of Gujarat's overseas trade, its Hindu merchant caste profited so much from related commercial activities that their wealth and luxurious lives became the envy of other Indians.

More southerly cities on the well-watered Malabar Coast of India imitated Gujarat's success. Calicut (KAL-ih-cut) (modern name Kozhikode) and other coastal cities prospered from local cotton, grains, and spices. They also served as clearing-houses for the long-distance trade of the Indian Ocean. The zamorin (ZAH-much-ruhn) (ruler) of Calicut presided over a loose federation of its Hindu rulers that united the coastal region, but steep mountains known as the Western Ghats cut the coast off from the inland areas on the Deccan Plateau. As in eastern Africa and Arabia, rulers tolerated religious and ethnic groups who contributed to commercial profits. Most trading activity lay in the hands of Muslims, many originally from Iran and Arabia, who intermarried with local Indian Muslims. Jewish merchants also operated from Malabar's trading cities.

Southeast Asia

At the eastern end of the Indian Ocean, the Strait of Malacca between the Malay Peninsula and the island of Sumatra provided the principal passage into the South China Sea (see Map 14.2). As trade increased in the fourteenth and fifteenth centuries, this commercial choke point became the site of political rivalry. The mainland kingdom of Siam controlled most of the upper Malay Peninsula, while the Java-based kingdom of Majapahit (mah-jah-PAH-heet) extended its dominion over the lower Malay Peninsula and much of Sumatra. Majapahit, however, could not suppress Chinese pirates based at the Sumatran city of Palembang (pah-lem-BONG) who preyed on ships sailing through the strait. In 1407, a fleet from China commanded by the admiral Zheng He (see Chapter 12) smashed the pirates' power and took their chief back home for trial.

Majapahit, weakened by internal struggles, could not take advantage of China's intervention, making the chief beneficiary the newer port of **Malacca** (or Melaka), which dominated the narrowest part of the strait. Under a prince from Palembang, Malacca

SECTION REVIEW

- Traversed by dhows and junks, the maritime trade network of the Indian Ocean tied together peoples of Asia, Africa, and Europe.

- Decentralized commercial interests rose throughout the network, including the Swahili city-states that exported African gold from Great Zimbabwe.

- Aden dealt in a variety of goods from Africa, Arabia, and Southeast Asia and traded with Zeila on the Red Sea.

- Despite political turmoil, the cities of Gujarat and the Malabar Coast prospered through agriculture, manufacture, and trade.

- Through astute alliances, Malacca grew into the predominant emporium of Southeast Asia.

had grown from an obscure fishing village into an important port through a series of astute alliances. Nominally subject to the king of Siam, Malacca also secured an alliance with China that was sealed by the visit of the imperial fleet in 1407. The conversion of an early ruler from Hinduism to Islam helped promote trade with Muslim merchants from Gujarat and elsewhere. Merchants also appreciated Malacca's security and low taxes.

Malacca served not just as a meeting point but also as an emporium for Southeast Asian products: rubies and musk from Burma, tin from Malaya, gold from Sumatra, cloves and nutmeg from the Moluccas (or Spice Islands, as Europeans later dubbed them). Shortly after 1500, when Malacca was at its height, one resident counted eighty-four languages spoken among the merchants gathered there, who came from as far away as Turkey, Ethiopia, and the Swahili Coast. Four officials administered the foreign merchant communities: one for the Gujaratis, one for other Indians and Burmese, one for Southeast Asians, and one for the Chinese and Japanese. Malacca's wealth and its cosmopolitan residents set the standard for luxury in Malaya for centuries to come.

Malacca Port city in the modern Southeast Asian country of Malaysia, founded about 1400 as a trading center on the Strait of Malacca.

SOCIAL AND CULTURAL CHANGE

■ *What social and cultural changes are reflected in the history of peoples living in tropical Africa and Asia during this period?*

As a result of state growth, commercial expansion, and the spread of Islam between 1200 and 1500, Muslim political and commercial elites grew in numbers and power. Religious agents sought converts both within and beyond the boundaries of Muslim states. Africa and India's local art, rituals, and even theological doctrines combined with those of Islam to form syncretic religious formations, often in the guise of Sufi brotherhoods, reminiscent of the syncretism of the Hellenistic period (see Chapter 4).

Architecture, Learning, and Religion

Social and cultural changes typically affected cities more than rural areas. As travelers often observed, wealthy merchants and ruling elites spent lavishly on mansions, palaces, and places of worship while the lives of common people were less affected. Most mosques, local pilgrimage sites, and Sufi shrines surviving from this period blend older traditions and new influences. For example, African Muslims produced Middle Eastern mosque designs in local building materials: sun-baked clay reinforced by wooden crossbeams in the western Sudan, masonry using blocks of coral on the Swahili Coast. Once their homelands came under Muslim rule, south Asian artisans were free to travel to newly Islamized regions like Gujarat and older Muslim lands like Afghanistan and Iran, bringing with them Hindu temple architectural ideas and sometimes material for Muslim places of worship. The congregational mosque at Cambay, built in 1325, utilized pillars, porches, and arches taken from sacked Hindu and Jain (jine) temples. The congregational mosque erected at the Gujarati capital of Ahmedabad (AH-muhd-ah-bahd) in 1423 had the open courtyard typical of mosques everywhere, but the surrounding verandas incorporated many Gujarati details and architectural conventions.

Mosques, churches, and temples were centers of education as well as prayer and ritual. Muslims promoted literacy among their sons (and sometimes their daughters) so that they could read sacred texts. In some lands south of the Sahara, Ethiopia excepted, Islam provided the first exposure to literate culture. In much of South Asia, literacy in Indo-European languages like Sanskrit and Dravidian languages like Tamil had been established many centuries before. Even there, however, a migration of Arabic and Persian vocabulary into local languages produced significant changes. Scholars adapted the Arabic alphabet to write local languages like Hausa in Mali and numerous tongues in the Malay Peninsula and island Southeast Asia.

Persian became the court language of the Delhi Sultanate, but **Urdu** (ER-doo), a Persian-influenced form of the local Hindustani tongue of northern India, eventually became an important literary language written in Arabic characters. Muslims also introduced paper into their new lands. This was an improvement over palm leaves and other fragile materials, but tropical humidity and insect life made preservation of written knowledge difficult nevertheless.

Muslim scholars everywhere studied the Quran along with Islamic law and theology. A few demonstrated a high level of interest in mathematics, medicine, science, and philosophy, partly derived from ancient Greek writings translated into Arabic (see Chapter 9). In sixteenth-century **Timbuktu** (see Map 14.1), over 150 schools taught the Quran while leading clerics taught advanced classes in mosques or homes. Books imported from North Africa brought high prices. Al-Hajj Ahmed, a scholar who died in Timbuktu in 1536, possessed some seven hundred volumes, an unusually large library for that time. In Southeast Asia, Malacca became a center of Islamic learning from which scholars spread Islam throughout the region. Other important centers of learning developed in Muslim India, particularly in Delhi, the capital.

Urdu A Persian-influenced literary form of Hindi written in Arabic characters and used as a literary language since the 1300s.

Timbuktu City on the Niger River in the modern country of Mali. It was founded by the Tuareg as a seasonal camp sometime after 1000. As part of the Mali Empire, Timbuktu became a major terminus of the trans-Saharan trade and a center of Islamic learning.

Even in conquered lands, Muslim rulers seldom required conversion. Example and persuasion by merchants and Sufis proved more effective in winning new believers. Muslim domination of long-distance trade assisted the adoption of Islam. Commercial transactions could take place across religious boundaries, but the common code of morality and law that Islam provided encouraged trust and drew many local merchants to Islam. From the major trading centers along the Swahili Coast, in the Sudan, in coastal India, and in Southeast Asia, Islam's influence spread along regional trade routes.

Islam also spread among rural peoples, such as the pastoral Fulani of West Africa and Somali. In Bengal, Muslim religious figures working for state officials oversaw the conversion of jungle into rice paddies and thereby gained converts among the people who came to work the land and inhabit the new villages. At first the new converts melded Islamic beliefs with Hindu traditions, seeing Muhammad, for example, as a manifestation of the god Vishnu. Over time, however, more standard versions of Islam gained headway.

Marriage also played a role. Single Muslim men traveling to and settling in tropical Africa and Asia often married local women. Their children grew up in the paternal faith because Islamic doctrine specified the transmission of religious identity in the male line. Some wealthy men had dozens of children from up to four wives and additional slave concubines. Servants and slaves in such households normally professed Islam.

In India, Muslim invasions eliminated the last strongholds of long-declining Buddhism, including, in 1196, the great Buddhist center of study at Nalanda (nuh-LAN-duh) in Bihar (bee-HAHR). Its manuscripts were burned, and thousands of monks were killed or driven into exile in Nepal and Tibet. With Buddhism reduced to a minor faith in the land of its birth, Islam emerged as India's second most important religion, displacing Hinduism as the elite religion in most of maritime Southeast Asia and slowly supplanting a variety of local cults. In mainland Southeast Asia, Buddhism and Islam vied for supremacy, with Islam prevailing in the south and Buddhism farther north in Thailand, Cambodia, and Burma (Myanmar).

Social and Gender Distinctions

A growth in slavery accompanied the rising prosperity of the elites. Military campaigns in India, according to Islamic sources, reduced hundreds of thousands of Hindu "infidels" to slavery. Delhi overflowed with slaves. Sultan Ala ud-Din owned 50,000 and Firuz Shah 180,000, including 12,000 skilled artisans. Sultan Tughluq sent 100 male slaves and 100 female slaves as a gift to the emperor of China in return for a similar gift.

When gold cut into the profitability of trans-Saharan trade, Mali and Bornu sent slaves across the Sahara to North Africa. The expanding Ethiopian Empire regularly sent captives to Aden traders at Zeila. Many eunuchs (castrated males) were included. According to modern estimates, Saharan and Red Sea traders sold about 2.5 million enslaved Africans between 1200 and 1500. African slaves from the Swahili Coast played conspicuous roles in the navies, armies, and administrations of some Indian states, especially in the fifteenth century. A few African slaves even reached China, where a source from about 1225 says rich families preferred gatekeepers with bodies "black as lacquer." Later Chinese paintings show Portuguese ships manned almost entirely by African seamen.

With "free" labor abundant and cheap, few slaves worked as farmers. In some places, hereditary castes of slaves dominated certain trades and military units. Indeed, the rulers of the Delhi Sultanate included a number of the powerful military caste of Turkish mamluk slaves (see Chapter 9). A slave general in the western Sudan named Askia Muhammad seized control of the Songhai Empire (Mali's successor) in 1493. Less fortunate slaves, like the men and women who mined copper in Mali, did hard menial work.

Wealthy households used many slave servants. Eunuchs guarded the harems of wealthy Muslims, but women predominated as household slaves, serving also as entertainers and concubines. Some rich men aspired to having a concubine from every part of the world. One of Firuz Shah's nobles reportedly had two thousand harem slaves, including women from Turkey and China.

Hindu commentaries suggest that the position of Hindu women may have improved somewhat. The ancient practice of sati (suh-TEE)—that is, of an upper-caste widow throwing herself on her husband's funeral pyre—remained a meritorious act strongly approved by social custom. But Ibn Battuta makes it clear that sati was strictly optional. Since the Hindu commentaries devote considerable attention to the rights of widows without sons to inherit their husbands' estates, one may even conclude that sati was rare.

A woman's male master—father, husband, or owner—determined her status, and Indian parents still gave their daughters in marriage before the age of puberty. But consummation of the marriage took place only when the young woman was ready. Wives faced far stricter rules of fidelity and chastity than their husbands and could be abandoned for any serious breach, but other offenses against law and custom usually brought lighter penalties than for men. Women seldom played active roles in commerce, administration, or religion.

Women involved themselves with child rearing, food preparation, and, when not prohibited by religious restrictions, brewing. In many parts of Africa, women commonly made beer from grains or bananas. These mildly alcoholic beverages played an important part in male rituals of hospitality and relaxation. Throughout tropical Africa and Asia, women toted heavy loads of food, firewood, and water balanced on their heads and did much of the farm work, as well as making clothing and clay pots. In India, women typically spun at home, leaving weaving to men now that the spinning wheel, possibly a local invention, reduced the cost of weaving by making the process faster. In West Africa, women often sold agricultural products, pottery, and other craftwork in the markets.

Differences between Muslims and Hindus on matters relating to gender were not as great as the formal religious texts of the two religious traditions would suggest. South Asian tradition tended to outweigh Muslim practices imported from Arabia and Persia, and African Islam showed similar inclinations in the area of gender. In Mali's capital, Ibn Battuta was appalled that Muslim women both free and slave did not completely cover their bodies and veil their faces when appearing in public. He considered their nakedness an offense to women's (and men's) modesty. Elsewhere in Mali, he berated a Muslim merchant from Morocco for permitting his wife to sit on a couch and chat with her male friend. The husband replied, "The association of women with men is agreeable to us and part of good manners, to which no suspicion attaches." Ibn Battuta refused to visit the merchant again.

THE WESTERN HEMISPHERE

■ *What were the key differences between the societies of Africa and Asia and the empires of the Aztecs and Inkas?*

Though isolated from the Eastern Hemisphere by oceans that were not crossed until the end of the fifteenth century, the tropical regions of the Western Hemisphere shared many of the climatic characteristics of the Old World tropics (see Chapter 7). However, the region's two most powerful urbanized empires, the Aztecs of Mexico and the Inka of Peru, developed at altitudes above 7,000 feet (11,265 meters), thus experiencing lower average rainfall and temperature than is common across the tropics. They also differed in being themselves centers of civilization rather than subsidiary to dominating political and economic powers located in temperate lands to the north or south.

Mesoamerica had witnessed a series of urbanized societies—Olmec, Maya, Toltec—from the

SECTION REVIEW

- Social and cultural life changed as a result of state formation, commercial expansion, and the spread of Islam.
- These changes mostly affected cities, where elites financed building programs, fostering hybrid styles of religious architecture.
- Islam spread mainly through peaceful adaptation and promoted education and scholarship.
- With rising prosperity came the expansion of slavery, which was endorsed by Islam.
- The position of Indian women seems to have improved, and the spread of Islam did not mean adoption of Arab gender customs.

second millennium B.C.E. onward, and the mountains and coastal deserts of the Andean region had an equally long sequence, including Moche, Tiwanaku, Wari, and Chimū (see Chapter 7). Apart from these advanced regions, which saw the rise of powerful empires between 1300 and 1500 C.E., most Western Hemisphere societies of the period subsisted at more basic levels as hunters and gatherers or village agriculturists.

Mesoamerica: The Aztecs

The Mexica (meh-SHE-ca) pushed into central Mexico from the north during the collapse of the Toltecs (see Chapter 7). When they arrived, the Mexica were organized as an **altepetl** (al-TEH-peh-tel)—an ethnic state led by a tlatoani (tlah-toh-AHN-ee) or ruler and the common political unit of the region. A group of **calpolli** (cal-POH-yee), each with up to a hundred families, served as the foundation of the altepetl, controlling land allocation, tax collection, and local religious life. Adapting to the political and social practices that they found among the urbanized agriculturalists of the valley, the Mexica first served their more powerful neighbors as serfs and mercenaries. As their strength grew, they relocated to small islands near the shore of Lake Texcoco.

Military successes allowed the Mexica to seize control of additional agricultural land along the lakeshore and to forge military alliances with neighboring altepetl. Once these more complex political and economic arrangements were in place, the Mexica-dominated alliance became the Aztec Empire. With increased economic independence, greater political security, and territorial expansion, the **Aztecs** transformed their political organization by introducing a monarchical system similar to that found in more powerful neighboring states. A council of powerful aristocrats selected new rulers from among male members of the ruling lineage. Once selected, the ruler had to renegotiate the submission of dependencies and then demonstrate his divine mandate by undertaking new military conquests. War acquired religious meaning, providing the ruler with legitimacy and increasing the prestige of successful warriors.

Around 1325 C.E. the Aztecs began the construction of their twin capitals, **Tenochtitlan** (teh-noch-TIT-lan) and Tlatelolco (tla-teh-LOHL-coh) (together the foundation for modern Mexico City). The population of Tenochtitlan and Tlatelolco combined with that of the cities and towns of the surrounding lakeshore was approximately 500,000 by 1500 C.E. Three causeways connected this island capital to the lakeshore. Planners laid out the urban center as a grid where canals and streets intersected at right angles to facilitate the movement of people and goods.

Although warfare gave increased power and privilege to males, women held substantial power and exercised broad influence in Aztec society. The roles of women and men were clearly distinguished, but women were held in high esteem. Scholars call this "gender complementarity." Following the birth of a boy, his umbilical cord was buried on the battlefield and he was given implements to signal his occupation or his role as a warrior. In the case of a girl, her umbilical cord was buried near the hearth and she was given weaving implements and female clothing. Women dominated the household and the markets, and sometimes served as teachers and priestesses. They were also seen as the founders of lineages, including the royal line.

Aztec military successes and territorial expansion allowed the warrior elite to seize land and peasant labor as spoils of war. In time, the royal family and highest-ranking members of the aristocracy possessed extensive estates that were cultivated by slaves and landless commoners. The lower classes received some material rewards from imperial expansion but lost their influence over decisions. Some commoners

---

altepetl An ethnic state in ancient Mesoamerica, the common political building block of that region.

calpolli A group of up to a hundred families that served as a social building block of an altepetl in ancient Mesoamerica.

Aztec The Mexica-dominated alliance that created a powerful empire in central Mexico (1325–1521).

Tenochtitlan Capital of the Aztec Empire, located on an island in Lake Texcoco. Its population was above 150,000 on the eve of the Spanish conquest. Mexico City was constructed on its ruins.

were able to achieve some social mobility through success on the battlefield.

However, by 1500 C.E. great inequalities in wealth and privilege characterized Aztec society. One of the Spaniards who participated in the conquest of the Aztec Empire remembered his first meeting with the Aztec ruler Moctezuma (mock-teh-ZU-ma) II (r. 1502–1520): "Many great lords walked before the great Montezuma [Moctezuma II], sweeping the ground on which he was to tread and laying down cloaks so that his feet should not touch the earth. Not one of these chieftains dared look him in the face."[3] While commoners lived in small dwellings and ate a limited diet of staples, members of the nobility lived in large, well-constructed, two-story houses and consumed a diet rich in animal protein.

A specialized class of merchants controlled long-distance trade. Given the absence of draft animals and wheeled vehicles in Mesoamerica, lightweight and valuable products like gold, jewels, feathered garments, cacao, and animal skins dominated this commerce. Merchants also provided political and military intelligence. Commerce took place without money or credit. Cacao beans, quills filled with gold, and cotton cloth were the standard units of value used to barter for goods. Aztec expansion integrated producers and consumers in the central Mexican economy. Hernán Cortés (1485–1547), the Spanish adventurer who eventually conquered the Aztecs, expressed his admiration for the abundance of the Aztec marketplace:

> One square in particular is twice as big as that of Salamanca and completely surrounded by arcades where there are daily more than sixty thousand folk buying and selling. Every kind of merchandise such as may be met with in every land is for sale. . . . There is nothing to be found in all the land which is not sold in these markets, for over and above what I have mentioned there are so many and such various things that on account of their very number . . . I cannot detail them.[4]

Although powerful and wealthy, merchants were never accepted into the ranks of the high nobility.

The Aztec state met the challenge of feeding an urban population of approximately 150,000 by efficiently organizing the labor of calpolli and of additional laborers sent by defeated peoples to expand agricultural land. Land reclamation centered on dikes more than 5 miles (9 kilometers) long by 23 feet (7 meters) wide that separated the fresh and salt water parts of Lake Texcoco. The dikes, whose construction consumed 4 million person-days, supported greater irrigation. Aztec **chinampas**—raised fields along lakeshores—contributed maize, fruits, and vegetables to the Tenochtitlan markets. The imposition of a **tribute system** on conquered peoples also helped relieve the capital's population pressure. Unlike the tribute system of Tang China, where tribute had a more symbolic character (see Chapter 11), one-quarter of the Aztec capital's food came from tribute payments of maize, beans, and other foods.

Religious rituals dominated public life in Tenochtitlan. As in other cultures of the Mesoamerican world, human sacrifice was common. Some scholars note that sacrifices took place before large crowds that included leaders from enemy and subject states, as well as the Aztec masses. The Aztecs worshiped numerous gods, most of which had a dual nature—both male and female. The chief god of the Mexica was Huitzilopochtli (wheat-zeel-oh-POSHT-lee) or southern hummingbird. Originally associated with war, it was later identified with the sun. Tenochtitlan was architecturally dominated by a great twin temple devoted to Huitzilopochtli and Tlaloc, the storm-god, symbolizing the two bases of the Aztec economy: war and agriculture.

---

[4]Hernando Cortéz, *Five Letters, 1519–1926*, trans. J. Bayard Morris (New York: Norton, 1991), 87.

chinampas Raised fields constructed along lakeshores in central Mexico to increase agricultural yields.

tribute system A system in which defeated peoples were forced to pay a tax in the form of goods and labor. The forced transfer of food, cloth, and other goods subsidized the development of large cities. An important component of the Aztec and Inka economies.

---

[3]Bernal Diaz del Castillo, *The Conquest of the New Spain*, trans. J.M. Cohen (London: Penguin Books, 1963), 217.

Werner Forman/Universal Images Group/Getty Images

Inka Tunic Andean weavers produced beautiful textiles from cotton and from the wool of llamas and alpacas. The Inka inherited this rich craft tradition and produced some of the world's most remarkable textiles. The quality and design of each garment indicated the weaver's rank and power in this society. This tunic was an outer garment for a powerful male.

The Andes: The Inka

In little more than a hundred years, the **Inka** developed a vast imperial state, which they called "Land of Four Corners." By 1525 the empire had a population of more than 6 million and stretched from the Maule River in Chile to northern Ecuador and from the Pacific coast across the Andes to the upper Amazon and, in the south, into Argentina. In the early fifteenth century, the Inka were one of many competing military powers in the southern highlands, an area of limited political significance after the collapse of Wari (see Chapter 7).

The Inka were traditional highland pastoralists whose prosperity and military strength depended on vast herds of llamas and alpacas. Centered in the valley of Cuzco, they were initially organized as a chiefdom based on reciprocal gift giving and the redistribution of food and textiles. Strong and resourceful leaders consolidated political authority in the 1430s and undertook ambitious military expansion.

The Inka state utilized Andean social customs and economic practices. Tiwanaku had used colonists to provide supplies of resources from distant, ecologically distinct zones. The Inka built on this legacy by

Inka Largest and most powerful Andean empire. Controlled the Pacific coast of South America from Ecuador to Chile from its capital of Cuzco.

conquering additional territories and increasing the scale of forced exchanges. Crucial to this process was the development of a large military. Unlike the peoples of Mesoamerica, who distributed specialized goods through markets and tribute relationships, Andean peoples used state power to broaden and expand the vertical exchange system that had permitted self-governing extended family groups called *ayllus* to exploit a range of ecological niches.

Collective efforts by mita labor, a system of forced service to the ruler (see Chapter 7), made the Inka Empire possible. Cuzco, the imperial capital, and the provincial cities, the royal court, the imperial armies, and the state's religious cults all rested on this foundation. The mita system also created the material surplus that provided the bare necessities for the old, weak, and ill of Inka society. Each ayllu contributed approximately one-seventh of its adult male population to meet these collective obligations. These draft laborers served as soldiers, construction workers, craftsmen, and runners to carry messages along post roads. They also drained swamps, terraced mountainsides, filled in valley floors, built and maintained irrigation works, and built storage facilities and roads. Inka laborers constructed 13,000 miles (20,930 kilometers) of road, facilitating military troop movements, administration, and trade.

The hereditary chiefs of ayllus, a group that included women, carried out local administrative and judicial functions. As the Inka expanded, they generally left local rulers in place. By doing so they risked rebellion, but they controlled these risks by a thinly veiled system of hostage taking and the use of military garrisons. Rulers of defeated regions sent their heirs to live at the Inka court in Cuzco, and representations of important local gods were brought to Cuzco to join the imperial pantheon. These measures promoted imperial integration while providing hostages to ensure the good behavior of subject peoples.

Conquests magnified the authority of the Inka ruler and led to the creation of an imperial bureaucracy drawn from his kinsmen. The royal family claimed descent from the sun, the primary Inka god. Members of the royal family lived in palaces main-

tained by armies of servants. Political and religious rituals dominated the lives of the ruler and his family and helped legitimize their authority. Because extending imperial boundaries by warfare was a king's duty, each new ruler began his reign with conquest.

Tenochtitlan, the Aztec capital, had a population of about 150,000 in 1520. At the height of Inka power in 1530, Cuzco had a population of less than 30,000. Nevertheless, Cuzco contained impressive buildings of carefully cut stones fitted together without mortar. The city was laid out in the shape of a giant puma (a mountain lion), and its center contained the palaces of rulers as well as the major temples. The richest was the Temple of the Sun, its interior lined with sheets of gold and its patio decorated with golden representations of llamas and corn. The ruler made every effort to awe and intimidate visitors and residents alike with a nearly continuous series of rituals, feasts, and sacrifices. Sacrifices of textiles, animals, and other goods sent as tribute dominated the city's calendar. The destruction of these valuable commodities, and a small number of human sacrifices, conveyed an impression of splendor and sumptuous abundance to validate the ruler's claimed descent from the sun.

Inka cultural achievement rested on the strong foundation of earlier Andean civilizations. We know that astronomical observation was a central concern of the priestly class, as in Mesoamerica. The collective achievements of Andean peoples were accomplished with a limited record-keeping system adapted from earlier Andean civilizations. Administrators used knotted colored cords, called **khipus** (KEY-pooz), for public administration, population counts, and tribute obligations. Inka weaving and metallurgy, also based on earlier regional development, was more advanced than in Mesoamerica. Inka craftsmen produced utilitarian tools and weapons of copper and bronze as well as decorative objects of gold and silver, while women produced textiles of extraordinary beauty from cotton and llama and alpaca wool.

khipus System of knotted colored cords used by preliterate Andean peoples to record information.

SECTION REVIEW

• The major centers of civilization of this period in the Western Hemisphere, although in the tropical zone, developed at altitudes around 7,000 feet and thus experienced more temperate climates.

• The Aztecs used conquest, trade, and an extensive irrigation system to build a mighty empire.

• Religion and sacrifice played an important role in Aztec life.

• The Inka relied on forced labor, conquest, and an extensive road system to hold together a diverse empire.

• Vertical exchange of products from different ecological niches benefited everyone in the empire.

• Luxury textiles and items of precious metals for the inka elite highlighted craft production.

Although the Inka did not introduce new technologies, they increased economic output and added to the region's prosperity. Ruling large populations in environmentally distinct regions allowed the Inka to multiply exchanges between ecological niches. But imperial economic and political expansion reduced equality and diminished local autonomy. The imperial elite, living in richly decorated palaces in Cuzco and other urban centers, were increasingly isolated from the masses. Even provincial nobility were held at arm's length. Commoners faced execution if they look directly at the ruler's face.

After only a century of regional dominance, the Inka Empire faced a crisis in 1525. The death of the ruler Huayna Capac at the conclusion of the conquest of Ecuador initiated a bloody struggle for the throne. The rivalry of two sons compelled both the professional military and the hereditary Inka elite to choose sides. The resulting civil war weakened the imperial state and ignited the resentments of regionalism and ethnic diversity on the eve of the arrival of Europeans.

CONCLUSION

Tropical Africa and Asia contained 40 percent of the world's population and over a quarter of its habitable land. Between 1200 and 1500, commercial, political, and cultural currents drew the region's peoples closer together. The Indian Ocean became the world's most important and richest trading area. The Delhi Sultanate brought the greatest political unity to India since the decline of the Guptas, and Mali extended the political and trading role pioneered by Ghana in the western Sudan. Trade and empire followed closely the enlargement of Islam's presence and the accompanying diversification of Islamic customs.

Yet many social and cultural practices remained stable. Most tropical Africans and Asians never ventured far outside the rural communities where their families had lived for generations. Their lives followed the patterns of agricultural or pastoral life, the cycle of religious observances, traditional occupational and kinship divisions, and the individual's passage through the stages of life from childhood to elder status. Village communities proved remarkably hardy. They might be ravaged by natural disaster or pillaged by advancing armies, but over time most recovered. Empires and kingdoms rose and fell, but village life endured.

In the Western Hemisphere, the powerful empires of the Aztecs and Inka rose in Mesoamerica and the Andean region, respectively. Each was heir to a series of preceding cultures, but they had in common an unprecedented territorial size. The Aztecs excelled at irrigation and trade, the Inka at labor organization and road building. Both empires were warlike and religious, and their success depended on the economic subordination of conquered peoples as well as specialized production in a variety of environmentally distinct regions.

CHAPTER REVIEW

TROPICAL AFRICA AND ASIA

■ *How did environmental differences shape cultural differences in tropical Africa and Asia?* (page 329)

By 1500 tropical Africa and Asia contained nearly 40 percent of the world's population but just over a quarter of its habitable land. Living in every type of ecosystem, from lush rain forests to arid deserts, tropical peoples had become intimately familiar with their environments, learning not merely to survive but also to prosper in them. African pastoralists tended herds of domestic animals in dry regions, while in Asia the more favorable soil and rainfall enabled farmers to cultivate rice, as well as grains and legumes.

NEW ISLAMIC EMPIRES

■ *Under what circumstances did the first Islamic empires arise in Africa and India?* (page 333)

The period from 1200 to 1500 saw the rise of the first powerful Islamic states outside the Middle East. Chief among these were the Delhi Sultanate, which brought South Asia its greatest political unity since the decline of the Guptas, and the Mali Empire in the western Sudan, which extended the political and trading role pioneered by Ghana. Mali was founded by an indigenous African dynasty that had earlier adopted Islam, while invading Turkish and Afghan Muslims founded the Delhi Sultanate.

INDIAN OCEAN TRADE

■ *How did cultural and ecological differences promote trade, and in turn how did trade and other contacts promote state growth and the spread of Islam?* (page 338)

Of greatest importance to the spread of Islam throughout tropical Africa and Asia was the Indian Ocean, which directly connected lands as distant as North and East Africa, Arabia, India, and Southeast Asia. Having mastered the seasonal monsoons, merchant sailors made the Indian Ocean the world's most important and richest trading area. A host of Muslim city-states arose: Kilwa along the Swahili Coast, Aden at the entrance to the Red Sea, Gujarat in India, and Malacca at the entrance to the South China Sea.

SOCIAL AND CULTURAL CHANGE

■ *What social and cultural changes are reflected in the history of peoples living in tropical Africa and Asia during this period?* (page 343)

With the enlargement of Islam's presence in the tropical world came changes that could be brutal as well as beneficial. Slavery, common in many parts of the world at this time, was an integral part of commerce and social life. A woman's status was largely determined by her father, husband, or owner, and women were generally precluded from holding important positions in religious or political life. Muslim culture in this period also brought great benefits, however. The centrality of the Quran in social life contributed to a rise in literacy, first in Arabic but later in native languages as well. Centers of higher education arose in which subjects such as mathematics, medicine, and science were significantly advanced.

THE WESTERN HEMISPHERE

■ *What were the key differences between the societies of Africa and Asia and the empires of the Aztecs and Inkas?* (page 345)

As the Western Hemisphere's long isolation drew to a close, the Aztecs and Inka used military conquest and political alliance to establish empires in Mesoamerica and the Andes. Divine monarchies that included human sacrifice, their societies were highly stratified and depended on the tribute system of defeated peoples, particularly labor obligations, food tribute, and exchange relationships, rather than their own techno-logical innovation. Unlike in the Eastern Hemisphere, these societies lived in diverse microclimates at high altitudes, a situation that contributed to specialized agricultural niches of such Western Hemisphere crops as cacao, corn, and squash—which were farmed using the methods and technologies of their predecessors. Large territories included roads for long-distance trade, though the absence of large domestic animals meant that transport and trade focused more on lightweight, high value goods than on the bulky cargos shipped on the Indian Ocean. While writing existed for the Aztecs, the Inka utilized khipus—knots on strings—to keep records and a barter system for trading.

Key Terms

Ibn Battuta (p. 329)

tropics (p. 329)

monsoon (p. 330)

Delhi Sultanate (p. 332)

Mali (p. 333)

Mansa Kankan Musa (p. 335)

Gujarat (p. 336)

dhows (p. 338)

Swahili Coast (p. 339)

Great Zimbabwe (p. 340)

Aden (p. 340)

Malacca (p. 342)

Urdu (p. 343)

Timbuktu (p. 343)

altepetl (p. 346)

calpolli (p. 346)

Aztec (p. 346)

Tenochtitlan (p. 346)

chinampas (p. 347)

tribute system (p. 347)

Inka (p. 348)

khipus (p. 349)

The Maritime Revolution

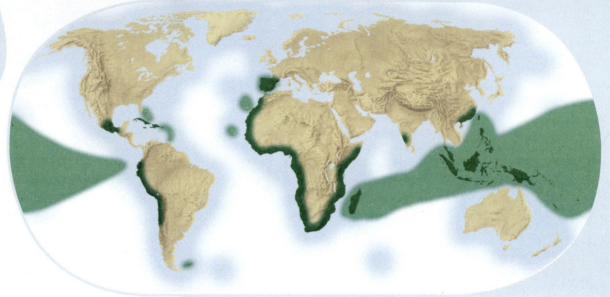

© Cengage Learning

n 1511 young Ferdinand Magellan sailed from Europe around the southern tip of Africa and eastward across the Indian Ocean as a member of the first Portuguese expedition to explore the East Indies (maritime Southeast Asia). Eight years later, this time in the service of Spain, he led an expedition that sought to reach the East Indies by sailing westward. By the middle of 1521 Magellan's expedition had achieved its goal by sailing across the Atlantic, rounding the southern tip of South America, and crossing the Pacific Ocean—but at a high price.

Of the five ships that had set out from Spain in 1519, only three made the long passage across the vast Pacific. Dozens of sailors died from starvation and disease during the voyage. In the Philippines, Magellan, having survived numerous mutinies during the voyage, died in battle on April 27, 1521, while aiding a local ruler who had promised to become a Christian.

To consolidate their dwindling resources, the expedition's survivors burned the least seaworthy of their remaining three ships and consolidated men and supplies. In the end only the *Victoria* made it home across the Indian Ocean and back to Europe. Nevertheless, the *Victoria*'s return to Spain on September 8, 1522, was a crowning example of Europeans' determination to make themselves masters of the oceans. A century of daring and dangerous voyages backed by the Portuguese crown had opened new routes through the South Atlantic to Africa, Brazil, and the rich trade of the Indian Ocean. Rival voyages sponsored by Spain since 1492 opened new contacts with the American continents. A maritime revolution was under way that would change the course of history.

This new maritime era marked the end of a long period when Asia had been the source of the most useful technologies and the most influential systems of belief. It was also home to the most powerful states and the richest overland and maritime trading networks. The success of European voyages of exploration in the following century would redirect the world's center of power, wealth, and innovation to the West.

This maritime revolution broadened and deepened contacts, alliances, and conflicts across ancient cultural boundaries. Some of these contacts ended tragically for individuals like Magellan. Some proved disastrous for entire populations: Amerindians, for instance, suffered conquest, colonization, and a rapid decline in numbers. And sometimes the results were mixed: Asians and Africans found both risks and opportunities in their new relations with Europe.

GLOBAL MARITIME EXPANSION BEFORE 1450

■ *What were the objectives and major accomplishments of the voyages of exploration undertaken by Chinese, Polynesians, and other non-Western peoples?*

By 1450 daring mariners had discovered and settled most of the islands of the Pacific, the Atlantic, and the Indian Ocean, and a great trading system united the peoples around the Indian Ocean. But no one had yet crossed the Pacific in either direction. Even the smaller Atlantic remained a barrier to contact between the Americas, Europe, and Africa. The inhabitants of Australia were also nearly cut off from contact with the rest of humanity. All this was about to change.

The Indian Ocean   Connected through trade, the archipelagos and coastal regions of Southeast Asia were divided politically, culturally, and religiously, but their languages all originated from a common Austronesian root. Scholars often use the term *Malayo Indonesians* or *Malay* to describe the early peoples of this maritime realm.

The region's sailors were highly skilled navigators, ship builders, and sail makers who influenced Chinese and Arab maritime advances. They discovered two direct sea routes between Sri Lanka and the South China Sea through the Straits of Malacca and Sunda, thus opening a profitable link to China's silk markets, and they also used the seasonal monsoon winds of the Indian Ocean to extend their voyages for thousands of miles, ultimately reaching East Africa and settling in Madagascar (see Chapter 8).

By the first century C.E. India and Southeast Asia were trading across the region for spices, gold, and aromatic woods, even sending spices as far west as Rome through Mediterranean intermediaries (see

Chapter 5). Their success attracted African, Arab, and Chinese merchants, creating a large, integrated, and highly profitable market in the centuries that followed. By 1000 the dhows (dow) of Arabs and Africans as well as Malay *jongs* and Chinese junks came together in the region's harbors for commerce.

The rise of Islam (see Chapter 9) gave Indian Ocean trade an important boost. The great Muslim cities of the Middle East provided a demand for valuable commodities, and networks of Muslim traders who shared a common language, ethic, and law actively spread their religion to distant trading cities. By 1400 there were Muslim trading communities all around the Indian Ocean. Chinese merchant communities were present as well.

Indian Ocean traders operated independently of the empires and states they served, but when Ming rulers overthrew Mongol rule in China, they became interested in these wealthy ports and reestablishing China's predominance and prestige abroad. The Ming moved to establish direct contacts with the peoples around the Indian Ocean, sending out seven imperial fleets between 1405 and 1433. Admiral Zheng He (jung huh) (1371–1435) commanded the expeditions. A Chinese Muslim with ancestral connections to the Persian Gulf, Zheng was a fitting emissary to the increasingly Muslim-dominated Indian Ocean Basin (see Chapter 14).

The enormous size of these expeditions, far larger than needed for exploration or promoting trade, indicates that the Ming sought to inspire awe. The first consisted of sixty-two specially built "treasure ships," large Chinese junks each about 300 feet long by 150 feet wide (90 by 45 meters). There were also at least a hundred smaller vessels. Each treasure ship had nine masts, twelve sails, many decks, and a carrying capacity of 3,000 tons (six times the capacity of Columbus's entire fleet). One expedition carried over 27,000 individuals, including infantry and cavalry troops. The ships were armed with small cannon, but highly accurate crossbows dominated most Chinese sea battles.

One Chinese-Arabic interpreter kept a journal recording local customs and beliefs. He observed new flora and fauna, noting exotic animals such as the black panther of Malaya and the tapir of Sumatra. In India he described the division of the coastal population into five classes, which correspond to the four Hindu varna and a separate Muslim class, and the fact that traders in the Indian port of Calicut (KAL-ih-kut) could perform error-free calculations by

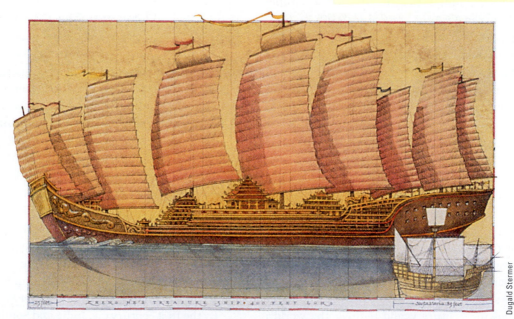

Chinese Junk This modern drawing shows how much larger the Chinese ships were compared to one of Vasco da Gama's vessels. Watertight interior bulkheads made junks the most seaworthy large ships of the fifteenth century. Sails made of pleated bamboo matting hung from the junk's masts, and a stern rudder provided steering. European ships of exploration, though smaller, were faster and more maneuverable.

Dugald Stermer

Chronology

	Pacific Ocean	Atlantic Ocean	Indian Ocean
Pre-1400	**300 B.C.E.–1200 C.E.** Polynesian settlement of Pacific islands **By 1000** Sporadic Polynesian contacts with American mainland **1200–1300** Polynesian societies in Hawaii, Tonga, and elsewhere develop clear class structures with hereditary chiefs	**770–1200** Viking voyages **1300s** Settlement of Madeira, Azores, Canaries **Early 1300s** Mali voyages	
1400		**1418–1460** Voyages of Henry the Navigator **1440s** Slaves from West Africa **1482** Portuguese at Gold Coast and Kongo **1486** Portuguese at Benin **1488** Bartolomeu Dias reaches Indian Ocean **1492** Columbus reaches Caribbean **1492–1500** Spanish conquer Hispaniola **1493** Columbus returns to Caribbean (second voyage) **1498** Columbus reaches mainland of South America (third voyage)	**1405–1433** Voyages of Zheng He **1497–1498** Vasco da Gama reaches India
1500	**1518** Smallpox arrives in Caribbean **1519–1522** Magellan expedition	**1500** Cabral reaches Brazil **1519–1521** Cortés conquers Aztec Empire **1531–1533** Pizarro conquers Inka Empire **1536** Rebellion of Inka in Peru	**1505** Portuguese bombard Swahili Coast cities **1510** Portuguese take Goa **1511** Portuguese take Malacca **1515** Portuguese take Hormuz **1535** Portuguese take Diu **1538** Portuguese defeat Ottoman fleet **1539** Portuguese aid Ethiopia

counting on their fingers and toes rather than using the Chinese abacus. After his return, the interpreter went on tour in China, telling of these exotic places and "how far the majestic virtue of [China's] imperial dynasty extended."[1]

---

[1]Ma Huan, *Ying-yai Sheng-lan: "The Overall Survey of the Ocean's Shores,"* ed. Feng Ch'eng-Chün, trans. J. V. G. Mills (Cambridge, England: Cambridge University Press, 1970), 180.

While curiosity about the region was likely one motive, the fact that the fleets visited major commercial ports suggests that expanding China's trade was an objective as well, and it appears that China's lavish gifts to local rulers stimulated the Swahili market for silk and porcelain. But interest in new contacts was not limited to the Chinese. At least three trading cities on the Swahili (swah-HEE-lee) Coast of East Africa sent delegations to China between 1415 and 1416.

Delegates from Malindi presented the Chinese emperor with a giraffe, creating quite a stir among normally reserved imperial officials. These African delegations may have encouraged more contacts because the next three of Zheng's voyages reached the African coast. Unfortunately, no documents record how Africans and Chinese reacted to each other.

Later Ming emperors would focus their attention on internal matters, facing opposition to the expeditions from some Chinese officials who opposed increased contact with peoples they regarded as barbarians incapable of making contributions to China. Such opposition caused a suspension in the voyages from 1424 to 1431. The final Chinese expedition sailed between 1432 and 1433. But long-established Chinese merchant communities continued as major participants in Indian Ocean trade. As the sultan of Malacca, one of the most prosperous trade centers (see Chapter 14), described the era in 1468, "We have learned that to master the blue oceans people must engage in commerce and trade. All the lands within the seas are united in one body. Life has never been so affluent in preceding generations as it is today."[2]

The Pacific Ocean

Around 3000 B.C.E. Austronesian-speaking seafarers from Southeast Asia reached the island of New Guinea. Contact with the island's original population eventually forged a new cultural identity between these peoples, called *Lapita* by archaeologists. Lapita settlers colonized the island chains of Melanesia (mel-uh-NEE-zhuh), reaching Tonga, Fiji, and Samoa around 1000 B.C.E. By 500 B.C.E. a linguistically and culturally distinct Polynesian culture had emerged from this Lapita origin.

While European sailors were still staying close to shore, Polynesians had mastered long-distance maritime exploration. Pushing east from Tonga, Samoa, and Fiji, they colonized the Marquesas (mar-KAY-suhs) and the Cook and Society archipelagos by approximately 300 B.C.E. Before 500 C.E. Polynesian colonies were established on the Hawaiian Islands 2,200 miles (3,541 kilometers) away. Colonists also

settled Easter Island, 2,300 miles (3,702 kilometers) to the southeast, by 800 C.E., and finally, New Zealand by 1200 C.E. Polynesian voyagers even made periodic contact with the mainland of South America after 1000 C.E., passing on the domesticated Asian chicken and returning with the sweet potato.

Both DNA and linguistic evidence make clear that the Polynesian settlement of the islands of the eastern Pacific was no accident, but rather part of a systematic cultural drive to discover new lands. Following voyages of reconnaissance, Polynesian mariners carried out colonizing expeditions in fleets of large double-hulled canoes that relied on scores of paddlers as well as sails. Their largest canoes reached 120 feet (37 meters) in length and carried crews of fifty. A wide platform connected the two hulls and permitted the transportation of animals and plants crucial to the success of distant and isolated settlements. Long-range expeditions took pigs, dogs, and chickens with them as well as domesticated plants such as taro, bananas, yams, and breadfruit. Their success depended upon reliably navigating thousands of miles of ocean using careful observation of the currents and stars as the crews searched for evidence of land (see Map 15.1).

While all Polynesian societies descended from the same culture and most depended on farming and fishing, differences in geography and climate led to varying colonization experiences. In Hawaii low-lying native forests were converted to farmland using controlled burns, and fishponds were built to increase fish yields. As a result, the Polynesian communities of Hawaii thrived into the era of European expansion. However, in Easter Island, among the most isolated of the Polynesian colonies, population growth led to total deforestation, soil erosion, intense resource competition, and, ultimately, a brutal cycle of warfare that drastically reduced the population. The hierarchical social and political structures that are in evidence throughout the Polynesian archipelagos and New Zealand around 1200–1300 led to chronic warfare elsewhere as well, as hereditary chiefs competed for resources.

The Atlantic Ocean

From the early Middle Ages, Viking raiders used their small, open ships to attack northern Europe's coastal settlements. Like the Polynesians, the Vikings

---

[2]Quotation in Craig A. Lockard, "'The Sea Common to All': Maritime Frontiers, Port Cities, and Chinese Traders in the Southeast Asian Age of Commerce, ca. 1400–1750," *Journal of World History* 21, no. 2 (2010): 228.

navigated by their knowledge of the heavens and the seas rather than by maps and other navigational devices. They first settled Iceland in 770, established a colony on Greenland in 982, and sighted North America in 986. Fifteen years later Leif Ericsson established a short-lived Viking settlement on the island of Newfoundland, which he called *Vinland*. When the climate turned colder after 1200, the settlements in Greenland declined and Vinland was abandoned.

Some southern Europeans applied their Mediterranean experience to Atlantic exploration. In the fourteenth century, Genoese and Portuguese expeditions settled the islands of Madeira (muh-DEER-uh), the Azores (A-zorz), and the Canaries.

There is some evidence that Africans also explored the Atlantic in this period. The Syrian geographer al-Umari (1301–1349) relates that when Mansa Kankan Musa (MAHN-suh KAHN-kahn MOO-suh), the ruler of the West African empire of Mali, passed through Egypt on his lavish pilgrimage to Mecca in 1324 (see Chapter 14), he told of Atlantic voyages undertaken by his predecessor, Mansa Muhammad. Muhammad had sent out four hundred vessels with men and supplies, telling them, "Do not return until you have reached the other side of the ocean or if you have exhausted your food or water." After a long time one canoe returned, reporting that the others were lost in a "violent current in the middle of the sea." Muhammad himself then set out at the head of a second, even larger, expedition, from which no one returned.

On the other side of the Atlantic, Amerindian voyagers from the Caribbean coast of South America colonized the West Indies. By the year 1000 the **Arawak** (AR-uh-wahk) (also called *Taino*) had followed the small islands of the Lesser Antilles (Barbados, Martinique, and Guadeloupe) to the Greater Antilles (Cuba, Hispaniola, Jamaica, and Puerto Rico) as well as to the Bahamas. The Carib followed the same route in later centuries, and by the late fifteenth century they had overrun most Arawak settlements in the Lesser Antilles and were raiding parts of the Greater Antilles. Both Arawak and Carib peoples also made contact with the North American mainland.

The transfer of maize cultivation to South America after its domestication in Mesoamerica suggests contact among Amerindian peoples, including the use of boats along the Pacific coast. After 100, mari-

SECTION REVIEW

- Polynesians explored and settled the eastern Pacific from the Marquesas to Hawaii and Easter Island.

- The Indian Ocean became a center of commerce and cultural exchange. Between 1405 and 1433 Chinese admiral Zheng He's seven expeditions established contacts with South Asian and African peoples.

- Vikings, Amerindians, and Africans also pursued long-distance explorations and settlement.

ners in two-masted balsa rafts as long as 36 feet (11 meters) were sailing north from the coast of Ecuador bringing pottery, jewelry made of copper as well as gold and silver, and textiles. The rafts could carry over 20 metric tons and ten or more crew members. Favorable winds and Pacific currents facilitated travel north, but these crafts were also capable of returning south, often with cargos of spondylus shells (a spiny bivalve considered sacred by ancient peoples). Through such contact metallurgy was introduced to Mesoamerica around 650.

EUROPEAN EXPANSION, 1400–1550

■ *In this era of long-distance exploration, did Europeans have any special advantages over other cultural regions?*

While the pace and intensity of maritime contacts increased in many parts of the world before 1450, it was the epic sea voyages sponsored by the European kingdoms of Portugal and Spain that launched the maritime revolution that would profoundly alter world history, ending the isolation of the Americas and increasing global interaction.

Overseas expansion arose from two related phenomena. First, Portuguese and Spanish rulers had strong economic, religious, and political motives to expand their influence. And second, improvements in maritime and military technologies gave them the means to master treacherous and unfamiliar ocean environments, seize control of existing maritime trade routes, and conquer new lands.

Arawak Amerindian peoples who inhabited the Greater Antilles of the Caribbean at the time of Columbus.

Map 15.1 **Exploration and Settlement in the Indian and Pacific Oceans Before 1500** Over many centuries, mariners originating in Southeast Asia gradually colonized the islands of the Pacific and Indian Oceans. The Chinese voyages led by Zheng He in the fifteenth century were lavish official expeditions. © Cengage Learning

Motives for Exploration

The immediate cause of the voyages in the fifteenth century was the ambitions and adventurous personalities of the rulers of Portugal and Spain, but the underlying causes were four trends evident in the countries of western Europe since about the year 1000: (1) the revival of urban life and trade, (2) the unique alliance between merchants and rulers, (3) a struggle with Islamic powers for dominance of the Mediterranean that mixed religious motives with the desire for trade, and (4) growing intellectual curiosity about the outside world.

By 1450 the city-states of northern Italy had well-established trade links to northern Europe, the Indian Ocean, and the Black Sea, and their merchant princes had also sponsored an intellectual and artistic Renaissance. The Italian trading states of Venice and Genoa maintained commercial ties in the Mediterranean that depended on lucrative alliances with Muslims from the East. Even after the expansion of the Ottoman Empire disrupted this trade, these cities did not take the lead in exploring the Atlantic. However, many individual Italians played leading roles in the Atlantic explorations.

In contrast, the Iberian kingdoms had been engaging in anti-Muslim warfare since the eighth century. By 1250 the Iberian kingdoms of Portugal, Castile, and Aragon had reconquered all the Muslim lands except the kingdom of Granada (see Chapter 13). The dynastic marriage of Isabella of Castile and Ferdinand of Aragon in 1469 facilitated the conquest of Granada in 1492 and the formation of Spain, sixteenth-century Europe's most powerful state.

Christian militancy continued to drive Portugal and Spain in their overseas ventures. But the Iberian rulers and their adventurous subjects also sought material returns. Their modest share of the Mediterranean trade made them more willing than the Italians to seek new routes to Africa and Asia via the Atlantic. Both kingdoms participated in the shipbuilding and the gunpowder revolutions that were under way in Atlantic Europe, and both were especially open to new geographical knowledge.

Portuguese Voyages

When the Muslim government of Morocco in northwestern Africa weakened in the fifteenth century, the Portuguese attacked, conquering the city of Ceuta (say-OO-tuh) in 1415. Despite the capture of several more ports along Morocco's Atlantic coast, they could not push inland and gain direct access to the gold trade. So they sought contact with the gold producers by sailing down the African coast.

Prince Henry (1394–1460), third son of the king of Portugal, had led the attack on Ceuta. Because from 1418 on he devoted the rest of his life to promoting exploration, he is known as **Henry the Navigator**. His official biographer emphasized Henry's desire to convert Africans to Christianity, make contact with Christian rulers in Africa, and launch joint crusades with them against the Ottomans. Profit also figured in his dreams. His initial explorations focused on Africa, but reaching India became the eventual goal of Portuguese explorers. While called "the Navigator," Henry himself never ventured far from home. Instead, he founded a research center at Sagres (SAH-gresh) to study navigation built on the pioneering efforts of Italian merchants and fourteenth-century Jewish cartographers, and to improve navigational instruments, including the magnetic compass, first developed in China, and the astrolabe, an instrument of Arab or Greek invention that enabled mariners to determine their latitude at sea by measuring the position of the sun or the stars. This center collected geographical information from sailors and travelers and sponsored new expeditions to explore the Atlantic. Henry's ships established permanent contact with the islands of Madeira in 1418 and with the Azores in 1439.

The Portuguese also developed a new type of long-distance sailing vessel. Large crews of oarsmen prevented Mediterranean galleys from carrying enough supplies for long voyages, and the square-rigged vessels of northern Europe could not sail into the wind. The Portuguese **caravel** (KAR-uh-vel) solved both problems. Much smaller than either the largest European ships or the Chinese junks, it could enter shallow coastal waters and explore upriver and yet also had the strength to weather ocean storms. When equipped with triangular lateen sails, caravels had great maneuverability and could sail at greater speeds into the wind. The addition of small cannon made them good fighting ships as well. The caravels' economy, speed, agility, and power justified a con-

temporary's claim that they were "the best ships that sailed the seas."[3]

Pioneering captains had to overcome the common fear that South Atlantic waters were boiling hot or contained ocean currents that would prevent any ship entering them from ever returning home. It took Prince Henry from 1420 to 1434 to coax an expedition to venture beyond southern Morocco (see Map 15.2). It would ultimately take the Portuguese four decades to cover the 1,500 miles (2,400 kilometers) from Lisbon to Sierra Leone (see-ER-uh lee-OWN); it then took only three additional decades to explore the remaining 4,000 miles (6,400 kilometers) to the southern tip of the African continent. With experience, navigators learned to return home speedily by sailing northwest into the Atlantic to the latitude of the Azores, where they picked up prevailing westerly winds. The knowledge that ocean winds tend to form large circular patterns helped later explorers discover many other ocean routes.

During the 1440s Portuguese raiders on the northwest coast of Africa and the Canary Islands began to return with slaves, finding a profitable market in an Iberia still recovering from the population losses of the Black Death. The total number of Africans captured or purchased on voyages exceeded eighty thousand by the end of the century and rose steadily thereafter. However, gold quickly became more important once the Portuguese contacted the trading networks that flourished in West Africa and reached across the Sahara. By 1457 enough African gold was coming back to Portugal for the kingdom to issue a new gold coin bearing a large cross and called the *cruzado*, another reminder of how deeply the Portuguese entwined religious and secular motives.

---

[3]Alvise da Cadamosto in *The Voyages of Cadamosto and Other Documents*, ed. and trans. G. R. Crone (London: Hakluyt Society, 1937), 2.

Henry the Navigator Portuguese prince who promoted the study of navigation and directed voyages of exploration down the western coast of Africa in the fifteenth century.

caravel A small, highly maneuverable three-masted ship used by the Portuguese and Spanish in the exploration of the Atlantic.

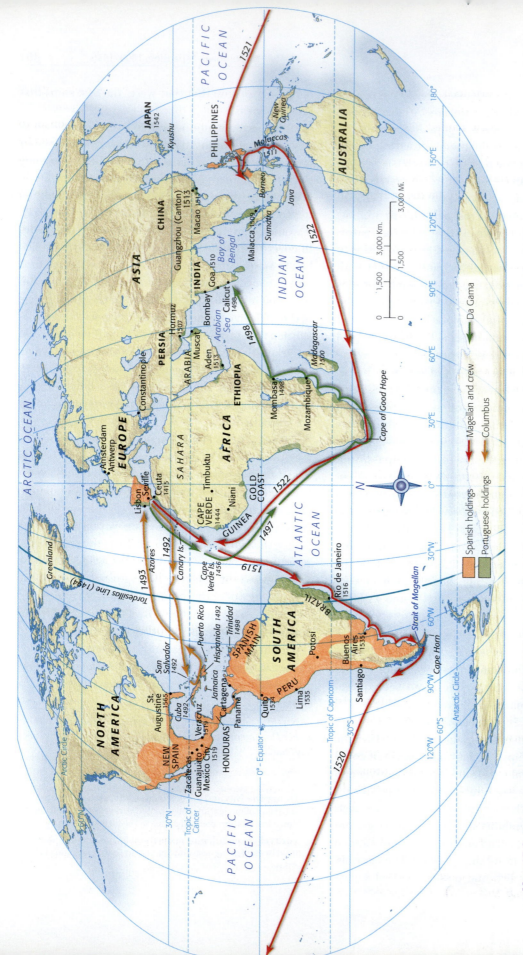

Map 15.2 **European Exploration, 1420–1542** Portuguese and Spanish explorers showed the possibility and practicality of inter-continental maritime trade. Before 1540 European trade with Africa and Asia was much more important than that with the Americas, but after the Spanish conquest of the Aztec and Inka Empires, transatlantic trade began to increase. Notice the Tordesillas line, which in theory separated the Spanish and Portuguese spheres of activity. © Cengage Learning

Royal sponsorship continued, but private commercial interests accelerated the pace of exploration. In 1469 a Lisbon merchant named Fernão Gomes purchased from the Crown the privilege of exploring 350 miles (550 kilometers) of African coast in return for a trade monopoly. He discovered the uninhabited island of São Tomé (sow toh-MAY) on the equator and following the example of the Venetians in the eastern Mediterranean converted it into a major producer of sugar dependent on slave labor. In the next century the island would serve as a model for the sugar plantations of Brazil and the Caribbean. Gomes also explored the Gold Coast, which became the headquarters of Portugal's West African trade.

The desire to find a passage around Africa to the rich spice trade of the Indian Ocean spurred the final thrust down the African coast. In 1488 Bartolomeu Dias rounded the southern tip of Africa and entered the Indian Ocean, and in 1497–1498 Vasco da Gama sailed around Africa and reached India. Then, in 1500, ships under the command of Pedro Alvares Cabral (kah-BRAHL) sailed too far west and accidentally reached the South American mainland, establishing Portugal's claim to Brazil. The gamble that Prince Henry had begun eight decades earlier was about to pay off handsomely.

Spanish Voyages

Spain's early discoveries owed more to haste and blind luck than to careful planning. Only in the last decade of the fifteenth century did the Spanish monarchs turn their attention from the conquest and organization of previously Muslim territories to overseas exploration. By that time, the Portuguese had already found their route to the India.

The leader of the overseas mission was Christopher Columbus (1451–1506), a Genoese mariner. His four voyages between 1492 and 1504 established the existence of a vast new world across the Atlantic. But Columbus refused to accept this momentous discovery, insisting he had found a shorter route to the Indian Ocean.

As a young man Columbus participated in Portuguese explorations along the African coast, but he dreamed of a shorter way to the riches of the East. By his reckoning (based on a serious misreading of a ninth-century Arab authority), the Canaries were a mere 2,400 nautical miles (4,450 kilometers) from Japan. The actual distance was five times greater.

It was not easy for Columbus to find a sponsor to underwrite his theory that Asia could be reached by sailing west. The Portuguese twice rejected his plan, and a Castilian commission questioned his geographical assumptions. Though more sympathetic, Queen Isabella rejected it, too. But his persistence paid off, and in 1492, the queen and her husband, King Ferdinand of Aragon, agreed to fund a modest expedition.

Columbus recorded in his log that he and his crew of ninety men "departed Friday the third day of August of the year 1492" toward "the regions of India." Their mission, the royal contract stated, was "to discover and acquire certain islands and mainland in the Ocean Sea." He carried letters of introduction from the Spanish sovereigns to Eastern rulers, including one to the "Grand Khan" (meaning the Chinese emperor), and brought along an Arabic interpreter. The expedition traveled in three small ships, the *Santa María*, the *Niña*, and the *Pinta*. The *Niña* and the *Pinta* were caravels.

Unfavorable headwinds had impeded other attempts to explore the Atlantic west of the Azores, but Columbus chose a southern route because he had learned in his earlier voyages along the African coast that there were west-blowing winds at the latitude of the Canaries. In October 1492 the expedition reached the islands of the Caribbean. Columbus called the inhabitants Indians because he believed he had reached the East Indies. His second voyage to the Caribbean in 1493 did nothing to change his mind. Even when, two months after Vasco da Gama reached India in 1498, Columbus first sighted the mainland of

Gold Coast Region of the Atlantic coast of West Africa occupied by modern Ghana; named for its gold exports to Europe from the 1470s onward.

Bartolomeu Dias Portuguese explorer who in 1488 led the first expedition to sail around the southern tip of Africa from the Atlantic and sight the Indian Ocean.

Vasco da Gama Portuguese explorer. In 1497–1498 he led the first naval expedition from Europe to sail to India, opening an important commercial sea route.

Christopher Columbus Genoese mariner who in the service of Spain led expeditions across the Atlantic, reestablishing contact between the peoples of the Americas and the Old World and opening the way to Spanish conquest and colonization.

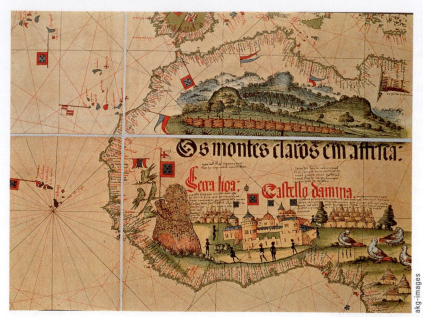

Os montes claros em affrica:

Serra lioa: **Castello damina.**

Portuguese Map of Western Africa, 1502 This map shows in great detail a section of African coastline that Portuguese explorers charted and named in the fifteenth century. The cartographer illustrated the African interior, which was almost completely unknown to Europeans, with drawings of birds and views of coastal sights: Sierra Leone (Serra lioa), named for a mountain shaped like a lion, and the Portuguese Castle of the Mine (Castello damina) on the Gold Coast.

akg-images

South America on his third voyage, he insisted it was part of Asia. But by then other Europeans were convinced that he had discovered islands and continents previously unknown to the Old World. Amerigo Vespucci's explorations, first on behalf of Spain and then for Portugal, led mapmakers to name the new continents "America," after him.

To prevent disputes about exploiting these lands and spreading Christianity among their peoples, Spain and Portugal agreed to split the world between them. The Treaty of Tordesillas (tor-duh-SEE-yuhs), negotiated by the pope in 1494, drew an imaginary line down the middle of the Atlantic Ocean. Lands east of the line in Africa and southern Asia were Portugal's to exploit; lands to the west in the Americas were reserved for Spain. Cabral's discovery of Brazil, however, gave Portugal a valid claim to the part of South America located east of the line.

Where would Spain's and Portugal's spheres of influence divide in the East? Given Europeans' ignorance of the earth's true size in 1494, it was not clear whether the Moluccas (muh-LOO-kuhz), the source of valuable spices in the East Indies, were on Portugal's or Spain's side of the Tordesillas line extended around the globe. The size of the Pacific Ocean would determine the boundary. In the end, the Moluccas turned out to lie well within Portugal's sphere, as Spain formally acknowledged in 1529.

In 1519 **Ferdinand Magellan** (ca. 1480–1521) sought to complete Columbus's interrupted westward voyage by sailing around the Americas and across the Pacific. Despite his death during this voyage on behalf of the king of Spain, Magellan was considered the first person to encircle the globe because a decade earlier he had sailed from Europe to the East Indies on an expedition sponsored by his native Portugal. His two voyages took him across the Tordesillas line and through the separate spheres claimed by Portugal and Spain; they also established the basis for Spanish colonization of the Philippines after 1564.

Columbus and those who followed in his wake laid the foundation for the colonial empires of Spain and other European nations. In turn, these empires promoted a major new trading network whose importance rivaled and eventually surpassed that of the Indian Ocean. Portugal's entry into the Indian Ocean led quickly to a major European presence and profit. Both the eastward and the westward voyages of exploration marked a tremendous expansion of Europe's role in world history.

Ferdinand Magellan Portuguese navigator who led the Spanish expedition of 1519–1522 that was the first to sail around the world.

ENCOUNTERS WITH EUROPE, 1450–1550

■ *What were the different outcomes of European interactions with Africa, India, and the Americas?*

European actions alone did not determine the global consequences of these new contacts. The ways in which Africans, Asians, and Amerindians perceived these visitors and interacted with them influenced developments as well. Everywhere indigenous peoples evaluated the Europeans as potential allies or enemies. In general,

Bronze Figure of Benin Ruler Both this prince and his horse are protected by chain mail introduced in the fifteenth century to Benin by Portuguese merchants. Antenna Gallery Dakar Senegal/ G.Dagli Orti/The Art Archive

Africans and Asians recognized the benefits and dangers of European contact. However, the long isolation of the Amerindians from the rest of the world made them vulnerable to European diseases, limiting their ability to resist European settlement.

Western Africa

Many Africans welcomed trade with the Portuguese, since it offered new markets for exports and access to imports cheaper than those transported overland from the Mediterranean. Miners in the hinterland, which the Portuguese had first visited in 1471, had long sold their gold to merchants from trading cities along the southern edge of the Sahara for transshipment to North Africa. Recognizing the possibility of more favorable terms, coastal Africans negotiated with the royal representative of Portugal, who arrived in 1482 seeking permission to erect a trading fort.

This Portuguese noble and his officers (likely including the young Christopher Columbus) were eager to make a proper impression. They dressed in their best clothes, erected a reception platform, celebrated a Catholic Mass, and signaled the start of negotiations with trumpets, tambourines, and drums. The African king, Caramansa, staged his entrance with equal ceremony, arriving with a large retinue of attendants and musicians. Through an African interpreter, the two leaders exchanged flowery speeches pledging goodwill and mutual benefit.

Caramansa then gave permission for a small trading fort, assured, he said, by the appearance of the royal delegate that they were honorable persons, unlike the "few, foul, and vile" Portuguese visitors of the previous decade.

Neither side made a show of force, but Caramansa warned that if the Portuguese acted aggressively, he and his people would move away, depriving their fort of food and trade. Trade at the post of Saint George of Elmina (the Arabic word for "seaport") enriched both sides. The Portuguese crown had soon purchased gold equal to one-tenth of the world's production at the time. In return, Africans received shiploads of goods brought by the Portuguese from Asia, Europe, and other parts of Africa.

After a century of aggressive expansion, the kingdom of Benin in the Niger Delta was near the peak of its power when it first encountered the Portuguese. Its oba (king) presided over an elaborate bureaucracy from a spacious palace in his large capital city, also known as Benin. In response to a Portuguese visit in 1486, the oba sent an ambassador to Portugal to learn more about these strangers. He then established a royal monopoly on Portuguese trade, selling pepper and ivory tusks (for export to Portugal) as well as stone beads, textiles, and prisoners of war (for resale at Elmina). In return, Portuguese merchants provided Benin with copper and brass, fine textiles, glass beads, and a horse for the king's royal procession. In the early sixteenth century, as the demand for slaves for the Portuguese sugar plantations on the nearby island of São Tomé grew, the oba first raised the price of slaves and then imposed restrictions that limited their sale.

Early contacts generally involved a mix of commercial, military, and religious exchanges. Some African rulers appreciated the advantage of European firearms. Because African religions were generally not exclusive, coastal rulers were also willing to test the value of the Christian practices promoted by the Portuguese. The rulers of Benin and Kongo, the two largest coastal kingdoms, accepted Portuguese missionaries and soldiers as allies in battle to determine the efficacy of the religion and the weaponry.

However, Portuguese efforts to persuade the king and nobles of Benin to accept the Catholic faith ultimately failed. Early kings showed some interest, but after 1538 rulers declined to receive more missionaries. They also closed the market in male slaves for the rest of the sixteenth century. We do not know why Benin chose to limit its contacts with the Portuguese, but the result makes clear that these rulers had the power to control their contacts with Europeans.

Farther south, on the lower Congo River, the manikongo (mah-NEE-KONG-goh) (king of Kongo) also sent delegates to Portugal, established a royal monopoly on trade, and expressed interest in missionary teachings. But here the royal family made Catholicism the kingdom's official faith. Lacking ivory and pepper, Kongo sold more slaves to acquire the goods brought by the Portuguese and to pay missionary expenses. Soon the royal trade monopoly broke down. In 1526 the Christian manikongo, Afonso I (r. 1506–ca. 1540), wrote to his royal "brother," the king of Portugal, begging for his help in stopping the trade because unauthorized Kongolese were kidnapping and selling people, even members of good families (see Diversity and Dominance: Kongo's Christian King). Alfonso received no reply from Portugal, whose interests were now concentrated in the Indian Ocean. Soon rebellion and the relocation of the slave trade from his kingdom to the south weakened the manikongo's authority.

Eastern Africa Different still were the reactions of the Muslim rulers of the coastal trading states of eastern Africa. As Vasco da Gama's fleet sailed up the coast in 1498, most rulers gave the Portuguese a cool reception, suspicious of the painted crusaders' crosses on their sails. The ruler of Malindi, however, saw the Portuguese as an ally who could help him expand Malindi's trade, and he provided da Gama with a pilot to guide him to India. The suspicions of the other rulers were proven correct seven years later when a Portuguese war fleet bombarded and looted most of the coastal cities of eastern Africa in the name of Christ and commerce, while sparing Malindi.

Christian Ethiopia also saw the benefit of an alliance with the Portuguese. In the fourteenth and fifteenth centuries, Ethiopian conflicts with Muslim states along the Red Sea increased. After the Ottoman Turks conquered Egypt and launched a fleet in the Indian Ocean to counter the Portuguese in 1517, the warlord of the Muslim state of Adal (now Djibouti) attacked Ethiopia. A decisive victory in 1529 put the Christian kingdom in jeopardy, making Portuguese support crucial.

For decades, delegations from Portugal and Ethiopia had explored a Christian alliance. Queen Helena of Ethiopia, who acted as regent for her young sons after her husband's death in 1478, sent a letter in 1509 to "our very dear and well-beloved brother," the king of Portugal, along with a gift of two tiny crucifixes said to be made of wood from the cross on which Christ was crucified. She proposed joining forces—her army and Portugal's fleet—to fight the Ottomans;

however, Helena's death in 1522 occurred before the alliance could be arranged. Ethiopia's situation then grew more desperate.

Finally, a small Portuguese force commanded by Vasco da Gama's son Christopher arrived to aid Ethiopia in 1539. With Portuguese help, another queen rallied the Ethiopians. Muslim forces captured and tortured to death Christopher da Gama, but they retreated when their own leader fell in battle. Portuguese aid helped save the Ethiopian kingdom from extinction, but a permanent alliance faltered because Ethiopian rulers refused to transfer their Christian affiliation from the patriarch of Alexandria to the Latin patriarch of Rome (the pope).

As these examples illustrate, African encounters with the Portuguese before 1550 varied considerably. Africans and Portuguese might become royal brothers, bitter opponents, or partners in a mutually profitable trade, but Europeans remained a minor presence in most of Africa in 1550. By then the Portuguese had become far more interested in the Indian Ocean trade.

Indian Ocean States

Vasco da Gama's arrival on the Malabar Coast of India in May 1498 did not impress the citizens of Calicut. The Chinese fleets of gigantic junks that had called at Calicut sixty-five years earlier dwarfed his four small ships, which were no larger than many of the dhows already filling the harbor. The samorin (ruler) of Calicut and his Muslim officials showed mild interest, but the gifts da Gama brought provoked derisive laughter: twelve pieces of fairly ordinary striped cloth, four scarlet hoods, six hats, and six wash basins. When da Gama tried to defend his gifts as those of an explorer, not a merchant, the samorin cut him short, asking whether he had come to discover men or stones: "If he had come to discover men, as he said, why had he brought nothing?"

Coastal rulers soon discovered that the Portuguese had no intention of remaining poor competitors in the Indian Ocean trade. Upon da Gama's return to Portugal in 1499, the jubilant King Manuel styled himself "Lord of the Conquest, Navigation, and Commerce of Ethiopia, Arabia, Persia, and India." Previously the Indian Ocean had been an open sea, used by merchants (and pirates) of all the surrounding coasts. Now the Portuguese crown intended to make it Portugal's sea, to be used on Portuguese terms alone.

Portugal's hope of controlling the Indian Ocean stemmed from the superiority of its ships and weapons, especially over the lightly armed merchant dhows. In 1505 a Portuguese fleet of eighty-one ships and some seven thousand men bombarded Swahili Coast cities. Indian ports were the next targets. Goa, on the west coast of India, fell to a well-armed fleet in 1510, becoming the base from which the Portuguese menaced the trading cities of Gujarat (goo-juh-RAHT) to the north and Calicut and other Malabar Coast cities to the south. The port of Hormuz, controlling entry to the Persian Gulf, fell in 1515. Aden, at the entrance to the Red Sea, successfully resisted, but the capture of the Gujarati port of Diu in 1535 consolidated Portuguese dominance of the western Indian Ocean.

Meanwhile, Portuguese explorers had reconnoitered the Bay of Bengal and the waters farther east. The city of Malacca (muh-LAH-kuh) on the strait between the Malay Peninsula and Sumatra became the focus of their attention. During the fifteenth century, Malacca had become the main entrepôt for the trade from China, Japan, India, the Southeast Asian mainland, and the Moluccas. The city's more than 100,000 residents spoke eighty-four different languages, including those of merchants from Cairo, Ethiopia, and the Swahili Coast. Many non-Muslim residents supported letting the Portuguese join its cosmopolitan trading community, perhaps hoping to offset the growing solidarity of Muslim traders. In 1511, however, the Portuguese seized Malacca with a force of a thousand fighting men, including three hundred recruited in southern India.

Force was not always necessary. On the China coast, local officials and merchants persuaded the imperial government to allow the Portuguese to establish a trading post at Macao (muh-COW) in 1557. Subsequently, Portuguese ships nearly monopolized trade between China and Japan.

Control of major port cities enabled the Portuguese to enforce their demands that all spices be carried in Portuguese ships, as well as goods on the major ocean routes such as between Goa and Macao. The Portuguese also tried to control and tax other Indian Ocean trade. Merchant ships entering and leaving their ports had to carry a Portuguese passport and

Kongo's Christian King

The new overseas voyages brought conquest to some and opportunities for fruitful borrowings and exchanges to others. The decision of the ruler of the kingdom of Kongo to adopt Christianity in 1491 added cultural diversity to Kongolese society and in some ways strengthened the hand of the king. From then on Kongolese rulers sought to introduce Christian beliefs and rituals while at the same time Africanizing Christianity to make it more intelligible to their subjects. In addition, the kings of Kongo sought a variety of more secular aid from Portugal, including schools and medicine. Trade with the Portuguese introduced new social and political tensions, especially in the case of the export trade in slaves for the Portuguese sugar plantations on the island of São Tomé to the north.

Two letters sent to King João (zhwao) III of Portugal in 1526 illustrate how King Afonso of Kongo saw his kingdom's new relationship with Portugal and the problems that resulted from it. (Afonso adopted that name when baptized as a young prince.) After the death of his father in 1506, Afonso successfully claimed the throne and ruled until 1542. His son Henrique became the first Catholic bishop of the Kongo in 1521.

These letters were written in Portuguese and penned by the king's secretary João Teixera (tay-SHER-uh), a Kongo Christian, who, like Afonso, had been educated by Portuguese missionaries.

6 July 1526

To the very powerful and excellent prince Dom João, our brother:

On the 20th of June just past, we received word that a trading ship from your highness had just come to our port of Sonyo. We were greatly pleased by that arrival for it had been many days since a ship had come to our kingdom, for by it we would get news of your highness, which many times we had desired to know, . . . and likewise as there was a great and dire need for wine and flour for the holy sacrament; and of this we had had no great hope for we have the same need frequently. And that, sir, arises from the great negligence of your highness's officials toward us and toward shipping us those things. . . .

Sir, your highness should know how our kingdom is being lost in so many ways that we will need to provide the needed cure, since this is caused by the excessive license given by your agents and officials to the men and merchants who come to this kingdom to set up shops with goods and many things which have been prohibited by us, and which they spread throughout our kingdoms and domains in such abundance that many of our vassals, whose submission we could once rely on, now act independently so as to get the things in greater abundance than we ourselves; whom we had formerly held content and submissive and under our vassalage and jurisdiction, so it is doing a great harm not only to the service of God, but also to the security and peace of our kingdoms and state.

And we cannot reckon how great the damage is, since every day the mentioned merchants are taking our people, sons of the land and the sons of our noblemen and vassals and our relatives, because the thieves and men of bad conscience grab them so as to have the things and wares of this kingdom that they crave; they grab them and bring them to be sold. In such a manner, sir, has been the corruption and deprivation that our land is becoming completely depopulated, and your highness should not deem this good nor in your service. And to avoid this we need from these kingdoms [of yours] no more than priests and a few people to teach in schools, and no other goods except wine and flour for the holy sacrament, which is why we beg of your highness to help and assist us in this matter. Order your agents to send here neither merchants nor wares, because it is our will that in these kingdoms there should not be any dealing in slaves nor outlet for them, for the reasons stated above. Again we beg your highness's agreement, since otherwise we cannot cure such manifest harm. May Our Lord in His mercy have your highness always under His protection and may you always do the things of His holy service. I kiss your hands many times.

From our city of Kongo. . . .

The King, Dom Afonso ➤

Very high and very powerful prince King of Portugal, our brother,

Sir, your highness has been so good as to promise us that anything we need we should ask for in our letters, and that everything will be provided. And so that there may be peace and health of our kingdoms, by God's will, in our lifetime. And as there are among us old folks and people who have lived for many days, many and different diseases happen so often that we are pushed to the ultimate extremes. And the same happens to our children, relatives, and people, because this country lacks physicians and surgeons who might know the proper cures for such diseases, as well as pharmacies and drugs to make them better. And for this reason many of those who had been already confirmed and instructed in the things of the holy faith of Our Lord Jesus Christ perish and die. And the rest of the people for the most part cure themselves with herbs and sticks and other ancient methods, so that they live putting all their faith in these herbs and ceremonies, and die believing that they are saved; and this serves God poorly.

And to avoid such a great error, I think, and inconvenience, since it is from God and from your highness that all the good and the drugs and medicines have come to us for our salvation, we ask your merciful highness to send us two physicians and two pharmacists and one surgeon, so that they may come with their pharmacies and necessary things to be in our kingdoms, for we have extreme need of each and every one of them. We will be very good and merciful to them, since sent by your highness, their work and coming should be for good. We ask your highness as a great favor to do this for us, because besides being good in itself it is in the service of God as we have said above.

Moreover, sir, in our kingdoms there is another great inconvenience which is of little service to God, and this is that many of our people, out of great desire for the wares and things of your kingdoms, which are brought here by your people, and in order to satisfy their disordered appetite, seize many of our people, freed and exempt men. And many times noblemen and the sons of noblemen, and our relatives are stolen, and they take them to be sold to the white men who are in our kingdoms and take them hidden or by night, so that they are not recognized. And as soon as they are taken by the white men, they are immediately ironed and branded with fire. And when they are carried off to be embarked, if they are caught by our guards, the whites allege that they have bought them and cannot say

from whom, so that it is our duty to do justice and to restore to the free their freedom. And so they went away offended.

And to avoid such a great evil we passed a law so that every white man living in our kingdoms and wanting to purchase slaves by whatever means should first inform three of our noblemen and officials of our court on whom we rely in this matter, namely Dom Pedro Manipunzo and Dom Manuel Manissaba, our head bailiff, and Gonçalo Pires, our chief supplier, who should investigate if the said slaves are captives or free men, and, if cleared with them, there will be no further doubt nor embargo and they can be taken and embarked. And if they reach the opposite conclusion, they will lose the aforementioned slaves. Whatever favor and license we give them [the white men] for the sake of your highness in this case is because we know that it is in your service too that these slaves are taken from our kingdom; otherwise we should not consent to this for the reasons stated above that we make known completely to your highness so that no one could say the contrary, as they said in many other cases to your highness, so that the care and remembrance that we and this kingdom have should not be withdrawn. . . .

We kiss your hands of your highness many times.

From our city of Kongo, the 18th day of October,

The King, Dom Afonso

QUESTIONS FOR ANALYSIS

1. What sorts of things does King Afonso desire from the Portuguese?
2. What is he willing and unwilling to do in return?
3. What problem with his own people has the slave trade created, and what has King Afonso done about it?
4. Does King Afonso see himself as an equal to King João or his subordinate? Do you agree with that analysis?

Source: From António Brásio, ed., *Monumenta Missionaria Africana: Africa Ocidental (1471–1531)* (Lisbon: Agência Geral do Ultramar, 1952), I: 468, 470–471, 488–491. Translated by David Northrup.

Portuguese in India In the sixteenth century Portuguese men moved to the Indian Ocean Basin to work as administrators and traders. This Indo-Portuguese drawing from about 1540 shows a Portuguese man speaking to an Indian woman, perhaps making a proposal of marriage.

Album/Art Resource, NY

pay customs duties. Portuguese patrols seized vessels that did not comply, confiscated their cargoes, and either killed the captain and crew or sentenced them to forced labor.

Reactions to this power grab varied. Like the emperors of China, the Mughal (MOO-gahl) emperors of India largely ignored Portugal's maritime intrusions. The Ottomans confronted the Christian intruders more aggressively. They supported Egypt's defensive efforts in 1501 and 1509 and then sent their own fleet into the Indian Ocean in 1538. However, Ottoman galleys proved no match for the faster, better-armed Portuguese vessels in the open ocean. They retained their advantage only in the Red Sea and Persian Gulf, where they controlled many ports.

Smaller trading states also could not challenge the Portuguese because their mutual rivalry kept them from forming a common front. Some cooperated with the Portuguese to safeguard their prosperity and security, while others engaged in evasion and resistance. When the merchants of Calicut put up sustained resistance, the Portuguese embargoed all trade with Aden, Calicut's principal trading partner, and centered their trade on the port of Cochin, which had once been a dependency of Calicut. Some Calicut merchants evaded their patrols, but Calicut's impor-

tance shrank as Cochin gradually became the major pepper-exporting port on the Malabar Coast.

Farther north, Gujarat initially resisted Portuguese attempts at monopoly and in 1509 joined Egypt's futile effort to sweep the Portuguese from the Arabian Sea. But in 1535, finding his state weakened by Mughal attacks, the ruler allowed the Portuguese to build a fort at Diu in return for their support. Once established, the Portuguese gradually extended their control, and by midcentury they were licensing and taxing all Gujarati ships. Even after the Mughals took control of Gujarat in 1572, the Mughal emperor Akbar permitted the Portuguese to continue their maritime monopoly in return for allowing one pilgrim ship a year to travel to Mecca without paying a fee.

The Portuguese never gained complete control of the Indian Ocean trade, but their domination of key ports and trade routes brought them considerable profits from spices and other luxury goods. The Portuguese broke the trading monopoly of Venice and Genoa by selling pepper at much lower prices.

The consequences flowing from these events were dramatic. The Portuguese were able to fund an aggressive colonization of Brazil, while Asian and East African traders were at the mercy of their warships. But because the Portuguese concentrated on maritime trade routes in Asia and Africa, Portugal had little impact on the Asian and African mainlands, in sharp contrast to what was occurring in the Americas.

The Americas

The Spanish and Portuguese monarchies had similar motives for expansion and used identical ships and weapons, but the Spanish established a territorial rather than a trading empire in the Americas. The outcomes had little to do with differences between the two kingdoms. Rather, the isolation of the Amerindian peoples was key, making their responses to outside contacts different from those of African and Indian Ocean peoples. Isolation had slowed the development of metallurgy and other militarily useful technologies in the Americas and also made these large populations more susceptible to new diseases. It was the spread of deadly new diseases, especially smallpox, among Amerindians after 1518 that weakened their ability to resist and facilitated Spanish and Portuguese occupation.

The first Amerindians to encounter Columbus were the Arawak of Hispaniola (modern Haiti and the Dominican Republic) in the Greater Antilles and the Bahamas to the north (see Map 15.2). They cultivated maize (corn), cassava (yuca), sweet potatoes, and hot peppers, as well as cotton and tobacco. Although the islands did not have large gold deposits and, unlike West Africans, the Arawak had not previously traded gold over long distances, the natives were skilled at working gold. They extended a cautious welcome, but they soon learned to tell exaggerated stories about gold in other places to persuade the Spanish to move on.

Columbus brought several hundred settlers, as well as missionaries, on his second trip to Hispaniola in 1493. The settlers provoked the Arawak by demanding indigenous labor to look for gold, stealing gold ornaments and food, and sexually assaulting native women. The Arawak rebelled in 1495 but were slaughtered by the tens of thousands, no match for Spanish horses, body armor, and steel swords. Thousands more were forced to labor for the Spanish. Meanwhile, cattle, pigs, and goats introduced by the settlers devoured the Arawaks' food crops, causing deaths from famine and disease, particularly smallpox. A governor appointed by the Spanish crown in 1502 institutionalized these demands by forcing the surviving Arawak to become laborers under the control of Spanish settlers.

The actions of the Spanish in the Antilles were similar to those used by the Spanish against the Muslims in previous centuries: they sought to serve God by defeating, controlling, and converting nonbelievers and to become rich in the process. Individual **conquistadors** (kon-KEY-stuh-dor) (conquerors) extended that pattern around the Caribbean. Some raided the Bahamas for gold and labor as both became scarce on Hispaniola. New expeditions searched for gold and Amerindian laborers across the Caribbean region, capturing thousands of Amerindians and relocating them to Hispaniola as slaves. The island of Borinquen (Puerto Rico) was conquered in 1508 and Cuba between 1510 and 1511.

An ambitious and ruthless nobleman, **Hernán Cortés** (kor-TEZ) (1485–1547) undertook a new expedition to the mainland. Cortés left Cuba in 1519 with six hundred fighting men to assault the Mexican mainland in search of slaves and trade. After learning of the rich Aztec Empire in central Mexico, he expanded the exploitation and conquest carried out in the Greater Antilles.

Many subject peoples resented the tribute payments, forced labor, and large-scale human sacrifices demanded by the Aztecs. Consequently, some embraced the Spanish as allies. The Aztecs also had powerful native enemies, including the Tlaxcalans (thlash-KAH-lans), who became crucial allies of Cortés. Individual Amerindians also calculated the potential benefit or threat represented by these strange visitors. Malintzin (mah-LEENT-zeen) (also called Malinche), a native woman given to Cortés shortly after his arrival in the Maya region, became his translator, key source of intelligence, and mistress. As peoples and as individuals, native allies were crucial to the Spanish campaign.

While the emperor **Moctezuma II** (mock-teh-ZOO-ma) (r. 1502–1520) hesitated to use force and

---

conquistadors Early-sixteenth-century Spanish adventurers who conquered Mexico, Central America, and Peru.

Hernán Cortés Spanish explorer and conquistador who led the conquest of Aztec Mexico in 1519–1521 for Spain.

Moctezuma II Aztec emperor who died while in custody of the Spanish conquistador Hernán Cortés.

Montezuma wearing on his back the royal standard of green Quetzal bird feathers, copied from a native artist (colour litho)/Private Collection/Peter Newark American Pictures/The Bridgeman Art Library

Coronation of Emperor Moctezuma This painting by an unnamed Aztec artist depicts the Aztec ruler's coronation. Moctezuma, his nose pierced by a bone, receives the crown from a prince in the palace at Tenochtitlan.

attempted diplomacy instead, Cortés pushed toward the Aztec capital of Tenochtitlan (teh-noch-TIT-lan). Spanish forces overcame opposition with firearms, cavalry tactics, and steel swords. As the Spanish approached his island capital, the emperor went out in a great procession, dressed in his finery, to welcome Cortés.

Despite Cortés's initial pledge of friendship, Moctezuma was quickly imprisoned. The Spanish looted his treasury, interfered with the city's religious rituals, and eventually massacred hundreds during a festival. The Aztecs rebelled, killing half the Spanish force and four thousand of Cortés's native allies. In the confusion Moctezuma also lost his life, either killed by the Spanish or in the Aztec attack.

The survivors, strengthened by Spanish reinforcements and aided by the Tlaxcalans, renewed their attack and captured Tenochtitlan in 1521. Their victory was aided by a smallpox epidemic that killed more of the city's defenders than did the fighting. One source remembered that the disease "spread over the people as a great destruction." Many Amerindians as well as Europeans blamed the devastating spread of

this disease on supernatural forces. Cortés and other Spanish leaders then led expeditions to the north and south accompanied by the Tlaxcalans and other indigenous allies. Everywhere epidemic disease, especially smallpox, helped crush indigenous resistance.

Meanwhile, Spanish settlers in Panama began hearing of another empire to the south. The Inka Empire stretched nearly 3,000 miles (5,000 kilometers) south of the equator along the Pacific coast (see Chapter 14). During its expansion, it had enforced labor demands and taxes on conquered peoples and exiled rebellious populations. When the Inka ruler Huayna Capac (WHY-nah KAH-pak) died in 1525, a civil war ensued as his sons fought for the throne. **Atahuallpa** (ah-tuh-WAHL-puh) (r. 1531–1533), the candidate of the northern army, defeated Huascar, the candidate of the royal court at Cuzco, but political leadership was weakened and the military

Atahuallpa Last ruling Inka emperor of Peru. He was executed by the Spanish.

Francisco Pizarro Spanish explorer who led the conquest of the Inka Empire of Peru in 1531–1533.

decimated. At this critical time **Francisco Pizarro** (pih-ZAHR-oh) (ca. 1478–1541) and his force of 180 men, thirty-seven horses, and two cannon entered the region.

Pizarro had come to the Americas in 1502 at the age of twenty-five to seek his fortune. He had participated in the conquest of Hispaniola and in Balboa's expedition across the Isthmus of Panama to the Pacific. In the 1520s he gambled his fortune on exploring the Pacific coast south of the equator, where he learned of the riches of the Inka. With a license from the king of Spain, he set out from Panama in 1531 to conquer them.

Having seen signs of the civil war after landing, Pizarro arranged to meet the Inka emperor, Atahuallpa, near the Andean city of Cajamarca (kah-hah-MAHR-kah) in November 1532. With supreme boldness and brutality, Pizarro's small band of armed men attacked Atahuallpa and his followers as they entered an enclosed courtyard. Though surrounded by an Inka army of at least forty thousand, the Spaniards were able to use their cannon to create confusion while their swords brought down thousands of the emperor's lightly armed retainers and servants.

Atahuallpa attempted to purchase his freedom. Noting the glee with which the Spaniards seized gold and silver, Atahuallpa offered what he thought would satisfy even the greediest among them: rooms filled to shoulder height with gold and silver. But after receiving 13,400 pounds (6,000 kilograms) of gold and 26,000 pounds (12,000 kilograms) of silver, the Spaniards still executed Atahuallpa. His death broke the unity of an empire already battered by civil war.

The Execution of Inka Ruler Atahuallpa

Felipe Guaman Poma de Ayala, a native Andean from the area of Huamanga in Peru, drew this representation of the execution. While Pizarro sentenced Atahuallpa to death by strangulation, not beheading, Guaman Poma's illustration forcefully made the point that Spain had imposed an arbitrary and violent government on the Andean people.

SECTION REVIEW

- African kingdoms reacted in various ways to the opportunities and threats created by the arrival of the Portuguese, but only Kongo embraced Christianity and accepted a large Portuguese military presence in the sixteenth century.

- The Portuguese used military force to consolidate a trade empire in the Indian Ocean.

- After the Spanish occupied the Caribbean, Cortés led an expedition that conquered the Aztecs, who were weakened by disease.

- The Spanish under Pizarro conquered the Inka Empire, already suffering from civil war, and then fell on each other; but surviving conquistadors continued to explore the Americas.

In 1533, the Spanish had taken Cuzco, but in 1536 Pizarro had to put down another massive native rebellion. The remaining Inka now retreated, creating a small kingdom in the mountains that lasted until 1572. In 1541, Pizarro himself met a violent death at the hands of Spanish rivals, but the conquest of the mainland continued. Incited by the fabulous wealth of the Aztecs and Inka, conquistadors extended Spanish conquest and exploration in South and North America, dreaming of new treasures.

CONCLUSION

The rapid expansion of European empires and the projection of European military power around the world, one of the most important events in world history, would have seemed unlikely in 1492. No European power matched the military and economic strength of China, and few could rival the Ottomans. Spain lacked strong national institutions and Portugal had a small population; both had limited resources. Because of these limitations, the monarchs of Spain and Portugal allowed their subjects greater initiative. While royal sponsorship was often crucial in the Portuguese contacts with Africa and the first voyages to Asia, many of the commercial and military expeditions were effectively organized and financed as private companies. Very often the kings of Spain and Portugal struggled to catch up with their restless and ambitious subjects, sometimes taking decades to establish royal control in new colonies.

The pace and character of European expansion in Africa and Asia were different than in the Americas. In Africa local rulers were generally able to limit European military power to coastal outposts and to control European trade. Only in the Kongo were the Portuguese able to project their power inland. When the Europeans arrived in the Indian Ocean, mature markets and specialized production for distant consumers already existed. Here Portuguese (and later Dutch and British) naval power allowed Europeans to harvest large profits and influence regional commercial patterns, but most indigenous populations continued to enjoy effective autonomy for centuries.

In the Americas, however, the terrible effects of epidemic disease and the destructiveness of the Spanish conquests led to the rapid creation of European settlements and the subordination of the surviving indigenous population. As we shall see in Chapter 16, American gold, silver, and sugar eventually produced great wealth but only through the introduction of new technologies, the imposition of oppressive forms of labor, most notably slavery, and the development of new roads and ports.

What gave the European maritime revolution unprecedented importance had more to do with what happened after 1550 than what happened prior. The overseas empires of the Europeans would endure longer than the Mongols' and would continue to expand for three centuries after 1600. Unlike the Chinese, the Europeans did not turn their backs on the world after an initial burst of exploration. Not content with dominance in the Indian Ocean trade, Europeans opened an Atlantic maritime network that grew to rival the Indian Ocean network in the wealth of its trade; they also pioneered trade across the Pacific. The maritime expansion, begun in the period from 1450 to 1550, marked the beginning of a new age of global interaction.

CHAPTER REVIEW

GLOBAL MARITIME EXPANSION BEFORE 1450

■ *What were the objectives and major accomplishments of the voyages of exploration undertaken by Chinese, Polynesians, and other non-Western peoples?* (page 355)

The voyages of exploration undertaken by the Malays, Chinese, and Polynesians pursued diverse objectives. Malay voyagers were crucial participants in the development of the rich and varied commerce of Southeast Asia and initiated connections between these markets and Arabia and Africa. The great voyages of the Chinese in the early fifteenth century were motivated by an interest in trade, curiosity, and the desire to project imperial power. For the Polynesians, the discovery and settlement of new lands was a recurring objective because most of the islands that were settled were too small to support large populations. The Vikings, Africans, and Amerindians all undertook long-distance explorations as well, although with fewer lasting consequences.

EUROPEAN EXPANSION, 1400–1550

■ *In this era of long-distance exploration, did Europeans have any special advantages over other cultural regions?* (page 359)

This projection of European influence between 1450 and 1550 was in some ways similar to that of other cultural regions in that it expanded commercial linkages, increased cross-cultural contacts, and served the ambitions of political leaders. But in the aftermath of several centuries of Spanish and Portuguese combat against Muslim kingdoms in Iberia, it was driven by unusually powerful urges to fight Muslims, acquire their riches, and spread Christianity. During those years European explorers opened new long-distance trade routes across the world's three major oceans, for the first time establishing regular contact among all the continents.

ENCOUNTERS WITH EUROPE, 1450–1550

■ *What were the different outcomes of European interactions with Africa, India, and the Americas?* (page 365)

Europeans created colonial empires in the Americas quite rapidly, while their progress in Africa and Asia was much slower. Many Amerindians welcomed the Spanish settlers at first, only to have the Spanish tax their labors, steal their food, introduce disease and warfare, and eventually subjugate them. In contrast, Portuguese visitors to Africa remained a minor presence in 1550. In some regions, the Portuguese were welcomed as trading partners; in others they were regarded as potential political and military allies. The real focus of the Portuguese was to capture the rich trade of the Indian Ocean. While they never gained complete control, they used their superior military strength to dominate key ports and major trade routes.

Key Terms

Arawak (p. 359)

Henry the Navigator (p. 361)

caravel (p. 361)

Gold Coast (p. 363)

Bartolomeu Dias (p. 363)

Vasco da Gama (p. 363)

Christopher Columbus (p. 363)

Ferdinand Magellan (p. 364)

conquistadors (p. 371)

Hernán Cortés (p. 371)

Moctezuma II (p. 371)

Atahuallpa (p. 372)

Francisco Pizarro (p. 372)

Climate and Population to 1500

During the millennia before 1500, human populations expanded in three momentous surges. The first occurred after 50,000 B.C.E. when humans emigrated from their African homeland to all of the inhabitable continents. After that, the global population remained steady for many millennia. During the second expansion, between about 5000 and 500 B.C.E., population rose from about 5 million to 100 million as agricultural societies spread around the world (see Figure 1). Population growth then slowed for several centuries before a third surge took world population to over 350 million by 1200 C.E. (Figure 2 shows population in China and Europe.)

For a long time historians tended to attribute these population surges to cultural and technological advances. Indeed, a great many changes in culture and technology are associated with adaptation to different climates and food supplies in the first surge and with the domestication of plants and animals in the second. However, historians have not found a cultural or technological change to explain the third surge, nor can they explain why creativity would have stagnated for long periods between the surges. Something else must have been at work.

Recently historians have begun to pay more attention to the impact of long-term variations in

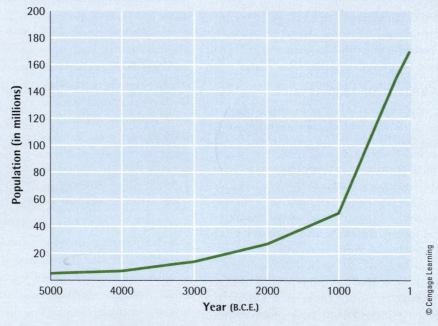

Figure 1 World Population, 5000–1 B.C.E.

global climate. By examining ice cores drilled out of glaciers, scientists have been able to compile records of thousands of years of climate change. The comparative width of tree rings from ancient forests has provided additional data on periods of favorable and unfavorable growth. Such evidence shows that cycles of population growth and stagnation followed changes in global climate.

Historians now believe that global temperatures were above normal for extended periods from the late 1100s to the late 1200s C.E. In the temperate lands where most of the world's people lived, above-normal temperatures meant a longer growing season, more bountiful harvests, and thus a more adequate and reliable food supply. The ways in which societies responded to the Medieval Warm Period (see Chapter 13) and the simultaneous cooling of the Middle East are as important as the climate change, but it is unlikely that human agency alone would have produced Europe's medieval surge. One notable response was that of the Vikings, who increased the size and range of their settlements in the North Atlantic, although their raids also caused death and destruction.

Some of the complexities involved in the interaction of human agency, climate, and other natural factors are also evident in the demographic changes that followed the Medieval Warm Period. During the 1200s the Mongol invasions caused death and disruption of agriculture across Eurasia. China's population, which had been over 100 million in 1200, declined by a third or more by 1300. The Mongol invasions did not cause harm west of Russia, but climate changes in the 1300s resulted in population losses in Europe. Unusually heavy rains caused crop failures and a prolonged famine in northern Europe from 1315 to 1319.

The freer movement of merchants within the Mongol Empire also facilitated the spread of disease across Eurasia, culminating in the great pandemic known as the Black Death in Europe. The demographic recovery under way in China was reversed. The even larger population losses in Europe may have been affected by the decrease in global temperatures to their lowest point in many millennia between 1350 and 1375. After 1400 improving economic conditions enabled population to recover more rapidly in Europe than in China, where the conditions of rural life remained harsh.

Because many other historical circumstances interact with changing weather patterns, historians have a long way to go in deciphering the role of climate in history. Nevertheless, it is a factor that can no longer be ignored.

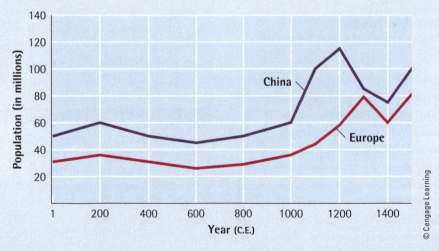

Figure 2 **Population in China and Europe, 1–1500** C.E.

GLOSSARY

Abbasid Caliphate Descendants of the Prophet Muhammad's uncle, al-Abbas, the Abbasids overthrew the Umayyad Caliphate and ruled an Islamic empire from their capital in Baghdad (founded 762) from 750 to 1258. (p. 215)

abolitionists Men and women who agitated for a complete end to slavery. Abolitionist pressure ended the British transatlantic slave trade in 1808 and slavery in British colonies in 1834. In the United States the activities of abolitionists were one factor leading to the Civil War (1861–1865). (p. 506)

Acheh Sultanate Muslim kingdom in northern Sumatra. Main center of Islamic expansion in Southeast Asia in the early seventeenth century, it declined after the Dutch seized Malacca from Portugal in 1641. (p. 443)

Aden Port city in the modern south Arabian country of Yemen. It has been a major trading center in the Indian Ocean since ancient times. (p. 340)

Adolf Hitler (1889–1945) Born in Austria, Hitler became a radical German nationalist during World War I. He led the National Socialist German Workers' Party—the Nazis—in the 1920s and became dictator of Germany in 1933. He led Europe into World War II. (p. 638)

African National Congress An organization dedicated to obtaining equal voting and civil rights for black inhabitants of South Africa. Founded in 1912 as the South African Native National Congress, it changed its name in 1923. Though it was banned and its leaders were jailed for many years, it eventually helped bring majority rule to South Africa. (p. 626)

Afrikaners South Africans descended from Dutch and French settlers of the seventeenth century. Their Great Trek founded new settler colonies in the nineteenth century. Though a minority among South Africans, they held political power after 1910, imposing a system of racial segregation called apartheid after 1949. (p. 540)

Agricultural Revolutions The change from food gathering to food production that occurred between ca. 8000 and 2000 B.C.E. Also known as the Neolithic Revolution. (p. 10)

agricultural revolution The transformation of farming that resulted in the eighteenth century from the spread of new crops, improvements in cultivation techniques and livestock breeding, and the consolidation of small holdings into large farms from which tenants and sharecroppers were forcibly expelled. (p. 472)

Akbar Most illustrious sultan of the Mughal Empire in India (r. 1556–1605). He expanded the empire and pursued a policy of conciliation with Hindus. (p. 438)

Akhenaten Egyptian pharaoh (r. 1353–1335 B.C.E.). He built a new capital at Amarna, fostered a new style of naturalistic art, and created a religious revolution by imposing worship of the sun-disk. (p. 34)

Albert Einstein (1879–1955) German physicist who developed the theory of relativity, which states that time, space, and mass are relative to each other and not fixed. (p. 610)

Alexander King of Macedonia in northern Greece. Between 334 and 323 B.C.E. he conquered the Persian Empire, reached the Indus Valley, founded many Greek-style cities, and spread Greek culture across the Middle East. Later known as Alexander the Great. (p. 100)

Alexander Nevskii Prince of Novgorod (r. 1236–1263). He submitted to the invading Mongols in 1240 and received recognition as the leader of the Russian princes under the Golden Horde. (p. 291)

Alexandria City on the Mediterranean coast of Egypt founded by Alexander. It became the capital of the Hellenistic kingdom of the Ptolemies. It contained the famous Library and the Museum, a center for leading scientific and literary figures. Its merchants engaged in trade with areas bordering the Mediterranean and the Indian Ocean. (p. 102)

All-India Muslim League Political organization founded in India in 1906 to defend the interests of India's Muslim minority. Led by Muhammad Ali Jinnah, it attempted to negotiate with the Indian National Congress. In 1940, the League began demanding a separate state for Muslims, to be called Pakistan. (p. 616)

altepetl An ethnic state in ancient Mesoamerica, the common political building block of that region. (p. 346)

amulet Small charm meant to protect the bearer from evil. Found frequently in archaeological excavations in Mesopotamia and Egypt, amulets reflect the religious practices of the common people. (p. 16)

Amur River This river valley was a contested frontier between northern China and eastern Russia until the settlement arranged in the Treaty of Nerchinsk (1689). (p. 459)

anarchism Movement of revolutionaries who wanted to abolish all private property and governments, usually by violence, and replace them with free associations of groups. (p. 575)

Anasazi Important culture of what is now the southwest United States (700–1300 C.E.). Centered on Chaco Canyon in New Mexico and Mesa Verde in Colorado, the Anasazi culture built multistory residences and worshiped in subterranean buildings called kivas. (p. 170)

aqueduct A conduit, either elevated or underground, that used gravity to carry water from a source to a location—usually a city—that needed it. The Romans built many aqueducts in a period of substantial urbanization. (p. 119)

Arawak Amerindian peoples who inhabited the Greater Antilles of the Caribbean at the time of Columbus. (p. 359)

Armenia One of the earliest Christian kingdoms, situated in eastern Anatolia and the western Caucasus and occupied by speakers of the Armenian language. (p. 204)

Ashikaga Shogunate The second of Japan's military governments headed by a shogun (a military ruler). Sometimes called the Muromachi Shogunate. (p. 302)

Ashoka Third ruler of the Mauryan Empire in India (r. 273–232 B.C.E.). He converted to Buddhism and broadcast his precepts on inscribed stones and pillars, the earliest surviving Indian writing. (p. 145)

Asian Tigers South Korea, Taiwan, Hong Kong, and Singapore, so called because their economies expanded so fast. (p. 675)

Atahuallpa Last ruling Inka emperor of Peru. He was executed by the Spanish. (p. 372)

Atatürk (1881–1938) The founder of modern Turkey. He distinguished himself as a war hero in World War I and expelled a Greek expeditionary army from Anatolia in 1921–1922. He replaced the Ottoman Empire with the Turkish Republic in 1923. As president, he pushed through a radical westernization and reform of Turkish society. (p. 599)

Atlantic system The network of trading links after 1500 that moved goods, wealth, people, and cultures around the Atlantic Basin. (p. 403)

Cuban Missile Crisis (1962) Brink-of-war confrontation between the United States and the Soviet Union over the latter's placement of nuclear-armed missiles in Cuba. (p. 662)

Culhuacán Multiethnic Mesoamerican state south of and historically connected with Teotihuacan. (p. 168)

cultural imperialism Domination of one culture over another by a deliberate policy or by economic or technological superiority. (p. 707)

Cultural Revolution (China) Campaign in China ordered by Mao Zedong to purge the Communist Party of his opponents and instill revolutionary values in the younger generation. (p. 675)

culture Socially transmitted patterns of action and expression. *Material culture* refers to physical objects such as dwellings, clothing, tools, and crafts. Culture also includes arts, beliefs, knowledge, and technology. (p. 5)

cuneiform A system of writing in which wedge-shaped symbols represented words or syllables. It originated in Mesopotamia and was used initially for Sumerian and Akkadian but later was adapted to represent other languages of western Asia. Literacy was confined to a relatively small group of administrators and scribes. (p. 15)

Cyrus Founder of the Achaemenid Persian Empire. Between 550 and 530 B.C.E. he conquered Media, Lydia, and Babylon. Revered in the traditions of both Iran and the subject peoples, he employed Persians and Medes in his administration and respected the institutions and beliefs of subject peoples. (p. 84)

daimyo Literally, "great name(s)." Japanese warlords and great landowners, whose armed samurai gave them control of the Japanese islands from the eighth to the later nineteenth century. Under the Tokugawa Shogunate they were subordinated to the imperial government. (p. 451)

Daoism Chinese school of thought, originating in the Warring States Period with Laozi. Daoism offered an alternative to the Confucian emphasis on hierarchy and duty, emphasizing instead understanding the "path" of nature. (p. 63)

Darius I Third ruler of the Persian Empire (r. 521–486 B.C.E.). He crushed the widespread initial resistance to his rule and gave major government posts to Persians rather than to Medes. He established a system of provinces and tribute, began construction of Persepolis, and expanded Persian control in the east (Pakistan) and west (northern Greece). (p. 85)

Decembrist revolt Abortive attempt by army officers to take control of the Russian government upon the death of Tsar Alexander I in 1825. (p. 523)

Declaration of the Rights of Man and of the Citizen Statement of fundamental political rights adopted by the French National Assembly at the beginning of the French Revolution. (p. 498)

deforestation The removal of trees faster than forests can replace themselves. (p. 392)

Delhi Sultanate Centralized Indian empire of varying extent, created by Muslim invaders. (p. 332)

democracy System of government in which all "citizens" (however defined) have equal political and legal rights, privileges, and protections, as in the Greek city-state of Athens in the fifth and fourth centuries B.C.E. (p. 90)

demographic transition A change in the rates of population growth. Before the transition, both birthrates and death rates are high, resulting in a slowly growing population; then the death rate drops but the birthrate remains high, causing a population explosion; finally the birthrate drops and the population growth slows down. This transition took place in Europe in the late nineteenth and early twentieth centuries, in North America and East Asia in the mid-twentieth century, and, most recently, in Latin America and South Asia. (p. 697)

Deng Xiaoping (1904–1997) Communist Party leader who forced Chinese economic reforms after the death of Mao Zedong. (p. 690)

dhows Characteristic cargo and passenger ships of the Arabian Sea. (p. 338)

Diaspora Greek word meaning "dispersal," used to describe the communities of a given ethnic group living outside their homeland. Jews, for example, spread from Israel to western Asia and Mediterranean lands in antiquity and today can be found throughout the world. (p. 46)

Dirty War Suppression of leftist groups by the Argentine military (1976–1983) characterized by the use of illegal imprisonment, torture, and executions. (p. 672)

division of labor A manufacturing technique that breaks down a craft into many simple and repetitive tasks that can be performed by unskilled workers. Pioneered in the manufacture of pottery and in other eighteenth-century factories, it greatly increased the productivity of labor and lowered the cost of manufactured goods. (p. 476)

driver A privileged male slave whose job was to ensure that a slave gang did its work on a plantation. (p. 417)

Druids The class of religious experts who conducted rituals and preserved sacred lore among some ancient Celtic peoples. (p. 74)

durbar An elaborate display of political power and wealth in British India in the nineteenth century, ostensibly in imitation of the pageantry of the Mughal Empire. (p. 549)

Dutch West India Company Trading company chartered by the Dutch government to conduct its merchants' trade in the Americas and Africa. (p. 419)

electricity A form of energy used in telegraphy from the 1840s on and for lighting, industrial motors, and railroads beginning in the 1880s. (p. 568)

electric telegraph A device for rapid, long-distance transmission of information over an electric wire. It was introduced in England and North America in the 1830s and 1840s and replaced telegraph systems that utilized visual signals such as semaphores. (p. 481)

Emiliano Zapata (1879–1919) Revolutionary and leader of peasants in the Mexican Revolution. He mobilized landless peasants in south-central Mexico in an attempt to seize and divide the lands of the wealthy landowners. Though successful for a time, he was ultimately defeated and assassinated. (p. 559)

Empress Dowager Cixi Empress of China and mother of Emperor Guangxi. She put her son under house arrest, supported antiforeign movements, and resisted reforms of the Chinese government and armed forces. (p. 583)

encomienda A grant of authority over a population of Amerindians in the Spanish colonies. It provided the grant holder with a supply of cheap labor and periodic payments of goods by the Amerindians. It obliged the grant holder to Christianize the Amerindians. (p. 405)

English Civil War (1642–1649) A conflict over royal versus parliamentary rights, caused by King Charles I's arrest of his parliamentary critics and ending with his execution. Its outcome checked the growth of royal absolutism and, with the Glorious Revolution of 1688 and the English Bill of Rights of 1689, ensured that England would be a constitutional monarchy. (p. 395)

Enlightenment A philosophical movement in eighteenth-century Europe that fostered the belief that one could reform society by discovering rational laws that governed social behavior and were just as scientific as the laws of physics. (p. 387, 491)

equites In ancient Italy, prosperous landowners second in wealth and status to the senatorial aristocracy. The Roman emperors allied with this group to counterbalance the influence of the old aristocracy and used the equites to staff the imperial civil service. (p. 112)

Estates General France's traditional national assembly with representatives of the three estates, or classes, in French society: the clergy, nobility, and commoners. The calling of the Estates General in 1789 led to the French Revolution. (p. 497)

Ethiopia East African highland nation lying east of the Nile River. (p. 204)

European Economic Community (Common Market) An organization promoting economic unity in Europe, formed in 1957 by consolidation of earlier, more limited, agreements. With the addition of many new nations it became the European Union (EU) in 1993. (p. 659)

Eva Duarte Perón (1919–1952) Wife of Juan Perón and champion of the poor in Argentina. She was a gifted speaker and popular political leader who campaigned to improve the life of the urban poor by founding schools and hospitals and providing other social benefits. (p. 623)

evolution The biological theory that, over time, changes occurring in plants and animals, mainly as a result of natural selection and genetic mutation, result in new species. (p. 5)

extraterritoriality The right of foreign residents in a country to live under the laws of their native country and disregard the laws of the host country. In the nineteenth and early twentieth centuries, European and American nationals living in certain areas of Chinese and Ottoman cities were granted this right. (p. 519)

Faisal I (1885–1933) Arab prince, leader of the Arab Revolt in World War I. The British made him king of Iraq in 1921, and he reigned under British protection until 1933. (p. 591)

Fascist Party Italian political party created by Benito Mussolini during World War I. It emphasized aggressive nationalism and was Mussolini's instrument for the creation of a dictatorship in Italy from 1922 to 1943. (p. 638)

Ferdinand Magellan Portuguese navigator who led the Spanish expedition of 1519–1522 that was the first to sail around the world. (p. 364)

fief In medieval Europe, land granted in return for a sworn oath to provide specified military service. (p. 238)

First Temple A monumental sanctuary built in Jerusalem by King Solomon in the tenth century B.C.E. to be the religious center for the Israelite god Yahweh. The Temple priesthood conducted sacrifices, received a tithe or percentage of agricultural revenues, and became economically and politically powerful. (p. 45)

Five-Year Plans Plans that Joseph Stalin introduced to industrialize the Soviet Union rapidly, beginning in 1928. They set goals for the output of steel, electricity, machinery, and most other products and were enforced by the police powers of the state. They succeeded in making the Soviet Union a major industrial power before World War II. (p. 631)

foragers People who support themselves by hunting wild animals and gathering wild edible plants and insects. (p. 8)

Francisco "Pancho" Villa (1877–1923) A popular leader during the Mexican Revolution. An outlaw in his youth, when the revolution started he formed a cavalry army in the north of Mexico and fought for the rights of the landless in collaboration with Emiliano Zapata. He was assassinated in 1923. (p. 559)

Francisco Pizarro Spanish explorer who led the conquest of the Inka Empire of Peru in 1531–1533. (p. 372)

Fujiwara Aristocratic family that dominated the Japanese imperial court between the ninth and twelfth centuries. (p. 272)

Funan An early complex society in Southeast Asia between the first and sixth centuries C.E. It was centered in the rich rice-growing region of southern Vietnam, and it controlled the passage of trade across the Malaysian isthmus. (p. 151)

gens de couleur Free men and women of color in Haiti. They sought greater political rights and later supported the Haitian Revolution. (p. 502)

gentry In China, the class of prosperous families, next in wealth below the rural aristocrats, from which the emperors drew their administrative personnel. Respected for their education and expertise, these officials became a privileged group and made the government more efficient and responsive than in the past. (p. 127)

gentry In England, the class of landholding families below the aristocracy. (p. 391)

George Washington Military commander of the American Revolution. He was the first elected president of the United States (1789–1797). (p. 495)

Getulio Vargas (1883–1954) Dictator of Brazil from 1930 to 1945 and from 1951 to 1954. Constitutionally barred from another term in 1938 and fearful of a military takeover, he suspended elections and created Estado Novo ("New State"), a dictatorship that emphasized industrialization and helped the urban poor but did little to alleviate the problems of the peasants. (p. 622)

Ghana First known kingdom in sub-Saharan West Africa between the sixth and thirteenth centuries C.E. Also the modern West African country once known as the Gold Coast. (p. 216)

Giuseppe Garibaldi Italian nationalist and revolutionary who conquered Sicily and Naples and added them to a unified Italy in 1860. (p. 576)

global elite culture At the beginning of the twenty-first century, the attitudes and outlook of well-educated, prosperous, Western-oriented people around the world, largely expressed in European languages, especially English. (p. 709)

globalization The economic, political, and cultural integration and interaction of all parts of the world brought about by increasing trade, travel, and technology. (p. 685)

global pop culture Popular cultural practices and institutions that have been adopted internationally, such as music, the Internet, television, food, and fashion. (p. 709)

Gold Coast Region of the Atlantic coast of West Africa occupied by modern Ghana; named for its gold exports to Europe from the 1470s onward. (p. 363)

Golden Horde Mongol khanate founded by Chinggis Khan's grandson Batu. It was based in southern Russia and quickly adopted both the Turkish language and Islam. Also known as the Kipchak Horde. (p. 288)

Gothic cathedrals Large churches originating in twelfth-century France; built in an architectural style featuring pointed arches, tall vaults and spires, flying buttresses, and large stained-glass windows. (p. 315)

Grand Canal The 1,100-mile (1,771-kilometer) waterway linking the Yellow and the Yangzi Rivers. It was begun in the Han period and completed during the Sui Empire. (p. 255)

Great Ice Age Geological era that occurred between ca. 2 million and 11,000 years ago. (p. 6)

"great traditions" Historians' term for a literate, well-institutionalized complex of religious and social beliefs and practices adhered to by diverse societies over a broad geographical area. (p. 199)

Great Western Schism A division in the Latin (Western) Christian Church between 1378 and 1415, when rival claimants to the papacy existed in Rome and Avignon. (p. 323)

Great Zimbabwe City, now in ruins (in the modern African country of Zimbabwe), whose many stone structures were built between about 1250 and 1450, when it was a trading center and the capital of a large state. (p. 340)

guild In medieval Europe, an association of men (rarely women), such as merchants, artisans, or professors, who worked in a particular trade and banded together to promote their economic and political interests. Guilds were also important in other societies, such as the Ottoman and Safavid Empires. (p. 314)

Gujarat Region of western India famous for trade and manufacturing; the inhabitants are called Gujaratis. (p. 336)

gunpowder A mixture of saltpeter, sulfur, and charcoal, in various proportions. The formula, brought to China in the 400s or 500s, was first used to make fumigators to keep away insect pests and evil spirits. In later centuries it was used to make explosives and grenades and to propel cannonballs, shot, and bullets. (p. 265)

Guomindang Nationalist political party founded on democratic principles by Sun Yat-sen in 1912. After 1925, the party was headed by Chiang Kai-shek, who turned it into an increasingly authoritarian movement. (p. 598)

Gupta Empire A powerful Indian state based, like its Mauryan predecessor, on a capital at Pataliputra in the Ganges Valley. It controlled most of the Indian subcontinent through a combination of military force and its prestige as a center of sophisticated culture. (p. 146)

Habsburg A powerful European family that provided many Holy Roman Emperors, founded the Austrian (later Austro-Hungarian) Empire, and ruled sixteenth- and seventeenth-century Spain. (p. 394)

hadith A tradition relating the words or deeds of the Prophet Muhammad; next to the Quran, the most important basis for Islamic law. (p. 221)

Haile Selassie (1892–1975) Emperor of Ethiopia (r. 1930–1974) and symbol of African independence. He fought the Italian invasion of his country in 1935 and regained his throne during World War II, when British forces expelled the Italians. He ruled Ethiopia as a traditional autocracy until he was overthrown in 1974. (p. 627)

Hammurabi Amorite ruler of Babylon (r. 1792–1750 B.C.E.). He conquered many city-states in southern and northern Mesopotamia and is best known for a code of laws, inscribed on a black stone pillar, illustrating the principles to be used in legal cases. (p. 17)

Han A term used to designate (1) the ethnic Chinese people who originated in the Yellow River Valley and spread throughout regions of China suitable for agriculture and (2) the dynasty of emperors who ruled from 206 B.C.E. to 220 C.E. (p. 126)

Hanseatic League An economic and defensive alliance of the free towns in northern Germany, founded about 1241 and most powerful in the fourteenth century. (p. 313)

Harappa Site of one of the great cities of the Indus Valley civilization of the third millennium B.C.E. It was located on the northwest frontier of the zone of cultivation (in modern Pakistan). (p. 134)

Hatshepsut Queen of Egypt (r. 1473–1458 B.C.E.). She dispatched a naval expedition to Punt (possibly northeast Sudan or Eritrea), the faraway source of myrrh. There is evidence of opposition to a woman as ruler, and after her death her name and image were frequently defaced. (p. 33)

Hebrew Bible A collection of sacred books containing diverse materials concerning the origins, experiences, beliefs, and practices of the Israelites. Most of the extant text was compiled by members of the priestly class in the fifth century B.C.E. and reflects the concerns and views of this group. (p. 43)

Hellenistic Age Historians' term for the era, usually dated 323–30 B.C.E., in which Greek culture spread across western Asia and northeastern Africa after the conquests of Alexander the Great. The period ended with the fall of the last major Hellenistic kingdom to Rome, but Greek cultural influence persisted until the spread of Islam in the seventh century C.E. (p. 101)

Henry the Navigator Portuguese prince who promoted the study of navigation and directed voyages of exploration down the western coast of Africa in the fifteenth century. (p. 361)

Hernán Cortés Spanish explorer and conquistador who led the conquest of Aztec Mexico in 1519–1521 for Spain. (p. 371)

Herodotus Heir to the technique of *historia* ("investigation/research") developed by Greeks in the late Archaic period. He came from a Greek community in Anatolia and traveled extensively, collecting information in western Asia and the Mediterranean lands. He traced the antecedents and chronicled the wars between the Greek city-states and the Persian Empire, thus originating the Western tradition of historical writing. (p. 92)

Hidden Imam Last in a series of twelve descendants of Muhammad's son-in-law Ali, whom Shi'ites consider divinely appointed leaders of the Muslim community. In occlusion since around 873, he is expected to return as a messiah at the end of time. (p. 434)

hieroglyphics A system of writing in which pictorial symbols represented sounds, syllables, or concepts. It was used for official and monumental inscriptions in ancient Egypt. Because of the long period of study required to master this system, literacy in hieroglyphics was confined to a relatively small group of scribes and administrators. (p. 23)

Hinduism A general term for a wide variety of beliefs and ritual practices that have developed in the Indian subcontinent since antiquity. Hinduism has roots in ancient Vedic, Buddhist, and south Indian religious concepts and practices. It spread along the trade routes to Southeast Asia. (p. 141)

Hipólito Irigoyen (1850–1933) Argentine politician, president of Argentina from 1916 to 1922 and 1928 to 1930. The first president elected by universal male suffrage, he began his presidency as a reformer but later became conservative. (p. 621)

Hiroshima City in Japan, the first to be destroyed by an atomic bomb, on August 6, 1945. The bombing hastened the end of World War II. (p. 644)

history The study of past events and changes in the development, transmission, and transformation of cultural practices. (p. 5)

Hittites A people from central Anatolia who established an empire in Anatolia and Syria in the Late Bronze Age. With wealth from the trade in metals and military power based on chariot forces, the Hittites vied with New Kingdom Egypt for control of Syria-Palestine before falling to unidentified attackers around 1200 B.C.E. (p. 32)

Holocaust Nazis' program during World War II to kill people they considered undesirable. Some 6 million Jews perished during the Holocaust, along with millions of Poles, Gypsies, communists, socialists, and others. (p. 648)

Holy Roman Empire Loose federation of mostly German states and principalities, headed by an emperor elected by the princes. It lasted from 962 to 1806. (p. 240, 394)

hominid The biological family that includes humans and humanlike primates. (p. 6)

Homo erectus An extinct human species. It evolved in Africa about 1.8 million years ago. (p. 7)

Homo habilis The first human species (now extinct). It evolved in Africa about 2.3 million years ago. (p. 6)

Homo sapiens The current human species. It evolved in Africa sometime between 400,000 and 100,000 years ago. (p. 8)

hoplite A heavily armored Greek infantryman of the Archaic and Classical periods who fought in the close-packed phalanx formation. Hoplite armies—militias composed of middle- and upper-class citizens supplying their own equipment—were for centuries superior to all other military forces. (p. 89)

horse collar Harnessing method that increased the efficiency of horses by shifting the point of traction from the animal's throat to the shoulders; its adoption favors the spread of horse-drawn plows and vehicles. (p. 248)

House of Burgesses Elected assembly in colonial Virginia, created in 1618. (p. 410)

humanists (Renaissance) European scholars, writers, and teachers associated with the study of the humanities (grammar, rhetoric, poetry, history, languages, and moral philosophy), influential in the fifteenth century and later. (p. 319)

Hundred Years' War (1337–1453) Series of campaigns over control of the throne of France, involving English and French royal families and French noble families. (p. 323)

Ibn Battuta Moroccan Muslim scholar, the most widely traveled individual of his time. He wrote a detailed account of his visits to Islamic lands from China to Spain and the western Sudan. (p. 329)

Il-khan A "secondary" or "peripheral" khan based in Persia. The Il-khans' khanate was founded by Hülegü, a grandson of Chinggis Khan, and was based at Tabriz in the Iranian province of Azerbaijan. It controlled much of Iran and Iraq. (p. 288)

import-substitution industrialization An economic system aimed at building a country's industry by restricting foreign trade. It was especially popular in Latin American countries such as Mexico, Argentina, and Brazil in the mid-twentieth century. It proved successful for a time but could not keep up with technological advances in Europe and North America. (p. 622)

indentured servant A migrant to British colonies in the Americas who paid for passage by agreeing to work for a set term ranging from four to seven years. (p. 410)

Indian Civil Service The elite professional class of officials who administered the government of British India. Originally composed exclusively of well-educated British men, it gradually added qualified Indians. (p. 551)

Indian National Congress A movement and political party founded in 1885 to demand greater Indian participation in government. Its membership was middle class, and its demands were modest until World War I. Led after 1920 by Mohandas K. Gandhi, it appealed increasingly to the poor, and it organized mass protests demanding self-government and independence. (p. 552)

Indian National Congress A movement and political party founded in 1885 to demand greater Indian participation in government. Its membership was middle class, and its demands were modest until World War I. Led after 1920 by Mohandas K. Gandhi, it appealed increasingly to the poor and organized mass protests demanding self-government and independence. (p. 616)

Indian Ocean Maritime System In premodern times, a network of seaports, trade routes, and maritime culture linking countries on the rim of the Indian Ocean from Africa to Indonesia. (p. 191)

indulgence The forgiveness of the punishment due for past sins, granted by the Catholic Church authorities as a reward for a pious act. Martin Luther's protest against the sale of indulgences is often seen as touching off the Protestant Reformation. (p. 382)

Industrial Revolution The transformation of the economy, the environment, and living conditions, occurring first in England in the eighteenth century, that resulted from the use of steam engines, the mechanization of manufacturing in factories, and innovations in transportation and communication. (p. 471)

Inka Largest and most powerful Andean empire. Controlled the Pacific coast of South America from Ecuador to Chile from its capital of Cuzco. (p. 348)

investiture controversy Dispute between the popes and the Holy Roman Emperors over who held ultimate authority over bishops in imperial lands. (p. 241)

Iron Age Historians' term for the period during which iron was the primary metal for tools and weapons. The advent of iron technology began at different times in different parts of the world. (p. 30)

iron curtain Winston Churchill's term for the Cold War division between the Soviet-dominated East and the U.S.-dominated West. (p. 660)

Iroquois Confederacy An alliance of five northeastern Amerindian peoples (six after 1722) that made decisions on military and diplomatic issues through a council of representatives. Allied first with the Dutch and later with the English, the Confederacy dominated the area from western New England to the Great Lakes. (p. 411)

Islam Religion expounded by the Prophet Muhammad on the basis of his reception of divine revelations, which were collected after his death into the Quran. In the tradition of Judaism and Christianity, and sharing much of their lore, Islam calls on all people to recognize one creator god—Allah—who rewards or punishes believers after death according to how they led their lives. (p. 211)

Israel In antiquity, the land between the eastern shore of the Mediterranean and the Jordan River, occupied by the Israelites from the early second millennium B.C.E. The modern state of Israel was founded in 1948. (p. 43)

James Watt Scot who invented the condenser and other improvements that made the steam engine a practical source of power for industry and transportation. The watt, an electrical measurement, is named after him. (p. 480)

Janissaries Infantry, originally of slave origin, armed with firearms and constituting the elite of the Ottoman army from the fifteenth century until the corps was abolished in 1826. (p. 429)

Jawaharlal Nehru (1889–1964) Indian statesman who succeeded Mohandas K. Gandhi as leader of the Indian National Congress. He negotiated the end of British colonial rule in India and became India's first prime minister (1947–1964). (p. 618)

Jesus A Jew from Galilee in northern Israel who sought to reform Jewish beliefs and practices. He was executed as a revolutionary by the Romans. Hailed as the Messiah and son of God by his followers, he became the central figure in Christianity, a belief system that developed in the centuries after his death. (p. 118)

joint-stock company A business, often backed by a government charter, that sold shares to individuals to raise money for its trading enterprises and to spread the risks (and profits) among many investors. (p. 391)

Joseph Stalin (1879–1953) Bolshevik revolutionary, head of the Soviet Communist Party after 1924, and dictator of the Soviet Union from 1928 to 1953. He led the Soviet Union with an iron fist, using Five-Year Plans to increase industrial production and terror to crush all opposition. (p. 631)

Josiah Wedgwood English industrialist whose pottery works were the first to produce fine-quality pottery by industrial methods. (p. 476)

Juan Perón (1895–1974) President of Argentina (1946–1955, 1973–1974). As a military officer, he championed the rights of labor. Aided by his wife Eva Duarte Perón, he was elected president in 1946. He built up Argentinean industry, became very popular among the urban poor, but harmed the economy. (p. 623)

junk A very large flatbottom sailing ship produced in the Tang, Song, and Ming Empires, specially designed for long-distance commercial travel. (p. 264)

Kamakura Shogunate The first of Japan's decentralized military governments (1185–1333). (p. 273)

kamikaze The "divine wind," which the Japanese credited with blowing Mongol invaders away from their shores in 1281. (p. 302)

Kangxi Qing emperor (r. 1662–1722). He oversaw the greatest expansion of the Qing Empire. (p. 458)

Karl Marx German journalist and philosopher, founder of the Marxist branch of socialism. He is known for two books: *Manifesto of the Communist Party* (1848) and *Das Kapital* (Vols. I–III, 1867–1894). (p. 573)

karma In Indian tradition, the residue of deeds performed in past and present lives that adheres to a "spirit" and determines what form it will assume in its next life cycle. The doctrines of karma and reincarnation were used by the elite in ancient India to encourage people to accept their social position and do their duty. (p. 139)

keiretsu Alliances of corporations and banks that dominate the Japanese economy. (p. 674)

khipus System of knotted colored cords used by preliterate Andean peoples to record information. (p. 173, 349)

Khubilai Khan Last of the Mongol Great Khans (r. 1260–1294) and founder of the Yuan Empire. (p. 294)

Kievan Russia State established at Kiev in Ukraine around 880 by Scandinavian adventurers asserting authority over a mostly Slavic farming population. (p. 229)

King Leopold II (1835–1909) King of Belgium (r. 1865–1909). He was active in encouraging the exploration of Central Africa and became the ruler of the Congo Free State (to 1908). (p. 544)

KLM Royal Dutch Airlines Oldest major airline, operating since 1920 in Europe and connecting to the Dutch East Indies in 1929. (p. 611)

Korean War (1950–1953) Conflict that began with North Korea's invasion of South Korea and that came to involve the United Nations (primarily the United States) allying with South Korea and the People's Republic of China allying with North Korea. (p. 661)

Koryo Korean kingdom founded in 918 and destroyed by a Mongol invasion in 1259. (p. 270)

Kush An Egyptian name for Nubia, the region alongside the Nile River south of Egypt, where an indigenous kingdom with its own distinctive institutions and cultural traditions arose beginning in the early second millennium B.C.E. (p. 68)

labor union An organization of workers in a particular industry or trade, created to defend the interests of members through strikes or negotiations with employers. (p. 573)

laissez faire The idea that government should refrain from interfering in economic affairs. The classic exposition of laissez-faire principles is Adam Smith's *Wealth of Nations* (1776). (p. 485)

lama In Tibetan Buddhism, a teacher. (p. 294)

Lázaro Cárdenas (1895–1970) President of Mexico (1934–1940). He brought major changes to Mexican life by distributing millions of acres of land to the peasants, bringing representatives of workers and farmers into the inner circles of politics, and nationalizing the oil industry. (p. 620)

League of Nations International organization founded in 1919 to promote world peace and cooperation but greatly weakened by the refusal of the United States to join. It proved ineffectual in stopping aggression by Italy, Japan, and Germany in the 1930s, and it was superseded by the United Nations in 1945. (p. 595)

Le Corbusier (1887–1965) Professional name of architect Charles-Éduard Jeanneret who led a modernist movement away from surface decoration and toward form following function. (p. 613)

Legalism In China, a political philosophy that emphasized the unruliness of human nature and justified state coercion and control. The ruling class invoked it to validate the authoritarian nature of the regime and its profligate expenditure of subjects' lives and labor. It was later superseded by a more benevolent Confucian doctrine of governmental moderation. (p. 62)

"legitimate" trade Exports from Africa in the nineteenth century that did not include the newly outlawed slave trade. (p. 548)

liberalism A political ideology that emphasizes the civil rights of citizens, representative government, and the protection of private property. This ideology, derived from the Enlightenment, was especially popular among the property-owning middle classes of Europe and North America. (p. 576)

Library of Ashurbanipal A large collection of writings drawn from the ancient literary, religious, and scientific traditions of Mesopotamia. It was assembled by the seventh-century B.C.E. Assyrian ruler Ashurbanipal. The many tablets unearthed by archaeologists constitute one of the most important sources of present-day knowledge of the long literary tradition of Mesopotamia. (p. 42)

Linear B A set of syllabic symbols, derived from the writing system of Minoan Crete, used in the Mycenaean palaces of the Late Bronze Age to write an early form of Greek. It was used primarily for palace records, and the surviving Linear B tablets provide substantial information about the economic organization of Mycenaean society and tantalizing clues about political, social, and religious institutions. (p. 37)

Li Shimin One of the founders of the Tang Empire and its second emperor (r. 626–649). He led the expansion of the empire into Inner Asia. (p. 256)

Little Ice Age A century-long period of cool climate that began in the 1590s. Its ill effects on agriculture in northern Europe were notable. (p. 391)

llama A hoofed animal indigenous to the Andes Mountains. It was the only domesticated beast of burden in the Americas before the arrival of Europeans. The use of llamas to transport goods made possible specialized production and trade among people living in different ecological zones and fostered the integration of these zones by Chavín and later Andean states. (p. 162)

loess A fine, light silt deposited by wind and water. It constitutes the fertile soil of the Yellow River Valley in northern China. (p. 58)

Long March (1934–1935) The 6,000-mile flight of Chinese communists from southeastern to northwestern China. The communists, led by Mao Zedong, were pursued by the Chinese army under orders from Chiang Kai-shek. The four thousand survivors of the march formed the nucleus of a revived communist movement that defeated the Guomindang after World War II. (p. 641)

ma'at Egyptian term for the concept of divinely created and maintained order in the universe. The divine ruler was the earthly guarantor of this order.   (p. 22)

Macartney mission The unsuccessful attempt by the British Empire to establish diplomatic relations with the Qing Empire.   (p. 462)

Mahabharata A vast epic chronicling the events leading up to a cataclysmic battle between related kinship groups in early India. It includes the Bhagavad-Gita.   (p. 146)

Mahayana Buddhism "Great Vehicle" branch of Buddhism followed in China, Japan, and Central Asia. The focus is on reverence for Buddha and for bodhisattvas, enlightened persons who have postponed nirvana to help others attain enlightenment.   (p. 141)

Malacca Port city in the modern Southeast Asian country of Malaysia, founded about 1400 as a trading center on the Strait of Malacca.   (p. 342)

Mali Empire created by indigenous Muslims in western Sudan of West Africa from the thirteenth to fifteenth century. It was famous for its role in the trans-Saharan gold trade.   (p. 333)

mamluks Under the Islamic system of military slavery, Turkish military slaves formed an important part of the armed forces of the Abbasid Caliphate of the ninth and tenth centuries. Mamluks eventually founded their own state, ruling Egypt and Syria (1250–1517).   (p. 216)

Manchu Federation of Northeast Asian peoples who founded the Qing Empire.   (p. 449)

Mandate of Heaven Chinese religious and political ideology developed by the Zhou, according to which it was the prerogative of Heaven, the chief deity, to grant power to the ruler of China and to take away that power if the ruler failed to conduct himself justly and in the best interests of his subjects.   (p. 62)

mandate system Allocation of former German colonies and Ottoman possessions to the victorious powers after World War I, to be administered under League of Nations supervision.   (p. 599)

manor In medieval Europe, a large, self-sufficient landholding consisting of the lord's residence (manor house), outbuildings, peasant village, and surrounding land.   (p. 237)

mansabs In India, grants of land given in return for service by rulers of the Mughal Empire.   (p. 438)

Mansa Kankan Musa Ruler of Mali (r. 1312–1337). His pilgrimage through Egypt to Mecca in 1324–1325 established the empire's reputation for wealth in the Mediterranean world.   (p. 335)

Mao Zedong (1893–1976) Leader of the Chinese Communist Party (1927–1976). He led the communists on the Long March (1934–1935) and rebuilt the Communist Party and Red Army during the Japanese occupation of China (1937–1945). After World War II, he led the communists to victory over the Guomindang.   (p. 641)

Margaret Sanger (1883–1966) American nurse and author; pioneer in the movement for family planning; organized conferences and established birth control clinics.   (p. 610)

Marie Curie (1867–1934) Twice winner of the Nobel Prize, the Polish Maria (Marie, in French) Sklodowska worked in Paris and, with her husband Pierre Curie, discovered the element radium and radioactivity, changing the knowledge of matter and the treatment of many diseases. In World War I, she convinced wealthy patrons to donate vehicles for use as X-Ray centers and traveled to aid doctors in detecting fractures and shrapnel in wounded soldiers.   (p. 613)

maroon A slave who ran away from his or her master. Often a member of a community of runaway slaves in the West Indies and South America.   (p. 418)

Marshall Plan U.S. program to support the reconstruction of western Europe after World War II. By 1961 more than $20 billion in economic aid had been dispersed.   (p. 658)

mass deportation The forcible removal and relocation of large numbers of people or entire populations. The mass deportations practiced by the Assyrian and Persian Empires were meant as a terrifying warning of the consequences of rebellion. They also brought skilled and unskilled labor to the imperial center.   (p. 41)

mass production The manufacture of many identical products by the division of labor into many small repetitive tasks. This method was introduced into the manufacture of pottery and into the spinning of cotton thread.   (p. 476)

Mauryan Empire The first state to unify most of the Indian subcontinent. It was founded by Chandragupta Maurya in 324 B.C.E. and survived until 184 B.C.E. From its capital at Pataliputra in the Ganges Valley it grew wealthy from taxes on agriculture, iron mining, and control of trade routes.   (p. 144)

Max Planck (1858–1947) German physicist who developed quantum theory and was awarded the Nobel Prize for physics in 1918.   (p. 610)

Maya Mesoamerican civilization concentrated in Mexico's Yucatán Peninsula and in Guatemala and Honduras but never unified into a single empire. Major contributions were in mathematics, astronomy, and development of the calendar.   (p. 165)

Mecca City in western Arabia; birthplace of the Prophet Muhammad and ritual center of the Islamic religion.   (p. 211)

mechanization The application of machinery to manufacturing and other activities. Among the first processes to be mechanized were the spinning of cotton thread and the weaving of cloth in late-eighteenth- and early-nineteenth-century England.   (p. 477)

medieval Literally "middle age," a term that historians of Europe use for the period from roughly 500 to 1300, signifying its intermediate point between Greco-Roman antiquity and the Renaissance.   (p. 229)

Medina City in western Arabia to which the Prophet Muhammad and his followers emigrated in 622 to escape persecution in Mecca.   (p. 212)

megaliths Structures and complexes of very large stones constructed for ceremonial and religious purposes in Neolithic times.   (p. 12)

Meiji Restoration The political program that followed the destruction of the Tokugawa Shogunate in 1868, in which a collection of young leaders set Japan on the path of centralization, industrialization, and imperialism.   (p. 578)

Memphis The capital of Old Kingdom Egypt, near the head of the Nile Delta. Early rulers were interred in the nearby pyramids.   (p. 23)

mercantilism European government policies of the sixteenth, seventeenth, and eighteenth centuries designed to promote overseas trade between a country and its colonies and accumulate precious metals by requiring colonies to trade only with their motherland country. The British system was defined by the Navigation Acts, the French system by laws known as the *Exclusif*.   (p. 418)

Meroë Capital of a flourishing kingdom in southern Nubia from the fourth century B.C.E. to the fourth century C.E. In this period Nubian culture shows more independence from Egypt and the influence of sub-Saharan Africa.   (p. 68)

Mexican Revolution A social revolution that developed haphazardly under ambitious but limited leaders, each representing a different segment of Mexican society. The revolution evolved into civil war for over ten years of armed struggle, but it established a constitution for Mexico.   (p. 558)

Miguel Hidalgo y Costilla Mexican priest who led the first stage of the Mexican independence war in 1810. He was captured and executed in 1811.   (p. 504)

Mikhail Gorbachev (b. 1931) Head of the Soviet Union from 1985 to 1991. His liberalization effort improved relations with the West, but he lost power after his reforms led to the collapse of the communist governments in eastern Europe.   (p. 680)

Ming Empire Empire based in China that Zhu Yuanzhang established after the overthrow of the Yuan Empire. The Ming emperor Yongle sponsored the building of the Forbidden City and the voyages of Zheng He. The later years of the Ming saw a slowdown in technological development and economic decline.   (p. 296)

Minoan Prosperous civilization on the Aegean island of Crete in the second millennium B.C.E. The Minoans engaged in far-flung commerce around the Mediterranean and exerted powerful cultural influences on the early Greeks.   (p. 36)

mita Andean labor system based on shared obligations to help kinsmen and work on behalf of the ruler and religious organizations.   (p. 173)

Moche Civilization of north coast of Peru (200–700 C.E.). An important Andean civilization that built extensive irrigation networks as well as impressive urban centers dominated by brick temples.   (p. 174)

Moctezuma II Aztec emperor who died while in custody of the Spanish conquistador Hernán Cortés.   (p. 371)

modernization The process of reforming political, military, economic, social, and cultural traditions in imitation of the early success of Western societies, often with little regard for accommodating local traditions in non-Western societies.   (p. 544)

Mohandas K. Gandhi (1869–1948) Leader of the Indian independence movement and advocate of nonviolent resistance. After being educated as a lawyer in England, he returned to India and became leader of the Indian National Congress in 1920. He appealed to the poor, led nonviolent demonstrations against British colonial rule, and was jailed many times. Soon after independence he was assassinated for attempting to stop Hindu-Muslim rioting.   (p. 617)

Mohenjo-Daro Largest of the cities of the Indus Valley civilization, centrally located in the extensive floodplain of the Indus River in contemporary Pakistan.   (p. 134)

moksha The Hindu concept of the spirit's "liberation" from the endless cycle of rebirths. There are various avenues—such as physical discipline, meditation, and acts of devotion to the gods—by which the spirit can distance itself from desire for the things of this world and be merged with the divine force that animates the universe.   (p. 139)

monasticism Living in a religious community apart from secular society and adhering to a rule stipulating chastity, obedience, and poverty. It was a prominent element of medieval Christianity and Buddhism. Monasteries were the primary centers of learning and literacy in medieval Europe.   (p. 241)

Mongols A people of this name is mentioned as early as the records of the Tang Empire, living as nomads in northern Eurasia. After 1206 they established an enormous empire under Chinggis Khan, linking western and eastern Eurasia.   (p. 281)

monotheism Belief in the existence of a single divine entity. Some scholars cite the devotion of the Egyptian pharaoh Akhenaten to Aten (sun-disk) and his suppression of traditional gods as the earliest instance. The Israelite worship of Yahweh developed into an exclusive belief in one god, and this concept passed into Christianity and Islam.   (p. 46)

monsoon Seasonal winds in the Indian Ocean caused by the differences in temperature between the rapidly heating and cooling landmasses of Africa and Asia and the slowly changing ocean waters. These strong and predictable winds have long been ridden across the open sea by sailors, and the large amounts of rainfall that they deposit on parts of India, Southeast Asia, and China allow for the cultivation of several crops a year.   (p. 137)

monsoon Seasonal winds in the Indian Ocean caused by the differences in temperature between the rapidly heating and cooling landmasses of Africa and Asia and the slowly changing ocean waters. These strong and predictable winds have long been ridden across the open sea by sailors, and the large amounts of rainfall that they deposit on parts of India, Southeast Asia, and China allow for the cultivation of several crops a year.   (p. 330)

most-favored-nation status A clause in a commercial treaty that awards to any later signatories all the privileges previously granted to the original signatories.   (p. 528)

movable type Type in which each individual character is cast on a separate piece of metal. It replaced woodblock printing, allowing for the arrangement of individual letters and other characters on a page, rather than requiring the carving of entire pages at a time. It may have been invented in Korea in the thirteenth century.   (p. 266)

Mughal Empire Muslim state (1526–1857) exercising dominion over most of India in the sixteenth and seventeenth centuries. Fragmentation of power and growth of English imperial strength marked the subsequent period.   (p. 437)

Muhammad Ali Jinnah (1876–1948) Indian Muslim politician who founded the state of Pakistan. A lawyer by training, he joined the All-India Muslim League in 1913. As leader of the League from the 1920s on, he negotiated with the British and the Indian National Congress for Muslim participation in Indian politics. From 1940 on, he led the movement for the independence of India's Muslims in a separate state of Pakistan, founded in 1947.   (p. 619)

Muhammad Ali Leader of Egyptian modernization in the early nineteenth century. He ruled Egypt as an Ottoman governor but had imperial ambitions. His descendants ruled Egypt until overthrown in 1952.   (p. 513)

Muhammad Arab prophet (570–632 C.E.); founder of religion of Islam.   (p. 211)

mummy A body preserved by chemical processes or special natural circumstances, often in the belief that the deceased will need it again in the afterlife.   (p. 26)

Muscovy The Russian principality that emerged gradually during the era of Mongol domination. The muscovite dynasty ruled without interruption from 1276 to 1598.   (p. 440)

Muslim An adherent of the Islamic religion; a person who "submits" (in Arabic, *Islam* means "submission") to the will of God.   (p. 211)

Mycenae Site of a fortified palace complex in southern Greece that controlled a Late Bronze Age kingdom. In ancient epic poems, Mycenae was the base of King Agamemnon, who commanded the Greeks besieging Troy. Contemporary archaeologists call the complex Greek society of the second millennium B.C.E. "Mycenaean."   (p. 37)

Napoleon Bonaparte General who overthrew the French Directory in 1799 and became emperor of the French in 1804. Failed to defeat Great Britain and abdicated in 1814. Returned to power briefly in 1815 but was defeated and died in exile.   (p. 500)

Nasir al-Din Tusi Persian mathematician and cosmologist whose academy near Tabriz provided a model for heavenly motions that helped to inspire the Copernican model of the solar system.   (p. 290)

National Assembly French Revolutionary assembly (1789–1791). The Estates General gave itself this title when it came together and demanded radical change. In 1789 it passed the Declaration of the Rights of Man and of the Citizen.   (p. 497)

nationalism A political ideology that stresses people's membership in a nation—a community defined by a common culture and history as well as by territory. In the late eighteenth and early nineteenth centuries, nationalism was a force for unity in western Europe. In the late nineteenth century it hastened the disintegration of the Austro-Hungarian and Ottoman Empires. In the twentieth century it provided the ideological foundation for scores of independent countries emerging from colonialism.   (p. 575)

nawab Technically, a semi-autonomous deputy of the Mughal emperor but often a Muslim prince allied to British India.   (p. 549)

Nazis German political party led by Adolf Hitler, emphasizing nationalism, racism, and war. When Hitler became chancellor of Germany in 1933, the Nazis became the only legal party and an instrument of Hitler's absolute rule. The party's formal name was National Socialist German Workers' Party.   (p. 638)

Neo-Assyrian Empire An empire extending from western Iran to Syria-Palestine, conquered by the Assyrians of northern Mesopotamia between the tenth and seventh centuries B.C.E. They used force and terror and exploited the wealth and labor of their subjects. They also preserved and continued the cultural and scientific developments of Mesopotamian civilization.   (p. 40)

Neo-Babylonian kingdom Under the Chaldaeans (nomadic kinship groups that settled in southern Mesopotamia in the early first millennium B.C.E.), Babylon again became a major political and cultural center in the seventh and sixth centuries B.C.E. After participating in the destruction of Assyrian power, the monarchs Nabopolassar and Nebuchadnezzar took over the southern portion of the Assyrian domains.   (p. 53)

neo-Confucianism Term used to describe new approaches to understanding classic Confucian texts that became the basic ruling philosophy of China from the Song period to the twentieth century.   (p. 265)

Neolithic The period of the Stone Age associated with the ancient Agricultural Revolution(s).   (p. 10)

New Economic Policy Policy proclaimed by Vladimir Lenin in 1923 to encourage the revival of the Soviet economy by allowing small private enterprises. Joseph Stalin ended the NEP in 1928 and replaced it with a series of Five-Year Plans.   (p. 595)

New France French colony in North America, with a capital in Quebec, founded in 1608. New France fell to the British in 1763.   (p. 412)

newly industrialized economies (NIEs) Rapidly growing new industrializing nations of the late twentieth century, including the Asian Tigers.   (p. 676)

new monarchies Historians' term for the monarchies in France, England, and Spain from 1450 to 1600. The centralization of royal power was increasing within more or less fixed territorial limits.   (p. 324)

nomads People without permanent, fixed places of residence, whose way of life and means of subsistence require them to periodically migrate, often with their herds of domesticated animals, to a familiar series of temporary seasonal encampments.   (p. 70)

nonaligned nations Developing countries that announced their neutrality in the Cold War.   (p. 665)

nongovernmental organizations (NGOs) Nonprofit international organizations devoted to investigating human rights abuses and providing humanitarian relief. Two NGOs won the Nobel Peace Prize in the 1990s: International Campaign to Ban Landmines (1997) and Doctors Without Borders (1999).   (p. 693)

North Atlantic Treaty Organization (NATO) Organization formed in 1949 as a military alliance of western European and North American states against the Soviet Union and its east European allies.   (p. 657)

Olmec The first Mesoamerican civilization. Between about 1200 and 400 B.C.E., the Olmec people of central Mexico created a vibrant civilization that included intensive agriculture, wide-ranging trade, ceremonial centers, and monumental construction. The Olmec had great cultural influence on later Mesoamerican societies.   (p. 158)

Oman Arab state based in Musqat, the main port in the southeast region of the Arabian peninsula. Oman succeeded Portugal as a power in the western Indian Ocean in the eighteenth century.   (p. 445)

Opium War War between Britain and the Qing Empire that was, in the British view, occasioned by the Qing government's refusal to permit the importation of opium into its territories. The victorious British imposed the one-sided Treaty of Nanking on China.   (p. 526)

Organization of Petroleum Exporting Countries (OPEC) Organization formed in 1960 by oil-producing states to promote their collective interest in generating revenue from oil.   (p. 678)

Ottoman Empire Islamic state founded by Osman in northwestern Anatolia around 1300. After the fall of the Byzantine Empire, the Ottoman Empire was based at Istanbul (formerly Constantinople) from 1453 to 1922. It encompassed lands in the Middle East, North Africa, the Caucasus, and eastern Europe.   (p. 293, 427)

Otto von Bismarck Chancellor (prime minister) of Prussia from 1862 until 1871, when he became chancellor of Germany. A conservative nationalist, he led Prussia to victory against Austria (1866) and France (1870) and was responsible for the creation of the German Empire in 1871.   (p. 577)

Paleolithic The period of the Stone Age associated with the evolution of humans.   (p. 7)

Panama Canal Ship canal cut across the Isthmus of Panama by U.S. Army engineers; it opened in 1914. It greatly shortened the sea voyage between the east and west coasts of North America. The United States turned the canal over to Panama on January 1, 2000.   (p. 560)

Pan-Slavism Movement among Russian intellectuals in the second half of the nineteenth century to identify culturally and politically with the Slavic peoples of eastern Europe.   (p. 522)

papacy The central administration of the Roman Catholic Church, of which the pope is the head.   (p. 240, 381)

papyrus A reed that grows along the banks of the Nile River in Egypt. From it was produced a coarse, paperlike writing medium used by the Egyptians and many other peoples in the ancient Mediterranean and Middle East.   (p. 23)

Parthians Iranian ruling dynasty between ca. 250 B.C.E. and 226 C.E.   (p. 189)

pastoralism A way of life dependent on moving large herds of small and large stock to new pastures and watering places throughout the year.   (p. 11)

patron/client relationship In ancient Rome, a fundamental social relationship in which the patron—a wealthy and powerful individual—provided legal and economic protection and assistance to clients, men of lesser status and means, and in return the clients supported the political careers and economic interests of their patron.   (p. 109)

Paul A Jew from the Greek city of Tarsus in Anatolia, he initially persecuted the followers of Jesus but, after receiving a revelation on the road to Syrian Damascus, became a Christian.

Taking advantage of his Hellenized background and Roman citizenship, he traveled throughout Syria-Palestine, Anatolia, and Greece, preaching the new religion and establishing churches. Finding his greatest success among pagans ("gentiles"), he began the process by which Christianity separated from Judaism. (p. 118)

pax Romana Literally, "Roman peace," it connoted the stability and prosperity that Roman rule brought to the lands of the Roman Empire in the first two centuries C.E. The movement of people and trade goods along Roman roads and safe seas allowed for the spread of cultural practices, technologies, and religious ideas. (p. 117)

Pearl Harbor Naval base in Hawaii attacked by Japanese aircraft on December 7, 1941. The sinking of much of the U.S. Pacific Fleet brought the United States into World War II. (p. 644)

Peloponnesian War A protracted (431–404 B.C.E.) and costly conflict between the Athenian and Spartan alliance systems that convulsed most of the Greek world. The war was largely a consequence of Athenian imperialism. Possession of a naval empire allowed Athens to fight a war of attrition. Ultimately, Sparta prevailed because of Athenian errors and Persian financial support. (p. 100)

perestroika Policy of "restructuring" that was the centerpiece of Mikhail Gorbachev's efforts to liberalize communism in the Soviet Union. (p. 680)

Pericles Aristocratic leader who guided the Athenian state through the transformation to full participatory democracy for all male citizens, supervised construction of the Acropolis, and pursued a policy of imperial expansion that led to the Peloponnesian War. He formulated a strategy of attrition but died from the plague early in the war. (p. 93)

Persepolis A complex of palaces, reception halls, and treasury buildings erected by the Persian kings Darius I and Xerxes in the Persian homeland. It is believed that the New Year's festival was celebrated here, as well as the coronations, weddings, and funerals of the Persian kings, who were buried in cliff-tombs nearby. (p. 86)

Persian Wars Conflicts between Greek city-states and the Persian Empire, ranging from the Ionian Revolt (499–494 B.C.E.) through Darius's punitive expedition that failed at Marathon (490 B.C.E.) and the defeat of Xerxes's massive invasion of Greece by the Spartan-led Hellenic League (480–479 B.C.E.). This first major setback for Persian arms launched the Greeks into their period of greatest cultural productivity. Herodotus chronicled these events in the first "history" in the Western tradition. (p. 94)

Peter the Great Russian tsar (r. 1689–1725). He enthusiastically introduced Western languages and technologies to the Russian elite and moved the capital from Moscow to the new city of St. Petersburg. (p. 441)

pharaoh The central figure in the ancient Egyptian state. Believed to be an earthly manifestation of the gods, he used his absolute power to maintain the safety and prosperity of Egypt. (p. 22)

Phoenicians Canaanites living on the coast of modern Lebanon and Syria in the first millennium B.C.E. From major cities such as Tyre and Sidon, Phoenician merchants and sailors explored the Mediterranean, engaged in widespread commerce, and founded Carthage and other colonies in the western Mediterranean. (p. 47)

pilgrimage Journey to a sacred shrine by Christians seeking to show their piety, fulfill vows, or gain absolution for sins. Other religions also have pilgrimage traditions, such as the Muslim pilgrimage to Mecca and the pilgrimages made by early Chinese Buddhists to India in search of sacred Buddhist writings. (p. 250)

Pilgrims Group of English Protestant dissenters who established Plymouth Colony in Massachusetts in 1620 to seek religious freedom after having lived briefly in the Netherlands. (p. 411)

polis The Greek term for a city-state, an urban center and the agricultural territory under its control. It was the characteristic form of political organization in southern and central Greece in the Archaic and Classical periods. Of the hundreds of city-states in the Mediterranean and Black Sea regions settled by Greeks, some were oligarchic, others democratic, depending on the powers delegated to the Council and the Assembly. (p. 89)

positivism A philosophy developed by the French Count of Saint-Simon. Positivists believed that social and economic problems could be solved by application of the scientific method, leading to continuous progress. Their ideas became popular in France and Latin America in the nineteenth century. (p. 485)

Potosí Located in Bolivia, one of the richest silver mining centers and most populous cities in colonial Spanish America. (p. 405)

printing press A mechanical device for transferring text or graphics from a woodblock or type to paper using ink. Presses using movable type first appeared in Europe in about 1450. (p. 321)

proletariat Industrial workers whose oppression was an example of how, according to *The Communist Manifesto*, history was dominated by class struggle between the workers who sold their labor for survival and those who owned the mills, factories, mines, or other means of industrial production and wealth (the bourgeoisie). (p. 485)

Protestant Reformation Religious reform movement within the Latin Christian Church beginning in 1519. It resulted in the "protesters" forming several new Christian denominations, including the Lutheran and Reformed Churches and the Church of England. (p. 382)

Ptolemies The Macedonian dynasty, descended from one of Alexander the Great's officers, that ruled Egypt for three centuries (323–30 B.C.E.). From their magnificent capital at Alexandria on the Mediterranean coast, the Ptolemies largely took over the system created by Egyptian pharaohs to extract the wealth of the land, rewarding Greeks and Hellenized non-Greeks serving in the military and administration. (p. 102)

Puritans English Protestant dissenters who believed that God predestined souls to Heaven or Hell before birth. They founded Massachusetts Bay Colony in 1629. (p. 411)

pyramid A large, triangular stone monument, used in Egypt and Nubia as a burial place for the king. The largest pyramids, erected during the Old Kingdom near Memphis, reflect the Egyptian belief that the proper and spectacular burial of the divine ruler would guarantee the continued prosperity of the land. (p. 22)

Qin A people and state in the Wei River Valley of eastern China that conquered rival states and created the first Chinese empire (221–206 B.C.E.). The Qin ruler, Shi Huangdi, standardized many features of Chinese society and ruthlessly marshaled subjects for military and construction projects, engendering hostility that led to the fall of his dynasty shortly after his death. The Qin framework was largely taken over by the succeeding Han dynasty. (p. 125)

Qing Empire Empire established in China by Manchus who overthrew the Ming Empire in 1644. At various times the Qing also controlled Manchuria, Mongolia, Turkestan, and Tibet. The last Qing emperor was overthrown in 1911. (p. 457)

Quran Book composed of divine revelations made to the Prophet Muhammad between roughly 610 and his death in 632; the sacred text of the religion of Islam. (p. 213)

railroads Networks of iron (later steel) rails on which steam (later electric or diesel) locomotives pulled long trains at high speeds. The first railroads were built in England in the 1830s. Their success caused a railroad-building boom throughout the world that lasted well into the twentieth century.   (p. 565)

Rajputs Members of a mainly Hindu warrior caste from northwest India. The Mughal emperors drew most of their Hindu officials from this caste, and Akbar married a Rajput princess.   (p. 438)

Ramesses II A long-lived ruler of New Kingdom Egypt (r. 1290–1224 B.C.E.). He reached an accommodation with the Hittites of Anatolia after a standoff in battle at Kadesh in Syria. He built on a grand scale throughout Egypt.   (p. 35)

Rashid al-Din Adviser to the Il-khan ruler Ghazan, who converted to Islam on Rashid's advice.   (p. 289)

recaptives Africans rescued by Britain's Royal Navy from the illegal slave trade of the nineteenth century and restored to free status.   (p. 548)

reconquest of Iberia Beginning in the eleventh century, military campaigns by various Iberian Christian states to recapture territory taken by Muslims. In 1492 the last Muslim ruler was defeated, and Spain and Portugal emerged as united kingdoms.   (p. 324)

Renaissance (European) A period of intense artistic and intellectual activity, said to be a "rebirth" of Greco-Roman culture. Usually divided into an Italian Renaissance, from roughly the mid-fourteenth to mid-fifteenth century, and a Northern (trans-Alpine) Renaissance, from roughly the early fifteenth to early seventeenth century.   (p. 318)

Revolutions of 1848 Democratic and nationalist revolutions that swept across Europe. The monarchy in France was briefly overthrown. In Germany, Austria, Italy, and Hungary the revolutions failed.   (p. 502)

Romanization The process by which the Latin language and Roman culture became dominant in the western provinces. Indigenous peoples in the provinces often chose to Romanize because of the political and economic advantages that it brought, as well as the allure of Roman success.   (p. 117)

Roman Principate A term used to characterize Roman government in the first three centuries C.E., based on the ambiguous title *princeps* ("first citizen") adopted by Augustus to conceal his military dictatorship.   (p. 112)

Roman Republic The period from 507 to 31 B.C.E., during which Rome was largely governed by the aristocratic Roman Senate.   (p. 109)

Roman Senate A council whose members were the heads of wealthy, landowning families. Originally an advisory body to the early kings, in the era of the Roman Republic the Senate effectively governed the Roman state and the growing empire. Under Senate leadership, Rome conquered an empire of unprecedented extent in the lands surrounding the Mediterranean Sea.   (p. 109)

Royal African Company A trading company chartered by the English government in 1672 to conduct its merchants' trade on the Atlantic coast of Africa.   (p. 419)

sacrifice A gift given to a deity, often with the aim of creating a relationship, gaining favor, and obligating the god to provide some benefit to the sacrificer, sometimes in order to sustain the deity and thereby guarantee the continuing vitality of the natural world.   (p. 91)

Saddam Husain (1937–2006) President of Iraq from 1979 until overthrown by the American invasion in 2003. Waged war on Iran from 1980 to 1988. His invasion of Kuwait was repulsed in the Persian Gulf War of 1991.   (p. 679)

Safavid Empire Iranian kingdom (1502–1722) established by Ismail Safavi, who declared Iran a Shi'ite state.   (p. 434)

Sahel Belt south of the Sahara; literally "coastland" in Arabic.   (p. 198)

Salvador Allende (1908–1973) Socialist president of Chile who was elected in 1970 and overthrown and killed by the military in 1973.   (p. 672)

samurai Literally "those who serve," the hereditary military elite of the Tokugawa Shogunate.   (p. 453)

Sandinistas Members of a leftist coalition that overthrew the Nicaraguan dictator Anastosio Somoza in 1979 and attempted to install a socialist economy. The United States financed an armed uprising against the Sandinista government. In 1990 the Sandinistas lost power after a national election.   (p. 672)

Sasanid Empire Iranian empire, established around 224, with a capital in Ctesiphon, Mesopotamia. The Sasanid emperors established Zoroastrianism as the state religion. Islamic Arab armies overthrew the empire around 651.   (p. 208)

satrap The governor of a province in the Achaemenid Persian Empire, often a relative of the king. He was responsible for protection of the province and for forwarding tribute to the central administration. Satraps in outlying provinces enjoyed considerable autonomy.   (p. 85)

savanna Tropical or subtropical grassland, either treeless or with occasional clumps of trees. Most extensive in sub-Saharan Africa but also present in South America.   (p. 199)

schism A formal split within a religious community.   (p. 232)

scholasticism A philosophical and theological system, associated with Thomas Aquinas, devised to reconcile Aristotelian philosophy and Roman Catholic theology in the thirteenth century.   (p. 319)

Scientific Revolution The intellectual movement in Europe, initially associated with planetary motion and other aspects of physics, that by the seventeenth century had laid the groundwork for modern science.   (p. 386)

scribe In the governments of many ancient societies, a professional position reserved for men who had undergone the lengthy training required to be able to read and write using cuneiform, hieroglyphics, or other early, cumbersome writing systems.   (p. 18)

Scythians Term used by the ancient Greeks for the nomadic peoples living on the steppe north of the Black and Caspian Seas.   (p. 71)

seasoning An often difficult period of adjustment to new climates, disease environments, and work routines, such as that experienced by slaves newly arrived in the Americas.   (p. 417)

"separate spheres" Nineteenth-century idea in Western societies that men and women, especially of the middle class, should have clearly differentiated roles in society: women as wives, mothers, and homemakers; men as breadwinners and participants in business and politics.   (p. 571)

sepoy A soldier in colonial India, especially in the service of the British.   (p. 549)

Sepoy Rebellion The revolt of Indian soldiers in 1857 against certain practices that violated religious customs; also known as the Sepoy Mutiny.   (p. 551)

Serbia The Ottoman province in the Balkans that rose up against Janissary control in the early 1800s. After World War II the central province of Yugoslavia.   (p. 514)

serf In medieval Europe, an agricultural laborer legally bound to a lord's property and obligated to perform set services for the lord. In Russia, later, some serfs worked as artisans and in factories; serfdom was not abolished there until 1861.   (p. 237, 441)

shaft graves A term used for the burial sites of elite members of Mycenaean Greek society in the mid-second millennium B.C.E. At the bottom of deep shafts lined with stone slabs, the bodies were laid out along with gold and bronze jewelry, implements, weapons, and masks.   (p. 37)

Shah Abbas I The fifth and most renowned ruler of the Safavid dynasty in Iran (r. 1587–1629). Abbas moved the royal capital to Isfahan in 1598.   (p. 435)

shamanism The practice of identifying special individuals (shamans) who will interact with spirits for the benefit of the community. Characteristic of the Korean kingdoms of the early medieval period and of early societies of Central Asia.   (p. 270)

Shang The dominant people in the earliest Chinese dynasty for which we have written records (ca. 1750–1045 B.C.E.).   (p. 60)

Shi Huangdi Founder of the short-lived Qin dynasty and creator of the Chinese Empire (r. 221–210 B.C.E.). He is remembered for his ruthless conquests of rival states, standardization of practices, and forcible organization of labor for military and engineering tasks. His tomb, with its army of life-size terracotta soldiers, has been partially excavated.   (p. 125)

Shi'ites Muslims belonging to the branch of Islam believing that God vests leadership of the community in a descendant of Muhammad's son-in-law Ali. Shi'ism is the state religion of Iran.   (p. 213)

Shi'ites Muslims belonging to the branch of Islam believing that God vests leadership of the community in a descendant of Muhammad's son-in-law Ali. Shi'ism is the state religion of Iran.   (p. 434)

Siberia The extreme northeastern sector of Asia, including the Kamchatka Peninsula and the present Russian coast of the Arctic Ocean, the Bering Strait, and the Sea of Okhotsk.   (p. 440)

Sigmund Freud (1856–1939) Austrian psychiatrist, founder of psychoanalysis. He argued that psychological problems were caused by traumas, especially sexual experiences in early childhood, that were repressed in later life. His ideas caused considerable controversy among psychologists and in the general public. Although his views on repressed sexuality are no longer widely accepted, his psychoanalytic methods are still very influential.   (p. 610)

Silk Road Caravan routes connecting China and the Middle East across Central Asia and Iran.   (p. 187)

Simón Bolívar The most important military leader in the struggle for independence in South America. Born in Venezuela, he led military forces there and in Colombia, Ecuador, Peru, and Bolivia.   (p. 504)

Slavophiles Russian intellectuals in the early nineteenth century who favored resisting western European influences and taking pride in the traditional peasant values and institutions of the Slavic peoples.   (p. 522)

"small traditions" Historians' term for a localized, usually nonliterate, set of customs and beliefs adhered to by a single society, often in conjunction with a "great tradition."   (p. 199)

socialism A political ideology that originated in Europe in the 1830s. Socialists advocated government protection of workers from exploitation by property owners and government ownership of industries. This ideology led to the founding of socialist or labor parties throughout Europe in the second half of the nineteenth century.   (p. 573)

Socrates Athenian philosopher (ca. 470–399 B.C.E.) who shifted the emphasis of philosophical investigation from questions of natural science to ethics and human behavior. He attracted young disciples from elite families but made enemies by revealing the ignorance and pretensions of others, culminating in his trial and execution by the Athenian state.   (p. 96)

Sokoto Caliphate A large Muslim state founded in 1809 in what is now northern Nigeria.   (p. 543)

Solidarity Polish trade union created in 1980 to protest working conditions and political repression. It began the nationalist opposition in eastern Europe.   (p. 681)

Song Empire Empire in central and southern China (960–1126) while the Liao people controlled the north. Empire in southern China (1127–1279; the "Southern Song") while the Jin people controlled the north. Distinguished for its advances in technology, medicine, astronomy, and mathematics.   (p. 263)

Spanish-American War U.S. war fought with Spain in 1898 over control of Cuba, ostensibly because of the sinking of a U.S. ship and also after reports of Spanish atrocities had fanned flames of American popular opinion. Won handily in three months, the war unofficially made Cuba a protectorate of the United States.   (p. 557)

Srivijaya A state based on the Indonesian island of Sumatra between the seventh and eleventh centuries C.E. It amassed wealth and power by a combination of selective adaptation of Indian technologies and concepts, control of the lucrative trade routes between India and China, and skillful showmanship and diplomacy in holding together a disparate realm of inland and coastal territories.   (p. 151)

Stalingrad City in Russia, site of a Red Army victory over the German army in 1942–1943. The Battle of Stalingrad was the turning point in the war between Germany and the Soviet Union. Today Volgograd.   (p. 644)

steam engine A machine that turns the energy released by burning fuel into motion. Thomas Newcomen built the first crude but workable steam engine in 1712. James Watt vastly improved his device in the 1760s and 1770s. Steam power was later applied to operating machinery in factories and to propelling ships and locomotives.   (p. 479)

steel A form of iron that is both durable and flexible. It was first mass-produced in the 1860s and quickly became the most widely used metal in construction, machinery, and railroad equipment.   (p. 567)

steppe An ecological region of grass- and shrub-covered plains that is treeless and too arid for agriculture.   (p. 70, 199)

stock exchange A place where shares in a company or business enterprise are bought and sold.   (p. 391)

Stone Age The historical period characterized by the production of tools from stone and other nonmetallic substances.   (p. 7)

submarine telegraph cables Insulated copper cables laid along the bottom of a sea or ocean for telegraphic communication. The first short cable was laid under the Hooghly River in Calcutta in 1839; the first successful transatlantic cable was laid in 1866.   (p. 567)

sub-Saharan Africa Portion of the African continent lying south of the Sahara.   (p. 195)

Suez Canal Ship canal dug across the Isthmus of Suez in Egypt, designed by Ferdinand de Lesseps. It opened to shipping in 1869 and shortened the sea voyage between Europe and Asia. Its strategic importance led to the British occupation of Egypt in 1882.   (p. 545)

Suleiman the Magnificent The most illustrious sultan of the Ottoman Empire (r. 1520–1566); also known as Suleiman Kanuni, "The Lawgiver." He significantly expanded the empire in the Balkans and eastern Mediterranean.   (p. 428)

Sumerians The people who dominated southern Mesopotamia through the end of the third millennium B.C.E.   (p. 15)

Sunnis Muslims belonging to branch of Islam believing that the community should select its own leadership. The majority religion in most Islamic countries.   (p. 214)

Sun Yat-sen (1867–1925) Chinese nationalist revolutionary, founder and leader of the Guomindang until his death. He attempted to create a liberal democratic political movement in China but was thwarted by military leaders.   (p. 597)

Swahili Bantu language with Arabic loanwords spoken in coastal regions of East Africa.   (p. 445)

Swahili Coast East African shores of the Indian Ocean between the Horn of Africa and the Zambezi River; from the Arabic *sawahil*, meaning "shores."   (p. 339)

Taiping Rebellion A Christian-inspired rural rebellion that threatened to topple the Qing Empire.   (p. 528)

Tamil kingdoms The kingdoms of southern India, inhabited primarily by speakers of Dravidian languages, which developed in partial isolation, and somewhat differently, from the Arya north. They produced epics, poetry, and performance arts. Elements of Tamil religious beliefs were merged into the Hindu synthesis.   (p. 146)

Tang Empire Empire unifying China and part of Inner Asia (618–907). The Tang emperors presided over a magnificent court at their capital, Chang'an.   (p. 256)

Tanzimat Restructuring reforms by the nineteenth-century Ottoman rulers, intended to move civil law away from the control of religious elites and make the military and the bureaucracy more efficient.   (p. 515)

tax farmers Private individuals or small partnerships who were given contracts to collect taxes for the government. In return tax farmers could keep whatever money they were able to collect above their tax obligation to the government.   (p. 397)

Tenochtitlan Capital of the Aztec Empire, located on an island in Lake Texcoco. Its population was above 150,000 on the eve of the Spanish conquest. Mexico City was constructed on its ruins.   (p. 346)

Teotihuacan A powerful city-state in central Mexico (100 B.C.E.–750 C.E.). Its population was about 150,000 at its peak in 600.   (p. 163)

terrorism Political belief that extreme and seemingly random violence will destabilize a government and permit the terrorists to gain political advantage. Though an old technique, terrorism gained prominence in the late twentieth century with the growth of worldwide mass media that, through their news coverage, amplified public fears of terrorist acts.   (p. 692)

theater-state Historians' term for a state that acquires prestige and power by developing attractive cultural forms and staging elaborate public ceremonies (as well as redistributing valuable resources) to attract and bind subjects to the center. Examples include the Gupta Empire in India and Srivijaya in Southeast Asia.   (p. 147)

Thebes Capital city of Egypt and home of the ruling dynasties during the Middle and New Kingdoms. Monarchs were buried across the river in the Valley of the Kings.   (p. 23)

Theravada Buddhism "Way of the Elders" branch of Buddhism followed in Sri Lanka and much of Southeast Asia. Theravada remains close to the original principles set forth by the Buddha; it downplays the importance of gods and emphasizes austerity and the individual's search for enlightenment.   (p. 141)

third-century crisis Historians' term for the political, military, and economic turmoil that beset the Roman Empire during much of the third century C.E.: frequent changes of ruler, civil wars, barbarian invasions, decline of urban centers, and near-destruction of long-distance commerce and the monetary economy. After 284 C.E. Diocletian restored order by making fundamental changes.   (p. 120)

Third World Term applied to a group of developing countries who professed nonalignment during the Cold War.   (p. 665)

Thomas Edison American inventor best known for inventing the electric light bulb, acoustic recording on wax cylinders, and motion pictures.   (p. 568)

Thomas Malthus (1766–1834) Eighteenth-century English intellectual who warned that population growth threatened the future generations because, in his view, it would always outstrip increases in agricultural production.   (p. 697)

three-field system A rotational system for agriculture in which two fields grow food crops and one lies fallow. It gradually replaced the two-field system in medieval Europe.   (p. 308)

Tibet Country centered on the high, mountain-bounded plateau north of India. Tibetan political power occasionally extended farther to the north and west between the seventh and thirteenth centuries.   (p. 259)

Timbuktu City on the Niger River in the modern country of Mali. It was founded by the Tuareg as a seasonal camp sometime after 1000. As part of the Mali Empire, Timbuktu became a major terminus of the trans-Saharan trade and a center of Islamic learning.   (p. 343)

Timur Member of a prominent family of the Mongols' Chagatai Khanate, Timur through conquest gained control over much of Central Asia and Iran. He consolidated the status of Sunni Islam as orthodox, and his descendants, the Timurids, maintained his empire for nearly a century and founded the Mughal Empire in India.   (p. 289)

Tiwanaku Name of capital city and empire centered on the region near Lake Titicaca in modern Bolivia (375–1000 C.E.).   (p. 175)

Tokugawa Shogunate The last of the three shogunates of Japan.   (p. 454)

Toltecs Powerful postclassic empire in central Mexico (900–1175 C.E.). It influenced much of Mesoamerica. Aztecs claimed ties to this earlier civilization.   (p. 168)

Toussaint L'Ouverture Leader of the Haitian Revolution. He freed the slaves and gained effective independence for Haiti despite military interventions by the British and French.   (p. 503)

trans-Saharan caravan routes Trading network linking North Africa with sub-Saharan Africa across the Sahara.   (p. 195)

Treaty of Nanking The treaty that concluded the Opium War. It awarded Britain a large indemnity from the Qing Empire, denied the Qing government tariff control over some of its own borders, opened additional ports of residence to Britons, and ceded the island of Hong Kong to Britain.   (p. 528)

Treaty of Versailles (1919) The treaty imposed on Germany by France, Great Britain, the United States, and other Allied powers after World War I. It demanded that Germany dismantle its military and give up some lands to Poland. It humiliated but did not weaken Germany.   (p. 595)

treaty ports Cities opened to foreign residents as a result of the forced treaties between the Qing Empire and foreign signatories. In the treaty ports, foreigners enjoyed extraterritoriality.   (p. 528)

tributary system A system in which, from the time of the Han Empire, countries in East and Southeast Asia not under the direct control of empires based in China nevertheless enrolled as tributary states, acknowledging the superiority of the emperors in China in exchange for trading rights or strategic alliances.   (p. 257)

tribute system A system in which defeated peoples were forced to pay a tax in the form of goods and labor. The forced transfer of food, cloth, and other goods subsidized the development of large cities. An important component of the Aztec and Inka economies. (p. 347)

trireme Greek and Phoenician warship of the fifth and fourth centuries B.C.E. It was sleek and light, powered by 170 oars arranged in three vertical tiers. Manned by skilled sailors, it was capable of short bursts of speed and complex maneuvers. (p. 95)

tropical rain forest High-precipitation forest zones of the Americas, Africa, and Asia lying between the Tropic of Cancer and the Tropic of Capricorn. (p. 199)

tropics Equatorial region between the Tropic of Cancer and the Tropic of Capricorn. It is characterized by generally warm or hot temperatures year-round, though much variation exists due to altitude and other factors. Temperate zones north and south of the tropics generally have a winter season. (p. 329)

Truman Doctrine Foreign policy initiated by U.S. president Harry Truman in 1947. It offered military aid to help Turkey and Greece resist Soviet military pressure and subversion. (p. 660)

tsar (czar) From Latin *caesar*, this Russian title for a monarch was first used in reference to a Russian ruler by Ivan III (r. 1462–1505). (p. 292, 440)

Tulip Period Last years of the reign of Ottoman sultan Ahmed III (1718–1730), during which European styles and attitudes became briefly popular in Istanbul. (p. 432)

tyrant The term the Greeks used to describe someone who seized and held power in violation of the normal procedures and traditions of the community. Tyrants appeared in many Greek city-states in the seventh and sixth centuries B.C.E., often taking advantage of the disaffection of the emerging middle class and, by weakening the old elite, unwittingly contributing to the evolution of democracy. (p. 90)

tzompantli Images of impaled skulls in scenes of human sacrifice included in the decoration of a prominent public buildings and temples in Tula. (p. 168)

Uighurs A group of Turkish-speakers who controlled their own centralized empire from 744 to 840 in Mongolia and Central Asia. (p. 259)

ulama Muslim religious scholars. From the ninth century onward, the primary interpreters of Islamic law and the social core of Muslim urban societies. (p. 219)

Umayyad Caliphate First hereditary dynasty of Muslim caliphs (661 to 750). From their capital at Damascus, the Umayyads ruled an empire that extended from Spain to India. Overthrown by the Abbasid Caliphate. (p. 213)

umma The community of all Muslims. A major innovation against the background of seventh-century Arabia, where traditionally kinship rather than faith had determined membership in a community. (p. 212)

United Nations International organization founded in 1945 to promote world peace and cooperation. It replaced the League of Nations. (p. 657)

Universal Declaration of Human Rights A 1948 United Nations covenant binding signatory nations to the observance of specified rights. (p. 693)

universities Degree-granting institutions of higher learning. Those that appeared in the countries of western Europe from about 1200 onward became the model of all modern universities. (p. 318)

Urdu A Persian-influenced literary form of Hindi written in Arabic characters and used as a literary language since the 1300s. (p. 343)

Usama bin Laden (1957–2011) Saudi-born Muslim extremist who funded the al-Qaeda organization that was responsible for several terrorist attacks, including those on the World Trade Center and the Pentagon in 2001. (p. 692)

varna/jati Two categories of social identity of great importance in Indian history. Varnas are the four major social divisions: the Brahmin priest class, the Kshatriya warrior/administrator class, the Vaishya merchant/farmer class, and the Shudra laborer class. Within the system of varnas are many jatis, regional groups of people who have a common occupational sphere and who marry, eat, and generally interact with other members of their group. (p. 138)

Vasco da Gama Portuguese explorer. In 1497–1498 he led the first naval expedition from Europe to sail to India, opening an important commercial sea route. (p. 363)

vassal In medieval Europe, a sworn supporter of a king or lord committed to rendering specified military service to that king or lord. (p. 238)

Vedas Early Indian sacred "knowledge"—the literal meaning of the term—long preserved and communicated orally by Brahmin priests and eventually written down. These religious texts, including the thousand poetic hymns to various deities contained in the *Rig Veda*, are our main source of information about the Vedic period (ca. 1500–500 B.C.E.). (p. 138)

Versailles The huge palace built for French king Louis XIV south of Paris. The palace symbolized both French power and the triumph of royal authority over the French nobility. (p. 396)

Victorian Age The reign of Queen Victoria of Great Britain (r. 1837–1901). The term is also used to describe late-nineteenth-century society, with its rigid moral standards and sharply differentiated roles for men and women and for middle-class and working-class people. (p. 570)

Vietnam War (1954–1975) Conflict pitting North Vietnam and South Vietnamese communist guerrillas against the South Vietnamese government, aided after 1961 by the United States. (p. 661)

Vladimir Lenin (1870–1924) Leader of the Bolshevik (later Communist) Party. He lived in exile in Switzerland until 1917, then returned to Russia to lead the Bolsheviks to victory during the Russian Revolution and the civil war that followed. (p. 592)

Wari Andean civilization culturally linked to Tiwanaku, perhaps beginning as a colony of Tiwanaku. (p. 175)

Warsaw Pact The 1955 treaty binding the Soviet Union and countries of eastern Europe in an alliance against the North Atlantic Treaty Organization. (p. 657)

western front A line of trenches and fortifications in World War I that stretched without a break from Switzerland to the North Sea. Scene of most of the fighting between Germany, on the one hand, and France and Britain, on the other. (p. 588)

Wilbur (1867–1912) and Orville (1871–1948) Wright American bicycle mechanics; the first to build and fly an airplane, at Kitty Hawk, North Carolina, December 7, 1903. (p. 611)

witch-hunt The pursuit of people suspected of witchcraft, especially in northern Europe in the late sixteenth and seventeenth centuries. (p. 385)

Women's Rights Convention An 1848 gathering of women angered by their exclusion from an international antislavery meeting. They met at Seneca Falls, New York, to discuss women's rights. (p. 507)

Woodrow Wilson (1856–1924) President of the United States (1913–1921) and a leading figure at the Paris Peace Conference of 1919. He was unable to persuade the U.S. Congress to ratify the Treaty of Versailles or join the League of Nations.   (p. 593)

World Bank A specialized agency of the United Nations that makes loans to countries for economic development, trade promotion, and debt consolidation. Its formal name is the International Bank for Reconstruction and Development.   (p. 658)

World Trade Organization (WTO) An international body established in 1995 to foster and bring order to international trade.   (p. 689)

Xiongnu A confederation of nomadic peoples living beyond the northwest frontier of ancient China. Chinese rulers tried a variety of defenses and stratagems to ward off these "barbarians," as they called them, and finally succeeded in dispersing the Xiongnu in the first century C.E.   (p. 129)

Yamagata Aritomo One of the leaders of the Meiji Restoration.   (p. 583)

yin/yang In Chinese belief, complementary factors that help to maintain the equilibrium of the world. Yang is associated with masculine, light, and active qualities; yin with feminine, dark, and passive qualities.   (p. 66)

Yongle The third emperor of the Ming Empire (r. 1403–1424). He sponsored the building of the Forbidden City, a huge encyclopedia project, the expeditions of Zheng He, and the reopening of China's borders to trade and travel.   (p. 296)

Young Ottomans Movement of young intellectuals to institute liberal reforms and build a feeling of national identity in the Ottoman Empire in the second half of the nineteenth century.   (p. 521)

Yuan Empire Empire created in China and Siberia by Khubilai Khan.   (p. 282)

Yuan Shikai (1859–1916) Chinese general and first president of the Chinese Republic (1912–1916). He stood in the way of the democratic movement led by Sun Yat-sen.   (p. 597)

Zen The Japanese word for a branch of Mahayana Buddhism based on highly disciplined meditation. It is known in Sanskrit as *dhyana*, in Chinese as *chan*, and in Korean as *son*.   (p. 265)

Zheng He An imperial eunuch and Muslim, entrusted by the Ming emperor Yongle with a series of state voyages that took his gigantic ships through the Indian Ocean, from Southeast Asia to Africa.   (p. 297)

Zhou The people and dynasty that took over the dominant position in north China from the Shang and created the concept of the Mandate of Heaven to justify their rule. The Zhou era, particularly the vigorous early period (1045–771 B.C.E.), was remembered in Chinese tradition as a time of prosperity and benevolent rule.   (p. 61)

ziggurat A massive pyramidal stepped tower made of mud bricks. It is associated with religious complexes in ancient Mesopotamian cities, but its function is unknown.   (p. 16)

Zoroastrianism A religion originating in ancient Iran that became the official religion of the Achaemenids. It centered on a single benevolent deity, Ahuramazda, who engaged in a struggle with demonic forces before prevailing and restoring a pristine world. It emphasized truth-telling, purity, and reverence for nature.   (p. 87)

Zulu A people of modern South Africa whom King Shaka united in 1818.   (p. 539)